THE WAITE GROUP®

OBJECT-ORIENTED PROGRAMMING IN C++

SECOND EDITION

ROBERT LAFORE

WAITE GROUP PRESS™
Corte Madera, California

Publisher: Mitchell Waite
Editor-in-Chief: Scott Calamar
Editorial Director: Joel Fugazzotto
Managing Editor: Joanne Miller
Content Editor: Harry Henderson
Copy Editor: Deirdre Greene
Technical Reviewer: Michael Radtke
Production Director: Julianne Ososke
Design and Production: Karen Johnston/Christi Payne Fryday
Illustrations: Frances Hasegawa
Cover Design: Michael Rogondino

Published by Waite Group Press™, 200 Tamal Plaza, Corte Madera, CA 94925.

Waite Group Press is distributed to bookstores and book wholesalers by Publishers Group West, Box 8843, Emeryville, CA 94662, 1-800-788-3123 (in California 1-510-658-3453).

Printed in the United States of America
94 95 96 97 • 10 9 8 7 6 5 4 3 2 1

Library of Congress Cataloging in Publication Data
Lafore, Robert (Robert W.)
The Waite Group's object-oriented programming in C++ / Robert Lafore. —2nd Ed.
p. cm.
Rev. ed. of: Object-oriented programming in Turbo C++.
Includes index
ISBN: 1-878739-73-5
1. Object-oriented programming (Computer science) 2. C++ (Computer program language) 3. Borland C++. 4. Turbo C++.
I. Lafore, Robert (Robert W.). Object-oriented programming in Turbo C++. II. Waite Group. III. Title:
QA76.64.L32 1994
005.13'3—dc20 94-26405
CIP

DEDICATION

This book is dedicated to GGL and her indomitable spirit.

ABOUT THE AUTHOR

Robert Lafore has been writing books about computer programming since 1982. His best-selling titles include *Assembly Language Programming for the IBM PC and XT, C Programming Using Turbo C++*, and *Microsoft C Programming for the PC*. Mr. Lafore holds degrees in mathematics and electrical engineering, and has been active in programming since the days of the PDP-5, when 4K of main memory was considered luxurious. His interests include hiking, windsurfing, and recreational mathematics.

ACKNOWLEDGMENTS

SECOND EDITION

My thanks to the following professors—users of this book as a text at their respective colleges and universities—for their help in planning the second edition: Dave Bridges, Frank Cioch, Jack Davidson, Terrence Fries, Jimmie Hattemer, Jack Van Luik, Kieran Mathieson, Bill McCarty, Anita Millspaugh, Ian Moraes, Jorge Prendes, Steve Silva, and Edward Wright.

I would like to thank the many readers of the first edition who wrote in with corrections and suggestions, many of which were invaluable.

At Waite Group Press, Joanne Miller has ably ridden herd on my errant scheduling and filled in as academic liaison, and Scott Calamar, as always, has made sure that everyone knew what they were doing. Deirdre Greene provided an uncannily sharp eye as copy editor.

Thanks too to Mike Radtke and Harry Henderson for their expert technical reviews.

Special thanks to Edward Wright, of Western Oregon State College, for reviewing and experimenting with the new exercises.

FIRST EDITION

My primary thanks go to Mitch Waite, who poured over every inch of the manuscript with painstaking attention to detail and made a semi-infinite number of helpful suggestions. Bill McCarty of Azusa Pacific University reviewed the content of the manuscript and its suitability for classroom use, suggested many excellent improvements, and attempted to correct my dyslexic spelling. George Leach ran all the programs, and, to our horror, found several that didn't perform correctly in certain circumstances. I trust these problems have all been fixed; if not, the fault is entirely mine. Scott Calamar of The Waite Group dealt with the myriad organizational aspects of writing and producing this book; his competence and unfailing good humor were an important ingredient in its completion. I would also like to thank Nan Borreson of Borland for supplying the latest releases of the software (among other useful tidbits), Harry Henderson for reviewing the exercises, Louise Orlando of The Waite Group for ably shepherding the book through production, Merrill Peterson of Matrix Productions for coordinating the most trouble-free production run I've ever been involved with, Juan Vargas for the innovative design, and Frances Hasegawa for her uncanny ability to decipher my sketches and produce beautiful and effective art.

PREFACE TO THE SECOND EDITION

The first edition of this book, which appeared in 1991, has been well received by educational institutions, industry, and programming enthusiasts. However, many changes have taken place in C++ in the last several years, and that edition was beginning to show its age. In this new edition we attempt to bring the book up to date with current C++ developments. We've added a chapter to cover the two major additions to C++, templates and exceptions. Numerous smaller subjects, such as the syntax for static member variables and runtime type identification, have been revised or added. The chapter on stream input/output has been revised and almost doubled in size. New examples have been added throughout, including a new emphasis on using C++ for simulation programs, as exemplified by the molecule program in Chapter 11 and the elevator program in Chapter 15. We've also changed the emphasis from programming in the older Turbo C++ environment to programming with the more sophisticated Borland C++ compiler (although we still provide all the material to use Turbo C++).

With all this, we've tried hard to keep the book as easy to read as the first edition.

TABLE OF CONTENTS

CONTENTS

INTRODUCTION

Object-oriented programming (OOP) is the most dramatic innovation in software development in the last decade. It ranks in importance with the development of the first higher-level languages at the dawn of the computer age. Sooner or later every programmer will be affected by the object-oriented approach to program design.

ADVANTAGES OF OOP

Why is everyone so excited about OOP? The chief problem with computer programs is complexity. Large programs are probably the most complicated entities ever created by humans. Because of this complexity, programs are prone to error, and software errors can be expensive and even life threatening (in air-traffic control, for example). Object-oriented programming offers a new and powerful way to cope with this complexity. Its goal is clearer, more reliable, more easily maintained programs.

LANGUAGES AND DEVELOPMENT PLATFORMS

Of the object-oriented programming languages, C++ is by far the most popular; if you want to learn C++, there are no better tools than Borland C++ and its lower-priced cousin, Turbo C++. These products provide a complete, easy-to-use development environment. They are also among the best platforms for professional software developers.

WHAT THIS BOOK DOES

This book teaches object-oriented programming with the C++ programming language, using either Borland C++ or Turbo C++. It is suitable for professional programmers, students, and kitchen-table enthusiasts.

NEW CONCEPTS

OOP involves concepts that are new to programmers of traditional languages such as Pascal, BASIC, and C. These ideas, such as data hiding, encapsulation, and polymorphism, lie at the heart of object-oriented programming. But it's easy to lose sight of these concepts when discussing the specifics of an object-oriented language. Many books overwhelm the reader with the details of language features, while ignoring the reason these features exist. This book attempts to keep an eye on the big picture and relate the details to the larger concepts.

THE GRADUAL APPROACH

We take a gradual approach in this book, starting with very simple programming examples and working up to full-fledged object-oriented applications. We introduce new concepts slowly so that you will have time to digest one idea before going on to the next. We use figures whenever possible to help clarify new ideas. There are questions and programming exercises at the end of most chapters to enhance the book's usefulness in the classroom. Answers to the questions and to the first few (starred) exercises can be found in Appendix D. The exercises vary in difficulty so as to pose a variety of challenges for the student.

WHAT YOU NEED TO KNOW TO USE THIS BOOK

To use this book, you should have some experience with at least one computer language, such as Pascal, BASIC, or FORTRAN. Thus we will assume that you know what variables are and that you are familiar with basic programming constructions such as loops and decisions.

You do not need to know the C language to use this book. Many books on C++ assume that you already know C, but this one does not. It teaches C++ from the ground up. If you do know C, it won't hurt, but you may be surprised at how little overlap there is between C and C++.

If you're using Borland C++, you should be familiar with Microsoft Windows. You should be familiar with menus and dialog boxes, and know how to use the Program Manager and File Manager.

If you're using Turbo C++, you should have some experience with MS-DOS. You should know how to list, copy, and delete files, and how to move around in the directory structure and perform other DOS-related activities. You don't need to know anything about Windows to use Turbo C++.

SOFTWARE AND HARDWARE

Here's the software and hardware you'll need for this book.

First, you should have either Borland C++, version 4.5 or later, or Turbo C++ for DOS, version 3.0 or later.

Borland C++ is Borland's flagship product. In its newest incarnation it runs under Microsoft Windows, but you can use it to develop either DOS or Windows programs. This book uses DOS program examples, so you don't need many of the features of Borland C++ that deal with Windows development. Borland C++ is a fast, easily learned system that's fun to use.

Turbo C++ for DOS runs under DOS and generates DOS programs; it has nothing to do with Windows. It lacks several minor features of Borland C++ that are relevant to this book. Most notably it does not (at least as of this writing) include the C++ exception feature. Also, the debugger is less oriented toward C++ development. However, these deficiencies are not major and can easily be ignored, especially if cost is important; Turbo C++ is much cheaper than Borland C++.

Earlier versions of both Borland C++ and Turbo C++ are compatible with most of the programs in this book, so don't worry too much if your compiler isn't completely up to date.

A potentially confusing fact: Both Borland C++ and Turbo C++ can be used to develop programs in the C language as well as in C++. However, we will not be concerned with the C language in this book.

Borland C++ requires a PC (IBM-compatible) computer capable of running Windows 3.1 or later. This typically means an 80386 or better processor, a color display (preferably VGA or better), at least 8 MB of memory, and a mouse. You'll need a hard disk with between 40 and 105 MB of free space.

Turbo C++ is less demanding of hardware since it runs on DOS-only systems. It needs MS-DOS 4.0 or higher, at least 640K of memory, a hard disk, and a floppy disk drive. The hard disk should have somewhat more than 6 MB of free space. (Turbo C++ will also run in a Windows DOS box.) Most of the examples in this book need only a character-based display, but Chapter 11 requires a graphics display, as do a few other examples. These graphics examples aren't critical to learning C++, so a character display is adequate for this book. Turbo C++ can accommodate a mouse; in fact, a mouse is very convenient. However, it is not necessary; you can perform all operations from the keyboard.

GO FOR IT!

You may have heard that C++ is difficult to learn. It's true that it might be a little more challenging than BASIC, but it's really quite similar to other languages, with two or three "grand ideas" thrown in. These new ideas are fascinating in themselves, and we think you'll have fun learning about them. They are also becoming part of the programming culture; they're something everyone should know a little bit about, like evolution and psychoanalysis. We hope this book will help you enjoy learning about these new ideas, at the same time that it teaches you the details of programming in C++.

A NOTE TO TEACHERS

Teachers, and others who already know C, may be interested in some details of the approach we use in this book and how it's organized.

 TREAT C++ AS A SEPARATE LANGUAGE

It's important to emphasize that C and C++ are entirely separate languages. While it's true that their syntax is similar, C is actually a subset of C++. But the similarity is largely a historical accident. In fact, the basic approach in a C++ program is radically different than that in a C program.

We think that C++ is the language of the future—that it will become increasingly important in the years ahead and that it may soon surpass C as the most popular language for serious programmers. Thus we don't believe it is necessary or advantageous to teach C before teaching C++. Students who don't know C are saved the time and trouble of learning C and then learning C++, an inefficient approach. Students who already know C may be able to skim parts of some chapters, but they will find that a remarkable percentage of the material is new.

OPTIMIZE ORGANIZATION FOR OOP

We could have begun the book by teaching the procedural concepts common to C and C++, and moved on to the new OOP concepts once the procedural approach had been digested. That seemed counterproductive, however, since one of our goals is to begin true object-oriented programming as quickly as possible. Accordingly we provide a minimum of procedural groundwork before getting to objects in Chapter 7. Even the initial chapters are heavily steeped in C++, as opposed to C, usage.

We introduce some concepts earlier than is traditional in books on C. For example, structures are a key feature for understanding C++, since classes are syntactically an extension of structures. For this reason, we introduce structures in Chapter 5 so that they will be familiar when we discuss classes.

Some concepts, such as pointers, are introduced later than in traditional C books. It's not necessary to understand pointers to follow the essentials of OOP, and pointers are usually a stumbling block for C and C++ students. Therefore, we defer a discussion of pointers until the main concepts of OOP have been thoroughly digested.

SUBSTITUTE SUPERIOR C++ FEATURES

Some features of C have been superseded by new approaches in C++. For instance, the `printf()` and `scanf()` functions, input/output workhorses in C, are seldom used in C++ because `cout` and `cin` do a better job. Consequently we leave out detailed descriptions of `printf()` and `scanf()`. Similarly, `#define` constants and macros in C have been largely superseded by the `const` qualifier and `inline` functions in C++, and need to be mentioned only briefly.

MINIMIZE IRRELEVANT CAPABILITIES

Since the focus in this book is on object-oriented programming, we can leave out some features of C that are seldom used and are not particularly relevant to OOP. For instance, it isn't necessary to understand the C bit-wise operators (used to operate on individual bits) to learn object-oriented programming. These and a few other features can be dropped from our discussion, or mentioned only briefly, with no loss in understanding of the major features of C++.

The result is a book that focuses on the fundamentals of OOP, moving the reader gently but briskly toward an understanding of new concepts and their application to real programming problems.

PROGRAMMING EXERCISES

One of the major changes in the second edition is the addition of numerous exercises. Each of these involves the creation of a complete C++ program. There are roughly 12 exercises per chapter. Solutions to the first three or four exercises in each chapter are provided in Appendix D. For the remainder of the exercises, readers are on their own, although qualified instructors can obtain a complimentary disk with suggested solutions. Please write or fax a request to Waite Group Press on your institution's letterhead to :

OOP in C++ Instructor Companion Disk
Waite Group Press
200 Tamal Plaza
Corte Madera, CA 94925

or (415) 924-2576 (FAX)

The exercises vary considerably in their degree of difficulty. In each chapter the early exercises are fairly easy, while later ones are more challenging. Instructors will probably want to assign only those exercises suited to the level of a particular class.

1

The Big Picture

WHY WE NEED OBJECT-ORIENTED PROGRAMMING

PROCEDURAL VERSUS OBJECT-ORIENTED LANGUAGES

FEATURES OF OBJECT-ORIENTED LANGUAGES

INTRODUCTION TO CLASSES AND OBJECTS

INTRODUCTION TO INHERITANCE

C++ AND C

1

This book teaches you how to program in C++, a computer language that supports *object-oriented programming* (OOP). Why do we need OOP? What does it do that traditional languages like C, Pascal, and BASIC don't? What are the principles behind OOP? Two key concepts in OOP are *objects* and *classes*. What do these terms mean? What is the relationship between C++ and the older C language?

This chapter explores these questions and provides an overview of the features discussed in the balance of the book. What we say here will necessarily be rather general (although mercifully brief). If you find the discussion somewhat abstract, don't worry. The concepts we mention here will come into focus as we demonstrate them in detail in subsequent chapters.

Why Do We Need Object-Oriented Programming?

Object-oriented programming was developed because limitations were discovered in earlier approaches to programming. To appreciate what OOP does, we need to understand what these limitations are and how they arose from traditional programming languages.

Procedural Languages

Pascal, C, BASIC, FORTRAN, and similar languages are *procedural* languages. That is, each statement in the language tells the computer to *do* something: Get some input, add these numbers, divide by 6, display that output. A program in a procedural language is a *list of instructions*.

For very small programs, no other organizing principle (often called a *paradigm*) is needed. The programmer creates the list of instructions, and the computer carries them out.

Division into Functions

When programs become larger, a single list of instructions becomes unwieldy. Few programmers can comprehend a program of more than a few hundred statements unless it is broken down into smaller units. For this reason the *function* was adopted as a way to make programs more comprehensible to their human creators. (The term *function* is used in C++ and C. In other languages the same concept may be referred to as a *subroutine*, a *subprogram*, or a *procedure*.) A program is divided into functions, and (ideally, at least) each function has a clearly defined purpose and a clearly defined interface to the other functions in the program.

The idea of breaking a program into functions can be further extended by grouping a number of functions together into a larger entity called a *module*, but the principle is similar: a grouping of components that carries out specific tasks.

Dividing a program into functions and modules is one of the cornerstones of *structured programming*, the somewhat loosely defined discipline that has influenced programming organization for several decades.

Problems with Structured Programming

As programs grow ever larger and more complex, even the structured programming approach begins to show signs of strain. You may have heard about, or been involved in, horror stories of program development. The project is too complex, the schedule slips, more programmers are added, complexity increases, costs skyrocket, the schedule slips further, and disaster ensues. (See *The Mythical Man-Month*, by Frederick P. Brooks, Jr., Addison-Wesley, 1982, for a vivid description of this process.)

Analyzing the reasons for these failures reveals that there are weaknesses in the procedural paradigm itself. No matter how well the structured programming approach is implemented, large programs become excessively complex.

What are the reasons for this failure of procedural languages? One of the most crucial is the role played by data.

Data Undervalued

In a procedural language, the emphasis is on doing things—read the keyboard, invert the vector, check for errors, and so on. The subdivision of a program into functions continues this emphasis. Functions do things just as single program statements do. What they do may be more complex or abstract, but the emphasis is still on the action.

What happens to the data in this paradigm? Data is, after all, the reason for a program's existence. The important part of an inventory program isn't a function that displays the data, or a function that checks for correct input; it's the inventory data itself. Yet data is given second-class status in the organization of procedural languages.

For example, in an inventory program, the data that makes up the inventory is probably read from a disk file into memory, where it is treated as a global variable. By *global* we mean that the variables that constitute the data are declared outside of any function, so they are accessible to all functions. These functions perform various operations on the data. They read it, analyze it, update it, rearrange it, display it, write it back to the disk, and so on.

We should note that most languages, such as Pascal and C, also support *local* variables, which are hidden within a single function. But local variables are not useful for important data that must be accessed by many different functions. Figure 1-1 shows the relationship between global and local variables.

Now suppose a new programmer is hired to write a function to analyze this inventory data in a certain way. Unfamiliar with the subtleties of the program, the programmer creates a function that accidentally corrupts the data. This is easy to do, because every function has complete access to the data. It's like leaving your personal papers in the lobby of your apartment building: Anyone can change or destroy them. In the same way, global data can be corrupted by functions that have no business changing it.

Another problem is that, since many functions access the same data, the way the data is stored becomes critical. The arrangement of the data can't be changed without modifying all the functions that access it. If you add new data items, for example, you'll need to modify all the functions that access the data so that they can also access these new items. It will be hard to find all such functions, and even harder to modify all of them correctly. It's similar to what happens when your

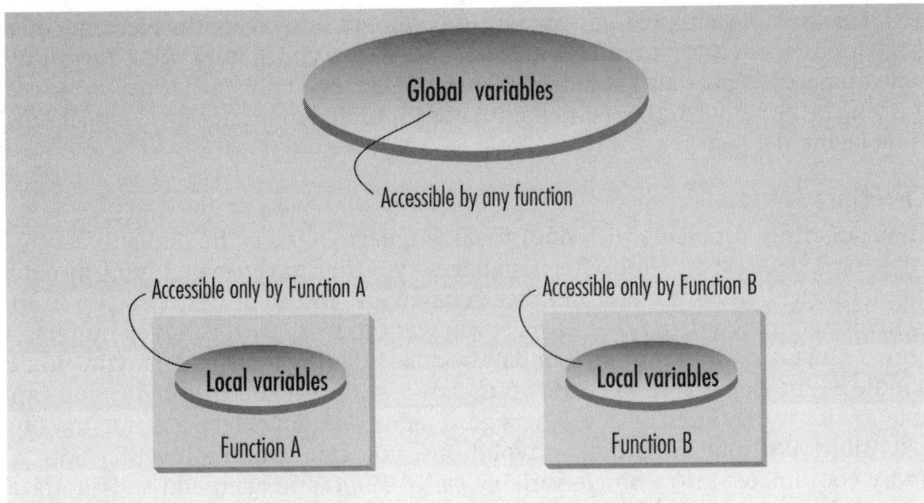

Figure 1-1 Global and Local Variables

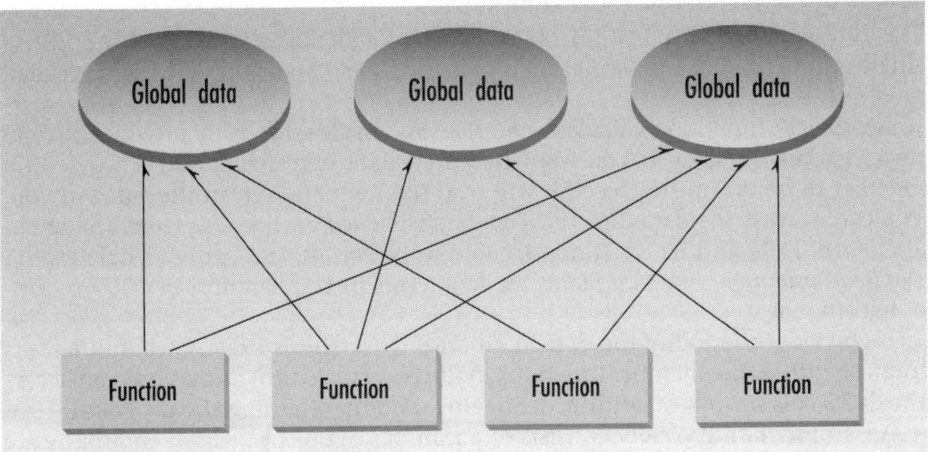

Figure 1-2 The Procedural Paradigm

local supermarket moves the bread from aisle 4 to aisle 12. Everyone who patronizes the supermarket must figure out where the bread has gone, and adjust their shopping habits accordingly. The relationship of functions and data in procedural programs is shown in Figure 1-2.

What is needed is a way to restrict access to the data, to *hide* it from all but a few critical functions. This will protect the data, simplify maintenance, and offer other benefits as well (as we'll see).

Relationship to the Real World

Procedural programs are often difficult to design. The problem is that their chief components—functions and data structures—don't model the real world very well. For example, suppose you are writing a program to create the elements of a graphics user interface: menus, windows, and so on. Quick now, what functions will you need? What data structures? The answers are not obvious, to say the least. It would be better if windows and menus corresponded more closely to actual program elements.

New Data Types

There are other problems with traditional languages. One is the difficulty of creating new data types. Computer languages typically have several built-in data types: integers, floating-point numbers, characters, and so on. What if you want to invent your own data type? Perhaps you want to work with complex numbers, or two-dimensional coordinates, or dates—quantities the built-in data types don't handle easily. Being able to create your own types is called *extensibility*; you can extend the capabilities of the language. Traditional languages are not usually extensible. Without unnatural convolutions, you can't bundle together both x and y coordinates into a single variable called *Point*, and then add and subtract values of this type. The result is that traditional programs are more complex to write and maintain.

The Object-Oriented Approach

The fundamental idea behind object-oriented languages is to combine into a single unit both *data* and *the functions that operate on that data*. Such a unit is called an *object*.

An object's functions, called *member functions* in C++, typically provide the only way to access its data. If you want to read a data item in an object, you call a member function in the object. It will read the item and return the value to you. You can't access the data directly. The data is *hidden*, so it is safe from accidental alteration. Data and its functions are said to be *encapsulated* into a single entity. *Data encapsulation* and *data hiding* are key terms in the description of object-oriented languages.

If you want to modify the data in an object, you know exactly what functions interact with it: the member functions in the object. No other functions can access the data. This simplifies writing, debugging, and maintaining the program.

A C++ program typically consists of a number of objects, which communicate with each other by calling one another's member functions. The organization of a C++ program is shown in Figure 1-3.

We should mention that what are called *member functions* in C++ are called *methods* in some other object-oriented (OO) languages (such as Smalltalk, one of the first OO languages). Also, data items are referred to as *instance variables*. Calling an object's member function is referred to as *sending a message* to the object. These terms are not usually used in C++.

An Analogy

You might want to think of objects as departments—such as sales, accounting, personnel, and so on—in a company. Departments provide an important approach to corporate organization. In most companies (except very small ones), people don't work on personnel problems one day, the payroll the next, and then go out in the field as salespeople the week after. Each department has its own personnel,

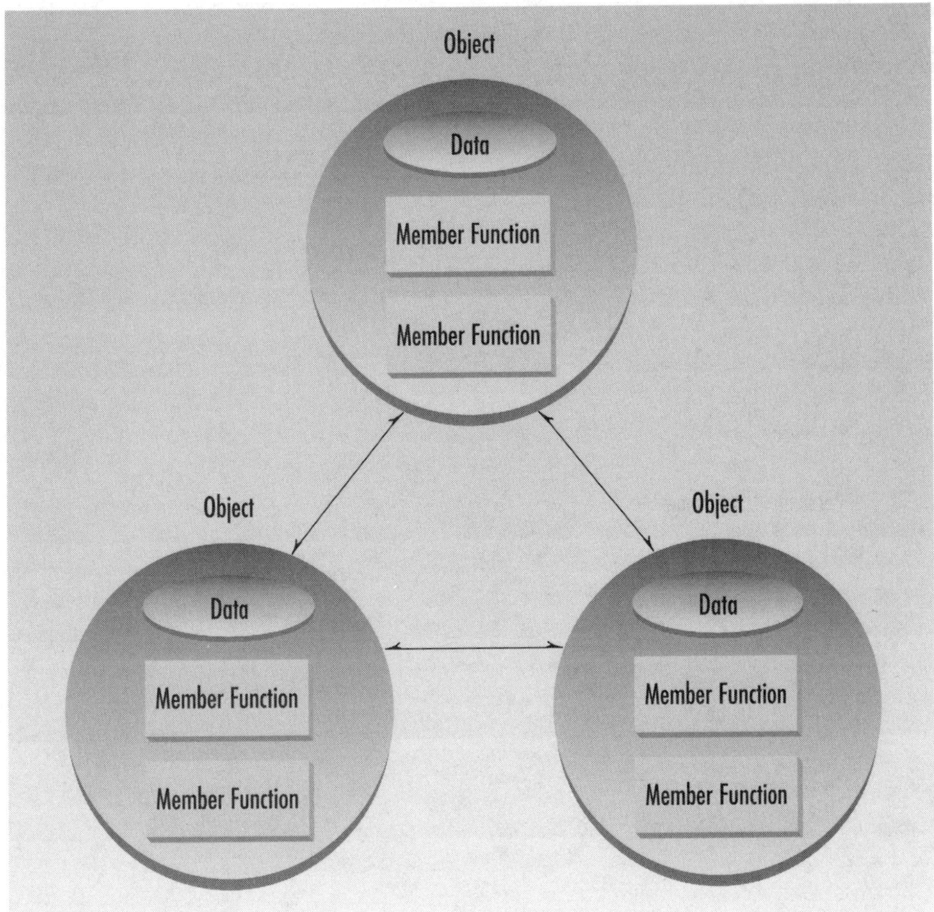

Figure 1-3 The Object-Oriented Paradigm

with clearly assigned duties. It also has its own data: payroll, sales figures, personnel records, inventory, or whatever, depending on the department.

The people in each department control and operate on that department's data. Dividing the company into departments makes it easier to comprehend and control the company's activities, and helps maintain the integrity of the information used by the company. The payroll department, for instance, is responsible for the payroll data. If you are from the sales department, and you need to know the total of all the salaries paid in the southern region in July, you don't just walk into the payroll department and start rummaging through file cabinets. You send a memo to the appropriate person in the department, and then you wait for that person to access the data and send you a reply with the information you want. This ensures that the data is accessed accurately and that it is not corrupted by inept outsiders. (This view of corporate organization is shown in Figure 1-4.) In the same way, objects provide an approach to program organization, while helping to maintain the integrity of the program's data.

Sales Department
Sales data
Sales Manager
Secretary
Personnel Department
Personnel data
Personnel Manager
Personnel Staff
Finance Department
Financial data
Chief Financial Officer
Financial Assistant

Figure 1-4 The Corporate Paradigm

OOP: An Approach to Organization

Keep in mind that object-oriented programming is not primarily concerned with the details of program operation. Instead, it deals with the overall organization of the program. Most individual program statements in C++ are similar to statements in procedural languages, and many are identical to statements in C. Indeed, an entire member function in a C++ program may be very similar to a procedural function in C. It is only when you look at the larger context that you can determine whether a statement or a function is part of a procedural C program or an object-oriented C++ program.

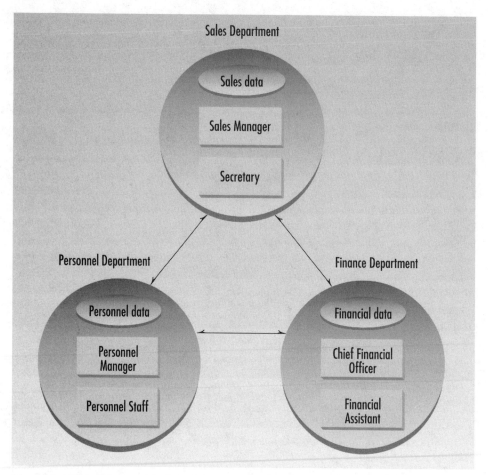

Characteristics of Object-Oriented Languages

Let's briefly examine a few of the major elements of object-oriented languages in general, and C++ in particular.

Objects

When you approach a programming problem in an object-oriented language, you no longer ask how the problem will be divided into functions, but how it will be divided into objects. Thinking in terms of objects, rather than functions, has a surprisingly helpful effect on how easily programs can be designed. This results from the close match between objects in the programming sense and objects in the real world.

What kinds of things become objects in object-oriented programs? The answer to this is limited only by your imagination, but here are some typical categories to start you thinking:

- Physical objects
  Automobiles in a traffic-flow simulation
  Electrical components in a circuit-design program
  Countries in an economics model
  Aircraft in an air-traffic-control system

- Elements of the computer-user environment
  Windows
  Menus
  Graphics objects (lines, rectangles, circles)
  The mouse, keyboard, disk drives, printer

- Data-storage constructs
  Customized arrays
  Stacks
  Linked lists
  Binary trees

- Human entities
  Employees
  Students
  Customers
  Salespeople

- Collections of data
  An inventory
  A personnel file
  A dictionary
  A table of the latitudes and longitudes of world cities

- User-defined data types
  Time
  Angles
  Complex numbers
  Points on the plane

- Components in computer games
  Ghosts in a maze game

Positions in a board game (chess, checkers)
Animals in an ecological simulation
Opponents and friends in adventure games

The match between programming objects and real-world objects is the happy result of combining data and functions: The resulting objects offer a revolution in program design. No such close match between programming constructs and the items being modeled exists in a procedural language.

Classes

In OOP we say that objects are *members of classes*. What does this mean? Let's look at an analogy. Almost all computer languages have built-in data types. For instance, a data type `int`, meaning *integer*, is predefined in C++ (as we'll see in Chapter 3). You can declare as many variables of type `int` as you need in your program:

```
int day;
int count;
int divisor;
int answer;
```

In a similar way, you can define many objects of the same *class*, as shown in Figure 1-5. A class serves as a plan, or template. It specifies what data and what functions will be included in objects of that class. Defining the class doesn't create any objects, just as the mere existence of a type `int` doesn't create any variables.

A class is thus a collection of similar objects. This fits our nontechnical understanding of the word *class*. Prince, Sting, and Madonna are members of the class of rock musicians. There is no one person called "rock musician," but specific people with specific names are members of this class if they possess certain characteristics.

Inheritance

The idea of classes leads to the idea of *inheritance*. In our daily lives, we use the concept of classes as divided into subclasses. We know that the class of animals is divided into mammals, amphibians, insects, birds, and so on. The class of vehicles is divided into cars, trucks, buses, and motorcycles.

The principle in this sort of division is that each subclass shares common characteristics with the class from which it's derived. Cars, trucks, buses, and motorcycles all have wheels and a motor; these are the defining characteristics of vehicles. In addition to the characteristics shared with other members of the class, each subclass also has its own particular characteristics: Buses, for instance, have seats for many people, while trucks have space for hauling heavy loads.

This idea is shown in Figure 1-6. Notice in the figure that features A and B, which are part of the base class, are common to all the derived classes, but that each derived class also has features of its own.

In a similar way, an OOP class can be divided into subclasses. In C++ the original class is called the *base class*; other classes can be defined that share its characteristics, but add their own as well. These are called *derived classes*.

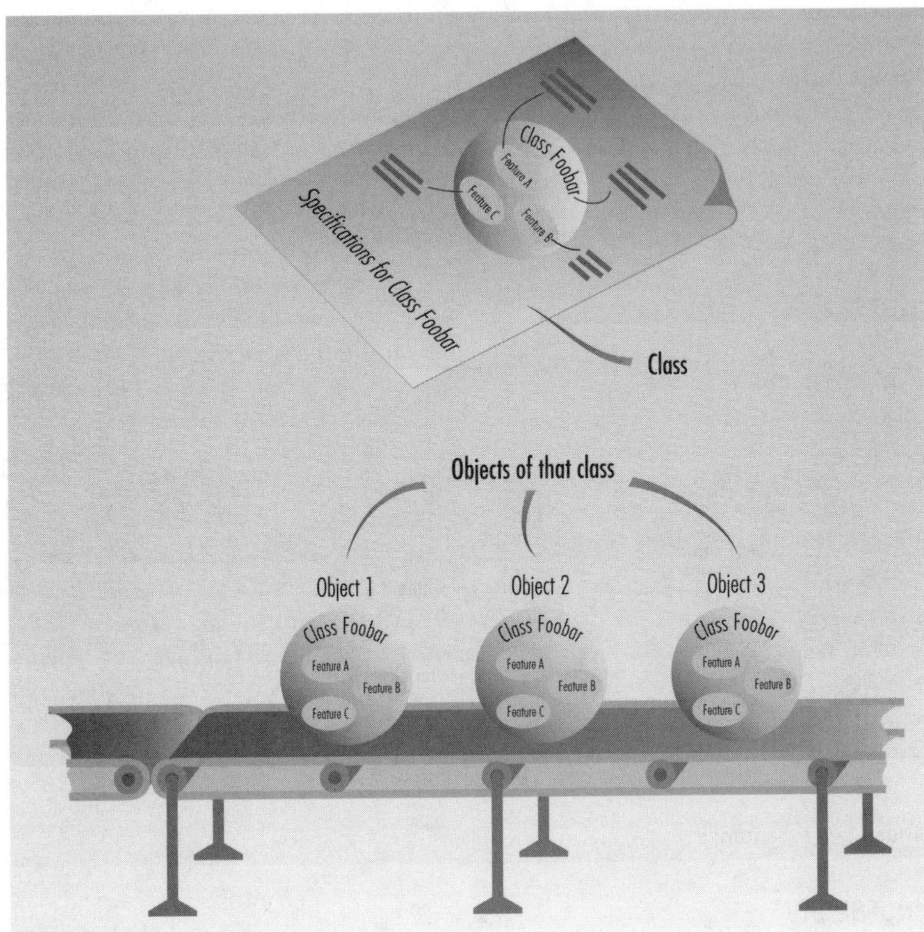

Figure 1-5 A Class and Its Objects

Don't confuse the relation of objects to classes, on the one hand, with the relation of a base class to derived classes, on the other. Objects, which exist in the computer's memory, each embody the exact characteristics of their class, which serves as a template. Derived classes inherit some characteristics from their base class, but add new ones of their own.

Inheritance is somewhat analogous to using functions to simplify a traditional procedural program. If we find that three different sections of a procedural program do almost exactly the same thing, we recognize an opportunity to extract the common elements of these three sections and put them into a single function. The three sections of the program can call the function to execute the common actions, and they can perform their own individual processing as well. Similarly, a base class contains elements common to a group of derived classes. As functions do in a procedural program, inheritance shortens an object-oriented program and clarifies the relationship among program elements.

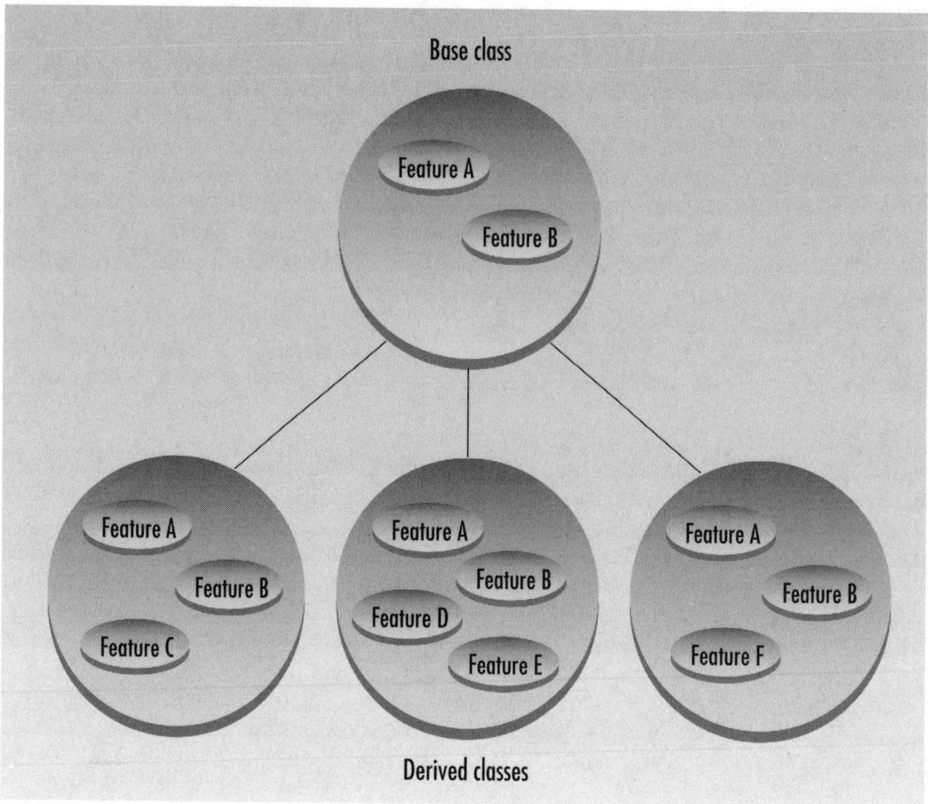

Figure 1-6 Inheritance

Reusability

Once a class has been written, created, and debugged, it can be distributed to other programmers for use in their own programs. This is called *reusability*. It is similar to the way a library of functions in a procedural language can be incorporated into different programs.

However, in OOP, the concept of inheritance provides an important extension to the idea of reusability. A programmer can take an existing class and, without modifying it, add additional features and capabilities to it. This is done by deriving a new class from the existing one. The new class will inherit the capabilities of the old one, but is free to add new features of its own.

For example, you might have written (or purchased from someone else) a class that creates a menu system, such as that used in the Turbo C++ Integrated Development Environment (IDE). This class works fine, and you don't want to change it, but you want to add the capability to make some menu entries flash on and off. To do this, you simply create a new class that inherits all the capabilities of the existing one but adds flashing menu entries.

The ease with which existing software can be reused is a major benefit—possibly *the* major benefit—of OOP. Many companies find that reusing classes on a second project provides a major return on their original investment. We'll have more to say about this in Chapters 10 and 15.

Creating New Data Types

One of the benefits of objects is that they give the programmer a convenient way to construct new data types. Suppose you work with two-dimensional positions (such as x and y coordinates, or latitude and longitude) in your program. You would like to express operations on these positional values with normal arithmetic operations, such as

```
position1 = position2 + origin
```

where the variables `position1`, `position2`, and `origin` each represent a *pair* of independent numerical quantities. By creating a class that incorporates these two values, and declaring `position1`, `position2`, and `origin` to be objects of this class, we can, in effect, create a new data type. Many features of C++ are intended to facilitate the creation of new data types in this manner.

Polymorphism and Overloading

Note that the `=` (equal) and `+` (plus) operators, used in the position arithmetic shown above, don't act the same way they do in operations on built-in types like `int`. The objects `position1` and so on are not predefined in C++, but are programmer-defined objects of class `Position`. How do the `=` and `+` operators know how to operate on objects? The answer is that we can define new operations for these operators. These operators will be member functions of the `Position` class.

Using operators or functions in different ways, depending on what they are operating on, is called *polymorphism* (one thing with several distinct forms). When an existing operator, such as `+` or `=`, is given the capability to operate on a new data type, it is said to be *overloaded*. Overloading is a kind of polymorphism; it is also an important feature of OOP.

C++ and C

C++ is derived from the C language. Strictly speaking, it is a superset of C: Almost every correct statement in C is also a correct statement in C++, although the reverse is not true. The most important elements added to C to create C++ are concerned with classes, objects, and object-oriented programming. (C++ was originally called "C with classes.") However, C++ has many other new features as well, including an improved approach to input/output (I/O) and a new way to write comments. Figure 1-7 shows the relationship of C and C++.

In fact, the practical differences between C and C++ are larger than you might think. Although you *can* write a program in C++ that looks like a program in C, hardly anyone does. C++ programmers not only make use of the new features of C++, they also emphasize the traditional C features in different proportions than do C programmers.

If you already know C, you will have a head start in learning C++ (although you may also have some bad habits to unlearn), but much of the material will be new.

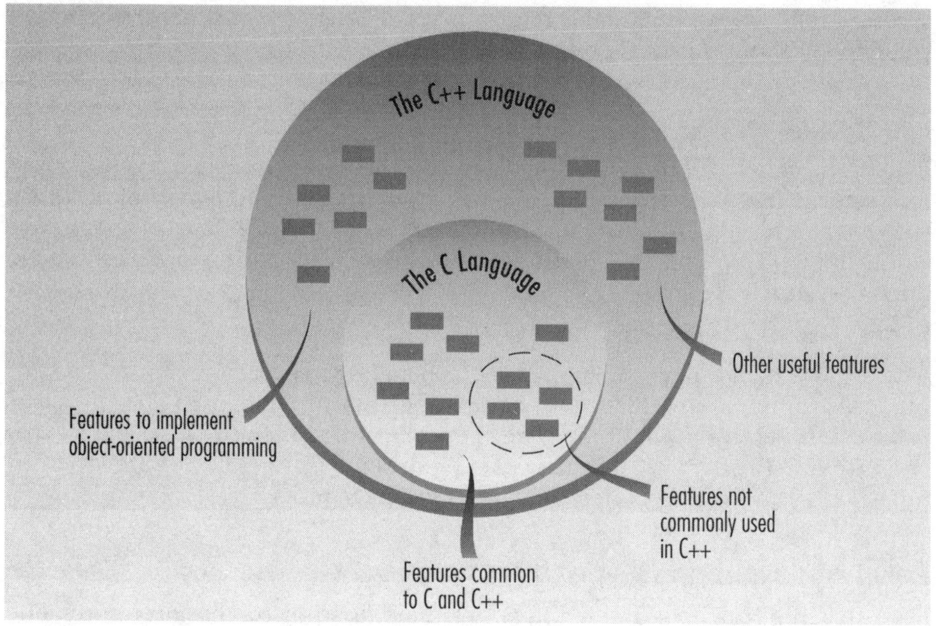

Figure 1-7 The Relationship Between C and C++

Laying the Groundwork

Our goal is to help you begin writing OOP programs as soon as possible. However, as we noted, much of C++ is inherited from C, so while the overall structure of a C++ program may be OOP, down in the trenches you need to know some old-fashioned procedural fundamentals. Chapters 3 through 6 therefore deal with the "traditional" aspects of C++, many of which are also found in C. You will learn about variables and I/O, about control structures like loops and decisions, and about functions themselves. You will also learn about structures in general, since the same syntax that's used for structures is used for classes.

If you already know C, you might be tempted to skip these chapters. However, you will find that there are many differences, some obvious and some rather subtle, between C and C++. Our advice is to read these chapters, skimming what you know, and concentrating on the ways C++ differs from C.

The specific discussion of OOP starts in Chapter 7, when we begin to explore objects and classes. From then on the examples will be object oriented.

Summary

OOP is a way of organizing programs. The emphasis is on the way programs are designed, not on the details of individual operators. In particular, OOP programs are organized around objects, which contain both data and functions that act on that data. A class is a template for a number of objects.

C++ is a superset of C. It adds to the C language the capability to implement OOP. It also adds a variety of other features. In addition, the emphasis is changed in C++, so that some features common to C, although still available in C++, are seldom used, while others are used far more frequently. The result is a surprisingly different language.

The general concepts discussed in this chapter will become more concrete as you learn more about the details of C++. You may want to refer back to this chapter as you progress further into this book.

Questions

Answers to questions can be found in Appendix D. Note: Throughout this book, multiple-choice questions can have more than one correct answer.

1. Pascal, BASIC, and C are p__________ languages, while C++ is an o__________ language.
2. A widget is to the blueprint for a widget as an object is to
   a. a member function.
   b. a class.
   c. an operator.
   d. a data item.
3. The two major components of an object are __________ and functions that __________.
4. In C++, a function contained within a class is called
   a. a member function.
   b. an operator.
   c. a class function.
   d. a method.
5. Protecting data from access by unauthorized functions is called __________.
6. Which of the following are good reasons to use an object-oriented language?
   a. You can define your own data types.
   b. Program statements are simpler than in procedural languages.
   c. An OO program can be taught to correct its own errors.
   d. It's easier to conceptualize an OO program.
7. __________ model entities in the real world more closely than do functions.
8. True or false: A C++ program is similar to a C program except for the details of coding.
9. Bundling data and functions together is called __________.

10. When a language has the capability to produce new data types, it is said to be
    a. reprehensible.
    b. encapsulated.
    c. overloaded.
    d. extensible.
11. True or false: You can easily tell, from any two lines of code, whether a program is written in C or C++.
12. The ability of a function or operator to act in different ways on different data types is called __________.
13. A normal C++ operator that acts in special ways on newly defined data types is said to be
    a. glorified.
    b. encapsulated.
    c. classified.
    d. overloaded.
14. Memorizing the new terms used in C++ is
    a. critically important.
    b. something you can return to later.
    c. the key to wealth and success.
    d. completely irrelevant.

2

Using Borland or Turbo C++

SETTING UP BORLAND C++ OR TURBO C++

YOUR FIRST C++ PROGRAM

USING THE INTEGRATED DEVELOPMENT ENVIRONMENT

EDITING, COMPILING, AND LINKING

2

Borland C++ and Turbo C++ provide almost ideal platforms for learning C++. Their Integrated Development Environment (IDE) puts all the tools you need for C++ program development into a single, convenient screen display. In this chapter we describe how to install both these products and write C++ programs using them. As we noted in the Introduction, we describe the Windows-hosted version of Borland C++, not the older version that ran under DOS; and we cover the version of Turbo C++ that runs under DOS, not Windows. Specifically, we describe Borland C++ version 4.5, and Turbo C++ for DOS, version 3.0.

Earlier versions of both Borland C++ and Turbo C++ are compatible with most of the example programs in this book; but we don't cover their installation procedures in this chapter. New versions of Borland C++ appear from time to time; it's likely that they will work in substantially the same way as the current version, although installation details may differ.

DOS Targets and EasyWin

Before describing how to install Borland C++ and Turbo C++, we should explain our general approach to developing C++ programs.

It's far easier to write C++ programs that run in the DOS environment than those that run under Windows; programming for Windows is something of a black art. Thus when you are learning a new programming language it makes sense to learn how to write for a DOS *target* (the environment the program will run under), even if you plan later in your career to program for Windows (or for some other platform). Thus this book describes programs that run under DOS. This makes it easier to focus on C++ and object-oriented programming.

This approach is not a problem with Turbo C++ for DOS, which runs under DOS and generates only DOS programs.

Things are slightly more complicated with Borland C++. Borland C++ always operates in Windows, but it can create programs that run on several different platforms, including various flavors of DOS and Windows. Our ultimate target is normal DOS programs. However, for development and experimentation in Borland C++, it turns out it's more convenient to create a special kind of Windows program that acts (almost) like a DOS program. This is called an *EasyWin* program. It runs under Windows, but you program it as if it is a DOS program.

There are several advantages to the EasyWin approach. First, you don't need to switch graphics modes when running your program, since EasyWin programs run in a regular Windows window. This means you don't lose the contents of the output screen when you switch back to the IDE after running the program. Second, the program can be debugged with the debugger built into Borland C++, rather than the stand-alone Turbo debugger for DOS. The built-in debugger is considerably more convenient to use, and seems to work more reliably.

However, if you want to create versions of your programs that actually run under DOS, or if you want to use DOS graphics and other DOS-only functions, you will want to create a DOS target rather than an EasyWin target.

The result is that we recommend installing Borland C++ to so that it can create both Windows (EasyWin) and DOS programs. We'll describe Borland C++ installation first, then Turbo C++ installation.

Installing Borland C++

In this section we describe how to install Borland C++ for both Windows and DOS targets.

To begin, start Windows. Put the Install disk (disk 1, if you're using floppies) in the appropriate drive. Before you do anything else, read the file called INSTALL.TXT (or something similar) that you'll find on the disk or CD. It will give you detailed instructions about the exact installation procedure. (The install process also gives you a chance to read this file.)

Run The Install Program

In general, you simply run the program called INSTALL from the floppy disk or CD, using Window's Run command. Specify the appropriate drive letter and path: `a:install` for floppies or `d:\install\install` for the CD (or whatever drive letters are appropriate on your system).

Borland C++ Installation Dialog

The first choice the INSTALL program gives you appears in a dialog called *Borland C++ Installation*. You can choose one of the following radio buttons:

- Full
- Custom
- CD-Only

The sections below describe the results of choosing Full or Custom. This dialog also lets you specify a different drive, although the INSTALL program has probably already guessed the correct one. You will be asked if the directory name \BC45\ is acceptable for Borland C++. Normally you can accept this choice. (This directory name will be different for different versions of Borland C++.)

Full-Scale Installation

If you have well over 100 MB of hard disk space that you don't mind devoting to Borland C++, choose *Full* in the *Borland C++ Installation* dialog. Things will be simple from now on. If you're loading from floppy disks, simply feed them in one after the other as requested by the prompts on the screen. Have a cup of coffee handy and call up Solitaire to pass the time. Read Borland's little signposts and watch the speedometer needle advance toward 100%. If you're loading from CD-ROM, things will go far more quickly and you don't need to oversee the process.

This full-scale installation will allow you to develop programs for any target platform, including Windows and DOS, using all the Borland C++ features.

Custom Installation

On the other hand, you may want to save hard disk space by installing only the minimum number of files necessary for EasyWin and DOS program development. In this case, choose Custom in the *Borland C++ Installation* dialog. You won't be able to develop real Windows programs with this installation, but if you don't want to program in Windows anyway, why waste the space? The installation described here takes about 50 MB. Installation is faster, too.

Borland C++ Target Platforms

If you've selected Custom installation, you'll see a dialog box labelled *Borland C++ Target Platforms*. There are three check boxes in this dialog:

- 16-bit Windows
- 32-bit Windows
- DOS

You want 16-bit Windows, so you can develop EasyWin programs, and DOS, so you can develop DOS programs. You don't need 32-bit Windows, so uncheck it. Leave all directory names unchanged throughout the installation process.

Borland C++ Tools

The next dialog, *Borland C++ Tools*, allows you to choose the general categories of software components you'll use for program development. There is a single check box:

- Command-line Tools

There are also five buttons:

- Debuggers
- Visual Tools
- Libraries
- Examples
- Help

Uncheck *Command-line Tools*. Push each of the five buttons in turn to call up dialog boxes with additional options, described in the next five sections.

Debuggers Button

The next dialog, *Borland C++ Debuggers*, has three check boxes:

- Turbo Debugger
- Remote Debugging
- Turbo Profiler

You don't need remote debugging or the profiler, so uncheck these boxes but keep *Turbo Debugger*, which you will find useful to debug EasyWin programs.

Visual Tools Button

The *Borland C++ Visual Tools* dialog is where you specify the Integrated Development Environment, which will be your "home" for developing C++ programs. Here are the choices in this dialog:

- Integrated Development Environment (IDE)
- Resource Workshop
- Winsight
- Control 3D Look
- Winspector
- Miscellaneous Tools

The only item you need to check here is the first one, for the IDE. However, when you check this box, the *Resource Workshop* box is checked automatically, although you don't need it for EasyWin or DOS programs. You can uncheck everything else.

Libraries Button

The *Borland C++ Libraries* dialog has five check boxes:

- Run-time Libraries
- Object Windows Libraries
- Object Components Libraries
- Class Libraries
- OLE

Each of these check boxes causes another dialog to be called up. (Will these dialogs never end?) You need check only two of them: *Run-time Libraries* and *Class Libraries*. Uncheck everything else.

Next you'll see the *Borland C++ Run-time Libraries* dialog. There are several choices to be made here. In one list you'll see four choices:

- Header Files
- Static Libraries
- Dynamic Libraries
- Graphics (BGI)

You don't need Dynamic Libraries, so uncheck this box. You do need Header Files, Static Libraries and Graphics. You can also chose the memory models you want. The choices are:

- Tiny
- Small

- Compact
- Medium
- Large
- Huge

Most of the programs in this book can be developed using the Small memory model. Programs that use Borland's Class Library, described in Chapter 17, should be written with the Large memory model. You don't need any of the other models, so you can uncheck Tiny, Compact, Medium and Huge. We'll discuss memory models later in this chapter.

In the *Borland C++ Class Libraries* dialog you'll see these choices:

- Static Class Libraries
- Dynamic Class Libraries
- Class Libraries Source
- Obsolete Class Libraries

You only need the first of these: Static Class Libraries. Uncheck the other three.

Borland C++ Examples

The *Borland C++ Examples* dialog allows you to install various kinds of example programs. The choices are:

- Object Windows
- Object Components
- Class Libraries
- Turbo Profiler
- Windows
- DOS
- IDE

You don't need any of these to use this book, but at some point you may find the Class Libraries and the DOS examples interesting, so you can check these if you aren't too tight on hard disk space.

Borland C++ OnLine Help

You can install online help of various kinds, all of which will be accessible from the Help menu in the IDE. Here are the choices:

- BCW and Library Reference
- BC DOS and Library Reference
- ObjectWindows
- Object Components

- Win32 and Windows 3.1 Reference
- Resource Workshop
- Visual Utilities
- Class Library Reference
- Creating Windows
- OpenHelp
- Documentation

You need four of these: the *BCW and Library Reference,* the *BC DOS and Library Reference*, the *Class Library Reference* and *Documentation*. You can uncheck everything else, since it applies to full-scale Windows programming.

Completing the Installation

When you've finished the customization process, the INSTALL program will start the installation process. From now on, if you're loading from floppy disks, you feed in the disks as requested by the prompts. The installation program will take care of figuring out what files you need and loading them onto your hard disk. Many of the disks will not contain any relevant files, but you must nevertheless feed them through in order. If you're loading from CD-ROM, you can walk away and let INSTALL do its job automatically.

Follow any additional instructions from the INSTALL program, and you're done.

Installing Turbo C++

Turbo C++ provides an automated installation procedure similar to Borland C++. In general, you need only follow the prompts and answer the questions. However, as with Borland C++, you can reduce the amount of hard disk space your system requires by making the appropriate choices at the beginning of the installation process.

To begin the installation process, put Disk 1 into the appropriate drive. From the DOS prompt, enter `a:install` (or `b:install` if appropriate).

Full-Scale Installation

A full-scale installation requires about 11 MB of free disk space, which on newer computers is not very much. If you don't mind using this much space, simply follow the instructions provided by the INSTALL program, and feed the diskettes in one after the other, as requested by the prompts.

Custom Installation

If you're using an older computer with a 30 or 40 MB hard disk you may find it worthwhile to customize the installation. You can reduce the amount of hard disk space to somewhat more than 5 MB.

After a few preliminary questions, you'll see a window with the line

```
Options... [IDE CMD LIB CLASS BGI HELP EXMPL]
```

Highlight this line by pressing the arrow keys, and press (ENTER). You'll see a table with various options, most of which are marked Yes. Change this table so it looks like this:

```
IDE & Tools                 Yes
CmdLine Compiler & Tools    No
Install Class Library       Yes
Install BGI Library         Yes
Unpack Examples             Packed
Help Files                  Yes
Memory Models               [ S L ]
```

Highlight the appropriate line with the arrow keys, and press (ENTER) to change the selection. (ESC) takes you back to the previous window.

You do need the IDE; it's the heart of Turbo C++.

You don't need the command-line compiler. It's useful only in specialized situations.

You will need the class library for Chapter 17.

You will need the BGI (Borland Graphics Interface) library for Chapter 11.

You may want to look at the program examples, but you can do this even if they're packed, which takes less room.

Most of the programs in this book can be developed using the Small memory model. (See the discussion of memory models next.) However, the examples in Chapter 17, on Borland's class library, require the Large (or Medium) model. A separate window appears when you press (ENTER) for this line, and you can select each memory model individually. Set `Install Small/Tiny` and `Large` to `Yes`, and change all the other choices to `No` (unless you know you're going to need them for some other project).

When you've set up these options correctly, select `Start Installation`. You'll be asked to insert each diskette in turn.

Memory Models

In the installation procedure for both Borland C++ and Turbo C++ you are asked what memory models you want to use. In this section we review what memory models are and how to choose an appropriate one.

C++ uses library routines to perform such tasks as I/O, graphics, and math operations. You'll need many of these routines for the examples in this book. Unfortunately, each routine comes in five different versions. Why is this? The segmented architecture of the 80x86 microprocessor is the culprit. This segmented architecture is used for all programs created for a 16-bit environment, which includes traditional DOS and Windows environments.

A program consists of code (executable statements) and data. Code or data that fits within a segment, which can be up to 64K bytes long, executes quickly. When code or data exceeds the 64K limit, it must be accessed in a less efficient way, and the program executes more slowly. Depending on the size of the code and data in the program, the developer must select a memory model large enough to accommodate the program, but not unnecessarily large, lest execution speed be reduced.

Table 2-1 summarizes the memory models and the number of 64K segments available with each one.

Memory model	Code segments	Data segments	Segments for one data item
Tiny	(one for both code and data)		one
Small	one	one	one
Medium	many	one	one
Compact	one	many	one
Large	many	many	one
Huge	many	many	many

Table 2-1 Memory Available with Different Memory Models

The Tiny model must squeeze both code and data into a single 64K segment. The Small, Medium, Compact, and Large models offer different combinations of segments. The Huge memory model is similar to the Large model, but allows a single data item (such as an array) to occupy several segments.

A set of library routines is available for each memory model (except for Tiny, which uses the same routines as the Small model). Which library routines you use depends on what memory model you decide to use for your program. For example, if your program requires more data than will fit in one 64K segment, but the code is less than a segment, you'll need to use the Compact memory model, so you'll need the library routines for that model.

When you install Borland C++ or Turbo C++, you can specify which memory models you plan to use, and the installation program will create library files containing the appropriate routines. If you don't specify particular memory models, the routines for all the models will be installed on your hard disk by default. Since the files containing these routines take up considerable disk space, you may not want to choose this default.

Borland C++ Preliminaries

In this section we'll discuss how to prepare Borland C++ for typing in and creating a C++ program. (Turbo C++ Preliminaries follow in the next section.) As we noted earlier, we will focus on the EasyWin format, which is a special kind of DOS program that runs directly under Windows. EasyWin programs are almost identical to real DOS programs, and easier to develop under Borland C++. In the section "Real DOS Programs" at the end of this chapter we'll describe how to create standalone DOS programs.

Starting Borland C++

Borland C++ loads a great many separate programs. You don't need to worry about most of them at this point. However, you may find it useful to access the index to all the Borland documentation by double-clicking on the Master Index icon MINDEX.HLP. Most of the other programs are called up automatically by Borland C++.

Double click on the Borland C++ icon BCW.EXE (or BORLAND C++). A window will appear with the title *Borland C++*. This window provides the IDE (Integrated Development Environment) in which you will create C++ programs. Everything is accessible from it: the editor, the compiler, the linker, a help system, and a debugger. Figure 2-1 shows the initial Borland C++ screen.

Besides the usual menus, Borland C++ uses a speed bar (not shown in the figure), with icons for the most-used menu choices. We'll describe the menu-based approach to the IDE, but as you gain proficiency you may want to experiment with the speed bar as well.

Projects

All program development in Borland C++ is based on *projects*. A project is (roughly speaking) a list of instructions to Borland C++ that specifies how the program will be created. These instructions are stored in a file with the .IDE extension. Using a project for a simple one-file program is optional in Turbo C++ (and older versions of Borland C++) but in the Windows-hosted Borland C++ it's essential. One reason for using the project feature is to tell Borland C++ what target you want for your program: will it be a DOS program or a Windows program?

To start, select *New Project* from the Project menu. This brings up a dialog called *New Project*. There are quite a few decisions to be made in this dialog.

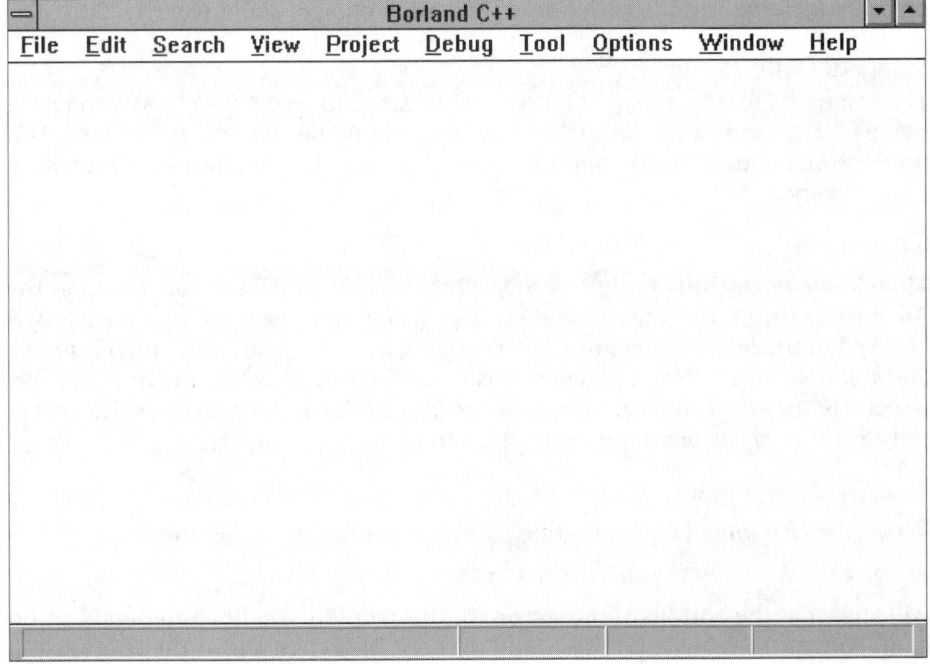

Figure 2-1 Initial Borland C++ Screen

Naming the Project

Type the path and filename of the program you want to create into the field called *Project Path and Name*. The name you use will be given to your program's .EXE file. In this chapter we're going to create a program called FIRST. Its executable file will be FIRST.EXE. Assume it will be placed in a directory called \TCPP\CHAP2\. Since you are specifying a project file, it has the .IDE extension. Assuming you're using the C: drive, you would type

```
c:\tcpp\chap2\first.ide
```

The Target Name window will change automatically to show the program name, FIRST.

The Target Type

Normally the target of the development process is a program or application. However, you can develop several other things with Borland C++ that aren't exactly programs: various kinds of libraries and help files. You can also create an EasyWin program. These choices are listed in the Target Type list box. For the time being we'll concentrate on creating an EasyWin program, so click on *EasyWin*.

Platform and Model

Once you select the EasyWin target type, the Platform list box will now have only one choice: *Windows 3.x (16)*. The *Target Model* (meaning the memory model to be used with this target) will let you choose from *Small*, *Medium*, *Compact* and *Large*. Choose *Small*. (If you followed the installation instructions, this and Large are the only libraries you installed anyway, so the other choices won't work.)

Standard Libraries

The Standard Libraries group of buttons will change to reflect the choices you have made for the target and platform. *Class Library* and *Run-time* will be selected. You don't normally need *Class Library* or *Diagnostic* (which is unchecked) so uncheck *Class Library*.

Initial Nodes

There's one more thing to do before leaving the New Project dialog. Click on the Advanced button. In the *Advanced Options* dialog make sure the *.cpp Node* box is checked in the *Initial Nodes* group. We're going to be programming in C++, not C, and *cpp Node* (not *c Node*) specifies this. You don't need an .RC file or a .DEF file, which are for full-scale Windows programs, so uncheck these boxes. Click on *OK* in the *Advanced Options* dialog and *OK* in the *New Project* dialog.

The Project Window

When the *New Project* dialog is gone, another window with the title

```
Project: c:\tcpp\chap2\first.ide
```

will appear at the bottom of the screen. In this window you'll see an organization chart containing icons for FIRST.EXE and FIRST.CPP. This chart shows the relationship between the various files in your program. The file that is your goal is the executable FIRST.EXE. There's only one file that contributes to that result (at least only one that is displayed here) and that's FIRST.CPP. This is the source file for your program.

You can manipulate the files in the Project window directly by clicking on them with the right (not the left) mouse button. This brings up a menu with various possibilities. For example, you can delete an unwanted node, or add a new one. In general—unless you've made a mistake—you won't need to use this feature.

Directories

Your executable (.EXE) file and various intermediate files will be placed automatically in the directory you specified in the New Project window.

You are now ready to create the source file FIRST.CPP by typing it in. You can also load the source files directly from the disk provided with this book, but at this point it will probably help you to focus on the syntax of C++ if you type the programs in by hand. Skip ahead to the section called Your First Program.

Turbo C++ Preliminaries

Because it can only develop DOS programs, Turbo C++ does not require you to use the project feature. Thus it's easier to get it ready to develop C++ programs.

To start Turbo C++, move to the directory in which you plan to do your C++ program development. It's best if you don't develop programs in the TC directory. You should create a separate directory for C++ development. From this directory, enter `TC` at the DOS prompt:

```
C:\TCPP\CHAP2>tc
```

The IDE screen will appear as shown in Figure 2-2.

It contains a menu bar on top, a status line on the bottom, and an empty Edit window with the title `NONAME00.CPP`. That's it. You're ready to type in a program.

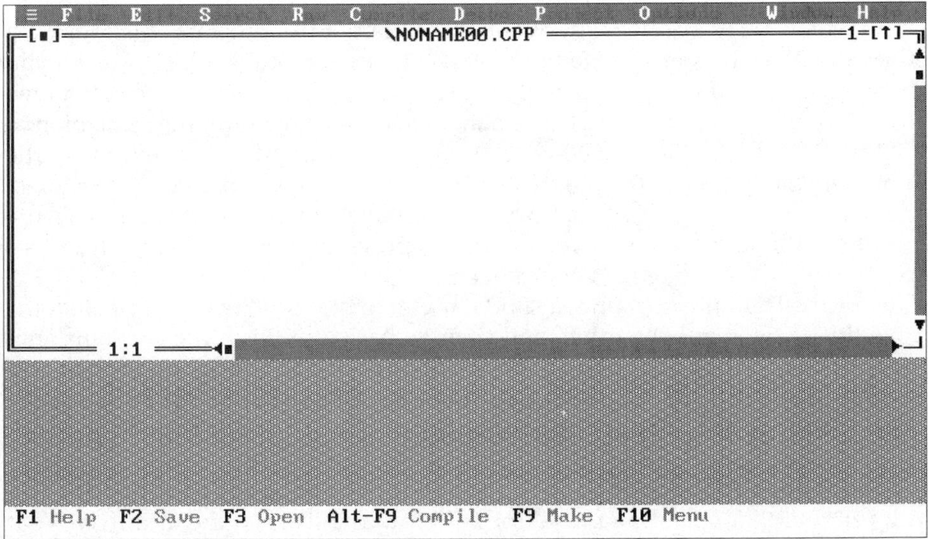

Figure 2-2 The Initial Turbo C++ Screen

Your First Program

This section applies whether you're using Borland C++ or Turbo C++. You should have arrived here after reading the "Preliminaries" section for your particular compiler. In this section we explain how to name, type in, and save the source file for your program. You'll also get your first exposure to an actual C++ program.

Naming Your Program

If you don't already have an Edit window on your screen, select *New* from the File menu to create one. Initially this Edit window should have the title NONAME00.CPP. You need to change this name. You can use the *Save as* selection from the File menu to do this. In the text field in the resulting dialog box, enter the name of your first program's source file, FIRST.CPP. (You can use uppercase or lowercase letters.) The new name will appear at the top of the Edit window.

In Turbo C++ (not Borland C++) the name you type here determines whether you're going to be working with the C compiler or the C++ compiler. Make sure the extension on the filename is .CPP, not .C. This is the only way Turbo C++ knows which compiler to use. In Borland C++ you selected the language in the *Initial Node* box.

Using the Editor

The cursor should now be positioned in the upper-left corner of the Edit window. You can start typing your program. Here it is:

```
#include <iostream.h>
void main()
   {
   cout << "Every age has a language of its own";
   }
```

We won't worry at this point about the syntax of the program. Instead, we'll concentrate on the steps needed to turn it into an executable file. However, you should make sure the program is typed in correctly. Note especially the use of lowercase letters for `main` and `cout`, the paired braces `{` and `}`, and the semicolon at the end of the longest line. Spell `void`, `main`, and `cout` correctly. Don't forget the quotation marks around the phrase `"Every age has a language of its own"` (a quote from the nineteenth-century English travel writer Augustus Hare). Figure 2-3 shows the Borland C++ screen with the program typed in. (The Turbo C++ screen is similar, although it's in character mode.)

Incidentally, some programmers find it useful to type both braces of a pair at the same time, one above the other, and then go back and fill in the program lines between them. This makes it less likely you'll forget the second brace. In this short example it doesn't matter, but when there are many statements between the braces, this approach may save you some grief.

Editor Commands

You will find that operating the editor built into the IDE is quite intuitive. What you type will appear on the screen, and you can use the arrow keys to move the cursor anywhere in the edit window. Pressing the (ENTER) key inserts a new line and

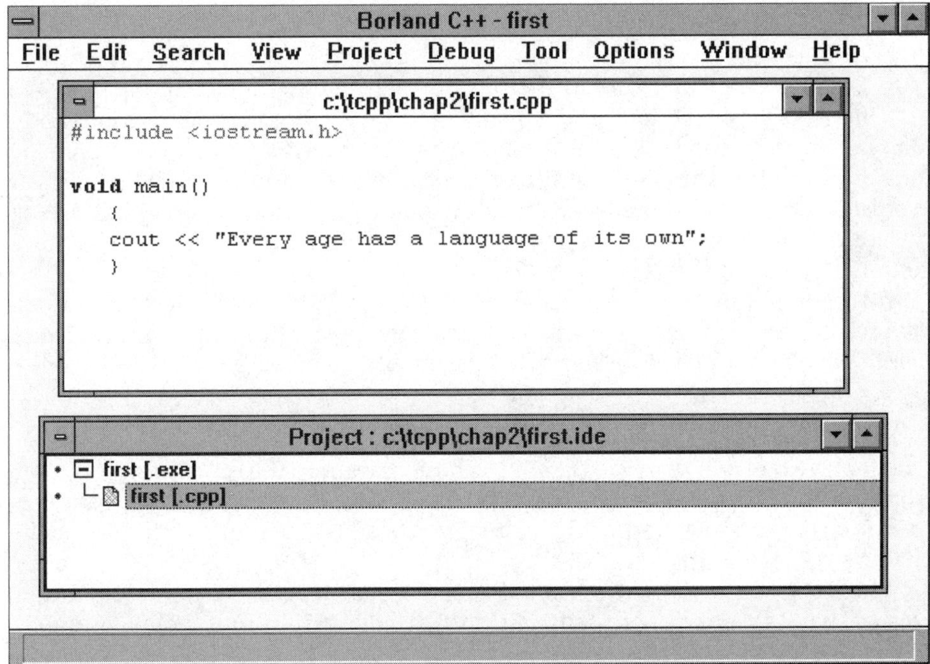

Figure 2-3 The FIRST.CPP File in the Edit Window

drops the cursor to the start of the line. The BACKSPACE key deletes the character to the left of the cursor.

Here is a list of some of the more important cursor commands:

Keyboard key	Action
↑	Cursor up one line
↓	Cursor down one line
←	Cursor left one character
→	Cursor right one character
CTRL-←	Cursor left one word
CTRL-→	Cursor right one word
HOME	Cursor to start of line
END	Cursor to end of line
PGUP	Scroll one screen up
PGDN	Scroll one screen down
ENTER	Insert line, go to next line
BACKSPACE	Delete character to left of cursor
DEL	Delete character under cursor
INS	Toggle insert/write-over

You can select text in the usual way by dragging the mouse pointer across it. The selected text can then be cut or copied to the clipboard, and pasted from the clipboard to a new location (or a new file) using the commands on the Edit menu.

Editor Help

You can use the Help menu to obtain more information about the editor.

In Borland C++, select *Contents* from the Help menu, and then click on—in sequence—*Keyboard, Default,* and *Editor.* You will see a list of keyboard commands. Many of these are derived from the old WordStar control commands, which are formed by holding the CTRL key and pressing one or more other keys. If you know Wordstar, you'll have a head start in using some of the more complex features of the editor. Clicking on *See Also* will show other editor commands such as block commands, and how to search for text.

In Turbo C++, from the Help menu select Contents and then select *Editor Commands.* You can now choose from several categories of editor commands, such as *Block Commands, Cursor Movement Commands,* and so on.

Saving Your Program

Once you've typed in your program, you should save it to the disk by selecting *Save* from the File menu. It's good to do this before compiling and running your program, so that if a bug crashes the system you won't lose your source file (or the changes you made since the last save).

Whenever you save a new version of your program, a backup file is automatically created that contains the previous version. This file is given the .BAK extension.

Compiling and Linking

The program that you type into the Edit window is the *source file.* When it is saved to disk, it is an ASCII file similar to that generated by a word processor. It has the .CPP file extension. If you're not familiar with compiled languages, the process of transforming a source file into an executable program may seem rather mysterious.

Remember that a source file is not an executable program; it is only the instructions on how to create a program. Transforming your source file into an executable program requires two steps.

First, you must *compile* the source file into an object file. The object file, which has an .OBJ extension, contains machine-language instructions that can be executed by the computer. However, these instructions are not complete. A second step, called *linking,* is required. The linking step is necessary because an executable program almost always consists of more than one object file. Linking combines several object files into a single executable program.

Why does a program consist of more than one object file? There are two major reasons. First, the programmer may have divided the program into several source files. Each of these source files is then compiled into a separate object file, and these object files must be linked together. We'll have more to say about multiple-file programs in Chapter 15. For now, our programs will consist of a single source file. Second, the library routines we mentioned earlier come in object-file form and must be combined with the user-written program.

Thus turning your source file into an executable file is a two-step process. First you compile your source file into an object file, and then you link it with the necessary library routines. Figure 2-4 shows the relationship between compiling and linking. Let's see how to use the IDE to compile and link your program.

Compiling

In Borland C++ you can compile whatever source file is in an active edit window (or selected in the Project window) by selecting *Compile* from the Project menu. A window called *Compile Status* will appear. An entry called *Lines* will change as compiling progresses. When the process is finished, the window (if you're a careful typist) will show that `Warnings` and `Errors` are `0`. (We'll talk about compilation errors later in this chapter.)

In Turbo C++, select *Compile* from the Compile menu. A window called *Compiling* will record program lines and errors.

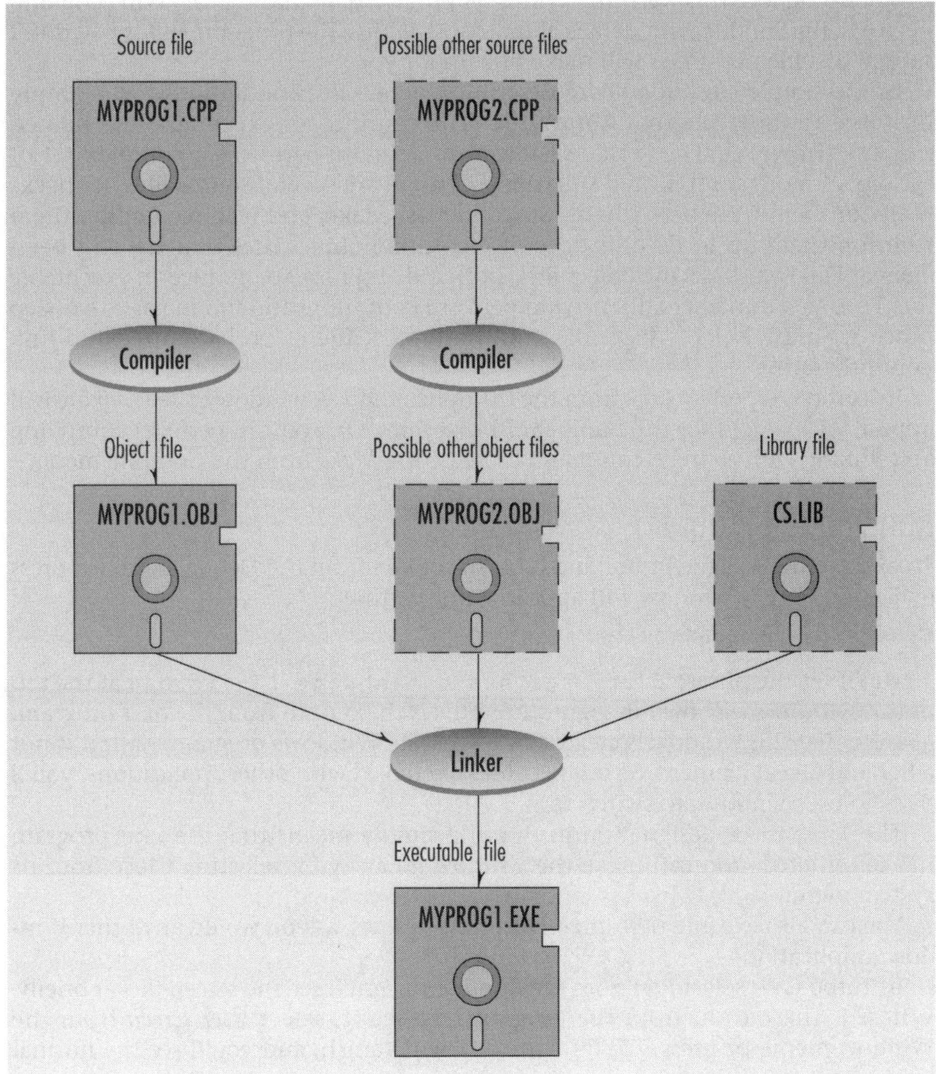

Figure 2-4 Compiling and Linking

As we noted, compilation creates an object file, which has the .OBJ file extension. The object file in our case is FIRST.OBJ.

Linking

To link your object file in Borland C++, select *Make All* from the Project menu. Now the *Compile Status* window (which should really retitle itself the *Link Status* window at this point) shows one warning in the Link column. Clicking on OK will bring up the Message window, with the line

```
Linker Warning: no module definition file specified: using defaults
```

You can ignore this warning. Windows programs, including EasyWin program, need a definition file with details about constructing the program, but if you don't supply this file the linker will make one up for you.

In the simple situation we're describing here, selecting Build All will simply link the FIRST.OBJ file to a library file. The result is an executable file named FIRST.EXE. However, The Make All selection actually performs a complex set of actions in more complicated situations. If there are several source files, it checks if any of them have been altered since the last Make, and if so recompiles them to bring them up to date. It doesn't recompile object files that haven't been altered. Finally it links the object files, both old and new, to produce an executable file. Thus you don't actually need to perform compiling and linking as a two-step process. Simply select Make All from the Project file to both compile and link your program.

In Turbo C++, select *Link* from the Compile menu. A window called *Linking* will appear, with a field for the number of link errors. Or, you can perform compiling and linking with a single command by selecting *Make* from the Compile menu.

Running the Program

To execute the .EXE file in Borland C++, select *Run* from the Debug menu (or press CTRL-F9). A new window will appear, with the title

```
[Inactive C:\TCPP\CHAP2\FIRST.EXE]
```

You'll see the phrase `Every age has a language of its own` at the top of this window, as shown in Figure 2-5. This is the output from the FIRST program.

Note that this window is created by a separate Windows program, FIRST; it is not a Borland C++ document. So if it becomes overlayed with other applications, you'll need to use Windows to switch to it.

The `Inactive` designation in the title simply means that the FIRST program has terminated. You can make the window go away by selecting Close from its system menu.

You can also execute FIRST directly from Windows, as you would any other Windows application.

In Turbo C++, select *Run* from the Run menu. You'll see the screen flicker briefly. Where is the output from the program? To see it, select *User screen* from the Window menu, or press ALT-F5. The IDE will vanish, and you'll see the normal DOS screen, with the following display:

```
C:\TCPP\CHAP2>tc
Every age has a language of its own
```

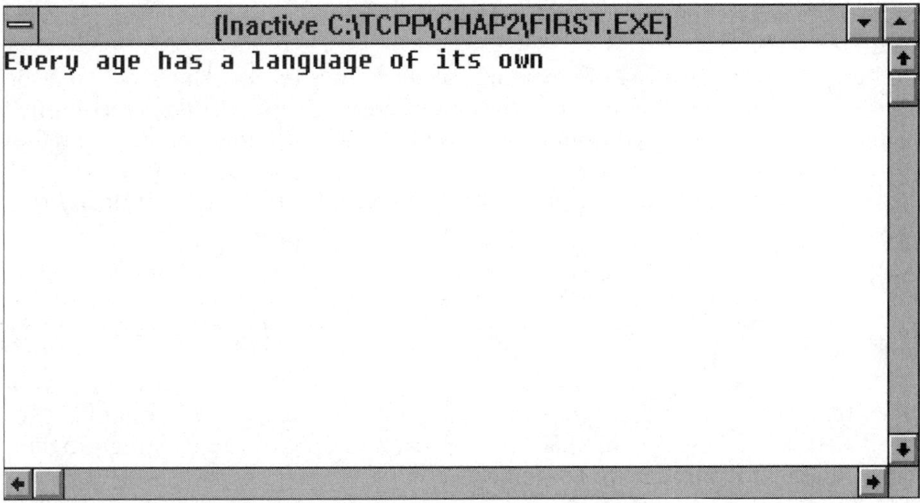

Figure 2-5 Output Window for the FIRST Program in Borland C++

As you can see, the program has displayed the phrase in quotation marks on the output screen. To return to the IDE, press any key.

Exiting from the IDE

To exit from the IDE, select *Exit* (or *Quit* in Turbo C++) from the File menu. If you haven't saved the latest revision to your program, and you try to exit, Borland C++ or Turbo C++ will give you a chance to correct your mistake.

Files

Borland C++ generates quite a few files during the build process. You can see what these files are using the File Manager. Here's a brief description of what they do.

- FIRST.CPP is the source file you typed in.
- FIRST.BAK is the previous version of the source file (if any).
- FIRST.OBJ is the object file created by the compiler.
- FIRST.EXE is the executable file created by the linker from the object files and library files.
- FIRST.IDE records the relationship of the files used in a project, and the target type.
- FIRST.~DE is a backup of the .IDE file.
- FIRST.CSM records information about precompiled header files.
- FIRST.DSW records desktop information for the IDE, such as what windows are open.

If you've saved your source file more than once there will be a file called FIRST.BAK. When a file already exists with the same name as the source file you are saving, it is renamed with the .BAK extension before the current file is saved. Sooner or later, a time will come when your .CPP file is mistakenly erased, and you will be glad this feature exists.

The purpose of the .CSM file may appear quite mysterious. The IOSTREAM.H file referred to in the first line of FIRST.CPP is an example of a *header file*. Precompiled header files speed up the compilation process. We'll learn more about header files as we go along.

Turbo C++, being a simpler product, generates only the first four of the files shown.

Opening an Existing Project or File

Once a program has been written and saved to disk, you can open it again to make additional changes.

Borland C++ always thinks in terms of projects. Turbo C++ thinks in terms of files. (Turbo C++ can use projects too, but they aren't necessary for simple programs with a single source file.) So the approach to opening an existing program is a little different for the two compilers.

In Borland C++ you can open a previously-saved project by selecting *Open Project* from the Project menu and double-clicking on the appropriate IDE file. Note that opening the source file is a separate operation. If it was open when you closed the project, it will be opened automatically and installed in an edit window when you open the project. Otherwise, you'll need to select *Open* from the File menu and double-click on the appropriate .CPP file in the box.

In Turbo C++ there are two ways to open a file. If you're invoking Turbo C++ from the DOS prompt, you can simply add the name of the .CPP source file on the command line, as in

```
C:\TCPP\CHAP2>tc first.cpp
```

Don't forget the .CPP extension. When Turbo C++ executes, it will open an Edit window containing this file.

If you have already started Turbo C++ and you want to open a file, select *Open* from the File menu and double-click on the desired .CPP file name. An Edit window containing the file will appear. Now you can edit the source file, and compile, link, and execute the program as before.

Note that, in both Borland C++ and Turbo C++, several Edit windows can be open on the IDE screen at the same time. You can move them around and resize them so that you can see parts of two files at the same time. You can also cut and paste text between two Edit windows. See the Help menu for details on these features.

To make an Edit window disappear from the screen in Borland C++, choose *Close* from its system menu. In Turbo C++, click on the square in the window's upper-left corner or press ALT-F3. In Turbo C++ you will probably want to close any open Edit windows before quitting. The IDE remembers which windows were open when you quit, and opens them when you restart it. If you don't close files before quitting, you may find an excessive number of open windows accumulating on the screen.

Errors

No one writes error-free computer programs every time (or even most of the time). It may be that you were unclear on the syntax of a particular statement, or that you made a typing error. Such errors can be discovered by the compiler or by the linker, or by various run-time routines that the compiler builds into your program automatically.

Of course there are also conceptual errors that the system can't identify. You can't detect them until you run the program and realize that it isn't doing what you expected.

Compiler Errors

Suppose you have forgotten to type the semicolon at the end of the statement in FIRST.CPP. The result will be that, when you compile the file, the Compile Status window in Borland C++ or the Compiling window in Turbo C++, instead of displaying the *Success* message, will show a positive number—in this case, 2—in the Errors field.

Click OK in the Edit Status window. A Message window will appear at the bottom of the screen. It will contain the following lines:

```
Error FIRST.CPP 6: Statement missing ; in function main()
Error FIRST.CPP 6: Compound statement missing } in function main()
```

Often one typing mistake will lead the compiler to issue several error messages, as happens here. It sees that the semicolon is missing, and this leads it to believe that a closing brace is missing as well.

In the Edit window, the program line with the closing brace is highlighted, and the brace itself is highlighted in a different color. This indicates the place where the compiler found the error. When it got to the brace, it realized that there should have been a semicolon earlier, so it signaled the errors at that point. The Borland C++ screen will now resemble the one in Figure 2-6.

If you correct the error, your next attempt should compile correctly.

Linker Errors

Errors can also appear during the linking process. For instance, suppose you spell the word `main` as `Main`. (Remember that C++ is case-sensitive.) The program will compile correctly, but when you build or link it, the Compile Status (or Linker) window will show a link error. Now the Message window will display a line something like:

```
Linker Error: Undefined symbol _main
```

The linker must find a function called *main*; without this, it cannot create an executable file. The linker does not highlight the offending line in the source file, so you may sometimes have difficulty in tracking down such errors. However, in this case the problem should be obvious.

Run-time Errors

A comparatively small number of errors do not reveal themselves until the program executes. These errors include division by 0, stack overflow, and the dreaded *null pointer assignment*. We'll have more to say about run-time errors later on.

Conceptual Errors

It's too soon at this point to dwell on the complexities of debugging. After all, you

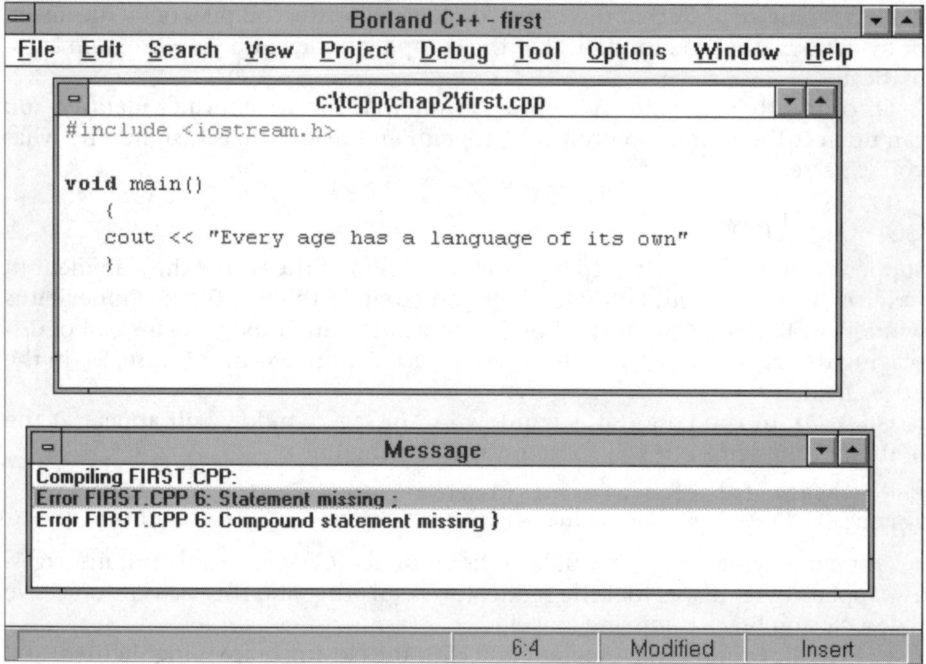

Figure 2-6 Error in FIRST

need to know how to write a program before you have any bugs to find. However, at some point in your study of C++ you'll want to know something about debugging. Accordingly, in Appendix F we've included a short explanation of how to use the Borland C++ and Turbo C++ debuggers.

DOS Programs in Borland C++

The process we described above for Borland C++ develops an EasyWin .EXE file; a DOS program that runs only in Windows. If you try to run it directly under DOS, you'll receive the message `This program must be run under Microsoft Windows.`

EasyWin works fine for most of the programs in this book, and you don't need to worry about anything else yet. However, at some point in the future you will need to create real DOS programs. This is necessary if you want to run program on DOS computers that don't have Windows, or if you plan to use Borland graphics (BGI) functions (as we do in Chapter 11), or if you use certain DOS-only library functions (as we do in the HORSE program of Chapter 13 and a few other places). Here's how to change the development process to produce stand-alone DOS programs. We'll use the FIRST program as our example. (This section doesn't apply to Turbo C++.)

Creating a DOS Executable

You may first want to make sure that the EasyWin version of your program compiles, links and runs correctly, if that's possible, since debugging is easier for

EasyWin programs. Then activate the Project window (not the menu). Using the right mouse button, click on the uppermost node, `first[.exe.]`, shown in this window.

Select *TargetExpert* from this menu. A dialog with this name will appear. It is similar to the *New Project* dialog you called up originally from the Project menu. However, TargetExpert allows you to change an existing project. You'll see that the previous *Target Type* is shown: *EasyWin*. Click on *Application* instead. Select *DOS (Standard)* from the *Platform* list, and *Small* from the *Target Model* list. In the Standard Libraries group, *Run-time* and *Emulation* should be checked. (Emulation works whether your microprocessor has a floating point processor or not. If you're sure your program will always run a computer with floating point, you could choose *Floating Point* for a small improvement in .EXE file size.) Make sure the boxes marked *Class Library BGI*, and *Alternate Startup* are not checked. You don't need BGI (unless you're using graphics functions, as in Chapter 11), or the Class Library (unless you're using the Borland library classes, as in Chapter 17).

Click on *OK*. The program will be automatically rebuilt for the new target type, in this case DOS. The .EXE file will now be a pure DOS program.

Running a DOS Executable

To run the DOS version of your program on a Windows machine you can execute it using the DOS box (activated from the *MS-DOS Prompt* icon) within Windows. Either way, you will see the program's output on the character-based DOS screen:

```
C:\TCPP\CHAP2>first
Every age has a language of its own.
C:\TCPP\CHAP2>
```

This new version of the .EXE file is portable to any DOS-only computer.

It's possible to run a DOS program directly from Borland C++, by selecting Run from the Debug menu. However, at least in FIRST and other simple programs, the output window won't stay on the screen long enough to see the results. As soon as the program terminates, the character-mode output window vanishes and the screen reverts back to graphics mode. (There are ways to keep the DOS output window on the screen, such as inserting statements that pause the program until you press a key, or using the `delay()` function, but we're not ready for these complexities yet.)

Summary

You've learned a few details about how to install Borland C++ or Turbo C++. You've also learned how to start up your system, type in the text of your source file, compile the source file into an object file, and link the object file into an executable file. You now know how to execute your program, how to view the results on the output screen, and how to deal with errors detected by the compiler or linker. In the next chapter we'll begin our exploration of C++ itself.

3

C++ Programming Basics

C++ PROGRAM STRUCTURE

VARIABLES

INPUT/OUTPUT WITH `cout` AND `cin`

ARITHMETIC OPERATORS

ASSIGNMENT AND INCREMENT OPERATORS

3

In any language there are some fundamentals you need to know before you can write even the most elementary programs. This chapter introduces three such fundamentals: basic program construction, variables, and input/output (I/O). It also touches on a variety of other language features, including comments, arithmetic operators, the increment operator, data conversion, and library functions.

Most of these topics are not conceptually difficult, but you may find that the style in C++ is a little austere compared with, say, BASIC or Pascal. Before you learn what it's all about, a C++ program may remind you more of a mathematics formula than a computer program. Don't worry about this. You'll find that as you gain familiarity with C++, it starts to look less forbidding, while other languages begin to seem unnecessarily fancy and verbose.

Basic Program Construction

Let's look more closely at the FIRST program introduced in Chapter 2. Here it is again:

```
#include <iostream.h>

void main()
   {
   cout << "Every age has a language of its own";
   }
```

Despite its small size, this program demonstrates a great deal about the construction of C++ programs. Let's examine it in detail.

Functions

Functions are one of the fundamental building blocks of C++. The FIRST program consists almost entirely of a single function called `main()`. The only part of this program that is not part of the function is the first line—the one that starts with `#include`. (We'll see what this line does in a moment.)

We noted in Chapter 1 that a function can be part of a class, in which case it is called a *member* function. However, functions can also exist independent of classes. We are not yet ready to talk about classes, so we will show functions that are separate stand-alone entities, as `main()` is here.

Function Name

The parentheses following the word `main` are the distinguishing feature of a function. Without the parentheses the compiler would think that `main` refers to a variable or to some other program element. When we discuss functions in the text, we'll follow the same convention that C++ uses: We'll put parentheses following the function name. Later on we'll see that the parentheses aren't always empty. They're used to hold function *arguments*: values passed from the calling program to the function.

The word `void` preceding the function name indicates that this particular function does not have a return value. Don't worry about this now; we'll learn about return values and type `void` in Chapter 6.

Braces and the Function Body

The *body* of a function is surrounded by braces (sometimes called *curly brackets*). These braces play the same role as the **BEGIN** and **END** keywords in Pascal: They surround or *delimit* a block of program statements. Every function must use this pair of braces. In this example there is only one statement within the braces: the line starting with `cout`. However, a function body can consist of many statements.

Always Start with `main()`

When you run a C++ program, the first statement executed will be at the beginning of a function called `main()`. The program may consist of many functions, classes, and other program elements, but on startup, control always goes to `main()`. If there is no function called `main()` in your program, the linker will signal an error.

In most C++ programs, as we'll see later, `main()` calls member functions in various objects to carry out the program's real work. The `main()` function may also contain calls to other stand-alone functions. This is shown in Figure 3-1.

Program Statements

The program *statement* is the fundamental unit of C++ programming. There's only one statement in the FIRST program: the line

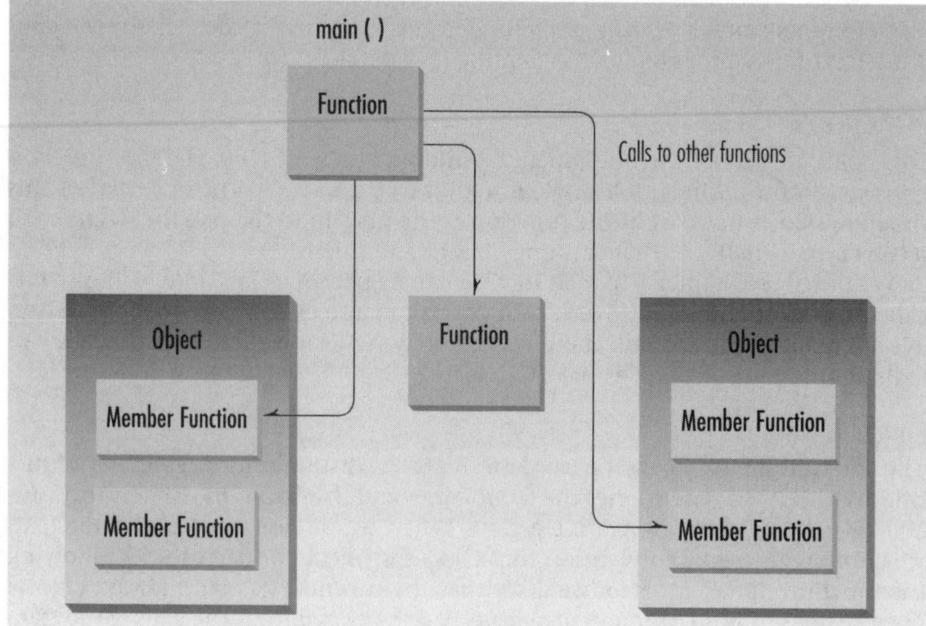

Figure 3-1 Objects, Functions, and `main ()`

```
cout << "Every age has a language of its own";
```

This statement tells the computer to display the quoted phrase. Most statements tell the computer to do something. In this respect, statements in C++ are similar to statements in other languages. In fact, as we've noted, the majority of statements in C++ are identical to statements in C.

A semicolon signals the end of the statement. This is a crucial part of the syntax but easy to forget. In some languages (like BASIC), the end of a statement is signaled by the end of the line, but that's not true in C++. If you leave out the semicolon, the compiler will signal an error.

Whitespace

Actually, the C++ compiler ignores whitespace almost completely. *Whitespace* is defined as spaces, carriage returns, linefeeds, tabs, vertical tabs, and formfeeds. These characters are invisible to the compiler. You can put several statements on one line, separated by any number of spaces or tabs, or you can run a statement over two or more lines. It's all the same to the compiler. Thus the FIRST program could be written this way:

```
#include <iostream.h>

void main () { cout
<<
"Every age has a language of its own"
; }
```

We don't recommend this syntax—it's nonstandard and hard to read—but it does compile correctly.

There are actually several exceptions to the rule that whitespace is invisible to the compiler. The first line of the program, starting with `#include`, is a *preprocessor directive*, which must be written on one line. Also, string constants, such as `"Every age has a language of its own"` cannot be broken into separate lines. (If you need a long string constant, you can insert a backslash (\) at the line break, or divide the string into two separate strings, each surrounded by quotes.)

Output Using `cout`

As you have seen, the statement

```
cout << "Every age has a language of its own";
```

causes the phrase in quotation marks to be displayed on the screen. How does this work? A complete description of this statement requires an understanding of objects, operator overloading, and other topics we won't discuss until later in the book, but here's a brief preview.

The identifier `cout` (pronounced "C out") is actually an *object*. It is predefined in C++ to correspond to the *standard output stream*. A *stream* is an abstraction that refers to a flow of data. The standard output stream normally flows to the screen display—although it can be redirected to other output devices. We'll discuss streams (and redirection) in Chapter 14.

The operator `<<` is called the *insertion* or *put to* operator. It directs the contents of the variable on its right to the object on its left. In FIRST it directs the string constant "`Every age has a language of its own`" to `cout`, which sends it to the display.

(If you know C, you'll recognize `<<` as the *left-shift* bit-wise operator and wonder how it can also be used to direct output. In C++, operators can be *overloaded*. That is, they can perform different activities, depending on the context. We'll learn about overloading in Chapter 9.)

Although the concepts behind the use of `cout` and `<<` may be obscure at this point, using them is easy. They'll appear in almost every example program. Figure 3-2 shows the result of using `cout` and the insertion operator `<<`.

String Constants

The phrase in quotation marks, `"Every age has a language of its own"`, is an example of a *string constant*. As you probably know, a constant, unlike a variable, cannot be given new values as the program runs. Its value is set when the program is written, and it retains this value throughout the program's existence.

As we'll see later, C++ (like C) takes a rather ambivalent attitude toward strings. On the one hand there is no real string variable type; instead you use an array of type `char` to hold string variables. On the other hand C++ recognizes string constants, surrounded by quotation marks as shown. We'll learn more about strings in Chapter 8.

Preprocessor Directives

The first line of the FIRST program,

```
#include <iostream.h>
```

might look like a program statement, but it's not. It isn't part of a function body and doesn't end with a semicolon, as program statements must. Instead, it starts with a number sign (`#`). It's called a *preprocessor directive*. Recall that program statements are instructions to the computer. A preprocessor directive, on the other hand, is an instruction to the compiler itself. A part of the compiler called the *preprocessor* deals with these directives before it begins the real compilation process.

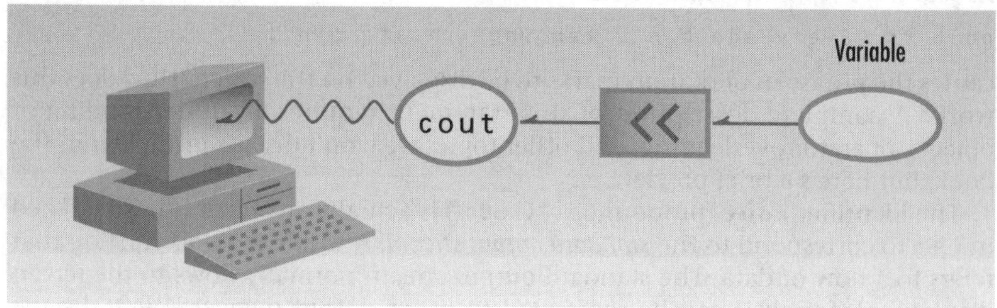

Figure 3-2 Output with `cout`

The #include Directive

The preprocessor directive #include tells the compiler to insert another file into your source file. In effect, the #include directive is replaced by the contents of the file indicated. Using an #include directive to insert another file into your source file is similar to pasting a block of text into a document with your word processor.

Header Files

In the FIRST example, the preprocessor directive #include tells the compiler to add the source file IOSTREAM.H to the FIRST.CPP source file before compiling. Why do this? IOSTREAM.H is an example of a *header file* (sometimes called an *include file*). It contains declarations that are needed by the cout identifier and the << operator. Without these declarations, the compiler won't recognize cout and will think << is being used incorrectly. (In C, header files are often optional; in C++ they're always necessary.)

If you want to see what's in IOSTREAM.H, you can go to the \bc4\include directory (tc\include in Turbo C++) and use the DOS TYPE command (or the IDE editor) to examine the file. The contents won't make much sense at this point, but you will at least prove to yourself that IOSTREAM.H is a source file, written in normal ASCII characters.

We'll return to the topic of header files at the end of this chapter, when we introduce library functions.

#include is only one of many preprocessor directives, all of which can be identified by the initial # sign. The use of preprocessor directives is not as common in C++ as it is in C, but we'll look at a few additional examples as we go along.

Comments

Comments are an important part of any program. They help the person writing a program, and anyone else who must read the source file, understand what's going on. The compiler ignores comments, so they do not add to the file size or execution time of the executable program.

Comment Syntax

Let's rewrite our FIRST program, incorporating comments into our source file:

```
// comments.cpp
// demonstrates comments
#include <iostream.h>             // preprocessor directive

void main()                       // function name
   {                              // start function body
   cout << "Every age has a language of its own";  // statement
   }                              // end function body
```

Comments start with a double slash symbol (//) and terminate at the end of the line. (This is one of the exceptions to the rule that the compiler ignores whitespace.)

A comment can start at the beginning of the line or on the same line following a program statement. Both possibilities are shown in the COMMENTS example.

When to Use Comments

Comments are almost always a good thing. Most programmers don't use enough of them. If you're tempted to leave out comments, remember that not everyone is as smart as you; they may need more explanation than you do about what your program is doing. Also, you may not be as smart next month, when you've forgotten key details of your program's operation, as you are today.

Use comments to explain to the person looking at the listing what you're trying to do. The details are in the program statements themselves, so the comments should concentrate on the big picture, clarifying your reasons for using a certain statement.

Alternative Comment Syntax

There's a second comment style available in C++:

```
/* this is an old-style comment */
```

This type of comment (the only comment available in C) begins with the `/*` character pair and ends with `*/` (*not* with the end of the line). These symbols are harder to type (since `/` is lowercase while `*` is uppercase) and take up more space on the line, so this style is not generally used in C++. However, it has advantages in special situations. You can write a multiline comment with only two comment symbols:

```
/* this
is a
potentially
very long
multiline
comment
*/
```

This is a good approach to making a comment out of a large text passage, since it saves inserting the `//` symbol on every line.

You can also insert a `/* */` comment anywhere within the text of a program line:

```
func1()
   {  /* empty function body */  }
```

If you attempt to use the `//` style comment in this case, the closing brace won't be visible to the compiler—since a `//` style comment runs to the end of the line—and the code won't compile correctly.

Integer Variables

Variables are the most fundamental part of any language. A variable is a symbolic name that can be given a variety of values. Variables are stored in particular places in the computer's memory. When a variable is given a value, that value is actually placed in the memory space occupied by the variable. Most popular languages use the same general variable types, such as integers, floating-point numbers, and characters, so you are probably already familiar with the ideas behind them.

Integer variables represent integer numbers like 1; 30,000; and –27. Such numbers are used for counting discrete numbers of objects. Unlike floating-point numbers, integers have no fractional part; you can express the idea of *four* using integers, but not *four and one-half.*

Defining Integer Variables

Integer variables exist in several sizes, but the most commonly used is type `int`. This type requires 2 bytes of storage (in MS-DOS computers) and holds numbers in the range –32,768 to 32,767. Figure 3-3 shows an integer variable in memory.

While type `int` occupies 2 bytes in MS-DOS computers, it may occupy 4 bytes on some other systems.

Here's a program that defines and uses several variables of type `int`:

```
// intvars.cpp
// demonstrates integer variables
#include <iostream.h>

void main()
   {
   int var1;                 // define var1
   int var2;                 // define var2

   var1 = 20;                // assign value to var1
   var2 = var1 + 10;         // assign value to var2
   cout << "var1+10 is ";    // output text
   cout << var2;             // output value of var2
   }
```

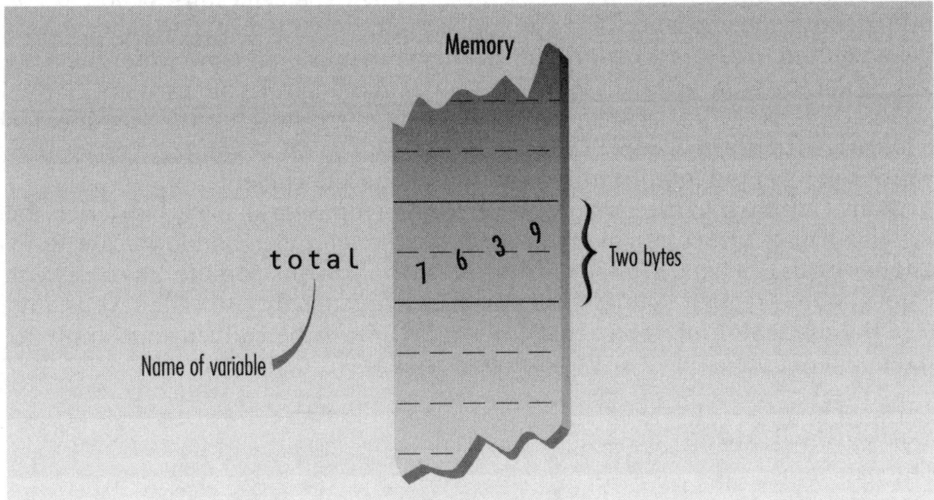

Figure 3-3 Variable of Type `int` in Memory

Type this program into the IDE, compile and link it, and then run it. Examine the output window. The statements

```
int var1;
int var2;
```

define two integer variables, `var1` and `var2`. The keyword `int` signals the type of variable. These statements, which are called *definitions*, must terminate with a semicolon, like other program statements.

You must define a variable before using it. However, you can place variable definitions anywhere in a program. It's not necessary to define variables before the first executable statement (as you must do in C).

Declarations and Definitions

Let's digress for a moment to note a subtle distinction between the terms *definition* and *declaration* as applied to variables.

A *declaration* introduces a variable's name (such as `var1`) into a program and specifies its type. If a declaration also sets aside memory for the variable, it is called a *definition*. The statements

```
int var1;
int var2;
```

in the INTVARS program are definitions because they set aside memory for `var1` and `var2`. We'll be concerned mostly with declarations that are also definitions; but in Chapter 15, when we discuss multifile programs, we'll see examples of declarations that are not definitions.

Variable Names

The program INTVARS uses variables named `var1` and `var2`. What are the rules for naming variables? You can use upper- and lowercase letters, and the digits from 1 to 9. You can also use the underscore (_). The first character must be a letter or underscore. Names can be as long as you like, but only the first 32 characters will be recognized. The compiler distinguishes between upper- and lowercase letters, so `Var` is not the same as `var` or `VAR`. (These same naming rules are used in C.)

You can't use a C++ *keyword* as a variable name. A keyword is the identifier for a language feature, like `int`, `class`, `if`, `while`, and so on. A complete list of keywords can be found in Appendix B and in Borland's documentation.

Many C++ programmers follow the convention of using all lowercase letters for variable names. Other programmers use a mixture of upper- and lowercase, as in `IntVar` or `dataCount`. Whichever approach you use, it's good to be consistent throughout a program. Names in all uppercase are generally reserved for constants (see the discussion of `const` that follows). These same conventions apply to naming other program elements such as classes and functions.

Assignment Statements

The statements

```
var1 = 20;
var2 = var1 + 10;
```

assign values to the two variables. The equal sign =, as you might guess, causes the value on the right to be assigned to the variable on the left. The = in C++ is equivalent to the := in Pascal or the = in BASIC. In the first line shown here, `var1`, which previously had no value, is given the value 20.

Integer Constants

The number 20 is an *integer constant*. Constants don't change during the course of the program. An integer constant consists of numerical digits. There can be no decimal point in an integer constant, and it must lie within the range of integers.

In the second program line shown here, the plus sign (+) adds the value of `var1` and 10, in which 10 is another constant. The result of this addition is then assigned to `var2`.

Output Variations

The statement

```
cout << "var1+10 is ";
```

displays a string constant, as we've seen before. The next statement,

```
cout << var2;
```

displays the value of the variable `var2`. As you can see in your output window, the output of the program is

```
var1+10 is 30
```

Note that `cout` and the `<<` operator know how to treat an integer and a string differently. If we send them a string, they print it as text. If we send them an integer, they print it as a number. This may seem obvious, but it is another example of operator overloading, a key feature of C++. (C programmers will remember that such functions as `printf()` need to be told not only the *variable* to be displayed, but the *type* of the variable as well, which makes the syntax far less intuitive.)

As you can see, the output of the two `cout` statements appears on the same line on the output screen. In fact, if you run the program again, you'll see that the new output continues to appear on the same line:

```
var1+10 is 30var1+10 is 30
```

No linefeed is inserted automatically. If you want to start on a new line, you must do it yourself. We'll see how in a moment.

Character Variables

We've seen one kind of integer variable, type `int`. Another integer variable is type `char`. This type stores integers that range in value from –128 to 127. Variables of this type occupy only 1 byte of memory. Character variables are sometimes used to store numbers that confine themselves to this limited range, but they are more commonly used to store ASCII characters.

As you probably know, the ASCII character set is a way of representing characters such as `'a'`, `'B'`, `'$'`, `'3'`, and so on, as numbers. These numbers range from 0 to 127. (Most MS-DOS computers extend this range to 255 to accommodate various foreign-language and graphics characters.) Appendix A shows the ASCII character set.

Character Constants

Character constants use single quotation marks around a character, as shown in the previous paragraph. (Note that this differs from string constants, which use double quotation marks.) When the C++ compiler encounters such a character constant, it translates it into the corresponding ASCII code and stores that number in the program. The constant `'a'` appearing in a program, for example, will be stored as 97, as shown in Figure 3-4.

Character variables can be assigned character constants as values. The following program shows some examples of character constants and variables.

```
// charvars.cpp
// demonstrates character variables

#include <iostream.h>         // for cout, etc.

void main()
   {
   char charvar1 = 'A';       // define char variable as character
   char charvar2 = '\t';      // define char variable as tab

   cout << charvar1;          // display character
   cout << charvar2;          // display character
   charvar1 = 'B';            // set char variable to char constant
   cout << charvar1;          // display character
   cout << '\n';               // display newline character
   }
```

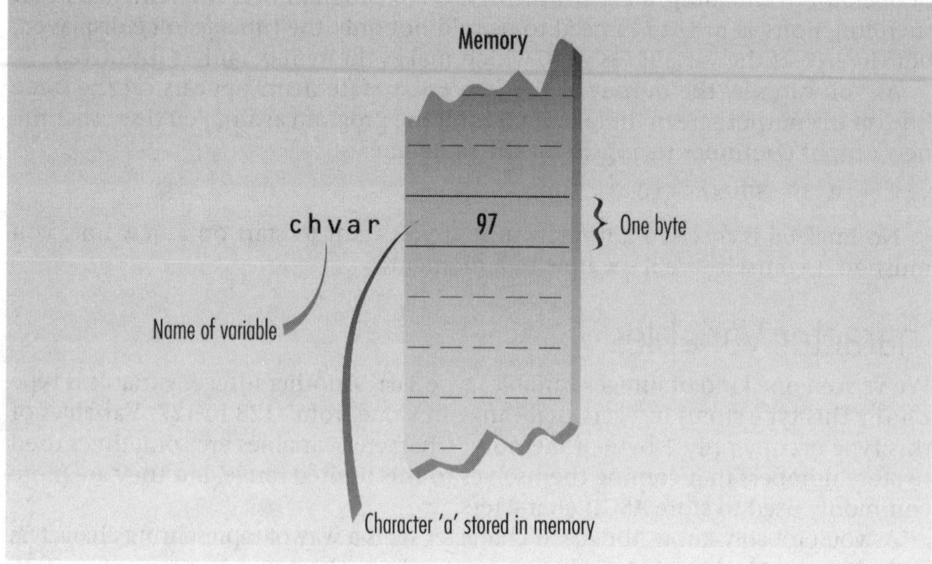

Figure 3-4 Variable of Type `char` in Memory

Initialization

Variables can be initialized at the same time they are defined. In this program two variables of type `char`—`charvar1` and `charvar2`—are initialized to the character constants `'A'` and `'\t'`.

Escape Sequences

This second character constant, `'\t'`, is an odd one. It is called an *escape sequence*, since the backslash causes an "escape" from the normal way characters are interpreted. In this case the `t` is interpreted not as the character 't' but as the tab character. A tab causes printing to continue at the next tab stop. Tab stops are positioned every eight spaces.

Another character constant, `'\n'`, is sent directly to `cout` in the last line of the program. This is the escape sequence for the *newline* character. This character causes both a carriage return and linefeed, so that the next character to be printed appears at the beginning of the next line down. This is by far the most frequently used escape sequence.

Escape sequences can be used in both character and string constants. Table 3-1 shows a list of common escape sequences.

Since the backslash, the single quotation marks, and the double quotation marks all have specialized meanings when used in constants, they must be represented by escape sequences. Here's an example of a quoted phrase in a string constant:

```
cout << "\"Run, Spot, run,\" she said.";
```

Sometimes you need to represent a character constant that doesn't appear on the keyboard, such as the graphics characters above ASCII code 127. To do this, you

Escape sequence	Character
\a	Bell (beep)
\b	Backspace
\f	Formfeed
\n	Newline
\r	Return
\t	Tab
\\	Backslash
\'	Single quotation mark
\"	Double quotation marks
\xdd	Hexadecimal representation

Table 3-1 Common Escape Sequences

can use the '\xdd' representation, where each d stands for a hexadecimal digit. If you want to print a solid rectangle, for example, you'll find such a character listed as decimal number 178, which is hexadecimal number B2 in the ASCII table. This character would be represented by the character constant '\xB2'. We'll see some examples of this later.

The CHARVARS program prints the value of charvar1 ('A') and the value of charvar2 (a tab). It then sets charvar1 to a new value ('B'), prints that, and finally prints the newline. The output looks like this:

```
A       B
```

Input with cin

Now that we've seen some variable types in use, let's see how a program accomplishes input. The next example program asks the user for a temperature in degrees Fahrenheit, converts it to Celsius, and displays the result.

```
// fahren.cpp
// demonstrates cin, newline
#include <iostream.h>

void main()
   {
   int ftemp;

   cout << "Enter temperature in fahrenheit: ";
   cin >> ftemp;
   int ctemp = (ftemp-32) * 5 / 9;
   cout << "Equivalent in Celsius is:  " << ctemp << '\n';
   }
```

The statement

```
cin >> ftemp;
```

causes the program to wait for the user to type in a number. The resulting number is placed in the variable ftemp. The keyword cin (pronounced "C in") is an object, predefined in C++ to correspond to the standard input stream. This stream represents data coming from the keyboard (unless it has been redirected). The >> is the *extraction* or *get from* operator. It takes the value from the stream object on its left and places it in the variable on its right.

Here's some sample interaction with the program:

```
Enter temperature in fahrenheit: 212
Equivalent in Celsius is: 100
```

Figure 3-5 shows input using cin and the extraction operator >>. (Incidentally, don't enter a number with leading zeros, like 032, or cin will interpret it as an octal number.)

Variables Defined at Point of Use

The FAHREN program has several new wrinkles besides its input capability. Look closely at the listing. Where is the variable ctemp defined? Not at the beginning of the program, but in the next-to-the-last line, where it's used to store the result

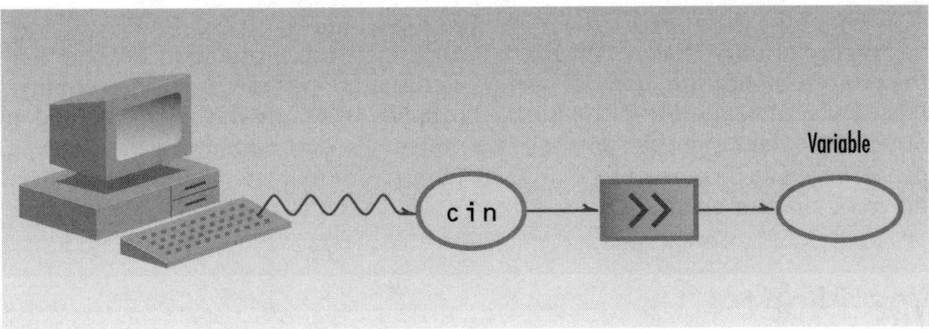

Figure 3-5 Input with `cin`

of the arithmetic operation. As we noted earlier, you can define variables throughout a program, not just at the beginning. (Many languages, including C, require all variables to be defined before the first executable statement.)

Defining variables where they are used can make the listing easier to understand, since you don't need to refer repeatedly to the start of the listing to find the variable definitions. However, the practice should be used with discretion. Variables that are used in many places in a function are probably better defined at the start of the function.

Cascading <<

The insertion operator `<<` is used repeatedly in the second `cout` statement in FAHREN. This is perfectly legal. The program first sends the phrase *Equivalent in celsius is:* to `cout`, then it sends the value of `ctemp`, and finally the newline character `'\n'`.

The extraction operator `>>` can be cascaded with `cin` in the same way, allowing the user to enter a series of values. However, this capability is not used so often, since it eliminates the opportunity to prompt the user between inputs.

Expressions

Any arrangement of variables and operators that specifies a computation is called an *expression*. Thus, `alpha+12` and `(alpha-37)*beta/2` are expressions. When the computations specified in the expression are performed, the result is usually a value. Thus if `alpha` is 7, the first expression shown has the value 19.

Parts of expressions may also be expressions. In the second example, `alpha-37` and `beta/2` are expressions. Even single variables and constants, like `alpha` and `37`, are considered to be expressions.

Note that expressions aren't the same as statements. Statements tell the compiler to do something and terminate with a semicolon, while expressions specify a computation. There can be several expressions in a statement.

Precedence

Note the parentheses in the expression

```
(ftemp-32) * 5 / 9
```

Without the parentheses, the multiplication would be carried out first, since * has higher priority than -. With the parentheses, the subtraction is done first, then the multiplication, since all operations inside parentheses are carried out first. Precedence and parentheses are normally applied this same way in algebra and in other computer languages, so their use probably seems quite natural. However, precedence is an important topic in C++. We'll return to it later when we introduce different kinds of operators.

Type `float`

We've talked about type `int` and type `char`, both of which represent numbers as integers—that is, numbers without a fractional part. Now let's examine a different way of storing numbers: as *floating-point* variables.

Floating-point variables represent numbers with a decimal place—like 3.1415927, 0.0000625, and –10.2. They have both an integer part, to the left of the decimal point, and a fractional part, to the right. Floating-point variables represent *real numbers*, which are used for measurable quantities like distance, area, and temperature and typically have a fractional part.

There are three kinds of floating-point variables in C++: type `float`, type `double`, and type `long double`. Let's look at the smallest of these, type `float`.

Type `float` stores numbers in the range 3.4×10^{-38} to 3.4×10^{38}, with a precision of seven digits. It occupies 4 bytes in memory, as shown in Figure 3-6.

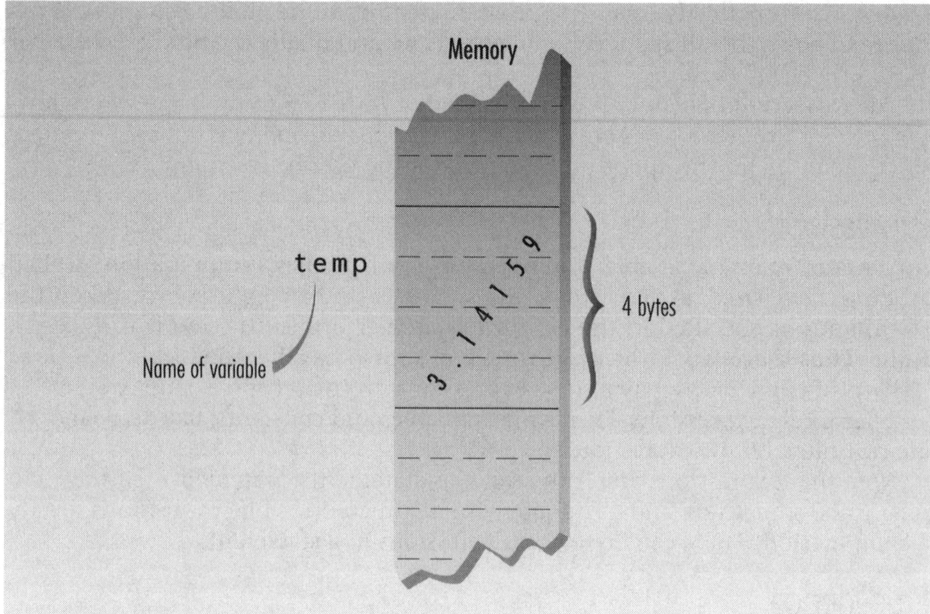

Figure 3-6 Variable of Type `float` in Memory

The following example program prompts the user to type in a floating-point number representing the radius of a circle. It then calculates and displays the circle's area.

```
// circarea.cpp
// demonstrates floating point variables
#include <iostream.h>                           // for cout, etc.

void main()
   {
   float rad;                                   // variable of type float
   const float PI = 3.14159;                    // type const float

   cout << "Enter radius of circle: ";          // prompt
   cin >> rad;                                  // get radius
   float area = PI * rad * rad;                 // find area
   cout << "Area is " << area << endl;          // display answer
   }
```

Here's a sample interaction with the program:

```
Enter radius of circle: 0.5
Area is 0.785398
```

This is the area in square feet of a 12-inch LP record (which has a radius of 0.5 feet). At one time this was an important quantity for manufacturers of vinyl.

Floating-Point Constants

The number 3.14159 in CIRCAREA is an example of a *floating-point constant*. The decimal point signals that it is a floating-point constant, and not an integer. This number is written in normal decimal notation.

You can also write floating-point constants using exponential notation. For example, the number 1234.56 would be written 1.23456E3 in exponential notation. This is the same as 1.23456 times 10^3. The number following the E is called the *exponent*. It indicates how many places the decimal point must be moved to change the number to ordinary decimal notation.

The exponent can be positive or negative. The exponential number 6.35239E–5 is equivalent to 0.0000635239 in decimal notation. This is the same as 6.35239 times 10^{-5}.

The `const` Qualifier

Besides demonstrating variables of type `float`, the CIRCAREA example also introduces the qualifier `const`. The keyword `const` (for *constant*) precedes the data type of a variable. It specifies that the value of a variable *will not change* throughout the program. Any attempt to alter the value of a variable defined with this qualifier will elicit an error message from the compiler.

The qualifier `const` ensures that your program does not inadvertently alter a variable that you intended to be a constant, such as the value of PI in CIRCAREA. It also reminds anyone reading the listing that the variable is not intended to change.

Variables with this qualifier are sometimes named in all uppercase, as a reminder that they are constants.

The #define Directive

Although the construction is not popular in C++, constants can also be specified using the preprocessor directive `#define`. This directive sets up an equivalence between an identifier and a text phrase. For example, the line

```
#define PI 3.14159
```

appearing at the beginning of your program specifies that the identifier `PI` will be replaced by the text `3.14159` throughout program. This construction has long been popular in C. However, you can't specify the data type of the constant using `#define`, which can lead to program bugs; so even in C `#define` is being superseded by `const` used with normal variables.

Manipulators

Manipulators are operators used with the insertion operator `<<` to modify—or manipulate—the way data is displayed. We'll look at two of the most common here: `endl` and `setw`.

The endl Manipulator

The last `cout` statement in the CIRCAREA program ends with an unfamiliar word: `endl`. This is a manipulator that causes a linefeed to be inserted into the stream. It has the same effect as sending the `'\n'` character, but is perhaps somewhat clearer.

The setw Manipulator

You can think of each value displayed by `cout` as occupying a *field*: an imaginary box with a certain width. The default field is just wide enough to hold the value. That is, the integer 567 will occupy a field three characters wide, and the string `"pajamas"` will occupy a field seven characters wide. However, in certain situations this may not lead to optimal results. Here's an example. The WIDTH1 program prints the names of three cities in one column, and their populations in another.

```
// width1.cpp
// demonstrates need for setw manipulator
#include <iostream.h>

void main()
   {
   long pop1=2425785, pop2=47, pop3=9761;

   cout << "LOCATION " << "POP." << endl
        << "Portcity " << pop1 << endl
        << "Hightown " << pop2 << endl
        << "Lowville " << pop3 << endl;
   }
```

Here's the output from this program:

```
LOCATION POP.
Portcity 2425785
Hightown 47
Lowville 9761
```

Unfortunately, this format makes it hard to compare the numbers; it would be better if they lined up to the right. Also, we had to insert spaces into the names of the cities to separate them from the numbers. This is an inconvenience.

Here's a variation of this program, WIDTH2, that uses the `setw` manipulator to eliminate these problems by specifying field widths for the names and the numbers:

```
// width2.cpp
// demonstrates setw manipulator
#include <iostream.h>
#include <iomanip.h>        // for setw

void main()
   {
   long pop1=2425785, pop2=47, pop3=9761;

   cout << setw(8) << "LOCATION" << setw(12)
                                 << "POPULATION" << endl
        << setw(8) << "Portcity" << setw(12) << pop1 << endl
        << setw(8) << "Hightown" << setw(12) << pop2 << endl
        << setw(8) << "Lowville" << setw(12) << pop3 << endl;
   }
```

The `setw` manipulator causes the number (or string) that follows it in the stream to be printed within a field `n` characters wide, where `n` is the argument to `setw(n)`. The value is right-justified within the field. Figure 3-7 shows how this looks.

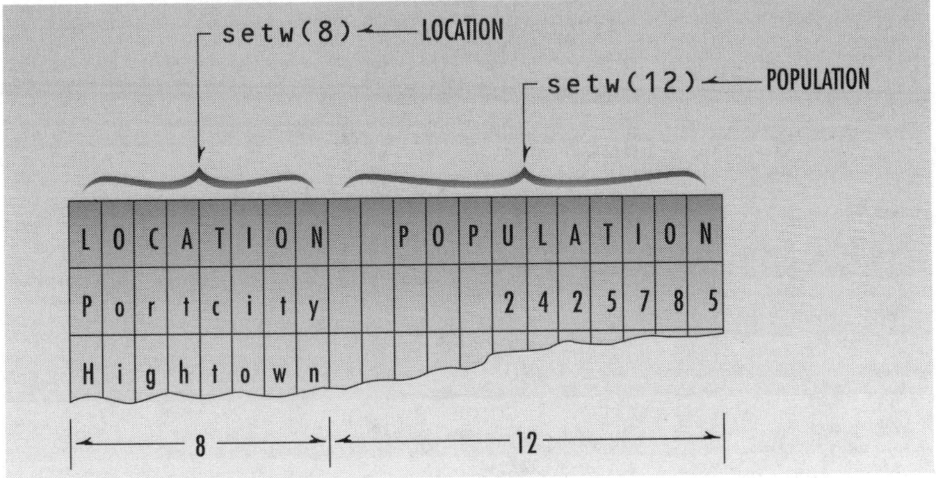

Figure 3-7 Field widths and `setw`

Here's the output of WIDTH2:

```
LOCATION   POPULATION
Portcity      2425785
Hightown           47
Lowville         9761
```

Type long

Besides the use of `setw`, there are several new aspects to the WIDTH1 and WIDTH2 programs. First, we've used a new data type: `long`. This is the third of the integer types, after `char` and `int`. Type `long` can also be written as `long int`; these mean the same thing. Type `long` can hold integers in the range –2,147,483,648 to 2,147,483,647. It's used when type `int` is too small for the values being stored. In WIDTH1 and WIDTH2, the population figures exceed the upper limit of type `int`—32,767—so type `long` must be used. Variables of type `long` occupy 4 bytes of memory (twice as much as type `int`), as shown in Figure 3-8.

If you want to create a constant of type `long`, use the letter `L` following the numerical value, as in

```
longvar = 7678L; // assigns long constant 7678 to longvar
```

If a constant's value is greater than 65,535, it is interpreted as type `long` whether you use the `L` or not.

Cascading the Insertion Operator

Note that there's only one `cout` statement in WIDTH1 and WIDTH2, although it's written on multiple lines. In doing this, we take advantage of the fact that the

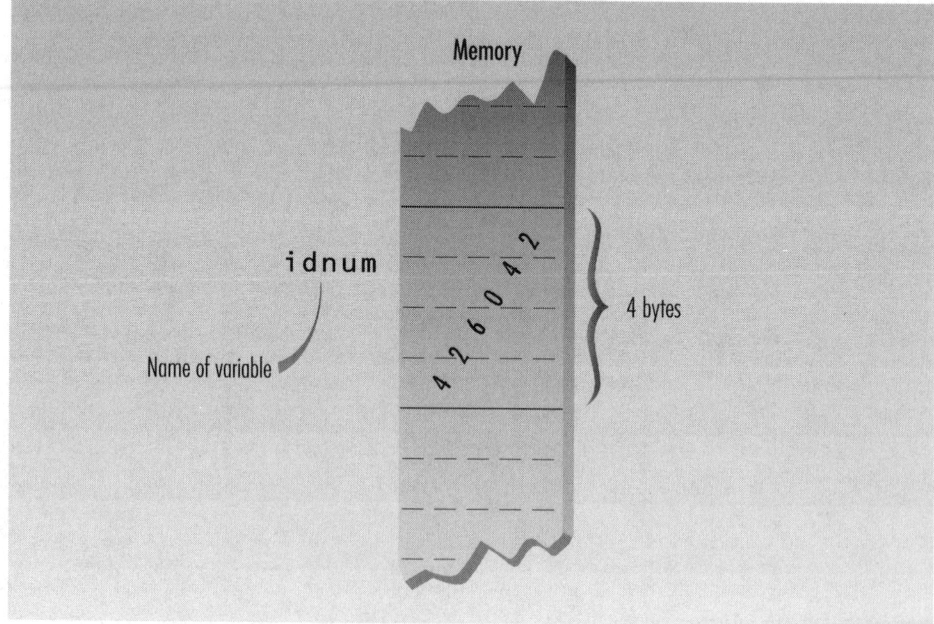

Figure 3-8 Variable of Type `long` in Memory

compiler ignores whitespace, and that the insertion operator can be cascaded. The effect is the same as using four separate statements, each beginning with `cout`.

Multiple Definitions

We initialized the variables `pop1`, `pop2`, and `pop3` to specific values at the same time we defined them. This is similar to the way we initialized `char` variables in the CHARVARS example. Here, however, we've defined and initialized all three variables on one line, using the same `long` keyword and separating the variable names with commas. This saves space where a number of variables are all the same type.

The IOMANIP.H Header File

The declarations for the manipulators are not in the usual IOSTREAM.H header file, but in a separate header file called IOMANIP.H. When you use these manipulators you must `#include` this header file in your program, as we do in the WIDTH2 example.

Variable Type Summary

Our program examples so far have covered four data types—`int`, `char`, `float`, and `long`. There are two others we haven't seen yet: `double` and `long double`. Let's pause now to summarize these data types. Table 3-2 shows the keyword used to define the type, the numerical range the type can accommodate, the digits of precision (in the case of floating-point numbers), and the bytes of memory occupied in the MS-DOS environment.

There are three integer types: `char`, `int`, and `long`; and three floating-point types: `float`, `double`, and `long double`.

In theory there is another integer type not shown here: `short`. In the MS-DOS environment, `short` is identical to `int`, so it is seldom used. However, on some computer systems `short` is smaller than `int`.

Type `double` occupies 8 bytes, twice as much memory as type `float`, and stores floating-point numbers with much larger range and precision. It stands for *double*

Keyword	Numerical range		Digits of	Bytes of
	low	high	precision	memory
char	–128	127	n/a	1
int	–32,768	32,767	n/a	2
long	–2,147,483,648	2,147,483,647	n/a	4
float	3.4×10^{-38}	3.4×10^{38}	7	4
double	1.7×10^{-308}	1.7×10^{308}	15	8
long double	3.4×10^{-4932}	1.1×10^{4932}	19	10

Table 3-2 Basic C++ Variable Types

precision floating point. It's used when type `float` is too small or insufficiently precise. Floating-point type `long double` occupies 10 bytes, and has only slightly greater range and precision than type `double`. However, it offers compatibility with the 80-bit numbers used in the optional math coprocessor chip (the 8087, 80287, 80387, and so on). It is usually used in conjunction with the math coprocessor. Figure 3-9 shows types `double` and `long double`.

Remember that integer type `long` extracts a performance penalty compared with type `int`. It is slower in arithmetic operations, and it occupies more memory, making your program larger. Similarly, the floating-point types `double` and `long double` are slower and larger than type `float`. You should use the smallest variable type that stores the values you're using in your program.

`unsigned` Data Types

By eliminating the sign of the character and integer types, you can change their range to start at 0 and include only positive numbers. This allows them to

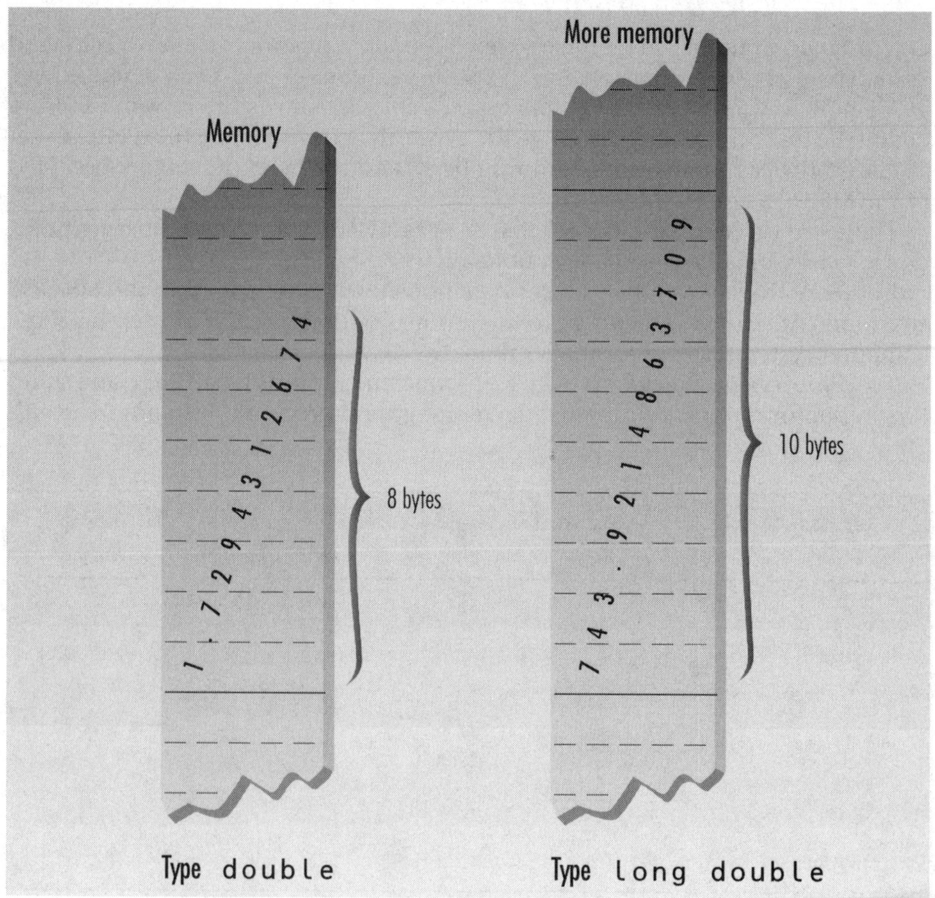

Figure 3-9 Variables of Type `double` and `long double`

Keyword	Numerical range		Bytes of
	low	high	memory
unsigned char	0	255	1
unsigned int	0	65,535	2
unsigned long	0	4,294,967,295	4

Table 3-3 Unsigned Integer Types

represent numbers twice as big as the signed type. Table 3-3 shows the unsigned versions.

The `unsigned` types are used when the quantities represented are always positive—such as when representing a count of something—or when the positive range of the signed types is not quite large enough.

To change an integer type to an unsigned type, precede the data type keyword with the keyword `unsigned`. For example, an unsigned variable of type `char` would be defined as

```
unsigned char ucharvar;
```

Exceeding the range of signed types can lead to obscure program bugs. These bugs can sometimes be eliminated by using unsigned types. For example, the following program stores the constant 25000 both as an `int` in `signedVar` and as an `unsigned int` in `unsignVar`.

```
// signtest.cpp
// tests signed and unsigned integers
#include <iostream.h>

void main()
   {
   int signedVar = 25000;              // signed: -32768 to 32767
   unsigned int unsignVar = 25000;     // unsigned: 0 to 65535

   signedVar = (signedVar * 2) / 3;    // calculation exceeds range
   unsignVar = (unsignVar * 2) / 3;    // calculation within range

   cout << "signedVar = " << signedVar << endl;   // wrong: -5178
   cout << "unsignVar = " << unsignVar << endl;   // ok: 16666
   }
```

The program multiplies both variables by 2, then divides them by 3. Although the result is 2/3 of the original number, the intermediate calculation is larger than the original number. This is a common situation, but it can lead to trouble. In SIGNTEST we expect that two-thirds the original value, or 16666, will be restored to both variables. Unfortunately, in `signedVar` the multiplication created a result—50,000—that exceeded the range of the `int` variable (–32768 to 32767). Here's the output:

```
signedVar = -5178
unsignVar = 25000
```

The signed variable now displays an incorrect answer, while the unsigned variable, which is large enough to hold the intermediate result of the multiplication, records the result correctly. The moral is this: Be careful that all values generated in your program are within the range of the variables that hold them. (The results may be different on non-MS-DOS computers, which may use more bytes for type `int`.)

Type Conversion

C++, like C, is more forgiving than some languages in the way it treats expressions involving several different data types. As an example, consider the MIXED program:

```
// mixed.cpp
// shows mixed expressions
#include <iostream.h>

void main()
   {
   int count = 7;
   float avgWeight = 155.5;

   double totalWeight = count * avgWeight;
   cout << "totalWeight=" << totalWeight << endl;
   }
```

Here a variable of type `int` is multiplied by a variable of type `float` to yield a result of type `double`. This program compiles without error; the compiler considers it normal that you want to multiply (or perform any other arithmetic operation on) numbers of different types.

Not all languages are this relaxed. Some don't permit mixed expressions, and would flag as an error the line that performs the arithmetic in MIXED. Such languages assume that when you mix types you're making a mistake, and they try to save you from yourself. C++ and C, however, assume that you must have a good reason for doing what you're doing, and they help carry out your intentions. This is one reason for the popularity of C++ and C. They give you more freedom.

Automatic Conversions

Let's consider what happens when the compiler confronts such mixed-type expressions as that in MIXED. Types are considered "higher" or "lower," based roughly on the order shown in Table 3-4.

When two operands of different types are encountered in the same expression, the lower-type variable is converted to the type of the higher-type variable. Thus in MIXED, the `int` value of `count` is converted to type `float` and stored in a temporary variable before being multiplied by the `float` variable `avgWeight`. The result (still of type `float`) is then converted to `double` so that it can be assigned to the `double` variable `totalWeight`. This process is shown in Figure 3-10.

These conversions take place invisibly, and ordinarily you don't need to think too much about them; C++ automatically does what you want. However, when we

Data type	Order
long double	Highest
double	
float	
long	
int	
char	Lowest

Table 3-4 Order of Data Types

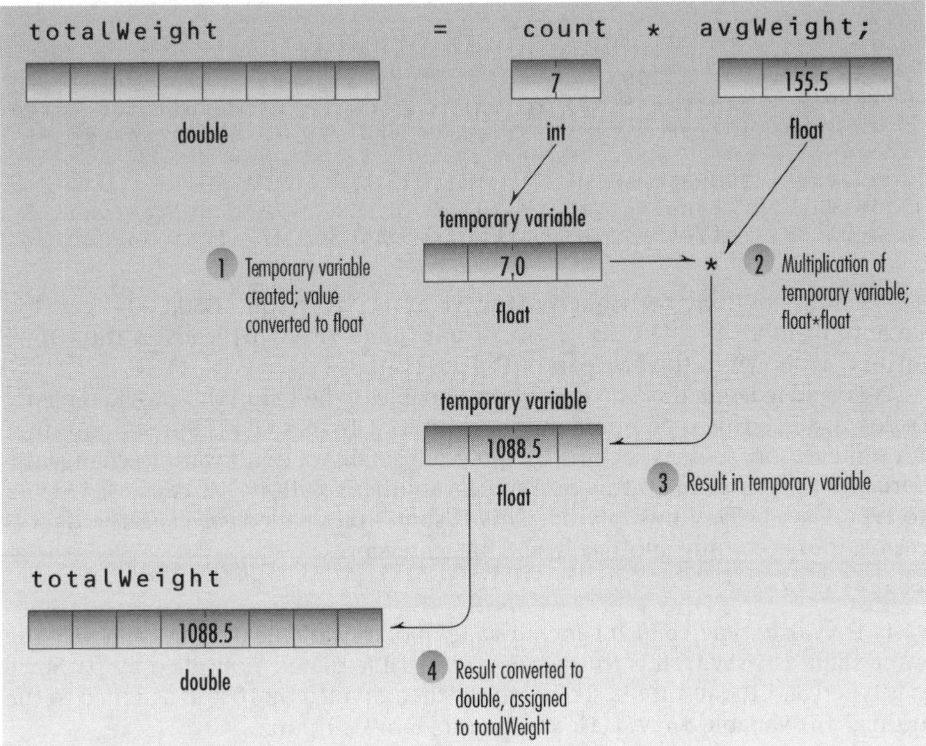

Figure 3-10 Data Conversion

start to use objects, we will in effect be defining our own data types. We may want to use these new data types in mixed expressions, just as we use normal variables in mixed expressions. When this is the case, we must be careful to create our own conversion routines to change objects of one type into objects of another. The compiler won't do it for us, as it does here with the built-in data types.

Casts

Casts sounds like something to do with classes in India, but in C++ the term applies to data conversions specified by the programmer, as opposed to the automatic data conversions we just described. What are casts for? Sometimes a programmer needs to convert a value from one type to another in a situation where the compiler will not do it automatically. Recall that in the SIGNTEST example, an intermediate result exceeded the capacity of the variable type, resulting in an erroneous result. We fixed the problem by using `unsigned int` instead of `int`. This worked because the intermediate result—50,000—would fit in the range of the unsigned variable.

But suppose an intermediate result won't fit the unsigned type either. In such a case we might be able to solve the problem by using a cast. Here's an example:

```
// cast.cpp
// tests signed and unsigned integers
#include <iostream.h>

void main()
   {
   int intVar = 25000;                    // signed: -32768 to 32767
   intVar = (intVar * 10) / 10;                   // result too large
   cout << "intVar = " << intVar << endl;   // wrong answer

   intVar = 25000;
   intVar = ( long(intVar) * 10) / 10;      // cast to long
   cout << "intVar = " << intVar << endl;   // right answer
   }
```

When we multiply the variable `intVar` by 10, the result—250,000—is far too large to fit in a variable of type `int` or `unsigned int`. This leads to the wrong answer, as shown in the first part of the program.

We could redefine the data type of the variables to be `long`; this provides plenty of room, since this type holds numbers up to 2,147,483,647. But suppose that for some reason, such as keeping the program small, we don't want to change the variables to type `long`. In this case there's another solution: We can cast `intVar` to type `long` before multiplying. This is sometimes called *coercion*; the data is *coerced* into becoming another type. The expression

```
long(intVar)
```

casts `intVar` to type `long`. It generates a temporary variable of type `long` with the same value as `intVar`. It is this temporary variable that is multiplied by 10. Since it is type `long`, the result fits. This result is then divided by 10 and assigned to the normal `int` variable `intVar`. Here's the program's output:

```
intVar = -1214
intVar = 25000
```

The first answer, without the cast, is wrong; but in the second answer, the cast produces the correct result.

You can use another syntax for casts. You can say

```
(long)intVar
```

with the parentheses around the type rather than around the variable. This is the only syntax acceptable in C, but in C++ the first approach (called *functional notation*) is preferred, because it is similar to the way other parts of C++, such as functions, are written.

The compiler gives you a warning message for this program: "Conversion may lose significant digits." This occurs when the coerced `long` is turned back into an `int`. You can ignore this message.

Arithmetic Operators

As you have probably gathered by this time, C++ uses the four normal arithmetic operators `+`, `-`, `*`, and `/` for addition, subtraction, multiplication, and division. These operators work on all the data types, both integer and floating-point. They are used in much the same way as in other languages, and are closely analogous to their use in algebra. However, there are some other arithmetic operators whose use is not so obvious.

The Remainder Operator

There is a fifth arithmetic operator that works only with integer variables (types `char`, `int`, and `long`). It's called the *remainder* operator, and is represented by `%`, the percent symbol. This operator (also called the *modulus* operator) finds the remainder when one number is divided by another. The REMAIND program demonstrates the effect.

```
// remaind.cpp
// demonstrates remainder operator
#include <iostream.h>

void main()
   {
   cout <<  6 % 8 << endl     // 6
        <<  7 % 8 << endl     // 7
        <<  8 % 8 << endl     // 0
        <<  9 % 8 << endl     // 1
        << 10 % 8 << endl;    // 2
   }
```

Here the numbers 6 through 10 are divided by 8, using the remainder operator. The answers are 6, 7, 0, 1, and 2—the remainders of these divisions. The remainder operator is used in a wide variety of situations. We'll show examples as we go along.

A note about precedence: In the expression

```
cout << 6 % 8
```

the remainder operator is evaluated first because it has higher precedence than the `<<` operator. If it did not, we would need to put parentheses around `6 % 8` to ensure it was evaluated before being acted on by `<<`.

Arithmetic Assignment Operators

C++ offers several ways to shorten and clarify your code. One of these is the *arithmetic assignment operator*. While not a key feature of the language, this operator is commonly used, and it helps to give C++ listings their distinctive appearance.

The following kind of statement is common in most languages.

```
total = total + item;   // adds "item" to "total"
```

In this situation you add something to an existing value (or you perform some other arithmetic operation on it). But the syntax of this statement offends those for whom brevity is important, because the name `total` appears twice. So C++ offers a condensed approach: the arithmetic assignment operator, which combines an arithmetic operator and an assignment operator and eliminates the repeated operand. Here's a statement that has exactly the same effect as the one above:

```
total += item;   // adds "item" to "total"
```

Figure 3-11 emphasizes the equivalence of the two forms.

There are arithmetic assignment operators corresponding to all the arithmetic operations: `+=`, `-=`, `*=`, `/=`, and `%=` (and some other operators as well). The following example shows the arithmetic assignment operators in use:

```
// assign.cpp
// demonstrates arithmetic assignment operators
#include <iostream.h>

void main()
   {
   int ans = 27;
   ans += 10;                // same as: ans = ans + 10;
   cout << endl << ans;
   ans -= 7;                 // same as: ans = ans - 7;
```

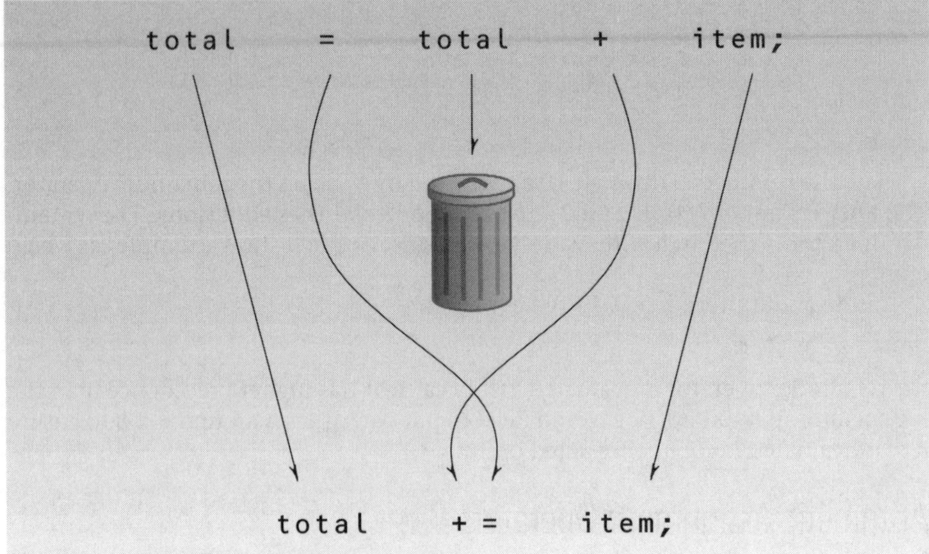

Figure 3-11 Arithmetic Assignment Operator

```
    cout << endl << ans;
    ans *= 2;                    // same as: ans = ans * 2;
    cout << endl << ans;
    ans /= 3;                    // same as: ans = ans / 3;
    cout << endl << ans;
    ans %= 3;                    // same as: ans = ans % 3;
    cout << endl << ans;
    }
```

Here's the output from this program:

```
37
30
60
20
2
```

You don't need to use arithmetic assignment operators in your code, but they are a common feature of the language; they'll appear in numerous examples in this book.

Increment Operators

Here's an even more specialized operator. You often need to add 1 to the value of an existing variable. You can do this the "normal" way:

```
count = count + 1;    // adds 1 to "count"
```

Or you can use an arithmetic assignment operator:

```
count += 1;    // adds 1 to "count"
```

But there's an even more condensed approach:

```
++count;    // adds 1 to "count"
```

The `++` operator *increments* (adds 1 to) its argument.

Prefix and Postfix

As if this weren't weird enough, the increment operator can be used in two ways: as a *prefix*, meaning that the operator precedes the variable; and as a *postfix*, meaning that the operator follows the variable. What's the difference? Often a variable is incremented within a statement that performs some other operation on it. For example,

```
totalWeight = avgWeight * ++count;
```

The question here is: Is the multiplication performed before or after `count` is incremented? In this case `count` is incremented first. How do we know that? Because prefix notation is used: `++count`. If we had used postfix notation, `count++`, the multiplication would have been performed first, then `count` would have been incremented. This is shown in Figure 3-12.

Here's an example that shows both the prefix and postfix versions of the increment operator:

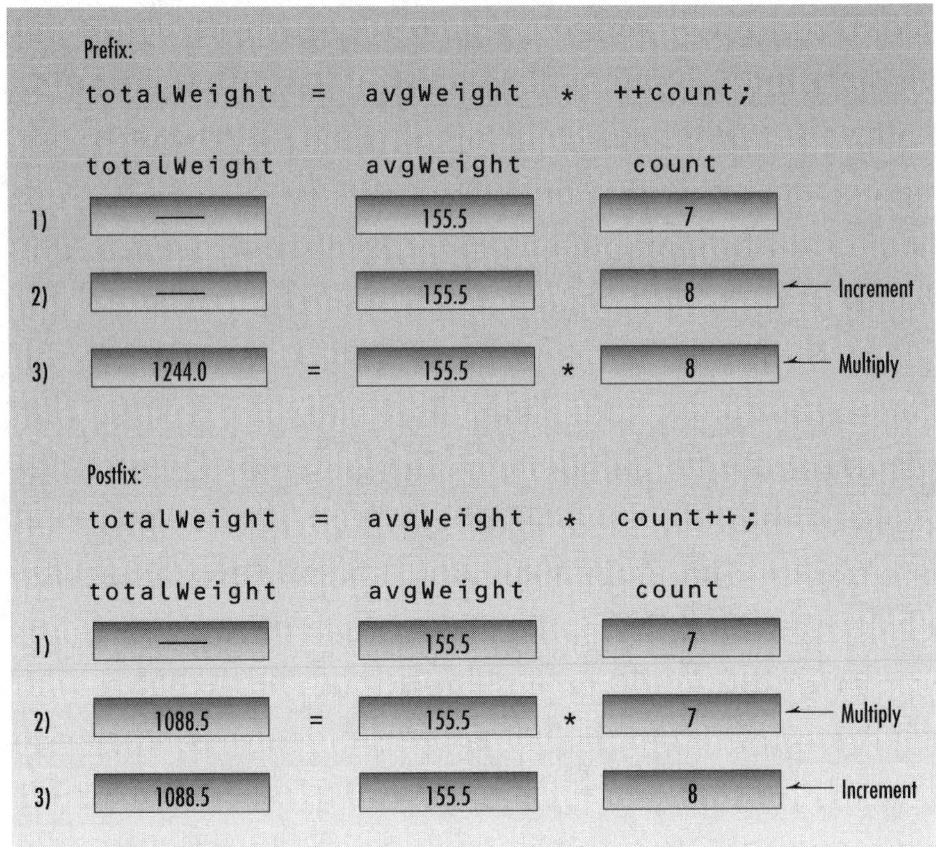

Figure 3-12 The Increment Operator

```
// increm.cpp
// demonstrates the increment operator
#include <iostream.h>

void main()
   {
   int count = 10;

   cout << "count=" << count << endl;     // displays 10
   cout << "count=" << ++count << endl;   // displays 11 (prefix)
   cout << "count=" << count << endl;     // displays 11
   cout << "count=" << count++ << endl;   // displays 11 (postfix)
   cout << "count=" << count << endl;     // displays 12
   }
```

Here's the program's output:

```
count=10
count=11
count=11
count=11
count=12
```

The first time `count` is incremented, the prefix `++` operator is used. This causes the increment to happen at the beginning of the statement evaluation, before the output operation has been carried out. When the value of the expression `++count` is displayed, it has already been incremented, and `<<` sees the value 11. The second time `count` is incremented, the postfix `++` operator is used. When the expression `count++` is displayed, it retains its unincremented value of 11. Following the completion of this statement, the increment takes effect, so that in the last statement of the program we see that `count` has acquired the value 12.

The Decrement (--) Operator

The decrement operator, `--`, behaves very much like the increment operator, except that it subtracts 1 from its operand. It can also be used in both prefix and postfix forms.

Library Functions

Many activities in C++ are carried out by *library functions*. These functions perform file access, mathematical computations, graphics, memory management, and data conversion, among other things. We don't want to dig too deeply into library functions before we explain how functions work (see Chapter 6), but you can use simple library functions without a thorough understanding of their operation. Here's a preview.

The next example, SQRT, uses the library function `sqrt()` to calculate the square root of a number entered by the user.

```
// sqrt.cpp
// demonstrates sqrt() library function
#include <iostream.h>               // for cout, etc.
#include <math.h>                   // for sqrt()
void main()
   {
   double number, answer;           // sqrt() requires type double
   cout << "Enter a number: ";
   cin >> number;                   // get the number
   answer = sqrt(number);           // find square root
   cout << "Square root is "
        << answer << endl;          // display it
   }
```

The program first obtains a number from the user. This number is then used as an *argument* to the `sqrt()` function, in the statement

```
answer = sqrt(number);
```

An argument is the input to the function; it is placed inside the parentheses following the function name. The function then processes the argument and *returns* a value; this is the output from the function. In this case the return value is the square root of the original number. *Returning a value* means that the function expression takes on this value, which can then be assigned to another variable—in this case `answer`. The program then displays this value. Here's some output from the program:

```
Enter a number: 1000
Square root is 31.622777
```

Multiplying 31.622777 by itself on your pocket calculator will verify that this answer is pretty close.

The arguments to a function, and their return values, must be the correct data type. You can find what these data types are by looking at the description of the library function in the Borland library documentation, which describes each of the hundreds of library functions. For `sqrt()`, the description specifies both an argument and a return value of type `double`, so we use variables of this type in the program.

Header Files

As with `cout` and other such objects, you must `#include` a header file that contains various declarations describing any library functions you use. In the documentation for the `sqrt()` function, you'll see that the specified header file is MATH.H. In SQRT the preprocessor directive

```
#include <math.h>
```

takes care of incorporating this header file into our source file.

If you don't include the appropriate header file when you use a library function, you'll get an error message like this from the compiler: *Function 'sqrt' should have a prototype in function main( ).*

Library Files

We mentioned earlier that a file containing library functions and objects will usually be linked to your program to create an executable file. This is true for all the programs in this chapter, since they use `cout` and other objects. If you're using the Small memory model, this library file is called CS.LIB (where the S indicates *Small*). The `sqrt()` function is also found in this file. It is extracted from the file automatically by the linker, and the proper connections are made so that it can be called (that is, invoked or accessed) from the SQRT program.

Header Files and Library Files

The relationship between library files and header files can be confusing, so let's review it. To use a library function like `sqrt()`, you must link the library file CS.LIB to your program. The appropriate functions from the library file are then connected to your program by the linker.

However, that's not the end of the story. The functions in your source file need to know the names and types of the functions and other elements in the library file. They are given this information in a header file. Each header file contains information for a particular group of functions. The functions themselves are in CS.LIB, but the information about them is scattered throughout a number of header files. The IOSTREAM.H header file contains information for various I/O functions and objects, including `cout`, while the MATH.H header file contains information for mathematics functions like `sqrt()`. If you were using memory management functions, you would include MEMORY.H, while string functions would require STRING.H, and so on.

Figure 3-13 shows the relationship of header files and library files to the other files used in program development.

The use of header files is common in C++. Whenever you use a library function or a predefined object or operator, you will need to use a header file that contains appropriate declarations.

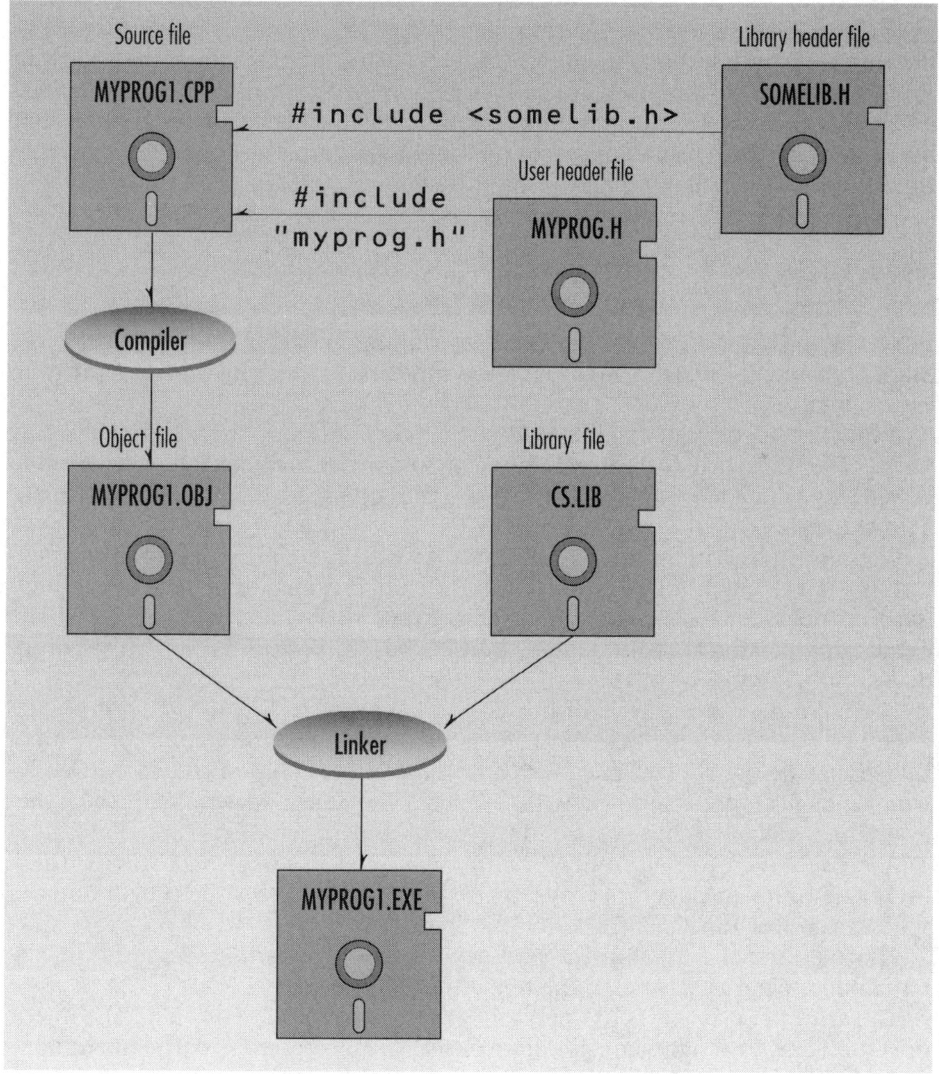

Figure 3-13 Header and Library Files

Two Ways to Use `#include`

We should mention that you can use `#include` in two ways. The angle brackets < and > surrounding the filenames IOSTREAM.H and MATH.H in the SQRT example indicate that the compiler should begin searching for these files in the standard INCLUDE directory. This directory holds the header files supplied by Borland for the system. You can see what Borland C++ thinks this directory is (and change it if you want) by selecting *Project* from the Options menu and clicking on *Directories*. In Turbo C++ select *Directory* from the Options menu.

Instead of angle brackets around the filename, you can also use quotation marks, as in

```
#include "myheader.h"
```

Quotation marks instruct the compiler to begin its search for the header file in the *current* directory; this is usually the directory that contains the source file. You normally use quotation marks for header files you write yourself (a situation we'll explore in Chapter 15). Quotation marks or angle brackets work in any case, but making the appropriate choice speeds up the compilation process slightly by giving the compiler a hint about where to find the file.

Summary

In this chapter we've learned that a major building block of C++ programs is the *function*. A function named `main()` is always the first one executed when a program is executed.

A function is composed of *statements*, which tell the computer to do something. Each statement ends with a semicolon. A statement may contain one or more *expressions*, which are sequences of variables and operators that usually evaluate to a specific value.

Output is most commonly handled in C++ with the `cout` object and `<<` insertion operator, which together cause variables or constants to be sent to the standard output device—usually the screen. Input is handled with `cin` and the extraction operator `>>`, which cause values to be received from the standard input device—usually the keyboard.

Six major data types are built into C++: `char`, `int`, and `long int` are the integer types; and `float`, `double`, and `long double` are the floating-point types. All of these types are signed. Unsigned versions of the integer types, signaled by the keyword `unsigned`, hold numbers twice as large. The `const` keyword stipulates that a variable's value will not change in the course of a program.

A variable is converted from one type to another in mixed expressions (those involving different data types) and by casting, which allows the programmer to specify a conversion.

C++ employs the usual arithmetic operators `+`, `-`, `*`, and `/`. In addition, the remainder operator, `%`, returns the remainder of integer division.

The arithmetic assignment operators `+=`, `+-`, and so on perform an arithmetic operation and an assignment simultaneously. The increment and decrement operators `++` and `--` increase or decrease a variable by 1.

Preprocessor directives consist of instructions to the compiler, rather than to the computer. The `#include` directive tells the compiler to insert another file into the present source file, and the `#define` directive tells it to substitute one thing for another.

If you use a library function in your program, the code for the function is in a library file, which is automatically linked to your program. A header file containing the function's declaration must be inserted into your source file with an `#include` statement.

Questions

Answers to questions can be found in Appendix D.

1. Dividing a program into functions
   - a. is the key to object-oriented programming.
   - b. makes the program easier to conceptualize.
   - c. may reduce the size of the program.
   - d. makes the program run faster.
2. A function name must be followed by __________.
3. A function body is delimited by __________.
4. Why is the `main()` function special?
5. A C++ instruction that tells the computer to do something is called a __________.
6. Write an example of a normal C++ comment and an example of an old-fashioned `/*` comment.
7. An expression
   - a. usually evaluates to a numerical value.
   - b. indicates the emotional state of the program.
   - c. always occurs outside a function.
   - d. may be part of a statement.
8. Specify how many bytes are occupied by the following data types in Borland C++ and Turbo C++:
   - a. Type `int`
   - b. Type `long double`
   - c. Type `float`
   - d. Type `long`
9. True or false: A variable of type `char` can hold the value 301.

10. What kind of program elements are the following?
    a. `12`
    b. `'a'`
    c. `4.28915`
    d. `JungleJim`
    e. `JungleJim()`
11. Write statements that display on the screen
    a. the character 'x'.
    b. the name *Jim.*
    c. the number 509.
12. True or false: In an assignment statement, the value on the left of the equal sign is always equal to the value on the right.
13. Write a statement that displays the variable `george` in a field 10 characters wide.
14. What header file must you `#include` with your source file to use `cout` and `cin`?
15. Write a statement that gets a numerical value from the keyboard and places it in the variable `temp`.
16. What header file must you `#include` with your program to use `setw`?
17. Three exceptions to the rule that the compiler ignores whitespace are __________, __________, and __________.
18. True or false: It's perfectly all right to use variables of different data types in the same arithmetic expression.
19. The expression `11%3` evaluates to __________.
20. An arithmetic assignment operator combines the effect of what two operators?
21. Write a statement that uses an arithmetic assignment operator to increase the value of the variable `temp` by 23. Write the same statement without the arithmetic assignment operator.
22. The increment operator increases the value of a variable by how much?
23. Assuming `var1` starts with the value 20, what will the following code fragment print out?

```
cout << var1--;
cout << ++var1;
```

24. In the examples we've seen so far, header files have been used for what purpose?

25. If you use the Small memory model, what library file must be linked to your program to provide standard library functions?

Exercises

Answers to the starred exercises can be found in Appendix D.

1.* Assuming there are 7.481 gallons in a cubic foot, write a program that asks the user to enter a number of gallons, and then displays the equivalent in cubic feet.

2.* Write a program that generates the following table:

```
1990       135
1991      7290
1992     11300
1993     16200
```

Use a single `cout` statement for all output.

3.* Write a program that generates the following output:

```
10
20
19
```

Use an integer constant for the 10, an arithmetic assignment operator to generate the 20, and a decrement operator to generate the 19.

4. Write a program that displays your favorite poem. Use an appropriate escape sequence for the line breaks. If you don't have a favorite poem, you can borrow this one by Ogden Nash:

```
Candy is dandy,
But liquor is quicker.
```

5. A library function, `islower()`, takes a single character (a letter) as an argument and returns a nonzero integer if the letter is lowercase, or zero if it is uppercase. This function requires the header file CTYPE.H. Write a program that allows the user to enter a letter, and then displays either zero or nonzero, depending on whether a lowercase or uppercase letter was entered. (See the SQRT program for clues.)

6. On a certain day the British pound was equivalent to $1.487 U.S., the French franc was $0.172, the German deutschemark was $0.584, and the Japanese yen was $0.00955. Write a program that allows the user to enter an amount in

dollars, and then displays this value converted to these four other monetary units.

7. You can convert temperature from degrees Celsius to degrees Fahrenheit by multiplying by 9/5 and adding 32. Write a program that allows the user to enter a floating-point number representing degrees Celsius, and then displays the corresponding degrees Fahrenheit.

8. When a value is smaller than a field specified with `setw()`, the unused locations are, by default, filled in with spaces. The manipulator `setfill()` takes a single character as an argument and causes this character to be substituted for spaces in the empty parts of a field. Rewrite the WIDTH program so that the characters on each line between the location name and the population number are filled in with periods instead of spaces, as in

```
Portcity.....2425785
```

9. If you have two fractions, `a/b` and `c/d`, their sum can be obtained from the formula

```
 a       c          a*d + b*c
--- +  ---    =    -----------
 b       d             b*d
```

For example, 1/4 plus 2/3 is

```
 1       2          1*3 + 4*2         3 + 8          11
--- +  ---    =    -----------   =   -------    =    ----
 4       3             4*3              12            12
```

Write a program that encourages the user to enter two fractions, and then displays their sum in fractional form. (You don't need to reduce it to lowest terms.) The interaction with the user might look like this:

```
Enter first fraction: 1/2
Enter second fraction: 2/5
Sum = 9/10
```

You can take advantage of the fact that the extraction operator (>>) can be chained to read in more than one quantity at once:

```
cin >> a >> dummychar >> b;
```

10. In the heyday of the British empire, Great Britain used a monetary system based on pounds, shillings, and pence. There were 20 shillings to a pound, and 12 pence to a shilling. The notation for this old system used the pound sign, £, and two decimal points, so that, for example, £5.2.8 meant 5 pounds, 2 shillings, and 8 pence. (*Pence* is the plural of *penny*.) The new monetary system, introduced in the 1950s, consists of only pounds and pence, with 100 pence to a pound (like U.S. dollars and cents). We'll call this new system *decimal pounds*.

Thus £5.2.8 in the old notation is £5.13 in decimal pounds (actually £5.1333333). Write a program to convert the old pounds-shillings-pence format to decimal pounds. An example of the user's interaction with the program would be

```
Enter pounds: 7
Enter shillings: 17
Enter pence: 9
Decimal pounds = £7.89
```

In both Borland C++ and Turbo C++, you can use the hex character constant `'\x9c'` to represent the pound sign (£). In Borland C++, you can put the pound sign into your program directly by pasting it from the Windows *Character Map* accessory.

11. By default, output is right-justified in its field. You can left-justify text output using the manipulator `setiosflags(ios::left)`. (For now, don't worry what this new notation means.) Use this manipulator, along with `setw()`, to help generate the following output:

```
Last name First name   Street address      Town    State
-----------------------------------------------------------
Jones      Bernard     109 Pine Lane       Littletown   MI
O'Brian    Coleen      42 E. 99th Ave.     Bigcity      NY
Wong       Harry       121-A Alabama St.   Lakeville    IL
```

12. Write the inverse of Exercise 10, so that the user enters an amount in Great Britain's new decimal-pounds notation (pounds and pence), and the program converts it to the old pounds-shillings-pence notation. An example of interaction with the program might be

```
Enter decimal pounds: 3.51
Equivalent in old notation = £3.10.2.
```

Make use of the fact that if you assign a floating-point value (say 12.34) to an integer variable, the decimal fraction (0.34) is lost; the integer value is simply 12. Use a cast to avoid a compiler warning. You can use statements like

```
float decpounds;      // input from user (new-style pounds)
int pounds;           // old-style (integer) pounds
float decfrac;        // decimal fraction (smaller than 1.0)

pounds = int(decpounds);          // remove decimal fraction
decfrac = decpounds - pounds;     // regain decimal fraction
```

You can then multiply `decfrac` by 20 to find shillings. A similar operation obtains pence.

4

Loops and Decisions

RELATIONAL OPERATORS

for, while, AND do LOOPS

if AND if...else STATEMENTS

THE switch STATEMENT

THE CONDITIONAL OPERATOR

LOGICAL OPERATORS

4

Not many programs execute all their statements in strict order from beginning to end. Most programs (like many humans) decide what to do in response to changing circumstances. The flow of control jumps from one part of the program to another, depending on calculations performed in the program. Program statements that cause such jumps are called control statements. There are two major categories: loops and decisions.

How many times a loop is executed, or whether a decision results in the execution of a section of code, depends on whether certain expressions are true or false. These expressions typically involve a kind of operator called a relational operator, which compares two values. Since the operation of loops and decisions is so closely involved with these operators, we'll examine them first.

Relational Operators

A relational operator compares two values. The values can be any built-in C++ data type, such as `char`, `int`, and `float`, or—as we'll see later—they can be user-defined classes. The comparison involves such relationships as equal to, less than, and greater than. The result of the comparison is true or false; for example, either two values are equal (true), or they're not (false).

Our first program, RELAT, demonstrates relational operators in a comparison of integer variables and constants.

```
// relat.cpp
// demonstrates relational operators
#include <iostream.h>

void main()
   {
   int numb;

   cout << "Enter a number: ";
   cin >> numb;
   cout << "numb<10  is " << (numb < 10)  << endl;
   cout << "numb>10  is " << (numb > 10)  << endl;
   cout << "numb==10 is " << (numb == 10) << endl;
   }
```

This program performs three kinds of comparisons between 10 and a number entered by the user. Here's the output when the user enters 20:

```
Enter a number: 20
numb<10  is 0
numb>10  is 1
numb==10 is 0
```

The first expression is true if `numb` is less than 10. The second expression is true if `numb` is greater than 10, and the third is true if `numb` is equal to 10. As you can see from the output, the C++ compiler considers that a true expression has the value 1, while a false expression has the value 0. Some languages have special Boolean variables to represent true and false values, but C++ does not. It uses the integer values 0 and 1 instead.

Here's the complete list of C++ relational operators:

Operator	Meaning
>	Greater than
<	Less than
==	Equal to
!=	Not equal to
>=	Greater than or equal to
<=	Less than or equal to

Now let's look at some expressions that use relational operators, and also look at the value of each expression. The first two lines are assignment statements that set the values of the variables `harry` and `jane`. You might want to hide the comments with your old Jose Canseco baseball card and see if you can predict which expressions evaluate to true and which to false.

```
jane = 44;           // assignment statement
harry = 12;          // assignment statement
(jane == harry)      // false
(harry <= 12)        // true
(jane > harry)       // true
(jane >= 44)         // true
(harry != 12)        // false
(7 < harry)          // true
(0)                  // false (by definition)
(44)                 // true (since it's not 0)
```

Note that the equal operator, ==, uses two equal signs. A common mistake is to use a single equal sign—the assignment operator—as a relational operator. This is a nasty bug, since the compiler won't notice anything wrong. However, your program won't do what you want.

Although C++ generates a 1 to indicate true, it assumes that any value other than 0 (such as –7 or 44) is true; only 0 is false. Thus, the last expression in the list is true.

Now let's see how these operators are used in typical situations. We'll examine loops first, then decisions.

Loops

Loops cause a section of your program to be repeated a certain number of times. The repetition continues while a condition is true. When the condition becomes false, the loop ends and control passes to the statements following the loop.

There are three kinds of loops in C++: the `for` loop, the `while` loop, and the `do` loop.

The `for` Loop

The `for` loop is (for many people, anyway) the easiest to understand of the C++ loops. All its loop-control elements are gathered in one place, while in the other loop constructions they are scattered about the program, which can make it harder to unravel how these loops work. Also, the `for` loop is a key concept in other languages; for a long time it was the *only* loop construction available in BASIC, for example.

The `for` loop executes a section of code a fixed number of times. It's usually (although not always) used when you know, before entering the loop, how many times you want to execute the code.

Here's an example, FORDEMO, that displays the squares of the numbers from 0 to 14:

```
// fordemo.cpp
// demonstrates simple FOR loop
#include <iostream.h>

void main()
   {
   int j;                          // define a loop variable

   for(j=0; j<15; j++)             // loop from 0 to 14,
      cout << j * j << "  ";       // displaying the square of j
   }
```

Here's the output:

```
0  1  4  9  16  25  36  49  64  81  100  121  144  169  196
```

How does this work? The `for` statement controls the loop. It consists of the keyword `for`, followed by parentheses that contain three expressions separated by semicolons:

```
for(j=0; j<15; j++)
```

These three expressions are the *initialization expression*, the *test expression*, and the *increment expression*, as shown in Figure 4-1.

These three expressions usually (but not always) involve the same variable, which we call the *loop variable*. In the FORDEMO example the loop variable is `j`. It's defined before the loop begins.

The *body* of the loop is the code to be executed each time through the loop. Repeating this code is the *raison d'être* for the loop. In this example the loop body consists of a single statement:

```
cout << j * j << "  ";
```

This statement prints out the square of `j`, followed by two spaces. The square is found by multiplying `j` by itself. As the loop executes, `j` goes through the sequence 0, 1, 2, 3, and so on up to 14; so the squares of these numbers are displayed—0, 1, 4, 9, up to 196.

Note that the `for` statement is not followed by a semicolon. That's because the `for` statement and the loop body are *together* considered to be a program statement. This is an important detail. If you put a semicolon after the `for` statement, the compiler will think there is no loop body, and the program will do things you don't expect.

Let's see how the three expressions in the `for` statement control the loop.

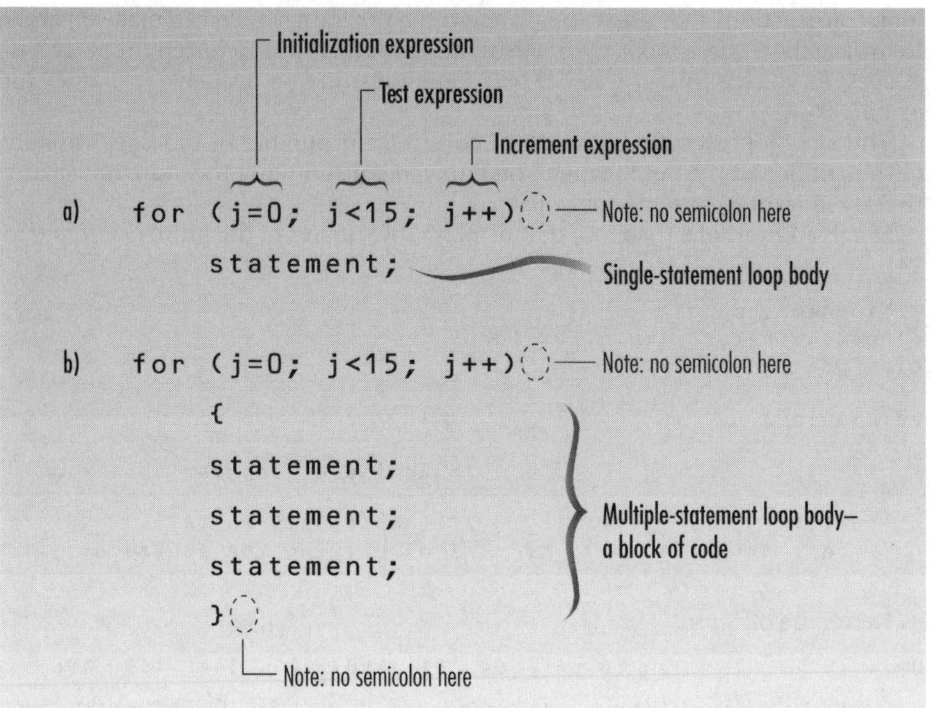

Figure 4-1 Syntax of the `for` Loop

The Initialization Expression

The initialization expression is executed only once, when the loop first starts. It gives the loop variable an initial value. In the FORDEMO example it sets `j` to 0.

The Test Expression

The test expression usually involves a relational operator. It is evaluated each time through the loop, just before the body of the loop is executed. It determines whether the loop will be executed again. If the test expression is true, the loop is executed one more time. If it's false, the loop ends, and control passes to the statements following the loop. In the FORDEMO example there are no statements following the loop, so the program ends when the test expression becomes false.

The Increment Expression

The increment expression changes the value of the loop variable, often by incrementing it. It is always executed at the end of the loop, after the loop body has been executed. Here the increment operator `++` adds 1 to `j` each time through the loop. Figure 4-2 shows a flowchart of a `for` loop's operation.

How Many Times?

The loop in the FORDEMO example executes exactly 15 times. The first time, `j` is 0. This is ensured in the initialization expression. The last time through the loop, `j` is 14. This is determined by the test expression `j<15`. When `j` becomes 15, the

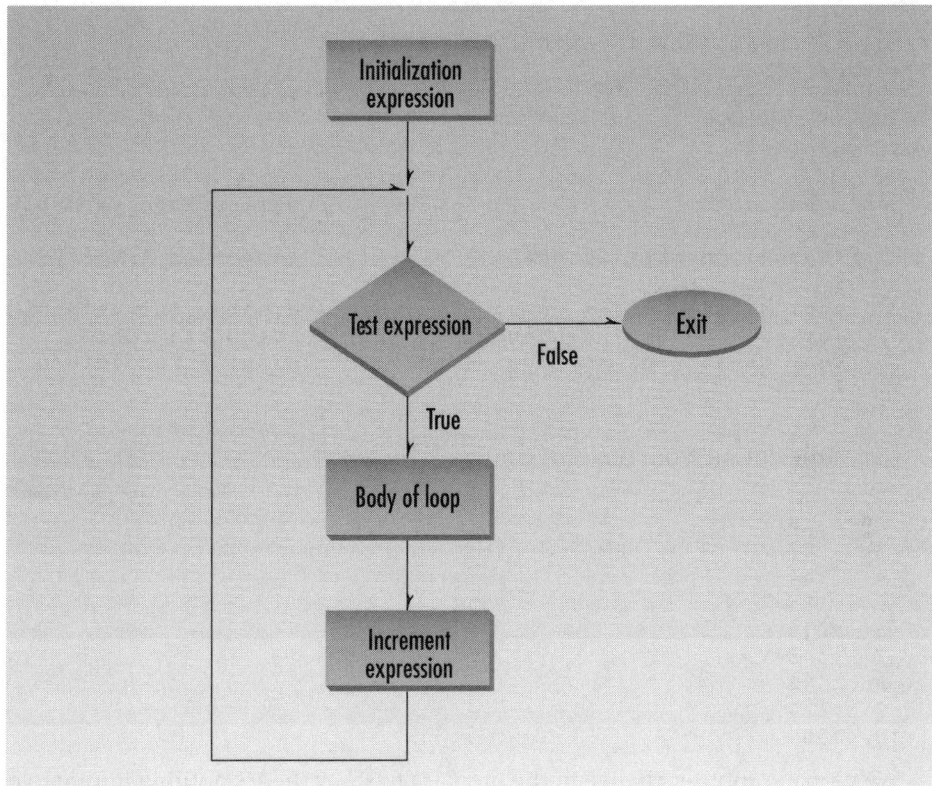

Figure 4-2 Operation of the `for` Loop

loop terminates; the loop body is not executed when `j` has this value. The arrangement shown is commonly used to do something a fixed number of times: start at 0, use a test expression with the less-than operator and a value equal to the desired number of iterations, and increment the loop variable after each iteration.

Here's another `for` loop example:

```
for(count=0; count<100; count++)
  // loop body
```

How many times will the loop body be repeated here? Exactly 100 times, with `count` going from 0 to 99.

Multiple Statements in Loop Body

Of course you may want to execute more than one statement in the loop body. Multiple statements are delimited by braces, just as functions are. Note that there is no semicolon following the final brace of the loop body, although there are semicolons following the individual statements in the loop body. See Figure 4-1b for the syntax of a multistatement `for` loop.

The next example, CUBELIST, uses three statements in the loop body. It prints out the cubes of the numbers from 1 to 10, using a two-column format.

```
// cubelist.cpp
// lists cubes from 1 to 10
#include <iostream.h>
#include <iomanip.h>                        // for setw

void main()
   {
   int numb;                                // define loop variable

   for(numb=1; numb<=10; numb++)            // loop from 1 to 10
      {
      cout << setw(4) << numb;              // display 1st column
      int cube = numb*numb*numb;            // calculate cube
      cout << setw(6) << cube << endl;      // display 2nd column
      }
   }
```

Here's the output from the program:

```
   1     1
   2     8
   3    27
   4    64
   5   125
   6   216
   7   343
   8   512
   9   729
  10  1000
```

We've made another change in the program to show there's nothing immutable about the format used in the last example. The loop variable is initialized to 1, not to 0, and it ends at 10, not at 9, by virtue of <=, the less-than-or-equal-to operator. The effect is that the loop body is executed 10 times, with the loop variable running from 1 to 10 (not from 0 to 9).

Blocks and Variable Visibility

The loop body, which consists of braces delimiting several statements, is called a *block* of code. One important aspect of a block is that a variable defined inside the block is not visible outside it. *Visible* means that program statements can access or "see" the variable. (We'll discuss visibility further in Chapter 6.) In CUBELIST we define the variable `cube` inside the block, in the statement

```
int cube = numb*numb*numb;
```

You can't access this variable outside the block; it's only visible within the braces. Thus if you placed the statement

```
cube = 10;
```

after the loop body, the compiler would signal an error because the variable `cube` would be undefined outside the loop.

One advantage of restricting the visibility of variables is that the same variable name can be used within different blocks in the same program. (Defining variables inside a block, as we did in CUBELIST, is common in C++ but is not popular in C.)

Indentation and Loop Style

Good programming style dictates that the loop body be indented—that is, shifted right, relative to the loop statement (and to the rest of the program). In the FORDEMO example one line is indented, and in CUBELIST the entire block, including the braces, is indented. This indentation is an important visual aid to the programmer: It makes it easy to see where the loop body begins and ends. The compiler doesn't care whether you indent or not (at least there's no way to tell if it cares).

There is a common variation on the style we use for loops in this book. We show the braces aligned vertically, but some programmers prefer to place the opening brace just after the loop statement, like this:

```
for(numb=1; numb<=10; numb++)  {
   cout << setw(4) << numb;
   int cube = numb*numb*numb;
   cout << setw(6) << cube << endl;
   }
```

This saves a line in the listing but makes it more difficult to read, since the opening brace is harder to see and harder to match with the corresponding closing brace.

Debugging Features

You can use the debugging features built into Borland C++ and Turbo C++ to create a dramatic animated display of loop operation. The key feature is *single-stepping.* The IDE makes this easy. Open a project for the program to be debugged, and an *Edit* window containing the source file. (In Turbo C++ you don't need to open a project.) Now simply press the (F8) function key. If necessary, the program will be recompiled. Then the first line of the program will be highlighted. The highlighted line is the line about to be executed. Each time you press (F8), the highlight moves to the next line.

Single-Stepping in CUBELIST

Try this with CUBELIST. Open an *Edit* window on CUBELIST.CPP, make sure the window is active, and press (F8). The first executable line will be highlighted. (Preprocessor directions and variable declarations are not considered executable.) Continue to press (F8). When you enter the `for` loop, you can watch the highlight cycle through the statements in the loop body.

The Watch Window

As you're single-stepping, you'll often find it useful to see how the values of certain variables change. To do this you can open a *Watch window.* Select *Add Watch* from the Debug menu. (In Turbo C++ select *Watches* from the Debug menu, and from the submenu select *Add watch.*) In the resulting dialog box, enter the name of the variable to be watched; in this case, enter `numb`. A window called *Watch* will appear; it will display the value of `numb`. As you step through the loop, the value of `numb` will change, and these changes will be reflected in the *Watch* window. You can add as many variables as you like to the *Watch* window; they will all be displayed.

Single-stepping and the *Watch* window are powerful debugging tools. If your loop doesn't behave as you think it should, you can use these features to monitor the values of key variables as you step through the loop. Usually the source of the problem will become clear.

for Loop Variations

The increment expression doesn't need to increment the loop variable; it can perform any operation it likes. In the next example it *decrements* the loop variable. This program, FACTOR, asks the user to type in a number, and then calculates the factorial of this number. (The factorial is calculated by multiplying the original number by all the positive integers smaller than itself. Thus the factorial of 5 is 5*4*3*2*1, or 120.)

```
// factor.cpp
// calculates factorials, demonstrates FOR loop
#include <iostream.h>

void main()
   {
   unsigned int numb;
   unsigned long fact=1;                // long for larger numbers

   cout << "\nEnter a number: ";
   cin >> numb;                         // get number

   for(int j=numb; j>0; j--)            // multiply 1 by
      fact *= j;                        // numb, numb-1, ..., 2, 1
   cout << "Factorial is " << fact;     // result is factorial
   }
```

In this example the initialization expression sets `j` to the value entered by the user. The test expression causes the loop to execute as long as `j` is greater than 0. The increment expression decrements `j` after each iteration.

We've used type `unsigned long` for the factorial, since the factorials even of small numbers are very large, as can be seen in the following output:

```
Enter a number: 10
Factorial is 3628800
```

Even using type `unsigned long`, the largest number you can use for input is 12.

Variables Defined in for Statements

There's another wrinkle in this program: The loop variable `j` is defined inside the `for` statement:

```
for(int j=numb; j>0; j--)
```

This is a common construction in C++. It defines the variable as close as possible to its point of use in the listing. Variables defined in the loop statement this way are visible from the point of definition onward in the listing (unlike variables defined within a block, which are visible only within the block).

Multiple Initialization and Test Expressions

You can put more than one expression in the initialization part of the `for` statement, separating the different expressions by commas. You can also have more than one increment expression, although you can have only one test expression. Here's an example:

```
for( j=0, alpha=100; j<50; j++, beta-- )
   {
   // body of loop
   }
```

This example has a normal loop variable `j`, but it also initializes another variable, `alpha`, and increments a third, `beta`. The variables `alpha` and `beta` don't need to have anything to do with each other, or with `j`. Multiple initialization expressions and multiple increment expressions are separated by commas.

We'll avoid using such multiple expressions. While this approach can make the listing more concise, it also tends to decrease its readability. It's always possible to use stand-alone statements to achieve the same effect.

The `while` Loop

The `for` loop does something a fixed number of times. What happens if you don't know how many times you want to do something before you start the loop? In this case a different kind of loop may be used: the `while` loop.

The next example, ENDON0, asks the user to enter a series of numbers. When the number entered is 0, the loop terminates. Notice that there's no way for the program to know in advance how many numbers will be typed before the 0 appears; that's up to the user.

```
// endon0.cpp
// demonstrates WHILE loop
#include <iostream.h>

void main()
   {
   int n = 99;            // make sure n isn't initialized to 0

   while( n != 0 )        // loop until n is 0
      cin >> n;           // read a number into n
   }
```

Here's some sample output. The user enters numbers, and the loop continues until 0 is entered, at which point the program terminates.

```
1
27
33
144
9
0
```

The `while` loop looks like a simplified version of the `for` loop. It contains a test expression but no initialization or increment expressions. Figure 4-3 shows the syntax of the `while` loop.

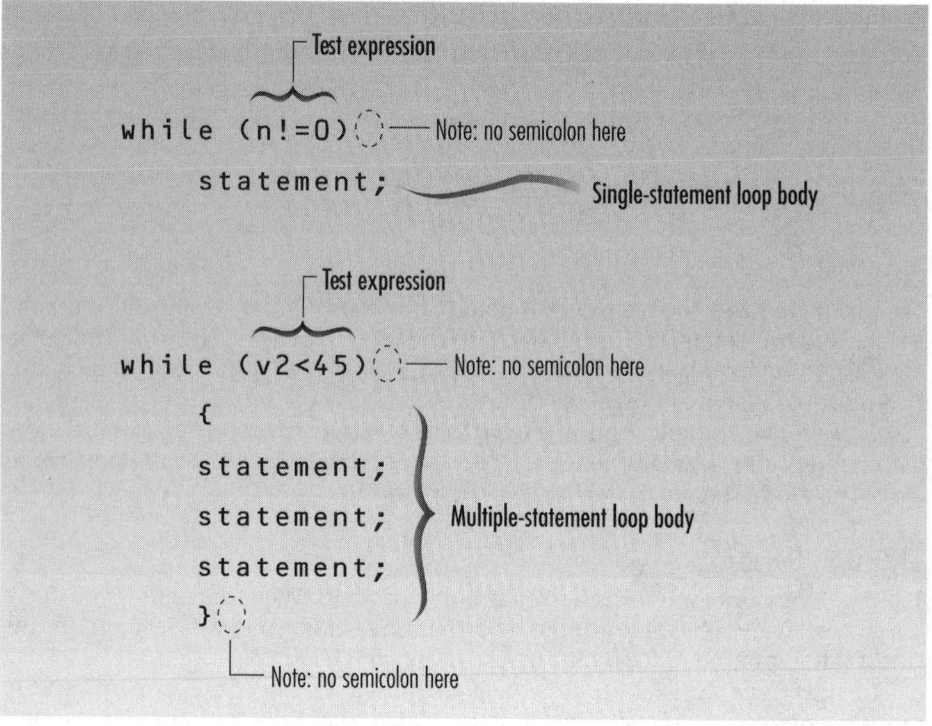

Figure 4-3 Syntax of the `while` Loop

As long as the test expression is true, the loop continues to be executed. In ENDON0, the text expression

```
n != 0
```

is true until the user enters 0.

Figure 4-4 shows the operation of a `while` loop. The simplicity of the `while` loop is a bit illusory. Although there is no initialization expression, the loop variable (`n` in ENDON0) must be initialized before the loop begins. The loop body must also contain some statement that changes the value of the loop variable; otherwise the loop would never end. In ENDON0 it's `cin>>n;`.

Multiple Statements in `while` Loop

The next example, WHILE4, uses multiple statements in a `while` loop. It's a variation of the CUBELIST program shown earlier with a `for` loop, but it calculates the fourth power, instead of the cube, of a series of integers. Let's assume that in this program it's important to put the results in a column four digits wide. To ensure that the results fit this column width, we must stop the loop before the results become larger than 9999. Without prior calculation we don't know what number will generate a result of this size, so we let the program figure it out. The test expression in the `while` statement terminates the program before the powers become too large.

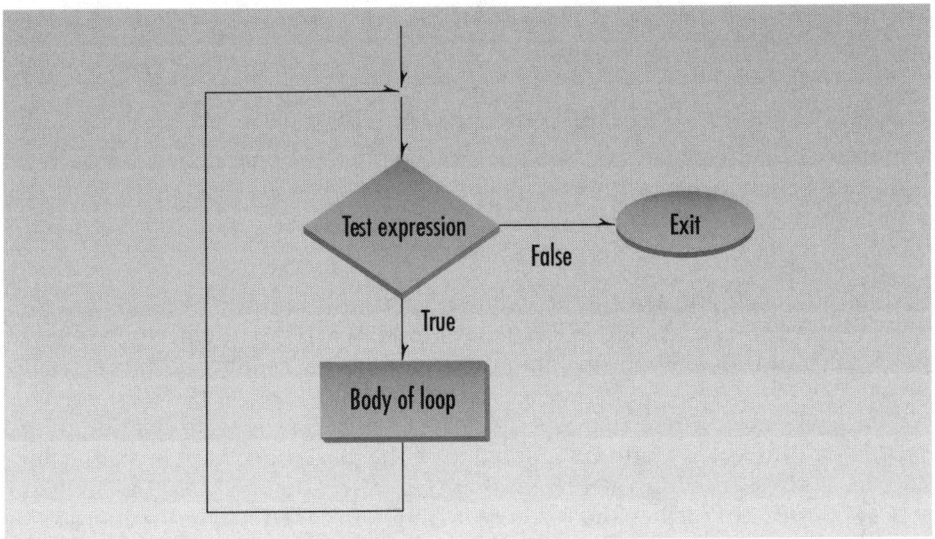

Figure 4-4 Operation of the `while` Loop

```
// while4.cpp
// prints numbers raised to fourth power
#include <iostream.h>
#include <iomanip.h>                // for setw

void main()
   {
   int pow=1;                       // power initially 1
   int numb=1;                      // numb goes from 1 to ???

   while( pow<9999 )                // loop while power < 4 digits
      {
      cout << setw(2) << numb;             // display number
      cout << setw(5) << pow << endl;      // display fourth power
      ++numb;                       // get ready for next power
      pow = numb*numb*numb*numb;           // calculate fourth power
      }
   }
```

To find the fourth power of `numb`, we simply multiply it by itself four times. Each time through the loop we increment `numb`. But we don't use `numb` in the test expression in `while`; instead, the resulting value of `pow` determines when to terminate the loop. Here's the output:

```
 1    1
 2   16
 3   81
 4  256
 5  625
 6 1296
 7 2401
 8 4096
 9 6561
```

The next number would be 10,000—too wide for our four-digit column; but by this time the loop has terminated.

Precedence: Arithmetic and Relational Operators

The next program touches on the question of operator precedence. It generates the famous sequence of numbers called *the Fibonacci series*. Here are the first few terms of the series:

```
1  1  2  3  5  8  13  21  34  55
```

Each term is found by adding the two previous ones: 1+1 is 2, 1+2 is 3, 2+3 is 5, 3+5 is 8, and so on. The Fibonacci series has applications in amazingly diverse fields, from sorting methods in computer science to the number of spirals in sunflowers.

One of the most interesting aspects of the Fibonacci series is its relation to the *golden ratio*. The golden ratio is supposed to be the ideal proportion in architecture and art, and was used in the design of ancient Greek temples. As the Fibonacci series is carried out further and further, the ratio of the last two terms approaches closer and closer to the golden ratio. Here's the listing for FIBO.CPP:

```
// fibo.cpp
// demonstrates WHILE loops using fibonacci series
#include <iostream.h>

void main()
   {                                 // largest unsigned long
   const unsigned long limit = 4294967295;
   unsigned long next=0;             // next-to-last term
   unsigned long last=1;             // last term

   while( next < limit / 2 )         // don't let results get too big
      {
      cout << last << "  ";          // display last term
      long sum = next + last;        // add last two terms
      next = last;                   // variables move forward
      last = sum;                    //    in the series
      }
   }
```

Here's the output:

```
1  1  2  3  5  8  13  21  34  55  89  144  233  377  610  987
1597  2584  4181  6765  10946  17711  28657  46368  75025  121393
196418  317811  514229  832040  1346269  2178309  3524578
5702887  9227465  14930352  24157817  39088169  63245986
102334155  165580141  267914296  433494437  701408733  1134903170
1836311903  2971215073
```

For you temple builders, the ratio of the last two terms gives an approximation of the golden ratio as 0.618033988—close enough for government work.

The FIBO program uses type `unsigned long`, the type that holds the largest positive integers. The test expression in the `while` statement terminates the loop before the numbers exceed the limit of this type. We define this limit as a `const` type, since it doesn't change. We must stop when `next` becomes larger than half the limit, otherwise `sum` would exceed the limit.

The test expression uses two operators:

```
(next < limit / 2)
```

Our intention is to compare `next` with the result of `limit/2`. That is, we want the division to be performed before the comparison. We could put parentheses around the division, to ensure that it's performed first.

```
(next < (limit/2) )
```

But we don't need the parentheses. Why not? Because arithmetic operators have a higher precedence than relational operators. This guarantees that `limit/2` will be evaluated before the comparison is made, even without the parentheses. We'll summarize the precedence situation later in this chapter, when we look at logical operators.

The do Loop

In a `while` loop, the test expression is evaluated at the *beginning* of the loop. If the test expression is false when the loop is entered, the loop body won't be executed at all. In some situations this is what you want. But sometimes you want to guarantee that the loop body is executed at least once, no matter what the initial state of the test expression. When this is the case you should use the `do` loop, which places the test expression at the *end* of the loop.

Our example, DIVDO, invites the user to enter two numbers: a dividend (the top number in a division) and a divisor (the bottom number). It then calculates the quotient (the answer) and the remainder, using the / and % operators, and prints out the result.

```
// divdo.cpp
// demonstrates DO loop
#include <iostream.h>

void main()
   {
   long dividend, divisor;
   char ch;

   do                                       // start of do loop
      {                                     // do some processing
      cout << "Enter dividend: "; cin >> dividend;
      cout << "Enter divisor: ";  cin >> divisor;
      cout << "Quotient is " << dividend / divisor;
      cout << ", remainder is " << dividend % divisor;

      cout << "\nDo another? (y/n): ";    // do it again?
      cin >> ch;
      }
   while( ch != 'n' );                     // loop condition
   }
```

Most of this program resides within the `do` loop. First, the keyword `do` marks the beginning of the loop. Then, as with the other loops, braces delimit the body of the loop. Finally a `while` statement provides the test expression and terminates the loop. This `while` statement looks much like the one in a `while` loop, except for its position at the end of the loop and the fact that it ends with a semicolon (which is easy to forget!). The syntax of the `do` loop is shown in Figure 4-5.

Following each computation, DIVDO asks if the user wants to do another. If so, the user enters a `'y'` character, and the test expression

```
ch != 'n'
```

remains true. If the user enters `'n'`, the test expression becomes false and the loop terminates. Figure 4-6 charts the operation of the `do` loop. Here's an example of DIVDO's output:

```
Enter dividend: 11
Enter divisor: 3
Quotient is 3, remainder is 2
Do another? (y/n): y
Enter dividend: 222
Enter divisor: 17
Quotient is 13, remainder is 1
Do another? (y/n): n
```

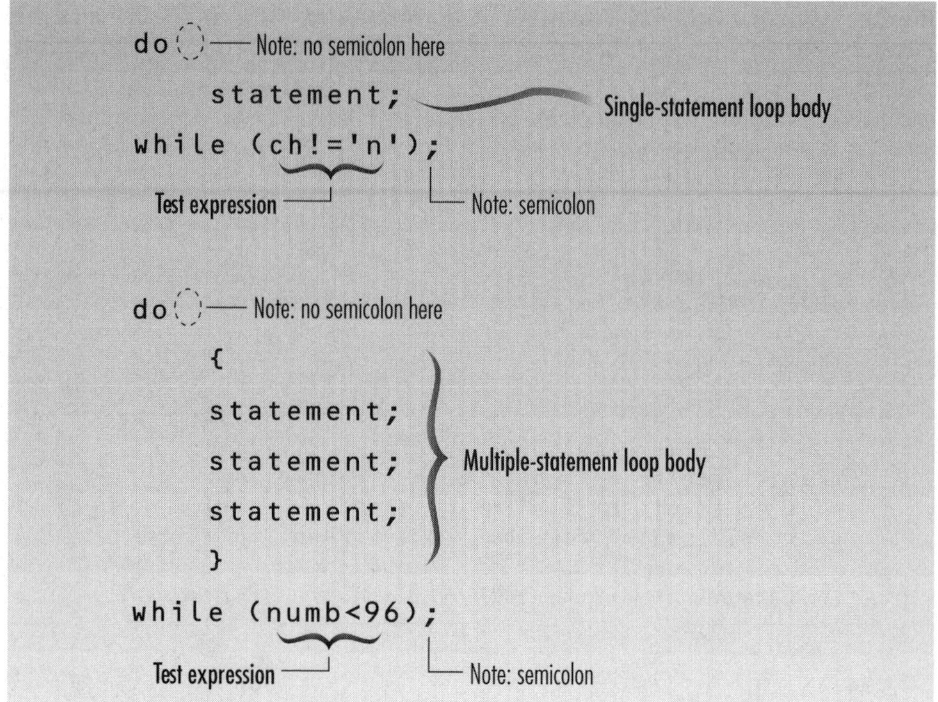

Figure 4-5 Syntax of the do Loop

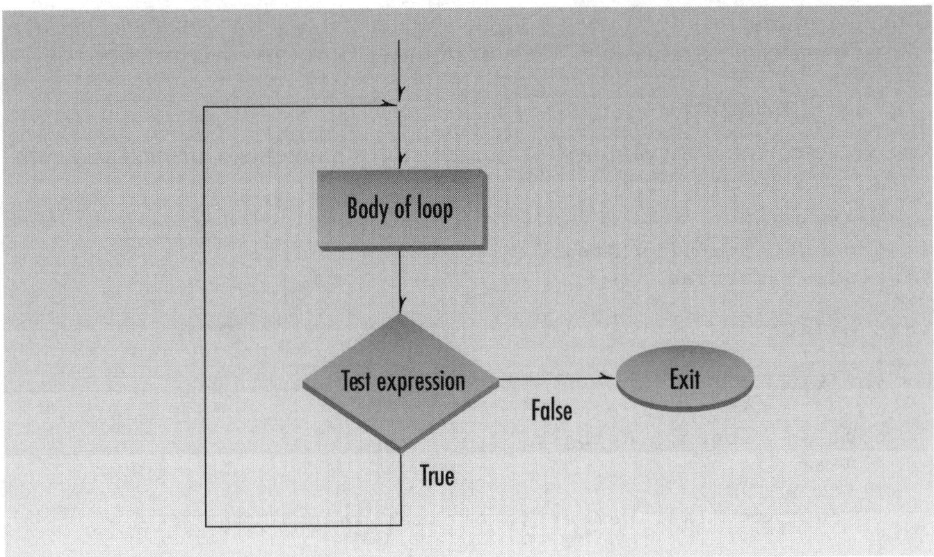

Figure 4-6 Operation of the `do` Loop

When to Use Which Loop

We've made some general statements about how loops are used. The `for` loop is appropriate when you know in advance how many times the loop will be executed. The `while` and `do` loops are used when you don't know in advance when the loop will terminate; the `while` loop when you may not want to execute the loop body even once, and the `do` loop when you're sure you want to execute the loop body at least once.

These criteria are somewhat arbitrary. Which loop type to use is more a matter of style than of hard-and-fast rules. You can actually make any of the loop types work in almost any situation. You should choose the type that makes your program the clearest and easiest to follow.

Decisions

The decisions in a loop always relate to the same question: Should we do this (the loop body) again? As humans we would find it boring to be so limited in our decision-making processes. We need to decide, not only whether to go to work again today (continuing the loop), but also whether to buy a red shirt or a green one (or no shirt at all), whether to take a vacation, and if so, in the mountains or by the sea.

Programs also need to make these one-time decisions. In a program a decision causes a one-time jump to a different part of the program, depending on the value of an expression. Decisions can be made in C++ in several ways. The most important is with the `if...else` statement, which chooses between two alternatives. This statement can be used without the `else`, as a simple `if` statement. Another decision statement, `switch`, creates branches for multiple alternative sections of code, depending on the value of a single variable. Finally the *conditional operator* is used in specialized situations. We'll examine each of these constructions.

The if Statement

The if statement is the simplest of the decision statements. Our next program, IFDEMO, provides an example.

```
// ifdemo.cpp
// demonstrates IF statement
#include <iostream.h>

void main()
   {
   int x;

   cout << "Enter a number: ";
   cin >> x;
   if( x > 100 )
      cout << "That number is greater than 100\n";
   }
```

The if keyword is followed by a test expression in parentheses. The syntax of the if statement is shown in Figure 4-7. As you can see, the syntax of if is very much like that of while. The difference is that the statements following the if are executed only once if the test expression is true; the statements following while

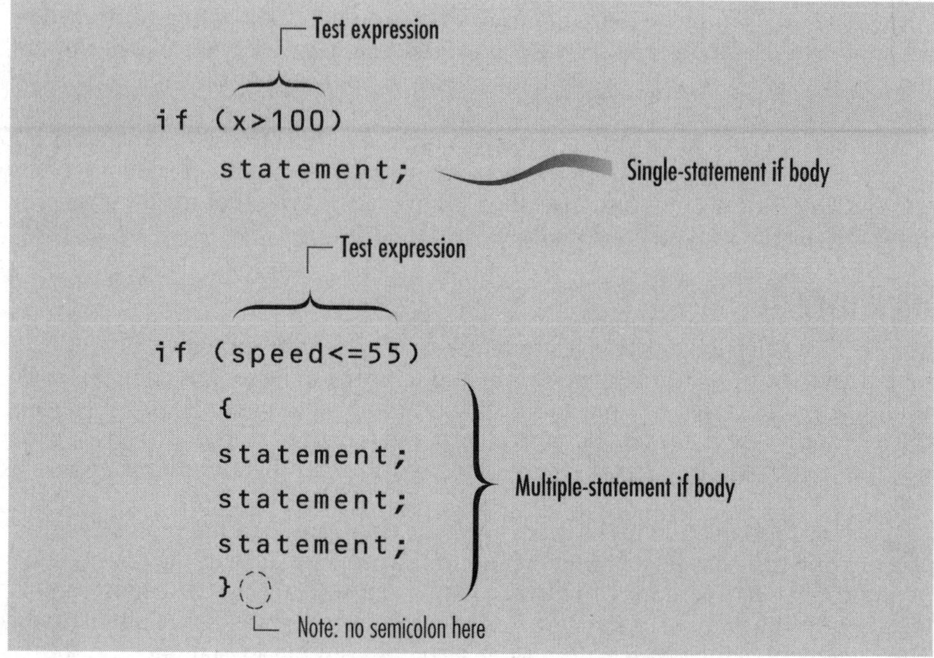

Figure 4-7 Syntax of the if Statement

are executed repeatedly until the test expression becomes false. Figure 4-8 shows the operation of the `if` statement.

Here's an example of the IFDEMO program's output when the number entered by the user is greater than 100:

```
C>if
Enter a number: 2000
That number is greater than 100
C>
```

If the number entered is not greater than 100, the program will terminate without printing anything.

Multiple Statements in the if Body

As in loops, the code in an `if` body can consist of a single statement—as shown in the IFDEMO example—or a block of statements delimited by braces. This variation on IFDEMO, called IF2, shows how that looks.

```
// if2.cpp
// demonstrates IF with multiline body
#include <iostream.h>

void main()
   {
   int x;
   cout << "Enter a number: ";
   cin >> x;
   if( x > 100 )
```

(continued on next page)

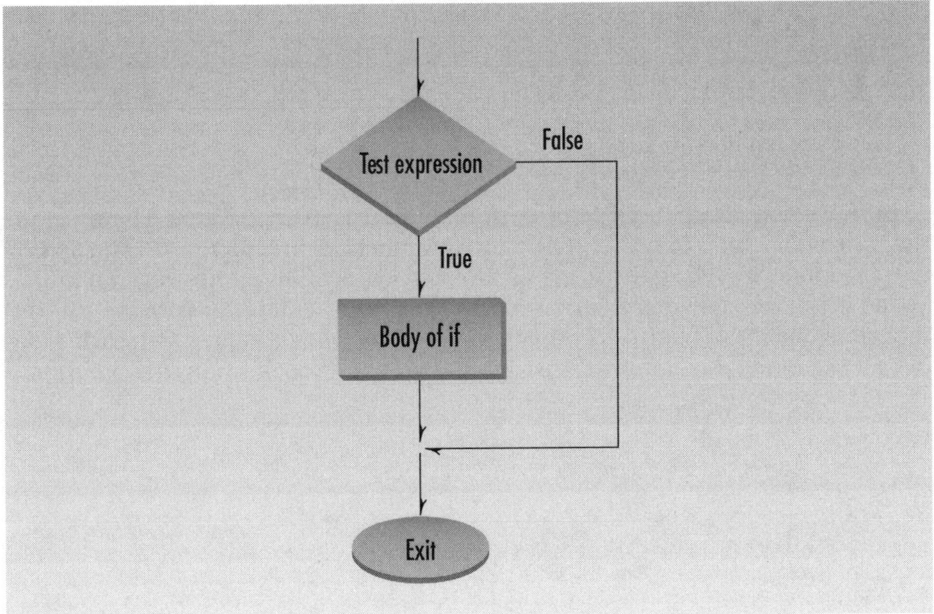

Figure 4-8 Operation of the `if` Statement

(continued from previous page)

```
      {
      cout << "The number " << x;
      cout << " is greater than 100\n";
      }
   }
```

Here's some output from IF2:

```
Enter a number: 12345
The number 12345 is greater than 100
```

Nesting ifs Inside Loops

The loop and decision structures we've seen so far can be nested inside one another. You can nest `if`s inside loops, loops inside `if`s, `if`s inside `if`s, and so on. Here's an example, PRIME, that nests an `if` within a `for` loop. This example tells you if a number you enter is a prime number. (Prime numbers are integers divisible only by themselves and 1. The first few primes are 1, 3, 5, 7, 11, 13, 17.)

```
// prime.cpp
// demonstrates IF statement with prime numbers
#include <iostream.h>
#include <process.h>      // for exit()

void main()
   {
   unsigned long n, j;

   cout << "Enter a number: ";
   cin >> n;                         // get number to test
   for(j=2; j < n/2; j++)            // divide by every integer from
      if(n%j == 0)                   // 2 on up; if remainder is 0,
         {                           // it's divisible by j
         cout << "It's not prime; divisible by " << j << endl;
         exit(0);                    // exit from the program
         }
   cout << "It's prime\n";
   }
```

In this example the user enters a number that is assigned to `n`. The program then uses a `for` loop to divide `n` by all the numbers from 2 up to `n/2`. The divisor is `j`, the loop variable. If any value of `j` divides evenly into `n`, then `n` is not prime. When a number divides evenly into another, the remainder is 0; we use the remainder operator `%` in the `if` statement to test for this condition with each value of `j`. If the number is not prime, we tell the user and we exit from the program.

Here's some output:

```
C>prime
Enter a number: 13
It's prime
C>prime
Enter a number: 22229
It's prime
C>prime
Enter a number: 22231
It's not prime; divisible by 11
```

(Beware: If you enter a number that is substantially larger than those shown and it happens to be prime, the program will take a long time to execute.)

Notice that there are no braces around the loop body. This is because the `if` statement, and the statements in *its* body, are considered to be a single statement.

Library Function `exit()`

When PRIME discovers that a number is not prime, it exits immediately, since there's no use proving more than once that a number isn't prime. This is accomplished with the library function `exit()`. This function causes the program to terminate, no matter where it is in the listing. It has no return value. Its single argument, 0 in our example, is returned to the operating system when the program exits. (This value is useful in batch files, where you can use the ERRORLEVEL value to query the return value provided by `exit()`. The value 0 is normally used for a successful termination; other numbers indicate errors.)

The `if...else` Statement

The `if` statement lets you do something if a condition is true. If it isn't true, nothing happens. But suppose we want to do one thing if a condition is true, and do something else if it's false. That's where the `if...else` statement comes in. It consists of an `if` statement, followed by a statement or block of statements, followed by the keyword `else`, followed by *another* statement or block of statements. The syntax is shown in Figure 4-9.

Here's a variation of our IF example, with an `else` added to the `if`:

```
// ifelse.cpp
// demonstrates IF...ELSE statement
#include <iostream.h>

void main()
   {
   int x;

   cout << "\nEnter a number: ";
   cin >> x;
   if( x > 100 )
      cout << "That number is greater than 100\n";
   else
      cout << "That number is not greater than 100\n";
   }
```

If the test expression in the `if` statement is true, the program prints one message; if it isn't, it prints the other.

Here's some output:

```
C>ifelse
Enter a number: 300
That number is greater than 100
C>ifelse
Enter a number: 3
That number is not greater than 100
C>
```

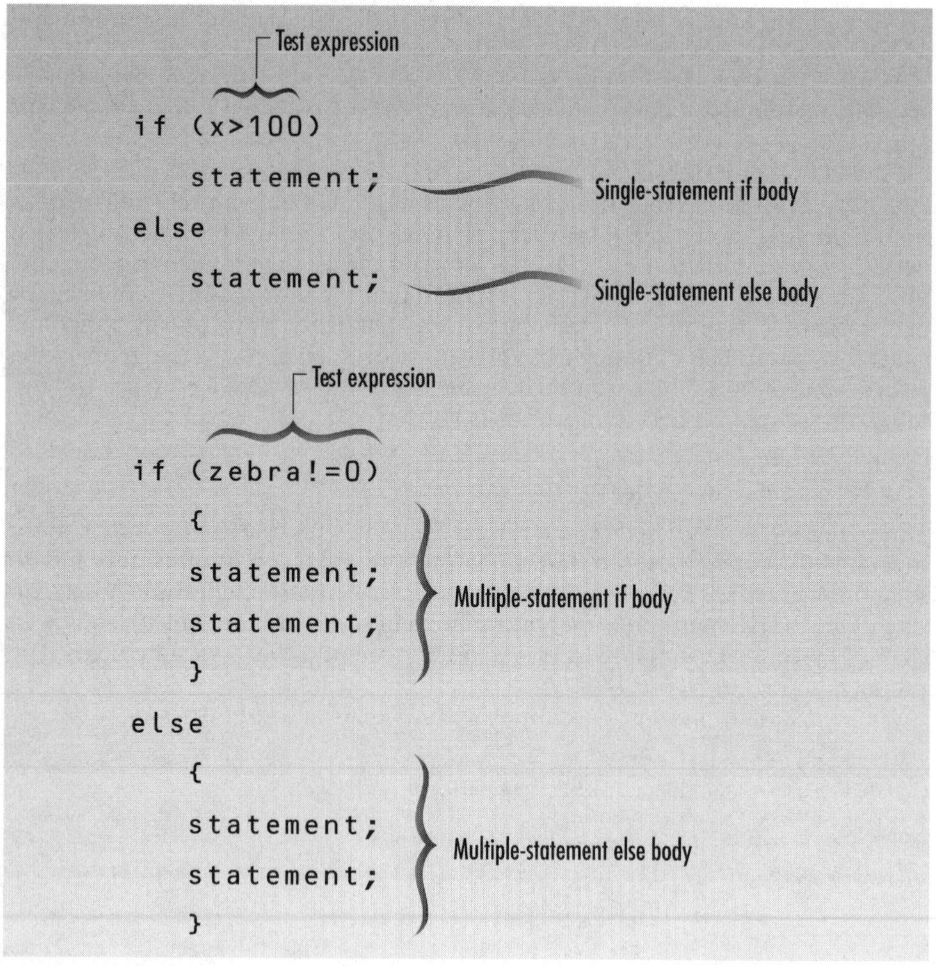

Figure 4-9 Syntax of the `if...else` Statement

The operation of the `if...else` statement is shown in Figure 4-10.

The `getche()` Library Function

Our next example shows an `if...else` statement embedded in a `while` loop. It also introduces a new library function: `getche()`. This program, CHCOUNT, counts the number of words and the number of characters in a phrase typed in by the user.

```
// chcount.cpp
// counts characters and words typed in
#include <iostream.h>
#include <conio.h>              // for getche()

void main()
   {
```

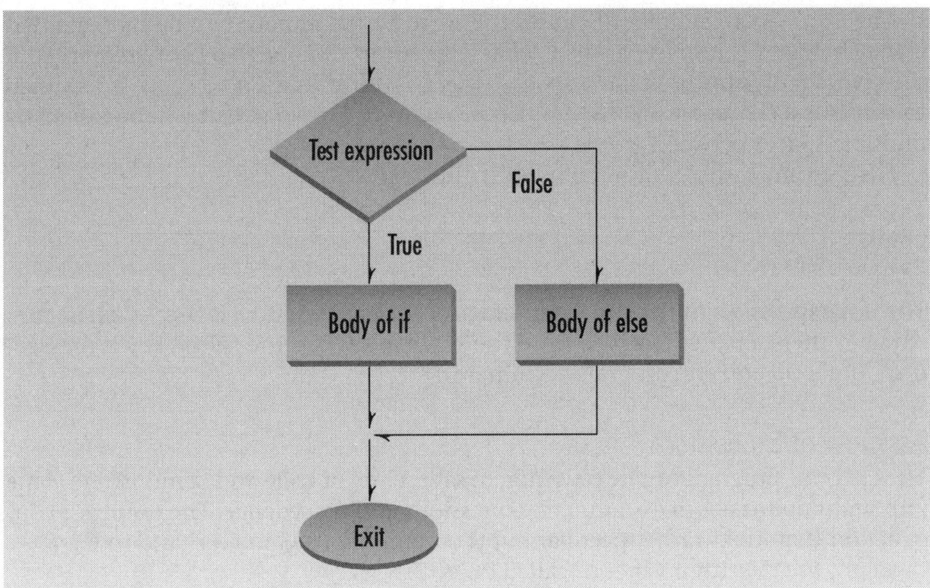

Figure 4-10 Operation of the `if...else` Statement

```
   int chcount=0;                  // counts non-space characters
   int wdcount=1;                  // counts spaces between words
   char ch = 'a';                  // ensure it isn't '\r'

   while( ch != '\r' )             // loop until Enter typed
      {
      ch = getche();               // read one character
      if( ch==' ' )                // if it's a space
         wdcount++;                // count a word
      else                         // otherwise,
         chcount++;                // count a character
      }                            // display results
      cout << "\nWords=" << wdcount << endl
           << "Letters=" << (chcount-1) << endl;
   }
```

So far we've used only `cin` and `>>` for input. That approach requires that the user always press the (ENTER) key to inform the program that the input is complete. This is true even for single characters: The user must type the character, then press (ENTER). However, as in the present example, a program often needs to process each character typed by the user without waiting for an (ENTER). The `getche()` library function performs this service. It returns each character typed, as soon as it's typed. It takes no arguments, and requires the CONIO.H header file. In CHCOUNT the value of the character returned from `getche()` is assigned to `ch`. (The `getche()` function echoes the character to the screen. That's why there's an `e` at the end of `getche`. Another function, `getch()`, is similar to `getche()` but doesn't echo the character to the screen.)

The `if...else` statement causes the word count `wdcount` to be incremented if the character is a space, and the character count `chcount` to be incremented if the character is anything *but* a space. Thus anything that *isn't* a space is assumed to count as a character. (Note that this program is fairly naïve; it will be fooled by multiple spaces between words.)

Here's some sample interaction with CHCOUNT:

```
For while and do
Words=4
Letters=13
```

The test expression in the `while` statement checks to see if `ch` is the '\r' character, which is the character received from the keyboard when the (ENTER) key is pressed. If so, the loop and the program terminate.

Assignment Expressions

The CHCOUNT program can be rewritten to save a line of code and demonstrate some important points about assignment expressions and precedence. The result is a construction that looks rather peculiar but is commonly used in C++ (and in C).

Here's the rewritten version, called CHCNT2:

```
// chcnt2.cpp
// counts characters and words typed in
#include <iostream.h>
#include <conio.h>                 // for getche()

void main()
   {
   int chcount=0;
   int wdcount=1;                  // space between two words
   char ch;

   while( (ch=getche()) != '\r' )  // loop until Enter typed
      {
      if( ch==' ' )                // if it's a space
         wdcount++;                // count a word
      else                         // otherwise,
         chcount++;                // count a character
      }                            // display results
      cout << "\nWords=" << wdcount << endl
           << "Letters=" << chcount << endl;
   }
```

The value returned by `getche()` is assigned to `ch` as before, but this entire assignment expression has been moved inside the test expression for `while`. The assignment expression is compared with `'\r'` to see if the loop should terminate. This works because the entire assignment expression takes on the value used in the assignment. That is, if `getche()` returns `'a'`, then not only does `ch` take on the value `'a'`, but the expression

```
(ch=getche())
```

also takes on the value `'a'`. This is then compared with `'\r'`.

The fact that assignment expressions have a value is also used in statements such as

```
x = y = z = 0;
```

This is perfectly legal in C++. First, `z` takes on the value 0, then `z = 0` takes on the value 0, which is assigned to `y`. Then the expression `y = z = 0` likewise takes on the value 0, which is assigned to `x`.

The parentheses around the assignment expression in

```
(ch=getche())
```

are necessary because the assignment operator = has a lower precedence than the relational operator `!=`. Without the parentheses the expression would be evaluated as

```
while( ch = (getche() != '\r') )    // not what we want
```

which would assign a true or false value to `ch`; not what we want.

The `while` statement in CHCNT2 provides a lot of power in a small space. It is not only a test expression (checking `ch` to see if it's `'\r'`); it also gets a character from the keyboard and assigns it to `ch`. It's also not easy to unravel the first time you see it.

Nested `if...else` Statements

Remember adventure games? You move your "character" around an imaginary landscape, and discover castles, sorcerers, treasure, and so on. This program, ADIFELSE, models a small part of an adventure game.

```
// adifelse.cpp
// demonstrates IF...ELSE with adventure program
#include <iostream.h>
#include <conio.h>          // for getche()

void main()
   {
   char dir='a';
   int x=10, y=10;

   cout << "Type Enter to quit\n";
   while( dir != '\r' )             // until Enter is typed
      {
      cout << "\nYour location is " << x << ", " << y;
      cout << "\nPress direction key (n, s, e, w): ";
      dir = getche();               // get character
      if( dir=='n')                 // go north
         y--;
      else
         if( dir=='s' )             // go south
            y++;
         else
            if( dir=='e' )          // go east
               x++;
```

(continued on next page)

(continued from previous page)

```
            else
               if( dir=='w' )    // go west
                  x--;
      }  // end while
   }  // end main
```

When the game starts, you find yourself on a barren moor. You can go one "unit" north, south, east, or west, while the program keeps track of where you are and reports your position, which starts at coordinates 10,10. Unfortunately, nothing exciting happens to your character, no matter where you go; the moor stretches almost limitlessly in all directions, as shown in Figure 4-11. We'll try to provide a little more excitement to this game later on.

Here's some sample interaction with ADIFELSE:

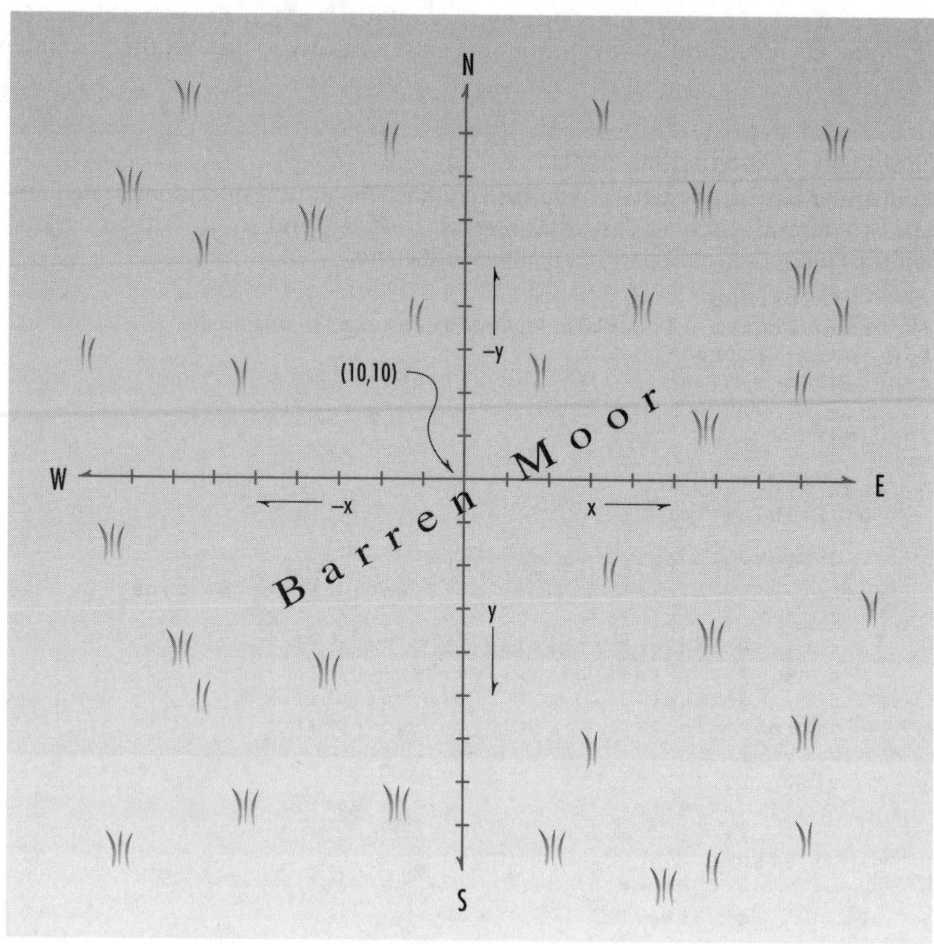

Figure 4-11 The Barren Moor

```
Your location is 10, 10
Press direction key (n, s, e, w): n
Your location is 10, 9
Press direction key (n, s, e, w): e
Your location is 11, 9
Press direction key (n, s, e, w):
```

You can press the ENTER key to exit from the program.

This program may not cause a sensation in the video arcades, but it does demonstrate one way to handle multiple branches. It uses an `if` statement nested inside an `if...else` statement, which is nested inside another `if...else` statement, which is nested inside yet another `if...else` statement. If the first test condition is false, the second one is examined, and so on until all four have been checked. If any one proves true, the appropriate action is taken—changing the x or y coordinate—and the program exits from all the nested decisions. Such a nested group of `if...else` statements is called a *decision tree*.

Matching the `else`

There's a potential problem in nested `if...else` statements: You can inadvertently match an `else` with the wrong `if`. BADELSE provides an example

```
// badelse.cpp
// demonstrates ELSE matched with wrong IF
#include <iostream.h>

void main()
   {
   int a, b, c;
   cout << "Enter a, b, and c:\n";
   cin >> a >> b >> c;

   if( a==b )
      if( b==c )
         cout << "a, b, and c are the same";
   else
      cout << "a and b are different";
   }
```

We've used multiple values with a single `cin`. Press ENTER following each value you type in; the three values will be assigned to `a`, `b`, and `c`.

What happens if you enter `2`, then `3`, and then `3`? Variable `a` is 2, and `b` is 3. They're different, so the first test expression is false, and you would expect the `else` to be invoked, printing *a and b are different*. But in fact nothing is printed. Why not? Because the `else` is matched with the wrong `if`. The indentation would lead you to believe that the `else` is matched with the first `if`, but in fact it goes with the second `if`. Here's the rule: An `e` is matched with the last `if` that doesn't have its own `else`.

Here's a corrected version:

```
if(a==b)
   if(b==c)
      cout << "a, b, and c are the same";
   else
      cout << "b and c are different";
```

We changed the indentation and also the phrase printed by the `else` body. Now if you enter 2, 3, 3, nothing will be printed. But entering 2, 2, 3 will cause the output

```
b and c are different
```

If you really want to pair an `else` with an earlier `if`, you can use braces around the inner `if`:

```
if(a==b)
   {
   if(b==c)
      cout << "a, b, and c are the same";
   }
else
   cout << "a and b are different";
```

Here the `else` is paired with the first `if`, as the indentation indicates. The braces make the material within them invisible to the following `else`.

The `else...if` Construction

The nested `if...else` statements in the ADIFELSE program look clumsy and can be hard—for humans—to interpret, especially if they are nested more deeply than shown. However there's another approach to writing the same statements. We need only reformat the program, obtaining the next example, ADELSEIF.

```
// adelseif.cpp
// demonstrates ELSE...IF with adventure program
#include <iostream.h>
#include <conio.h>        // for getche()

void main()
   {
   char dir='a';
   int x=10, y=10;

   cout << "Type Enter to quit\n";
   while( dir != '\r' )           // until Enter is typed
      {
      cout << "\nYour location is " << x << ", " << y;
      cout << "\nPress direction key (n, s, e, w): ";
      dir = getche();             // get character
      if( dir=='n')               // go north
         y--;
      else if( dir=='s' )         // go south
         y++;
      else if( dir=='e' )         // go east
         x++;
      else if( dir=='w' )         // go west
         x--;
      }  // end while
   }  // end main
```

The compiler sees this as identical to ADIFELSE, but we've rearranged the `if`s so they directly follow the `else`s. The result looks almost like a new keyword: `else if`. The program goes down the ladder of `else...if`s until one of the test expressions is true. It then executes the following statement and exits from the ladder. This format is clearer and easier to follow than the `if...else` approach.

The `switch` Statement

If you have a large decision tree, and all the decisions depend on the value of the same variable, you will probably want to consider a `switch` statement instead of a series of `if...else` or `else...if` constructions. Here's a simple example called PLATTERS that will appeal to nostalgia buffs:

```
// platters.cpp
// demonstrates SWITCH statement
#include <iostream.h>

void main()
   {
   int speed;                          // turntable speed

   cout << "\nEnter 33, 45, or 78: ";
   cin >> speed;                       // user enters speed
   switch(speed)                       // selection based on speed
      {
      case 33:                         // user entered 33
         cout << "LP album\n";
         break;
      case 45:                         // user entered 45
         cout << "Single selection\n";
         break;
      case 78:                         // user entered 78
         cout << "Obsolete format\n";
         break;
      }
   }
```

This program prints one of three possible messages, depending on whether the user inputs the number `33`, `45`, or `78`. The keyword `switch` is followed by a *switch variable* in parentheses.

```
switch(speed)
```

Braces then delimit a number of `case` statements. Each `case` keyword is followed by a constant, which is not in parentheses but is followed by a colon.

```
case 33:
```

The data type of the case constants should match that of the switch variable. Figure 4-12 shows the syntax of the `switch` statement.

Before entering the switch, the program should assign a value to the switch variable. This value will usually match a constant in one of the `case` statements. When this is the case (pun intended!), the statements immediately following the keyword `case` will be executed, until a `break` is reached.

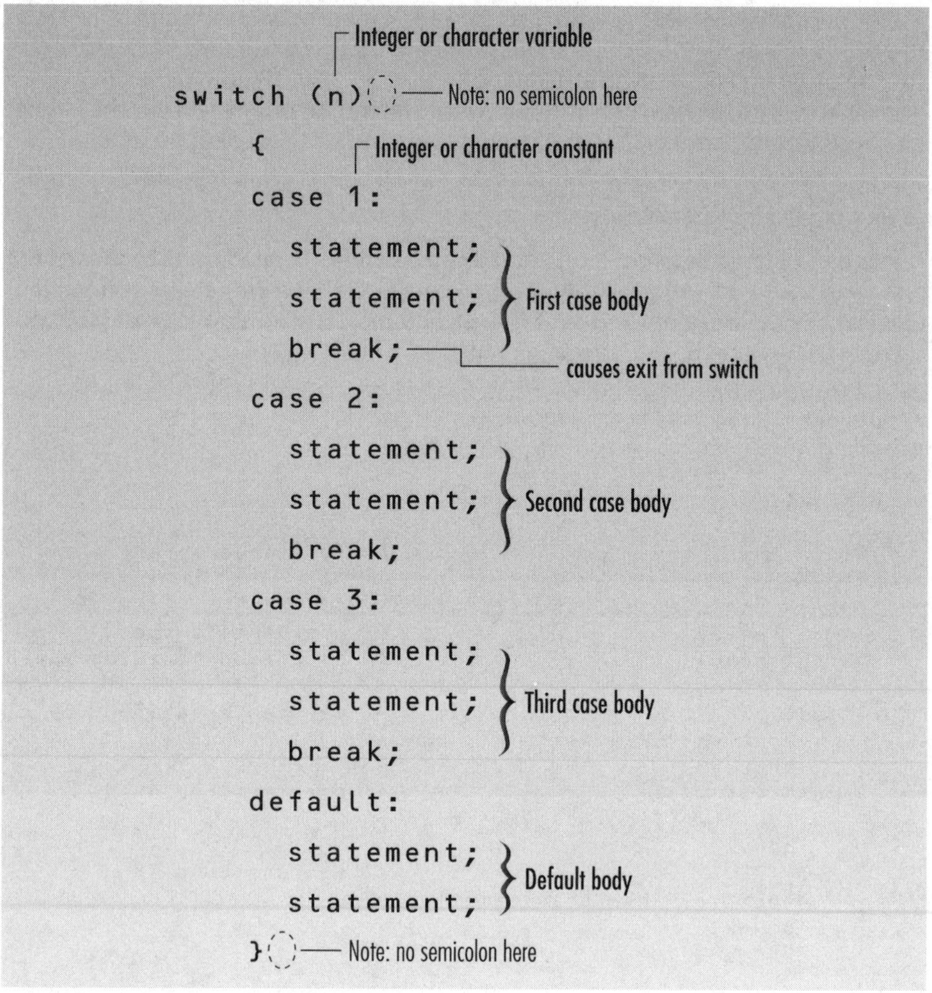

```
              ┌ Integer or character variable
switch (n)( )── Note: no semicolon here
   {              ┌ Integer or character constant
   case 1:
      statement;  )
      statement;  } First case body
      break;──────┘── causes exit from switch
   case 2:
      statement;  )
      statement;  } Second case body
      break;      )
   case 3:
      statement;  )
      statement;  } Third case body
      break;      )
   default:
      statement;  } Default body
      statement;  )
   }( )── Note: no semicolon here
```

Figure 4-12 Syntax of the `switch` Statement

Here's an example of PLATTER's output:

```
Enter 33, 45, or 78: 45
Single selection
```

The `break` Statement

PLATTERS has a `break` statement at the end of each `case` section. The `break` keyword causes the entire `switch` statement to exit. Control goes to the first statement following the end of the `switch` construction, which in PLATTERS is the end of the program. Don't forget the `break`; without it, control passes down (or "falls through") to the statements for the next `case`, which is usually not what you want (although sometimes it's useful).

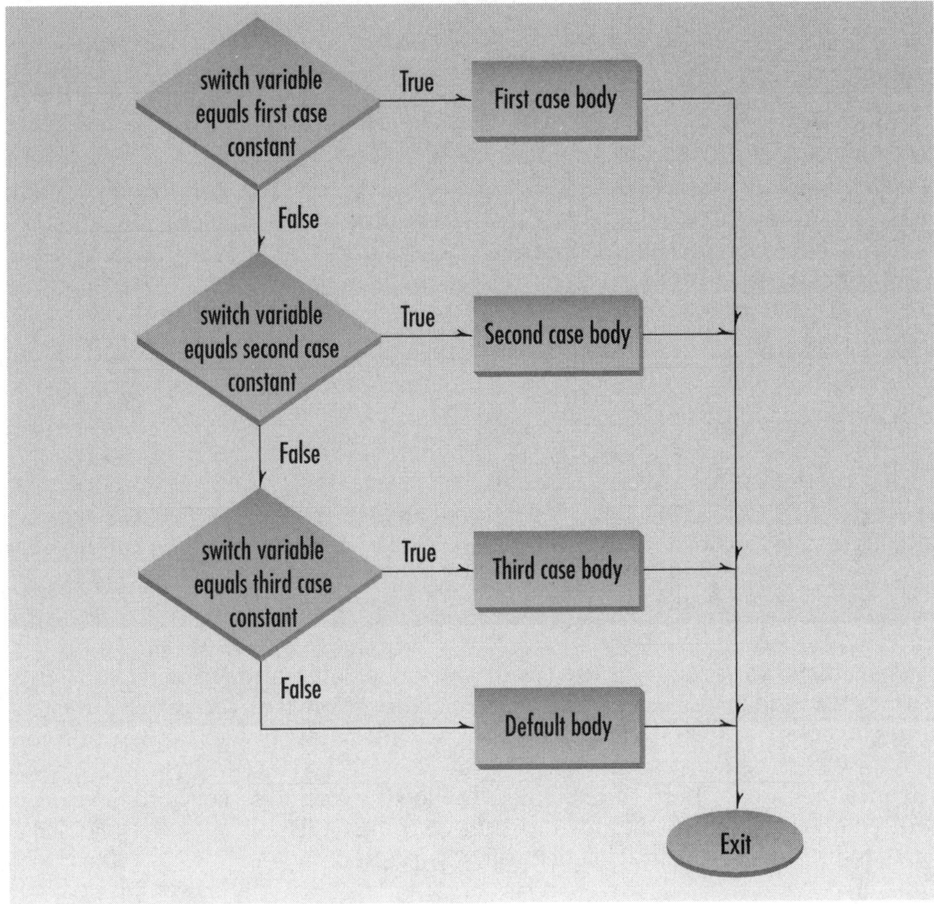

Figure 4-13 Operation of the `switch` Statement

If the value of the switch variable doesn't match any of the `case` constants, then control passes to the end of the switch without doing anything. The operation of the `switch` statement is shown in Figure 4-13.The `break` keyword is also used to escape from loops; we'll discuss this soon.

`switch` Statement with Character Variables

The PLATTERS example shows a `switch` statement based on a variable of type `int`. You can also use type `char`. Here's our ADELSEIF program rewritten as ADSWITCH:

```
// adswitch.cpp
// demonstrates SWITCH with adventure program
#include <iostream.h>
#include <conio.h>        // for getche()
```

(continued on next page)

(continued from previous page)

```
void main()
   {
   char dir='a';
   int x=10, y=10;

   while( dir != '\r' )
      {
      cout << "\nYour location is " << x << ", " << y;
      cout << "\nEnter direction (n, s, e, w): ";
      dir = getche();                            // get character
      switch(dir)                                // switch on it
         {
         case 'n':  y--; break;                  // go north
         case 's':  y++; break;                  // go south
         case 'e':  x++; break;                  // go east
         case 'w':  x--; break;                  // go west
         case '\r': cout << "Exiting\n"; break;  // Enter key
         default:   cout << "Try again\n";       // unknown char
         }  // end switch
      }  // end while
   }  // end main
```

A character variable `dir` is used as the switch variable, and character constants `'n'`, `'s'`, and so on are used as the case constants. (Note that you can use integers and characters as switch variables, as shown in the last two examples, but you can't use floating-point numbers.)

Since they are so short, the statements following each `case` keyword have been written on one line, which makes for a more compact listing. We've also added a `case` to print an exit message when (ENTER) is pressed.

The `default` Keyword

In the ADSWITCH program, where you expect to see the last `case` at the bottom of the `switch` construction, you instead see the keyword `default`. This keyword gives the `switch` construction a way to take an action if the value of the loop variable doesn't match any of the `case` constants. Here we use it to print `Try again` if the user types an unknown character. No `break` is necessary after `default`, since we're at the end of the `switch` anyway.

A `switch` statement is a common approach to *parsing* (figuring out) input entered by the user. Each of the possible characters is represented by a `case`.

It's a good idea to use a `default` statement in all `switch` statements, even if you don't think you need it. A construction such as

```
default:
   cout << "Error: incorrect input to switch"; break;
```

alerts the programmer (or the user, if the programmer doesn't catch the bug) that something has gone wrong in the operation of the program. In the interest of brevity we don't always include such a `default` statement, but you should, especially in serious programs.

switch versus if...else

When do you use a series of `if...else` (or `else...if`) statements, and when do you use a `switch` statement? In an `if...else` construction you can use a series of expressions that involve unrelated variables and are as complex as you like. For example:

```
if( SteamPressure*Factor > 56 )
   // statements
else if( VoltageIn + VoltageOut < 23000)
   // statements
else if( day==Thursday )
   // statements
else
   // statements
```

In a `switch` statement, however, all the branches are selected by the same variable; the only thing distinguishing one branch from another is the value of this variable. You can't say

```
case a<3:
   // do something
   break;
```

The case constant must be an integer or character constant, like `3` or `'a'`, or an expression that evaluates to a constant, like `'a'+32`.

When these conditions are met, the `switch` statement is very clean—easy to write and to understand. It should be used whenever possible, especially when the decision tree has more than a few possibilities.

The Conditional Operator

Here's a strange sort of decision operator. It exists because of a common programming situation: A variable is given one value if something is true and another value if it's false. For example, here's an `if...else` statement that gives the variable `min` the value of `alpha` or the value of `beta`, depending on which is smaller:

```
if( alpha < beta )
   min = alpha;
else
   min = beta;
```

This sort of construction is so common that the designers of C++ (actually the designers of C, long ago) invented a compressed way to express it: the *conditional operator*. This operator consists of two symbols, which operate on three operands. It's the only such operator in C++; other operators operate on one or two operands. Here's the equivalent of the same program fragment, using a conditional operator:

```
min = (alpha<beta) ? alpha : beta;
```

The part of this statement to the right of the equal sign is called the *conditional expression*:

```
(alpha<beta) ? alpha : beta   // conditional expression
```

The question mark and the colon make up the conditional operator. The expression before the question mark,

```
(alpha<beta)
```

is the test expression. It and `alpha` and `beta` are the three operands.

If the test expression is true, then the entire conditional expression takes on the value of the operand following the question mark: `alpha` in this example. If the test expression is false, the conditional expression takes on the value of the operand following the colon: `beta`. The parentheses around the test expression aren't needed for the compiler, but they're customary; they make the statement easier to read (and it needs all the help it can get). Figure 4-14 shows the syntax of the conditional statement, and Figure 4-15 shows its operation.

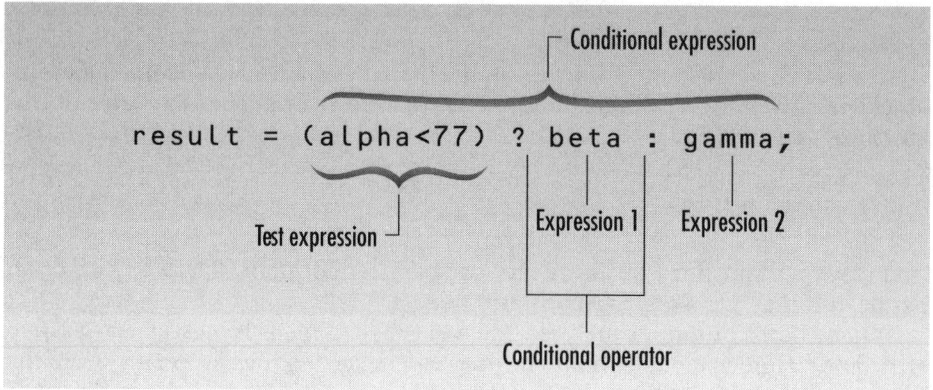

Figure 4-14 Syntax of the Conditional Operator

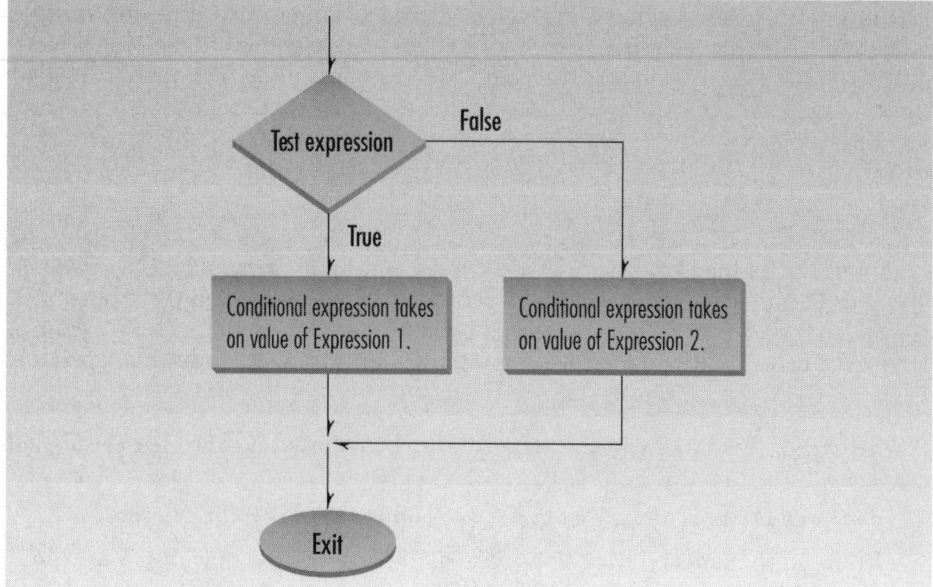

Figure 4-15 Operation of the Conditional Operator

The conditional expression can be assigned to another variable, or used anywhere a value can be. In this example it's assigned to the variable `min`.

Here's another example: a statement that uses a conditional operator to find the absolute value of a variable `n`. (The absolute value of a number is the number with any negative sign removed, so it's always positive.)

```
absvalue = n<0 ? -n : n;
```

If `n` is less than 0, the expression becomes `-n`, a positive number. If `n` is not less than 0, the expression remains `n`. The result is the absolute value of `n`, which is assigned to `absvalue`.

Here's a program, CONDI.CPP, that uses the conditional operator to print an `x` every eight spaces in a line of text. You might use this to see where the tab stops are on your screen.

```
// condi.cpp
// prints 'x' every 8 columns
// demonstrates conditional operator
#include <iostream.h>

void main()
   {
   for(int j=0; j<80; j++)              // for every column,
      {                                 // ch is 'x' if column is
      char ch = (j%8) ? ' ' : 'x';      // multiple of 8, and
      cout << ch;                       // ' ' (space) otherwise
      }
   }
```

Some of the right side of the output is lost because of the page width, but you can probably imagine it:

```
x       x       x       x       x       x       x       x       x
```

As `j` cycles through the numbers from 0 to 79, the remainder operator causes the expression `(j % 8)` to become false—that is, 0—only when `j` is a multiple of 8. So the conditional expression

```
(j%8) ? ' ' : 'x'
```

has the value `' '` when `j` is not a multiple of 8, and the value `'x'` when it is.

You may think this is terse, but we could have combined the two statements in the loop body into one, eliminating the `ch` variable:

```
cout << ( (j%8) ? ' ' : 'x' );
```

Hotshot C++ (and C) programmers love this sort of thing—getting a lot of bang from very little code. But you don't need to strive for concise code if you don't want to. Sometimes it becomes so obscure it's not worth the effort. Even using the conditional operator is optional: An `if...else` statement and a few extra program lines will accomplish the same thing.

Logical Operators

So far we've seen two families of operators (besides the oddball conditional operator). First are the arithmetic operators `+`, `-`, `*`, `/`, and `%`. Second are the relational operators `<`, `>`, `<=`, `>=`, `==`, and `!=`.

Let's examine a third family of operators, called *logical operators*. These operators allow you to logically combine Boolean (true/false) values. For example, *today is a weekday* has a Boolean value, since it's either true or false. Another Boolean expression is *Maria took the car*. We can connect these expressions logically: *If today is a weekday, and Maria took the car, then I'll have to take the bus*. The logical connection here is the word *and*, which provides a true or false value to the combination of the two phrases. Only if they are both true will I have to take the bus.

Logical AND Operator

Let's see how logical operators combine Boolean expressions in C++. Here's an example, ADVENAND, that uses a logical operator to spruce up the adventure game from the ADSWITCH example. We'll bury some treasure at coordinates (7,11) and see if the player can find it.

```
// advenand.cpp
// demonstrates AND logical operator
#include <iostream.h>
#include <process.h>                    // for exit()
#include <conio.h>                      // for getche()
void main()
   {
   char dir='a';
   int x=10, y=10;

   while( dir != '\r' )
      {
      cout << "\nYour location is " << x << ", " << y;
      cout << "\nEnter direction (n, s, e, w): ";
      dir = getche();                   // get direction
      switch(dir)
         {
         case 'n': y--; break;          // update coordinates
         case 's': y++; break;
         case 'e': x++; break;
         case 'w': x--; break;
         }
      if( x==7 && y==11 )               // if x is 7 and y is 11
         {
         cout << "\nYou found the treasure!\n";
         exit(0);                       // exit from program
         }
      }  // end switch
   }  // end main
```

The key to this program is the `if` statement

```
if( x==7 && y==11 )
```

The test expression will be true only if *both* `x` is 7 *and* `y` is 11. The logical AND operator `&&` joins the two relational expressions to achieve this result.

Notice that parentheses are not necessary around the relational expressions.

```
( (x==7) && (y==11) )   // inner parentheses not necessary
```

This is because the relational operators have higher precedence than the logical operators.

Here's some interaction as the user arrives at these coordinates:

```
Your location is 7, 10
Enter direction (n, s, e, w): s
You found the treasure!
```

There are three logical operators in C++:

Operator	Effect
&&	Logical AND
||	Logical OR
!	Logical NOT

There is no logical XOR (exclusive OR) operator in C++.

Let's look at examples of the || and ! operators.

Logical OR Operator

Suppose in the adventure game you decide there will be dragons if the user goes too far east or too far west. Here's an example, ADVENOR, that uses the logical OR operator to implement this frightening impediment to free adventuring. It's a variation on the ADVENAND program.

```
// advenor.cpp
// demonstrates OR logical operator
#include <iostream.h>
#include <process.h>                // for exit()
#include <conio.h>                  // for getche()
void main()
   {
   char dir='a';
   int x=10, y=10;

   while( dir != '\r' )             // quit on Enter key
      {
      cout << "\n\nYour location is " << x << ", " << y;

      if( x<5 || x>15 )             // if x west of 5 OR east of 15
         cout << "\nBeware: dragons lurk here";

      cout << "\nEnter direction (n, s, e, w): ";
      dir = getche();               // get direction
      switch(dir)
         {
         case 'n': y--; break;      // update coordinates
         case 's': y++; break;
         case 'e': x++; break;
         case 'w': x--; break;
         }
      }
   }
```

The expression

```
x<5 || x>15
```

is true whenever either `x` is less than 5 (the player is too far west), or `x` is greater than 15 (the player is too far east). Again, the `||` operator has lower precedence than the relational operators `<` and `>`, so no parentheses are needed in this expression.

Logical NOT Operator

The logical NOT operator `!` is a unary operator—that is, it takes only one operand. (Almost all the operators we've seen thus far are binary operators; they take two operands. The conditional operator is the only ternary operator in C++.) The effect of the `!` is that the logical value of its operand is reversed: If something is true, `!` makes it false; if it is false, `!` makes it true.

For example, `(x==7)` is true if `x` is equal to 7, but `!(x==7)` is true if `x` is *not* equal to 7. (In this situation you could use the relational *not equals* operator, `x != 7`, to achieve the same effect.)

A True/False Value for Every Integer Variable

We may have given you the impression that for an expression to have a true/false value, it must involve a relational operator. But in fact, every integer expression has a true/false value, even if it is only a single variable. The expression `x` is true whenever `x` is not 0, and false when `x` is 0. Applying the `!` operator to this situation, we can see that the `!x` is true whenever `x` *is* 0, since it reverses the truth value of `x`.

Let's put these ideas to work. Imagine in your adventure game that you want to place a mushroom on all the locations where both `x` and `y` are a multiple of 7. (As you probably know, mushrooms, when consumed by the player, confer magical powers.) The remainder when `x` is divided by 7, which can be calculated by `x%7`, is 0 only when `x` is a multiple of 7. So to specify the mushroom locations, we can write

```
if( x%7==0 && y%7==0 )
   cout << "There's a mushroom here.\n";
```

However, remembering that expressions are true or false even if they don't involve relational operators, you can use the `!` operator to provide a more concise format.

```
if( !(x%7) && !(y%7) )    // if not x%7 and not y%7
```

This has exactly the same effect.

We've said that the logical operators `&&` and `||` have lower precedence than the relational operators. Why then do we need parentheses around `x%7` and `y%7`? Because, even though it is a logical operator, `!` is a unary operator, which has higher precedence than relational operators.

Precedence Summary

Lets summarize the precedence situation for the operators we've seen so far. The operators higher on the list have higher precedence than those lower down. Operators with higher precedence are evaluated before those with lower precedence. Operators on the same row have equal precedence. You can force an expression to be evaluated first by placing parentheses around it.

Operator type	Operators
Unary	!, ++, --, −
Arithmetic	Multiplicative *, /, % Additive +, −
Relational	inequality <, >, <=, >= equality ==, !=
Logical	and && or ||
Conditional	?:
Assignment	=, +=, =, *=, /=, %=

Other Control Statements

There are several other control statements in C++. We've already seen one, `break`, used in `switch` statements, but it can be used other places as well. Another statement, `continue`, is used only in loops, and a third, `goto`, should be avoided. Let's look at these statements in turn.

The `break` Statement

The `break` statement causes an exit from a loop, just as it does from a `switch` statement. The next statement after the `break` is executed is the statement following the loop. Figure 4-16 shows the operation of the `break` statement.

To demonstrate `break`, here's a program, SHOWPRIM, that displays the distribution of prime numbers in graphical form:

```
// showprim.cpp
// displays prime number distribution
#include <iostream.h>
#include <conio.h>                    // for getche()

void main()
   {
   const unsigned char WHITE = 219;     // solid color (primes)
   const unsigned char GRAY  = 176;     // gray (non primes)
   unsigned char ch;
                                       // for each screen position
   for(int count=0; count<80*25-1; count++)
      {
      ch = WHITE;                     // assume it's prime
      for(int j=2; j<count; j++)      // divide by every integer from
         if(count%j == 0)             // 2 on up; if remainder is 0,
            {
            ch = GRAY;                // it's not prime
            break;                    // break out of inner loop
            }
      cout << ch;                     // display the character
      }
   getche();                          // freeze screen until keypress
   }
```

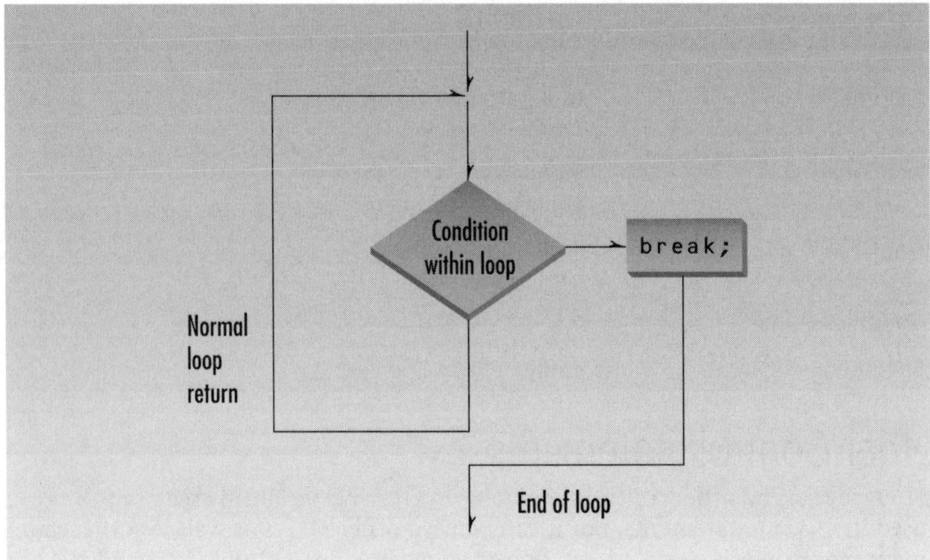

Figure 4-16 Operation of the `break` Statement

In effect every position on the screen is numbered, from 0 to 1999 (which is 80*25–1). If the number at a particular position is prime, the position is colored white (or whatever color your monitor displays); if it's not prime, it's colored gray.

Figure 4-17 shows the display. Strictly speaking, 0 is not considered a prime, but it's shown as white to avoid complicating the program. Think of the columns across the top as being numbered from 0 to 79. Notice that no primes (except 2) appear in even-numbered columns, since they're all divisible by 2. Is there a pattern to the other numbers? The mathematics world will be very excited if you find a pattern that allows you to predict whether any given number is prime.

When the inner `for` loop determines that a number is not prime, it sets the character `ch` to GRAY, and then executes `break` to escape from the inner loop. (We don't want to exit from the entire program, as in the PRIME example, since we have a whole series of numbers to work on.)

Notice that `break` only takes you out of the *innermost* loop. This is true no matter what constructions are nested inside each other: `break` only takes you out of the construction in which it's embedded. If there were a `switch` within a loop, a `break` in the `switch` would only take you out of the `switch`, not out of the loop.

The last `cout` statement prints the character, and then the loop continues, testing the next number for primeness.

IBM Extended Character Set

This program uses two characters from the *extended IBM character set*, the characters represented by the numbers from 128 to 255, as shown in Appendix A. The value 219 represents a solid-colored block (white on a black-and-white monitor), while 176 represents a gray block.

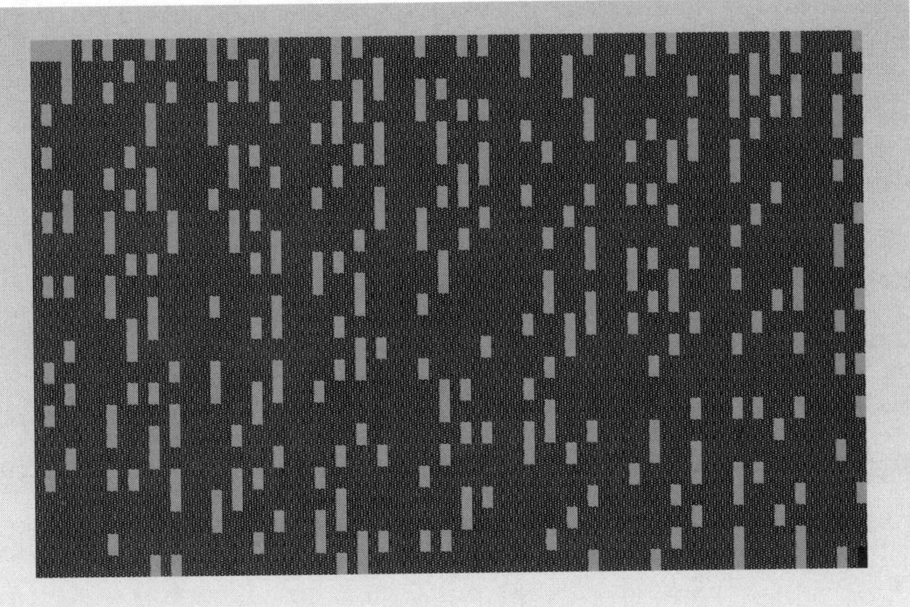

Figure 4-17 Output of SHOWPRIM Program

The SHOWPRIM example uses `getche()` in the last line, to keep the DOS prompt from scrolling the screen up when the program terminates. It freezes the screen until you press a key.

We use type `unsigned char` for the character variables in SHOWPRIM, since it goes up to 255. Type `char` only goes up to `127`.

The `continue` Statement

The `break` statement takes you out of the bottom of a loop. Sometimes, however, you want to go back to the top of the loop when something unexpected happens. Executing `continue` has this effect. Figure 4-18 shows the operation of `continue`.

Here's a variation on the DIVDO example. This program, which we saw earlier in this chapter, does division, but it has a fatal flaw: If the user inputs `0` as the divisor, the program undergoes catastrophic failure and terminates with the runtime error message *Divide error*. The revised version of the program, DIVDO2, deals with this situation more gracefully.

```
// divdo2.cpp
// demonstrates CONTINUE statement
#include <iostream.h>

void main()
   {
   long dividend, divisor;
   char ch;
```

(continued on next page)

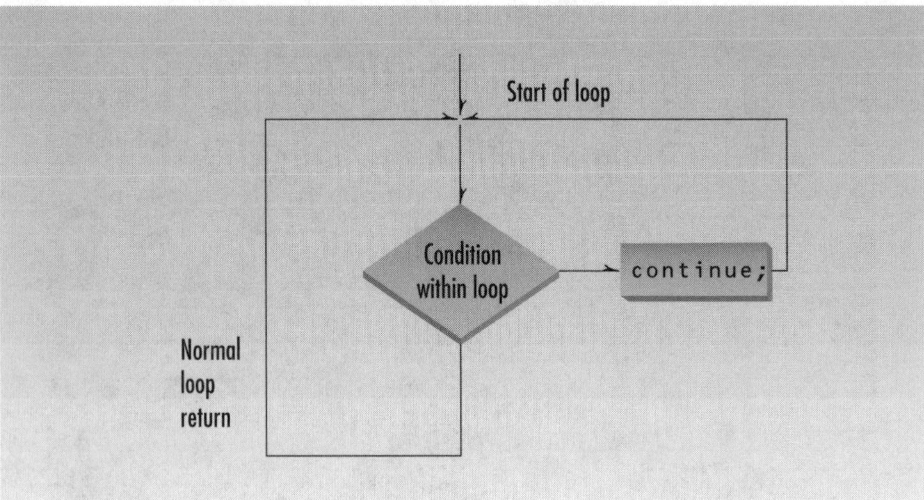

Figure 4-18 Operation of the `continue` Statement

(continued from previous page)

```
do
   {
   cout << "Enter dividend: "; cin >> dividend;
   cout << "Enter divisor: ";  cin >> divisor;
   if( divisor == 0 )                   // if attempt to
      {                                 // divide by 0,
      cout << "Illegal divisor\n";      // display message
      continue;                         // go to top of loop
      }
   cout << "Quotient is " << dividend / divisor;
   cout << ", remainder is " << dividend % divisor;

   cout << "\nDo another? (y/n): ";
   cin >> ch;
   }
while( ch != 'n' );
}
```

If the user inputs `0` for the divisor, the program prints an error message and, using `continue`, returns to the top of the loop to issue the prompts again. Here's some sample output:

```
Enter dividend: 10
Enter divisor: 0
Illegal divisor
Enter dividend:
```

A `break` statement in this situation would cause an exit from the `do` loop and the program, an unnecessarily harsh response.

The `goto` Statement

We'll mention the `goto` statement here for the sake of completeness—not because it's a good idea to use it. If you've had any exposure to structured programming principles, you know that `goto`s can quickly lead to "spaghetti" code that is difficult to understand and debug. There is almost never any need to use `goto`, as is demonstrated by its absence in the program examples in this book.

With that lecture out of the way, here's the syntax. You insert a *label* in your code at the desired destination for the `goto`. The label is always terminated by a colon. The keyword `goto`, followed by this label name, then takes you to the label. The following code fragment demonstrates this approach.

```
goto SystemCrash;
// other statements
SystemCrash:
// control will begin here following goto
```

Summary

Relational operators compare two values to see if they're equal, if one is larger than the other, and so on. The result is a logical or Boolean value, which is true or false. False is indicated by 0, and true by any other number.

There are three kinds of loops in C++. The `for` loop is most often used when you know in advance how many times you want to execute the loop. The `while` loop and `do` loops are used when the condition causing the loop to terminate arises within the loop, with the `while` loop not necessarily executing at all, and the `do` loop always executing at least once.

A loop body can be a single statement or a block of multiple statements delimited by braces. A variable defined within a block is visible only within that block.

There are four kinds of decision-making statements. The `if` statement does something if a test expression is true. The `if...else` statement does one thing if the test expression is true, and another thing if it isn't. The `else...if` construction is a way of rewriting a ladder of nested `if...else` statements to make it more readable. The `switch` statement branches to multiple sections of code, depending on the value of a single variable. The conditional operator simplifies returning one value if a test expression is true, and another if it's false.

The logical AND and OR operators combine two Boolean expressions to yield another one, and the logical NOT operator changes a Boolean value from true to false, or from false to true.

The `break` statement sends control to the end of the innermost loop or switch in which it occurs. The `continue` statement sends control to the top of the loop in which it occurs. The `goto` statement sends control to a label.

Precedence specifies which kinds of operations will be carried out first. The order is unary, arithmetic, relational, logical, conditional, assignment.

Questions

Answers to questions can be found in Appendix D.

1. A relational operator
   a. assigns one operand to another.
   b. yields a Boolean result.
   c. compares two operands.
   d. logically combines two operands.
2. Write an expression that uses a relational operator to return true if the variable `george` is not equal to `sally`.
3. Is –1 true or false?
4. Name and describe the usual purpose of three expressions in a `for` statement.
5. In a `for` loop with a multistatement loop body, semicolons should appear following
   a. the `for` statement itself.
   b. the closing brace in a multistatement loop body.
   c. each statement within the loop body.
   d. the test expression.
6. True or false: The increment expression in a `for` loop can decrement the loop variable.
7. Write a `for` loop that displays the numbers from 100 to 110.
8. A block of code is delimited by __________.
9. A variable defined within a block is visible
   a. from the point of definition onward in the program.
   b. from the point of definition onward in the function.
   c. from the point of definition onward in the block.
   d. throughout the function.
10. Write a `while` loop that displays the numbers from 100 to 110.
11. True or false: Relational operators have a higher precedence than arithmetic operators.
12. How many times is the loop body executed in a `do` loop?
13. Write a `do` loop that displays the numbers from 100 to 110.
14. Write an `if` statement that prints `Yes` if a variable `age` is greater than 21.

15. The library function `exit()` causes an exit from
    a. the loop in which it occurs.
    b. the block in which it occurs.
    c. the function in which it occurs.
    d. the program in which it occurs.
16. Write an `if...else` statement that displays `Yes` if a variable `age` is greater than 21, and displays `No` otherwise.
17. The `getche()` library function
    a. returns a character when any key is pressed.
    b. returns a character when (ENTER) is pressed.
    c. displays a character on the screen when any key is pressed.
    d. does not display a character on the screen.
18. What is the character obtained from `cin` when the user presses the (ENTER) key?
19. An `else` always matches the __________ `if`, unless the `if` is __________.
20. The `else...if` construction is obtained from a nested `if...else` by __________.
21. Write a `switch` statement that prints `Yes` if a variable `ch` is `'y'`, prints `No` if `ch` is `'n'`, and prints `Unknown response` otherwise.
22. Write a statement that uses a conditional operator to set `ticket` to 1 if `speed` is greater than 55, and to 0 otherwise.
23. The `&&` and `||` operators
    a. compare two numeric values.
    b. combine two numeric values.
    c. compare two Boolean values.
    d. combine two Boolean values.
24. Write an expression involving a logical operator that is true if `limit` is 55 and `speed` is greater than 55.
25. Arrange in order of precedence (highest first) the following kinds of operators: logical, unary, arithmetic, assignment, relational, conditional.
26. The `break` statement causes an exit
    a. only from the innermost loop.
    b. only from the innermost switch.
    c. from all loops and switches.
    d. from the innermost loop or switch.

27. Executing the `continue` operator from within a loop causes control to go to __________.

28. The `goto` statement causes control to go to
   a. an operator.
   b. a label.
   c. a variable.
   d. a function.

Exercises

Answers to the starred exercises can be found in Appendix D.

1.* Assume you want to generate a table of multiples of any given number. Write a program that allows the user to enter the number, and then generates the table, formatting it into 10 columns and 20 lines. Interaction with the program should look like this (only the first three lines are shown):

```
Enter a number: 7
     7    14    21    28    35    42    49    56    63    70
    77    84    91    98   105   112   119   126   133   140
   147   154   161   168   175   182   189   196   203   210
```

2.* Write a temperature-conversion program that gives the user the option of converting Fahrenheit to Celsius or Celsius to Fahrenheit. Then carry out the conversion. Use floating-point numbers. Interaction with the program might look like this:

```
Type 1 to convert Fahrenheit to Celsius,
     2 to convert Celsius to Fahrenheit: 1
Enter temperature in Fahrenheit: 70
In Celsius that's 21.111111
```

3.* Operators such as >>, which read input from the keyboard, must be able to convert a series of digits into a number. Write a program that does the same thing. It should allow the user to type up to six digits, and then display the resulting number as a type `long` integer. The digits should be read individually, as characters, using `getche()`. Constructing the number involves multiplying the existing value by 10 and then adding the new digit. (Hint: Subtract 48 or '0' to go from ASCII to a numerical digit.)

Here's some sample interaction:

```
Enter a number: 123456
Number is: 123456
```

4.* Create the equivalent of a four-function calculator. The program should request the user to enter a number, an operator, and another number. (Use floating point.) It should then carry out the specified arithmetical operation: adding, subtracting, multiplying, or dividing the two numbers. Use a `switch` statement to select the operation. Finally, display the result.

When it finishes the calculation, the program should ask if the user wants to do another calculation. The response can be `'y'` or `'n'`. Some sample interaction with the program might look like this:

```
Enter first number, operator, second number: 10 / 3
Answer = 3.333333
Do another (y/n)? y
Enter first number, operator, second number: 12 + 100
Answer = 112
Do another (y/n)? n
```

5. Use `for` loops to construct a program that displays a pyramid of Xs on the screen. The pyramid should look like this

```
    X
   XXX
  XXXXX
 XXXXXXX
XXXXXXXXX
```

except that it should be 20 lines high, instead of the 5 lines shown here. One way to do this is to nest two inner loops, one to print spaces and one to print Xs, inside an outer loop that steps down the screen from line to line.

6. Modify the FACTOR program in this chapter so that it repeatedly asks for a number and calculates its factorial, until the user enters 0, at which point it terminates. You can enclose the relevant statements in FACTOR in a `while` loop or a `do` loop to achieve this effect.

7. Write a program that calculates how much money you'll end up with if you invest an amount of money at a fixed interest rate, compounded yearly. Have the user furnish the initial amount, the number of years, and the yearly interest rate in percent. Some interaction with the program might look like this:

```
Enter initial amount: 3000
Enter number of years: 10
Enter interest rate (percent per year): 5.5
At the end of 10 years, you will have 5124.43 dollars.
```

At the end of the first year you have 3000 + (3000 * 0.055), which is 3165. At the end of the second year you have 3165 + (3165 * 0.055), which is 3339.08. Do this as many times as there are years. A `for` loop makes the calculation easy.

8. Write a program that repeatedly asks the user to enter two money amounts expressed in old-style British currency: pounds, shillings, and pence. (See Exercises 10 and 12 in Chapter 3.) The program should then add the two amounts and display the answer, again in pounds, shillings, and pence. Use a `do` loop that asks the user if the program should be terminated. Typical interaction might be

```
Enter first amount: £5.10.6
Enter second amount: £3.2.6
Total is £8.13.0
Do you wish to continue (y/n)?
```

To add the two amounts, you'll need to carry 1 shilling when the pence value is greater than 11, and carry 1 pound when there are more than 19 shillings.

9. Suppose you give a dinner party for six guests, but your table seats only four. In how many ways can four of the six guests arrange themselves at the table? Any of the six guests can sit in the first chair. Any of the remaining five can sit in the second chair. Any of the remaining four can sit in the third chair, and any of the remaining three can sit in the fourth chair. (The last two will have to stand.) So the number of possible arrangements of six guests in four chairs is 6*5*4*3, which is 360. Write a program that calculates the number of possible arrangements for any number of guests and any number of chairs. (Assume there will never be fewer guests than chairs.) Don't let this get too complicated. A simple `for` loop should do it.

10. Write another version of the program from Exercise 7 so that, instead of finding the final amount of your investment, you tell the program the final amount and it figures out how many years it will take, at a fixed rate of interest compounded yearly, to reach this amount. What sort of loop is appropriate for this problem? (Don't worry about fractional years, use an integer value for the year.)

11. Create a three-function calculator for old-style English currency, where money amounts are specified in pounds, shillings, and pence. (See Exercises 10 and 12 in Chapter 3.) The calculator should allow the user to add or subtract two money amounts, or to multiply a money amount by a floating-point number. (It doesn't make sense to multiply two money amounts; there is no such thing as square money. We'll ignore division. Use the general style of the ordinary four-function calculator in Exercise 4 in this chapter.)

12. Create a four-function calculator for fractions. (See Exercise 9 in Chapter 3, and Exercise 4 in this chapter.) Here are the formulas for the four arithmetic operations applied to fractions:

Addition:	`a/b + c/d = (a*d + b*c) / (b*d)`
Subtraction:	`a/b - c/d = (a*d - b*c) / (b*d)`
Multiplication:	`a/b * c/d = (a*c) / (b*d)`
Division:	`a/b / c/d = (a*d) / (b*c)`

The user should type the first fraction, an operator, and a second fraction. The program should then display the result and ask if the user wants to continue.

5

Structures

STRUCTURE SPECIFIERS AND DEFINITIONS

ACCESSING STRUCTURE MEMBERS

NESTED STRUCTURES

STRUCTURES AS OBJECTS AND DATA TYPES

ENUMERATED DATA TYPES

5

We've seen variables of simple data types, such as `float`, `char`, and `int`. Variables of such types represent one item of information: a height, an amount, a count, and so on. But just as groceries are organized into bags, employees into departments, and words into sentences, it's often convenient to organize simple variables into more complex entities. The C++ construction called the *structure* is one way to do this.

The first part of this chapter is devoted to structures. In the second part we'll look at a related topic: the enumerated data type.

Structures

A structure is a collection of simple variables. The variables in a structure can be of different types: Some can be `int`, some can be `float`, and so on. (This is unlike the array, which we'll meet later, in which all the variables must be the same type.) The data items in a structure are called the *members* of the structure.

In books on C programming, structures are often considered an advanced feature and are introduced toward the end of the book. However, for C++ programmers, structures are one of the two important building blocks in the understanding of objects and classes. In fact, the syntax of a structure is almost identical to that of a class. A structure (as typically used) is a collection of data, while a class is a collection of both data and functions. So by learning about structures we'll be paving the way for an understanding of classes and objects. Structures in C++ (and C) serve a similar purpose to *records* in BASIC and Pascal.

A Simple Structure

Let's start off with a structure that contains three variables: two integers and a floating-point number. This structure represents an item in a widget company's parts inventory. It is a template for information about a single widget part. The company makes several kinds of widgets, so the widget model number is the first member of the structure. The number of the part itself is the next member, and the final member is the part's cost. (Those of you who consider part numbers unexciting need to open your eyes to the romance of commerce.)

The program PARTS specifies the structure `part`, defines a structure variable of that type called `part1`, assigns values to its members, and then displays these values.

```
// parts.cpp
// uses parts inventory to demonstrate structures
#include <iostream.h>

struct part                 // specify a structure
   {
   int modelnumber;         // ID number of widget
   int partnumber;          // ID number of widget part
   float cost;              // cost of part
   };
```

(continued on next page)

(continued from previous page)

```
void main()
   {
   part part1;                  // define a structure variable

   part1.modelnumber = 6244;    // give values to structure members
   part1.partnumber = 373;
   part1.cost = 217.55;
                                // display structure members
   cout << "\nModel "  << part1.modelnumber;
   cout << ", part "   << part1.partnumber;
   cout << ", costs $" << part1.cost;
   }
```

The program's output looks like this:

```
Model 6244, part 373, costs $217.55
```

The PARTS program has three main aspects: specifying the structure, defining a structure variable, and accessing the members of the structure. Let's look at each of these.

Specifying the Structure

The structure *specifier* tells how the structure is organized: It specifies what members the structure will have. Here it is:

```
struct part
   {
   int modelnumber;
   int partnumber;
   float cost;
   };
```

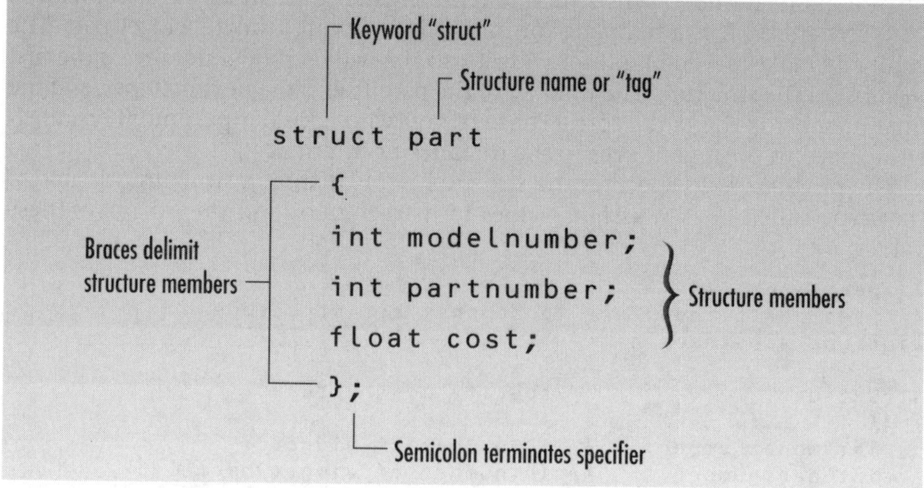

Figure 5-1 Syntax of the Structure Specifier

This construction is often called a structure *declaration*. However, the word declaration is also used in another sense—as we'll see later—so for clarity we'll use the word specifier.

Syntax of the Structure Specifier

The keyword `struct` introduces the specifier. Next comes the *structure name* or *tag*, which is `part`. The declarations of the structure members—`modelnumber`, `partnumber`, and `cost`—are enclosed in braces. A semicolon follows the closing brace, terminating the entire structure. Note that this use of the semicolon for structures is unlike the usage for a block of code. As we've seen, blocks of code, which are used in loops, decisions, and functions, are also delimited by braces. However, they don't use a semicolon following the final brace. Figure 5-1 shows the syntax of the structure specifier.

Use of the Structure Specifier

The specifier serves as a blueprint for the creation of variables of type `part`. The specifier does not itself define any variables; that is, it does not set aside any space in memory or name any variables. It's merely a specification for how such structure variables will look when they are defined. This is shown in Figure 5-2.

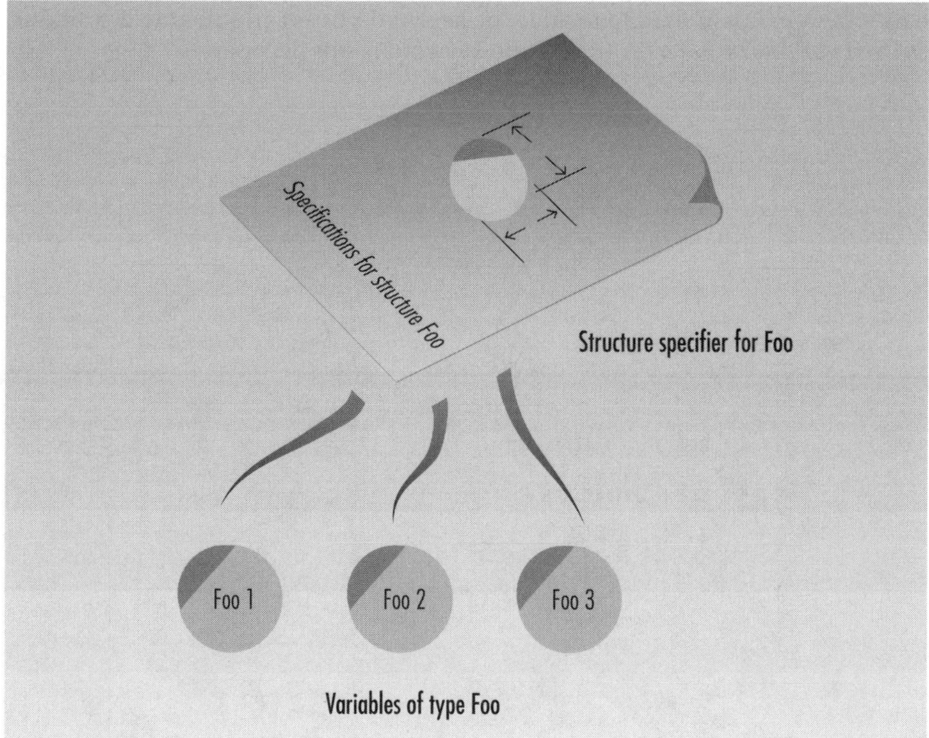

Figure 5-2 Structures and Structure Variables

It's not accidental that this description sounds like the distinction we noted between classes and objects in Chapter 1. As we'll see, an object has the same relationship to its class that a variable of a structure type has to the structure specifier.

Defining a Structure Variable

The first statement in `main()`,

```
part part1;
```

defines a variable, called `part1`, of type structure `part`. This definition reserves space in memory for `part1`. How much space? Enough to hold all the members of `part1`—namely `modelnumber`, `partnumber`, and `cost`. In this case there will be 2 bytes for each of the two `int`s, and 4 bytes for the `float`. Figure 5-3 shows how `part1` looks in memory.

In some ways we can think of the `part` structure as the specification for a new data type. This will become clearer as we go along, but notice that the format for defining a structure variable is the same as that for defining a built-in data type such as `int`:

```
part part1;
int var1;
```

This similarity is not accidental. One of the aims of C++ is to make the syntax and the operation of user-defined data types as similar as possible to that of built-in data types. (In C you need to include the keyword `struct` in structure definitions, as in `struct part part1;`. In C++ the keyword is not necessary.)

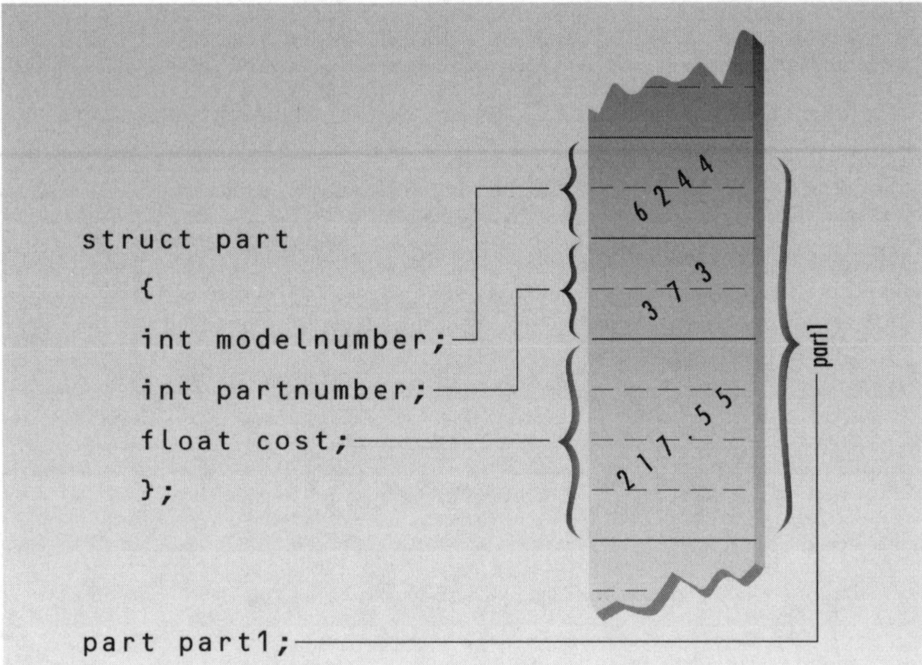

Figure 5-3 Structure Members in Memory

Accessing Structure Members

Once a structure variable has been defined, its members can be accessed using something called the *dot operator*. Here's how the first member is given a value:

```
part1.modelnumber = 6244;
```

The structure member is written in three parts: the name of the structure variable (`part1`); the dot operator, which consists of a period (`.`); and the member name (`modelnumber`). This means "the `modelnumber` member *of* `part1`."

Remember that the first component of an expression involving the dot operator is the name of the specific structure variable (`part1` in this case), not the name of the structure specifier (`part`). The variable name must be used to distinguish one variable from another when there is more than one, such as `part1`, `part2`, and so on, as shown in Figure 5-4.

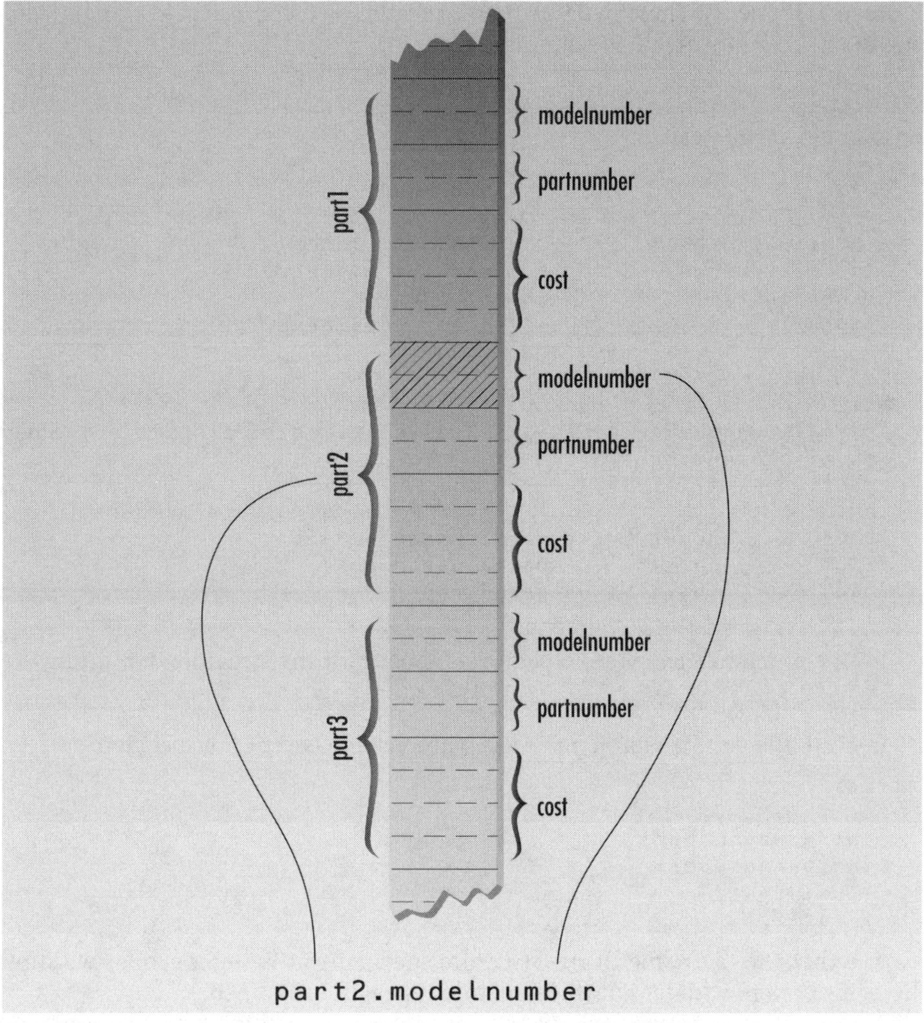

Figure 5-4 The Dot Operator

Structure members are treated just like other variables. In the statement `part1.modelnumber = 6244;`, the member is given the value 6244 using a normal assignment operator. The program also shows members used in `cout` statements such as:

```
cout << "\nModel " << part1.modelnumber;
```

These statements output the values of the structure members.

Other Structure Features

Structures are surprisingly versatile. Let's look at some additional features of structure syntax and usage.

Combining Specifier and Definition

In the PARTS example we showed the structure specifier and the definition as two separate statements. These two statements can also be combined into a single statement, as shown in the next example, PARTSCOM.

```
// partscom.cpp
// uses parts inventory to demonstrate structures
#include <iostream.h>

struct                    // no tag needed
   {
   int modelnumber;       // ID number of widget
   int partnumber;        // ID number of widget part
   float cost;            // cost of part
   } part1;               // definition goes here

void main()
   {
   part1.modelnumber = 6244;  // give values to structure members
   part1.partnumber = 373;
   part1.cost = 217.55;
                              // display structure members
   cout << "\nModel "  << part1.modelnumber;
   cout << ", part "   << part1.partnumber;
   cout << ", costs $" << part1.cost;
   }
```

In this program there is no separate statement for the structure definition:

```
part part1;
```

Instead, the variable name `part1` is placed at the end of the specifier:

```
struct
   {
   int modelnumber;
   int partnumber;
   float cost;
   } part1;
```

Notice that the tag name in the structure specifier can be removed, as we show here, if no more variables of this structure type will be defined.

Merging the structure specification and definition this way is a shorthand approach that can save a few program lines. Generally it is less clear and less flexible than using separate specifiers and definitions.

Initializing Structure Members

The next example shows how structure members can be initialized when the structure is defined. It also demonstrates that you can have more than one variable of a given structure type (we hope you suspected this all along).

Here's the listing for PARTINIT:

```
// partinit.cpp
// shows initialization of structure variables
#include <iostream.h>

struct part                 // specify a structure
   {
   int modelnumber;         // ID number of widget
   int partnumber;          // ID number of widget part
   float cost;              // cost of part
   };

void main()
   {
   part part1 = { 6244, 373, 217.55 };   // initialize variable
   part part2;                           // define variable
                                 // display first variable
   cout << "\nModel "  << part1.modelnumber;
   cout << ", part "   << part1.partnumber;
   cout << ", costs $" << part1.cost;

   part2 = part1;                // assign first variable to second
                                 // display second variable
   cout << "\nModel "  << part2.modelnumber;
   cout << ", part "   << part2.partnumber;
   cout << ", costs $" << part2.cost;
   }
```

This program defines two variables of type `part`: `part1` and `part2`. It initializes `part1`, prints out the values of its members, assigns `part1` to `part2`, and prints out its members.

Here's the output:

```
Model 6244, part 373, costs $217.55
Model 6244, part 373, costs $217.55
```

Not surprisingly the same output is repeated, since one variable is made equal to the other.

Initializing Structure Variables

The `part1` structure variable's members are initialized when the variable is defined:

```
part part1 = { 6244, 373, 217.55 };
```

The values to be assigned to the structure members are surrounded by braces and separated by commas. The first value in the list is assigned to the first member, the second to the second member, and so on.

Structure Variables in Assignment Statements

As can be seen in PARTINIT, one structure variable can be assigned to another:

```
part2 = part1;
```

The value of each member of `part1` is assigned to the corresponding member of `part2`. Since a large structure can have dozens of members, such an assignment statement can require the computer to do a considerable amount of work.

Note that one structure variable can be assigned to another only when they are of the same structure type. If you try to assign a variable of one structure type to a variable of another type, the compiler will complain.

A Measurement Example

Let's see how a structure can be used to group a different kind of information. If you've ever looked at an architectural drawing, you know that (at least in the United States) distances are measured in feet and inches. The length of a living room, for example, might be given as 12'–8", meaning 12 feet 8 inches. The hyphen isn't a negative sign; it merely separates the feet from the inches. This is part of the English system of measurement. (We'll make no judgment here on the merits of English versus metric.) Figure 5-5 shows typical length measurements in the English system.

Suppose you want to create a drawing or architectural program that uses the English system. It will be convenient to store distances as two numbers, representing feet and inches. The next example, ENGLSTRC, gives an idea of how this could be done using a structure. This program will show how two measurements of type `Distance` can be added together.

```
// englstrc.cpp
// demonstrates structures using English measurements
#include <iostream.h>

struct Distance                    // English distance
   {
   int feet;
   float inches;
   };

void main()
   {
   Distance d1, d3;                  // define two lengths
   Distance d2 = { 11, 6.25 }; // define & initialize one length

                                     // get length d1 from user
   cout << "\nEnter feet: ";  cin >> d1.feet;
   cout << "Enter inches: ";  cin >> d1.inches;

                                     // add lengths d1 and d2 to get d3
   d3.inches = d1.inches + d2.inches;  // add the inches
   d3.feet = 0;                        // (for possible carry)
   if(d3.inches >= 12.0)               // if total exceeds 12.0,
      {                                // then decrease inches
      d3.inches -= 12.0;               // by 12.0 and
      d3.feet++;                       // increase feet
```

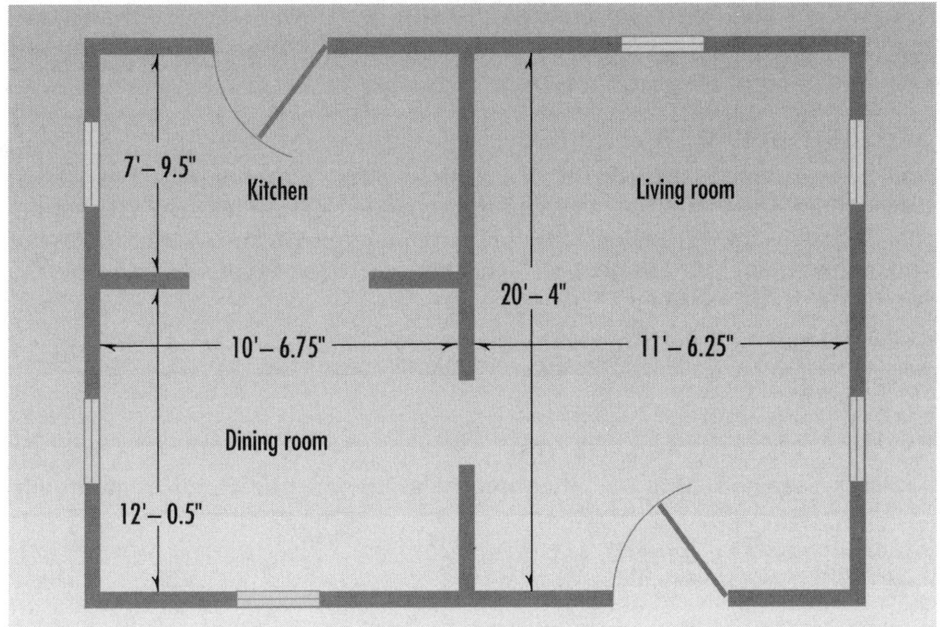

Figure 5-5 Measurements in the English System

```
    }                                   // by 1
    d3.feet += d1.feet + d2.feet;       // add the feet

                                    // display all lengths
    cout << d1.feet << "\'-" << d1.inches << "\" + ";
    cout << d2.feet << "\'-" << d2.inches << "\" = ";
    cout << d3.feet << "\'-" << d3.inches << "\"\n";
    }
```

Here the structure `Distance` has two members: `feet` and `inches`. The `inches` variable may have a fractional part, so we'll use type `float` for it. Feet are always integers, so we'll use type `int` for them.

We define two such distances, `d1` and `d3`, without initializing them, while we initialize another, `d2`, to 11'–6.25". The program asks the user to enter a distance in feet and inches, and assigns this distance to `d1`. (The inches value should be smaller than 12.0.) It then adds the distance `d1` to `d2`, obtaining the total distance `d3`. Finally the program displays the two initial distances and the newly calculated total distance. Here's some output:

```
Enter feet: 10
Enter inches: 6.75
10'-6.75" + 11'-6.25" = 22'-1"
```

Notice that we can't add the two distances with a program statement like

```
d3 = d1 + d2;    // can't do this in ENGLSTRC
```

Why not? Because there is no routine built into C++ that knows how to add variables of type `Distance`. The `+` operator works with built-in types like `float`, but not with types we define ourselves, like `Distance`. (However, one of the benefits of using classes, as we'll see, is the ability to add and perform other operations on user-defined data types.)

Structures Within Structures

You can nest structures within other structures. Here's a variation on the ENGLSTRC program that shows how this looks. In this program we want to create a data structure that stores the dimensions of a typical room: its length and width. Since we're working with English distances, we'll use two variables of type `Distance` as the length and width variables.

```
struct Room
   {
   Distance length;
   Distance width;
   }
```

Here's a program, ENGLAREA, that uses the `Room` structure to represent a room.

```
// englarea.cpp
// demonstrates nested structures
#include <iostream.h>

struct Distance                       // English distance
   {
   int feet;
   float inches;
   };

struct Room                           // rectangular area
   {
   Distance length;                   // length of rectangle
   Distance width;                    // width of rectangle
   };

void main()
   {
   Room dining;                           // define a room

   dining.length.feet = 13;               // assign values to room
   dining.length.inches = 6.5;
   dining.width.feet = 10;
   dining.width.inches = 0.0;

                                          // convert length & width
   float l = dining.length.feet + dining.length.inches/12;
   float w = dining.width.feet  + dining.width.inches/12;
                                          // find area and display it
   cout << "\nDining room area is " << l * w
        << " square feet" ;
   }
```

This program defines a single variable—`dining`—of type `Room`, in the line

```
Room dining;  // variable dining of type Room
```

It then assigns values to the various members of this structure.

Accessing Nested Structure Members

Because one structure is nested inside another, we must apply the dot operator twice to access the structure members.

```
dining.length.feet = 13;
```

In this statement, `dining` is the name of the structure variable, as before; `length` is the name of a member in the outer structure (`Room`); and `feet` is the name of a member of the inner structure (`Distance`). The statement means "take the `feet` member of the `length` member of the variable `dining` and assign it the value 13." Figure 5-6 shows how this works.

Once values have been assigned to members of `dining`, the program calculates the floor area of the room, as shown in Figure 5-7.

To find the area, the program converts the length and width from variables of type `Distance` to variables of type `float`, `l`, and `w`, representing distances in

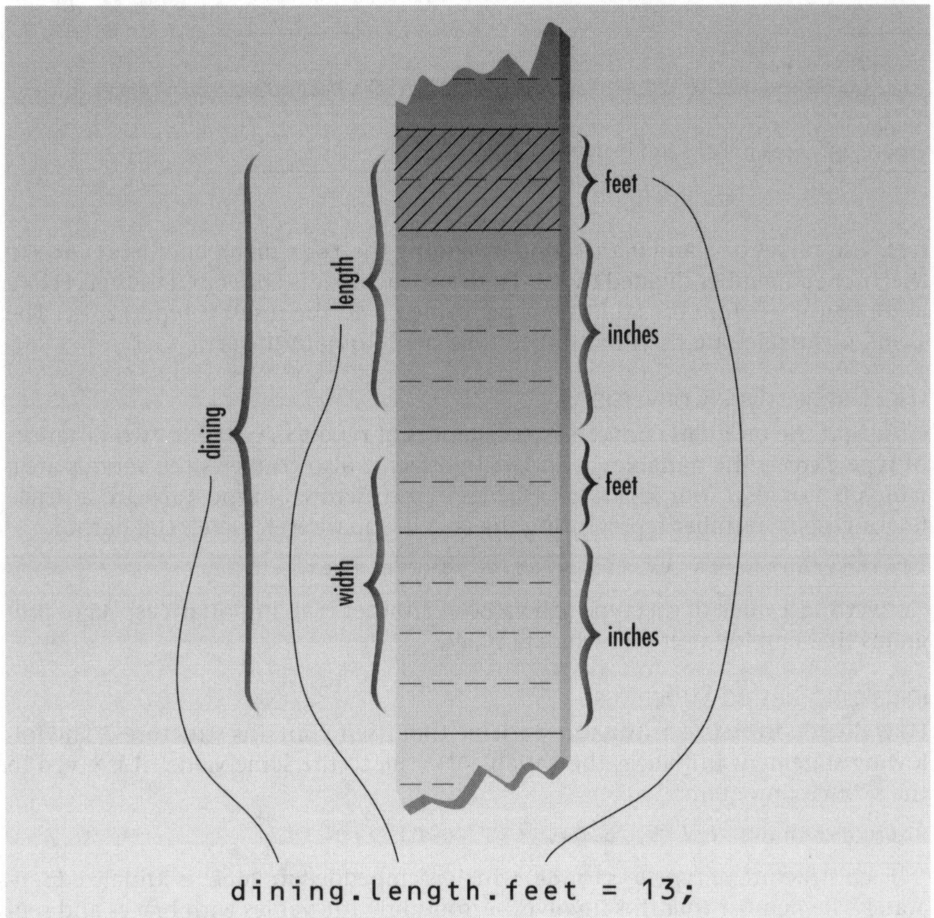

Figure 5-6 Dot Operator and Nested Structures

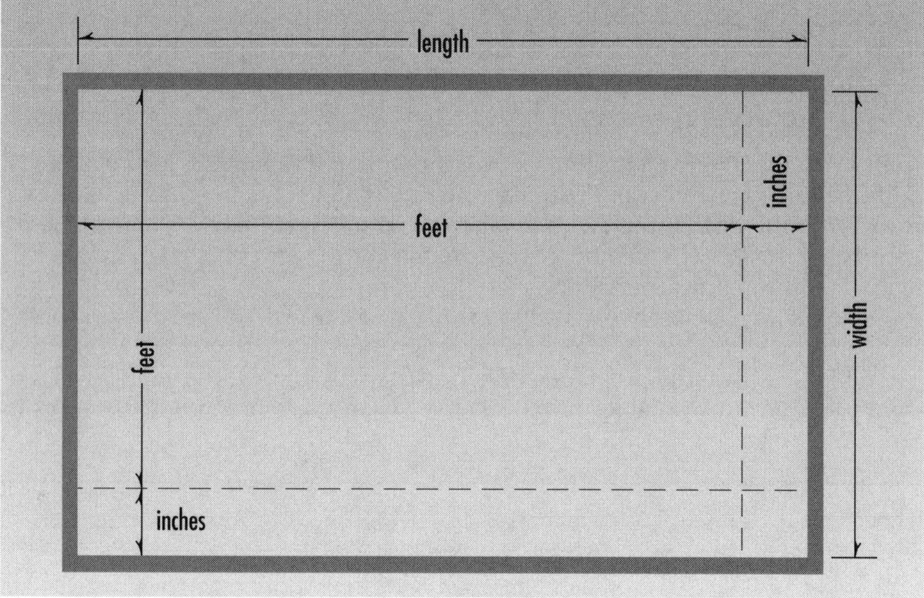

Figure 5-7 Area in Feet and Inches

feet. The values of `l` and `w` are found by adding the `feet` member of `Distance` to the `inches` member divided by 12. The `feet` member is converted to type `float` automatically before the addition is performed, and the result is type `float`. The `l` and `w` variables are then multiplied together to obtain the area.

User-Defined Type Conversions

Note that the program converts two distances of type `Distance` to two distances of type `float`: the variables `l` and `w`. In effect it also converts the room's area, which is stored as four separate variables in a structure of type `Room`, to a single floating-point number representing the area in square feet. Here's the output:

```
Dining room area is 135.416672 square feet
```

Converting a value of one type to a value of another is an important aspect of programs that employ user-defined data types.

Initializing Nested Structures

How do you initialize a structure variable that itself contains structures? The following statement initializes the variable `dining` to the same values it is given in the ENGLAREA program:

```
Room dining = { {13, 6.5}, {10, 0.0} };
```

Each structure of type `Distance`, which is embedded in `Room`, is initialized separately. Remember that this involves surrounding the values with braces and separating them with commas. The first `Distance` is initialized to

```
{13, 6.5}
```

and the second to

```
{10, 0.0}
```

These two `Distance` values are then used to initialize the `Room` variable, again surrounding them with braces and separating them by commas.

Depth of Nesting

In theory, structures can be nested to any depth. In a program that designs apartment buildings, you might find yourself with statements like

```
apartment1.laundry_room.washing_machine.width.feet
```

A Card-Game Example

Let's examine a different kind of example. This one uses a structure to model a playing card. The program imitates a game played by cardsharps (professional gamblers) at carnivals. The cardsharp shows you three cards, then places them face down on the table and interchanges their positions several times. If you can guess correctly where a particular card is, you win. Everything is in plain sight, yet the cardsharp switches the cards so rapidly and confusingly that the player (the "mark") almost always loses track of the card and loses the game (which is, of course, played for money).

Here's the structure the program uses to represent a playing card:

```
struct card
   {
   int number;
   int suit;
   };
```

This structure uses separate members to hold the number of the card and the suit. The number runs from 2 to 14, where 11, 12, 13, and 14 represent the jack, queen, king, and ace, respectively (this is the order used in poker). The suit runs from 0 to 3, where these four numbers represent clubs, diamonds, hearts, and spades.

Here's the listing for CARDS:

```
// cards.cpp
// demonstrates structures using playing cards
#include <iostream.h>

const int clubs = 0;
const int diamonds = 1;
const int hearts = 2;
const int spades = 3;

const int jack = 11;
const int queen = 12;
const int king = 13;
const int ace = 14;

struct card
   {
   int number;    // 2 to 10, jack, queen, king, ace
```

(continued on next page)

(continued from previous page)

```
   int suit;      // clubs, diamonds, hearts, spades
   };

void main()
   {
   card temp, chosen, prize;                        // define cards
   int position;

   card card1 = { 7, clubs };                       // initialize card1
   cout << "Card 1 is the 7 of clubs\n";

   card card2 = { jack, hearts };                   // initialize card2
   cout << "Card 2 is the jack of hearts\n";

   card card3 = { ace, spades };                    // initialize card3
   cout << "Card 3 is the ace of spades\n";

   prize = card3;                // copy this card, to remember it

   cout << "I'm swapping card 1 and card 3\n";
   temp = card3; card3 = card1; card1 = temp;

   cout << "I'm swapping card 2 and card 3\n";
   temp = card3; card3 = card2; card2 = temp;

   cout << "I'm swapping card 1 and card 2\n";
   temp = card2; card2 = card1; card1 = temp;

   cout << "Now, where (1, 2, or 3) is the ace of spades? ";
   cin >> position;

   switch (position)
      {
      case 1: chosen = card1; break;
      case 2: chosen = card2; break;
      case 3: chosen = card3; break;
      }
   if(chosen.number == prize.number &&           // compare cards
                       chosen.suit == prize.suit)
      cout << "That's right!  You win!\n";
   else
      cout << "Sorry. You lose.\n";
   }
```

Here's some sample interaction with the program:

```
Card 1 is the 7 of clubs
Card 2 is the jack of hearts
Card 3 is the ace of spades
I'm swapping card 1 and card 3
I'm swapping card 2 and card 3
I'm swapping card 1 and card 2
Now, where (1, 2, or 3) is the ace of spades? 3
Sorry. You lose.
```

In this case the hapless mark chose the wrong card (the right answer is 2).

The program begins by defining a number of variables of type `const` for the face card and suit values. (Not all these variables are used in the program; they're included for completeness.) Next the `card` structure is specified. The program then defines three uninitialized variables of type `card`: `temp`, `chosen`, and `prize`. It also defines three cards—`card1`, `card2`, and `card3`—which it initializes to three arbitrary card values. It prints out the values of these cards for the user's information. It then sets a card variable, `prize`, to one of these card values as a way of remembering it. This card is the one whose location the player will be asked to guess at the end of the game.

Next the program rearranges the cards. It swaps the first and third cards, the second and third cards, and the first and second cards. Each time it tells the user what it's doing. (If you find the program too easy, you can add more such statements to further shuffle the cards. Flashing the statements on the screen for a limited time would also increase the challenge.)

Finally the program asks the player what position a particular card is in. It sets a card variable, `chosen`, to the card in this position, and then compares `chosen` with the `prize` card. If they match, it's a win for the player; if not, it's a loss.

Notice how easy swapping cards is.

```
temp = card3;   card3 = card1;   card1 = temp;
```

Although the cards represent structures, they can be moved around very naturally, thanks to the ability of the assignment operator = to work with structures.

Unfortunately, just as structures can't be added, they also can't be compared. You can't say

```
if( chosen == prize )                    // not legal yet
```

because there's no routine built into the == operator that knows about the `card` structure. But, as with addition, this problem can be solved with operator overloading, as we'll see later.

Structures and Classes

We must confess to having misled you slightly on the capabilities of structures. It's true that structures are usually used to hold data only, and classes are used to hold both data and functions. However, in C++, structures can in fact hold both data and functions. (In C they can hold only data.) The syntactical distinction between structures and classes in C++ is minimal, so they can in theory be used interchangeably. But most C++ programmers use structures as we have in this chapter, exclusively for data. Classes are usually used to hold both data and functions, as we'll see in Chapter 7.

Enumerated Data Types

As we've seen, structures can be looked at as a way to provide user-defined data types. Another approach to defining your own data type is the *enumerated data type*. This feature of C++ is somewhat less crucial than structures. You can write perfectly good object-oriented programs in C++ without knowing anything about enumerated data types. However, they are very much in the spirit of C++, in that, by allowing you to define your own data types, they can simplify and clarify your programming. C++ programmers use enumerated types frequently. (C programmers use them less often.) Enumerated types exist in Pascal.

Days of the Week

Enumerated types work when you know in advance a finite (usually short) list of values that a data type can take on. Here's an example program, DAYENUM, that uses an enumerated data type for the days of the week:

```
// dayenum.cpp
// demonstrates enum types
#include <iostream.h>
                                        // specify enum type
enum days_of_week { Sun, Mon, Tue, Wed, Thu, Fri, Sat };

void main()
   {
   days_of_week day1, day2;     // define variables
                                // of type days_of_week
   day1 = Mon;                  // give values to
   day2 = Thu;                  // variables

   int diff = day2 - day1;      // can do integer arithmetic
   cout << "Days between = " << diff << endl;

   if(day1 < day2)              // can do comparisons
      cout << "day1 comes before day2\n";
   }
```

An `enum` specifier defines the set of all names that will be permissible values of the type. These permissible values are called *members*. The `enum` type `days_of_week` has seven members: `Sun`, `Mon`, `Tue`, and so on, up to `Sat`. Figure 5-8 shows the syntax of an `enum` specifier.

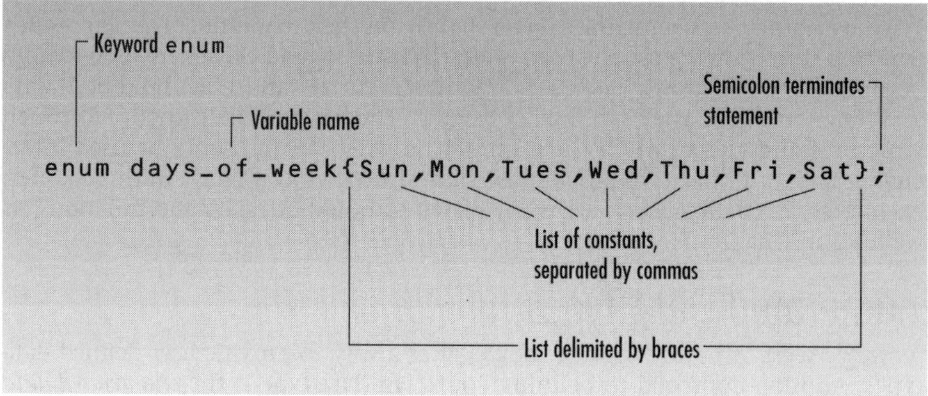

Figure 5-8 Syntax of `enum` Specifier

Enumerated means that all the values are listed. This is unlike the specification of an `int`, for example, which is given in terms of a range of possible values. In an `enum` you must give a specific name to every possible value. Figure 5-9 shows the difference between an `int` and an `enum`.

Once you've specified the data type `days_of_week` as shown, you can define variables of this type. DAYENUM has two such variables, `day1` and `day2`, defined in the statement

```
days_of_week  day1, day2;
```

(In C you must use the keyword `enum` before the type name, as in

```
enum days_of_week day1, day2;
```

In C++ this isn't necessary.)

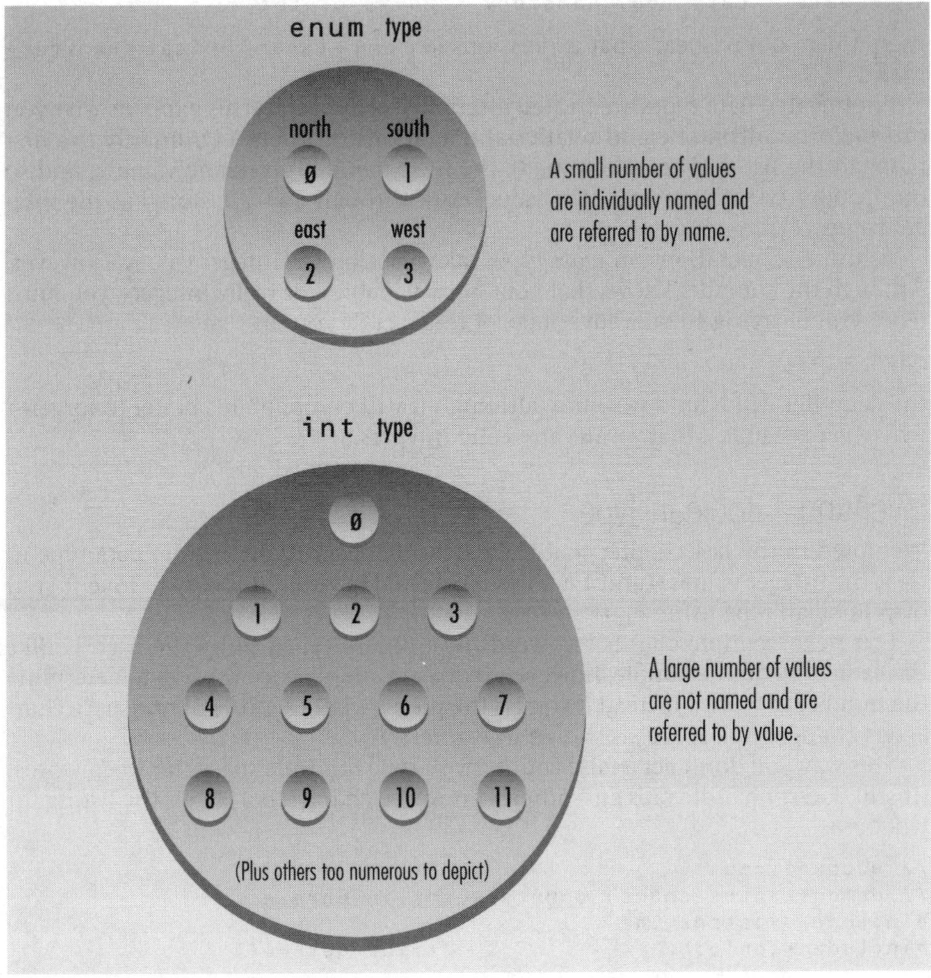

Figure 5-9 Usage of `int`s and `enum`s

Variables of an enumerated type, like day1 and day2, can be given any of the values listed in the enum specifier. In the example we give them the values Mon and Thu. You can't use values that weren't listed in the specifier. Such statements as

```
day1 = halloween;
```

are illegal.

You can use the standard arithmetic operators on enum types. In the program we subtract two values. You can also use the comparison operators, as we show. Here's the program's output:

```
Days between = 3
day1 comes before day2
```

The use of arithmetic and relational operators doesn't make much sense with some enum types. For example, if you have the specifier

```
enum pets { cat, dog, hamster, canary, ocelot };
```

then it may not be clear what expressions like dog + canary or (cat < hamster) mean.

Enumerated data types are treated internally as integers. (This explains why you can perform arithmetic and relational operations on them.) Ordinarily the first name in the list is given the value 0, the next name is given the value 1, and so on. In the DAYENUM example, the values Sun through Sat are stored as the integer values 0 through 6.

Arithmetic operations on enum types take place on the integer values. However, although the compiler knows that your enum variables are really integers, you must be careful of trying to take advantage of this fact. If you say

```
day1 = 5;
```

the compiler will issue a warning (although it will compile). It's better to forget—whenever possible—that enums are really integers.

Inventing a Boolean Type

We noted in the last chapter that there is no Boolean (false or true) data type in C++; the integer values 0 and 1 are used instead. However, it is easy to invent your own Boolean type using enum.

Our next example counts the words in a phrase typed in by the user. Unlike the earlier CHCOUNT example, however, it doesn't simply count spaces to determine the number of words. Instead it counts the places where a string of nonspace characters changes to a space, as shown in Figure 5-10.

This way you don't get a false count if you type multiple spaces between words. (It still doesn't handle tabs and other whitespace characters.) Here's the listing for WDCOUNT:

```
// wdcount.cpp
// demonstrates enums, counts words in phrase
#include <iostream.h>
#include <conio.h>                  // for getche()

enum boolean { false, true };       // false=0, true=1
```

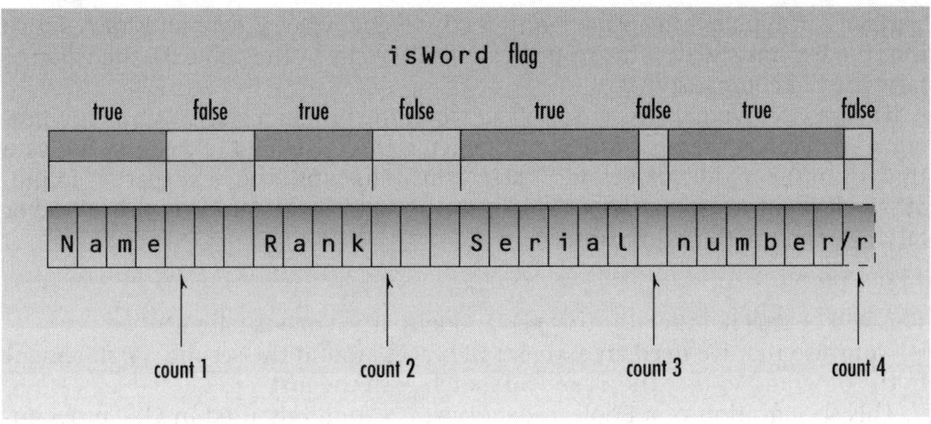

Figure 5-10 Operation of WDCOUNT Program

```
void main()
   {
   boolean isWord = false;        // true when in a word,
                                  // false when in whitespace
   char ch = 'a';                 // character read from keyboard
   int wordcount = 0;             // number of words read

   do
      {
      ch = getche();                       // get character
      if(ch==' ' || ch=='\r')              // if whitespace,
         {
         if( isWord )                      // and doing a word,
            {                              // then it's end of word
            wordcount++;                   // count the word
            isWord = false;                // reset flag
            }
         }                                 // otherwise, it's
      else                                 // normal character
         if( !isWord )                     // if start of word,
            isWord = true;                 // then set flag
      } while( ch != '\r' );               // quit on Enter key
   cout << "\n--Word count is " << wordcount << "--\n";
   }
```

The program cycles in a `do` loop, reading characters from the keyboard. It passes over (nonspace) characters until it finds a space. At this point it counts a word. Then it passes over spaces until it finds a character, and again counts characters until it finds a space. Doing this requires the program to remember whether it's in the middle of a word, or in the middle of a string of spaces. It remembers this with the variable `isWord`. This variable is defined to be of type `boolean`. This type is specified in the statement

```
enum boolean { false, true };
```

Variables of type `boolean` have only two possible values: *false* and *true*. Notice that the list starts with *false*, so this value will be given the value 0—the value of false used in comparisons.

The `isWord` variable is set to `false` when the program starts. When the program encounters the first nonspace character, it sets `isWord` to `true` to indicate that it's in the middle of a word. It keeps this value until the next space is found, at which point it's set back to `false`. Notice that, since `isWord` is either true or false, we can use the expression

```
if( isWord )
```

This will be true if `isWord` is true (1), and false if `isWord` is false (0).

Note also that we need an extra set of braces around the second `if` statement in the program, so that the `else` will match with the first `if`.

This specification of a Boolean data type is commonly used in C++ programming when flags and similar variables must be defined.

Organizing the Cards

Here's another example of `enum` types. Remember that in the CARDS program earlier in this chapter we defined a group of constants of type `const int` to represent a card's suits.

```
const int clubs = 0;
const int diamonds = 1;
const int hearts = 2;
const int spades = 3;
```

This sort of list is somewhat clumsy. Let's revise the CARDS program to use enumerated data types instead. Here's the listing for CARDENUM:

```
// cardenum.cpp
// demonstrates the enumerated data type
#include <iostream.h>

const int jack = 11;  // 2 through 10 are unnamed integers
const int queen = 12;
const int king = 13;
const int ace = 14;

enum Suit { clubs, diamonds, hearts, spades };

struct card
   {
   int number;           // 2 to 10, jack, queen, king, ace
   Suit suit;            // clubs, diamonds, hearts, spades
   };

void main()
   {
   card temp, chosen, prize;                       // define cards
   int position;

   card card1 = { 7, clubs };                      // initialize card1
   cout << "Card 1 is the seven of clubs\n";
```

```
   card card2 = { jack, hearts };             // initialize card2
   cout << "Card 2 is the jack of hearts\n";

   card card3 = { ace, spades };              // initialize card3
   cout << "Card 3 is the ace of spades\n";

   prize = card3;                  // copy this card, to remember it

   cout << "I'm swapping card 1 and card 3\n";
   temp = card3; card3 = card1; card1 = temp;

   cout << "I'm swapping card 2 and card 3\n";
   temp = card3; card3 = card2; card2 = temp;

   cout << "I'm swapping card 1 and card 2\n";
   temp = card2; card2 = card1; card1 = temp;

   cout << "Now, where (1, 2, or 3) is the ace of spades? ";
   cin >> position;

   switch (position)
      {
      case 1: chosen = card1; break;
      case 2: chosen = card2; break;
      case 3: chosen = card3; break;
      }
   if(chosen.number == prize.number &&           // compare cards
                        chosen.suit == prize.suit)
      cout << "That's right!  You win!\n";
   else
      cout << "Sorry. You lose.\n";
   }
```

Here the set of definitions for suits used in CARDS has been replaced by an `enum` specifier:

```
enum Suit { clubs, diamonds, hearts, spades };
```

This is a cleaner approach than using `const` variables. We know exactly what the possible values of the suit are; attempts to use other values, as in

```
card1.suit = 5;
```

result in warnings from the compiler.

Specifying Integer Values

We said that in an `enum` specifier the first name was given the integer value 0, the second the value 1, and so on. This ordering can be altered by using an equal sign to specify a starting point other than 0. For example, if you want the suits to start with 1 instead of 0, you can say

```
enum Suit { clubs=1, diamonds, hearts, spades };
```

Subsequent names are given values starting at this point, so `diamonds` is 2, `hearts` is 3, and `spades` is 4.

Not Perfect

One annoying aspect of `enum` types is that they are not recognized by C++ input/output (I/O) statements. As an example, what do you think the following code fragment will cause to be displayed?

```
enum direction { north, south, east, west };
direction dir1 = south;
cout << dir1;
```

Did you guess the output would be `south`? That would be nice, but C++ I/O treats variables of `enum` types as integers, so the output would be `1`.

Other Examples

Here are some other examples of enumerated data specifiers, to give you a feeling for possible uses of this feature:

```
enum months { Jan, Feb, Mar, Apr, May, Jun,
              Jul, Aug, Sep, Oct, Nov, Dec };

enum switch { off, on };

enum meridian { am, pm };

enum chess { pawn, knight, bishop, rook, queen, king };

enum coins { penny, nickel, dime, quarter, half-dollar, dollar }
```

We'll see other examples in future programs.

Summary

We've covered two topics in this chapter: structures and the enumerated data type. Structures are an important component of C++, since their syntax is the same as that used in classes. In fact, classes are nothing more than structures that include functions. Structures are typically used to group several data items together to form a single entity. A structure specifier lists the variables that make up the structure. Definitions then set aside memory for structure variables. Structure variables are treated as indivisible units in some situations (such as setting one structure variable equal to another), but in other situations their members are accessed individually (often using the dot operator).

The enumerated data type is a programmer-defined type that is limited to a fixed list of values. A specifier gives the type a name and specifies the permissible values. Definitions then create variables of this type. Internally the compiler treats enumerated variables as integers.

Structures should not be confused with enumerated data types. Structures are a powerful and flexible way of grouping a diverse collection of data into a single entity. An enumerated data type allows the definition of variables that can take on a fixed set of values that are listed (enumerated) in the type's specifier.

Questions

Answers to questions can be found in Appendix D.

1. A structure brings together a group of
   a. items of the same data type.
   b. related data items.
   c. integers with user-defined names.
   d. variables.
2. True or false: A structure and a class use similar syntax.
3. The closing brace of a structure is followed by a _________.
4. Write a structure specification that includes three variables—all of type `int`—called `hrs`, `mins`, and `secs`. Call this structure `time`.
5. True or false: A structure specifier creates space in memory for a variable.
6. When accessing a structure member, the identifier to the left of the dot operator is the name of
   a. a structure member.
   b. a structure tag.
   c. a structure variable.
   d. the keyword `struct`.
7. Write a statement that sets the `hrs` member of the `time2` structure variable equal to 11.
8. If you have three variables defined to be of type `struct time`, and this structure contains three `int` members, how many bytes of memory do the variables use together?
9. Write a definition that initializes the members of `time1`—which is a variable of type `struct time`, as defined in Question 4—to `hrs` = 11, `mins` = 10, `secs` = 59.
10. True or false: You can assign one structure variable to another, provided they are of the same type.
11. Write a statement that sets the variable `temp` equal to the `paw` member of the `dogs` member of the `fido` variable.
12. An enumerated data type brings together a group of
    a. items of different data types.
    b. related data variables.

c. integers with user-defined names.

d. constant values.

13. Write a statement that declares an enumerated data type called `players` with the values B1, B2, SS, B3, RF, CF, LF, P, and C.

14. Assuming the `enum` type `players` as declared in Question 13, define two variables `joe` and `tom`, and assign them the values LF and P, respectively.

15. Assuming the statements of Questions 13 and 14, state whether each of the following statements is legal.

   a. `joe = QB;`

   b. `tom = SS;`

   c. `LF = tom;`

   d. `difference = joe - tom;`

16. The first three members of an `enum` type are normally represented by the values __________, __________, and __________.

17. Write a statement that declares an enumerated data type called `speeds` with the values `obsolete`, `single`, and `album`. Give these three names the integer values 78, 45, and 33.

18. State the reason why

```
enum boolean{ false, true };
```

is better than

```
enum boolean{ true, false };
```

Exercises

Answers to the starred exercises can be found in Appendix D.

1.* A phone number, such as (212) 767-8900, can be thought of as having three parts: the area code (212), the exchange (767), and the number (8900). Write a program that uses a structure to store these three parts of a phone number separately. Call the structure `phone`. Create two structure variables of type `phone`. Initialize one, and have the user input a number for the other one. Then display both numbers. The interchange might look like this:

```
Enter your area code, exchange, and number: 415 555 1212
My number is (212) 767-8900
Your number is (415) 555-1212
```

2.*. A point on the two-dimensional plane can be represented by two numbers: an x coordinate and a y coordinate. For example, (4,5) represents a point 4 units to the right of the origin along the x axis, and 5 units up the y axis. The sum of two points can be defined as a new point whose x coordinate is the sum of the x coordinates of the two points, and whose y coordinate is the sum of their y coordinates.

Write a program that uses a structure called `point` to model a point. Define three points, and have the user input values to two of them. Then set the third point equal to the sum of the other two, and display the value of the new point. Interaction with the program might look like this:

```
Enter coordinates for p1: 3 4
Enter coordinates for p2: 5 7
Coordinates of p1+p2 are: 8, 11
```

3.* Create a structure called `Volume` that uses three variables of type `Distance` (from the ENGLSTRC example) to model the volume of a room. Initialize a variable of type `Volume` to specific dimensions, then calculate the volume it represents, and print out the result. To calculate the volume, convert each dimension from a `Distance` variable to a variable of type `float` representing feet and fractions of a foot, and then multiply the resulting three numbers.

4. Create a structure called `employee` that contains two members: an employee number (type `int`) and the employee's compensation (in dollars; type `float`). Ask the user to fill in this data for three employees, store it in three variables of type `struct employee`, and then display the information for each employee.

5. Create a structure of type `date` that contains three members: the month, the day of the month, and the year, all of type `int`. (Or use day-month-year order if you prefer.) Have the user enter a date in the format 12/31/97, store it in a variable of type `struct date`, then retrieve the values from the variable and print them out in the same format.

6. We said earlier that C++ I/O statements don't automatically understand the values of enumerated data types. Instead, the (>>) and (<<) operators think of such variables simply as integers. You can overcome this limitation by using `switch` statements to translate between the user's way of expressing an enumerated variable and the actual values of the enumerated variable. For example, imagine an enumerated type with values that indicate an employee type within an organization:

```
enum etype { laborer, secretary, manager, accountant, executive,
researcher };
```

Write a program that first allows the user to specify a type by entering its first letter ('l', 's', 'm', and so on), then stores the type chosen as a value of a variable of type `enum etype`, and finally displays the complete word for this type.

```
Enter employee type (first letter only)
   laborer, secretary, manager,
   accountant, executive, researcher): a
Employee type is accountant.
```

You'll probably need two `switch` statements: one for input and one for output.

7. Add a variable of type `enum etype` (see Exercise 5), and another variable of type `struct date` (see Exercise 3) to the `employee` class of Exercise 4. Organize the resulting program so that the user enters four items of information for each of three employees: an employee number, the employee's compensation, the employee type, and the date of first employment. The program should store this information in three variables of type `employee`, and then display their contents.

8. Start with the fraction-adding program of Exercise 9 in Chapter 3. This program stores the numerator and denominator of two fractions before adding them, and may also store the answer, which is also a fraction. Modify the program so that all fractions are stored in variables of type `struct fraction`, whose two members are the fraction's numerator and denominator (both type `int`). All fraction-related data should be stored in structures of this type.

9. Create a structure called `time`. Its three members, all type `int`, should be called `hours`, `minutes`, and `seconds`. Write a program that prompts the user to enter a time value in hours, minutes, and seconds. This can be in 12:59:59 format, or each number can be entered at a separate prompt (`Enter hours`, etc.). The program should then store the time in a variable of type `struct time`, and finally print out the total number of seconds (which should be type `long`) represented by this `time` value:

```
long totalsecs = (long)t1.hours*3600 + t1.minutes*60 + t1.seconds
```

10. Create a structure called `sterling` that stores money amounts in the old-style British system discussed in Exercises 8 and 11 in Chapter 4. The members could be called `pounds` (type `long`), `shillings` (type `int`), and `pence` (type `int`). The program should request the user to enter a money amount in new-style decimal pounds (type `double`), convert it to the old-style system, store it in a variable of type `struct sterling`, and then display this amount in pounds-shillings-pence format.

11. Use the `time` structure from Exercise 9, and write a program that obtains two `time` values from the user in 12:59:59 format, stores them in `struct time` variables, converts each one to seconds (type `long`), adds these quantities, converts the result back to hours-minutes-seconds, stores the result in a `time` structure, and finally displays the result in 12:59:59 format.

12. Revise the four-function fraction calculator program of Exercise 12 in Chapter 4 so that each fraction is stored internally as a variable of type `struct fraction`, as discussed in Exercise 8 in this chapter.

6

Functions

FUNCTION DEFINITIONS AND DECLARATIONS

ARGUMENTS AND RETURN VALUES

REFERENCE ARGUMENTS

OVERLOADED FUNCTIONS

DEFAULT ARGUMENTS

STORAGE CLASSES

6

A function groups a number of program statements into a unit and gives it a name. This unit can then be invoked from other parts of the program.

The most important reason to use functions is to aid in the conceptual organization of a program. Dividing a program into functions is, as we discussed in Chapter 1, one of the major principles of structured programming. (However, object-oriented programming provides other, more powerful ways to organize programs.)

Another reason to use functions (and the reason they were invented, long ago) is to reduce program size. Any sequence of instructions that appears in a program more than once is a candidate for being made into a function. The function's code is stored in only one place in memory, even though the function is executed many times in the course of the program. Figure 6-1 shows how a function is invoked from different sections of a program.

Functions in C++ (and C) serve the same purpose as subroutines and functions in BASIC, and procedures and functions in Pascal.

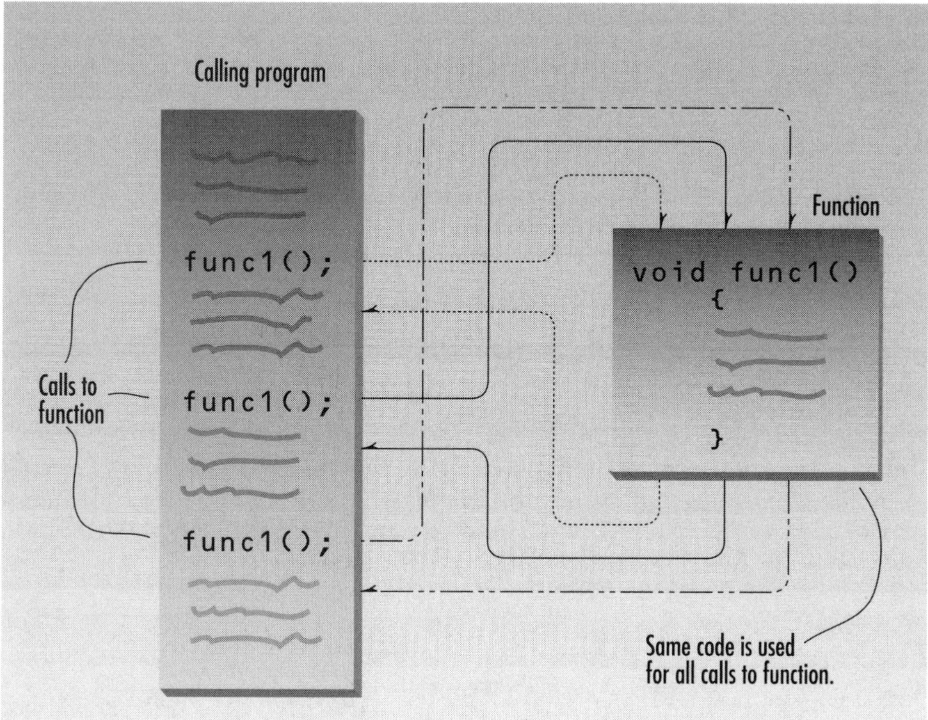

Figure 6-1 Flow of Control to Function

Simple Functions

Our first example demonstrates a simple function whose purpose is to print a line of 45 asterisks. The example program generates a table, and lines of asterisks are used to make the table more readable. Here's the listing for TABLE:

```
// table.cpp
// demonstrates simple function
#include <iostream.h>

void starline();                                 // function declaration
                                                 //    (prototype)
void main()
   {
   starline();                                   // call to function
   cout << "Data type   Range" << endl;
   starline();                                   // call to function
   cout << "char        -128 to 127" << endl
        << "int         -32,768 to 32,767" << endl
        << "double      -2,147,483,648 to 2,147,483,647" << endl;
   starline();                                   // call to function
   }

// starline()
// function definition
void starline()                                  // function declarator
   {
   for(int j=0; j<45; j++)                       // function body
      cout << '*';
   cout << endl;
   }
```

The output from the program looks like this:

```
*********************************************
Data type   Range
*********************************************
char        -128 to 127
int         -32,768 to 32,767
double      -2,147,483,648 to 2,147,483,647
*********************************************
```

The program consists of two functions: `main()` and `starline()`. You've already seen many programs that use `main()` alone. What other components are necessary to add a function to the program? There are three: the function declaration, the calls to the function, and the function definition.

The Function Declaration

Just as you can't use a variable without first telling the compiler what it is, you also can't use a function without telling the compiler about it. The most common approach is to *declare* the function at the beginning of the program. In the TABLE program, the function `starline()` is declared in the line

```
void starline();
```

The declaration tells the compiler that at some later point we plan to present a function called *starline*. The keyword `void` specifies that the function has no return value, and the empty parentheses indicate that it takes no arguments. (You can also use the keyword `void` in parentheses to indicate that the function takes no arguments, as is often done in C, but leaving them empty is the more common practice in C++.) We'll have more to say about arguments and return values soon.

Notice that the function declaration is terminated with a semicolon. It is a complete statement in itself.

Function declarations are also called *prototypes*, since they provide a model or blueprint for the function. They tell the compiler, "a function that looks like this is coming up later in the program, so it's all right if you see references to it before you see the function itself."

Calling the Function

The function is *called* (or invoked, or executed) three times from `main()`. Each of the three calls looks like this:

```
starline();
```

This is all we need to call the function: the function name, followed by parentheses. The syntax of the call is very similar to that of the declaration, except that the return type is not used. The call is terminated by a semicolon. Executing the call statement causes the function to execute; that is, control is transferred to the function, the statements in the function definition (which we'll examine in a moment) are executed, and then control returns to the statement following the function call.

The Function Definition

Finally we come to the function itself, which is referred to as the function *definition*. The definition contains the actual code for the function. Here's the definition for `starline()`:

```
void starline()                    // declarator
   {
   for(int j=0; j<45; j++)         // function body
      cout << '*';
   cout << endl;
   }
```

The definition consists of a line called the *declarator*, followed by the function body. The function body is composed of the statements that make up the function, delimited by braces.

The declarator must agree with the declaration: It must use the same function name, have the same argument types in the same order (if there are arguments), and have the same return type.

Notice that the declarator is *not* terminated by a semicolon. As with loops, the entire function definition—including the declarator, opening brace, function body, and closing brace—is considered to be one program statement. Figure 6-2 shows the syntax of the function declaration, function call, and function definition.

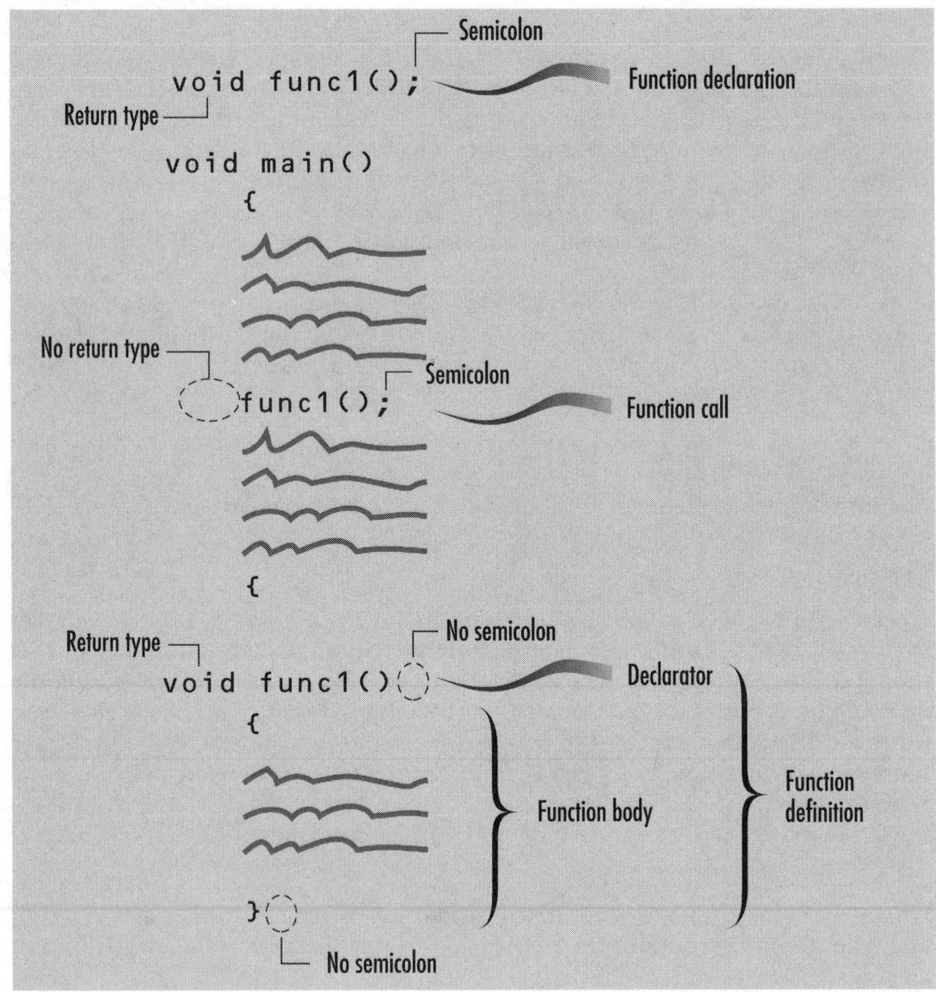

Figure 6-2 Function Syntax

When the function is called, control is transferred to the first statement in the function body. The other statements in the function body are then executed, and when the closing brace is encountered, control returns to the calling program.

Table 6-1 summarizes the different function components.

Comparison with Library Functions

We've already seen some library functions in use. We have embedded calls to library functions, such as

```
ch = getche();
```

in our program code. Where are the declaration and definition for this library function? The declaration is in the header file specified at the beginning of the program (CONIO.H, for `getche()`). The definition (compiled into executable code) is in the

Component	Purpose	Example
Declaration (prototype)	Specifies function name, argument types, and return value. Alerts compiler (and programmer) that function is coming up later.	`void func ();`
Call	Causes the function to be executed.	`func ();`
Definition	The function itself. Contains the lines of code that constitute the function.	`void func (); { // lines of code }`
Declarator	First line of definition.	`void func ()`

Table 6-1 Function Components

library file CS.LIB (or a similar file). When we use a library function we don't need to write the declaration or definition.

But when we write our own functions, the declaration and definition are part of our source file, as we've shown in the TABLE example. (Things get more complicated in multifile programs, as we'll discuss in Chapter 15.)

Eliminating the Declaration

We should note that you can eliminate the function declaration if the function definition (the function itself) appears in the listing before the first call to the function. For example, we could rewrite TABLE to produce TABLE2, in which the function definition appears first.

```
// table2.cpp
// demonstrates function definition preceding function calls
#include <iostream.h>
                                      // no function declaration

// starline()                         // function definition
void starline()
   {
   for(int j=0; j<45; j++)
      cout << '*';
   cout << endl;
   }

void main()                           // main follows function
   {
   starline();                        // call to function
   cout << "Data type   Range" << endl;
   starline();                        // call to function
   cout << "char        -128 to 127" << endl
```

(continued on next page)

(continued from previous page)

```
        << "int         -32,768 to 32,767" << endl
        << "double      -2,147,483,648 to 2,147,483,647" << endl;
   starline();                              // call to function
   }
```

This approach is simpler for short programs, in that it removes the declaration, but it is less flexible. To use this technique when there are more than a few functions, the programmer must give considerable thought to arranging the functions so that each one appears before it is called by any other. Sometimes this is impossible. Also, many programmers prefer to place `main()` first in the listing, since it is where execution begins. In general we'll stick with the first approach, using declarations and starting the listing with `main()`.

Passing Arguments to Functions

An argument is a piece of data (an `int` value, for example) passed from a program to the function. Arguments allow a function to operate with different values, or even to do different things, depending on the requirements of the program calling it.

Passing Constants

As an example, let's suppose we decide that the `starline()` function in the last example is too rigid. Instead of a function that always prints 45 asterisks, we want a function that will print any character any number of times.

Here's a program, TABLEARG, that incorporates just such a function. We use arguments to pass the character to be printed and the number of times to print it.

```
// tablearg.cpp
// demonstrates function arguments
#include <iostream.h>

void repchar(char, int);                       // function declaration

void main()
   {
   repchar('-', 43);                           // call to function
   cout << "Data type   Range" << endl;
   repchar('=', 23);                           // call to function
   cout << "char        -128 to 127" << endl
        << "int         -32,768 to 32,767" << endl
        << "double      -2,147,483,648 to 2,147,483,647" << endl;
   repchar('-', 43);                           // call to function
   }

// repchar()
// function definition
void repchar(char ch, int n)                   // function declarator
   {
   for(int j=0; j<n; j++)                      // function body
      cout << ch;
   cout << endl;
   }
```

The new function is called `repchar()`. Its declaration looks like this:

```
void repchar(char, int);    // declaration specifies data types
```

The items in the parentheses are the data types of the arguments that will be sent to `repchar()`: `char` and `int`.

In the function call, specific values—constants in this case—are inserted in the appropriate place in the parentheses:

```
repchar('-', 43);    // function call specifies actual values
```

This statement instructs `repchar()` to print a line of 43 dashes. The values supplied in the call must be of the types specified in the declaration: the first argument, the '–' character, must be of type `char`; and the second argument, the number 43, must be of type `int`. The types in the declaration and the definition must also agree.

The next call to `repchar()`,

```
repchar('=', 23);
```

tells it to print a line of 23 equal signs. The third call again prints 43 dashes. Here's the output from TABLEARG:

```
-------------------------------------------
Data type   Range
=======================
char        -128 to 127
int         -32,768 to 32,767
double      -2,147,483,648 to 2,147,483,647
-------------------------------------------
```

The calling program supplies arguments, such as '–' and 43, to the function. The variables used within the function to hold the argument values are called *parameters*; in `repchar()` they are `ch` and `n`. (We should note that many programmers use the terms *argument* and *parameter* interchangeably.) The declarator in the function definition specifies both the data types and the names of the parameters:

```
void repchar(char ch, int n)   // declarator specifies parameter
                               // names and data types
```

These parameter names, `ch` and `n`, are used in the function as if they were normal variables. Placing them in the declarator is equivalent to defining them with statements like

```
char ch;
int n;
```

When the function is called, its parameters are automatically initialized to the values passed by the calling program.

Passing Variables

In the TABLEARG example the arguments were constants: '–', 43, and so on. Let's look at an example where variables, instead of constants, are passed as arguments. This program, VARARG, incorporates the same `repchar()` function as did TABLEARG, but lets the user specify the character and the number of times it should be repeated.

```
// vararg.cpp
// demonstrates variable arguments
#include <iostream.h>

void repchar(char, int);                        // function declaration

void main()
   {
   char chin;
   int nin;

   cout << "Enter a character: ";
   cin >> chin;
   cout << "Enter number of times to repeat it: ";
   cin >> nin;
   repchar(chin, nin);
   }

// repchar()
// function definition
void repchar(char ch, int n)                    // function declarator
   {
   for(int j=0; j<n; j++)                       // function body
      cout << ch;
   cout << endl;
   }
```

Here's some sample interaction with VARARG:

```
Enter a character: +
Enter number of times to repeat it: 20
++++++++++++++++++++
```

Here `chin` and `nin` in `main()` are used as arguments to `repchar()`:

```
repchar(chin, nin);    // function call
```

The data types of variables used as arguments must match those specified in the function declaration and definition, just as they must for constants. That is, `chin` must be a `char`, and `nin` must be an `int`.

Passing by Value

In VARARG the particular values possessed by `chin` and `nin` when the function call is executed will be passed to the function. As it did when constants were passed to it, the function creates new variables to hold the values of these variable arguments. The function gives these new variables the names and data types of the parameters specified in the declarator: `ch` of type `char` and `n` of type `int`. It initializes these parameters to the values passed. They are then accessed like other variables by statements in the function body.

Passing arguments in this way, where the function creates copies of the arguments passed to it, is called *passing by value*. We'll explore another approach, passing by reference, later in this chapter. Figure 6-3 shows how new variables are created in the function when arguments are passed by value.

Passing Structure Variables

Entire structures can be passed as arguments to functions. The next example features a function that uses an argument of type `Distance`, the same structure type we saw in several programs in Chapter 5. Here's the listing for ENGLDISP:

```
// engldisp.cpp
// demonstrates passing structure as argument
#include <iostream.h>

struct Distance                    // English distance
   {
   int feet;
   float inches;
   };

void engldisp( Distance );          // declaration

void main()
   {
   Distance d1, d2;                 // define two lengths
```

(continued on next page)

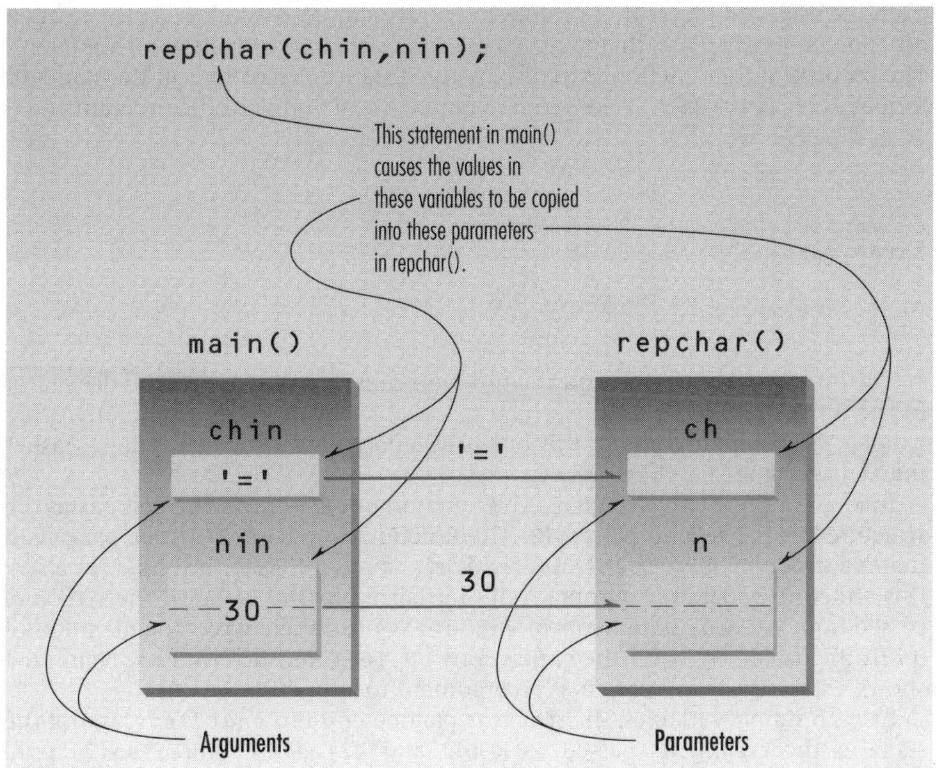

Figure 6-3 Passing by Value

(continued from previous page)

```
                                        // get length d1 from user
    cout << "\nEnter feet: ";    cin >> d1.feet;
    cout << "Enter inches: ";    cin >> d1.inches;

                                        // get length d2 from user
    cout << "\nEnter feet: ";    cin >> d2.feet;
    cout << "Enter inches: ";    cin >> d2.inches;

    cout << "\nd1 = ";
    engldisp(d1);                       // display length 1
    cout << "\nd2 = ";
    engldisp(d2);                       // display length 2
}

// engldisp()
// display structure of type Distance in feet and inches
void engldisp( Distance dd )     // parameter dd of type Distance
    {
    cout << dd.feet << "\'-" << dd.inches << "\"";
    }
```

The main() part of this program accepts two distances in feet-and-inches format from the user, and places these values in two structures, d1 and d2. It then calls a function, engldisp( ), that takes a Distance structure variable as an argument. The purpose of the function is to display the distance passed to it in the standard format, such as 10'–2.25". Here's some sample interaction with the program:

```
Enter feet: 6
Enter inches: 4

Enter feet: 5
Enter inches: 4.25

d1 = 6'-4"
d2 = 5'-4.25"
```

The function declaration and the function calls in main(), and the declarator in the function body, treat the structure variables just as they would any other variable used as an argument; this one just happens to be type Distance, rather than a basic type like char or int.

In main() there are two calls to the function engldisp(). The first passes the structure d1; the second passes d2. The function engldisp() uses a parameter that is a structure of type Distance, which it names dd. As with simple variables, this structure variable is automatically initialized to the value of the structure passed from main(). Statements in engldisp() can then access the members of dd in the usual way, with the expressions dd.feet and dd.inches. Figure 6-4 shows a structure being passed as an argument to a function.

As with simple variables, the structure parameter dd in engldisp() is not the same as the arguments passed to it (d1 and d2). Thus, engldisp() could (although it doesn't do so here) modify dd without affecting d1 and d2. That is, if engldisp() contained statements like

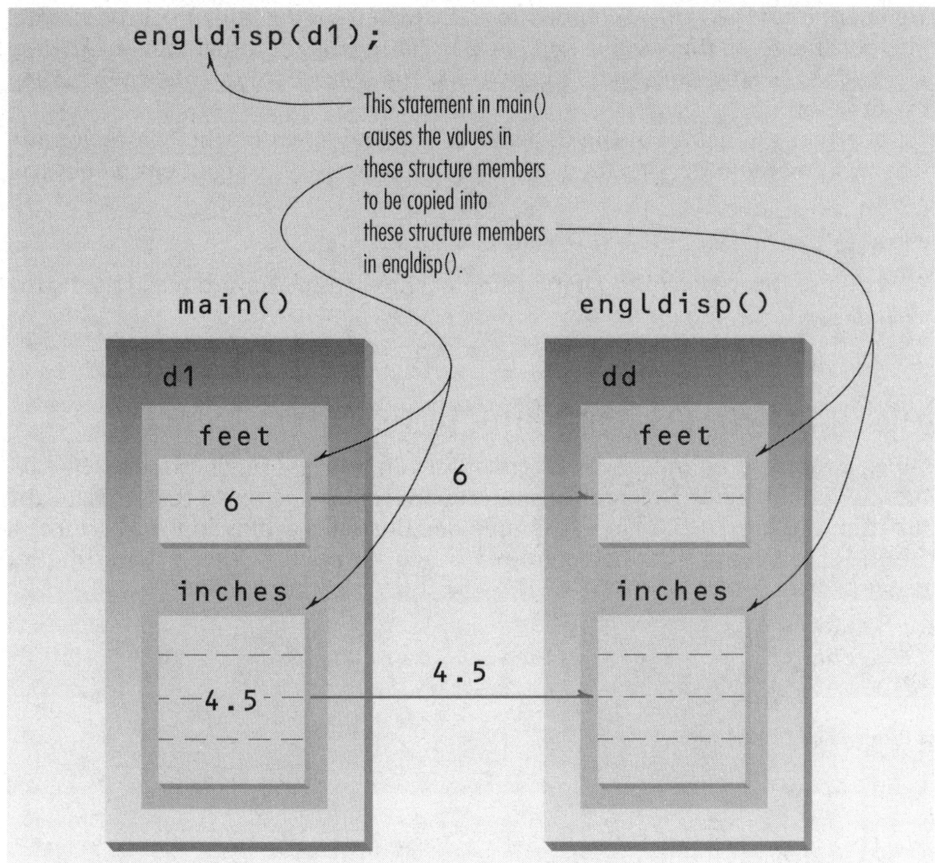

Figure 6-4 Structure Passed As Argument

```
dd.feet = 2;
dd.inches = 3.25;
```

this would have no effect on `d1` or `d2` in `main()`.

Names in the Declaration

Here's a way to increase the clarity of your function declarations. The idea is to insert meaningful names in the declaration, along with the data types. For example, suppose you were using a function that displayed a point on the screen. You could use a declaration with only data types,

```
void display_point(int, int);  // declaration
```

but a better approach is

```
void display_point(int horiz, int vert);  // declaration
```

These two declarations mean exactly the same thing to the compiler. However, the first approach, with `(int, int)`, doesn't contain any hint about which argument is for the vertical coordinate and which is for the horizontal coordinate. The advantage of the second approach is clarity for the programmer: Anyone seeing this declaration is more likely to use the correct arguments when calling the function.

Note that the names in the declaration have no effect on the names you use when calling the function. You are perfectly free to use any argument names you want:

```
display_point(x, y);   // function call
```

We'll use this name-plus-datatype approach when it seems to make the listing clearer.

Returning Values from Functions

When a function completes its execution, it can return a single value to the calling program. Usually this return value consists of an answer to the problem the function has solved. The next example demonstrates a function that returns a weight in kilograms after being given a weight in pounds. Here's the listing for CONVERT:

```
// convert.cpp
// demonstrates return values, converts pounds to kg
#include <iostream.h>

float lbstokg(float);

void main()
   {
   float lbs, kgs;

   cout << "\nEnter your weight in pounds: ";
   cin >> lbs;
   kgs = lbstokg(lbs);
   cout << "Your weight in kilograms is " << kgs;
   }

// lbstokg()
// converts pounds to kilograms
float lbstokg(float pounds)
   {
   float kilograms =  0.453592 * pounds;
   return kilograms;
   }
```

Here's some sample interaction with this program:

```
Enter your weight in pounds: 182
Your weight in kilograms is 82.553741
```

When a function returns a value, the data type of this value must be specified. The function declaration does this by placing the data type, `float` in this case, before the function name in the declaration and the definition. Functions in earlier program examples returned no value, so the return type was `void`. In the

CONVERT program, the function `lbstokg()` (*pounds to kilograms*, where `lbs` means pounds) returns type `float`, so the declaration is

```
float lbstokg(float);
```

The first `float` specifies the return type. The `float` in parentheses specifies that an argument to be passed to `lbstokg()` is also of type `float`.

When a function returns a value, the call to the function

```
lbstokg(lbs)
```

is considered to be an expression that takes on the value returned by the function. We can treat this expression like any other variable; in this case we use it in an assignment statement:

```
kgs = lbstokg(lbs);
```

This causes the variable `kgs` to be assigned the value returned by `lbstokg()`.

The `return` Statement

The function `lbstokg()` is passed an argument representing a weight in pounds, which it stores in the parameter `pounds`. It calculates the corresponding weight in kilograms by multiplying this pounds value by a constant; the result is stored in the variable `kilograms`. The value of this variable is then returned to the calling program using a `return` statement:

```
return kilograms;
```

Notice that both `main()` and `lbstokg()` have a place to store the kilogram variable: `kgs` in `main()`, and `kilograms` in `lbstokg()`. When the function returns, the value in kilograms is copied into `kgs`. The calling program does not access the `kilograms` variable in the function; only the value is returned. This process is shown in Figure 6-5.

While many arguments may be sent to a function, only one argument may be returned from it. This is a limitation when you need to return more information. However, there are other approaches to returning multiple variables from functions. One is to pass arguments by reference, which we'll look at later in this chapter.

You should always include a function's return type in the function declaration. If the function doesn't return anything, use the keyword `void` to indicate this fact. If you don't use a return type in the declaration, the compiler will assume that the function returns an `int` value. For example, the declaration

```
somefunc();    // declaration -- assumes return type is int
```

tells the compiler that `somefunc()` has a return type of `int`.

The reason for this is historical, based on usage in early versions of C. In practice you shouldn't take advantage of this default type. Always specify the return type explicitly, even if it's `int`. This keeps the listing consistent and readable.

Eliminating Unnecessary Variables

The CONVERT program contains several variables that are used in the interest of clarity but are not really necessary. A variation of this program, CONVERT2, shows how expressions can often be used in place of variables.

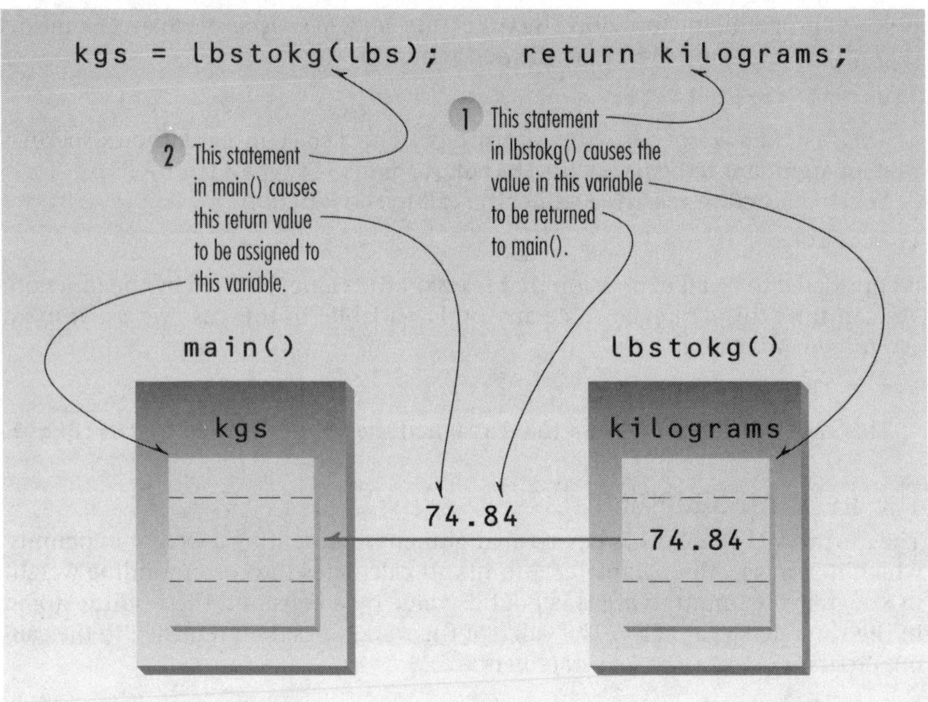

Figure 6-5 Returning a Value

```
// convert2.cpp
// eliminates unnecessary variables
#include <iostream.h>

float lbstokg(float);

void main()
   {
   float lbs;

   cout << "\nEnter your weight in pounds: ";
   cin >> lbs;
   cout << "Your weight in kilograms is " << lbstokg(lbs);
   }

// lbstokg()
// converts pounds to kilograms
float lbstokg(float pounds)
   {
   return 0.453592 * pounds;
   }
```

In `main()` the variable `kgs` from the CONVERT program has been eliminated. Instead the expression `lbstokg(lbs)` is inserted directly into the `cout` statement:

```
cout << "Your weight in kilograms is " << lbstokg(lbs);
```

Also in the `lbstokg()` function, the variable `kilograms` is no longer used. The expression `0.453592*pounds` is inserted directly into the `return` statement:

```
return 0.453592 * pounds;
```

The calculation is carried out and the resulting value is returned to the calling program, just as the value of a variable would be.

For clarity, programmers often put parentheses around the expression used in a `return` statement:

```
return (0.453592 * pounds);
```

Even when not required by the compiler, extra parentheses in an expression don't do any harm, and they may help make the listing easier for us poor humans to read.

Experienced C++ (and C) programmers will probably prefer the concise form of CONVERT2 to the more verbose CONVERT. However, CONVERT2 is not so easy to understand, especially for the nonexpert. The brevity-versus-clarity issue is a question of style, depending on your personal preference and on the expectations of those who will be reading your listing.

Returning Structure Variables

We've seen that structures can be used as arguments to functions. You can also use them as return values. Here's a program, RETSTRC, that incorporates a function that adds variables of type structure `Distance` and returns a value of this same type:

```
// retstrc.cpp
// demonstrates returning a structure
#include <iostream.h>

struct Distance                        // English distance
   {
   int feet;
   float inches;
   };

Distance addengl(Distance, Distance);  // declarations
void engldisp(Distance);

void main()
   {
   Distance d1, d2, d3;               // define three lengths
                                      // get length d1 from user
   cout << "\nEnter feet: ";   cin >> d1.feet;
   cout << "Enter inches: ";   cin >> d1.inches;
                                      // get length d2 from user
   cout << "\nEnter feet: ";   cin >> d2.feet;
   cout << "Enter inches: ";   cin >> d2.inches;

   d3 = addengl(d1, d2);              // d3 is sum of d1 and d2
```

(continued on next page)

(continued from previous page)

```
   engldisp(d1); cout << " + ";  // display all lengths
   engldisp(d2); cout << " = ";
   engldisp(d3); cout << "\n";
   }

// addengl()
// adds two structures of type Distance, returns sum
Distance addengl( Distance dd1, Distance dd2 )
   {
   Distance dd3;       // define a new structure for sum

   dd3.inches = dd1.inches + dd2.inches;  // add the inches
   dd3.feet = 0;                          // (for possible carry)
   if(dd3.inches >= 12.0)                 // if inches >= 12.0,
      {                                   // then decrease inches
      dd3.inches -= 12.0;                 // by 12.0 and
      dd3.feet++;                         // increase feet
      }                                   // by 1
   dd3.feet += dd1.feet + dd2.feet;       // add the feet
   return dd3;                            // return structure
   }

// engldisp()
// display structure of type Distance in feet and inches
void engldisp( Distance dd )
   {
   cout << dd.feet << "\'-" << dd.inches << "\"";
   }
```

The program asks the user for two lengths, in feet-and-inches format, adds them together by calling the function `addengl()`, and displays the results using the `engldisp()` function introduced in the ENGLDISP program. Here's some output from the program:

```
Enter feet: 4
Enter inches: 5.5

Enter feet: 5
Enter inches: 6.5

4'-5.5" + 5'-6.5" = 10'-0"
```

The `main()` part of the program adds the two lengths, each represented by a structure of type `Distance`, by calling the function `addengl`:

```
d3 = addengl(d1, d2);
```

This function returns the sum of `d1` and `d2`, and the result is assigned to the structure `d3`.

Internally, the `addengl()` function must create a new variable of type `Distance` to hold the results of its calculation. It can't simply return an expression, as in

```
return dd1+dd2;    // doesn't make sense
```

because the process of adding the two structures actually takes several steps: The inches are added separately from the feet. Instead the values of the individual members of `dd3` are calculated, and then `dd3` is returned to the calling program with the statement

```
return dd3;
```

The result is assigned to `d3` in the calling program.

Besides showing how structures are used as return values, this program also shows two functions (three if you count `main()`) used in the same program. You can arrange the functions in any order. The only rule is that the function declarations must appear in the listing before any calls are made to the functions.

Reference Arguments

A reference provides an alias—a different name—for a variable. By far the most important use for references is in passing arguments to functions.

We've seen examples of function arguments passed by value. When arguments are passed by value, the called function creates a new variable of the same type as the argument and copies the argument's value into it. As we noted, the function cannot access the original variable in the calling program, only the copy it created. Passing arguments by value is useful when the function does not need to modify the original variable in the calling program. In fact, it offers insurance that the function cannot harm the original variable.

Passing arguments by reference uses a different mechanism. Instead of a value being passed to the function, a reference to the original variable, in the calling program, is passed. (It's actually the address of the variable that is passed, although you don't need to know this.)

The primary advantage of passing by reference is that the function can access the actual variables in the calling program. Among other benefits, this provides a mechanism for returning more than one value from the function back to the calling program.

Passing Simple Data Types by Reference

The next example, REF, shows a simple variable passed by reference.

```
// ref.cpp
// demonstrates passing by reference
#include <iostream.h>

void main()
   {
   void intfrac(float, float&, float&);       // prototype
   float number, intpart, fracpart;           // float variables
   do
      {
      cout << "\nEnter a real number: ";      // number from user
      cin >> number;
      intfrac(number, intpart, fracpart);     // find int and frac
      cout << "Integer part is " << intpart   // print them
           << ", fraction part is " << fracpart;
```

(continued on next page)

(continued from previous page)

```
      } while( number != 0 );                    // exit loop on 0
   }
// intfrac()
// finds integer and fractional parts of real number
void intfrac(float n, float& intp, float& fracp)
   {
   intp = float( long(n) );   // convert to long, back to float
   fracp = n - intp;          // subtract integer part
   }
```

The `main()` part of this program asks the user to enter a number of type `float`. The program will separate this number into an integer and a fractional part. That is, if the user's number is 12.456, the program should report that the integer part is 12.0 and the fractional part is 0.456. To find these values, `main()` calls the function `intfrac()`. Here's some sample interaction:

```
Enter a real number: 99.44
Integer part is 99, fractional part is 0.44
```

The `intfrac()` function finds the integer part by converting the number (which was passed to the parameter `n`) into a variable of type `long int` with a cast, using the expression

```
long(n)
```

This effectively chops off the fractional part of the number, since integers (of course) store only the integer part. The result is then converted back to type `float` with another cast:

```
float( long(n) )
```

The fractional part is simply the original number less the integer part. (We should note that a library function, `fmod()`, performs a similar function for type `double`.)

The `intfrac()` function can find the integer and fractional parts, but how does it pass them back to `main()`? It could use a `return` statement to return one value but not both. The problem is solved using reference arguments. Here's the declarator for the function:

```
void intfrac(float n, float& intp, float& fracp)
```

Reference arguments are indicated by the ampersand (`&`) following the data type:

```
float& intp
```

The `&` indicates that `intp` is an alias—another name—for whatever variable is passed as an argument. In other words, when you use the name `intp` in the `intfrac()` function, you are really referring to `intpart` in `main()`. The `&` can be taken to mean *reference to*, so

```
float& intp
```

means `intp` *is a reference to the* `float` *variable passed to it*. Similarly, `fracp` is an alias for—or a reference to—`fracpart`.

The function declaration echoes the usage of the ampersand in the definition:

```
void intfrac(float, float&, float&);    // ampersands
```

As in the definition, the ampersand follows those arguments that are passed by reference.

The ampersand is *not* used in the function call:

```
intfrac(number, intpart, fracpart);    // no ampersands
```

From the function call alone, there's no way to tell whether an argument will be passed by reference or by value.

While `intpart` and `fracpart` are passed by reference, the variable `number` is passed by value. `intp` and `intpart` are different names for the same place in memory, as are `fracp` and `fracpart`. On the other hand, since it is passed by value, the parameter `n` in `intfrac()` is a separate variable into which the value of `number` is copied. It can be passed by value because the `intfrac()` function doesn't need to modify `number`. Figure 6-6 shows how reference arguments work.

(C programmers should not confuse the ampersand that is used to mean *reference to* with the same symbol used to mean *address of*. These are different usages. We'll discuss the *address of* meaning of `&` when we talk about pointers in Chapter 12.)

A More Complex Pass by Reference

Here's a somewhat more complex example of passing simple arguments by reference. Suppose you have pairs of numbers in your program and you want to be sure that the smaller one always precedes the larger one. To do this you call a function, `order()`, which checks two numbers passed to it by reference and swaps the originals if the first is larger than the second. Here's the listing for REFORDER:

```
// reforder.cpp
// orders two arguments passed by reference
#include <iostream.h>

void main()
   {
   void order(int&, int&);          // prototype

   int n1=99, n2=11;                // this pair not ordered
   int n3=22, n4=88;                // this pair ordered

   order(n1, n2);                   // order each pair of numbers
   order(n3, n4);

   cout << endl << "n1=" << n1;     // print out all numbers
   cout << endl << "n2=" << n2;
   cout << endl << "n3=" << n3;
   cout << endl << "n4=" << n4;
   }
void order(int& numb1, int& numb2)   // orders two numbers
   {
   if(numb1 > numb2)                   // if 1st larger than 2nd,
      {
      int temp = numb1;                // swap them
      numb1 = numb2;
      numb2 = temp;
      }
   }
```

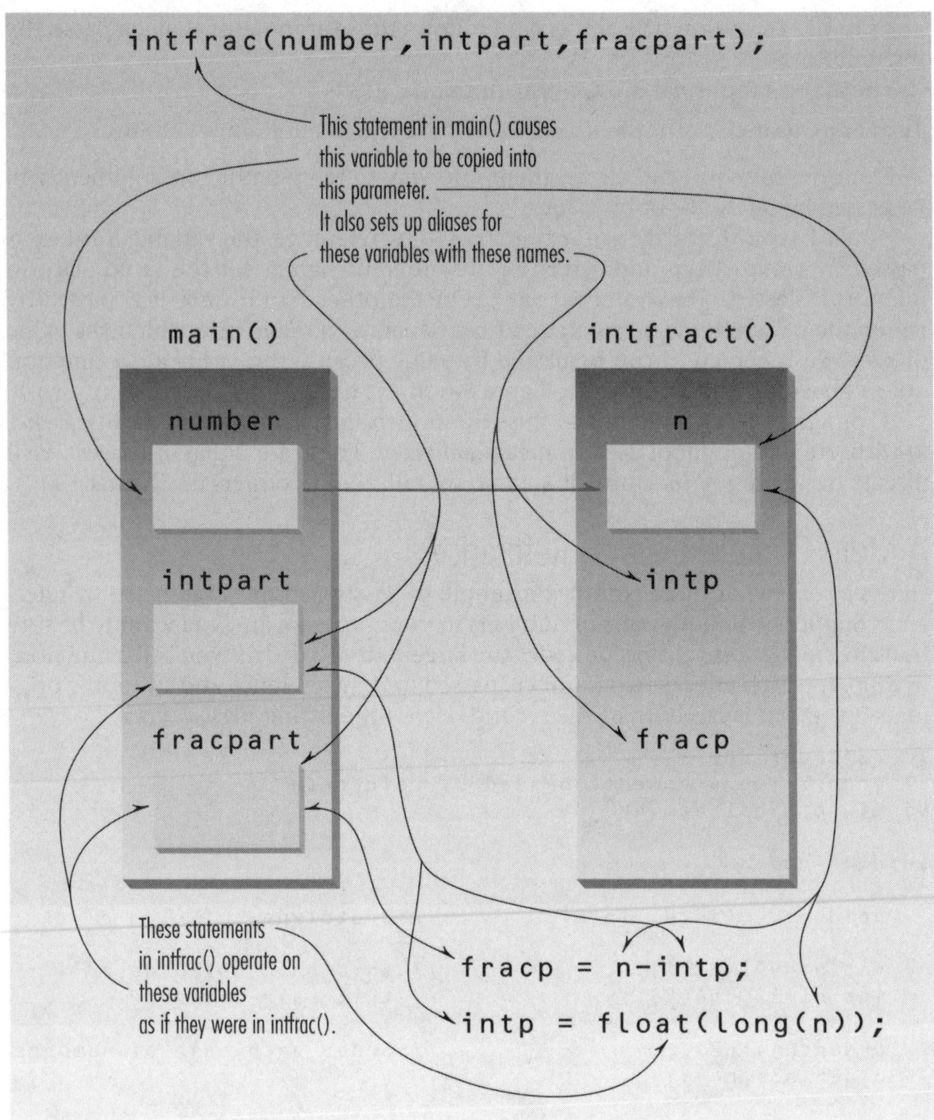
intfrac(number,intpart,fracpart);
This statement in main() causes
this variable to be copied into
this parameter.
It also sets up aliases for
these variables with these names.
main()
intfract()
number
n
intpart
intp
fracpart
fracp
These statements
in intfrac() operate on
these variables
as if they were in intfrac().
fracp = n-intp;
intp = float(long(n));

Figure 6-6 Passing by Reference

In `main()` there are two pairs of numbers—the first pair not ordered and the second pair ordered. The `order()` function is called once for each pair, and then all the numbers are printed out. The output reveals that the first pair has been swapped while the second pair hasn't. Here it is:

```
n1=11
n2=99
n3=22
n4=88
```

In the `order()` function the first variable is called `numb1` and the second is `numb2`. If `numb1` is greater than `numb2` the function stores `numb1` in `temp`, puts `numb2` in `numb1`, and finally puts `temp` back in `numb2`. Remember that `numb1` and `numb2` are simply different names for whatever arguments were passed; in this case, `n1` and `n2` on the first call to the function, and `n2` and `n3` on the second call. The effect is to check the ordering of the original arguments in the calling program and swap them if necessary.

Using reference arguments in this way is a sort of remote-control operation. The calling program tells the function what variables in the calling program to operate on, and the function modifies these variables without ever knowing their real names. It's as if you called the house painters and then sat back and watched as your dining room walls mysteriously changed color.

Passing Structures by Reference

You can pass structures by reference just as you can simple data types. Here's a program, REFERST, that performs scale conversions on values of type `Distance`. A scale conversion involves multiplying a group of distances by a factor. If a distance is 6'–8", and a scale factor is 0.5, the new distance is 3'–4". Such a conversion might be applied to all the dimensions of a building to make the building shrink but remain in proportion.

```
// referst.cpp
// demonstrates passing structure by reference
#include <iostream.h>

struct Distance                              // English distance
   {
   int feet;
   float inches;
   };

void scale( Distance&, float );              // function
void engldisp( Distance );                   // declarations

void main()
   {
   Distance d1 = { 12, 6.5 };                // initialize d1 and d2
   Distance d2 = { 10, 5.5 };

   cout << "\nd1 = "; engldisp(d1);          // display old d1 and d2
   cout << "\nd2 = "; engldisp(d2);

   scale(d1, 0.5);                           // scale d1 and d2
   scale(d2, 0.25);

   cout << "\nd1 = "; engldisp(d1);          // display new d1 and d2
   cout << "\nd2 = "; engldisp(d2);
   }

// scale()
// scales value of type Distance by factor
void scale( Distance& dd, float factor)
```

(continued on next page)

(continued from previous page)

```
   {
   float inches = (dd.feet*12 + dd.inches) * factor;
   dd.feet = inches / 12;
   dd.inches = inches - dd.feet * 12;
   }

// engldisp()
// display structure of type Distance in feet and inches
void engldisp( Distance dd )   // parameter dd of type Distance
   {
   cout << dd.feet << "\'-" << dd.inches << "\"";
   }
```

REFERST initializes two `Distance` variables—`d1` and `d2`—to specific values, and displays them. Then it calls the `scale()` function to multiply `d1` by 0.5 and `d2` by 0.25. Finally, it displays the resulting values of the distances. Here's the program's output:

```
d1 = 12'-6.5"
d2 = 10'-5.5"
d1 = 6'-3.25"
d2 = 2'-7.375"
```

Here are the two calls to the function `scale()`:

```
scale(d1, 0.5);
scale(d2, 0.25);
```

The first call causes `d1` to be multiplied by 0.5, the second causes `d2` to be multiplied by 0.25. Notice that these changes take place directly to `d1` and `d2`. The function doesn't return anything; the operation is performed directly on the `Distance` argument, which is passed by reference to `scale`. (Since only one value is changed in the calling program, you could rewrite the function to pass the argument by value and return the scaled value. Calling the function would look like this:

```
d1 = scale(d1, 0.5);
```

However, this is inelegant and unnecessarily verbose.)

Notes on Passing by Reference

Passing arguments by reference is also possible in Pascal and BASIC. References don't exist in C, where pointers serve a somewhat similar purpose, although often less conveniently. Reference arguments were introduced into C++ to provide flexibility in a variety of situations involving objects as well as simple variables.

The third way to pass arguments to functions, besides by value and by reference, is to use pointers. We'll explore this when we discuss pointers in Chapter 12.

Overloaded Functions

An overloaded function appears to perform different activities depending on the kind of data sent to it. Overloading is like the joke about the famous scientist who insisted that the thermos bottle was the greatest invention of all time. Why? "It's a miracle device," he said. "It keeps hot things hot, but cold things it keeps cold. How does it know?"

It may seem equally mysterious how an overloaded function knows what to do. It performs one operation on one kind of data but another operation on a different kind. Let's clarify matters with some examples.

Different Numbers of Arguments

Recall the `starline()` function in the TABLE example and the `repchar()` function from the TABLEARG example, both shown earlier in this chapter. The `starline()` function printed a line using 45 asterisks, while `repchar()` used a character and a line length that were both specified when the function was called. We might imagine a third function, `charline()`, that always prints 45 characters but that allows the calling program to specify the character to be printed. These three functions—`starline()`, `repchar()`, and `charline()`—perform similar activities but have different names. For programmers using these functions, that means three names to remember and three places to look them up if they are listed alphabetically in an application's *Function Reference* documentation.

It would be far more convenient to use the same name for all three functions, even though they each have different arguments. Here's a program, OVERLOAD, that makes this possible:

```
// overload.cpp
// demonstrates function overloading
#include <iostream.h>

void repchar();
void repchar(char);
void repchar(char, int);

void main()
   {
   repchar();
   repchar('=');
   repchar('+', 30);
   }

// repchar()
// displays 45 asterisks
void repchar()
   {
   for(int j=0; j<45; j++)    // always loops 45 times
      cout << '*';            // always prints asterisk
   cout << endl;
   }

// repchar()
// displays 45 copies of specified character
void repchar(char ch)
   {
   for(int j=0; j<45; j++)    // always loops 45 times
      cout << ch;             // prints specified character
   cout << endl;
   }
```

(continued on next page)

(continued from previous page)

```
// repchar()
// displays specified number of copies of specified character
void repchar(char ch, int n)
   {
   for(int j=0; j<n; j++)    // loops n times
      cout << ch;            // prints specified character
   cout << endl;
   }
```

This program prints out three lines of characters. Here's the output:

```
*********************************************
=============================================
++++++++++++++++++++++++++++++
```

The first two lines are 45 characters long, and the third is 30.

The program contains three functions with the same name. There are three declarations, three function calls, and three function definitions. What keeps the compiler from becoming hopelessly confused? It uses the number of arguments, and their data types, to distinguish one function from another. In other words, the declaration

```
void repchar();
```

which takes no arguments, describes an entirely different function than the declaration

```
void repchar(char);
```

which takes one argument of type `char`, or the declaration

```
void repchar(char, int);
```

which takes one argument of type `char` and another of type `int`.

The compiler, seeing several functions with the same name but different numbers of arguments, could decide the programmer had made a mistake (which is what it would do in C). Instead, it very tolerantly sets up a separate function for every such definition. Which one of these functions will be called depends on the number of arguments supplied in the call. Figure 6-7 shows this process.

Different Kinds of Arguments

In the OVERLOAD example we created several functions with the same name but different numbers of arguments. The compiler can also distinguish between overloaded functions with the same number of arguments, provided their type is different. Here's a program, OVERENGL, that uses an overloaded function to display a quantity in feet-and-inches format. The single argument to the function can be either a structure of type `Distance` (as used in the ENGLDISP example) or a simple variable of type `float`. Different functions are used depending on the type of argument.

```
// overengl.cpp
// demonstrates overloaded functions
#include <iostream.h>
```

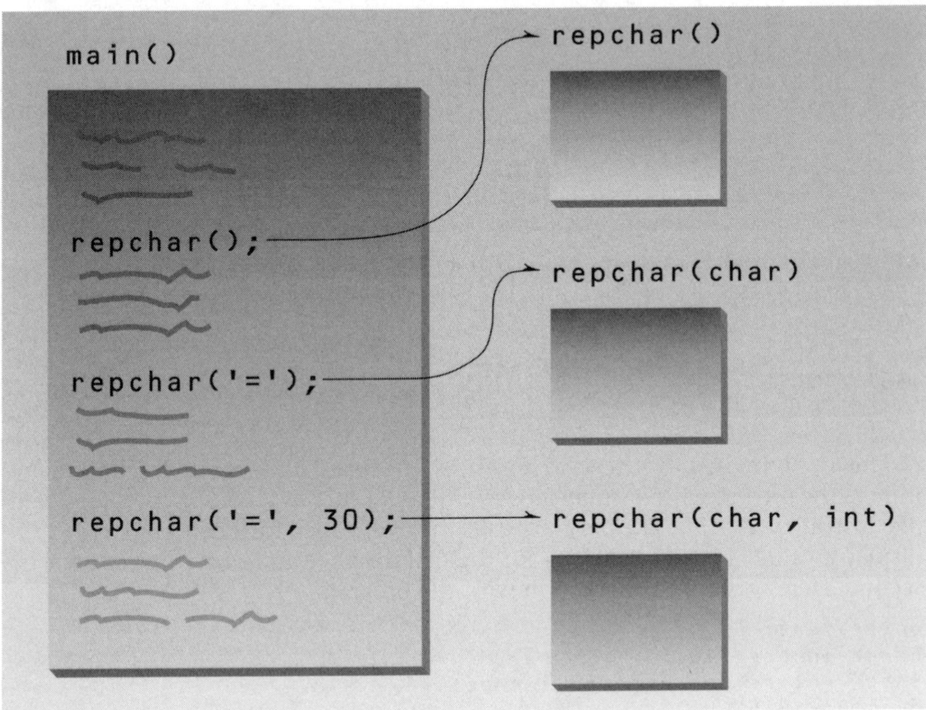

Figure 6-7 Overloaded Functions

```
struct Distance                    // English distance
   {
   int feet;
   float inches;
   };

void engldisp( Distance );          // declarations
void engldisp( float );

void main()
   {
   Distance d1;                     // distance of type Distance
   float d2;                        // distance of type float
                                    // get length d1 from user
   cout << "\nEnter feet: ";  cin >> d1.feet;
   cout << "Enter inches: ";  cin >> d1.inches;
                                    // get length d2 from user
   cout << "Enter entire distance in inches: "; cin >> d2;
   cout << "\nd1 = ";
   engldisp(d1);                    // display length 1
   cout << "\nd2 = ";
   engldisp(d2);                    // display length 2
}
```

(continued on next page)

(continued from previous page)

```
// engldisp()
// display structure of type Distance in feet and inches
void engldisp( Distance dd )    // parameter dd of type Distance
   {
   cout << dd.feet << "\'-" << dd.inches << "\"";
   }

// engldisp()
// display variable of type float in feet and inches
void engldisp( float dd )    // parameter dd of type float
   {
   int feet = dd / 12;
   float inches = dd - feet*12;
   cout << feet << "\'-" << inches << "\"";
   }
```

The user is invited to enter two distances, the first with separate feet and inches inputs, the second with a single large number for inches (109.5 inches, for example, instead of 9'–1.5"). The program calls the overloaded function `engldisp()` to display a value of type `Distance` for the first distance and of type `float` for the second. Here's a sample interaction with the program:

```
Enter feet: 5
Enter inches: 10.5
Enter entire distance in inches: 76.5
d1 = 5'-10.5"
d2 = 6'-4.5"
```

Notice that, while the different versions of `engldisp()` do similar things, the code is quite different. The version that accepts the all-inches input has to convert to feet and inches before displaying the result.

Overloaded functions can simplify the programmer's life by reducing the number of function names to be remembered. As an example of the complexity that arises when overloading is not used, consider the Borland C++ library routines for finding the absolute value of a number. Because these routines must work with C (which does not allow overloading) as well as with C++, there must be separate versions of the absolute value routine for each data type. There are four of them: `abs()` for type `int`, `cabs()` for complex numbers, `fabs()` for type `double`, and `labs()` for type `long int`. In C++, a single name, `abs()`, would suffice for all these data types.

As we'll see later, overloaded functions are also useful for handling different types of objects.

Inline Functions

We mentioned that functions save memory space because all the calls to the function cause the same code to be executed; the function body need not be duplicated in memory. When the compiler sees a function call, it normally generates a jump to the function. At the end of the function it jumps back to the instruction following the call, as we show in Figure 6-1.

While this sequence of events may save memory space, it takes some extra time. There must be an instruction for the jump to the function (actually the assembly-language instruction CALL), instructions for saving registers, instructions for pushing arguments onto the stack in the calling program and removing them from the stack in the function (if there are arguments), instructions for restoring registers, and an instruction to return to the calling program. The return value (if any) must also be dealt with. All these instructions slow down the program.

To save execution time in short functions, you may elect to put the code in the function body directly in line with the code in the calling program. That is, each time there's a function call in the source file, the actual code from the function is inserted, instead of a jump to the function. The difference between a function and inline code is shown in Figure 6-8.

Long sections of repeated code are generally better off as normal functions: The savings in memory space is worth the comparatively small sacrifice in execution speed. But making a short section of code into a function may result in little savings in memory space, while imposing just as much time penalty as a larger function. In fact, if a function is very short, the instructions necessary to call it may take up as much space as the instructions within the function body, so that there is not only a time penalty but a space penalty as well.

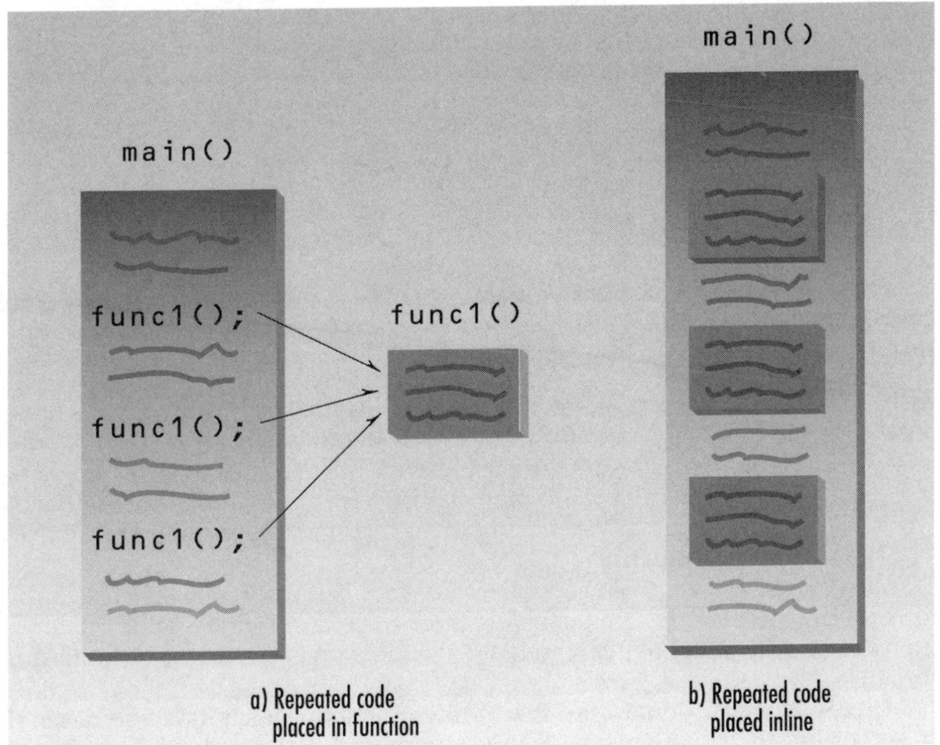

Figure 6-8 Functions Versus Inline Code

In such cases you could simply repeat the necessary code in your program, inserting the same group of statements wherever it was needed. The trouble with repeatedly inserting the same code is that you lose the benefits of program organization and clarity that come with using functions. The program may run faster and take less space, but the listing is longer and more complex.

The solution to this quandary is the *inline function*. This kind of function is written like a normal function in the source file but compiles into inline code instead of into a function. The source file remains well organized and easy to read, since the function is shown as a separate entity. However, when the program is compiled, the function body is actually inserted into the program wherever a function call occurs.

Functions that are very short, say one or two statements, are candidates to be inlined. Here's INLINE, a variation on the CONVERT2 program. It inlines the `lbstokg()` function.

```
// inline.cpp
// demonstrates inline functions
#include <iostream.h>

// lbstokg()                                      // definition of
// converts pounds to kilograms                   // inline function
inline float lbstokg(float pounds)                // (must precede calls
   {                                              // to it)
   return 0.453592 * pounds;
   }

void main()                                       // main() must follow any
   {                                              // inline definitions
   float lbs;

   cout << "\nEnter your weight in pounds: ";
   cin >> lbs;
   cout << "Your weight in kilograms is " << lbstokg(lbs);
   }
```

It's easy to make a function inline: All you need is the keyword `inline` in the function definition:

```
inline float lgstokg(float pounds)
```

However, there are some subtleties to using inline functions. The compiler must have seen the function definition (not just the declaration) before it gets to the first function call. This is because it must insert the actual code into the program, not just instructions to call the function. In INLINE we must place the definition of `lbstokg()` before `main()`. When you do this the function declaration is unnecessary and can be eliminated.

You should be aware that the `inline` keyword is actually just a *request* to the compiler. Sometimes the compiler will ignore the request and compile the function as a normal function. It might decide the function is too long to be inline, for instance.

(C programmers should note that inline functions largely take the place of `#define` macros in C. They serve the same purpose but provide better type checking and do not need special care with parentheses, as macros do.)

Default Arguments

Surprisingly, a function can be called without specifying all its arguments. This won't work on just any function: The function declaration must provide default values for those arguments that are not specified.

Here's an example, a variation on the OVERLOAD program, that demonstrates this effect. In OVERLOAD we used three different functions with the same name to handle different numbers of arguments. The present example, MISSARG, achieves the same effect in a different way.

```
// missarg.cpp
// demonstrates missing and default arguments
#include <iostream.h>

void repchar(char='*', int=45);     // prototype with
                                    // default arguments

void main()
   {
   repchar();              // prints 45 asterisks
   repchar('=');           // prints 45 equal signs
   repchar('+', 30);       // prints 30 plus signs
   }

// repchar()
// displays line of characters
void repchar(char ch, int n)  // defaults supplied if necessary
   {
   for(int j=0; j<n; j++)   // loops n times
      cout << ch;           // prints ch
   cout << endl;
   }
```

In this program the function `repchar()` takes two arguments. It's called three times from `main()`. The first time it's called with no arguments, the second time with one, and the third time with two. Why do the first two calls work? Because the called function provides *default arguments*, which will be used if the calling program doesn't supply them. The default arguments are specified in the prototype to `repchar()`:

```
void repchar(char='*', int=45);   // prototype (declaration)
```

The default argument follows an equal sign, which is placed directly after the type name. You can also use variable names, as in

```
void repchar(char reptChar='*', int numberReps=45);
```

If one argument is missing when the function is called, it is assumed to be the last argument. The `repchar()` function assigns the value of the single argument to the `ch` parameter and uses the default value 45 for the `n` parameter.

If both arguments are missing, the function assigns the default value '*' to `ch` and the default value 45 to `n`. Thus the three calls to the function all work, even though each has a different number of arguments.

Remember that missing arguments must be the trailing arguments—those at the end of the argument list. You can leave out the last three arguments, but you can't leave out the next-to-last and then put in the last. This is reasonable; how would the compiler know which arguments you meant, if you left out some in the middle? (Missing arguments could have been indicated with commas, but commas are notoriously subject to misprints, so the designers of C++ ignored this possibility.) Not surprisingly, the compiler will flag an error if you leave out arguments for which the function does not provide default values.

Default arguments are useful if you don't want to go to the trouble of writing arguments that, for example, almost always have the same value. They are also useful in cases where, after a program is written, the programmer decides to increase the capability of a function by adding another argument. Using default arguments means that the existing function calls can continue to use the old number of arguments, while new function calls can use more.

Variables and Storage Classes

Now that we know about functions, we can explore a feature of C++ that's related to the interaction of variables and functions: the *storage class*. The storage class of a variable determines which parts of the program can access it and how long it stays in existence. We'll look at variables with three storage classes—automatic, external, and static.

Automatic Variables

So far all the variables we've used in example programs have been defined inside the function in which they are used. That is, the definition occurs inside the braces that delimit the function body:

```
void somefunc()
   {
   int somevar;            // variables defined within
   float othervar;         // the function body
   // other statements
   }
```

Variables may be defined inside `main()` or inside other functions; the effect is similar, since `main()` is a function. Variables defined within a function body are called *automatic variables*. Actually, a keyword, `auto`, can be used to specify an automatic variable. You would say

```
void somefunc()
   {
   auto int somevar;           // same as int somevar
   auto float othervar;        // same as float othervar
   // other statements
   }
```

However, since this is the default, there is seldom any need to use the `auto` keyword. Variables defined within a function are automatic anyway.

Let's look at the two important characteristics of automatic variables—lifetime and visibility.

Lifetime

An automatic variable is not created until the function in which it is defined is called. (More accurately, we can say that variables defined within any block of code are not created until the block is executed.) In the program fragment just given, the variables `somevar` and `othervar` don't exist until the `somefunc()` function is called. That is, there is no place in memory where their values are stored; they are undefined. When control is transferred to `somefunc()`, the variables are created and memory space is set aside for them. Later, when `somefunc()` exits and control is returned to the calling program, the variables are destroyed and their values are lost. The name *automatic* is used because the variables are automatically created when a function is called and automatically destroyed when it returns.

The time period between the creation and destruction of a variable is called its *lifetime* (or sometimes its *duration*). The lifetime of an automatic variable coincides with the time when the function in which it is defined is executing.

The idea behind limiting the lifetime of variables is to save memory space. If a function is not executing, the variables it uses during execution are presumably not needed. Removing them frees up memory that can then be used by other functions.

Visibility

A variable's *visibility* describes where within a program it can be accessed. It can be referred to in statements in some parts of the program; in others, attempts to access it lead to an *unknown variable* error message. The word *scope* is also used to describe visibility. The scope of a variable is that part of the program where the variable is visible.

Automatic variables are only `visible`, meaning they can only be accessed, within the function in which they are defined. Suppose you have two functions in a program:

```
void somefunc()
   {
   int somevar;      // automatic variables
   float othervar;

   somevar = 10;     // ok
   othervar = 11;    // ok
   nextvar = 12;     // illegal: not visible in somefunc()
   }

void otherfunc()
   {
   int nextvar;      // automatic variable

   somevar = 20;     // illegal: not visible in otherfunc()
   othervar = 21;    // illegal: not visible in otherfunc()
   nextvar = 22;     // ok
   }
```

The variable `nextvar` is invisible in function `somefunc()`, and the variables `somevar` and `othervar` are invisible in `otherfunc()`.

Limiting the visibility of variables helps organize and modularize the program. You can be confident that the variables in one function are safe from accidental alteration by other functions because the other functions can't see them. This is an important part of structured programming, the methodology for organizing old-fashioned procedural programs. Limiting visibility is also an important part of object-oriented programming.

In the case of automatic variables, lifetime and visibility coincide: These variables exist only while the function in which they are defined is executing, and are only visible within this function. For some storage classes, however, lifetime and visibility are not the same.

Initialization

When an automatic variable is created, the compiler does not try to initialize it. Thus it will start off with an arbitrary value, which may be 0 but probably will be something else. If you want it initialized, you must do it explicitly, as in

```
int n = 33;
```

then it will start off with this value.

Automatic variables are sometimes called *local* variables, since they are visible only locally, in the function where they are defined.

External Variables

The next major storage class is *external*. While automatic variables are defined within functions, external variables are defined outside of (external to) any function. An external variable is visible to all the functions in a program. More precisely, it is visible to all those functions that follow the variable's definition in the listing. Usually you want external variables to be visible to all functions, so you put their declarations at the beginning of the listing. External variables are also called *global* variables, since they are known by all the functions in a program.

Here's a program, EXTERN, in which three functions all access an external variable.

```
// extern.cpp
// demonstrates external variables
#include <iostream.h>
#include <conio.h>            // for getch()

char ch = 'a';                // external variable ch

void getachar();              // function declarations
void putachar();

void main()
   {
   while( ch != '\r' )        // main() accesses ch
      {
      getachar();
      putachar();
      }
   }
```

```
void getachar()                    // getachar() accesses ch
   {
   ch = getch();
   }

void putachar()                    // putachar() accesses ch
   {
   cout << ch;
   }
```

One function in EXTERN, `getachar()`, reads characters from the keyboard. It uses the library function `getch()`, which is like `getche()` except that it doesn't echo the character typed to the screen (hence the absence of the final `e` in the name). A second EXTERN function, `putachar()`, displays each character on the screen. The effect is that what you type is displayed in the normal way:

```
I'm typing in this line of text
```

The significant thing about this program is that the variable `ch` is not defined in any of the functions. Instead it is defined at the beginning of the file, before the first function. It is an external variable. Any function that follows the definition of `ch` in the listing can access it—in this case all the functions in EXTERN: `main()`, `getachar()`, and `putachar()`. Thus the visibility of `ch` is the entire source file.

Role of External Variables

The external storage class is used when a variable must be accessible to more than one function in a program. In procedural programs external variables are often the most important variables in the program. However, as we noted in Chapter 1, external variables create organizational problems for the very reason that they can be accessed by any function. The wrong functions may access them, or functions may access them incorrectly. In an object-oriented program, there is less necessity for external variables.

Initialization

If an external variable is initialized by the program, as in

```
int exvar = 199;
```

this initialization takes place when the file is first loaded but not thereafter. If an external variable is not initialized explicitly by the program—for example, if it is defined as

```
int exvar;
```

—then it is initialized automatically to 0 when it is created. (This is unlike automatic variables, which are not initialized and probably contain random or "garbage" values when they are created.)

Lifetime and Visibility

External variables exist for the life of the program. That is, memory space is set aside for them when the program begins, and continues in existence until the program ends.

External variables are visible in the file in which they are defined, starting at the point where they are defined. If `ch` were defined following `main()` but before `getachar()`, it would be visible in `getachar()` and `putachar()`, but not in `main()`.

Static Variables

We'll touch on another storage class: *static*. Here we are concerned with static automatic variables. There are static external variables, but they are meaningful only in multifile programs, which we don't examine until Chapter 15.

A static automatic variable has the visibility of a local variable but the lifetime of an external variable. Thus it is visible only inside the function in which it is defined, but it remains in existence for the life of the program.

Static automatic variables are used when it's necessary for a function to remember a value when it is not being executed; that is, between calls to the function. In the next example, a function, `getavg()`, calculates a running average. It remembers the total of the numbers it has averaged before, and how many there were. Each time it receives a new number, sent as an argument from the calling program, it adds this number to the total, adds 1 to a count, and returns the new average by dividing the total by the count. Here's the listing for STATIC:

```
// static.cpp
// demonstrates static variables
#include <iostream.h>

float getavg(float);                        // prototype

void main()
   {
   float data=1, avg;

   while( data != 0 )
      {
      cout << "Enter a number: ";
      cin >> data;
      avg = getavg(data);
      cout << "New average is " << avg << endl;
      }
   }

// getavg()
// finds average of old plus new data
float getavg(float newdata)
   {
   static float total = 0;  // static variables are initialized
   static int count = 0;    // only once per program

   count++;                 // increment count
   total += newdata;        // add new data to total
   return total / count;    // return the new average
   }
```

Here's some sample interaction:

```
Enter a number: 10
New average is 10  <------- total is 10, count is 1
Enter a number: 20
New average is 15  <------- total is 30, count is 2
Enter a number: 30
New average is 20  <------- total is 60, count is 3
```

The static variables `total` and `count` in `getavg()` retain their values after `getavg()` returns, so they're available the next time it's called.

Initialization

When static variables are initialized, as `total` and `count` are in `getavg()`, the initialization takes place only once—the first time their function is called. They are not reinitialized on subsequent calls to the function, as ordinary automatic variables are.

Storage

If you're familiar with the architecture of MS-DOS computers, you might be interested to know that automatic variables are stored in the stack segment, while external and static variables are stored in the data segment.

Table 6-2 summarizes the lifetime, visibility, and some other aspects of automatic, static automatic, and external variables.

Returning by Reference

Now that we know about external variables, we can examine a rather odd-looking C++ feature. Besides passing values by reference, you can also *return* a value by reference. Why you would want to do this may seem obscure. The primary reason is to allow you to use a function call *on the left side of the equal sign*. This is a somewhat bizarre concept, so let's look at an example. The RETREF program shows the mechanism.

	automatic	static auto	external
Visibility	function	function	file
Lifetime	function	program	program
Initialized value	not initialized	0	0
Storage	stack segment	data segment	data segment
Purpose	variables used by a single function	same as auto, but must retain value when function terminates	variables used by several functions

Table 6-2 Storage Types

```
// retref.cpp
// returning reference values
#include <iostream.h>

int x;                        // global variable
int& setx();                  // function declaration

void main()
   {                          // set x to a value, using
   setx() = 92;               // function call on left side
   cout << "\nx=" << x;       // display new value in x
   }

int& setx()
   {
   return x;                  // returns the value to be modified
   }
```

In this program the function `setx()` is declared with a reference type, `int&`, as the return type:

```
int& setx();
```

This function contains the statement

```
return x;
```

where `x` has been defined as an external variable. Now—and this is what looks so strange—you can put a call to this function on the left side of the equal sign:

```
setx() = 92;
```

The result is that the variable returned by the function is assigned the value on the right side of the equal sign. That is, `x` is given the value 92. The output from the program,

```
x=92
```

verifies that this assignment has taken place.

Function Calls on the Left of the Equal Sign

Does this still sound obscure? Remember that an ordinary function—one that returns a value—can be used as if it were a value:

```
y=squareroot(x);
```

Here whatever value `squareroot(x)` has (like 27.2) is assigned to `y`. The function is treated as if it were a *value*. A function that returns a reference, on the other hand, is treated as if it were a *variable*. It returns an alias to a variable, namely the variable in the function's `return` statement. In RETREF.C the function `setx()` returns a reference to the variable `x`. When this function is called, it's treated *as if it were* the variable `x`. Thus it can be used on the left side of an equal sign.

There are two corollaries to this. One is that you can't return a constant from a function that returns by reference. In `setx()`, you can't say

```
int& setx()
   {
   return 3;
   }
```

If you try this the compiler will complain that you need an *"lvalue,"* that is, something that can go on the left side of the equal sign: a variable and not a constant.

More subtly, you can't return a reference to an automatic variable:

```
int& setx()
   {
   int x = 3;
   return x;      // error
   }
```

What's wrong with this? The problem is that a function's automatic variables are (probably) destroyed when the function returns, and it doesn't make sense to return a reference to something that no longer exists.

Don't Worry Yet

Of course, the question remains why one would ever want to use a function call on the left of an equal sign. In procedural programming there probably isn't too much use for this technique. As in the above example, there are easier ways to achieve the same result. However, when we cover overloaded operators in Chapter 9, we'll find that returning by reference is an indispensable technique. Until then, keep it in the back of your mind.

Summary

Functions provide a way to help organize programs, and to reduce program size, by giving a block of code a name and allowing it to be executed from other parts of the program. Function declarations (prototypes) specify what the function looks like, function calls transfer control to the function, and function definitions contain the statements that make up the function. The function declarator is the first line of the definition.

Arguments can be sent to functions either by value, where the function works with a copy of the argument, or by reference, where the function works with the original argument in the calling program.

Functions can return only one value. Functions ordinarily return a value, but they can also return a reference, which allows the function call to be used on the left side of an assignment statement. Arguments and return values can be either simple data types or structures.

An overloaded function is actually a group of functions with the same name. Which of them is executed when the function is called depends on the type and number of arguments supplied in the call.

An inline function looks like a normal function in the source file but inserts the function's code directly into the calling program. Inline functions execute faster but may require more memory than normal functions unless they are very small.

If a function uses default arguments, calls to it need not include all the arguments shown in the declaration. Default values supplied by the function are used for the missing arguments.

Variables possess a characteristic called the storage class. The most common storage class is automatic. Variables of this class exist only while the function in which they are defined is executing, and are visible only within that function. External variables exist for the life of a program and can be visible throughout an entire file. Static automatic variables exist for the life of a program but are visible only in their own function.

In Chapter 5 we examined one of the two major parts of objects: structures, which are collections of data. In this chapter we explored the second part: functions. Now we're ready to put these two components together to create objects, the subject of Chapter 7.

Questions

Answers to questions can be found in Appendix D.

1. A function's single most important role is to
   - a. give a name to a block of code.
   - b. reduce program size.
   - c. accept arguments and provide a return value.
   - d. help organize a program into conceptual units.
2. A function itself is called the function d_________.
3. Write a function called `foo()` that displays the word *foo*.
4. A one-statement description of a function is referred to as a function d_________ or a p_________.
5. The statements that carry out the work of the function constitute the function _________.
6. A program statement that invokes a function is a function _________
7. The first line of a function definition is referred to as the _________.
8. A function argument is
   - a. a variable in the function that receives a value from the calling program.
   - b. a way that functions resist accepting the calling program's values.
   - c. a value sent to the function by the calling program.
   - d. a value returned by the function to the calling program.
9. True or false: When arguments are passed by value, the function works with the original arguments in the calling program.

10. What is the purpose of using argument names in a function declaration?

11. Which of the following can legitimately be passed to a function?

    a. A constant
    b. A variable
    c. A structure
    d. A header file

12. What is the significance of empty parentheses in a function declaration?

13. How many values can be returned from a function?

14. True or false: When a function returns a value, the entire function call can appear on the right side of the equal sign and be assigned to another variable.

15. Where is a function's return type specified?

16. A function that doesn't return anything has return type ________.

17. Here's a function:

```
int times2(int a)
   {
   return (a*2);
   }
```

    Write a `main()` program that includes everything necessary to call this function.

18. When an argument is passed by reference,

    a. a variable is created in the function to hold the argument's value.
    b. the function cannot access the argument's value.
    c. a temporary variable is created in the calling program to hold the argument's value.
    d. the function accesses the argument's original value in the calling program.

19. What is the principle reason for passing arguments by reference?

20. Overloaded functions

    a. are a group of functions with the same name.
    b. all have the same number and types of arguments.
    c. make life simpler for programmers.
    d. may fail unexpectedly due to stress.

21. Write declarations for two overloaded functions named `bar()`. They both return type `int`. The first takes one argument of type `char`, and the second takes two arguments of type `char`. If this is impossible, say why.

22. In general, an inline function executes ________ than a normal function, but requires ________ memory.

23. Write the declarator for an inline function named `foobar()` that takes one argument of type `float` and returns type `float`.

24. A default argument has a value that

    a. may be supplied by the calling program.
    b. may be supplied by the function.
    c. must have a constant value.
    d. must have a variable value.

25. Write a declaration for a function called `blyth()` that takes two arguments and returns type `char`. The first argument is type `int`, and the second is type `float` with a default value of 3.14159.

26. Storage class is concerned with the ________ and ________ of a variable.

27. What functions can access an external variable that appears in the same file with them?

28. What functions can access an automatic variable?

29. A static automatic variable is used to

    a. make a variable visible to several functions.
    b. make a variable visible to only one function.
    c. conserve memory when a function is not executing.
    d. retain a value when a function is not executing.

30. In what unusual place can you use a function call when a function returns a value by reference?

Exercises

Answers to the starred exercises can be found in Appendix D.

1.* Refer to the CIRCAREA program in Chapter 3. Write a function called `circarea()` that finds the area of a circle in a similar way. It should take an argument of type `float` and return an argument of the same type. Write a `main()` function that gets a radius value from the user, calls `circarea()`, and displays the result.

2.* Raising a number `n` to a power `p` is the same as multiplying `n` by itself `p` times. Write a function called `power()` that takes a `double` value for `n` and an `int` value for `p`, and returns the result as a `double` value. Use a default argument of 2 for `p`, so that if this argument is omitted, the number will be squared. Write a `main()` function that gets values from the user to test this function.

3.* Write a function called `zeroSmaller()` that is passed two `int` arguments by reference and then sets the smaller of the two numbers to 0. Write a `main()` program to exercise this function.

4.* Write a function that takes two `Distance` values as arguments and returns the larger one. Include a `main()` program that accepts two `Distance` values from the user, compares them, and displays the larger. (See the RETSTRC program for hints.)

5. Write a function called `hms_to_secs()` that takes three `int` values—for hours, minutes, and seconds—as arguments, and returns the equivalent time in seconds (type `long`). Create a program that exercises this function by repeatedly obtaining a time value in hours, minutes, and seconds from the user (format 12:59:59), calling the function, and displaying the value of seconds it returns.

6. Start with the program from Exercise 11, Chapter 5, which adds two `struct time` values. Keep the same functionality, but modify the program so that it uses two functions. The first, `time_to_secs()`, takes as its only argument a structure of type `time`, and returns the equivalent in seconds (type `long`). The second function, `secs_to_time()`, takes as its only argument a time in seconds (type `long`), and returns a structure of type `time`.

7. Start with the `power ()` function of Exercise 2, which works only with type `double`. Create a series of overloaded functions with the same name that, in addition to `double`, also work with types `char`, `int`, `long`, and `float`. Write a `main()` program that exercises these overloaded functions with all argument types.

8. Write a function called `swap()` that interchanges two `int` values passed to it by the calling program. (Note that this function swaps the values of the variables in the calling program, not those in the function.) You'll need to decide how to pass the arguments. Create a `main()` program to exercise the function.

9. This exercise is similar to Exercise 8, except that instead of two `int` variables, have the `swap()` function interchange two `struct time` values (see Exercise 6).

10. Write a function that, when you call it, displays a message telling how many times it has been called: `I have been called 3 times`, or whatever. Write a `main()` program that calls this function at least 10 times. Try implementing this function in two different ways. First, use an external variable to store the count. Second, use a local static variable. Which is more appropriate? Why can't you use an automatic variable?

11. Write a program, based on the `sterling` structure of Exercise 10 in Chapter 5, that obtains from the user two money amounts in old-style British format (£9:19:11), adds them, and displays the result, again in old-style format. Use

three functions. The first should obtain a pounds-shillings-pence value from the user and return the value as a structure of type `sterling`. The second should take two arguments of type `sterling` and return a value of the same type, which is the sum of the arguments. The third should take a `sterling` structure as its argument and display its value.

12. Revise the four-function fraction calculator from Exercise 12, Chapter 5, so that it uses functions for each of the four arithmetic operations. They can be called `fadd()`, `fsub()`, `fmul()`, and `fdiv()`. Each of these functions should take two arguments of type `struct fraction`, and return an argument of the same type.

7

Objects and Classes

OBJECTS AND CLASSES

MEMBER FUNCTIONS AND DATA

`private` AND `public`

CONSTRUCTORS AND DESTRUCTORS

OBJECTS IN THE REAL WORLD

WHEN TO USE OBJECTS

7

And now, the topics you've all been waiting for: objects and classes. The preliminaries are out of the way. We've learned about structures, which provide a way to group data elements. We've examined functions, which organize program actions into named entities. In this chapter we'll put these ideas together. We'll introduce several classes, starting with simple ones and working toward more complicated examples. We'll focus first on the details of classes and objects. At the end of the chapter we'll take a wider view, discussing what is to be gained by using the OOP approach.

As you read this chapter you may want to refer back to the concepts introduced in Chapter 1.

A Simple Class

Our first program contains a class and two objects of that class. Although it's simple, the program demonstrates the syntax and general features of classes in C++. Here's the listing for the SMALLOBJ program:

```
// smallobj.cpp
// demonstrates a small, simple object
#include <iostream.h>

class smallobj                   // specify a class
   {
   private:
      int somedata;              // class data
   public:
      void setdata(int d)        // member function to set data
         { somedata = d; }
      void showdata()            // member function to display data
         { cout << "\nData is " << somedata; }
   };

void main()
   {
   smallobj s1, s2;     // define two objects of class smallobj

   s1.setdata(1066);    // call member function to set data
   s2.setdata(1776);

   s1.showdata();       // call member function to display data
   s2.showdata();
   }
```

The class `smallobj` specified in this program contains one data item and two member functions. These functions provide the only access to the data item from outside the class. The first member function sets the data item to a value, and the second displays the value. (This may sound like Greek, but we'll see what these terms mean as we go along.)

Placing data and functions together into a single entity is the central idea of object-oriented programming. This is shown in Figure 7-1.

Classes and Objects

Recall from Chapter 1 that an object has the same relationship to a class that a variable has to a data type. An object is said to be an *instance* of a class, in the same way my 1954 Chevrolet is an instance of a vehicle. In SMALLOBJ, the class—whose name is `smallobj`—is specified in the first part of the program. Later, in `main()`, we define two objects—`s1` and `s2`—that are instances of that class.

Each of the two objects is given a value, and each displays its value. Here's the output of the program:

```
Data is 1066 <———— object s1 displayed this
Data is 1776 <———— object s2 displayed this
```

We'll begin by looking in detail at the first part of the program—the specification for the class `smallobj`. Later we'll focus on what `main()` does with objects of this class.

Specifying the Class

Here's the specifier for the class `smallobj`, copied from the SMALLOBJ listing:

```
class smallobj                    // specify a class
   {
```

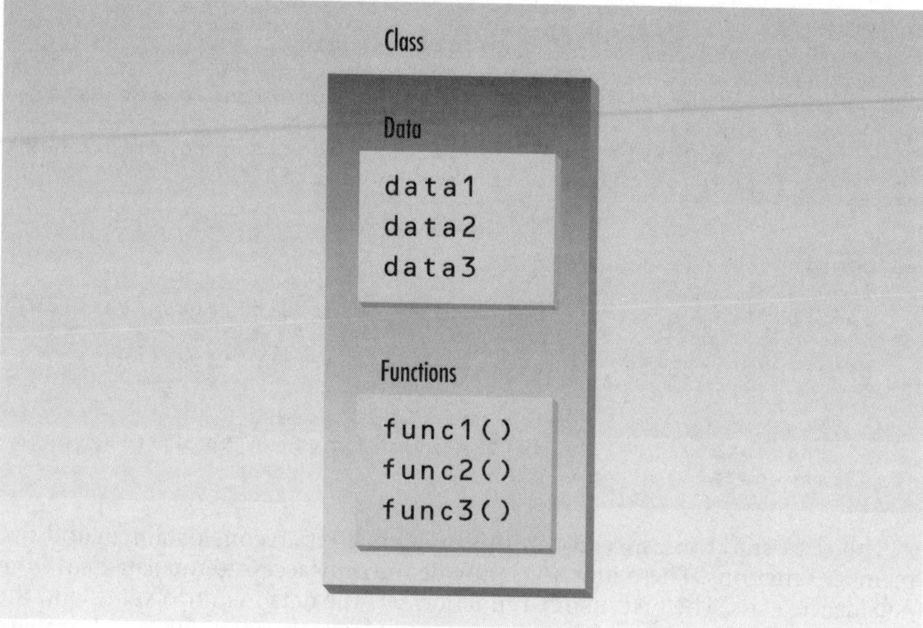

Figure 7-1 Classes Contain Data and Functions

```
private:
   int somedata;              // class data
public:
   void setdata(int d)        // member function to set data
      { somedata = d; }
   void showdata()            // member function to display data
      { cout << "\nData is " << somedata; }
};
```

The specifier starts with the keyword `class`, followed by the class name—`smallobj` in this example. Like a structure, the body of the class is delimited by braces and terminated by a semicolon. (Don't forget the semicolon. Remember, data constructs like structures and classes end with a semicolon, while control constructs like functions and loops do not.)

`private` and `public`

The body of the class contains two unfamiliar keywords: `private` and `public`. What is their purpose?

A key feature of object-oriented programming is *data hiding*. This term does not refer to the activities of particularly paranoid programmers; rather it means that data is concealed within a class, so that it cannot be accessed mistakenly by functions outside the class. The primary mechanism for hiding data is to put it in a class and make it *private*. Private data or functions can only be accessed from within the class. Public data or functions, on the other hand, are accessible from outside the class. This is shown in Figure 7-2.

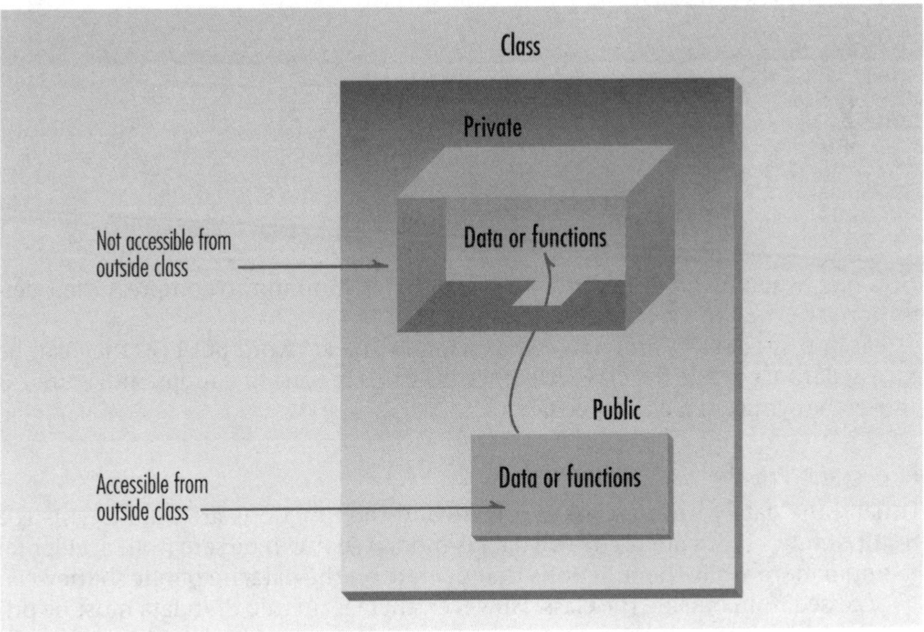

Figure 7-2 Private and Public

Hidden from Whom?

Don't confuse data hiding with the security techniques used to protect computer databases. To provide a security measure you might, for example, require a user to supply a password before granting access to a database. The password is meant to keep unauthorized or malevolent users from altering (or often even reading) the data.

Data hiding, on the other hand, is designed to protect well-intentioned programmers from honest mistakes. Programmers who really want to can figure out a way to access `private` data, but they will find it hard to do so by accident.

Class Data

The `smallobj` class contains one data item: `somedata`, which is of type `int`. There can be any number of data items in a class, just as there can be any number of data items in a structure. The data item `somedata` follows the keyword `private`, so it can be accessed from within the class, but not from outside.

Member Functions

Member functions are functions that are included within a class. (In some object-oriented languages, such as Smalltalk, member functions are called *methods*; some writers use this term in C++ as well.) There are two member functions in `smallobj`: `setdata()` and `showdata()`. The function bodies of these functions have been written on the same line as the braces that delimit them. You could also use the more traditional format for these function definitions:

```
void setdata(int d)
   {
   somedata = d;
   }
```

and

```
void showdata()
   {
   cout << "\nData is " << somedata;
   }
```

However, when member functions are small, it is common to compress their definitions this way to save space.

Because `setdata()` and `showdata()` follow the keyword `public`, they can be accessed from outside the class. We'll see how this is done in a moment. Figure 7-3 shows the syntax of a class specifier.

Public and Private

Usually the data within a class is private and the functions are public. This is a result of how classes are used. The data is hidden so it will be safe from accidental manipulation, while the functions that operate on the data are public so they can be accessed from outside the class. However, there is no rule that data must be private and functions public; in some circumstances you may find you'll need to use private functions and public data.

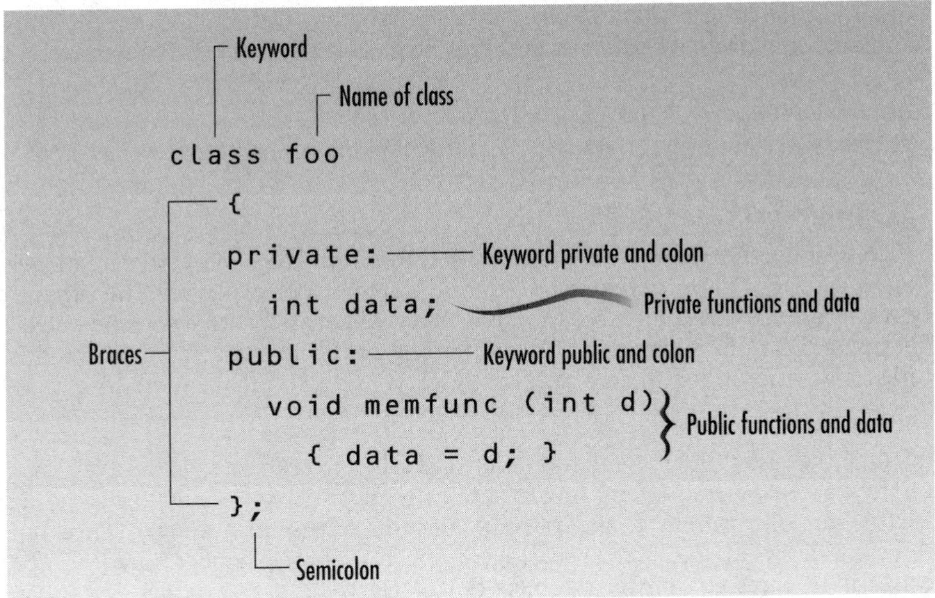

Figure 7-3 Syntax of a Class Specifier

Member Functions Within Class Specifier

The member functions in the `smallobj` class perform operations that are quite common in classes: setting and retrieving the data stored in the class. The `setdata()` function accepts a value as a parameter and sets the `somedata` variable to this value. The `showdata()` function displays the value stored in `somedata`.

Note that the member functions `setdata()` and `showdata()` are *definitions*: The actual code for the function is contained within the class specification. Member functions defined inside a class this way are created as *inline* functions by default. (Inline functions were discussed in Chapter 6.) We'll see later that it is also possible to *declare* a function within a class but to *define* it elsewhere. Functions defined outside the class are not normally inline.

Using the Class

Now that the class is specified, let's see how `main()` makes use of it. We'll see how objects are defined, and, once defined, how their member functions are accessed.

Defining Objects

The first statement in `main()`,

```
smallobj s1, s2;
```

defines two objects, `s1` and `s2`, of class `smallobj`. Remember that the specification for the class `smallobj` does not create any objects. It only describes how they will look when they are created, just as a structure specifier describes how a structure will look but doesn't create any structure variables. It is the definition that actually creates objects that can be used by the program. Defining an object is similar to defining a variable of any data type: Space is set aside for it in memory.

Calling Member Functions

The next two statements in `main()` call the member function `setdata()`:

```
s1.setdata(1066);
s2.setdata(1776);
```

These statements don't look like normal function calls. Why are the object names `s1` and `s2` connected to the function names with a period? This strange syntax is used to call a member function that is associated with a specific object. Because `setdata()` is a member function of the `smallobj` class, it must always be called in connection with an object of this class. It doesn't make sense to say

```
setdata(1066);
```

by itself, because a member function is always called to act on a specific object, not on the class in general. Attempting to access the class this way would be like trying to drive the blueprint of a car. Not only does this statement not make sense, but the compiler will issue an error message if you attempt it. Member functions of a class can be accessed only by an object of that class.

To use a member function, the dot operator (the period) connects the object name and the member function. The syntax is similar to the way we refer to structure members, but the parentheses signal that we're executing a member function rather than referring to a data item. The dot operator is also called the *class member access operator*.

The first call to `setdata()`,

```
s1.setdata(1066);
```

executes the `setdata()` member function of the `s1` object. This function sets the variable `somedata` in object `s1` to the value 1066. The second call,

```
s2.setdata(1776);
```

causes the variable `somedata` in `s2` to be set to 1776. Now we have two objects whose `somedata` variables have different values, as shown in Figure 7-4.

Similarly, the following two calls to the `showdata()` function will cause the two objects to display their values:

```
s1.showdata();
s2.showdata();
```

Messages

Some object-oriented languages, such as Smalltalk, refer to calls to member functions as *messages*. Thus the call

```
s1.showdata();
```

can be thought of as sending a message to `s1` telling it to display itself. The term *message* is not a formal part of C++, but it is a useful idea to keep in mind as we discuss member functions. Talking about messages emphasizes that objects are discrete entities and that we communicate with them by calling their member

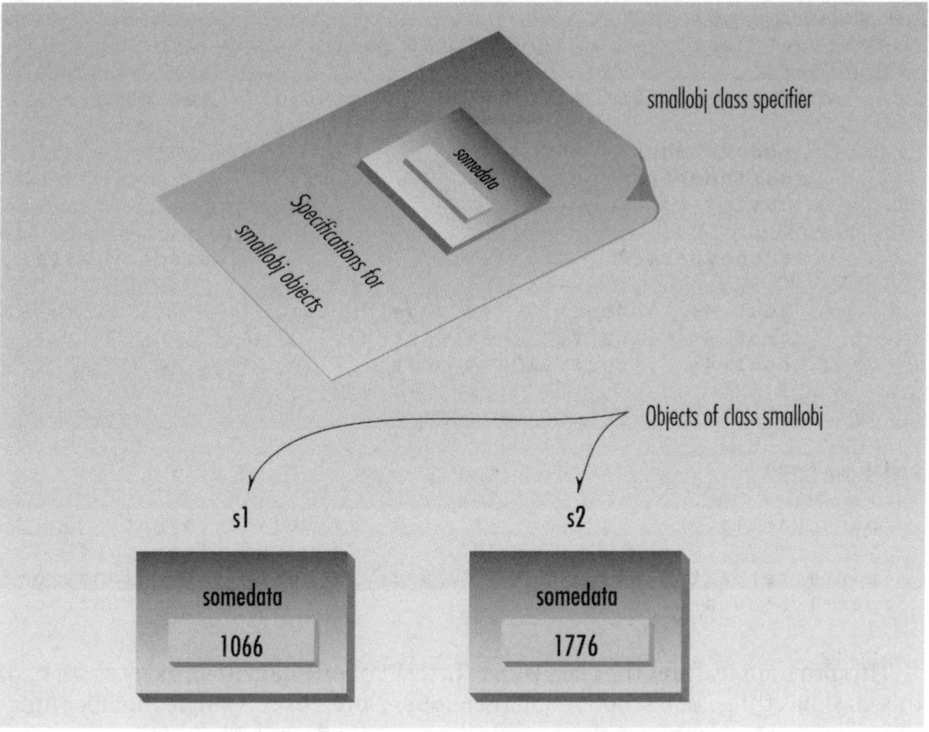

Figure 7-4 Two Objects of Class `smallobj`

functions. Referring to the analogy with company organization in Chapter 1, it's like sending a message to the secretary in the sales department to get a list of products sold in the southwest distribution area.

C++ Objects As Physical Objects

The `smallobj` class in the last example had only one data item. Let's examine an example of a somewhat more ambitious class. (These are not the same ambitious classes discussed in political science courses.) We'll create a class based on the structure for the widget parts inventory, last seen in such examples as PARTS in Chapter 5. Here's the listing for OBJPART:

```
// objpart.cpp
// widget part as an object
#include <iostream.h>

class part                    // specify an object
   {
   private:
      int modelnumber;      // ID number of widget
      int partnumber;       // ID number of widget part
```

(continued on next page)

(continued from previous page)

```
      float cost;          // cost of part
   public:
      void setpart(int mn, int pn, float c)  // set data
         {
         modelnumber = mn;
         partnumber = pn;
         cost = c;
         }
      void showpart()                          // display data
         {
         cout << "\nModel "  << modelnumber;
         cout << ", part "   << partnumber;
         cout << ", costs $" << cost;
         }
   };

void main()
   {
   part part1;                             // define object
                                           //    of class part
   part1.setpart(6244, 373, 217.55);       // call member function
   part1.showpart();                       // call member function
   }
```

This program features the class `part`. Instead of one data item, as SMALLOBJ had, this class has three: `modelnumber`, `partnumber`, and `cost`. A single member function, `setpart()`, supplies values to all three data items at once. Another function, `showpart()`, displays the values stored in all three items.

In this example only one object of type `part` is created: `part1`. The member function `setpart()` sets the three data items in this part to the values 6244, 373, and 217.55. The member function `showpart()` then displays these values. Here's the output:

```
Model 6244, part 373, costs $217.55
```

This is a somewhat more realistic example than SMALLOBJ. If you were designing an inventory program you might actually want to create a class something like `part`. It's an example of a C++ object representing a physical object in the real world—a widget part.

C++ Objects As Data Types

Here's another kind of entity C++ objects can represent: variables of a user-defined data type. We'll use objects to represent distances measured in the English system, as discussed in Chapter 5. Here's the listing for ENGLOBJ:

```
// englobj.cpp
// objects using English measurements
#include <iostream.h>

class Distance                          // English Distance class
   {
   private:
      int feet;
```

```
      float inches;
   public:
      void setdist(int ft, float in)    // set distance to args
         { feet = ft; inches = in; }

      void getdist()                    // get length from user
         {
         cout << "\nEnter feet: ";  cin >> feet;
         cout << "Enter inches: ";  cin >> inches;
         }

      void showdist()                   // display distance
         { cout << feet << "\'-" << inches << '\"'; }
   };

void main()
   {
   Distance dist1, dist2;               // define two lengths

   dist1.setdist(11, 6.25);             // set dist1

   dist2.getdist();                     // get dist2 from user

                                        // display lengths
   cout << "\ndist1 = ";  dist1.showdist();
   cout << "\ndist2 = ";  dist2.showdist();
   }
```

In this program, the class `Distance` contains two data items, `feet` and `inches`. This is similar to the `Distance` structure seen in examples in Chapter 5, but here the class `Distance` also has three member functions: `setdist()`, which uses arguments to set `feet` and `inches`; `getdist()`, which gets values for `feet` and `inches` from the user at the keyboard; and `showdist()`, which displays the distance in feet-and-inches format.

The value of an object of class `Distance` can thus be set in either of two ways. In `main()` we define two objects of class `Distance`: `dist1` and `dist2`. The first is given a value using the `setdist()` member function with the arguments 11 and 6.25, and the second is given a value that is supplied by the user. Here's a sample interaction with the program:

```
Enter feet: 10
Enter inches: 4.75

dist1 = 11'-6.25"   ←——— provided by arguments
dist2 = 10'-4.75"   ←——— input by the user
```

Constructors

The ENGLOBJ example shows two ways to give values to the data items in an object. Sometimes, however, it's convenient if an object can initialize itself when it's first created, without the need to make a separate call to a member function. Automatic initialization is carried out using a special member function called a *constructor*. A constructor is a member function that is executed automatically whenever an object is created.

A Counter Example

As an example, we'll create a class of objects that might be useful as a general-purpose programming element. A *counter* is a variable that counts things. Maybe it counts file accesses, or the number of times the user presses the ENTER key, or the number of customers entering a bank. Each time such an event takes place, the counter is incremented (1 is added to it). The counter can also be accessed to find the current count.

Let's assume that this counter is important in the program and must be accessed by many different functions. In procedural languages such as C, a counter would probably be implemented as an external variable. However, as we noted in Chapter 1, external variables may be modified accidentally. This example, COUNTER, provides a counter variable that can be modified only through its member functions.

```
// counter.cpp
// object represents a counter variable
#include <iostream.h>

class Counter
   {
   private:
      unsigned int count;                    // count
   public:
      Counter()        { count = 0; }        // constructor
      void inc_count() { count++; }          // increment count
      int get_count()  { return count; }     // return count
   };

void main()
   {
   Counter c1, c2;                          // define and initialize

   cout << "\nc1=" << c1.get_count();      // display
   cout << "\nc2=" << c2.get_count();

   c1.inc_count();                          // increment c1
   c2.inc_count();                          // increment c2
   c2.inc_count();                          // increment c2

   cout << "\nc1=" << c1.get_count();      // display again
   cout << "\nc2=" << c2.get_count();
   }
```

The `Counter` class has one data item: `count`, of type `unsigned int` (since the count is always positive). It has three member functions: `Counter()`, which we'll look at in a moment; `inc_count()`, which adds 1 to `count`; and `get_count()`, which returns the current value of `count`.

Automatic Initialization

When an object of type `Counter` is first created, we want its `count` to be initialized to 0. After all, most counts start at 0. We could provide a `set_count()` function to do this and call it with an argument of 0, or we could provide a `zero_count()` function, which would always set `count` to 0. However, such functions would need to be executed every time we created a `Counter` object.

```
Counter c1;          // every time we do this,
c1.zero_count();     // we must do this too
```

It's more convenient, especially when there are a great many objects of a given class, to cause each object to initialize itself. In the `Counter` class, the constructor `Counter()` does this. This function is called automatically whenever a new object of type `Counter` is created. Thus in `main()` the statement

```
Counter c1, c2;
```

creates two objects of type `Counter`. As each is created, its constructor, `Counter()`, is executed. This function sets the `count` variable to 0. So the effect of this single statement is to not only create two objects, but also to initialize their `count` variables to 0.

Same Name As the Class

There are some unusual aspects of constructor functions. First, it is no accident that they have exactly the same name (`Counter` in this example) as the class of which they are members. This is how the compiler knows they are constructors.

Second, no return type is used for constructors. Why not? Since the constructor is called automatically by the system, there's no program for it to return anything to; a return value wouldn't make sense.

Messing with the Format

Note that, in writing the functions in this example, we've compressed them so they occupy only one line each:

```
Counter()   { count = 0; }
```

This is just the same (as far as the compiler is concerned) as the normal function syntax

```
Counter()
   {
   count = 0;
   }
```

The `main()` part of this program exercises the `Counter` class by creating two counters, `c1` and `c2`. It causes the counters to display their initial values, which—as arranged by the constructor—are 0. It then increments `c1` once and `c2` twice, and again causes the counters to display themselves (noncriminal behavior in this context). Here's the output:

```
c1=0
c2=0
c1=1
c2=2
```

If this isn't enough proof that the constructor is operating as advertised, we can rewrite the constructor to print a message when it executes.

```
Counter()  {  count = 0;  cout << "I'm the constructor\n";  }
```

Now the program's output looks like this:

```
I'm the constructor
I'm the constructor
c1=0
c2=0
c1=1
c2=2
```

As you can see, the constructor is executed twice—once for `c1` and once for `c2`—when the statement

```
Counter c1, c2;
```

is executed in `main()`.

Do-It-Yourself Data

Constructors are pretty amazing when you think about it. Whoever writes language compilers (for C or BASIC or even for C++) must execute the equivalent of a constructor when the user defines a variable. If you define an `int`, for example, somewhere there's a constructor allocating 2 bytes of memory for it. If we can write our own constructors we can start to take over some of the tasks of a compiler writer. This is one step on the path to creating our own data types, as we'll see later.

Destructors

We've seen that a special member function—the constructor—is called automatically when an object is first created. You might guess that another function is called automatically when an object is destroyed. This is indeed the case. Such a function is called a *destructor*. A destructor has the same name as the constructor (which is the same as the class name) but preceded by a tilde:

```
class Foo
   {
   private:
      int data;
   public:
      Foo() { data = 0; }   // constructor (same name as class)
      ~Foo()  { }           // destructor (same name with tilde)
   };
```

Like constructors, destructors do not have a return value. They also take no arguments (the assumption being that there's only one way to destroy an object).

The most common use of destructors is to deallocate memory that was allocated for the object by the constructor. We'll investigate these activities in Chapter 12. Until then we won't have much use for destructors.

Objects as Function Arguments

Our next program adds some embellishments to the ENGLOBJ example. It also demonstrates some new aspects of classes: constructor overloading, defining member functions outside the class, and—perhaps most importantly—objects as function arguments. Here's the listing for ENGLCON:

```
// englcon.cpp
// constructors, adds objects using member function
#include <iostream.h>

class Distance                          // English Distance class
   {
   private:
      int feet;
      float inches;
   public:
      Distance()                        // constructor (no args)
         { }
      Distance(int ft, float in)  // constructor (two args)
         { feet = ft; inches = in; }

      void getdist()                    // get length from user
         {
         cout << "\nEnter feet: ";  cin >> feet;
         cout << "Enter inches: ";  cin >> inches;
         }

      void showdist()                   // display distance
         { cout << feet << "\'-" << inches << '\"'; }

      void add_dist( Distance, Distance );    // declaration
   };
                                        // add lengths d2 and d3
void Distance::add_dist(Distance d2, Distance d3)
   {
   inches = d2.inches + d3.inches;  // add the inches
   feet = 0;                        // (for possible carry)
   if(inches >= 12.0)               // if total exceeds 12.0,
      {                             // then decrease inches
      inches -= 12.0;               // by 12.0 and
      feet++;                       // increase feet
      }                             // by 1
   feet += d2.feet + d3.feet;       // add the feet
   }

void main()
   {
   Distance dist1, dist3;           // define two lengths
   Distance dist2(11, 6.25);        // define and initialize dist2

   dist1.getdist();                 // get dist1 from user
   dist3.add_dist(dist1, dist2);    // dist3 = dist1 + dist2

                                    // display all lengths
   cout << "\ndist1 = ";  dist1.showdist();
   cout << "\ndist2 = ";  dist2.showdist();
   cout << "\ndist3 = ";  dist3.showdist();
   }
```

This program starts with a distance set to an initial value and adds to it a distance supplied by the user to obtain the sum of the distances. It then displays all three distances:

```
Enter feet: 17
Enter inches: 5.75

dist1 = 17'-5.75"
dist2 = 11'-6.25"
dist3 = 29'-0"
```

Let's see how the new features in this program are implemented.

Overloaded Constructors

It would be nice to be able to give variables of type `Distance` a value when they are first created. That is, we would like to use definitions like

```
Distance width(5, 6.25);
```

which defines an object, `width`, and simultaneously initializes it to a value of 5 for `feet` and 6.25 for `inches`.

To do this we write a constructor like this:

```
Distance(int ft, float in)
   { feet = ft; inches = in; }
```

This sets the class data `feet` and `inches` to whatever values are passed as arguments to the constructor. So far so good.

However, we also want to define variables of type `Distance` without initializing them, as we did in ENGLOBJ.

```
Distance dist1, dist2;
```

In that program there was no constructor, but our definitions worked just fine. How could they work without a constructor? Because an implicit constructor was built into the program automatically by the compiler and it created the objects, even though we didn't define it in the class.

Unfortunately, once we define one constructor, we must also define the implicit constructor. So we need the definition

```
Distance()
   { }         // no function body, doesn't do anything
```

in class `Distance`. The empty braces mean that the function doesn't do anything; it's just there to satisfy the compiler.

Since there are now two constructors with the same name, `Distance()`, we say the constructor is overloaded. Which of the two constructors is executed when an object is created depends on how many arguments are used in the definition:

```
Distance length;            // calls first constructor
Distance width(11, 6.0);    // calls second constructor
```

The Default Copy Constructor

You can also initialize an object with another object of the same type. Surprisingly, you don't need to create a special constructor for this; one is already built into all classes. It's called the *default copy constructor.* It's a one-argument constructor whose argument is an object of the same class as the constructor. The ECOPYCON program shows how it works.

```
// ecopycon.cpp
// initialize with object, using default copy constructor
#include <iostream.h>

class Distance                          // English Distance class
   {
   private:
      int feet;
      float inches;
   public:
      Distance()                        // constructor (no args)
         { }
                                        // note: no one-arg constructor

      Distance(int ft, float in)        // constructor (two args)
         { feet = ft; inches = in; }

      void getdist()                    // get length from user
         {
         cout << "\nEnter feet: ";  cin >> feet;
         cout << "Enter inches: ";  cin >> inches;
         }

      void showdist()                   // display distance
         { cout << feet << "\'-" << inches << '\"'; }
   };

void main()
   {
   Distance dist1(11, 6.25);            // two-arg constructor
   Distance dist2(dist1);               // one-arg constructor
   Distance dist3 = dist1;              // also one-arg constructor

                                        // display all lengths
   cout << "\ndist1 = ";  dist1.showdist();
   cout << "\ndist2 = ";  dist2.showdist();
   cout << "\ndist3 = ";  dist3.showdist();
   }
```

We initialize `dist1` to the value of 11'-6.25" using the two-argument constructor. The we create two more objects of type `Distance`, `dist2` and `dist3`. Both these are initialized to the value of `dist1` using the default copy constructor. The object `dist2` is initialized using the statement

```
Distance dist2(dist1);
```

This causes the default copy constructor for the `Distance` class to perform a member-by-member copy of `dist1` into `dist2`. Surprisingly, a different format has exactly the same effect, causing `dist1` to be copied member-by-member into `dist3`:

```
Distance dist3 = dist1;
```

Although this looks like an assignment statement, it is not. Both formats invoke the copy constructor, and can be used interchangeably. Here's the output from the program:

```
dist1 = 11'-6.25"
dist2 = 11'-6.25"
dist3 = 11'-6.25"
```

This shows that the `dist2` and `dist3` objects have been initialized to the same value as `dist1`. In Chapter 13 we discuss how to create your own custom copy constructor by overloading the default.

Member Functions Defined Outside the Class

So far we've seen member functions that were defined inside the class specifier. This need not always be the case. ENGLCON shows a member function, `add_dist()`, that is not defined within the `Distance` class specifier. It is only declared inside the class, with the statement

```
void add_dist(Distance, Distance);
```

This tells the compiler that this function is a member of the class but that it will be defined outside the class specifier, someplace else in the listing.

In ENGLCON the function is defined immediately after the class specifier. It is adapted from the ENGLSTRC program in Chapter 5:

```
                                 // add lengths d2 and d3
void Distance::add_dist(Distance d2, Distance d3)
   {
   inches = d2.inches + d3.inches;   // add the inches
   feet = 0;                        // (for possible carry)
   if(inches >= 12.0)               // if total exceeds 12.0,
      {                             // then decrease inches
      inches -= 12.0;               // by 12.0 and
      feet++;                       // increase feet
      }                             // by 1
   feet += d2.feet + d3.feet;       // add the feet
   }
```

The declarator in this definition contains some unfamiliar syntax. The function name, `add_dist()`, is preceded by the class name, `Distance`, and a new symbol—the double colon (`::`). This symbol is called the *scope resolution operator*. It is a way of specifying what class something is associated with. In this situation it means *the* `add_dist()` *member function of the* `Distance` *class*. Figure 7-5 shows its usage.

Objects As Arguments

Now we can see how ENGLCON works. The distances `dist1` and `dist3` are created using the constructor that takes no arguments; this constructor does not do any initialization. The distance `dist2` is created with the constructor that takes two arguments, and is initialized to the values passed in these arguments. A value is obtained for `dist1` by calling the member function `getdist()`, which obtains values from the user.

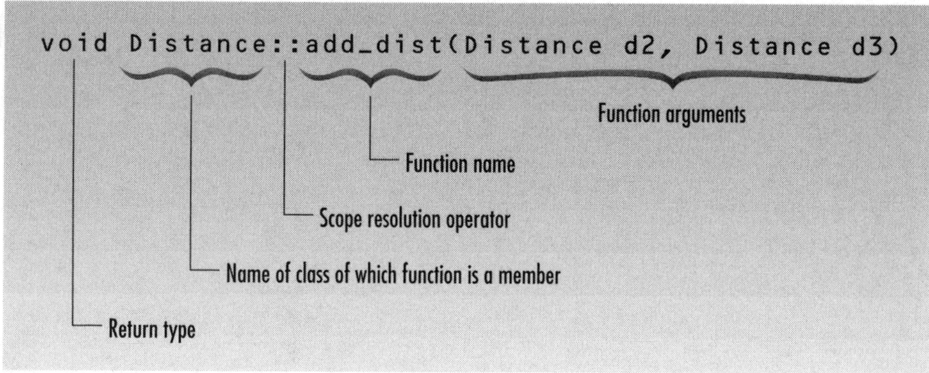

Figure 7-5 The Scope Resolution Operator

Now we want to add `dist1` and `dist2` to obtain `dist3`. The function call in `main()`,

```
dist3.add_dist(dist1, dist2);
```

does this. The two distances to be added, `dist1` and `dist2`, are supplied as arguments to `add_dist()`. The syntax for arguments that are objects is the same as that for arguments that are simple data types like `int`: The object name is supplied as the argument. Since `add_dist()` is a member function of the `Distance` class, it can access the private data in any object of class `Distance` supplied to it as an argument, using names like `dist1.inches` and `dist2.feet`.

Close examination of `add_dist()` emphasizes some important truths about member functions. When a member function is called, it is given access to only one object: *the object of which the function is a member*. In the following statement in ENGLCON, what objects can `add_dist()` access?

```
dist3.add_dist(dist1, dist2);
```

It can access `dist1` and `dist2`, because they are supplied as arguments. It can also access `dist3`, because it is a member function of `dist3`. You might think of `dist3` as a sort of phantom argument; the member function always has access to it, even though it is not supplied as an argument. That's what this statement means: "Execute the `add_dist()` member function of `dist3`." When the variables `feet` and `inches` are referred to within this function, they refer to `dist3.feet` and `dist3.inches`. In Chapter 12 we'll see that a member function can refer to the entire object of which it is a member with the keyword `this`. The term `this` emphasizes the close relationship between a function and the object of which it is a member.

Notice that the result is not returned by the function. The return type of `add_dist()` is `void`. The result is stored automatically in the `dist3` object. Figure 7-6 shows the two distances `dist1` and `dist2` being added together, with the result stored in `dist3`.

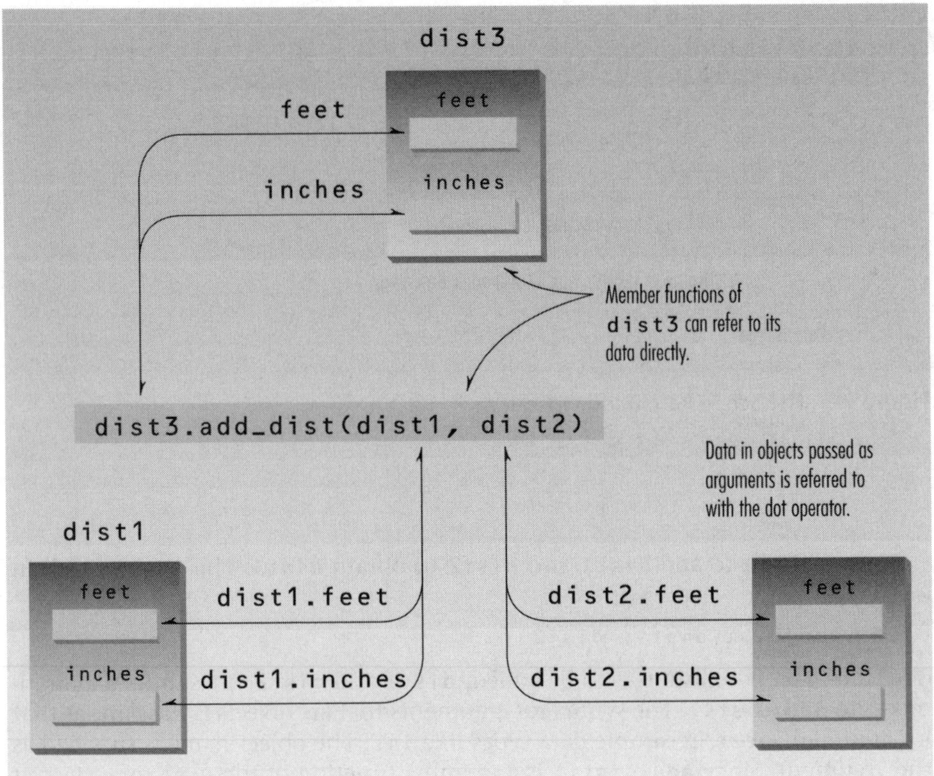

Figure 7-6 Result in this Object

Returning Objects from Functions

In the ENGLCON example we saw objects being passed as arguments to functions. Now we'll see an example of a function that returns an object. We'll modify the ENGLCON program to produce ENGLRET:

```
// englret.cpp
// function returns value of type Distance
#include <iostream.h>

class Distance                              //English Distance class
   {
   private:
      int feet;
      float inches;
   public:
      Distance()                            // constructor (no args)
         { feet = 0; inches = 0.0; }
      Distance(int ft, float in)            // constructor (two args)
         { feet = ft; inches = in; }
```

```
      void getdist()                    // get length from user
         {
         cout << "\nEnter feet: ";  cin >> feet;
         cout << "Enter inches: ";  cin>> inches;
         }

      void showdist()                   // display distance
         { cout << feet << "\'-" << inches << '\"'; }

      Distance add_dist( Distance );  // add
   };
                                        // add this distance to d2
Distance Distance::add_dist(Distance d2)   // return the sum
   {
   Distance temp;                           // temporary variable
   temp.inches = inches + d2.inches;        // add the inches
   if(temp.inches >= 12.0)                  // if total exceeds 12.0,
      {                                     // then decrease inches
      temp.inches -= 12.0;                  // by 12.0 and
      temp.feet = 1;                        // increase feet
      }                                     // by 1
   temp.feet += feet + d2.feet;             // add the feet
   return temp;
   }

void main()
   {
   Distance dist1, dist3;                  // define two lengths
   Distance dist2(11, 6.25);               // define, initialize dist2

   dist1.getdist();                        // get dist1 from user
   dist3 = dist1.add_dist(dist2);          // dist3 = dist1 + dist2

                                           // display all lengths
   cout << "\ndist1 = ";  dist1.showdist();
   cout << "\ndist2 = ";  dist2.showdist();
   cout << "\ndist3 = ";  dist3.showdist();
   }
```

From the user's viewpoint, ENGLRET operates just the same as ENGLCON. In fact, the program is very similar to ENGLCON, but the differences reveal how functions work with objects. In ENGLCON, two distances were passed to `add_dist()` as arguments, and the result was stored in the object of which `add_dist()` was a member, namely `dist3`. In ENGLRET, one distance, `dist2`, is passed to `add_dist()` as an argument. It is added to the object, `dist1`, of which `add_dist()` is a member, and the result is returned from the function. In `main()` the result is assigned to `dist3`, in the statement

```
dist3 = dist1.add_dist(dist2);
```

The effect is the same as the corresponding statement in ENGLCON, but it is more natural looking, since the assignment operator, =, is used in a natural way. In Chapter 9 we'll see how to use the arithmetic + operator to achieve the even more obvious expression

```
dist3 = dist1 + dist2;
```

ENGLCON and ENGLRET perform the same operation, but they do it differently. Here's the add_dist() function from ENGLRET:

```
                                            // add this distance to d2
Distance Distance::add_dist(Distance d2)      // return the sum
   {
   Distance temp;                           // temporary variable
   temp.inches = inches + d2.inches;        // add the inches
   if(temp.inches >= 12.0)                  // if total exceeds 12.0,
      {                                     // then decrease inches
      temp.inches -= 12.0;                  // by 12.0 and
      temp.feet = 1;                        // increase feet
      }                                     // by 1
   temp.feet += feet + d2.feet;             // add the feet
   return temp;
   }
```

Compare this with the same function in ENGLCON. As you can see, there are some subtle differences. In the ENGLRET version, a temporary object of class Distance is created. This object holds the sum until it can be returned to the calling program. The sum is calculated by adding two distances. The first is the object of which add_dist() is a member, dist1. Its member data is accessed as feet and inches. The second is the object passed as an argument, dist2. Its member data is accessed as d2.feet and d2.inches. The result is stored in temp and accessed as temp.feet and temp.inches. The temp object is then returned by the function using the statement

```
return temp;
```

and the statement in main() assigns it to dist3. Notice that dist1 is not modified; it simply supplies data to add_dist(). Figure 7-7 shows how this looks.

How Many Arguments?

Let's review how argument and return value usage differs between member functions and ordinary nonmember functions. Let's call a function's return value and its arguments its *operands*. We'll be talking here, for member functions, about operands that are objects of the same class as the function. That is, for member functions of class Distance, we're talking only about operands of type Distance, not other types like int.

Here's the rule: There is always one less operand for a member function than there is for a normal nonmember function. Why? Because, for a member function, the object of which it is a member is already directly accessible to it, so it need not be an operand.

Thus a normal function that adds two values and returns a result would be written

```
v3 = sumfunc(v1, v2);        // three operands
```

For member functions, there are two ways to format the equivalent operation:

```
obj3.sumfunc(obj2, obj3);  // two operands, sumfunc() is member of obj3
```

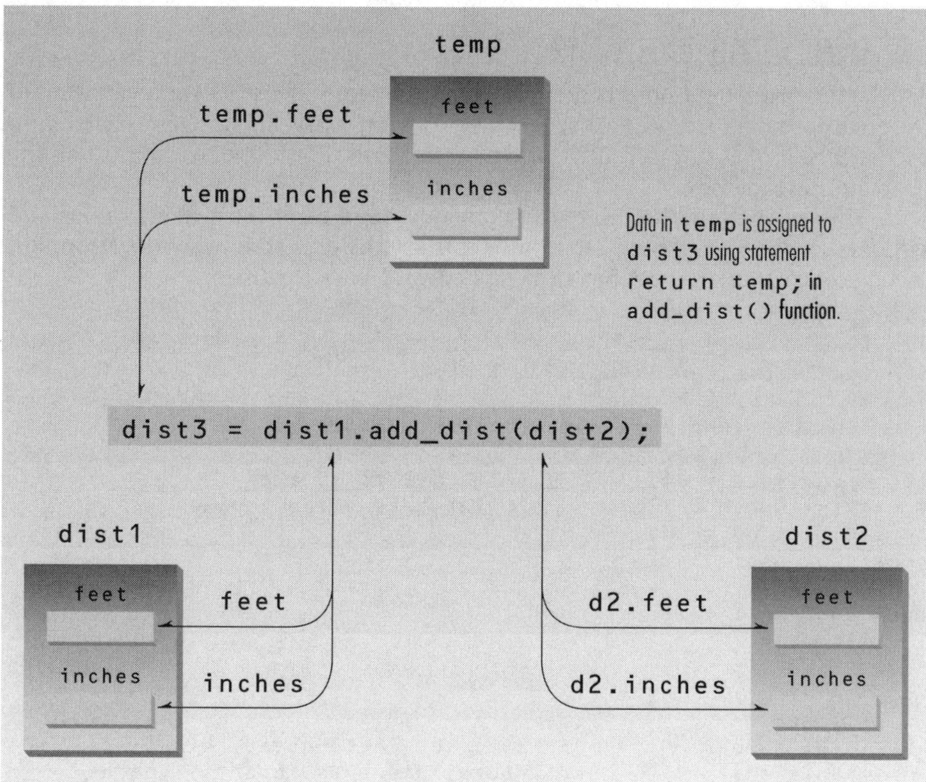

Figure 7-7 Result Returned from Temporary Object

or

```
obj3 = obj2.sumfunc(obj3); // two operands, sumfunc() is member of obj2
```

In both cases there are only two operands, because `sumfunc()` is a member of the third object. You've already seen an example of this in the two ways the `add_dist()` function was implemented in the ENGLECON and ENGLERET programs.

The same situation applies to functions that operate on only one variable to produce a result. For example, a nonmember function that squares a quantity has two operands.

```
v2 = square(v1);              // two operands
```

On the other hand, a member version of this function can be written either as

```
obj2 = obj1.square();       // one operand, square() is member of obj1
```

or as

```
obj2.square(obj1);          // one operand, square() is member of obj2
```

This difference between member and nonmember functions goes a long way in explaining how member functions are formatted.

A Card-Game Example

As a larger example of objects modeling the real world, let's look at a variation of the CARDS program from Chapter 5. This program, CARDOBJ, has been rewritten to use objects. It does not introduce any new concepts, but it does use almost all the programming ideas we've discussed up to this point.

As the CARDS example did, CARDOBJ creates three cards with fixed values and switches them around in an attempt to confuse the user about their location. But in CARDOBJ each card is an object of class `card`. Here's the listing:

```
// cardobj.cpp
// cards as objects
#include <iostream.h>

enum Suit { clubs, diamonds, hearts, spades };

const int jack = 11;          // from 2 to 10 are
const int queen = 12;         // integers without names
const int king = 13;
const int ace = 14;

enum Boolean { false, true };

class card
   {
   private:
      int number;          // 2 to 10, jack, queen, king, ace
      Suit suit;           // clubs, diamonds, hearts, spades
   public:
      card ()                        // constructor (no-arg)
         { }
      card (int n, Suit s)           // constructor (2-args)
          { suit = s; number = n; }
      void display();                // display card
      Boolean isEqual(card);         // same as another card?
   };

void card::display()                 // display the card
   {
   if( number >= 2 && number <= 10 )
      cout << number << " of ";
   else
      switch(number)
         {
         case jack:  cout << "jack of ";  break;
         case queen: cout << "queen of "; break;
         case king:  cout << "king of ";  break;
         case ace:   cout << "ace of ";   break;
         }
   switch(suit)
      {
      case clubs:    cout << "clubs"; break;
      case diamonds: cout << "diamonds"; break;
```

```
      case hearts:   cout << "hearts"; break;
      case spades:   cout << "spades"; break;
      }
   }

Boolean card::isEqual(card c2)    // return true if cards equal
   {
   return ( number==c2.number && suit==c2.suit ) ? true : false;
   }

void main()
   {
   card temp, chosen, prize;       // define various cards
   int position;

   card card1( 7, clubs );         // define & initialize card1
   cout << "\nCard 1 is the ";
   card1.display();                // display card1

   card card2( jack, hearts );     // define & initialize card2
   cout << "\nCard 2 is the ";
   card2.display();                // display card2
   card card3( ace, spades );      // define & initialize card3
   cout << "\nCard 3 is the ";
   card3.display();                // display card3
   prize = card3;                  // prize is the card to guess
   cout << "\nI'm swapping card 1 and card 3";
   temp = card3; card3 = card1; card1 = temp;
   cout << "\nI'm swapping card 2 and card 3";
   temp = card3; card3 = card2; card2 = temp;

   cout << "\nI'm swapping card 1 and card 2";
   temp = card2; card2 = card1; card1 = temp;

   cout << "\nNow, where (1, 2, or 3) is the ";
   prize.display();                // display prize card
   cout << "? ";
   cin >> position;                // get user's guess of position

   switch (position)
      {                            // set chosen to user's choice
      case 1: chosen = card1; break;
      case 2: chosen = card2; break;
      case 3: chosen = card3; break;
      }
   if( chosen.isEqual(prize) )     // is chosen card the prize?
      cout << "That's right!  You win!";
   else
      cout << "Sorry. You lose.";
   cout << "  You chose the ";
   chosen.display();               // display chosen card
   cout << endl;
   }
```

There are two constructors in class card. The first, which takes no arguments, is used in main() to create the cards temp, chosen, and prize, which are not initialized. The second constructor, which takes two arguments, is used to create card1, card2, and card3 and to initialize them to specific values. Besides the constructors, card has two other member functions, both defined outside the class. The display() function takes no arguments; it simply displays the card object of which it is a member, using the number and suit data items in the card. The isEqual() function checks whether the card is equal to a card supplied as an argument.The statement in main()

```
chosen.display();
```

displays the card chosen by the user.

The isEqual() member function uses the conditional operator to compare the card of which it is a member with a card supplied as an argument. This function could also have been written with an if...else statement,

```
if( number==c2.number && suit==c2.suit )
   return true;
else
   return false;
```

but the conditional operator is more compact.

In isEqual() the argument is called c2 as a reminder that there are two cards in the comparison: The first card is the object of which isEqual() is a member. The expression

```
if( chosen.isEqual(prize) )
```

in main() compares the card chosen with the card prize.

Here's the output when the user guesses an incorrect card:

```
Card 1 is the 7 of clubs
Card 2 is the jack of hearts
Card 3 is the ace of spades
I'm swapping card 1 and card 3
I'm swapping card 2 and card 3
I'm swapping card 1 and card 2
Now, where (1, 2, or 3) is the ace of spades? 1
Sorry, you lose. You chose the 7 of clubs
```

Structures and Classes

The examples so far in this book have portrayed structures as a way to group data and classes as a way to group both data and functions. In fact, you can use structures in almost exactly the same way that you use classes. The only formal difference between class and struct is that in a class the members are private by default, while in a structure they are public by default.

Here's the format we've been using for classes:

```
class foo
   {
   private:
      int data1;
   public:
```

```
        void func();
    };
```

Since in classes `private` is the default, this keyword is unnecessary. You can just as well write

```
class foo
    {
        int data1;
    public:
        void func();
    };
```

and the `data1` will still be private. Many programmers prefer this style. We like to include the `private` keyword because it offers a small increase in clarity.

If you want to use a structure to accomplish the same thing as this class, you can dispense with the keyword `public`, provided you put the public members before the private ones:

```
struct foo
    {
        void func();
    private:
        int data1;
    };
```

since public is the default. However, in most situations programmers use structures to group data, and classes to group data and functions.

Classes, Objects, and Memory

We've probably given you the impression that each object created from a class contains separate copies of that class's data and member functions. This is a good first approximation, since it emphasizes that objects are complete, self-contained entities, designed using the class specifier. The mental image here is of cars (objects) rolling off an assembly line, each one made according to a blueprint (the class specifier).

However, things are not quite so simple. It's true that each object has its own separate data items. (In some object-oriented languages, such as Smalltalk, a data item that is part of a class is called an *instance variable*, since there is an instance of it for each object created.)

On the other hand, contrary to what you may have been led to believe, all the objects in a given class use the same member functions. The member functions are created and placed in memory only once—when they are defined in the class specifier. This makes sense; there's really no point in duplicating all the member functions in a class every time you create another object of that class, since the functions for each object are identical. The data items, however, will hold different values, so there must be a separate instance of each data item in each object. Data is therefore placed in memory when each object is defined, so there is a set for each object. Figure 7-8 shows how this looks.

In the SMALLOBJ example there are two objects of type `smallobj`, so there are two instances of `somedata` in memory. However, there is only one instance of the functions `setdata()` and `showdata()`. These functions are shared by all the

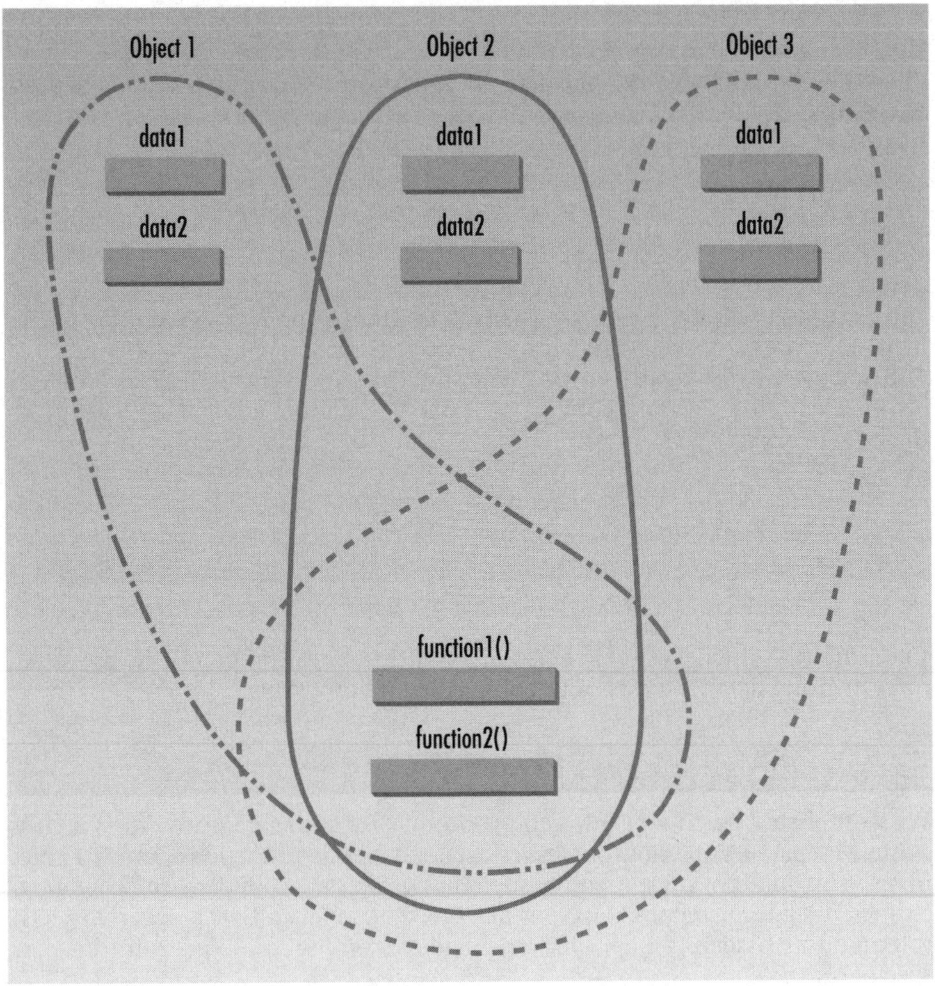

Figure 7-8 Objects, Data, Functions, and Memory

objects of the class. There is no conflict because (at least in a single-tasking system) only one function is executed at a time.

In most situations you don't need to know that there is only one member function for an entire class. It's simpler to visualize each object as containing both its own data and its own member functions. But in some situations, such as in estimating the size of an executing program, it's helpful to know what's happening behind the scenes.

Static Class Data

Having said that each object contains its own separate data, we must now amend that slightly. If a data item in a class is defined as `static`, then only one such item is created for the entire class, no matter how many objects there are. A static data item is useful when all objects of the same class must share a common item of information. A member variable defined as `static` has characteristics similar to a normal static variable: It is visible only within the class, but its lifetime is the entire program. (See Chapter 6 for a discussion of static variables.) However, while a normal static variable is used to retain information between calls to a function, static class member data is used to share information among the objects of a class.

Uses of Static Class Data

Why would you want to use static member data? As an example, suppose an object needed to know how many other objects of its class were in the program. In a road-racing game, for example, a race car might want to know how many other cars were still in the race. In this case a static variable `count` could be included as a member of the class. All the objects would have access to this variable. It would be the same variable for all of them; they would all see the same count.

As another example, in the HORSE example in Chapter 13, a horse-race program, the horses all need to know the time elapsed so far in the race. We could use an external variable for this, but since it applies only to horses, it makes more sense to make it a static member of the `horse` class.

Sometimes it's important for every object in a class to be able to access data in another object. The race cars might want to know where the other race cars are, for example. Static data can be used for this situation as well, by storing a pointer to each object. This allows each object to access the data in all the others. (We'll discuss pointers in Chapter 12, and see an example of their use for this purpose in the ELEV program in Chapter 15.)

An Example of Static Class Data

Here's a simple example, STATDATA, that demonstrates a simple static data member:

```
// statdata.cpp
// static class data
#include <iostream.h>
class foo
   {
   private:
      static int count;     // only one data item for all objects
                            // note: *declaration* only!
   public:
      foo() { count++; }    // increments count when object created
      int getcount()  { return count; }      // returns count
   };
int foo::count;             // *definition* of count

void main()
   {
   foo f1, f2, f3;          // create three objects

   cout << "\ncount is " << f1.getcount();  // each object
   cout << "\ncount is " << f2.getcount();  // sees the same
   cout << "\ncount is " << f3.getcount();  // value of count
   }
```

The class `foo` in this example has one data item, `count`, which is type `static int`. The constructor for this class causes `count` to be incremented. In `main()` we define three objects of class `foo`. Since the constructor is called three times, `count` is incremented three times. Another member function, `getcount()`, returns the value in `count`. We call this function from all three objects, and—as we expected—each prints the same value. Here's the output:

```
count is 3    <------- static data
count is 3
count is 3
```

If we had used an ordinary automatic variable—as opposed to a static variable—for `count`, each constructor would have incremented its own private copy of `count` once, and the output would have been

```
count is 1    <------- automatic data
count is 1
count is 1
```

Static class variables are not used often, but they are important in special situations, and knowing about them helps clarify how the more common automatic variables work. Figure 7-9 shows how static variables compare with automatic variables.

Separate Declaration and Definition

Static member data requires an unusual format. Ordinary variables are declared (the compiler is told about their name and type) and defined (the compiler sets aside memory to hold the variable) in the same statement. Static member data, on the other hand, requires two separate statements. The variable's declaration appears in the class specifier, but the variable is actually defined outside the class, in much the same way as an external variable.

Why is this two-part approach used? If static member data were defined inside the class specification (as it actually was in early versions of C++), it would violate the idea that a class specification is only a declaration and does not set aside any memory. Putting the definition of static member data outside of the class also serves to emphasize that the memory space for such data is allocated only once, at the beginning of the program, and that one static member variable is accessed by an entire class; each object does not have its own version of the variable, as it would with ordinary member data. In this way a static member variable is more like a global variable.

It's easy to handle static data incorrectly, and the compiler is not helpful about such errors. If you include the declaration of a static variable but forget its definition, there will be no warning from the compiler. Everything looks fine until you get to the linker, which will tell you that you're trying to reference an undeclared external variable. This happens even if you include the definition, but forget the class name (the `foo::` in the STATDATA example).

What Does It All Mean?

Now that you've been introduced to classes and objects, you may wonder what benefit they really offer. After all, as you can see by comparing several of the

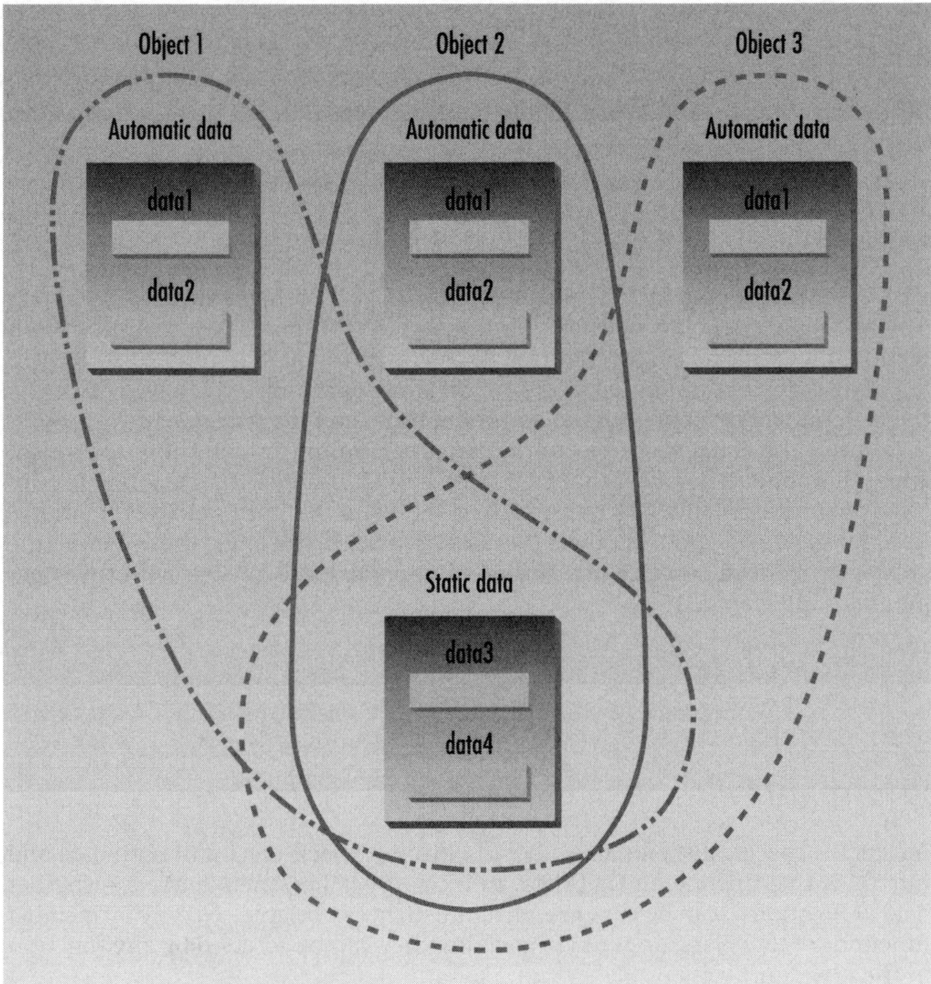

Figure 7-9 Static Versus Automatic Member Variables

programs in this chapter with those in Chapter 5, it's possible to do the same sorts of things with a procedural approach as it is with objects.

One benefit of OOP that you may have glimpsed already is the close correspondence between the real-world things being modeled *by* the program and the C++ objects *in* the program. A widget part object represents a widget part, a card object represents a card, and so on. In C++ everything about a widget part is included in its class description—the part number and other data items, and the functions necessary to access and operate on this data. This makes it easy to conceptualize a programming problem. You figure out what parts of the problem can be most usefully represented as objects, and then put all the data and functions connected with that object into the class specification. If you're using a C++ class to represent a playing card, you put into this class the data items that represent the value of the card, and also the functions to set value, retrieve it, display it, compare it, and so on.

In a procedural program, by contrast, the external variables and functions connected with a real-world object are distributed all over the listing; they don't form a single, easily grasped unit.

In some situations it may not be obvious what parts of a real-life situation should be made into objects. If you're writing a program that plays chess, for instance, what are the objects? The chessmen, the squares on the board, or possibly entire board positions? There are no hard and fast rules for this sort of analysis. Often you proceed by trial and error. You break a problem into objects in one way and write trial class specifiers for these objects. If the classes seem to match reality in a useful way, you continue. If they don't, you may need to start over, selecting different entities to be classes. The more experience you have with OOP, the easier it will be to break a programming problem into classes.

Some of the benefits of object-oriented programming are probably not apparent at this point. Remember that OOP was devised to cope with the complexity of large programs. Smaller programs, such as the examples in this chapter, have less need for the organizational power that OOP provides. The larger the program, the greater the benefit. Some of this power will become more obvious with the larger programs in Chapter 15.

Summary

A class is a specification for a number of objects. Objects consist of both data and functions that operate on that data. In a class specifier, the members—whether data or functions—can be `private`, meaning they can be accessed only by member functions of that class, or `public`, meaning they can be accessed by any function in the program.

A member function is a function that is a member of a class. Member functions have access to an object's private data, while nonmember functions do not.

A constructor is a member function, with the same name as its class, that is executed every time an object of the class is created. A constructor has no return type but can take arguments. It is often used to give initial values to object data members. Constructors can be overloaded, so an object can be initialized in different ways.

A destructor is a member function with the same name as its class but preceded by a tilde (~). It is called when an object is destroyed. A destructor takes no arguments and has no return value.

There is a separate copy of the data members for each object that is created from a class, but there is only one copy of a class's member functions. A data item can be restricted to a single instance for all objects of a class by making it `static`.

One reason to use OOP is the close correspondence between real-world objects and OOP classes. There are no rules on how to break a programming problem into classes. Often trial and error is necessary.

Questions

Answers to questions can be found in Appendix D.

1. What is the purpose of a class specifier (declaration)?
2. A _________ has the same relation to an _________ that a basic data type has to a variable of that type.
3. In a class specifier, data or functions designated `private` are accessible
    a. to any function in the program.
    b. only if you know the password.
    c. to member functions of that class.
    d. only to public members of the class.
4. Write a class specifier that creates a class called `leverage` with one private data member, `crowbar`, of type `int` and one public function whose declaration is `void pry()`.
5. True or false: Data items in a class must be private.
6. Write a statement that defines an object called `lever1` of the `leverage` class described in Question 4.
7. The dot operator (or class member access operator) connects the following two entities (reading from left to right):
    a. A class member and a class object
    b. A class object and a class
    c. A class and a member of that class
    d. A class object and a member of that class
8. Write a statement that executes the `pry()` function in the `lever1` object, as described in Questions 4 and 6.
9. Member functions defined inside a class specifier are _________ by default.
10. Write a member function called `getcrow()` for the `leverage` class described in Question 4. This function should return the value of the `crowbar` data. Assume the function is defined within the class specifier.
11. A constructor is executed automatically when an object is _________.
12. A constructor's name is the same as _________.
13. Write a constructor that initializes to 0 the `crowbar` data, a member of the `leverage` class described in Question 4. Assume the constructor is defined within the class specifier.

14. True or false: In a class you can have more than one constructor with the same name.

15. A member function can always access the data
    a. in the object of which it is a member.
    b. in the class of which it is a member.
    c. in any object of the class of which it is a member.
    d. in the public part of its class.

16. Assume the member function `getcrow()` described in Question 10 is defined outside the class specifier. Write the declaration that goes inside the class specifier.

17. Write a revised version of the `getcrow()` member function from Question 10 that is defined outside the class specifier.

18. The only technical difference between structures and classes in C++ is that _________.

19. If three objects of a class are defined, how many copies of that class's data items are stored in memory? How many copies of its member functions?

20. *Sending a message* to an object is the same as _________.

21. Classes are useful because they
    a. are removed from memory when not in use.
    b. permit data to be hidden from other classes.
    c. bring together all aspects of an entity in one place.
    d. can closely model objects in the real world.

22. True or false: There is a precise methodology for dividing a real-world programming problem into classes.

Exercises

Answers to the starred exercises can be found in Appendix D.

1.* Create a class that imitates part of the functionality of the basic data type `int`. Call the class `Int` (note different spelling). The only data in this class is an `int` variable. Include member functions to initialize an `Int` to 0, to initialize it to an `int` value, to display it (it looks just like an `int`), and to add two `Int` values.

    Write a program that exercises this class by creating two initialized and one uninitialized `Int` values, adding these two initialized values and placing the response in the uninitialized value, and then displaying this result.

2.* Imagine a tollbooth at a bridge. Cars passing by the booth are expected to pay a 50¢ toll. Mostly they do, but sometimes a car goes by without paying. The tollbooth keeps track of the number of cars that have gone by, and of the total amount of money collected.

Model this tollbooth with a class called `tollBooth`. The two data items are a type `unsigned int` to hold the total number of cars, and a type `double` to hold the total amount of money collected. A constructor initializes both of these to 0. A member function called `payingCar()` increments the car total and adds 0.50 to the cash total. Another function, called `nopayCar()`, increments the car total but adds nothing to the cash total. Finally, a member function called `display()` displays the two totals.

Include a program to test this class. This program should allow the user to push one key to count a paying car, and another to count a nonpaying car. Pushing the (ESC) key should cause the program to print out the total cars and total cash and then exit.

3.* Create a class called `time` that has separate `int` member data for hours, minutes, and seconds. One constructor should initialize this data to 0, and another should initialize it to fixed values. Another member function should display it, in 11:59:59 format. The final member function should add two objects of type `time` passed as arguments.

A `main()` program should create two initialized `time` objects and one that isn't initialized. Then it should add the two initialized values together, leaving the result in the third `time` variable. Finally it should display the value of this third variable.

4. Create an `employee` class, basing it on Exercise 4 of Chapter 5. The member data should comprise an `int` for storing the employee number, and a `float` for storing the employee's compensation. Member functions should allow the user to enter this data and display it. Write a `main()` that allows the user to enter data for three employees and display it.

5. Start with the `date` structure in Exercise 5 in Chapter 5, and transform it into a `date` class. Its member data should consist of three `int`s: `month`, `day`, and `year`. It should also have two member functions: `getdate()`, which allows the user to enter a date in 12/31/97 format, and `showdate()`, which displays the date.

6. Extend the `employee` class of Exercise 4 to include a `date` class (see Exercise 5) and an `etype enum` (see Exercise 6 in Chapter 5). An object of the `date` class should be used to hold the date of first employment; that is, the date when

the employee was hired. The `etype` variable should hold the employee's type: laborer, secretary, manager, and so on. These two items will be private member data in the `employee` specification, just like the employee number and salary. You'll need to extend the `getemploy()` and `putemploy()` functions to obtain this new information from the user and display it. These functions will probably need `switch` statements to handle the `etype` variable. Write a `main()` program that allows the user to enter data for three `employee` variables, which then displays this data.

7. In ocean navigation, locations are measured in degrees and minutes of latitude and longitude. Thus if you're lying off the mouth of Papeete Harbor in Tahiti, your location is 149 degrees 34.8 minutes west longitude, and 17 degrees 31.5 minutes south latitude. This is written as 149°34.8' W, 17°31.5' S. There are 60 minutes in a degree. (An older system also divided a minute into 60 seconds, but the modern approach is to use decimal minutes instead.) Longitude is measured from 0 to 180 degrees, east or west from Greenwich, England, to the international dateline in the Pacific. Latitude is measured from 0 to 90 degrees, north or south from the equator to the poles.

   Create a class `angle` that includes three member variables: an `int` for degrees, a `float` for minutes, and a `char` for the direction letter (N, S, E, or W). This class can hold either a latitude variable or a longitude variable. Write one member function to obtain an angle value (in degrees and minutes) and a direction from the user, and a second to display the angle value in 179°59.9' E format. Also write a three-argument constructor. Write a `main()` program that displays an angle initialized with the constructor, and then, within a loop, allows the user to input any angle value, and then displays the value. The hex character constant `'\xF8'` prints a degree (°) symbol.

8. Create a class that includes a data member that holds a "serial number" for each object created from the class. That is, the first object created will be numbered 1, the second 2, and so on.

   To do this, you'll need another data member that records a count of how many objects have been created so far. (This member should apply to the class as a whole; not to individual objects. What keyword specifies this?) Then, as each object is created, its constructor can examine this count member variable to determine the appropriate serial number for the new object.

   Add a member function that permits an object to report its own serial number. Then write a `main()` program that creates three objects and queries each one about its serial number. They should respond `I am object number 2`, and so on.

9. Transform the `fraction` structure from Exercise 8, Chapter 5, into a `fraction` class. Member data is the fraction's numerator and denominator. Member functions should accept input from the user in the form `3/5`, and output the fraction's value in the same format. Another member function should add two fraction values. Write a `main()` program that allows the user to repeatedly input two fractions, and which then displays their sum. After each operation ask if the user wants to continue.

10. Create a class called `ship` that incorporates a ship's number and location. Use the approach of Exercise 8 to number each `ship` object as it is created. Use two variables of the `angle` class from Exercise 7 to represent the ship's latitude and longitude. A member function of the `ship` class should get a position from the user and store it in the object; another should report the serial number and position. Write a `main()` program that creates three ships, asks the user to input the position of each, and then displays each ship's number and position.

11. Modify the four-function fraction calculator of Exercise 12, Chapter 6, to use a `fraction` class rather than a structure. There should be member functions for input and output, as well as for the four arithmetical operations. While you're at it, you might as well install the capability to reduce fractions to lowest terms. Here's a member function that will reduce the `fraction` object of which it is a member to lowest terms. It finds the greatest common divisor (gcd) of the fraction's numerator and denominator, and uses this gcd to divide both numbers.

```
void fraction::lowterms()       // change ourself to lowest terms
   {
   long tnum, tden, temp, gcd;

   tnum = labs(num);            // use non-negative copies
   tden = labs(den);            //    (needs math.h)
   if( tnum!=0 && tden==0 )     // check for n/0
      { cout << "Illegal fraction: division by 0"; exit(1); }
   else if( tnum==0 )           // check for 0/n
      { num=0; den = 1; return; }

   // this 'while' loop finds the gcd of tnum and tden
   while(tnum != 0)
      {
      if(tnum < tden)           // ensure numerator larger
         { temp=tnum; tnum=tden; tden=temp; }  // swap them
      tnum = tnum - tden;       // subtract them
      }
   gcd = tden;                  // this is greatest common divisor
   num = num / gcd;             // divide both num and den by gcd
   den = den / gcd;             // to reduce frac to lowest terms
   }
```

You can call this function at the end of each arithmetic function, or just before you perform output. You'll also need the usual member functions: four arithmetic operations, input, and display. You may find a two-argument constructor useful.

12. Note that one advantage of the OOP approach is that an entire class can be used, without modification, in a different program. Use the `fraction` class from Exercise 11 in a program that generates a multiplication table for fractions. Let the user input a denominator, and then generate all combinations of two such fractions that are between 0 and 1, and multiply them together. Here's an example of the output if the denominator is 6:

```
        1/6     1/3     1/2     2/3     5/6
-----------------------------------------
1/6     1/36    1/18    1/12    1/9     5/36
1/3     1/18    1/9     1/6     2/9     5/18
1/2     1/12    1/6     1/4     1/3     5/12
2/3     1/9     2/9     1/3     4/9     5/9
5/6     5/36    5/18    5/12    5/9     25/36
```

8

Arrays

ARRAY DEFINITIONS

ACCESSING ARRAY ELEMENTS

ARRAYS AS CLASS MEMBERS

ARRAYS OF OBJECTS

STRINGS

STRING INPUT/OUTPUT

8

In everyday life we commonly group similar objects into units. We buy peas by the can and eggs by the carton. In computer languages we also need to group together data items of the same type. The mechanism that accomplishes this in C++ is the *array*. Arrays can hold a few data items or tens of thousands. The data items grouped in an array can be simple types like `int` or `float`, or they can be user-defined types like structures and objects.

Arrays are like structures in that they both group a number of items into a larger unit. But while a structure usually groups items of different types, an array groups items of the same type. More importantly, the items in a structure are accessed by name, while those in an array are accessed by an index number. Using an index number to specify an item allows easy access to a large number of items.

Arrays exist in almost every computer language, including Pascal and BASIC. Arrays in C++ are similar to those in other languages, and identical to those in C.

In this chapter we'll look first at arrays of basic data types like `int` and `char`. Then we'll examine arrays used as data members in classes, and arrays used to hold objects. Thus this chapter is intended not only to introduce arrays, but to increase your understanding of object-oriented programming. We'll finish the chapter with an introduction to *strings*, which are arrays of type `char`.

Array Fundamentals

A simple example program will serve to introduce arrays. This program, REPLAY, creates an array of four integers representing the ages of four people. It then asks the user to enter four values, which it places in the array. Finally, it displays all four values.

```
// replay.cpp
// gets four ages from user, displays them

#include <iostream.h>

void main()
   {
   int age[4];                       // array 'age' of 4 ints

   cout << endl;
   for(int j=0; j<4; j++)            // get 4 ages
      {
      cout << "Enter an age: ";
      cin >> age[j];                 // access array element
      }
   for(j=0; j<4; j++)                // display 4 ages
      cout << "\nYou entered " << age[j];
   }
```

Here's a sample interaction with the program:

```
Enter an age: 44
Enter an age: 16
Enter an age: 23
Enter an age: 68

You entered 44
You entered 16
You entered 23
You entered 68
```

The first `for` loop gets the ages from the user and places them in the array, while the second reads them from the array and displays them.

Defining Arrays

Like other variables in C++, an array must be defined before it can be used to store information. And, like other definitions, an array definition specifies a variable type and a name. But it includes another feature: a size. The size specifies how many data items the array will contain. It immediately follows the name, and is surrounded by square brackets. Figure 8-1 shows the syntax of an array definition.

In the REPLAY example, the array is type `int`. The name of the array comes next, followed immediately by an opening bracket, the array size, and a closing bracket. The number in brackets must be a constant or an expression that evaluates to a constant, and should also be an integer. In the example we use the value 4.

Array Elements

The items in an array are called *elements* (in contrast to the items in a structure, which are called *members*). As we noted, all the elements in an array are of the same type; only the values vary. Figure 8-2 shows the elements of the array `age`.

Following the conventional (although in some ways backward) approach, memory grows downward in the figure. That is, the first array elements are on the top of the page; later elements extend downward.

Since each element in `age` is an integer, it occupies two bytes. As specified in the definition, the array has exactly four elements.

Notice that the first array element is numbered 0. Thus, since there are four elements, the last one is number 3. This is a potentially confusing situation; you might think the last element in a four-element array would be number 4, but it's not.

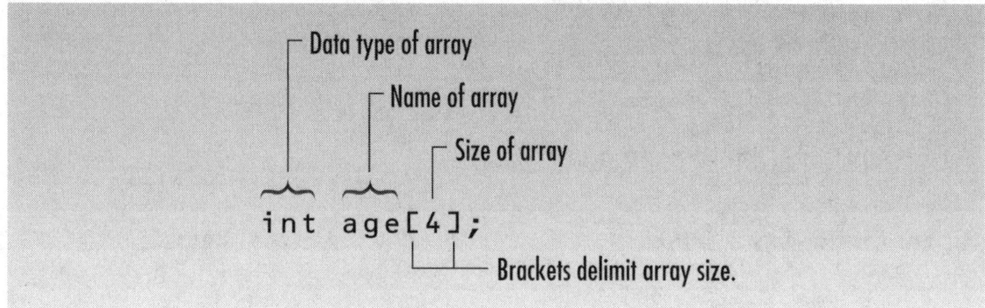

Figure 8-1 Syntax of Array Definition

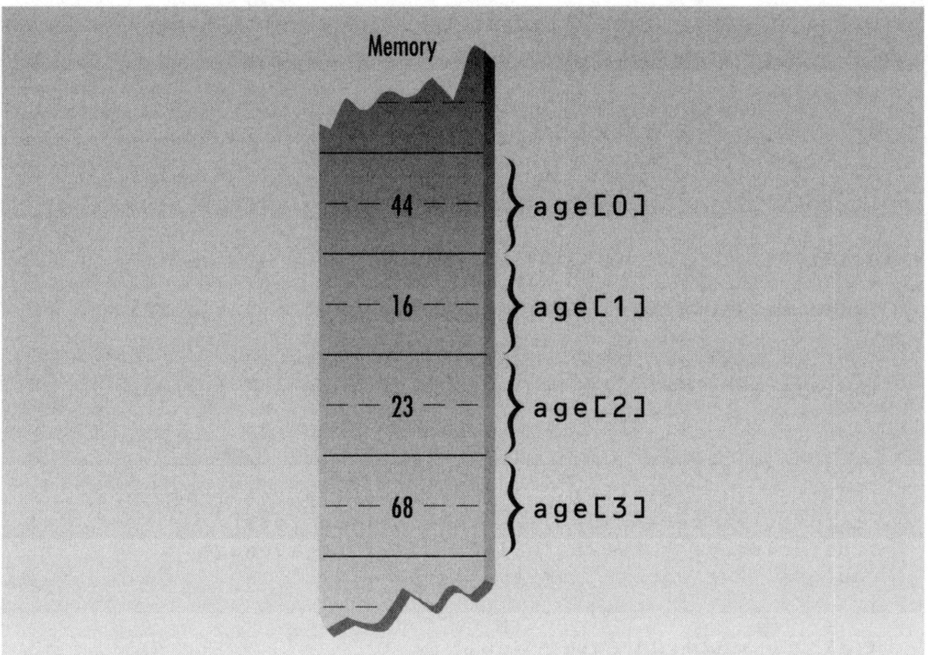

Figure 8-2 Array Elements

Accessing Array Elements

In the REPLAY example we access each array element twice. The first time, we insert a value into the array, with the line

```
cin >> age[j];
```

the second time, we read it out with the line

```
cout << "\nYou entered " << age[j];
```

In both cases the expression for the array element is

```
age[j]
```

This consists of the name of the array, followed by brackets delimiting a variable `j`. Which of the four array elements is specified by this expression depends on the value of `j`; `age[0]` refers to the first element, `age[1]` to the second, `age[2]` to the third, and `age[3]` to the fourth. The variable (or constant) in the brackets is called the array *index*.

Since `j` is the loop variable in both `for` loops, it starts at 0 and is incremented until it reaches 3, thereby accessing each of the array elements in turn.

Averaging Array Elements

Here's another example of an array at work. This one, SALES, invites the user to enter a series of six values representing widget sales for each day of the week (excluding Sunday), and then calculates the average of these values. We use an array of type `float` so that monetary values can be entered.

```
// sales.cpp
// averages a weeks's widget sales (6 days)
#include <iostream.h>

const int SIZE = 6;                 // number of array elements

void main()
   {
   float sales[SIZE];               // array of 6 variables

   cout << "\nEnter widget sales for 6 days\n";
   for(int j=0; j<SIZE; j++)        // put figures in array
      cin >> sales[j];

   float total = 0;
   for(j=0; j<SIZE; j++)            // read figures from array
      total += sales[j];            // to find total
   float average = total / SIZE;    // find average
   cout << "Average = " << average;
   }
```

Here's some sample interaction with SALES:

```
Enter widget sales for 6 days
352.64
867.70
781.32
867.35
746.21
189.45
Average = 634.11
```

A new detail in this program is the use of a `const` variable for the array size and loop limits. This variable is defined at the start of the listing:

```
const int SIZE = 6;
```

Using a variable (instead of a number, such as the 4 used in the last example) makes it easier to change the array size: Only one program line needs to be changed to change the array size, loop limits, and anywhere else the array size appears. The all-uppercase name reminds us that the variable cannot be modified in the program.

Initializing Arrays

You can give values to each array element when the array is first defined. Here's an example, DAYS, that sets 12 array elements in the array `days_per_month` to the number of days in each month.

```
// days.cpp
// shows days from start of year to date specified
#include <iostream.h>

void main()
```

```
{
int month, day, total_days;
int days_per_month[12] = { 31, 28, 31, 30, 31, 30,
                           31, 31, 30, 31, 30, 31 };
cout << "\nEnter month (1 to 12): ";  // get date
cin >> month;
cout << "Enter day (1 to 31): ";
cin >> day;
total_days = day;                      // separate days
for(int j=0; j<month-1; j++)           // add days each month
   total_days += days_per_month[j];
cout << "Total days from start of year is: " << total_days;
}
```

The program calculates the number of days from the beginning of the year to a date specified by the user. (Beware: It doesn't work for leap years.) Here's some sample interaction:

```
Enter month (1 to 12): 3
Enter day (1 to 31): 11
Total days from start of year is: 70
```

Once it gets the month and day values, the program adds the number of days to the total. Then it cycles through a loop, where it adds values from the `days_per_month` array to the `total_days` variable. The number of such values to add is one less than the number of months. For instance, if the user enters month 5, the values of the first four array elements (31, 28, 31, and 30) are added to the total.

The values to which `days_per_month` is initialized are surrounded by braces and separated by commas. They are connected to the array expression by an equal sign. Figure 8-3 shows the syntax.

Actually, we don't need to use the array size when we initialize all the array elements, since the compiler can figure it out by counting the initializing variables. Thus we can write

```
int days_per_month[] = { 31, 28, 31, 30, 31, 30,
                         31, 31, 30, 31, 30, 31 };
```

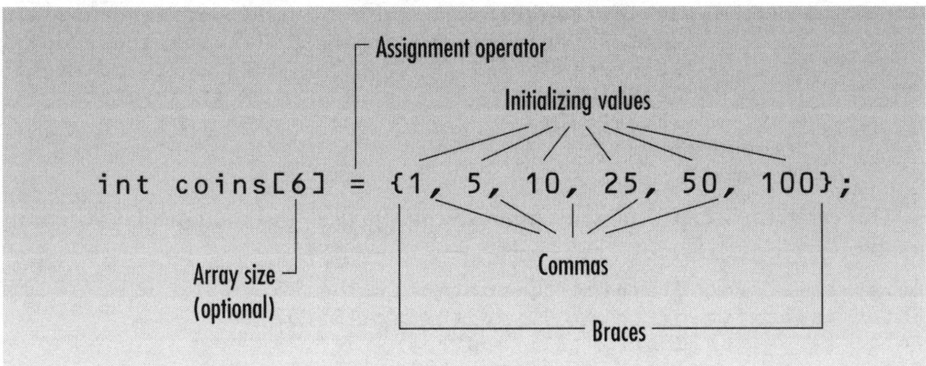

Figure 8-3 Syntax of Array Initialization

What happens if you do use an explicit array size, but it doesn't agree with the number of initializers? If there are too few initializers, the missing elements will be set to 0. If there are too many, an error is signaled.

Multidimensional Arrays

So far we've looked at arrays of one dimension: A single variable specifies each array element. But arrays can have higher dimensions. Here's a program, SALEMON, that uses a two-dimensional array to store sales figures for several districts and several months:

```
// salemon.cpp
// displays sales chart using 2-d array
#include <iostream.h>
#include <iomanip.h>                   // for setprecision, etc.

const int DISTRICTS = 4;               // array dimensions
const int MONTHS = 3;

void main()
   {
   int d, m;
   float sales[DISTRICTS][MONTHS];     // two-dimensional array
                                       // definition
   cout << endl;
   for(d=0; d<DISTRICTS; d++)          // get array values
      for(m=0; m<MONTHS; m++)
         {
         cout << "Enter sales for district " << d+1;
         cout << ", month " << m+1 << ": ";
         cin >> sales[d][m];           // put number in array
         }

   cout << "\n\n";
   cout << "                           Month\n";
   cout << "                 1          2          3";
   for(d=0; d<DISTRICTS; d++)
      {
      cout <<"\nDistrict " << d+1;
      for(m=0; m<MONTHS; m++)          // display array values
         cout << setiosflags(ios::fixed)        // not exponential
              << setiosflags(ios::showpoint)  // always use point
              << setprecision(2)              // digits to right
              << setw(10)                     // field width
              << sales[d][m];          // get number from array
      }  // end for(d)
   }  // end main
```

This program accepts the sales figures from the user and then displays them in a table.

```
Enter sales for district 1, month 1: 3964.23
Enter sales for district 1, month 2: 4135.87
Enter sales for district 1, month 3: 4397.98
Enter sales for district 2, month 1: 867.75
Enter sales for district 2, month 2: 923.59
```

```
Enter sales for district 2, month 3: 1037.01
Enter sales for district 3, month 1: 12.77
Enter sales for district 3, month 2: 378.32
Enter sales for district 3, month 3: 798.22
Enter sales for district 4, month 1: 2983.53
Enter sales for district 4, month 2: 3983.73
Enter sales for district 4, month 3: 9494.98

                          Month
                1           2           3
District 1   3964.23     4135.87     4397.98
District 2    867.75      923.59     1037.01
District 3     12.77      378.32      798.22
District 4   2983.53     3983.73     9494.98
```

Defining Multidimensional Arrays

The array is defined with two size specifiers, each enclosed in brackets:

```
float sales[DISTRICTS][MONTHS];
```

One way to think about this statement is that `sales` is an array of arrays. It is an array of `DISTRICTS` elements, each of which is an array of `MONTHS` elements. Figure 8-4 shows how this looks.

(Of course there can be arrays of dimensions higher than two. A three-dimensional array is an array of arrays of arrays. It is accessed with three indexes:

```
elem = dimen3[i][j][k];
```

This is entirely analogous to one- and two-dimensional arrays.

Accessing Multidimensional Array Elements

Array elements in two-dimensional arrays require two indexes:

```
sales[d][m]
```

Notice that each index has its own set of brackets. Don't write `sales[d,m]`; this works in some languages, but not in C++.

Formatting Numbers

The SALEMON program displays a table of dollar values. It's important that such values be formatted properly, so let's digress to see how this is done in C++. With dollar values you normally want to have exactly two digits to the right of the decimal point, and you want the decimal points of all the numbers in a column to line up. It's also nice if trailing zeros are displayed; you want 79.50, not 79.5.

Convincing the C++ I/O streams to do all this requires a little work. You've already seen the manipulator `setw()`, used to set the output field width. Formatting decimal numbers requires several additional manipulators.

Here's a statement that prints a floating-point number called `fpn` in a field 10 characters wide, with two digits to the right of the decimal point:

```
cout << setiosflags(ios::fixed)        // fixed (not exponential)
     << setiosflags(ios::showpoint)    // always show decimal point
     << setprecision(2)                // two decimal places
     << setw(10)                       // field width 10
     << fpn;                           // finally, the number
```

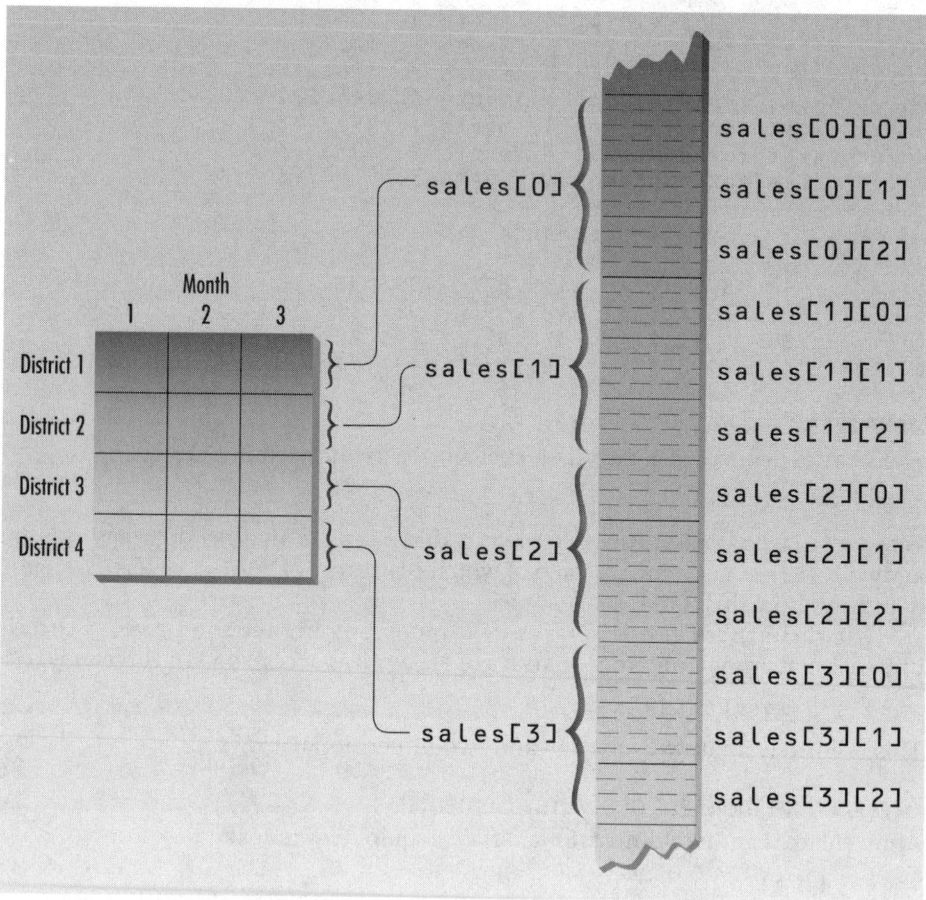

Figure 8-4 Two-Dimensional Array

A group of one-bit *formatting flags* in a `long int` in the `ios` class determines how formatting will be carried out. At this point we don't need to know what the `ios` class is, or the reasons for the exact syntax used with this class, to make the manipulators work.

We're concerned with two of the `ios` flags: `fixed` and `showpoint`. To set the flags, use the manipulator `setiosflags`, with the name of the flag as an argument. The name must be preceded by the class name, `ios`, and the scope resolution operator (`::`).

The first two lines of the `cout` statement set the `ios` flags. (If you need to unset—that is, clear—the flags at some later point in your program, you can use the `resetiosflags` manipulator.) The `fixed` flag prevents numbers from being printed in exponential format, such as 3.45e3. The `showpoint` flag specifies that there will always be a decimal point, even if the number has no fractional part: 123.00, instead of 123.

To set the precision to two digits to the right of the decimal place, use the `setprecision` manipulator, with the number of digits as an argument. We've already seen how to set the field width by using the `setw` manipulator. Once all these manipulators have been sent to `cout`, you can send the number itself; it will be displayed in the desired format.

We'll talk more about the ios formatting flags in Chapter 14.

Initializing Multidimensional Arrays

As you might expect, you can initialize multidimensional arrays. The only prerequisite is a willingness to type a lot of braces and commas. Here's a variation of the SALEMON program that uses an initialized array instead of asking for input from the user. This program is called SALEINIT.

```
// saleinit.cpp
// displays sales chart, initializes 2-d array
#include <iostream.h>
#include <iomanip.h>                // for setprecision, etc.

const int DISTRICTS = 4;            // array dimensions
const int MONTHS = 3;

void main()
   {
   int d, m;
                                    // initialize array elements
   float sales[DISTRICTS][MONTHS]
               = { {  1432.07,    234.50,    654.01 },
                   {   322.00,  13838.32,  17589.88 },
                   {  9328.34,    934.00,   4492.30 },
                   { 12838.29,   2332.63,     32.93 }  };
   cout << "\n\n";
   cout << "                          Month\n";
   cout << "            1         2         3";
   for(d=0; d<DISTRICTS; d++)
      {
      cout <<"\nDistrict " << d+1;
      for(m=0; m<MONTHS; m++)
         cout << setw(10) << setiosflags(ios::fixed)
              << setiosflags(ios::showpoint) << setprecision(2)
              << sales[d][m];  // access array element
      }
   }
```

Remember that a two-dimensional array is really an array of arrays. The format for initializing such an array is based on this fact. The initializing values for each subarray are enclosed in braces and separated by commas,

```
{ 1432.07, 234.50, 654.01 }
```

and then all four of these subarrays, each of which is an element in the main array, is likewise enclosed by braces and separated by commas, as can be seen in the listing.

Passing Arrays to Functions

Arrays can be used as arguments to functions. Here's an example, a variation of the SALEINIT program, that passes the array of sales figures to a function whose purpose is to display the data as a table. Here's the listing for SALEFUNC:

```
// salefunc.cpp
// passes array as argument
#include <iostream.h>
#include <iomanip.h>          // for setprecision, etc.

const int DISTRICTS = 4;      // array dimensions
const int MONTHS = 3;

void display( float[DISTRICTS][MONTHS] );  // prototype

void main()
   {                          // initialize two-dimensional array
   float sales[DISTRICTS][MONTHS]
                = {  {  1432.07,    234.50,    654.01 },
                     {   322.00, 13838.32, 17589.88 },
                     {  9328.34,    934.00,   4492.30 },
                     { 12838.29,   2332.63,     32.93 }  };

   display(sales);            // call function, array as argument
}  // end main

// display()
// function to display 2-d array passed as argument
void display( float funsales[DISTRICTS][MONTHS] )
   {
   int d, m;

   cout << "\n\n";
   cout << "                        Month\n";
   cout << "              1         2          3";

   for(d=0; d<DISTRICTS; d++)
      {
      cout <<"\nDistrict " << d+1;
      for(m=0; m<MONTHS; m++)
         cout << setiosflags(ios::fixed) << setw(10)
              << setiosflags(ios::showpoint) << setprecision(2)
              << funsales[d][m];    // array element
      }  // end for(d)
   }  // end display
```

Function Declaration with Array Argument

In a function declaration, array arguments are represented by the data type and sizes of the array. Here's the declaration of the `display()` function:

```
void display( float[DISTRICTS][MONTHS] );  // declaration
```

Actually, there is one unnecessary piece of information here. The following statement works just as well:

```
void display( float[][MONTHS] );    // declaration
```

Why doesn't the function need the size of the first dimension? Again, remember that a two-dimensional array is an array of arrays. The function first thinks of the argument as an array of districts. It doesn't need to know how many districts there are, but it does need to know how big each district element is, so it can calculate where a particular element is (by multiplying the bytes per element times the index). So we must tell it the size of each element, which is MONTHS, but not how many there are, which is DISTRICTS.

It follows that if we were declaring a function that used a one-dimensional array as an argument, we would not need to use the array size:

```
void somefunc( int elem[] );    // declaration
```

Function Call with Array Argument

When the function is called, only the name of the array is used as an argument.

```
display(sales);    // function call
```

This name (`sales` in this case) actually represents the memory *address* of the array. We aren't going to explore addresses in detail until Chapter 12 but here are a few preliminary points about them.

Using an address for an array argument is similar to using a reference argument, in that the values of the array elements are not duplicated (copied) into the function. (See the discussion of reference arguments in Chapter 6.) Instead, the function works with the original array, although it refers to it by a different name. This system is used for arrays because they can be very large; duplicating an entire array in every function that called it would be both time-consuming and wasteful of memory.

However, an address is not the same as a reference. No ampersand (`&`) is used with the array name in the function declaration. Until we discuss pointers, take it on faith that arrays are passed using their name alone, and that the function accesses the original array, not a duplicate.

Function Definition with Array Argument

In the function definition the declarator looks like this:

```
void display( float funsales[DISTRICTS][MONTHS] )   // declarator
```

The array argument uses the data type, a name, and the sizes of the dimensions. The array name used by the function (`funsales` in this example) can be different from the name that defines the array (`sales`), but they both refer to the same array. All the array dimensions must be specified (except in some cases the first one); the function needs them to access the array elements properly.

References to array elements in the function use the function's name for the array:

```
funsales[d][m]
```

But in all other ways the function can access array elements as if the array had been defined in the function.

Arrays of Structures

Arrays can contain structures as well as simple data types. Here's an example based on the `part` structure from Chapter 5.

```
// partaray.cpp
// structure variables as array elements
#include <iostream.h>

const int SIZE = 4;                 // number of parts in array

struct part                         // specify a structure
   {
   int modelnumber;                 // ID number of widget
   int partnumber;                  // ID number of widget part
   float cost;                      // cost of part
   };

void main()
   {
   int n;
   part apart[SIZE];                // define array of structures

   for(n=0; n<SIZE; n++)            // get values for all members
      {
      cout << endl;
      cout << "Enter model number: ";
      cin >> apart[n].modelnumber;       // get model number
      cout << "Enter part number: ";
      cin >> apart[n].partnumber;        // get part number
      cout << "Enter cost: ";
      cin >> apart[n].cost;              // get cost
      }
   for(n=0; n<SIZE; n++)            // show values for all members
      {
      cout << "\nModel " << apart[n].modelnumber;
      cout << "  Part "  << apart[n].partnumber;
      cout << "  Cost "  << apart[n].cost;
      }
   }
```

The user types in the model number, part number, and cost of a part. The program records this data in a structure. However, this structure is only one element in an array of structures. The program asks for the data for four different parts, and stores it in the four elements of the `apart` array. It then displays the information. Here's some sample input:

```
Enter model number: 44
Enter part number: 4954
Enter cost: 133.45

Enter model number: 44
Enter part number: 8431
Enter cost: 97.59
```

```
Enter model number: 77
Enter part number: 9343
Enter cost: 109.99

Enter model number: 77
Enter part number: 4297
Enter cost: 3456.55

Model 44   Part 4954   Cost 133.45
Model 44   Part 8431   Cost 97.59
Model 77   Part 9343   Cost 109.99
Model 77   Part 4297   Cost 3456.55
```

The array of structures is defined in the statement

```
part apart[SIZE];
```

This has the same syntax as that of arrays of simple data types. Only the type name, `part`, shows that this is an array of a more complex type.

Accessing a data item that is a member of a structure that is itself an element of an array involves a new syntax. For example,

```
apart[n].modelnumber
```

refers to the `modelnumber` member of the structure that is element `n` of the `apart` array. Figure 8-5 shows how this looks.

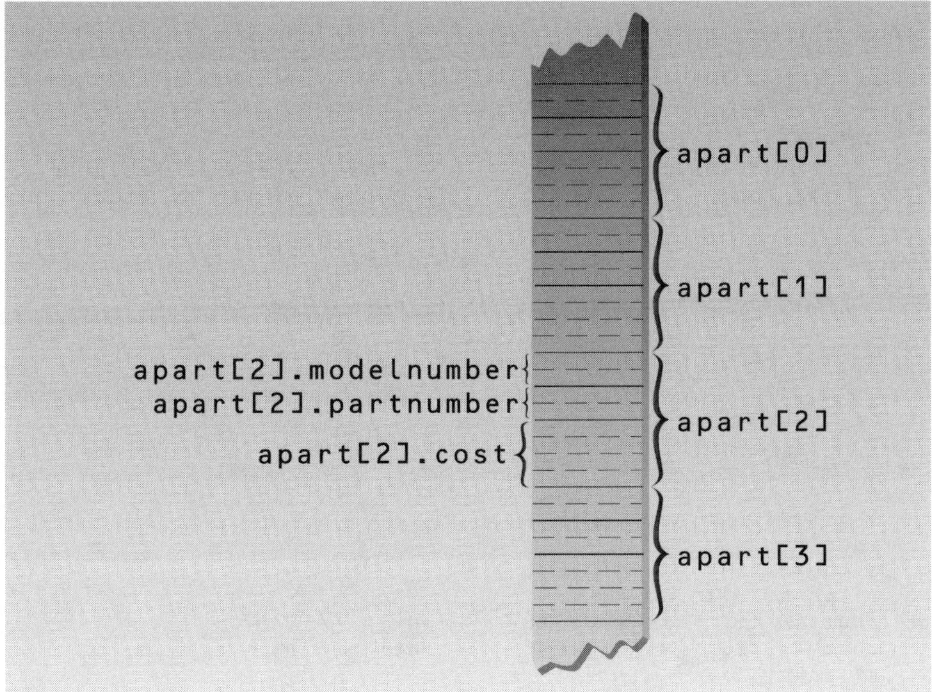

Figure 8-5 Array of Structures

Arrays of structures are a useful data type in a variety of situations. We've shown an array of car parts, but we could also store an array of personnel data (name, age, salary), an array of geographical data about cities (name, population, elevation), and many other types of data.

Arrays As Class Member Data

Arrays can be used as data items in classes. Let's look at an example that models a common computer data structure: the stack.

A stack works like the spring-loaded devices that hold trays in cafeterias. When you put a tray on top, the stack sinks down a little; when you take a tray off, it pops up. The last tray placed on the stack is always the first tray removed.

Stacks are one of the cornerstones of the architecture of the 80x86 microprocessor used in MS-DOS computers. As we mentioned earlier, functions pass their arguments and store their return address on the stack. This kind of stack is implemented partly in hardware and is most conveniently accessed in assembly language. However, stacks can also be created completely in software. Software stacks offer a useful storage device in certain programming situations, such as in parsing (analyzing) algebraic expressions.

Our example program, STAKARAY, creates a simple stack class.

```
// stakaray.cpp
// a stack as a class
#include <iostream.h>

const int MAX = 100;

class Stack
   {
   private:
      int st[MAX];                 // stack: array of integers
      int top;                     // number of top of stack
   public:
      Stack()                      // constructor
         { top = -1; }
      void push(int var)           // put number on stack
         { st[++top] = var; }
      int pop()                    // take number off stack
         { return st[top--]; }
   };

void main()
   {
   Stack s1;

   s1.push(11);
   s1.push(22);
   cout << "1: " << s1.pop() << endl;  // 22
   cout << "2: " << s1.pop() << endl;  // 11
   s1.push(33);
   s1.push(44);
   s1.push(55);
```

```
s1.push(66);
cout << "3: " << s1.pop() << endl;   // 66
cout << "4: " << s1.pop() << endl;   // 55
cout << "5: " << s1.pop() << endl;   // 44
cout << "6: " << s1.pop() << endl;   // 33
}
```

The stack itself consists of the array `st`. An `int` variable, `top`, indicates the index of the last item placed on the stack; the location of this item is the top of the stack. Figure 8-6 shows a stack.

Since memory grows downward in the figure, the top of the stack is at the bottom in the figure. When an item is added to the stack, the address in `top` is incremented to point to the new top of the stack. When an item is removed, the value in `top` is decremented. (We don't need to erase the old value left in memory when an item is removed; it just becomes irrelevant.)

To place an item on the stack—a process called *pushing* the item—you call the `push()` member function with the value to be stored as an argument. To retrieve (or *pop*) an item from the stack, you use the `pop()` member function, which returns the value of the item.

The `main()` program in STAKARAY exercises the `stack` class by creating an object, `s1`, of the class. It pushes two items onto the stack, and pops them off and displays

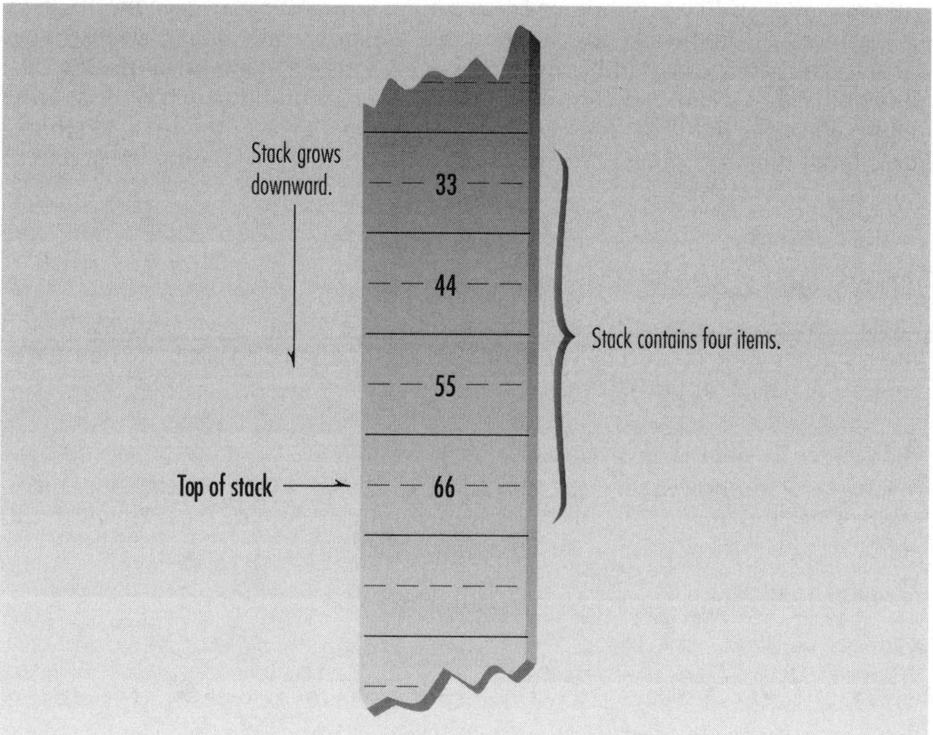

Figure 8-6 A Stack

them. Then it pushes four more items onto the stack, and pops them off and displays them. Here's the output:

```
1: 22
2: 11
3: 66
4: 55
5: 44
6: 33
```

As you can see, items are popped off the stack in reverse order; the last thing pushed is the first thing popped.

Notice the subtle use of prefix and postfix notation in the increment and decrement operators. The statement

```
st[++top] = var;
```

in the `push()` member function first increments `top` so that it points to the next available array element—one past the last element. It then assigns `var` to this location, which becomes the new top of the stack. The statement

```
return st[top--];
```

first returns the value it finds at the top of the stack, and then decrements `top` so that it points to the preceding element.

The `stack` class is an example of an important feature of object-oriented programming: using a class to implement a certain kind of data-storage mechanism. In Chapter 17, when we discuss the Borland container class library, we'll see that a stack is only one of a number of ways to store data. There are also queues, sets, linked lists, and so on. A data-storage scheme is chosen that matches the specific requirements of the program. Using a preexisting class to provide data storage means that the programmer does not need to waste time duplicating the details of a data-storage mechanism.

Arrays of Objects

We've seen how an object can contain an array. We can also reverse that situation and create an array of objects. We'll look at two situations: an array of English distances and a deck of cards.

Arrays of English Distances

In Chapter 7 we showed several examples of an English `Distance` class that incorporated feet and inches into an object representing a new data type. The next program, ENGLARAY, demonstrates an array of such objects.

```
// englaray.cpp
// objects using English measurements
#include <iostream.h>

const int MAX = 100;                    // maximum number of elements

class Distance                          // English Distance class
   {
   private:
```

```
      int feet;
      float inches;
   public:
      void getdist()                  // get length from user
         {
         cout << "\n   Enter feet: ";  cin >> feet;
         cout << "   Enter inches: ";  cin >> inches;
         }
      void showdist()                 // display distance
         { cout << feet << "\'-" << inches << '\"'; }
   };

void main()
   {
   Distance dist[MAX];                // array of distances
   int n=0;                           // count the entries
   char ans;                          // user response ('y' or 'n')

   cout << endl;
   do                                 // get distances from user
      {
      cout << "Enter distance number " << n+1;
      dist[n++].getdist();            // store distance in array
      cout << "Enter another (y/n)?: ";
      cin >> ans;
      }                               // quit if user types 'n'
   while( ans != 'n' );

   for(int j=0; j<n; j++)             // display all distances
      {
      cout << "\nDistance number " << j+1 << " is ";
      dist[j].showdist();
      }
   }
```

In this program the user types in as many distances as desired. After each distance is entered, the program asks if the user desires to enter another. If not, it terminates, and displays all the distances entered so far. Here's a sample interaction when the user enters three distances:

```
Enter distance number 1
   Enter feet: 5
   Enter inches: 4
Enter another (y/n)? y
Enter distance number 2
   Enter feet: 6
   Enter inches: 2.5
Enter another (y/n)? y
Enter distance number 3
   Enter feet: 5
   Enter inches: 10.75
Enter another (y/n)? n

Distance number 1 is 5'-4"
Distance number 2 is 6'-2.5"
Distance number 3 is 5'-10.75"
```

Of course, instead of simply displaying the distances already entered, the program could have averaged them, written them to disk, or operated on them in other ways. For simplicity, we avoid these embellishments.

Array Bounds

This program uses a `do` loop to get input from the user. This way the user can input data for as many structures of type `part` as seems desirable, up to `MAX`, the size of the array (which is set to 100).

Although it's hard to imagine anyone having the patience, what would happen if the user entered more than 100 distances? The answer is, something unpredictable but almost certainly bad. There is no bounds checking in C++ arrays. If the program inserts something beyond the end of the array, neither the compiler nor the runtime system will object. However, the renegade data will probably be written on top of other data or the program code itself. This may cause bizarre effects or crash the system completely.

The moral is that it is up to the programmer to deal with the array bounds checking. If it seems possible that the user will insert too much data for an array to hold, then the array should be made larger or some means of warning the user should be devised. For example, you could insert the following code at the beginning of the `do` loop in ENGLARAY:

```
if( n >= MAX )
   {
   cout << "\nThe array is full!!!";
   break;
   }
```

This causes a `break` out of the loop and prevents the array from overflowing.

Accessing Objects in an Array

The specification of the `Distance` class in this program is similar to that used in previous programs. However, in the `main()` program we define an array of such objects:

```
Distance dist[MAX];
```

Here the data type of the `dist` array is `Distance`, and it has `MAX` elements. Figure 8-7 shows what this looks like.

A class member function that is an array element is accessed similarly to a structure member that is an array element, as in the PARTARAY example. Here's how the `showdist()` member function of the `j`th element of the array `dist` is invoked:

```
dist[j].showdist();
```

As you can see, a member function of an object that is an array element is accessed using the dot operator: The array name followed by the index in brackets is joined, using the dot operator, to the member function name followed by parentheses. This is similar to accessing a structure (or class) data member, except that the function name and parentheses are used instead of the data name.

Notice that when we call the `getdist()` member function to put a distance into the array, we take the opportunity to increment the array index `n`:

```
dist[n++].getdist();
```

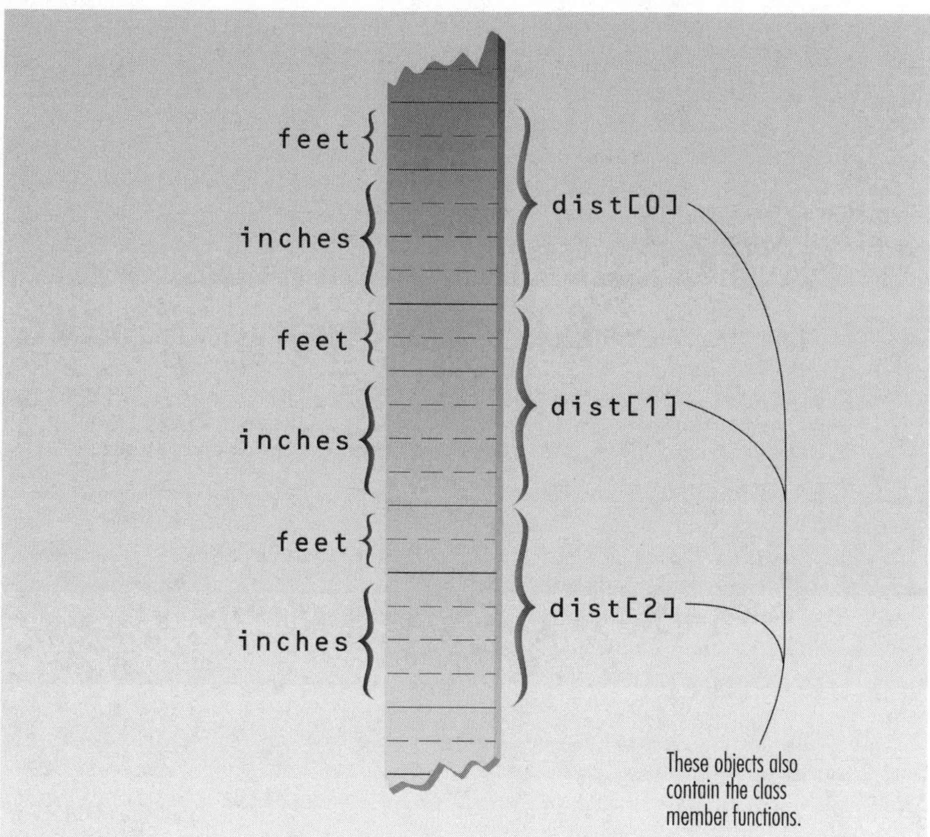

Figure 8-7 Array of Objects

This way the next group of data obtained from the user will be placed in the structure in the next array element in `dist`. The `n` variable must be incremented manually like this because we use a `do` loop instead of a `for` loop. In the `for` loop, the loop variable—which is incremented automatically—can serve as the array index.

Arrays of Cards

Here's another, somewhat longer, example of an array of objects. You will no doubt remember the CARDOBJ example from Chapter 7. We'll borrow the `card` class from that example, and group an array of 52 such objects together in an array, thus creating a deck of cards. Remember that, because this program uses DOS graphics characters for the four suits (spades, clubs, hearts, and diamonds), you must compile it to run directly under DOS, not EasyWin. Here's the listing for CARDARAY:

```
// cardaray.cpp
// cards as objects
// for IBM character set, build DOS target, not EasyWin
#include <iostream.h>
```

(continued on next page)

(continued from previous page)

```
#include <stdlib.h>          // for randomize(), rand
#include <time.h>            // for randomize()
#include <conio.h>           // for getche()

enum Suit { clubs, diamonds, hearts, spades };

const int jack = 11;         // from 2 to 10 are
const int queen = 12;        // integers without names
const int king = 13;
const int ace = 14;

class card
   {
   private:
      int number;          // 2 to 10, jack, queen, king, ace
      Suit suit;           // clubs, diamonds, hearts, spades
   public:
      card()                         // constructor
         { }
      void init(int n, Suit s)    // initialize card
         { suit = s; number = n; }
      void display();                // display card
   };

void card::display()                 // display the card
   {
   if( number >= 2 && number <= 10 )
      cout << number;
   else
      switch(number)
         {
         case jack:  cout << "J"; break;
         case queen: cout << "Q"; break;
         case king:  cout << "K"; break;
         case ace:   cout << "A"; break;
         }
   switch(suit)
      {
      case clubs:    cout << char(5); break;
      case diamonds: cout << char(4); break;
      case hearts:   cout << char(3); break;
      case spades:   cout << char(6); break;
      }
   }

void main()
   {
   card deck[52];

   cout << endl;
   for(int j=0; j<52; j++)
      {
      int num = (j % 13) + 2;  // cycles through 2 to 14, 4 times
      Suit su = Suit(j / 13);  // cycles through 0 to 3, 13 times
```

```
        deck[j].init(num, su);    // set card
        }

    cout << "\nOrdered deck:\n";
    for(j=0; j<52; j++)           // display ordered deck
        {
        deck[j].display();
        cout << "  ";
        if( !( (j+1) % 13) )      // newline every 13 cards
            cout << endl;
        }

    randomize();                  // seed random number generator
    for(j=0; j<52; j++)           // for each card in the deck,
        {
        int k = random(52);       // pick another card at random
        card temp = deck[j];      // and swap them
        deck[j] = deck[k];
        deck[k] = temp;
        }

    cout << "\nShuffled deck:\n";
    for(j=0; j<52; j++)           // display shuffled deck
        {
        deck[j].display();
        cout << ", ";
        if( !( (j+1) % 13) )      // newline every 13 cards
            cout << endl;
        }
    getche();                     // wait for keypress
    } // end main
```

Once we've created a deck, it's hard to resist the temptation to shuffle it. We display the cards in the deck, shuffle it, and then display it again. To conserve space we use the IBM graphics characters for the club, diamond, heart, and spade. Figure 8-8 shows the output from the program. This program incorporates several new ideas, so let's look at them in turn.

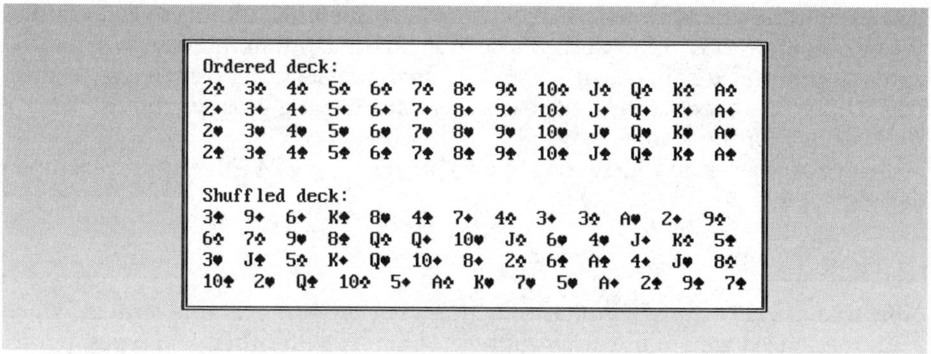

```
Ordered deck:
2♣  3♣  4♣  5♣  6♣  7♣  8♣  9♣  10♣  J♣  Q♣  K♣  A♣
2♦  3♦  4♦  5♦  6♦  7♦  8♦  9♦  10♦  J♦  Q♦  K♦  A♦
2♥  3♥  4♥  5♥  6♥  7♥  8♥  9♥  10♥  J♥  Q♥  K♥  A♥
2♠  3♠  4♠  5♠  6♠  7♠  8♠  9♠  10♠  J♠  Q♠  K♠  A♠

Shuffled deck:
3♠  9♦  6♦  K♠  8♥  4♠  7♦  4♣  3♦  3♣  A♥  2♦  9♣
6♣  7♣  9♥  8♠  Q♣  Q♦  10♥  J♣  6♥  4♥  J♦  K♣  5♠
3♥  J♠  5♣  K♦  Q♥  10♦  8♦  2♣  6♠  A♠  4♦  J♥  8♣
10♠  2♥  Q♠  10♣  5♦  A♣  K♥  7♥  5♥  A♦  2♠  9♠  7♠
```

Figure 8-8 Output of the CARDARAY Program

Use DOS Target for IBM Graphics Characters

There are several special IBM graphics characters in the range below ASCII code 32. (See Appendix A for a list of IBM ASCII codes.) In the `display()` member function of `card` we use codes 5, 4, 3, and 6 to create the characters for a club, a diamond, a heart, and a spade, respectively. Casting these numbers to type `char`, as in

```
char(5)
```

causes the `<<` operator to print them as characters rather than as numbers.

Since Windows does not use the IBM character set, you'll need to use an Application target type on a DOS standard platform when you build your program in Borland C++. The EasyWin approach won't work.

The Card Deck

The array of structures that constitutes the deck of cards is defined in the statement

```
card deck[52];
```

which creates an array called `deck`, consisting of 52 objects of type `card`. To display the `j`th card in the deck, we call the `display()` member function:

```
deck[j].display();
```

Random Numbers

It's always fun and sometimes even useful to generate random numbers. In this program we use them to shuffle the deck. Two steps are necessary to obtain random numbers in Borland or Turbo C++. First the random-number generator must be *seeded* or initialized. To do this we call the `randomize()` library function. This function uses the system time as the seed, so it requires two header files, STDLIB.H and TIME.H.

To actually generate a random number we call the `random()` library function. This function takes a single integer argument: the highest number, plus one, in the desired range. Thus if this argument is `max`, the function returns a random number in the range from 0 to max–1. To obtain a number in the range 0 to 51, we use the expression

```
random(52);
```

The resulting random number is then used as an index to swap two cards. We go through the `for` loop, swapping one card, whose index points to each card in 0-to-51 order, with another card, whose index is the random number. When all 52 cards have been exchanged with a random card, the deck is considered to be shuffled. This program could form the basis for a card-playing program, but we'll leave these details for the reader.

Arrays of objects are widely used in C++ programming. We'll see other examples as we go along.

Strings

Now that we have some familiarity with arrays, we can examine strings, which are a specialized way to use arrays of type `char`. As with other data types, strings can be variables or constants. We'll look at these two entities before going on to examine more complex string operations.

String Variables

Here's an example that defines a single string variable. It asks the user to enter a string, and places this string in the string variable. Then it displays the string. Here's the listing for STRINGIN:

```
// stringin.cpp
// simple string variable
#include <iostream.h>
const int MAX = 80;                     // max characters in string

void main()
   {
   char str[MAX];                       // string variable str

   cout << "\nEnter a string: ";
   cin >> str;                          // put string in str
   cout << "You entered: " << str;      // display string from str
   }
```

The definition of the string variable `str` looks like (and is) the definition of any array of type `char`:

```
char str[MAX];
```

We use the extraction operator `>>` to read a string from the keyboard and place it in the string variable `str`. This operator knows how to deal with strings; it understands that they are arrays of characters. If the user enters the string `"Amanuensis"` (one employed to copy manuscripts) in this program, the array `str` will look something like Figure 8-9.

Each character occupies 1 byte of memory. An important aspect of strings in C++ is that they must terminate with a byte containing 0. This is often represented by the character constant `'\0'`, which is a character with an ASCII value of 0. This terminating zero is called the *null* character. When the `<<` operator displays the string, it displays characters until it encounters the null character.

Avoiding Buffer Overflow

The STRINGIN program invites the user to type in a string. What happens if the user enters a string that is longer than the array used to hold it? As we mentioned earlier, there is no built-in mechanism in C++ to keep a program from inserting array elements outside an array. So an overly enthusiastic typist could end up crashing the system.

However, it is possible to tell the `>>` operator to limit the number of characters it places in an array. The SAFETYIN program demonstrates this approach.

```
// safetyin.cpp
// avoids buffer overflow with cin.width
#include <iostream.h>
#include <iomanip.h>                     // for setw
const int MAX = 20;                      // max characters in string

void main()
```

(continued on next page)

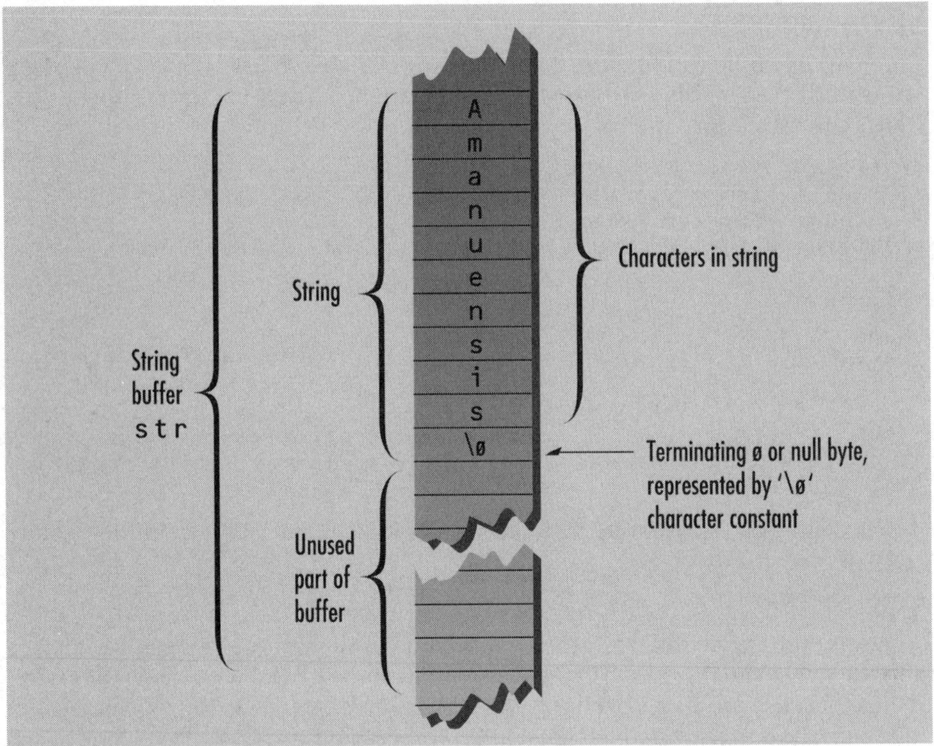

Figure 8-9 String Stored in String Variable

(continued from previous page)

```
   {
   char str[MAX];                        // string variable str

   cout << "\nEnter a string: ";
   cin >> setw(MAX) >> str;              // put string in str,
                                         // no more than MAX chars
   cout << "You entered: " << str;       // display string from str
   }
```

This program uses the `setw` manipulator to specify the maximum number of characters the input buffer can accept. The user may type more characters, but the `>>` operator won't insert them into the array. Actually, one character fewer than the number specified is inserted, so there is room in the buffer for the terminating null character. Thus, in SAFETYIN, a maximum of 19 characters are inserted. (Incidentally, DOS restricts you to 127 characters of character input.)

String Constants

You can initialize a string to a constant value when you define it. Here's an example, STRINIT, that does just that (with the first line of a Shakespearean sonnet):

```
// strinit.cpp
// initialized string
#include <iostream.h>
```

```
void main()
   {
   char str[] = "Farewell! thou art too dear for my possessing";

   cout << str;
   }
```

Here the string constant is written as a normal English phrase, delimited by quotes. This may seem surprising, since a string is an array of type `char`. In past examples you've seen arrays initialized to a series of values delimited by braces and separated by commas. Why isn't `str` initialized the same way? In fact you could use such a sequence of character constants:

```
char str[] = { 'F', 'a', 'r', 'e', 'w', 'e', 'l', 'l', ' ', 't', 'h',
```

and so on. Fortunately, the designers of C++ (and C) took pity on us and provided the shortcut approach shown in STRINIT. The effect is the same: The characters are placed one after the other in the array. As with all strings, the last character is a null (zero).

Reading Embedded Blanks

If you tried the STRINGIN program with strings that contained more than one word, you may have had an unpleasant surprise. Here's an example:

```
Enter a string: Law is a bottomless pit.
You entered: Law
```

Where did the rest of the phrase (a quotation from the Scottish writer John Arbuthnot, 1667–1735) go? It turns out that the extraction operator `>>` considers a space to be a terminating character. Thus it will read strings consisting of a single word, but anything typed after a space is thrown away.

To read text containing blanks we use another function, `cin::get()`. This syntax means a member function `get()` of the stream class of which `cin` is an object. The following example, BLANKSIN, shows how it's used.

```
// blanksin.cpp
// reads string with embedded blanks
#include <iostream.h>
const int MAX = 80;                     // max characters in string

void main()
   {
   char str[MAX];                       // string variable str

   cout << "\nEnter a string: ";
   cin.get(str, MAX);                   // put string in str
   cout << "You entered: " << str;      // display string from str
   }
```

The first argument to `cin::get()` is the array address where the string being input will be placed. The second argument specifies the maximum size of the array, thus automatically avoiding buffer overrun.

Using this function, the input string is now stored in its entirety.

```
Enter a string: Law is a bottomless pit.
You entered: Law is a bottomless pit.
```

There's a potential problem when you mix `cin.get()` with `cin` and the extraction operator (>>). We'll discuss this in Chapter 11, since it occurs most commonly in graphics-oriented programs.

Reading Multiple Lines

We may have solved the problem of reading strings with embedded blanks, but what about strings with multiple lines? It turns out that the `cin::get()` function can take a third argument to help out in this situation. This argument specifies the character that tells the function to stop reading. The default value for this argument is the newline (`'\n'`) character, but if you call the function with some other character for this argument, the default will be overridden by the specified character.

In the next example, LINESIN, we call the function with a dollar sign (`'$'`) as the third argument:

```
// linesin.cpp
// reads multiple lines, terminates on '$' character
#include <iostream.h>
const int MAX = 2000;                    // max characters in string

void main()
   {
   char str[MAX];                        // string variable str

   cout << "\nEnter a string:\n";
   cin.get(str, MAX, '$');               // terminate with $
   cout << "You entered:\n" << str;      // display string from str
   }
```

Now you can type as many lines of input as you want. The function will continue to accept characters until you enter the terminating character (or until you exceed the size of the array). Remember, you must still press (ENTER) after typing the `'$'` character. Here's a sample interaction with a poem from Thomas Carew, 1595–1639:

```
Enter a string:
Ask me no more where Jove bestows
When June is past, the fading rose;
For in your beauty's orient deep
These flowers, as in their causes, sleep.
$
You entered:
Ask me no more where Jove bestows
When June is past, the fading rose;
For in your beauty's orient deep
These flowers, as in their causes, sleep.
```

We terminate each line with (ENTER), but the program continues to accept input until we enter `'$'`.

Copying a String the Hard Way

The best way to understand the true nature of strings is to deal with them character by character. The following program does this.

```
// strcopy1.cpp
// copies a string using a for loop
#include <iostream.h>
#include <string.h>          // for strlen()
const int MAX = 80;          // size of str2 buffer
void main()
   {                                      // initialized string
   char str1[] = "Oh, Captain, my Captain! "
                 "our fearful trip is done";

   char str2[MAX];                        // empty string

   for(int j=0; j<strlen(str1); j++)      // copy strlen characters
      str2[j] = str1[j];                  //    from str1 to str2
   str2[j] = '\0';                        // insert null character
   cout << endl;
   cout << str2;                          // display str2

   }
```

This program creates a string constant, `str1`, and a string variable, `str2`. It then uses a `for` loop to copy the string constant to the string variable. The copying is done one character at a time, in the statement

```
str2[j] = str1[j];
```

Recall that the compiler concatenates two adjacent string constants into a single one.

This program also introduces string library functions. Because there are no string operators built into C++, strings must usually be manipulated using library functions. Fortunately there are many such functions. The one we use in this program, `strlen()`, finds the length of a string (that is, how many characters are in it). We use this length as the limit in the `for` loop so that the right number of characters will be copied. When string functions are used, the header file STRING.H must be `#included` in the program.

The copied version of the string must be terminated with a null. However, the string length returned by `strlen()` does not include the null. We could copy one additional character, but it's safer to insert the null overtly. We do this with the line

```
str2[j] = '\0';
```

If you don't insert this character, you'll find that the string printed by the program includes all sorts of weird characters following the string you want. The `<<` just keeps on printing characters, whatever they are, until by chance it encounters a `'\0'`.

Copying a String the Easy Way

Of course you don't need to use a `for` loop to copy a string. As you might have guessed, a library function will do it for you. Here's a revised version of the program, STRCOPY2, that uses the `strcpy()` function.

```
// strcopy2.cpp
// copies a string using strcpy() function
#include <iostream.h>
```

(continued on next page)

(continued from previous page)

```
#include <string.h>          // for strcpy()
const int MAX = 80;          // size of str2 buffer
void main()
   {
   char str1[] = "Tiger, tiger, burning bright\n"
                 "In the forests of the night";

   char str2[MAX];                         // empty string

   strcpy(str2, str1);                     // copy str1 to str2
   cout << endl;
   cout << str2;                           // display str2

   }
```

Note that you call this function like this:

```
strcpy(destination, source)
```

with the destination first. The right-to-left order is reminiscent of the format of normal assignment statements: The variable on the right is copied to the variable on the left.

Arrays of Strings

If there are arrays of arrays, of course there can be arrays of strings. This is actually quite a useful construction. Here's an example, STRARAY, that puts the names of the days of the week in an array:

```
// straray.cpp
// array of strings
#include <iostream.h>
const int DAYS = 7;                    // number of strings in array
const int MAX = 10;                    // maximum size of each string

void main()
   {                                   // array of strings
   char star[DAYS][MAX] = { "Sunday", "Monday", "Tuesday",
                            "Wednesday", "Thursday",
                            "Friday", "Saturday"  };
   for(int j=0; j<DAYS; j++)           // display every string
      cout << star[j] << endl;
   }
```

The program prints out each string from the array:

```
Sunday
Monday
Tuesday
Wednesday
Thursday
Friday
Saturday
```

Since a string is an array, it must be that `star`—an array of strings—is really a two-dimensional array. The first dimension of this array, `DAYS`, tells how many strings are in the array. The second dimension, `MAX`, specifies the maximum length of the strings (9 characters for "Wednesday" plus the terminating null makes 10). Figure 8-10 shows how this looks.

Notice that some bytes are wasted following strings that are less than the maximum length. We'll learn how to remove this inefficiency when we talk about pointers.

The syntax for accessing a particular string may look surprising:

```
star[j];
```

If we're dealing with a two-dimensional array, where's the second index? Since a two-dimensional array is an array of arrays, we can access elements of the "outer" array, each of which is an array (in this case a string), individually. To do this we don't need the second index. So `star[j]` is string number `j` in the array of strings.

Strings As Class Members

Strings frequently appear as members of classes. The next example, a variation of the OBJPART program in Chapter 7, uses a string to hold the name of the widget part.

```
// strpart.cpp
// string used in widget part object
#include <iostream.h>
#include <string.h>          // for strcpy()

class part
   {
   private:
      char partname[30];     // name of widget part
      int partnumber;        // ID number of widget part
      float cost;            // cost of part
```

(continued on next page)

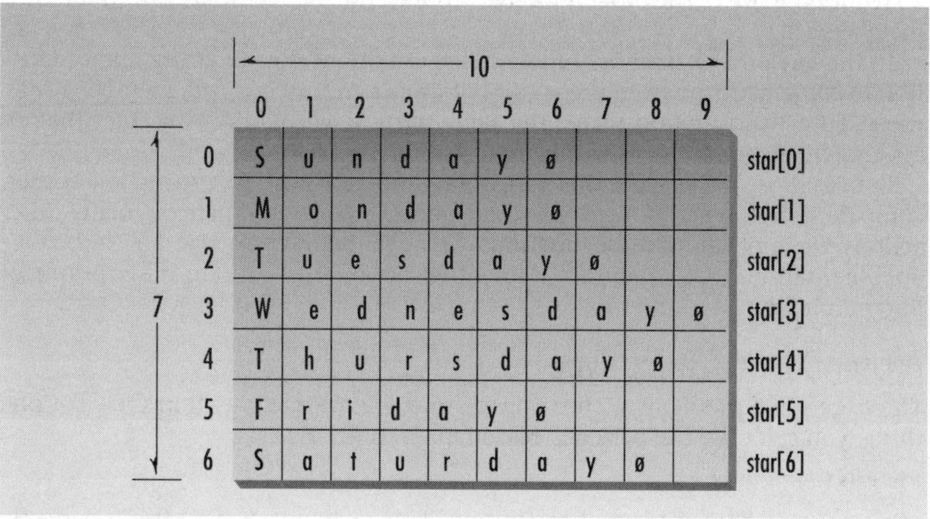

Figure 8-10 Array of Strings

(continued from previous page)

```
   public:
      void setpart(char pname[], int pn, float c)
         {
         strcpy(partname, pname);
         partnumber = pn;
         cost = c;
         }
      void showpart()                              // display data
         {
         cout << "\nName="    << partname;
         cout << ", number="  << partnumber;
         cout << ", cost=$"   << cost;
         }
   };

void main()
   {
   part part1, part2;

   part1.setpart("handle bolt", 4473, 217.55);
   part2.setpart("start lever", 9924, 419.25);
   cout << "\nFirst part: ";  part1.showpart();
   cout << "\nSecond part: "; part2.showpart();
   }
```

This program defines two objects of class `part`, and gives them values with the `setpart()` member function. Then it displays them with the `showpart()` member function. Here's the output:

```
First part:
Name=handle bolt, number=4473, cost=$217.55
Second part:
Name=start lever, number=9924, cost=$419.25
```

To reduce the size of the program we've dropped the model number from the class members.

In the `setpart()` member function, we use the `strcpy()` string library function to copy the string from the argument `pname` to the class data member `partname`. Thus this function serves the same purpose with string variables that an assignment statement does with simple variables.

Besides those we've seen, there are library functions to add a string to another, compare strings, search for specific characters in strings, and perform many other actions. Descriptions of these functions can be found in the Borland or Turbo C++ documentation. (See Appendix E for other books that contain descriptions of library functions.)

A User-Defined String Type

There are some problems with strings as they are normally used in C++. For one thing, you can't use the perfectly reasonable expression

```
strDest = strSrc;
```

to set one string equal to another. (In some languages, like BASIC, this is perfectly all right.) But if we define our own string type, using a C++ class, we can use just such assignment statements. (Many other string operations can be simplified as well, but we'll have to wait until we've learned about overloaded operators in Chapter 9 to see how this is done.)

The STROBJ program creates a class `String`. Here's the listing:

```
// strobj.cpp
// a string as a class
#include <iostream.h>
#include <string.h>          // for strcpy(), strcat()


const int SZ = 80;           // size of all Strings

class String
   {
   private:
      char str[SZ];
   public:
      String()                                  // constructor, no args
         { str[0] = '\0'; }
      String( char s[] )                        // constructor, one arg
         { strcpy(str, s); }
      void display()                            // display string
         { cout << str; }
      void concat(String s2)                    // add arg string to
        {                                       // this string
        if( strlen(str)+strlen(s2.str) < SZ )
           strcat(str, s2.str);
        else
           cout << "\nString too long";
        }
   };

void main()
   {
   String s1("Merry Christmas!  ");             // uses constructor 2
   String s2 = "Season's Greetings!";           // alternate form of 2
   String s3;                                   // uses constructor 1

   cout << "\ns1="; s1.display();               // display them all
   cout << "\ns2="; s2.display();
   cout << "\ns3="; s3.display();

   s3 = s1;                                     // assignment
   cout << "\ns3="; s3.display();               // display s3
   s3.concat(s2);                               // concatenation
   cout << "\ns3="; s3.display();               // display s3
   }
```

The `String` class contains a single data item: an array of type `char`. It may seem that our newly defined class is just the same as the original definition of a string: an array of type `char`. But, by making it a class, we have achieved some interesting benefits. Since an object can be assigned the value of another object of the same class, we can use statements like

```
s3 = s1;
```

as we do in `main()`, to set one `String` equal to another. We can also define our own member functions to deal with `Strings` (objects of class `String`).

In the STROBJ program all `Strings` have the same length: `SZ` characters (which we set to 80). There are two constructors. The first sets the first character in `str` to the null character, `'\0'`, so the string has a length of 0. This constructor is called with statements like

```
String s3;
```

The second constructor sets the `String` object to a "normal" (that is, not a `String`) string constant. It uses the `strcpy()` library function to copy the string constant into the object's data. It's called with statements like

```
String s1("Merry Christmas! ");
```

An alternative format for calling this constructor, which works with any one-argument constructor, is

```
String s1 = "Merry Christmas! ");
```

Whichever format is used, this constructor effectively converts a string to a `String`—that is, a normal string constant to an object of class `String`. A member function, `display()`, displays the `String`.

Another member function, `concat()`, concatenates (adds) one `String` to another. The original `String` is the object of which `concat()` is a member. To this `String` will be added the `String` passed as an argument. Thus the statement in `main()`,

```
s3.concat(s2);
```

causes `s2` to be added to the existing `s3`. Since `s2` has been initialized to "Season's Greetings!" and `s3` has been assigned the value of `s1`, which was "Merry Christmas!" the resulting value of `s3` is "Merry Christmas! Season's Greetings!"

The `concat()` function uses the `strcat()` C++ library function to do the concatenation. This library function adds the string specified in the second argument to the string specified in the first argument. The output from the program is

```
s1=Merry Christmas!
s2=Season's Greetings!
s3=                                      ←——— nothing here yet
s3=Merry Christmas!                      ←——— set equal to s1
s3=Merry Christmas! Season's Greetings!  ←——— s2 concatenated
```

If the two `Strings` given to the `concat()` function together exceed the maximum `String` length, then the concatenation is not carried out, and a message is sent to the user.

Summary

Arrays contain a number of data items of the same type. This type can be a simple data type, a structure, or a class. The items in an array are called elements. Elements are accessed by number; this number is called an index. Elements can be initialized to specific values when the array is defined. Arrays can have multiple dimensions. A two-dimensional array is an array of arrays. The address of an array can be used as an argument to a function; the array itself is not copied. Arrays can be used as member data in classes. Care must be taken to prevent data from being placed in memory outside an array.

Strings are arrays of type `char`. The last character in a string must be the null character, `'\0'`. String constants take a special form so that they can be written conveniently. A variety of string library functions are used to manipulate strings. An array of strings is an array of arrays of type `char`. Strings are frequently used as class members.

Questions

Answers to questions can be found in Appendix D.

1. An array element is accessed using
   a. a first-in–first-out approach.
   b. the dot operator.
   c. a member name.
   d. an index number.

2. All the elements in an array must be the _________ data type.

3. Write a statement that defines a one-dimensional array called `doubleArray` of type `double` that holds 100 elements.

4. The elements of a 10-element array are numbered from _________ to _________.

5. Write a statement that takes element `j` of array `doubleArray` and writes it to `cout` with the insertion operator.

6. Element `doubleArray[7]` is which element of the array?
   a. The sixth
   b. The seventh
   c. The eighth
   d. Impossible to tell

7. Write a statement that defines an array `coins` of type `int` and initializes it to the values of the penny, nickel, dime, quarter, half-dollar, and dollar.

8. When a multidimensional array is accessed, each array index is
   a. separated by commas.
   b. surrounded by brackets and separated by commas.
   c. separated by commas and surrounded by brackets.
   d. surrounded by brackets.

9. Write an expression that accesses element 4 in subarray 2 in a two-dimensional array called `twoD`.

10. True or false: In C++ there can be an array of four dimensions.

11. For a two-dimensional array of type `float`, called `flarr`, write a statement that declares the array and initializes the first subarray to 52, 27, 83; the second to 94, 73, 49; and the third to 3, 6, 1.

12. An array name, used in the source file, represents the __________ of the array.

13. When an array name is passed to a function, the function
    a. accesses exactly the same array as the calling program.
    b. accesses a copy of the array passed by the program.
    c. refers to the array using the same name as that used by the calling program.
    d. refers to the array using a different name than that used by the calling program.

14. Tell what this statement defines:

```
employee emplist[1000];
```

15. Write an expression that accesses a structure member called `salary` in a structure variable that is the 17th element in an array called `emplist`.

16. In a stack, the data item placed on the stack first is
    a. not given an index number.
    b. given the index number 0.
    c. the first data item to be removed.
    d. the last data item to be removed.

17. Write a statement that defines an array called `manybirds` that holds 50 objects of type `bird`.

18. True or false: The compiler will complain if you try to access array element 14 in a 10-element array.

19. Write a statement that executes the member function `cheep()` in an object of class `bird` that is the 27th element in the array `manybirds`.

20. A string in C++ is an __________ of type __________.

21. Write a statement that defines a string variable called `city` that can hold a string of up to 20 characters (this is slightly tricky).

22. Write a statement that defines a string constant, called `dextrose`, that has the value "C6H12O6-H2O".

23. True or false: The extraction operator (>>) stops reading a string when it encounters a space.

24. You can read input that consists of multiple lines of text using

    a. the normal `cout <<` combination.

    b. the `cin.get()` function with one argument.

    c. the `cin.get()` function with two arguments.

    d. the `cin.get()` function with three arguments.

25. Write a statement that uses a string library function to copy the string `name` to the string `blank`.

26. Write the specification for a class called `dog` that contains two data members: a string called `breed` and an `int` called `age`. (Don't include any member functions.)

Exercises

Answers to the starred exercises can be found in Appendix D.

1.* Write a function called `reversit()` that reverses a string (an array of `char`). Use a `for` loop that swaps the first and last characters, then the second and next-to-last characters, and so on. The string should be passed to `reversit()` as an argument.

Write a program to exercise `reversit()`. The program should get a string from the user, call `reversit()`, and print out the result. Use an input method that allows embedded blanks. Test the program with Napoleon's famous phrase, "Able was I ere I saw Elba."

2.* Create a class called `employee` that contains a name (an array of `char`) and an employee number (type `long`). Include a member function called `getdata()` to get data from the user for insertion into the object, and another function called `putdata()` to display the data. Assume the name has no embedded blanks.

Write a `main()` program to exercise this class. It should create an array of type `employee`, and then invite the user to input data for up to 100 employees. Finally, it should print out the data for all the employees.

3.* Write a program that calculates the average of up to 100 English distances input by the user. Create an array of objects of the `Distance` class, as in the ENGLARAY example in this chapter. To calculate the average, you can borrow the `add_dist()` member function from the ENGLCON example in Chapter 7. You'll also need a member function that divides a `Distance` value by an integer. Here's one possibility:

```
void Distance::div_dist(Distance d2, int divisor)
   {
   float fltfeet = d2.feet + d2.inches/12.0;
   fltfeet /= divisor;
   feet = int(fltfeet);
   inches = (fltfeet-feet) * 12.0;
   }
```

4. Start with a program that allows the user to input a number of integers, and then stores them in an `int` array. Write a function called `maxint()` that goes through the array, element by element, looking for the largest one. The function should take as arguments the address of the array and the number of elements in it, and return the index number of the largest element. The program should call this function and then display the largest element and its index number. (See the SALES program in this chapter.)

5. Start with the `fraction` class from Exercises 11 and 12 in Chapter 7. Write a `main()` program that obtains an arbitrary number of fractions from the user, stores them in an array of type `fraction`, averages them, and displays the result.

6. In the game of contract bridge, each of four players is dealt 13 cards, thus exhausting the entire deck. Modify the CARDARAY program in this chapter so that, after shuffling the deck, it deals four hands of 13 cards each. Each of the four players' hands should then be displayed.

7. One of the weaknesses of C++ for writing business programs is that it does not contain a built-in type for monetary values such as $173,698,001.32. Such a money type should be able to store a number with a fixed decimal point and about 17 digits of precision, which is enough to handle the national debt in dollars and cents. Fortunately, the built-in C++ type `long double` has 19 digits of precision, so we can use it as the basis of a money class, even though it uses a floating decimal. However, we'll need to add the capability to input and output money amounts preceded by a dollar sign and divided by commas into groups of three digits; this makes it much easier to read large numbers. As a first step toward developing such a class, write a function called `mstold()` that takes a *money string*, a string representing a money amount like

   ```
   "$1,234,567,890,123.99"
   ```

   as an argument, and returns the equivalent `long double`.

   You'll need to treat the money string as an array of characters, and go through it character by character, copying only digits (1 to 9) and the decimal point into another string. Ignore everything else, including the dollar sign and the commas. You can then use the `_atold()` library function (note the initial underscore; header file STDLIB.H or MATH.H) to convert the resulting pure string to a `long double`. Assume that money values will never be negative. Write a `main()` program to test `mstold()` by repeatedly obtaining a money string from the user and displaying the corresponding `long double`.

8. Another weakness of C++ is that it does not automatically check array indexes to see if they are in bounds. (This makes array operations faster but less safe.) We can use a class to create a safe array that checks the index of all array accesses.

Write a class called `safearay` that uses an `int` array of fixed size (call it `LIMIT`) as its only data member. There will be two member functions. The first, `putel()`, takes an index number and an `int` value as arguments and inserts the `int` value into the array at the index. The second, `getel()`, takes an index number as an argument and returns the `int` value of the element with that index.

```
safearay sa1;              // define a safearay object
int temp = 12345;          // define an int value
sa1.putel(7, temp);        // insert value of temp into array at index 7
temp = sa1.getel(7);       // obtain value from array at index 7
```

Both functions should check the index argument to make sure it is not less than 0 or greater than `LIMIT-1`. You can use this array without fear of writing over other parts of memory.

Using functions to access array elements doesn't look as eloquent as using the `[]` operator. In Chapter 9 we'll see how to overload this operator to make our `safearay` class work more like built-in arrays.

9. A *queue* is a data storage device much like a stack. The difference is that in a stack the last data item stored is the first one retrieved, while in a queue the first data item stored is the first one retrieved. That is, a stack uses a last-in-first-out (LIFO) approach, while a queue uses first-in-first-out (FIFO). A queue is like a line of customers in a bank: The first one to join the queue is the first one served.

Rewrite the STAKARAY program from this chapter to incorporate a class called `queue` instead of a class called `stack`. Besides a constructor, it should have two functions: one called `put()` to put a data item on the queue, and one called `get()` to get data from the queue. These are equivalent to `push()` and `pop()` in the `stack` class.

Both a queue and a stack use an array to hold the data. However, instead of a single `int` variable called `top`, as the stack has, you'll need two variables for a queue: one called `head`, to point to the head of the queue, and one called `tail` to point to the tail. Items are placed on the queue at the tail (like the last customer getting in line at the bank) and removed from the queue at the head. The tail will follow the head along the array as items are added and removed from the queue. This results in an added complexity: When either the tail or the head gets to the end of the array, it must "wrap around" to the beginning. Thus you'll need a statement like

```
if(tail == MAX-1)
   tail = -1;
```

to wrap the tail, and a similar one for the head. The array used in the queue is sometimes called a circular buffer, because the head and tail circle around it, with the data between them.

10. A matrix is a two-dimensional array. Create a class `matrix` that provides the same safety feature as the array class in Exercise 7; that is, it checks to be sure no array index is out of bounds. Make the member data in the `matrix` class a 10-by-10 array. A constructor should allow the programmer to specify the actual dimensions of the matrix (provided they're less than 10 by 10). The member functions that access data in the matrix will now need two index numbers: one for each dimension of the array. Here's what a fragment of a `main()` program that operates on such a class might look like:

```
matrix m1(3, 4);             // define a matrix object
int temp = 12345;            // define an int value
m1.putel(7, 4, temp);        // insert value of temp into matrix at 7,4
temp = m1.getel(7, 4);       // obtain value from matrix at 7,4
```

11. Refer back to the discussion of money strings in Exercise 6. Write a function called `ldtoms()` to convert a number represented as type `long double` to the same value represented as a money string. First you should check that the value of the original long double is not too large. We suggest that you don't try to convert any number greater than 9,999,999,999,999,990.00. Then convert the `long double` to a pure string (no dollar sign or commas) stored in memory, using an `ostrstream` object, as discussed earlier in this chapter. The resulting formatted string can go in a buffer called `ustring`.

You'll then need to start another string with a dollar sign; copy one digit from `ustring` at a time, starting from the left, and inserting a comma into the new string every three digits. Also, you'll need to suppress leading zeros. You want to display $3,124.95, for example, not $0,000,000,000,003,124.95. Don't forget to terminate the string with a `'\0'` character.

Write a `main()` program to exercise this function by having the user repeatedly input numbers in type `long double` format, and printing out the result as a money string.

12. Create a class called `bMoney`. It should store money amounts as a `long double`. Use the function `mstold()` to convert a money string entered as input into a `long double`, and the function `ldtoms()` to convert the `long double` to a money string for display. (See Exercises 6 and 10.) You can call the input and output member functions `getmoney()` and `putmoney()`. Write another member function that adds two `bMoney` amounts; you can call it `madd()`. Adding `bMoney` objects is easy: Just add the `long double` member data amounts in two `bMoney` objects. Write a `main()` program that repeatedly requests the user to enter two money strings, and then displays the sum as a money string. Here's how the class specifier might look:

```
class bMoney
   {
   private:
      long double money;
   public:
      bMoney();
      bMoney(char s[]);
      void madd(bMoney m1, bMoney m2);
      void getmoney();
      void putmoney();
   };
```

9

Operator Overloading

THE `operator` KEYWORD

OVERLOADING UNARY OPERATORS

OVERLOADING BINARY OPERATORS

CONSTRUCTORS AS CONVERSION ROUTINES

CONVERTING BETWEEN BASIC AND USER-DEFINED TYPES

THOUGHTS ON OVERLOADING

9

Operator overloading is one of the most exciting features of object-oriented programming. It can transform complex, obscure program listings into intuitively obvious ones. For example, statements like

```
d3.addobjects(d1, d2);
```

or the similar but equally obscure

```
d3 = d1.addobjects(d2);
```

can be changed to the much more readable

```
d3 = d1 + d2;
```

The rather forbidding term *operator overloading* refers to giving the normal C++ operators, such as `+`, `*`, `<=`, and `+=`, additional meanings when they are applied to user-defined data types. Normally

```
a = b + c;
```

works only with basic types like `int` and `float`, and attempting to apply it when `a`, `b`, and `c` are objects of a user-defined class will cause complaints from the compiler. However, using overloading, you can make this statement legal even when `a`, `b`, and `c` are user-defined types.

In effect, operator overloading gives you the opportunity to redefine the C++ language. If you find yourself limited by the way the C++ operators work, you can change them to do whatever you want. By using classes to create new kinds of variables, and operator overloading to create new definitions for operators, you can extend C++ to be, in many ways, a new language of your own design.

Another kind of operation, *data type conversion*, is closely connected with operator overloading. C++ handles the conversion of simple types, like `int` and `float`, automatically; but conversions involving user-defined types require some work on the programmer's part. We'll look at data conversions in the second part of this chapter.

Overloaded operators are not all beer and skittles. We'll discuss some of the dangers of their use at the end of the chapter.

Overloading Unary Operators

Let's start off by overloading a *unary operator*. As you may recall from Chapter 2, unary operators act on only one operand. (An operand is simply a variable acted on by an operator.) Examples of unary operators are the increment and decrement operators `++` and `--`, and the unary minus, as in `-33`.

In the COUNTER example in Chapter 7 we created a class `Counter` to keep track of a count. Objects of that class were incremented by calling a member function.

```
c1.inc_count();
```

That did the job, but the listing would have been more readable if we could have used the increment operator `++` instead.

```
++c1;
```

All dyed-in-the-wool C++ (and C) programmers would guess immediately that this expression increments `c1`.

Let's rewrite COUNTER to make this possible. Here's the listing for COUNTPP1:

```
// countpp1.cpp
// increment counter variable with ++ operator
#include <iostream.h>

class Counter
   {
   private:
      unsigned int count;                        // count
   public:
      Counter()           { count = 0; }         // constructor
      int get_count()     { return count; }      // return count
      void operator ++ ()   { ++count; }         // increment count
   };

void main()
   {
   Counter c1, c2;                          // define and initialize

   cout << "\nc1=" << c1.get_count();       // display
   cout << "\nc2=" << c2.get_count();

   ++c1;                                    // increment c1
   ++c2;                                    // increment c2
   ++c2;                                    // increment c2

   cout << "\nc1=" << c1.get_count();       // display again
   cout << "\nc2=" << c2.get_count();
   }
```

In this program we create two objects of class `Counter`: `c1` and `c2`. The counts in the objects are displayed; they are initially 0. Then, using the overloaded `++` operator, we increment `c1` once and `c2` twice, and display the resulting values. Here's the program's output:

```
c1=0   <------- counts are initially 0
c2=0
c1=1   <------- incremented once
c2=2   <------- incremented twice
```

The statements responsible for these operations are

```
++c1;
++c2;
++c2;
```

The `++` operator is applied once to `c1` and twice to `c2`. We use prefix notation in this example; we'll explore postfix later.

The `operator` Keyword

How do we teach a normal C++ operator to act on a user-defined operand? The keyword `operator` is used to overload the `++` operator in this declarator:

```
void operator ++ ()
```

The return type (`void` in this case) comes first, followed by the keyword `operator`, followed by the operator itself (`++`), and finally the argument list enclosed in parentheses (which are empty here). This declarator syntax tells the compiler to call this member function whenever the `++` operator is encountered, provided the operand (the variable operated on by the `++`) is of type `Counter`.

We saw in Chapter 6 that the only way the compiler can distinguish between overloaded functions is by looking at the data types and number of their arguments. In the same way, the only way it can distinguish between overloaded operators is by looking at the data type of their operands. If the operand is a basic type like an `int`, as in

```
++intvar;
```

then the compiler will use its built-in routine to increment an `int`. But if the operand is a `Counter` variable, then the compiler will know to use our user-written `operator++()` instead.

Operator Arguments

In `main()` the `++` operator is applied to a specific object, as in the expression `++c1`. Yet `operator++()` takes no arguments. What does this operator increment? It increments the `count` data in the object of which it is a member function. Since member functions can always access the particular object for which they've been called, this operator requires no arguments. This is shown in Figure 9-1.

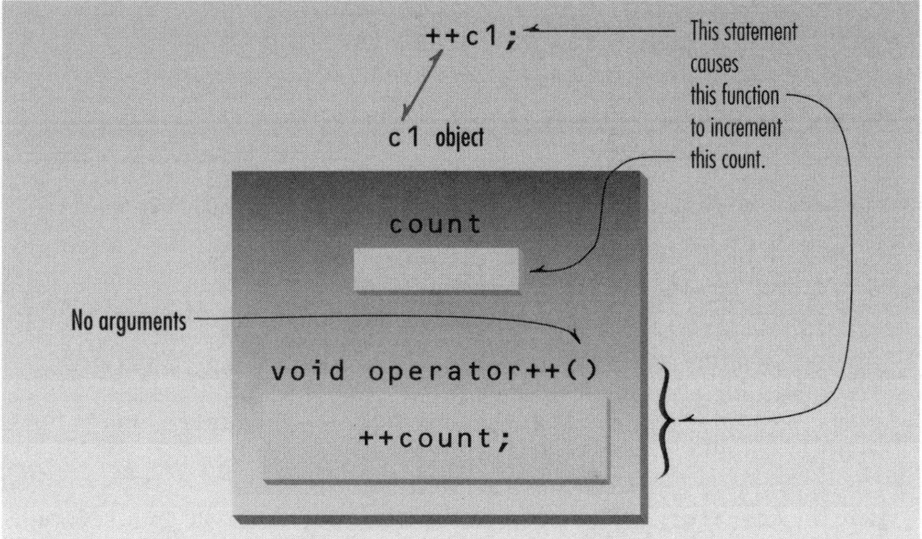

Figure 9-1 Overloaded Unary Operator: No Arguments

Operator Return Values

The `operator++()` function in the COUNTPP1 program has a subtle defect. You will discover it if you use a statement like this in `main()`:

```
c1 = ++c2;
```

The compiler will complain. Why? Because we have defined the `++` operator to have a return type of `void` in the `operator++()` function, while in the assignment statement it is being asked to return a variable of type `Counter`. That is, the compiler is being asked to return whatever value `c2` has after being operated on by the `++` operator, and assign this value to `c1`. So as defined in COUNTPP1, we can't use `++` to increment `Counter` objects in assignments; it must always stand alone with its operand. (Of course the normal `++` operator, applied to basic data types like `int`, would not have this problem.)

To make it possible to use our homemade `operator++()` in expressions, we must provide a way for it to return a value. The next program, COUNTPP2, does just that.

```
// countpp2.cpp
// increment counter variable with ++ operator, return value
#include <iostream.h>

class Counter
   {
   private:
      unsigned int count;                         // count
   public:
      Counter()          { count = 0; }           // constructor
      int get_count()    { return count; }        // return count
      Counter operator ++ ()                      // increment count
        {
        ++count;              // increment count
        Counter temp;         // make a temporary Counter
        temp.count = count;   // give it same value as this obj
        return temp;          // return the copy
        }
   };

void main()
   {
   Counter c1, c2;                                // c1=0, c2=0

   cout << "\nc1=" << c1.get_count();             // display
   cout << "\nc2=" << c2.get_count();

   ++c1;                                          // c1=1
   c2 = ++c1;                                     // c1=2, c2=2

   cout << "\nc1=" << c1.get_count();             // display again
   cout << "\nc2=" << c2.get_count();   // c2=3
   }
```

Here the `operator++()` function creates a new object of type `Counter`, called `temp`, to use as a return value. It increments the `count` data in its own object as before, then creates the new `temp` object and assigns `count` in the new object the same value as in its own object. Finally it returns the `temp` object. This has the desired effect. Expressions like

```
++c1
```

now return a value, so they can be used in other expressions, such as

```
c2 = ++c1;
```

as shown in `main()`, where the value returned from `c1++` is assigned to `c2`. The output from this program is

```
c1=0
c2=0
c1=2
c2=2
```

Nameless Temporary Objects

In COUNTPP2 we created a temporary object of type `Counter`, named `temp`, whose sole purpose was to provide a return value for the `++` operator. This required three statements.

```
Counter temp;           // make a temporary Counter object
temp.count = count;     // give it same value as this object
return temp;            // return it
```

There are more convenient ways to return objects from functions and overloaded operators. Let's examine another approach, as shown in the program COUNTPP3:

```
// countpp3.cpp
// increment counter variable with ++ operator
// uses unnamed temporary object
#include <iostream.h>

class Counter
   {
   private:
      unsigned int count;                        // count
   public:
      Counter()           { count = 0; }         // constructor  no args
      Counter(int c)      { count = c; }         // constructor, one arg
      int get_count()     { return count; }      // return count
      Counter operator ++ ()                     // increment count
        {
        ++count;                     // increment count, return
        return Counter(count);       // an unnamed temporary object
        }                            // initialized to this count
   };
void main()
   {
   Counter c1, c2;                               // c1=0, c2=0

   cout << "\nc1=" << c1.get_count();            // display
   cout << "\nc2=" << c2.get_count();
```

(continued on next page)

(continued from previous page)

```
   ++c1;                                        // c1=1
   c2 = ++c1;                                   // c1=2, c2=2

   cout << "\nc1=" << c1.get_count();      // display again
   cout << "\nc2=" << c2++.get_count();    // c2=3
   }
```

In this program a single statement,

```
return Counter(count);
```

does what all three statements did in COUNTPP2. This statement creates an object of type `Counter`. This object has no name; it won't be around long enough to need one. This unnamed object is initialized to the value provided by the argument `count`.

But wait: Doesn't this require a constructor that takes one argument? It does, and to make this statement work we sneakily inserted just such a constructor into the member function list in COUNTPP3.

```
Counter(int c)  { count = c; }  // constructor, one arg
```

Once the unnamed object is initialized to the value of `count`, it can then be returned. The output of this program is the same as that of COUNTPP2.

The approaches in both COUNTPP2 and COUNTPP3 involve making a copy of the original object (the object of which the function is a member), and returning the copy. (Another approach, as we'll see in Chapter 11, is to return the value of the original object using the `this` pointer.)

Postfix Notation

So far we've shown the increment operator used only in its prefix form.

```
++c1
```

What about postfix, where the variable is incremented after its value is used in the expression?

```
c1++
```

Versions of Borland C++ (and Turbo C++ later than 3.0) can handle postfix notation, with a slight change of format. We define two overloaded ++ operators, as shown in the POSTFIX program:

```
// postfix.cpp
// overloaded ++ operator in both prefix and postfix
#include <iostream.h>

class Counter
   {
   private:
      unsigned int count;                       // count
   public:
      Counter()         { count = 0; }      // constructor  no args
      Counter(int c)    { count = c; }      // constructor, one arg
      int get_count()   { return count; }  // return count

      Counter operator ++ ()          // increment count (prefix)
        {                             // increment count, then return
```

```
         return Counter(++count); // an unnamed temporary object
         }                        // initialized to this count

      Counter operator ++ (int)   // increment count (postfix)
         {                        // return an unnamed temporary
         return Counter(count++); // object initialized to this
         }                        // count, then increment count
   };

void main()
   {
   Counter c1, c2;                          // c1=0, c2=0

   cout << "\nc1=" << c1.get_count();       // display
   cout << "\nc2=" << c2.get_count();

   ++c1;                                    // c1=1
   c2 = ++c1;                               // c1=2, c2=2 (prefix)

   cout << "\nc1=" << c1.get_count();       // display
   cout << "\nc2=" << c2.get_count();

   c2 = c1++;                               // c1=3, c2=2 (postfix)

   cout << "\nc1=" << c1.get_count();       // display again
   cout << "\nc2=" << c2.get_count();
   }
```

Now there are two different declarators for overloading the `++` operator. The one we've seen before, for prefix notation, is

```
Counter operator ++ ()
```

The new one, for postfix notation, is

```
Counter operator ++ (int)
```

The only difference is the `int` in the parentheses. This `int` isn't really an argument, and it doesn't mean `int`. It's simply a signal to the compiler to create the postfix version of the operator. The designers of C++ are fond of recycling existing operators and keywords to play multiple roles, and `int` is the one they chose to indicate postfix. Here's the output from the program:

```
c1=0
c2=0
c1=2
c2=2
c1=3
c2=2
```

We saw the first four of these output lines in COUNTPP2 and COUNTPP3. But in the last two lines we see the results of the statement

```
c2=c1++;
```

Here `c1` is incremented to 3, but `c2` is assigned the value of `c1` before it is incremented, so `c2` retains the value 2.

Of course you can use this same approach with the decrement operator, (`--`).

Overloading Binary Operators

Binary operators can be overloaded just as easily as unary operators. We'll look at examples that overload arithmetic operators, comparison operators, and arithmetic assignment operators.

Arithmetic Operators

In the ENGLCON program in Chapter 7 we showed how two English **Distance** objects could be added using a member function **add_dist()**:

```
dist3.add_dist(dist1, dist2);
```

By overloading the **+** operator we can reduce this dense-looking expression to

```
dist3 = dist1 + dist2;
```

Here's the listing for ENGLPLUS, which does just this:

```
// englplus.cpp
// overloaded '+' operator adds two Distances
#include <iostream.h>

class Distance                          // English Distance class
   {
   private:
      int feet;
      float inches;
   public:
      Distance()                        // constructor (no args)
         { feet = 0; inches = 0.0; }
      Distance(int ft, float in)  // constructor (two args)
         { feet = ft; inches = in; }

      void getdist()                    // get length from user
         {
         cout << "\nEnter feet: ";  cin >> feet;
         cout << "Enter inches: ";  cin >> inches;
         }

      void showdist()                   // display distance
         { cout << feet << "\'-" << inches << '\"'; }

      Distance operator + ( Distance );  // add two distances
   };
                                        // add this distance to d2
Distance Distance::operator + (Distance d2)   // return the sum
   {
   int f = feet + d2.feet;              // add the feet
   float i = inches + d2.inches;  // add the inches
   if(i >= 12.0)                        // if total exceeds 12.0,
      {                                 // then decrease inches
      i -= 12.0;                        // by 12.0 and
      f++;                              // increase feet by 1
      }                                 // return a temporary Distance
```

```
   return Distance(f,i);          // initialized to sum
   }

void main()
   {
   Distance dist1, dist3, dist4;   // define distances
   dist1.getdist();                // get dist1 from user

   Distance dist2(11, 6.25);       // define, initialize dist2

   dist3 = dist1 + dist2;          // single '+' operator

   dist4 = dist1 + dist2 + dist3;  // multiple '+' operators

                                   // display all lengths
   cout << "\ndist1 = ";  dist1.showdist();
   cout << "\ndist2 = ";  dist2.showdist();
   cout << "\ndist3 = ";  dist3.showdist();
   cout << "\ndist4 = ";  dist4.showdist();
   }
```

To show that the result of an addition can be used in another addition as well as in an assignment, another addition is performed in `main()`. We add `dist1`, `dist2`, and `dist3` to obtain `dist4` (which should be double the value of `dist3`), in the statement

```
dist4 = dist1 + dist2 + dist3;
```

Here's the output from the program:

```
Enter feet: 10
Enter inches: 6.5

dist1 = 10'-6.5"     ←——— from user
dist2 = 11'-6.25"    ←——— initialized in program
dist3 = 22'-0.75"    ←——— dist1+dist2
dist4 = 44'-1.5"     ←——— dist1+dist2+dist3
```

In class `Distance` the declaration for the `operator+()` function looks like this:

```
Distance operator + ( Distance );
```

This function has a return type of `Distance`, and takes one argument of type `Distance`.

In expressions like

```
dist3 = dist1 + dist2;
```

it's important to understand how the return value and arguments of the operator relate to the objects. When the compiler sees this expression it looks at the argument types, and finding only type `Distance`, it realizes it must use the `Distance` member function `operator+()`. But what does this function use as its argument—`dist1` or `dist2`? And doesn't it need two arguments, since there are two numbers to be added?

Here's the key: The argument on the *left side* of the operator (`dist1` in this case) is the object of which the operator is a member function. The object on the *right* side of the operator (`dist2`) must be furnished as an argument to the operator.

The operator returns a value, which can be assigned or used in other ways; in this case it is assigned to `dist3`. Figure 9-2 shows how this looks.

In the `operator+()` function, the left operand is accessed directly—since this is the object of which the function is a member—using `feet` and `inches`. The right operand is accessed as function's argument, as `d2.feet` and `d2.inches`.

We can generalize and say that an overloaded operator always requires one less argument than its number of operands, since one operand is the object of which the operator is a member function. That's why unary operators require no arguments. (This rule does not apply to `friend` functions and operators, a C++ feature we'll discuss in Chapter 13.)

To calculate the return value of `operator+()` in ENGLPLUS, we first add the feet and inches from the two operands (adjusting for a carry if necessary). The resulting values, `f` and `i`, are then used to initialize a nameless `Distance` object, which is returned in the statement

```
return Distance(f, i);
```

This is similar to the construction used in COUNTPP3, except that the constructor takes two arguments instead of one. The statement

```
dist3 = dist1 + dist2;
```

in `main()` then assigns the value of the nameless `Distance` object to `dist3`. Compare this intuitively obvious statement with the use of a function call to perform the same task, as in the ENGLCON example in Chapter 7.

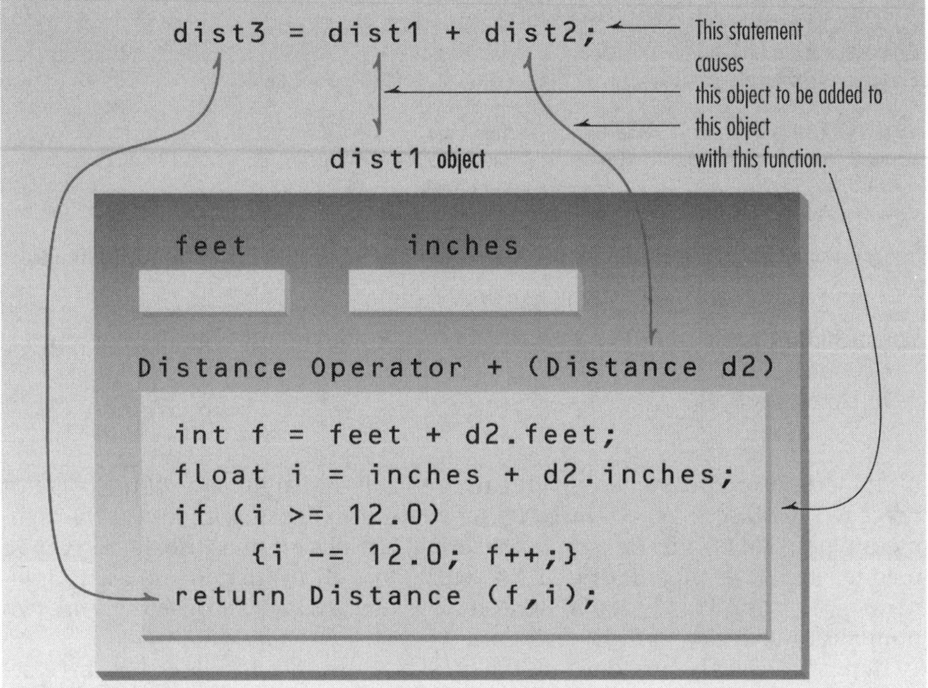

Figure 9-2 Overloaded Binary Operator: One Argument

Similar functions could be created to overload other operators in the `Distance` class, so you could subtract, multiply, and divide objects of this class in natural-looking ways.

Adding Polar Coordinates

Here's another example of operator overloading. Points on a plane are commonly specified with a pair of rectangular coordinates (x, y). Thus a point (4, 3) is located where x is 4 and y is 3, as shown in Figure 9-3.

There's another way to describe a point on the plane: using polar coordinates of the form (radius, angle). In this system a line called the `radius`, drawn from the origin to the point, and the angle this line makes with the positive x axis specify the point, as shown in Figure 9-4.

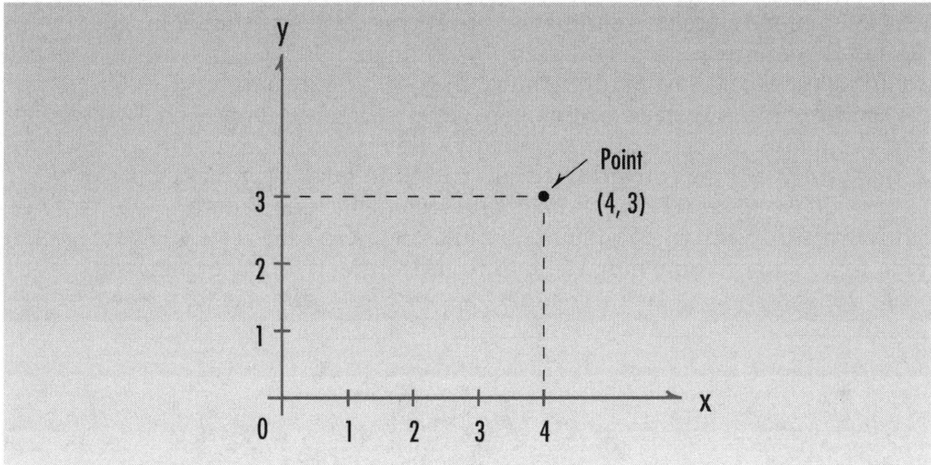

Figure 9-3 A Point in Rectangular Coordinates

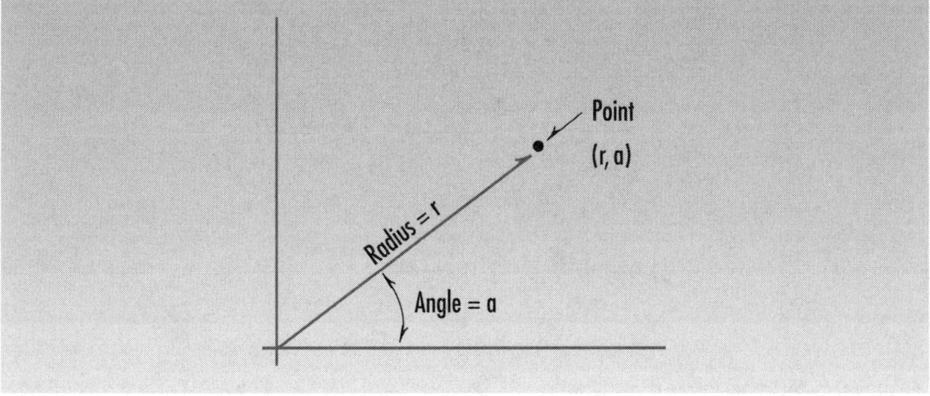

Figure 9-4 A Point in Polar Coordinates

Polar coordinates are handy for describing certain curves, such as spirals. They are commonly found on scientific calculators; pushing buttons performs conversions between polar and rectangular coordinates.

Our example program will show a class, `Polar`, that models polar coordinates. We'll use the overloaded `+` operator to add two objects of type `Polar`.

What does it mean to add two points on the two-dimensional plane? If the points are considered to be the end points of directed lines, they can show a distance and direction traveled, say by an airplane. If you fly north from Toledo 100 miles, and then fly east 50 miles, how far from Toledo are you, and in which direction? Adding two variables of type `Polar` solves this kind of problem, as shown in Figure 9-5.

Adding points expressed in polar coordinates requires several steps. It turns out it's easier to add points when they are expressed in rectangular coordinates. This is done by adding the x and y coordinates separately. Say you have two points expressed in rectangular coordinates—(4, 1) and (2, 3)—as shown in Figure 9-6a. To add the points, we first add their x coordinates: 4+2=6. Then we add their y coordinates: 1+3=4. The resulting point is (6, 4), as shown in Figure 9-6b.

Adding points in polar coordinates requires a three-step approach. First we convert the points to rectangular coordinates, then we add the points as described above, and finally we convert the result back into polar coordinates.

How do we convert between polar and rectangular coordinates? These conversions involve several trigonometric formulas. It doesn't matter if you've forgotten your trig; you need only plug values into the formulas to make them work.

To convert from polar to rectangular, use these formulas (expressed in C++ form):

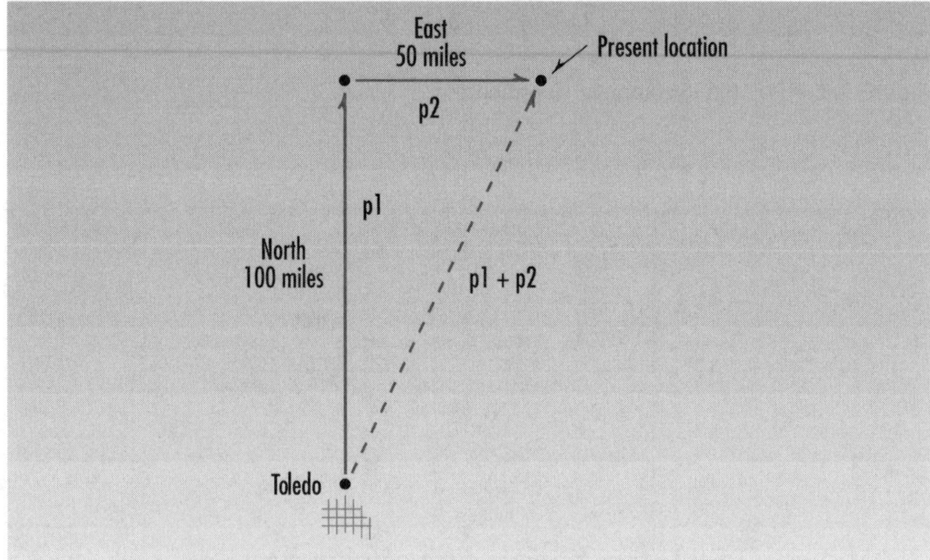

Figure 9-5 Adding Polar Coordinates

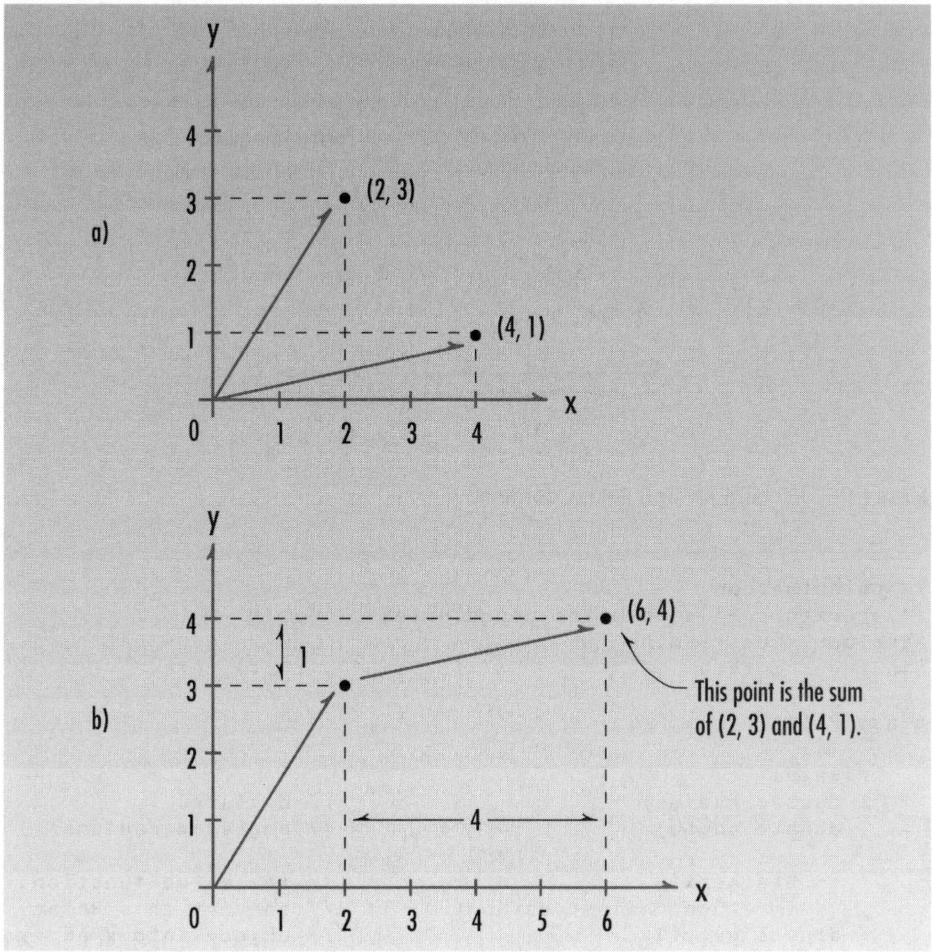

Figure 9-6 Adding Points in Rectangular Coordinates

```
x = radius * cos(angle);
y = radius * sin(angle);
```

The `cos()` and `sin()` (cosine and sine) functions are available as C++ library functions.

To convert back from rectangular to polar, use the formulas

```
angle = atan(y/x);
radius = sqrt(x*x + y*y);
```

The functions `atan()` (for arctangent) and `sqrt()` (for square root) are also library functions. The Pythagorean theorem is used to find the radius, and the arctangent of the x and y sides of the triangle is the angle, as shown in Figure 9-7.

The POLAPLUS program makes use of this three-step approach to add two points in polar coordinates. Here's the listing:

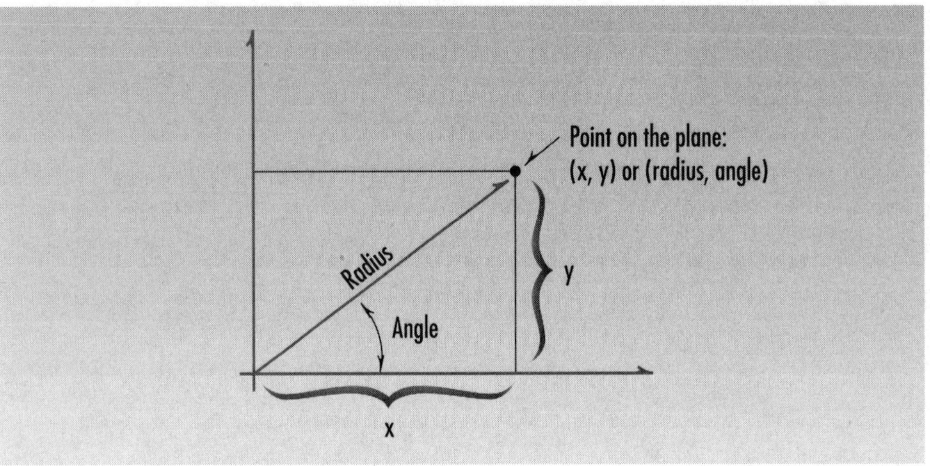

Figure 9-7 Rectangular and Polar Coordinates

```
// polaplus.cpp
// operator '+' with polar coordinates
#include <iostream.h>
#include <math.h>              // for sin(), cos(), etc.

class Polar
   {
   private:
      double radius;                        // distance
      double angle;                         // angle in radians

      double getx()                         // these two functions
         { return radius*cos(angle); }      // convert this Polar
      double gety()                         // object into x and y
         { return radius*sin(angle); }      // rectangular coords
   public:
      Polar()                               // constructor, no args
         { radius=0.0; angle=0.0; }
      Polar(float r, float a)               // constructor, two args
         { radius=r; angle=a; }
      void display()                        // display
         { cout << "("  << radius
                << ", " << angle << ")"; }
      Polar operator + (Polar p2)           // add two Polars
         {
         double x = getx() + p2.getx();     // add x and y coords
         double y = gety() + p2.gety();     // for this and p2
         double r = sqrt(x*x + y*y);        // convert new x and y
         double a = atan(y/x);              // to Polar
         return Polar(r, a);                // return temp Polar
         }
   };

void main()
```

```
{
Polar p1(10.0, 0.0);                // line to the right
Polar p2(10.0, 1.570796325);        // line straight up
Polar p3;                           // uninitialized Polar

p3 = p1 + p2;                       // add two Polars

cout << "\np1="; p1.display();      // display all Polars
cout << "\np2="; p2.display();
cout << "\np3="; p3.display();
}
```

The `Polar` class contains two data items: `radius` and `angle`. Since we'll be using C++ math library functions to operate on this data, and since these functions mostly use type `double`, we'll define `radius` and `angle` to be of this type. Angles are measured in radians. (There are 2*pi, or about 6.28, radians in a circle, so a radian is about 57 degrees.)

Constructors in `Polar` initialize a variable to 0 or initialize it to specified values. Another member function displays these values.

Two other member functions, `getx()` and `gety()`, convert polar coordinates to rectangular coordinates. These functions are needed because, as we noted, adding two points in polar coordinates involves converting to rectangular coordinates before adding. The `getx()` and `gety()` functions are made private because they don't need to be accessed from outside the class; they're only used internally.

The `operator+()` function adds two `Polar` variables. It does this by converting the `Polar` operands to rectangular coordinates, and adding the x coordinates to obtain `x` and the y coordinates to obtain `y`. The `x` and `y` variables are then used to find the `radius` and `angle` of the sum, which is returned.

In the `main()` part of POLAPLUS, one `Polar` variable is initialized to (10.0, 0.0). This represents a point located 10 units horizontally along the x axis. Another variable is initialized to (10.0, 1.570796325). Since these angles are measured in radians, this represents a point 10 units straight up on the y axis. (1.570796325 radians is 90 degrees.)

These two variables are then added, in the statement

```
p3 = p1 + p2;
```

The result should be a point at 45 degrees (half of 90), as shown in Figure 9-8.

Here's the actual output:

```
p1=(10, 0)                  ←——— point on x axis (0 degrees)
p2=(10, 1.570796325)        ←——— point on y axis (90 degrees)
p3=(14.142136, 0.785398)    ←——— point at 45 degree angle
```

The point (14.142136, 0.785398) is indeed at 45 degrees.

This example has shown how to overload only one operator: `+`. We could also overload the other arithmetic operators for the `Polar` type, so such coordinates could be subtracted, multiplied, divided, and so on.

Concatenating Strings

In C++ the `+` operator cannot normally be used to concatenate strings, as it can in some languages such as BASIC. That is, you can't say

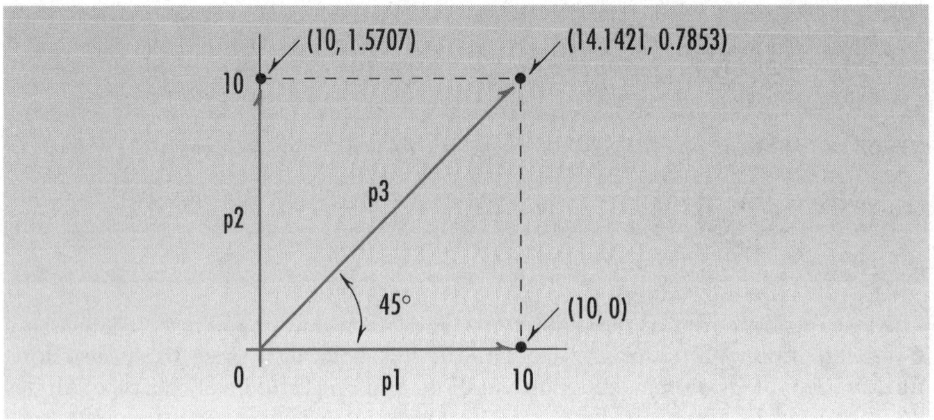

Figure 9-8 Representation of POLAPLUS Output

```
str3 = str1 + str2;
```

where `str1`, `str2`, and `str3` are string variables (arrays of type `char`), as in "cat" plus "bird" equals "catbird." However, if we use our own `String` class, as shown in the STROBJ program in Chapter 7, then we can overload the `+` operator to do such concatenation. This is another example of redefining the C++ language. Here's the listing for STRPLUS:

```
// strplus.cpp
// overloaded '+' operator concatenates strings
#include <iostream.h>
#include <string.h>        // for strcpy(), strcat()

const int SZ = 80;         // size of all String objects

class String               // user-defined string type
   {
   private:
      char str[SZ];                    // holds a string
   public:
      String()                         // constructor, no args
         { strcpy(str, ""); }
      String( char s[] )               // constructor, one arg
         { strcpy(str, s); }
      void display()                   // display the String
         { cout << str; }
      String operator + (String ss)   // add a String to another
         {
         if( strlen(str) + strlen(ss.str) < SZ )
            {
            String temp;                  // make a temporary String
            strcpy(temp.str, str);        // copy this string to temp
            strcat(temp.str, ss.str);     // add the argument string
            return temp;                  // return temp String
            }
         else
            cout << "\nString overflow";
```

```
      }
   };

void main()
   {
   String s1 = "\nMerry Christmas!  ";     // uses constructor 2
   String s2 = "Happy new year!";          // uses constructor 2
   String s3;                              // uses constructor 1

   s1.display();          // display strings
   s2.display();
   s3.display();

   s3 = s1 + s2;          // add s2 to s1, assign to s3

   s3.display();          // display s3
   }
```

The program first displays three strings separately. (The third is empty at this point, so nothing is printed when it displays itself.) Then the first two strings are concatenated and placed in the third, and the third string is displayed again. Here's the output:

```
Merry Christmas!  Happy new year!      ←——— s1, s2, and s3 (empty)
Merry Christmas!  Happy new year!      ←——— s3 after concatenation
```

By now the basics of overloading the + operator should be somewhat familiar. The declarator

```
String operator + (String ss)
```

shows that the + operator takes one argument of type `String` and returns an object of the same type. The concatenation process in `operator+()` involves creating a temporary object of type `String`, copying the string from our own `String` object into it, concatenating the argument string using the library function `strcat()`, and returning the resulting temporary string. Note that we can't use the

```
return String(string);
```

approach, where a nameless temporary `String` is created, because we need access to the temporary `String` not only to initialize it, but to concatenate the argument string to it.

We must be careful that we don't overflow the fixed-length strings used in the `String` class. To prevent such accidents in the `operator+()` function, we check that the combined length of the two strings to be concatenated will not exceed the maximum string length. If they do, we print an error message instead of carrying out the concatenation operation. (We could handle errors in other ways, like returning a 0 if an error occurred.)

Multiple Overloading

We've seen three different uses of the + operator: to add English distances, to add polar coordinates, and to concatenate strings. You could put all these classes together in the same program, and C++ would still know how to interpret the + operator: It selects the correct function to carry out the "addition" based on the type of operand.

Comparison Operators

Let's see how to overload a different kind of C++ operator: comparison operators.

Comparing Distances

In our first example we'll overload the *less than* operator `<` in the English `Distance` class, so that we can compare two distances. Here's the listing for ENGLESS:

```
// engless.cpp
// overloaded '<' operator compares two Distances
#include <iostream.h>

enum boolean { false, true };

class Distance                          // English Distance class
   {
   private:
      int feet;
      float inches;
   public:
      Distance()                        // constructor (no args)
         { feet = 0; inches = 0.0; }
      Distance(int ft, float in)        // constructor (two args)
         { feet = ft; inches = in; }
      void getdist()                    // get length from user
         {
         cout << "\nEnter feet: ";  cin >> feet;
         cout << "Enter inches: ";  cin >> inches;
         }
      void showdist()                   // display distance
         { cout << feet << "\'-" << inches << '\"'; }
      boolean operator < (Distance);    // compare distances
   };
                                        // compare this distance with d2
boolean Distance::operator < (Distance d2)   // return true or false
   {
   float bf1 = feet + inches/12;
   float bf2 = d2.feet + d2.inches/12;
   return (bf1 < bf2) ? true : false;
   }

void main()
   {
   Distance dist1;                      // define Distance dist1
   dist1.getdist();                     // get dist1 from user

   Distance dist2(6, 2.5);              // define and initialize dist2
                                        // display distances
   cout << "\ndist1 = ";  dist1.showdist();
   cout << "\ndist2 = ";  dist2.showdist();

   if( dist1 < dist2 )                  // overloaded '<' operator
      cout << "\ndist1 is less than dist2";
   else
      cout << "\ndist1 is greater than dist2";
   }
```

This program compares a distance entered by the user with a distance, 6'-2.5", initialized by the program. Depending on the result, it then prints one of two possible sentences. Here's some typical output:

```
Enter feet: 5
Enter inches: 11.5
dist1 = 5'-11.5"
dist2 = 6'-2.5"
dist1 is less than dist2
```

The approach used in the `operator<()` function in ENGLESS is similar to overloading the + operator in the ENGLPLUS program, except that here the `operator<()` function has a return type of `boolean` (defined in the `enum` statement at the beginning of the program). The return value is `false` or `true`, depending on the comparison of the two distances. The comparison is made by converting both distances to floating-point feet, and comparing them using the normal < operator. Remember that the statement

```
return (bf1 < bf2) ? true : false;
```

is the same as

```
if(bf1 < bf2)
   return true;
else
   return false;
```

Comparing Strings

Here's another example of overloading a comparison operator, this time the *equal* (==) operator. We'll use it to compare two strings, returning `true` if the strings are the same and `false` if they're different. Here's the listing for STREQUAL:

```
// strequal.cpp
// overloaded '==' operator compares strings
#include <iostream.h>
#include <string.h>          // for strcmp()

const int SZ = 80;           // size of all String objects
enum boolean { false, true };
class String                 // user-defined string type
   {
   private:
      char str[SZ];                        // holds a string
   public:
      String()                             // constructor, no args
         { strcpy(str, ""); }
      String( char s[] )                   // constructor, one arg
         { strcpy(str, s); }
      void display()                       // display a String
         { cout << str; }
      void getstr()                        // read a string
         { cin.get(str, SZ); }
      boolean operator == (String ss)  // check for equality
         {
         return ( strcmp(str, ss.str)==0 ) ? true : false;
```

(continued on next page)

(continued from previous page)

```
         }
   };

void main()
   {
   String s1 = "yes";
   String s2 = "no";
   String s3;

   cout << "\nEnter 'yes' or 'no': ";
   s3.getstr();                          // get String from user

   if(s3==s1)                            // compare with "yes"
      cout << "You typed yes\n";
   else if(s3==s2)                       // compare with "no"
      cout << "You typed no\n";
   else
      cout << "You didn't follow instructions\n";
   }
```

The `main()` part of this program uses the `==` operator twice, once to see if a string input by the user is "yes" and once to see if it's "no." Here's the output when the user types "yes":

```
Enter 'yes' or 'no': yes
You typed yes
```

The `operator==()` function uses the library function `strcmp()` to compare the two strings. This function returns 0 if the strings are equal, a negative number if the first is less than the second, and a positive number if the first is greater than the second. Here *less than* and *greater than* are used in their lexicographical sense to indicate whether the first string appears before or after the second in an alphabetized listing.

Other comparison operators, such as `<` and `>`, could also be used to compare the lexicographical value of strings. Or, alternatively, these comparison operators could be redefined to compare string lengths. Since you're the one defining how the operators are used, you can use any definition that seems appropriate to your situation.

Arithmetic Assignment Operators

Let's finish up our exploration of overloaded binary operators with an arithmetic assignment operator: the `+=` operator. Recall that this operator combines assignment and addition into one step. We'll use this operator to add one English distance to a second, leaving the result in the first. This is similar to the ENGLPLUS example shown earlier, but there is a subtle difference. Here's the listing for ENGLPLEQ:

```
// englpleq.cpp
// overloaded '+=' assignment operator
#include <iostream.h>

class Distance                         // English Distance class
```

```
   {
   private:
      int feet;
      float inches;
   public:
      Distance()                       // constructor (no args)
         { feet = 0; inches = 0.0; }
      Distance(int ft, float in)       // constructor (two args)
         { feet = ft; inches = in; }
      void getdist()                   // get length from user
         {
         cout << "\nEnter feet: ";  cin >> feet;
         cout << "Enter inches: ";  cin >> inches;
         }
      void showdist()                  // display distance
         { cout << feet << "\'-" << inches << '\"'; }
      void operator += ( Distance );
   };
                                       // add distance to this one
void Distance::operator += (Distance d2)
   {
   feet += d2.feet;                    // add the feet
   inches += d2.inches;                // add the inches
   if(inches >= 12.0)                  // if total exceeds 12.0,
      {                                // then decrease inches
      inches -= 12.0;                  // by 12.0 and
      feet++;                          // increase feet
      }                                // by 1
   }

void main()
   {
   Distance dist1;                     // define dist1
   dist1.getdist();                    // get dist1 from user
   cout << "\ndist1 = ";  dist1.showdist();

   Distance dist2(11, 6.25);           // define, initialize dist2
   cout << "\ndist2 = ";  dist2.showdist();
   dist1 += dist2;                     // dist1 = dist1 + dist2
   cout << "\nAfter addition,";
   cout << "\ndist1 = ";  dist1.showdist();
   }
```

In this program we obtain a distance from the user and add to it a second distance, initialized to 11'-6.25" by the program. Here's a sample of interaction with the program:

```
Enter feet: 3
Enter inches: 5.75
dist1 = 3'-5.75"
dist2 = 11'-6.25"
After addition,
dist1 = 15'-0"
```

In this program the addition is carried out in `main()` with the statement

```
dist1 += dist2;
```

This causes the sum of `dist1` and `dist2` to be placed in `dist1`.

Notice the difference between the function used here, `operator+=()`, and that used in ENGLPLUS, `operator+()`. In the earlier `operator+()` function, a new object of type `Distance` had to be created and returned by the function so it could be assigned to a third `Distance` object, as in

```
dist3 = dist1 + dist2;
```

In the `operator+=()` function in ENGLPLEQ, the object that takes on the value of the sum is the object of which the function is a member. Thus it is `feet` and `inches` that are given values, not temporary variables used only to return an object. The `operator+=()` function has no return value; it returns type `void`. A return value is not usually needed with arithmetic assignment operators like `+=`, because the result of the assignment operator is not assigned to anything. The operator is used alone, in expressions like the one in the program.

```
dist1 += dist2;
```

If you wanted to use this operator in more complex expressions, like

```
dist3 = dist1 += dist2;
```

then you would need to provide a return value. This can be done by ending the `operator+=()` function with a statement like

```
return Distance(feet, inches);
```

in which a nameless object is initialized to the same values as this object, and returned.

The Subscript Operator `[]`

The subscript operator, `[]`, which is normally used to access array elements, can be overloaded. This is useful if you want to modify the way arrays work in C++. For example, you might want to make a "safe" array: One that automatically checks the index numbers you use to access the array, to ensure they are not out of bounds.

To demonstrate the overloaded subscript operator, we must return to another topic, first mentioned in Chapter 6: returning values from functions by reference. To be useful, the overloaded subscript operator must return by reference. To see why this is true, we'll show three example programs that implement a safe array, each one using a different approach to inserting and reading the array elements:

- Separate `put()` and `get()` functions
- A single `access()` function using return by reference
- The overloaded `[]` operator using return by reference

All three programs create a class called `safearay`, whose only member data is an array of 100 `int` values, and all three check to ensure that all array accesses are within bounds. The `main()` program in each program tests the class by filling the safe array with values (each one equal to 10 times its array index) and then displaying them all to assure the user that everything is working as it should.

Separate `get()` and `put()` Functions

The first program provides two functions to access the array elements: `putel()` to insert a value into the array, and `getel()` to find the value of an array element. Both functions check the value of the index number supplied to ensure it's not out of bounds; that is, less than 0 or larger than the array size (minus 1). Here's the listing for ARROVER1:

```
// arrover1.cpp
// creates safe array (index values are checked before access)
// uses separate put and get functions

#include <iostream.h>
#include <process.h>          // for exit()
const int LIMIT = 100;        // array size

class safearay
   {
   private:
      int arr[LIMIT];
   public:
      void putel(int n, int elvalue)
         {
         if( n<0 || n>=LIMIT )
            { cout << "\nIndex out of bounds"; exit(1); }
         arr[n] = elvalue;
         }
      int getel(int n)
         {
         if( n<0 || n>=LIMIT )
            { cout << "\nIndex out of bounds"; exit(1); }
         return arr[n];
         }
   };

void main()
   {
   safearay sa1;

   for(int j=0; j<LIMIT; j++)   // insert elements
      sa1.putel(j, j*10);

   for(j=0; j<LIMIT; j++)       // display elements
      {
      int temp = sa1.getel(j);
      cout << "\nElement " << j << " is " << temp;
      }
   }
```

The data is inserted into the safe array with the `putel()` member function, and then displayed with `getel()`. This implements a safe array; you'll receive an error message if you attempt to use an out-of-bounds index. However, the format is a bit crude.

Single `access()` Function Returning by Reference

As it turns out, we can use the same member function both to insert data into the safe array and to read it out. The secret is to return the value from the function by reference. This means we can place the function on the left side of the equal sign, and the value on the right side will be assigned to the variable returned by the function, as explained in Chapter 6. Here's the listing for ARROVER2:

```
// arrover2.cpp
// creates safe array (index values are checked before access)
// uses one access() function for both put and get

#include <iostream.h>
#include <process.h>              // for exit()
const int LIMIT = 100;            // array size

class safearay
   {
   private:
      int arr[LIMIT];
   public:
      int& access(int n)      // note: return by reference
         {
         if( n<0 || n>=LIMIT )
            { cout << "\nIndex out of bounds"; exit(1); }
         return arr[n];
         }
   };

void main()
   {
   safearay sa1;

   for(int j=0; j<LIMIT; j++)      // insert elements
      sa1.access(j) = j*10;        // *left* side of equal sign

   for(j=0; j<LIMIT; j++)          // display elements
      {
      int temp = sa1.access(j); // *right* side of equal sign
      cout << "\nElement " << j << " is " << temp;
      }
   }
```

The statement

```
sa1.access(j) = j*10;       // *left* side of equal sign
```

causes the value j*10 to be placed in `arr[j]`, the return value of the function.

It's perhaps slightly more convenient to use the same function for input and output of the safe array than using separate functions; there's one less name to remember. But there's an even better way, with no names to remember at all.

Overloaded [] Operator Returning by Reference

To access the safe array using the same subscript ([]) operator that's used for normal C++ arrays, we overload the subscript operator in the safearay class. However, since this operator is commonly used on the left side of the equal sign, this overloaded function must return by reference, as we showed in the previous program. Here's the listing for ARROVER3:

```
// arrover3.cpp
// creates safe array (index values are checked before access)
// uses overloaded [] operator for both put and get

#include <iostream.h>
#include <process.h>           // for exit()
const int LIMIT = 100;         // array size

class safearay
   {
   private:
      int arr[LIMIT];
   public:
      int& operator [](int n)   // note: return by reference
         {
         if( n<0 || n>=LIMIT )
            { cout << "\nIndex out of bounds"; exit(1); }
         return arr[n];
         }
   };

void main()
   {
   safearay sa1;

   for(int j=0; j<LIMIT; j++)   // insert elements
      sa1[j] = j*10;            // *left* side of equal sign
   for(j=0; j<LIMIT; j++)       // display elements
      {
      int temp = sa1[j];        // *right* side of equal sign
      cout << "\nElement " << j << " is " << temp;
      }
   }
```

In this program we can use the natural subscript expressions

```
sa1[j] = j*10;
```

and

```
temp = sa1[j];
```

for input and output to the safe array.

Data Conversion

We've discussed how several kinds of operators can be overloaded, but we haven't looked at the assignment operator =. This is a rather special operator, with complex properties.

You already know that the = operator will assign a value from one variable to another, in statements like

```
intvar1 = intvar2;
```

where `intvar1` and `intvar2` are integer variables. You may also have noticed that = assigns the value of one user-defined object to another, provided they are of the same type, in statements like

```
dist3 = dist1 + dist2;
```

where the result of the addition, which is type `Distance`, is assigned to another object of type `Distance`, `dist3`. Normally, when the value of one object is assigned to another of the same type, the values of all the member data items are simply copied into the new object. The compiler doesn't need any special instructions to use = for the assignment of user-defined objects such as `Distance` objects.

Thus, assignments between types, whether they are basic types or user-defined types, are handled by the compiler with no effort on our part, provided that the same data type is used on both sides of the equal sign. But what happens when the variables on different sides of the = are of different types? This is a more thorny question, to which we will devote the balance of this chapter. We'll first review how the compiler handles the conversion of basic types, which it does automatically. Then we'll explore several situations where the compiler doesn't handle things automatically and we need to tell it what to do. These include conversions between basic types and user-defined types, and conversions between different user-defined types.

You might think it represents poor programming practice to convert routinely from one type to another. After all, languages such as Pascal go to considerable trouble to keep you from doing such conversions. However, the philosophy in C++ (and C) is that the flexibility provided by allowing conversions outweighs the dangers of making mistakes by allowing type mixing.

Conversions Between Basic Types

When we write a statement like

```
intvar = floatvar;
```

where `intvar` is of type `int` and `floatvar` is of type `float`, we are assuming that the compiler will call a special routine to convert the value of `floatvar`, which is expressed in floating-point format, to an integer format so that it can be assigned to `intvar`. There are of course many such conversions: from `float` to `double`, `char` to `float`, and so on. Each such conversion has its own routine, built into the compiler and called up when the data types on different sides of the = sign so dictate. We say such conversions are *implicit* because they aren't apparent in the listing.

Sometimes we want to force the compiler to convert one type to another. To do this we use the cast operator. For instance, to convert `float` to `int`, we could say

```
intvar = int(floatvar);
```

Casting provides *explicit* conversion: It's obvious in the listing that the `int()` conversion function will convert from `float` to `int`. However, such explicit conversions use the same built-in routines as implicit conversions.

Conversions Between Objects and Basic Types

When we want to convert between user-defined data types and basic types, we can't rely on built-in conversion routines, since the compiler doesn't know anything about user-defined types besides what we tell it. Instead, we must write these routines ourselves.

Our next example shows how to convert between a basic type and a user-defined type. In this example the user-defined type is (surprise!) the English `Distance` class from previous examples, and the basic type is `float`, which we use to represent meters, a unit of length in the metric measurement system.

The example shows conversion both from `Distance` to `float`, and from `float` to `Distance`. Here's the listing for ENGLCONV:

```
// englconv.cpp
// conversions: Distance to meters, meters to Distance
#include <iostream.h>

const float MTF = 3.280833;          // meters to feet

class Distance                       // English Distance class
   {
   private:
      int feet;
      float inches;
   public:
      Distance()                     // constructor (no args)
         { feet = 0; inches = 0.0; }
      Distance( float meters )       // constructor (one arg)
         {                           // convert meters to Distance
         float fltfeet = MTF * meters;  // convert to float feet
         feet = int(fltfeet);           // feet is integer part
         inches = 12*(fltfeet-feet);    // inches is what's left
         }
      Distance(int ft, float in)     // constructor (two args)
         { feet = ft; inches = in; }
      void getdist()                 // get length from user
         {
         cout << "\nEnter feet: ";  cin >> feet;
         cout << "Enter inches: ";  cin >> inches;
         }
      void showdist()                // display distance
         { cout << feet << "\'-" << inches << '\"'; }

      operator float()               // conversion function
         {                           // converts Distance to meters
         float fracfeet = inches/12;  // convert the inches
         fracfeet += float(feet);     // add the feet
         return fracfeet/MTF;         // convert to meters
         }
   };

void main()
```

(continued on next page)

(continued from previous page)

```
{
Distance dist1 = 2.35;            // uses 1-arg constructor to
                                  // convert meters to Distance
cout << "\ndist1 = "; dist1.showdist();

dist1 = 1.00;                     // this form also uses
                                  // 1-arg constructor
cout << "\ndist1 = ";  dist1.showdist();

Distance dist2(5, 10.25);         // uses 2-arg constructor

float mtrs = float(dist2);        // uses conversion function to
                                  // convert Distance to meters
cout << "\ndist2 = " << mtrs << " meters";

mtrs = dist1;                     // this form also uses
                                  // conversion function
cout << "\ndist1 = " << mtrs << " meters";
}
```

In `main()` the program first converts a fixed `float` quantity—2.35, representing meters—to feet and inches, using the one-argument constructor.

```
Distance dist1 = 2.35;
```

It converts a second quantity in meters to feet and inches in the statement

```
dist1 = 1.00;
```

Going in the other direction, it converts a `Distance` to meters in the statements

```
float mtrs =float(dist2);
```

and

```
mtrs = dist1;
```

Here's the output:

```
dist1 = 7'-8.519485"      <------- this is 2.35 meters
dist1 = 3'-3.369996"      <------- this is 1.0 meter
dist2 = 1.784354 meters   <------- this is 5'-10.25"
dist1 = 1 meter           <------- this is 3'-3.369996"
```

We've seen how conversions are performed using simple assignment statements in `main()`. Now let's see what goes on behind the scenes, in the `Distance` member functions.

Converting a user-defined type to a basic type requires a different approach than converting a basic type to a user-defined type. We'll see how both types of conversions are carried out in ENGLCONV.

From Basic to User-Defined

To go from a basic type—`float` in this case—to a user-defined type such as `Distance`, we use a constructor with one argument. Here's how it looks in ENGLCONV:

```
Distance(float meters)
   {
   float fltfeet = MTF * meters;
   feet = int(fltfeet);
   inches = 12 * (fltfeet-feet);
   }
```

This function is called when an object of type `Distance` is created with a single argument. The function assumes this argument represents meters. It converts the argument to feet and inches, and assigns the resulting values to the object. Thus the conversion from meters to `Distance` is carried out along with the creation of an object in the statement

```
Distance dist1 = 2.35;
```

But there is another way to perform the same conversion. In the program, after defining `dist1` and displaying its value, we then say

```
dist1 = 1.0;
```

What is the compiler to make of this? We're converting `float` to `Distance`, but we're not creating a new object. Surprisingly, the one-argument constructor will be called in this situation as well. Confronted with a statement that calls for a particular conversion, the compiler looks for any tool that might do the job. In this case it finds a constructor that converts `float` to `Distance`, so it applies it to the assignment situation, creating an unnamed temporary object with feet-and-inches values corresponding to 1.0 meter. It assigns this object to `dist1`, and voilà, `dist1` has been assigned the correct values, converted from meters.

Thus the compiler blurs the distinction between definition and assignment. If no overloaded = operator is available, it will look for a constructor to do the same job.

From User-Defined to Basic

What about going the other way, from a user-defined type to a basic type? The trick here is to overload the cast operator, creating something called a *conversion function*. Here's where we do that in ENGLCONV:

```
operator float()
   {
   float fracfeet = inches/12;
   fracfeet += float(feet);
   return fracfeet/MTF;
   }
```

This operator takes the value of the `Distance` object of which it is a member, converts this value to a `float` value representing meters, and returns this value.

This operator can be called like this:

```
mtrs = float(dist2);
```

This converts the `Distance` object `dist2` to its equivalent `float` value in meters.

Again the compiler uses the same conversion in assignment statements. You can say

```
mtrs = dist2;
```

This has exactly the same effect. When the compiler finds that you want to convert a user-defined type to a basic type, it looks for the appropriate conversion function. Here the compiler starts by looking for an overloaded = operator. But when it doesn't find one, it doesn't give up. It finds the conversion function and uses that instead.

Conversion Between Strings and `String` Objects

Here's another example that uses a one-argument constructor and a conversion function. It operates on the `String` class that we saw in such examples as STRPLUS earlier in this chapter.

```
// strconv.cpp
// convert between ordinary strings and class String
#include <iostream.h>
#include <string.h>          // for strcpy(), etc.

const int SZ = 80;           // size of all String objects

class String                 // user-defined string type
   {
   private:
      char str[SZ];                       // holds a string
   public:
      String()                            // constructor 0, no args
         { str[0] = '\0'; }

      String( char s[] )                  // constructor 1, one arg
         { strcpy(str, s); }              // convert string to String

      void display()                      // display the String
         { cout << str; }

      operator char*()                    // conversion function
         { return str; }                  // convert String to string
   };

void main()
   {
   String s1;                             // use constructor 0
   char xstr[] =                          // create and initialize string
            "\nJoyeux Noel! ";
   s1 = xstr;                             // use constructor 1
                                          // to convert string to String
   s1.display();                          // display String

   String s2 = "Bonne Annee!";            // uses constructor 1
                                          // to initialize String

   cout << (char*)s2;                     // use conversion function
                                          // to convert String to string
                                          // before sending to << op

   }
```

The one-argument constructor converts a normal string (an array of `char`) to an object of class `String`:

```
String(char s[])
   { strcpy(str, s); }
```

The string `s` is passed as an argument, and copied into the `str` data member in a newly created `String` object.

This conversion will be applied when a string is created, as in

```
String s2 = "Bonne Annee!";
```

or it will be applied in assignment statements, as in

```
s1 = xstr;
```

where `s1` is type `String` and `xstr` is a normal string.

A conversion function is used to convert from a `String` type to a normal string:

```
operator char*()
   { return str; }
```

The use of the asterisk in this expression means *pointer to*. We won't explore pointers until Chapter 12, but its use here is not hard to figure out. It means *pointer to* `char`, which is very similar to *array of type* `char`. Thus `char*` is similar to `char[]`. It's another way of specifying a string data type.

The conversion function is used by the compiler in the statement

```
cout << (char*)s2;
```

Here the `s2` variable is an argument supplied to the overloaded operator `<<`. Since the `<<` operator doesn't know anything about our user-defined `String` type, the compiler looks for a way to convert `s2` to a type that `<<` does know about. We specify the type we want to convert it to with the (`char*`) cast, so it looks for a conversion from `String` to string, finds our `operator char*()` function, and uses it to generate a normal string, which is then sent on to `<<` to be displayed. (The effect is similar to calling the `String::display()` function, but given the ease and intuitive clarity of displaying with `<<`, the `display()` function is redundant and could be removed.)

Here's the output from STRCONV:

```
Joyeux Noel! Bonne Annee!
```

The STRCONV example demonstrates that conversions take place automatically not only in assignment statements but in other appropriate places, such as in arguments sent to operators (like `<<`) or functions. If you supply an operator or a function with arguments of the wrong type, they will be converted to arguments of an acceptable type, provided you have defined such a conversion.

Conversions Between Objects of Different Classes

What about converting between objects of different user-defined classes? The same two methods just shown for conversion between basic types and user-defined types also apply to conversions between two user-defined types. That is, you can use a one-argument constructor or you can use a conversion function. The choice depends on whether you want to put the conversion routine in the class specifier of the source object or of the destination object. For example, suppose you say

```
objecta = objectb;
```

where `objecta` is a member of class `A` and `objectb` is a member of class `B`. Is the conversion routine located in `A` (the destination class, since `objecta` receives the value) or `B` (the source class)? We'll look at both cases.

Routine in Source Object

The next example program shows a conversion routine located in the source class. When the conversion routine is in the source class, it is commonly implemented as a conversion function.

The two classes used in the next program are `Rec` and `Polar`. We've already seen an example of the `Polar` class, in the POLAPLUS program earlier in this chapter. The `Rec` class is similar in that its objects are points in a two-dimensional plane. However, it uses a rectangular coordinate system, where the location of each point is specified by x and y coordinates. Its member functions are similar to those for `Polar` but are adapted to rectangular coordinates. Here's the listing for POLAREC1:

```
// polarec1.cpp
// converts from Polar to Rec using routines in Polar (source)
#include <iostream.h>
#include <math.h>                  // for sin(), cos(), etc.

class Rec
   {
   private:
      double xco;                          // x coordinate
      double yco;                          // y coordinate
   public:
      Rec()                                // constructor 0, no args
         { xco = 0.0; yco = 0.0; }
      Rec(double x, double y)              // constructor 2, two args
         { xco = x; yco = y; }
      void display()                       // display
         { cout << "("  << xco
                << ", " << yco << ")"; }
   };

class Polar
   {
   private:
      double radius;
      double angle;
   public:
      Polar()                              // constructor 0, no args
         { radius=0.0; angle=0.0; }
      Polar(double r, double a)            // constructor 2, two args
         { radius=r; angle=a; }
      void display()                       // display
         { cout << "("  << radius
                << ", " << angle << ")"; }
      operator Rec()                       // conversion function
         {                                 // Polar to Rect
```

```
        double x = radius * cos(angle);  // find x and y to
        double y = radius * sin(angle);  // initialize nameless
        return Rec(x, y);                // Rec for return
        }
   };

void main()
   {
   Rec rec;                             // Rec using constructor 0
   Polar pol(10.0, 0.785398);           // Polar using constructor 2

   rec = pol;                           // convert Polar to Rec
                                        // using conversion function
                                        // (or use  rec = Rect(pol);

   cout << "\npol="; pol.display();     // display original Polar
   cout << "\nrec="; rec.display();     // display equivalent Rect
   }
```

In the `main()` part of POLAREC1 we define an object of type `Rec`, called `rec`, which is not initialized. We also define an object of type `Polar`, called `pol`, which is initialized to a radius of 10.0 and an angle of 0.785398 radians (45 degrees).

Now we want to be able to assign the value of the `pol` object to `rec`, with the statement

```
rec = pol;
```

Since these objects are from different classes, the assignment involves a conversion, and—as we specified—in this program the conversion function is a member of the `Polar` class.

```
operator Rec()
   {
   double x = radius * cos(angle);
   double y = radius * sin(angle);
   return Rec(x, y);
   }
```

This function transforms the object of which it is a member to a `Rec` object, and returns this object, which `main()` then assigns to `rec`. Here's the output from POLAREC1:

```
pol=(10, 0.785398)
rec=(7.07107, 7.07107)
```

Routine in Destination Object

Let's see how the same conversion is carried out when the conversion routine is in the destination class. In this situation it's common to use a one-argument constructor. However, things are complicated by the fact that the constructor in the destination class must be able to access the data in the source class to perform the conversion. The data in `Polar`—the radius and angle—is private, so we must provide special functions to allow direct access to it.

Here's the listing for POLAREC2:

```
// polarec2.cpp
// converts Polar to Rec using routine in Rec (destination)
#include <iostream.h>
#include <math.h>                        // for sin(), cos(), etc.

class Polar                              // point, polar coordinates
   {
   private:
      double radius;                     // radius coord
      double angle;                      // angle coord (radians)
   public:
      Polar()                            // constructor, no args
         { radius=0.0; angle=0.0; }
      Polar(double r, double a)          // constructor, two args
         { radius=r; angle=a; }
      void display()                     // display
         { cout << "("  << radius
                << ", " << angle << ")"; }
      double getr()                      // these routines allow
         { return radius; }              // radius and angle to be
      double geta()                      // accessed from outside
         { return angle; }               // the class
   };

class Rec                                // point, rectangular coords
   {
   private:
      double xco;                        // x coordinate
      double yco;                        // y coordinate
   public:
      Rec()                              // constructor 0, no args
         { xco = 0.0; yco = 0.0; }
      Rec(double x, double y)            // constructor 2, two args
         { xco = x; yco = y; }
      Rec(Polar p)                       // constructor 1, one arg
         {                               //    Polar to Rec
         float r = p.getr();
         float a = p.geta();             // get r and a from Polar
         xco = r * cos(a);               // using getr() and geta()
         yco = r * sin(a);               // change to our xco and yco
         }
      void display()                     // display
         { cout << "("  << xco
                << ", " << yco << ")"; }
   };

void main()
   {
   Rec rec;                              // Rec using constructor 1
   Polar pol(10.0, 0.785398);            // Polar using constructor 2

   rec = pol;                            // convert Polar to Rec

   cout << "\npol="; pol.display();      // display original Polar
   cout << "\nrec="; rec.display();      // display converted Rec
   }
```

Here's the conversion routine, a one-argument constructor, from the `Rec` class:

```
Rec(Polar p)
   {
   float r = p.getr();
   float a = p.geta();
   xco = r * cos(a);
   yco = r * sin(a);
   }
```

This function sets the object of which it is a member to the rectangular coordinates that correspond to the polar coordinates of the object received as an argument.

To perform the conversion, this constructor must be able to access the data values of the `Polar` object sent as an argument. The `Polar` class contains the following two routines to allow this:

```
double getr()
   { return radius; }
double geta()
   { return angle; }
```

The `main()` part of POLAREC2 is the same as that in POLAREC1. The one-argument constructor again allows the `Polar` to `Rec` conversion to take place in the statement

```
rec = pol;
```

Conversions: When to Use What

When should you use the one-argument constructor in the destination class, as opposed to the conversion function in the source class? Sometimes the choice is made for you. If you have purchased a library of classes, you may not have access to their source code. If you use an object of such a class as the source in a conversion, then you'll have access only to the destination class, and you'll need to use a one-argument constructor. If the library class object is the destination, then you must use a conversion function in the source.

Pitfalls of Operator Overloading and Conversion

Operator overloading and type conversions give you the opportunity to create what amounts to an entirely new language. When `a`, `b`, and `c` are objects from user-defined classes, and `+` is overloaded, the statement

```
a = b + c;
```

means something quite different than it does when `a`, `b`, and `c` are variables of basic data types. The ability to redefine the building blocks of the language can be a blessing in that it can make your listing more intuitive and readable. It can also have the opposite effect, making your listing more obscure and hard to understand. Here are some guidelines.

Use Similar Meanings

Use overloaded operators to perform operations that are as similar as possible to those performed on basic data types. You could overload the `+` sign to perform subtraction, for example, but that would hardly make your listings more comprehensible.

Overloading an operator assumes that it makes sense to perform a particular operation on objects of a certain class. If we're going to overload the + operator in class X, then the result of adding two objects of class X should have a meaning at least somewhat similar to addition. For example, in this chapter we showed how to overload the + operator for the English `Distance` class. Adding two distances is clearly meaningful. We also overloaded + for the `String` class. Here we interpret the addition of two strings to mean placing one string after another to form a third. This also has an intuitively satisfying interpretation. But for many classes it may not be reasonable to talk about "adding" their objects. You probably wouldn't want to add two objects of a class called `employee` that held personal data, for example.

Use Similar Syntax

Use overloaded operators in the same way you use basic types. For example, if `alpha` and `beta` are basic types, the assignment operator in the statement

```
alpha += beta;
```

sets `alpha` to the sum of `alpha` and `beta`. Any overloaded version of this operator should do something analogous. It should probably do the same thing as

```
alpha = alpha + beta;
```

where the + is overloaded.

Some syntactical characteristics of operators can't be changed even if you want them to. As you may have discovered, you can't overload a binary operator to be a unary operator, or vice versa.

Show Restraint

Remember that if you have overloaded the + operator, anyone unfamiliar with your listing will need to do considerable research to find out what a statement like

```
a = b + c;
```

really means. If the number of overloaded operators grows too large, and if they are used in nonintuitive ways, then the whole point of using them is lost, and the listing becomes less readable instead of more. Use overloaded operators sparingly, and only when the usage is obvious. When in doubt, use a function instead of an overloaded operator, since a function name can state its own purpose. If you write a function to find the left side of a string, for example, you're better off calling it `getleft()` than trying to overload some operator like `&&` to do the same thing.

Avoid Ambiguity

Suppose you use both a one-argument constructor and a conversion function to perform the same conversion (`Polar` to `Rec`, for example). How will the compiler know which conversion to use? It won't. The compiler does not like to be placed in a situation where it doesn't know what to do, and it will signal an error. So avoid doing the same conversion in more than one way.

Not All Operators Can Be Overloaded

The following operators cannot be overloaded: the member access or dot operator (`.`), the scope resolution operator (`::`), and the conditional operator (`?:`). Also, the pointer-to-member operator (`.*`), which we have not yet encountered, cannot be overloaded.

Summary

In this chapter we've seen how the normal C++ operators can be given new meanings when applied to user-defined data types. The keyword `operator` is used to overload an operator, and the resulting operator will adopt the meaning supplied by the programmer.

Closely related to operator overloading is the issue of type conversion. Some conversions take place between user-defined types and basic types. Two approaches are used in such conversions: A one-argument constructor changes a basic type to a user-defined type, and a conversion function converts a user-defined type to a basic type. When one user-defined type is converted to another, either approach can be used.

Table 9-1 summarizes these conversions.

	Routine in destination	Routine in source
Basic to basic	(Built-in conversion functions)	
Basic to class	Constructor	NA
Class to basic	NA	Conversion function
Class to class	Constructor	Conversion function

Table 9-1 Type Conversions

Questions

Answers to questions can be found in Appendix D.

1. Operator overloading is
   - **a.** making C++ operators work with objects.
   - **b.** giving C++ operators more than they can handle.
   - **c.** giving new meanings to existing C++ operators.
   - **d.** making new C++ operators.
2. Assuming that class X does not use any overloaded operators, write a statement

that subtracts an object of class X, x1, from another such object, x2, and places the result in x3.

3. Assuming that class X includes a routine to overload the - operator, write a statement that would perform the same task as that specified in Question 2.

4. True or false: The >= operator can be overloaded.

5. Write a complete definition for an overloaded operator for the Counter class of the COUNTPP1 example that, instead of incrementing the count, decrements it.

6. How many arguments are required in the definition of an overloaded unary operator?

7. Assume a class C with objects obj1, obj2, and obj3. For the statement obj3 = obj1 - obj2 to work correctly, the overloaded - operator must
   a. take two arguments.
   b. return a value.
   c. create a named temporary object.
   d. use the object of which it is a member as an operand.

8. Write a complete definition for an overloaded ++ operator for the Distance class from the ENGLPLUS example. It should add 1 to the feet member data, and make possible statements like:

```
dist1++;
```

9. Repeat Question 8, except statements like the following should be allowed:

```
dist2 = dist1++;
```

10. When used in prefix form, what does the overloaded ++ operator do differently from what it does in postfix form?

11. Here are two declarators that describe ways to add two string objects:

```
void add(String s1, String s2)
String operator + (String s)
```

Match the following from the first declarator with the appropriate selection from the second:

function name (add) matches _________

return value (type void) matches _________

first argument (s1) matches _________

second argument (s2) matches _________

object of which function is a member matches _________.

a. argument (s)
b. object of which operator is a member
c. operator (+)
d. return value (type `String`)
e. no match for this item

12. When an object of type `Polar` is added to itself, the result is a radius ________ as long at the ________ angle.

13. When you overload an arithmetic assignment operator, the result
    a. goes in the object to the right of the operator.
    b. goes in the object to the left of the operator.
    c. goes in the object of which the operator is a member.
    d. must be returned.

14. Write the complete definition of an overloaded `++` operator that works with the `String` class from the STRPLUS example and has the effect of changing its operand to uppercase. You can use the library function `toupper()` (header file CTYPE.H), which takes as its only argument the character to be changed and returns the changed character (or the same character if no change is necessary).

15. To convert from a user-defined class to a basic type, you would most likely use
    a. a built-in conversion function.
    b. a one-argument constructor.
    c. an overloaded = operator.
    d. a conversion function that's a member of the class.

16. True or false: The statement `objA=objB;` will cause a compiler error if the objects are of different classes.

17. To convert from a basic type to a user-defined class, you would most likely use
    a. a built-in conversion function.
    b. a one-argument constructor.
    c. an overloaded = operator.
    d. a conversion function that's a member of the class.

18. True or false: If you've defined a constructor to handle definitions like `aclass obj = intvar;` you can also make statements like `obj = intvar;`.

19. If `objA` is in class A, and `objB` is in class B, and you want to say `objA = objB;`, and you want the conversion routine to go in class A, what type of conversion routine might you use?

20. True or false: The compiler won't object if you overload the * operator to perform division.

Exercises

Answers to starred exercises can be found in Appendix D.

1.* To the `Distance` class in the ENGLPLUS program in this chapter, add an overloaded - operator that subtracts two distances. It should allow statements like `dist3=dist1-dist2;`. Assume the operator will never be used to subtract a larger number from a smaller one (that is, negative distances are not allowed).

2.* Write a program that substitutes an overloaded += operator for the overloaded + operator in the STRPLUS program in this chapter. This operator should allow statements like

```
s1 += s2;
```

where `s2` is added (concatenated) to `s1` and the result is left in `s1`. The operator should also permit the results of the operation to be used in other calculations, as in

```
s3 = s1 += s2;
```

3.* Modify the `time` class from Exercise 3 in Chapter 7 so that instead of a function `add_time()` it uses the overloaded + operator to add two times. Write a program to test this class.

4.* Create a class `Int` based on Exercise 1 in Chapter 7. Overload all five integer arithmetic operators (+, -, *, /, and %) so that they operate on objects of type `Int`. If the result of any such arithmetic operation exceeds the normal range of `int`s—from -32,768 to 32,767—have the operator print a warning and terminate the program. Such a data type might be useful where mistakes caused by arithmetic overflow are unacceptable. Hint: To facilitate checking for overflow, perform the calculations using type `long`. Write a program to test this class.

5. Augment the `time` class referred to in Exercise 3 to include overloaded increment (++) and decrement (--) operators that operate in both prefix and postfix notation and return values. Add statements to `main()` to test these operators.

6. Add to the `time` class of Exercise 5 the ability to subtract two `time` values using the overloaded (-) operator, and to multiply a `time` value by a number of type `float`, using the overloaded (*) operator.

7. Modify the `fraction` class in the four-function fraction calculator from Exercise 11 in Chapter 7 so that it uses overloaded operators for addition, subtraction, multiplication, and division. (Remember the rules for fraction arithmetic in Exercise 12 in Chapter 4.) Also overload the == and != comparison operators, and use them to exit from the loop if the user enters 0/1, 0/1 for the values of the two input fractions. You may want to modify the `lowterms()` function so that it returns the value of its argument reduced to lowest terms. This makes it more useful in the arithmetic functions, where it can be applied just before the answer is returned.

8. Modify the bMoney class from Exercise 12 in Chapter 8 to include the following arithmetic operations, performed with overloaded operators:

```
bMoney = bMoney + bMoney
bMoney = bMoney - bMoney
bMoney = bMoney * long double  (price per widget times number of widgets)
long double = bMoney / bMoney  (total price divided by price per widget)
bMoney = bMoney / long double  (total price divided by number of widgets)
```

Notice that the / operator is overloaded twice. The compiler can distinguish between the two usages because the arguments are different. Remember that it's easy to perform arithmetic operations on bMoney objects by performing the same operation on their long double data.

Make sure the `main()` program asks the user to enter two money strings and a floating-point number. It should then carry out all five operations and display the results. This should happen in a loop, so the user can enter more numbers if desired.

Some money operations don't make sense: `bMoney * bMoney` doesn't represent anything real, since there is no such thing as square money; and you can't add `bMoney` to `long double` (what's dollars plus widgets?). To make it impossible to compile such illegal operations, don't include conversion functions for `bMoney` to `long double` or `long double` to `bMoney`. If you do, and you write an expression like

```
bmon2 = bmon1 + widgets;  // doesn't make sense
```

then the compiler will automatically convert `widgets` to `bMoney` and carry out the addition. Without them, the compiler will flag such conversions as an error, making it easier to catch conceptual mistakes.

There are some other plausible money operations that we don't yet know how to perform with overloaded operators, since they require an object on the right side of the operator but not the left:

```
long double * bMoney   // can't do this yet: bMoney only on right
long double / bMoney   // can't do this yet: bMoney only on right
```

We'll learn how to handle this situation when we discuss `friend` functions in Chapter 13.

9. Augment the `safearay` class in the ARROVER3 program in this chapter so that the user can specify both the upper and lower bound of the array (indexes running from 100 to 200, for example). Have the overloaded subscript operator check the index each time the array is accessed to ensure it is not out of bounds. You'll need to add a two-argument constructor that specifies the upper and lower bounds. Since we have not yet learned how to allocate memory dynamically, the member data will still be an array that starts at 0 and runs up to 99, but perhaps you can map the indexes for the `safearay` into different indexes in the real `int` array. For example, if the client selects a range from 100 to 175, you could map this into the range from `arr[0]` to `arr[75]`.

10. Augment the `Polar` class in the POLAPLUS program in this chapter to incorporate overloaded operators for subtraction, multiplication, and division, as well as addition. Multiplication and division require a constant (type `double`) as the second operand, not a `Polar`.

    Subtraction is similar to addition, except that the x and y coordinates are subtracted. Multiplication is easy: Just multiply the radius times the `double` value. For division, divide the radius by the `double` value. In both operations the angle is unchanged. Write a `main()` program to exercise all these operations with a variety of values.

11. Remember the `sterling` structure? We saw it in Exercise 10 in Chapter 3 and Exercise 11 in Chapter 6, among other places. Turn it into a class, with `pounds` (type `long`) `shillings` (type `int`) and `pence` (type `int`) data items. Create the following member functions:

    - no-argument constructor
    - one-argument constructor, taking type `double` (for converting from decimal pounds)
    - three-argument constructor, taking pounds, shillings, and pence
    - `getsterling()` to get an amount in pounds, shillings, and pence from the user, format £9.19.11
    - `putsterling()` to display an amount in pounds, shillings, and pence, format £9.19.11
    - addition (`sterling + sterling`) using overloaded + operator

- subtraction (`sterling - sterling`) using overloaded - operator
- multiplication (`sterling * double`) using overloaded * operator
- division (`sterling / sterling`) using overloaded / operator
- division (`sterling / double`) using overloaded / operator
- operator `double` (to convert to `double`)

To perform arithmetic, you could (for example) add each object's data separately: Add the pence, carry, add the shillings, carry, and so on. However, it's easier to use the conversion functions to convert both sterling objects to type double, perform the arithmetic on the doubles, and convert back to sterling. Thus the overloaded + operator looks like this:

```
sterling sterling::operator + (sterling s2)
   {
   return sterling( double(sterling(pounds, shillings, pence))
                   + double(s2) );
   }
```

This creates two temporary `double` variables, one derived from the object of which the function is a member, and one derived from the argument `s2`. These `double` variables are then added, and the result is converted back to `sterling` and returned.

Notice that we use a different philosophy with the `sterling` class than with the `bMoney` class. With `sterling` we use conversion functions, thus giving up the ability to catch illegal math operations but gaining simplicity in writing the overloaded math operators.

12. Write a program that incorporates both the `bMoney` class from Exercise 8 and the `sterling` class from Exercise 11. Write conversion functions to convert between `bMoney` and `sterling`, assuming that one pound (£1.0.0) equals fifty dollars ($50.00). This was the approximate exchange rate in the 19th century when the British Empire was at its height and the pounds-shillings-pence format was in use. Write a `main()` program that allows the user to enter an amount in either currency, and that then converts it to the other currency and displays the result. Minimize any modifications to the existing `bMoney` and `sterling` classes.

10

Inheritance

REASONS FOR INHERITANCE

BASE AND DERIVED CLASSES

ACCESS CONTROL

CLASS HIERARCHIES

MULTIPLE INHERITANCE

INHERITANCE AND PROGRAM DEVELOPMENT

10

Inheritance is probably the most powerful feature of object-oriented programming, after classes themselves. Inheritance is the process of creating new classes, called *derived* classes, from existing or *base* classes. The derived class inherits all the capabilities of the base class but can add embellishments and refinements of its own. The base class is unchanged by this process. The inheritance relationship is shown in Figure 10-1.

The arrow in Figure 10-1 goes in the opposite direction to what you might expect. If it pointed downward we would label it *inheritance*. However, the more common approach is to point the arrow up, from the derived class to the base class, and to think of it as a "derived from" arrow.

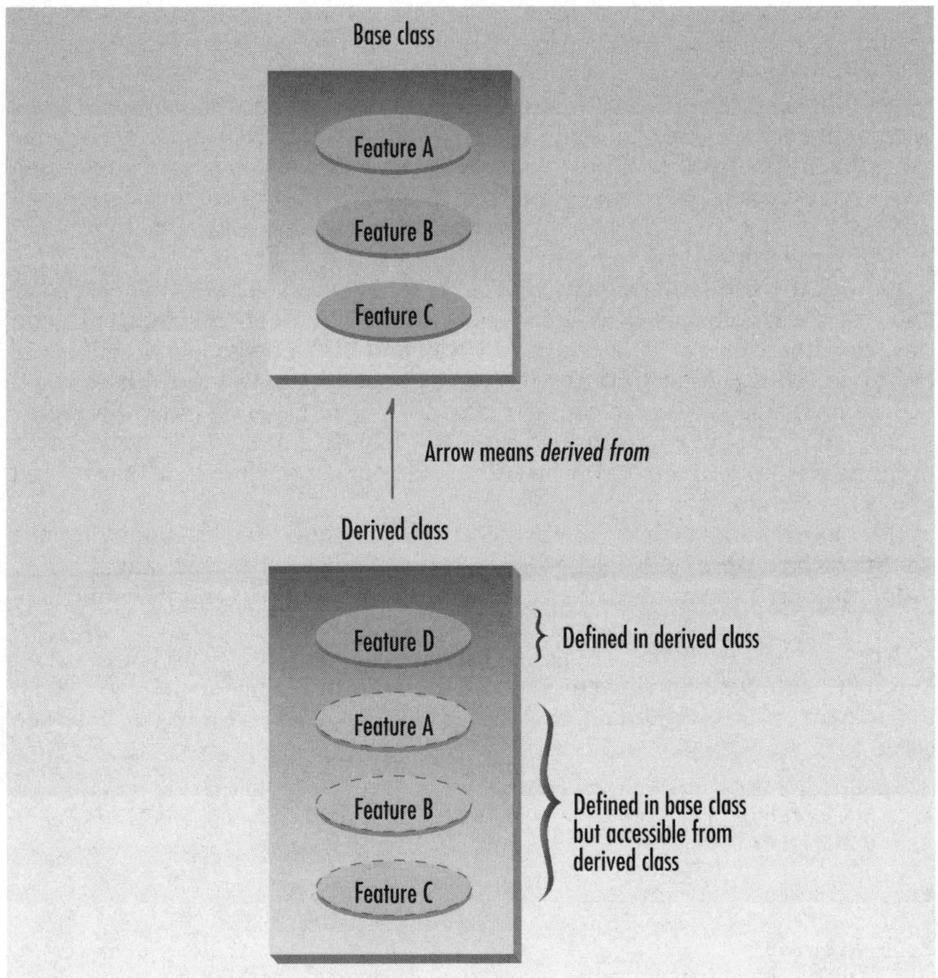

Figure 10-1 Inheritance

Inheritance is an essential part of OOP. Its big payoff is that it permits code *reusability*. Once a base class is written and debugged, it need not be touched again, but can nevertheless be adapted to work in different situations. Reusing existing code saves time and money and increases a program's reliability. Inheritance can also help in the original conceptualization of a programming problem, and in the overall design of the program.

An important result of reusability is the ease of distributing class libraries. A programmer can use a class created by another person or company, and, without modifying it, derive other classes from it that are suited to particular situations.

We'll examine these features of inheritance in more detail after we've seen some specific instances of inheritance at work.

Derived Class and Base Class

Remember the COUNTPP3 example from Chapter 9? This program used a class `Counter` as a general-purpose counter variable. A count could be initialized to 0 or to a specified number with constructors, incremented with the `++` operator, and read with the `get_count()` operator.

Let's suppose that we have worked long and hard to make the `Counter` class operate just the way we want, and we're pleased with the results, except for one thing. We really need a way to decrement the count. Perhaps we're counting people entering a bank, and we want to increment the count when they come in and decrement it when they go out, so that the count represents the number of people in the bank at any moment.

We could insert a decrement routine directly into the source code of the `Counter` class. However, there are several reasons why we might not want to do this. First, the `Counter` class works very well and has undergone many hours of testing and debugging. (Of course that's an exaggeration in this case, but it would be true in a larger and more complex class.) If we start fooling around with the source code for `Counter`, the testing process will need to be carried out again, and of course we may foul something up and spend hours debugging code that worked fine before we modified it.

In some situations there might be another reason for not modifying the `Counter` class: We might not have access to its source code, especially if it had been distributed as part of a class library. (We'll discuss this issue further in Chapter 15.)

To avoid these problems we can use inheritance to create a new class based on `Counter`, without modifying `Counter` itself. Here's the listing for COUNTEN, which includes a new class, `CountDn`, that adds a decrement operator to the `Counter` class:

```
// counten.cpp
// inheritance with Counter class
#include <iostream.h>

class Counter                          // base class
   {
   protected:                                 // NOTE: not private
      unsigned int count;                     // count
   public:
```

```
      Counter()         { count = 0; }     // constructor, no args
      Counter(int c)    { count = c; }     // constructor, one arg
      int get_count()   { return count; } // return count
      Counter operator ++ ()               // incr count (prefix)
        { return Counter(++count); }
   };

class CountDn : public Counter             // derived class
   {
   public:
      Counter operator -- ()               // decr count (prefix)
        { return Counter(--count); }
   };

void main()
   {
   CountDn c1;                           // c1 of class CountDn

   cout << "\nc1=" << c1.get_count();    // display c1

   ++c1; ++c1; ++c1;                     // increment c1
   cout << "\nc1=" << c1.get_count();    // display it

   --c1; --c1;                           // decrement c1
   cout << "\nc1=" << c1.get_count();    // display it
   }
```

The listing starts off with the `Counter` class, which (with one small exception, which we'll look at later) has not changed since its appearance in COUNTPP3. Notice that, for simplicity we haven't modelled this program on the POSTFIX program, which incorporated the second overloaded `++` operator to provide postfix notation.

Specifying the Derived Class

Following the `Counter` class in the listing is the specification for a new class, `CountDn`. This class incorporates a new function, `operator--()`, which decrements the count. However—and here's the key point—the new `CountDn` class inherits all the features of the `Counter` class. `CountDn` doesn't need a constructor or the `get_count()` or `operator++()` functions, because these already exist in `Counter`.

The first line of `CountDn` specifies that it is derived from `Counter`:

```
class CountDn : public Counter
```

Here we use a single colon (not the double colon used for the scope resolution operator), followed by the keyword `public` and the name of the base class `Counter`. This sets up the relationship between the classes. This line says `CountDn` *is derived from the base class* `Counter`. (We'll explore the effect of the keyword `public` later.) The relationship is shown in Figure 10-2.

Remember that the arrow in diagrams like this means *derived from*. The arrows point this way to emphasize that the derived class *refers to* functions and data in the base class, while the base class has no access to the derived class. Mathematicians call this kind of diagram a *directed acyclic graph*, or DAG (as in "DAGonnit, I drew the arrow the wrong way"). They are also called *inheritance trees*.

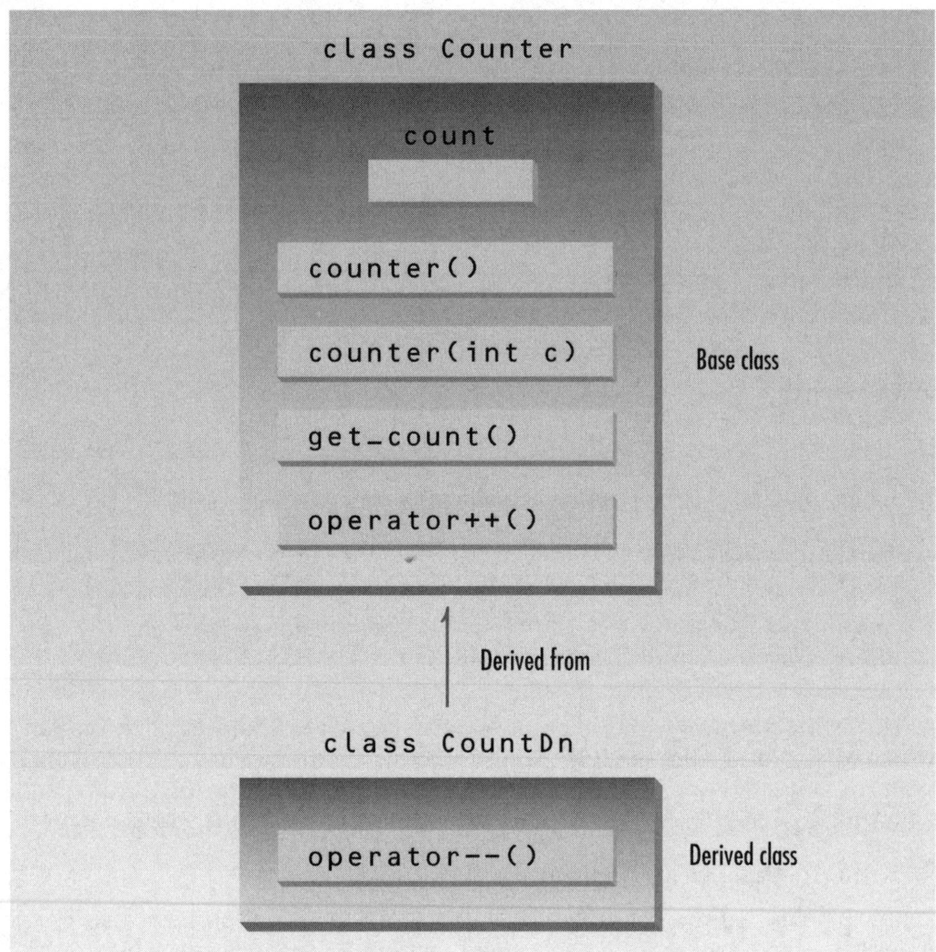

Figure 10-2 Class Hierarchy in COUNTEN

Accessing Base Class Members

An important topic in inheritance is knowing when a member function in the base class can be used by objects of the derived class. This is called *accessibility*. Let's see how the compiler handles the accessibility issue in the COUNTEN example.

Substituting Base Class Constructors

In the `main()` part of COUNTEN we create an object of class `CountDn`:

```
CountDn c1;
```

This causes `c1` to be created as an object of class `CountDn` and initialized to 0. But wait—how is this possible? There is no constructor in the `CountDn` class specifier, so what entity carries out the initialization? It turns out that—at least under certain circumstances—if you don't specify a constructor, the derived class will use an appropriate constructor from the base class. In COUNTEN there's no constructor in `CountDn`, so the compiler uses the no-argument constructor from `Count`.

This flexibility on the part of the compiler—using one function because another isn't available—appears regularly in inheritance situations. Generally the substitution is what you want, but sometimes it can be unnerving.

Substituting Base Class Member Functions

The object `c1` of the `CountDn` class also uses the `operator++()` and `get_count()` functions from the `Counter` class. The first is used to increment `c1`:

```
++c1;
```

and the second is used to display the count in `c1`:

```
cout << "\nc1=" << c1.get_count();
```

Again the compiler, not finding these functions in the class of which `c1` is a member, uses member functions from the base class.

Output of COUNTEN

In `main()` we increment `c1` three times, print out the resulting value, decrement `c1` twice, and finally print out its value again. Here's the output:

```
c1=0   <------ after initialization
c1=3   <------ after ++c1, ++c1, ++c1
c1=1   <------ after --c1, --c1
```

The `++` operator, the constructors, the `get_count()` function in the `Counter` class, and the `--` operator in the `CountDn` class all work with objects of type `CountDn`.

The `protected` Access Specifier

We have increased the functionality of a class without modifying it. Well, almost without modifying it. Let's look at the single change we made to the `Counter` class.

The data in the classes we've looked at so far, including `count` in the `Counter` class in the earlier COUNTPP3 program, have used the `private` access specifier.

In the `Counter` class in COUNTEN, `count` is given a new specifier: `protected`. What does this do?

Let's first review what we know about the access specifiers `private` and `public`. Class members (which can be data or functions) can always be accessed by functions *within their own class*, whether the members are private or public. But objects of a class defined *outside the class* can access class members only if the members are public. For instance, suppose an object `objA` is an instance of class `A`, and function `funcA()` is a member function of A. Then in `main()` (or any other function that is not a member of A) the statement

```
objA.funcA();
```

will not be legal unless `func()` is public. The object `objA` cannot access private members of class A. Private members are, well, *private*. This is shown in Figure 10-3.

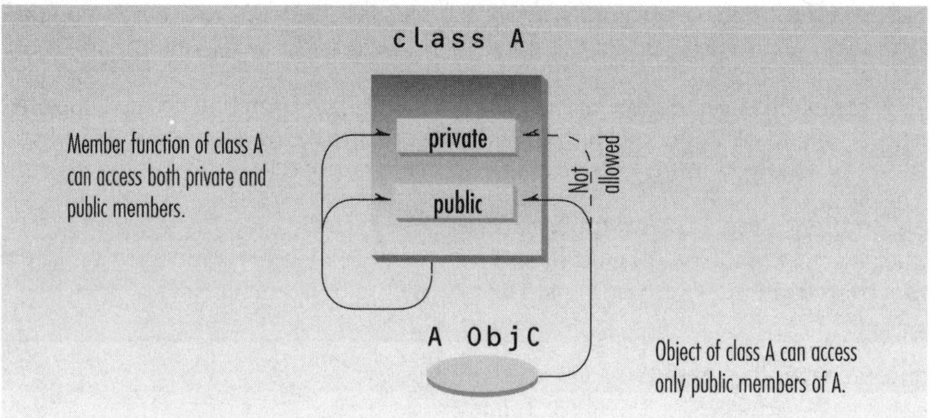

Figure 10-3 Access Specifiers Without Inheritance

This is all we need to know if we don't use inheritance. With inheritance, however, there is a whole raft of additional possibilities. The question that concerns us at the moment is, can member functions of the derived class access members of the base class? In other words, can `operator--()` in `CountDn` access `count` in `Counter`? The answer is that member functions can access members of the base class if the members are `public`, or if they are `protected`. They can't access `private` members.

We don't want to make `count public`, since that would allow it to be accessed by any function anywhere in the program and eliminate the advantages of data hiding. A `protected` member, on the other hand, can be accessed by member functions in its own class or—and here's the key—in any class derived from its own class. It can't be accessed from functions outside these classes, such as `main()`. This is just what we want. The situation is shown in Figure 10-4.

Table 10-1 summarizes the situation in a different way.

The moral is that if you are writing a class that you suspect might be used, at any point in the future, as a base class for other classes, then any data or functions that the derived classes might need to access should be made `protected` rather than `private`. This ensures that the class is "inheritance ready."

Access specifier	Accessible from own class	Accessible from derived class	Accessible from objects outside class
public	yes	yes	yes
protected	yes	yes	no
private	yes	no	no

Table 10-1 Inheritance and Accessibility

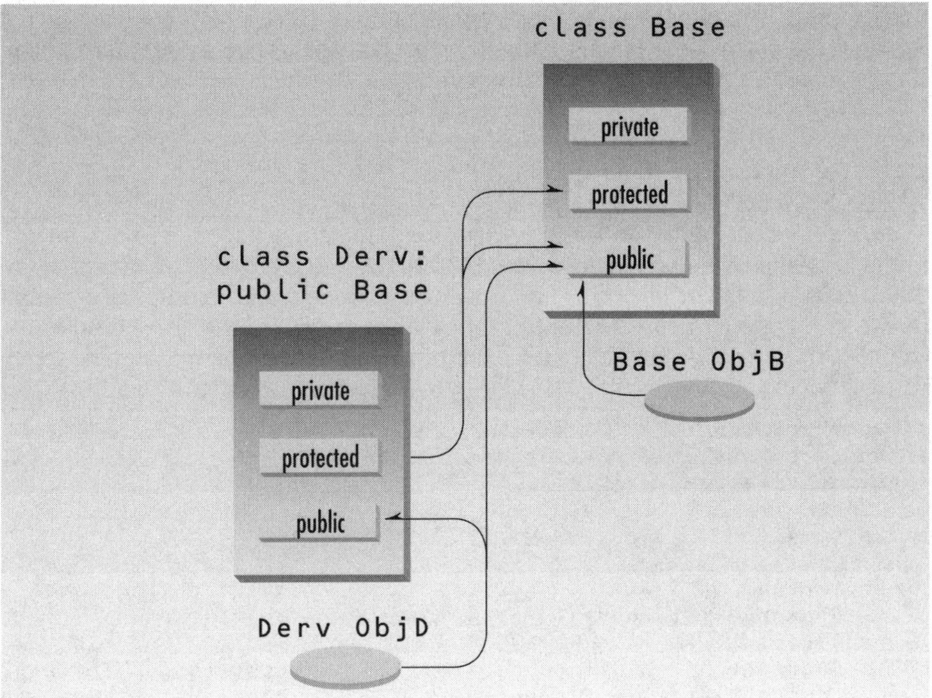

Figure 10-4 Access Specifiers with Inheritance

Dangers of `protected`

You should know that there's a disadvantage to making class members `protected`. Say you've written a class library, which you're distributing to the public. Any programmer who buys this library can access protected members of your classes simply by deriving other classes from them. This makes protected members considerably less secure than private members. To avoid corrupted data, it's often safer to force derived classes to access data in the base class using only public functions in the base class, just as ordinary `main()` programs must do. Using the `protected` specifier leads to simpler programming, so we rely on it—perhaps a bit too much—in the examples in this book. You'll need to weigh the advantages of `protected` against its disadvantages in your own programs.

Base Class Unchanged

Remember that, even if other classes have been derived from it, the base class remains unchanged. In the `main()` part of COUNTEN, we could define objects of type `Counter`:

```
Counter c2;   ←——— object of base class
```

Such objects would behave just as they would if `CountDn` didn't exist.

Note also that inheritance doesn't work in reverse. The base class and its objects don't know anything about any classes derived from the base class. In this example that means that objects of class `Counter`, such as `c2` defined here, can't use the `operator--()` function in `CountDn`. If you want a counter that you can decrement, it must be of class `CountDn`, not `Counter`.

Derived Class Constructors

There's a potential glitch in the COUNTEN program. What happens if we want to initialize a `CountDn` object to a value? Can the one-argument constructor in `Counter` be used? The answer is no. As we saw in COUNTEN, the compiler will substitute a no-argument constructor from the base class, but it draws the line at more complex constructors. To make such a definition work we must write a new set of constructors for the derived class. This is shown in the COUNTEN2 program.

```
// counten2.cpp
// constructors in derived class
#include <iostream.h>

class Counter
   {
   protected:                                     // NOTE: not private
      unsigned int count;                         // count
   public:
      Counter()         { count = 0; }            // constructor, no args
      Counter(int c)    { count = c; }            // constructor, one arg
      int get_count()   { return count; }         // return count
      Counter operator ++ ()                      // incr count (prefix)
        { return Counter(++count); }
   };

class CountDn : public Counter
   {
   public:
      CountDn() : Counter()                       // constructor, no args
        { }
      CountDn(int c) : Counter(c)                 // constructor, 1 arg
        { }
      CountDn operator -- ()                      // decr count (prefix)
        { return CountDn(--count); }
   };

void main()
   {
   CountDn c1;                                   // class CountDn
   CountDn c2(100);

   cout << "\nc1=" << c1.get_count();   // display
   cout << "\nc2=" << c2.get_count();   // display

   ++c1; ++c1; ++c1;                    // increment c1
   cout << "\nc1=" << c1.get_count();   // display it

   --c2; --c2;                          // decrement c2
   cout << "\nc2=" << c2.get_count();   // display it
```

```
   CountDn c3 = --c2;                    // create c3 from c2
   cout << "\nc3=" << c3.get_count();    // display c3
}
```

This program uses two new constructors in the `CountDn` class. Here is the one-argument constructor:

```
CountDn() : Counter()
   { }
```

This constructor has an unfamiliar feature: the colon followed by a function name. This construction causes the `CountDn()` constructor to call the `Counter()` constructor in the base class. In `main()`, when we say

```
CountDn c1;
```

the compiler will create an object of type `CountDn` and then call the `CountDn` constructor to initialize it. This constructor will in turn call the `Counter` constructor, which carries out the work. The `CountDn()` constructor could add additional statements of its own, but in this case it doesn't need to, so the function body between the braces is empty.

The statement

```
CountDn c2(100);
```

in `main()` uses the one-argument constructor in `CountDn`. This constructor also calls the corresponding constructor in the base class:

```
CountDn(int c) : Counter(c)   <-------- argument c is passed to Counter
   { }
```

This construction causes the argument `c` to be passed from `CountDn()` to `Counter()`, where it is used to initialize the object.

In `main()`, after initializing the `c1` and `c2` objects, we increment one and decrement the other and then print the results. The one-argument constructor is also used in an assignment statement.

```
CountDn c3 = --c2;
```

Overriding Member Functions

You can use member functions in a derived class that have the same name as those in the base class. You might want to do this so that calls in your program work the same way for objects of both base and derived classes.

Here's an example based on the STAKARAY program from Chapter 8. That program modeled a stack, a simple data storage device. It allowed you to push integers onto the stack and pop them off. However, STAKARAY had a potential flaw. If you tried to push too many items onto the stack, the program might bomb, since data would be placed in memory beyond the end of the `st[]` array. Or if you tried to pop too many items, the results would be meaningless, since you would be reading data from memory locations outside the array.

To cure these defects we've created a new class, `Stack2`, derived from `Stack`. Objects of `Stack2` behave in exactly the same way as those of `Stack`, except that you will be warned if you attempt to push too many items on the stack, or if you try to pop an item from an empty stack. Here's the listing for STAKEN:

```
// staken.cpp
// overloading functions in base and derived classes
#include <iostream.h>
#include <process.h>                 // for exit()

const int MAX = 3;                   // maximum size of stack

class Stack
   {
   protected:                        // NOTE: can't be private
      int st[MAX];                   // stack: array of integers
      int top;                       // index to top of stack
   public:
      Stack()                        // constructor
         { top = -1; }
      void push(int var)             // put number on stack
         { st[++top] = var; }
      int pop()                      // take number off stack
         { return st[top--]; }
   };

class Stack2 : public Stack
   {
   public:
      void push(int var)                // put number on stack
         {
         if(top >= MAX-1)               // error if stack full
            { cout << "\nError: stack is full"; exit(1); }
         Stack::push(var);              // call push() in Stack class
         }
      int pop()                         // take number off stack
         {
         if(top < 0)                    // error if stack empty
            { cout << "\nError: stack is empty"; exit(1); }
         return Stack::pop();           // call pop() in Stack class
         }
   };

void main()
   {
   Stack2 s1;

   s1.push(11);                        // push some values onto stack
   s1.push(22);
   s1.push(33);

   cout << endl << s1.pop();           // pop some values from stack
   cout << endl << s1.pop();
   cout << endl << s1.pop();
   cout << endl << s1.pop();           // woops, pops one too many...
   }
```

In this program the `Stack` class is just the same as it was in the STAKARAY program, except that the data members have been made `protected`.

Which Function Is Used?

The `Stack2` class contains two functions, `push()` and `pop()`. These functions have the same names, and the same argument and return types, as the functions in `Stack`. When we call these functions from `main()`, in statements like

```
s1.push(11);
```

how does the compiler know which of the two `push()` functions to use? Here's the rule: When the same function exists in both the base class and the derived class, the function in the derived class will be executed. (This is true of objects of the derived class. Objects of the base class don't know anything about the derived class and will always use the base class functions.) We say that the derived class function *overrides* the base class function. So in the statement above, since `s1` is an object of class `Stack2`, the `push()` function in `Stack2` will be executed, not the one in `Stack`.

The `push()` function in `Stack2` checks to see if the stack is full. If it is, it displays an error message and causes the program to exit. If it isn't, it calls the `push()` function in `Stack`. Similarly, the `pop()` function in `Stack2` checks to see if the stack is empty. If it is, it prints an error message and exits; otherwise, it calls the `pop()` function in `Stack`.

In `main()` we push three items onto the stack, but we pop four. The last pop elicits an error message.

```
33
22
11
Error: stack is empty
```

and terminates the program.

Scope Resolution with Overridden Functions

How do `push()` and `pop()` in `Stack2` access `push()` and `pop()` in `Stack`? They use the scope resolution operator, `::`, in the statements.

```
Stack::push(var);
```

and

```
return Stack::pop();
```

These statements specify that the `push()` and `pop()` functions in `Stack` are to be called. Without the scope resolution operator, the compiler would think the `push()` and `pop()` functions in `Stack2` were calling themselves, which—in this case—would lead to program failure. Using the scope resolution operator allows you to specify exactly what class the function is a member of.

Inheritance in the English `Distance` Class

Here's a somewhat more complex example of inheritance. So far in this book the various programs that used the English `Distance` class assumed that the distances to be represented would always be positive. This is usually the case in architectural drawings. However, if we were measuring, say, the water level of the Pacific Ocean as the tides varied, we might want to be able to represent negative feet-and-inches quantities. (Tide levels below mean-lower-low-water are called *minus tides*; they prompt clam diggers to take advantage of the larger area of exposed beach.)

Let's derive a new class from `Distance`. This class will add a single data item to our feet-and-inches measurements: a sign, which can be positive or negative. When we add the sign, we'll also need to modify the member functions so they can work with signed distances. Here's the listing for ENGLEN:

```
// englen.cpp
// inheritance using English Distances
#include <iostream.h>

class Distance                          // English Distance class
   {
   protected:                           // (could be private)
      int feet;
      float inches;
   public:
      Distance()                        // constructor (no args)
         { feet = 0; inches = 0.0; }
      Distance(int ft, float in)        // constructor (two args)
         { feet = ft; inches = in; }
      void getdist()                    // get length from user
         {
         cout << "\nEnter feet: ";  cin >> feet;
         cout << "Enter inches: ";  cin >> inches;
         }
      void showdist()                   // display distance
         { cout << feet << "\'-" << inches << '\"'; }
   };

enum posneg { pos, neg };  // for sign in DistSign

class DistSign : public Distance        // adds sign to Distance
   {
   private:
      posneg sign;                      // sign is pos or neg
   public:
                                        // constructor  (no args)
      DistSign() : Distance()           // call base constructor
         { sign = pos; }                // set the sign to +

                                        // constructor (2 or 3 args)
      DistSign(int ft, float in, posneg sg=pos) :
               Distance(ft, in)         // call base constructor
         { sign = sg; }                 // set the sign

      void getdist()                    // get length from user
         {
         Distance::getdist();           // call base getdist()
         char ch;                       // get sign from user
         cout << "Enter sign (+ or -): ";  cin >> ch;
         sign = (ch=='+') ? pos : neg;
         }
```

```
      void showdist()                     // display distance
         {
         cout << ( (sign==pos) ? "(+)" : "(-)" );  // show sign
         Distance::showdist();                     // ft and in
         }
   };

void main()
   {
   DistSign alpha;                        // no-arg constructor
   alpha.getdist();                       // get alpha from user

   DistSign beta(11, 6.25);               // 2-arg constructor

   DistSign gamma(100, 5.5, neg);         // 3-arg constructor

                                          // display all distances
   cout << "\nalpha = ";  alpha.showdist();
   cout << "\nbeta = ";  beta.showdist();
   cout << "\ngamma = ";  gamma.showdist();
   }
```

Here the `DistSign` class adds the functionality to deal with signed numbers. The `Distance` class in this program is just the same as in previous programs, except that the data is `protected`. Actually in this case it could be private, because none of the derived-class functions accesses it. However, it's safer to make it protected so that a derived-class function could access it if necessary.

Operation of ENGLEN

The `main()` program declares three different signed distances. It gets a value for `alpha` from the user and initializes `beta` to (+)11'-6.25" and `gamma` to (–)100'-5.5". We use parentheses around the sign to avoid confusion with the hyphen separating feet and inches. Here's some sample output:

```
Enter feet: 6
Enter inches: 2.5
Enter sign (+ or -): -

alpha = (-)6'-2.5"
beta = (+)11'-6.25"
gamma = (-)100'-5.5"
```

The `DistSign` class is derived from `Distance`. It adds a single variable, `sign`, which is of type `posneg`. The `sign` variable will hold the sign of the distance. The `posneg` type is defined in an `enum` statement to have two possible values: `pos` and `neg`.

Constructors in `DistSign`

`DistSign` has two constructors, mirroring those in `Distance`. The first takes no arguments, the second takes either two or three arguments. The third, optional, argument in the second constructor is a sign, either `pos` or `neg`. Its default value is `pos`. These constructors allow us to define variables (objects) of type `DistSign` in several ways.

Both constructors in `DistSign` call the corresponding constructors in `Distance` to set the feet-and-inches values. They then set the `sign` variable. The no-argument constructor always sets it to `pos`. The second constructor sets it to `pos` if no third-argument value has been provided, or to a value (`pos` or `neg`) if the argument is specified.

The arguments `ft` and `in`, passed from `main()` to the second constructor in `DistSign`, are simply forwarded to the constructor in `Distance`.

Member Functions in `DistSign`

Adding a sign to `Distance` has consequences for both its member functions. The `getdist()` function in the `DistSign` class must ask the user for the sign as well as for feet-and-inches values, and the `showdist()` function must display the sign along with the feet and inches. These functions call the corresponding functions in `Distance`, in the lines

```
Distance::getdist();
```

and

```
Distance::showdist();
```

These calls get and display the feet and inches values. The body of `getdist()` and `showdist()` in `DistSign` then go on to deal with the sign.

Abetting Inheritance

C++ is designed to make it efficient to create a derived class. Where we want to use parts of the base class, it's easy to do so, whether these parts are data, constructors, or member functions. Then we add the functionality we need to create the new improved class. Notice that in ENGLEN we didn't need to duplicate any code; instead we made use of the appropriate functions in the base class.

Class Hierarchies

In the examples so far in this chapter, inheritance has been used to add functionality to an existing class. Now let's look at an example where inheritance is used for a different purpose: as part of the original design of a program.

Our example models a database of employees of a widget company. We've simplified the situation so that only three kinds of employees are represented. Managers manage, scientists perform research to develop better widgets, and laborers operate the dangerous widget-stamping presses.

The database stores a name and an employee identification number for all employees, no matter what category they are. However, for managers, it also stores their titles and golf club dues. For scientists it stores the number of scholarly articles they have published. Laborers need no additional data beyond their names and numbers.

Our example program starts with a base class `employee`. This class handles the employee's last name and employee number. From this class three other classes are derived: `manager`, `scientist`, and `laborer`. The `manager` and `scientist` classes contain additional information about these categories of employee, and member functions to handle this information, as shown in Figure 10-5.

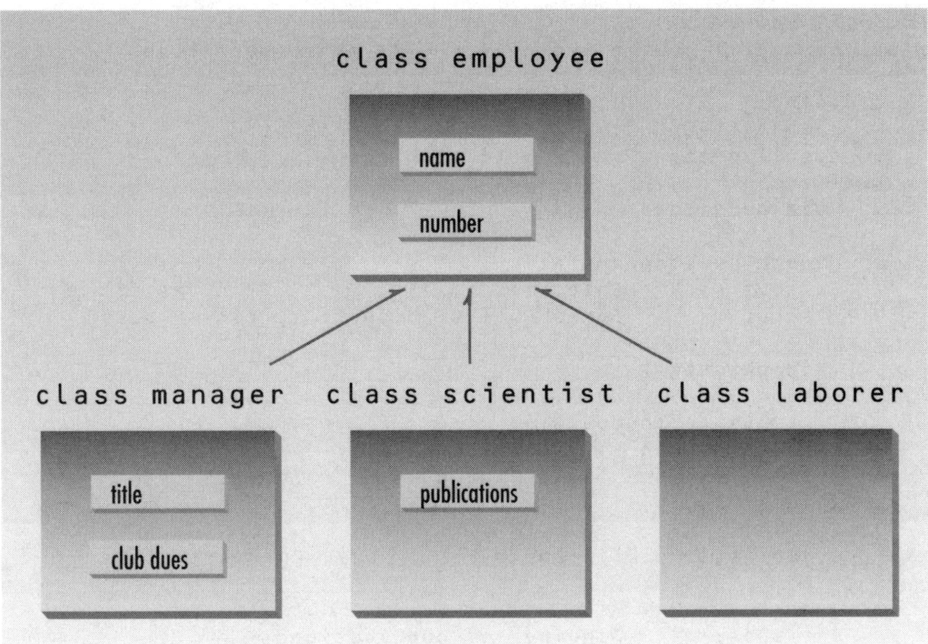

Figure 10-5 Class Hierarchy in EMPLOY

Here's the listing for EMPLOY:

```
// employ.cpp
// models employee database using inheritance
#include <iostream.h>

const int LEN = 80;             // maximum length of names

class employee                  // employee class
   {
   private:
      char name[LEN];           // employee name
      unsigned long number;     // employee number
   public:
      void getdata()
         {
         cout << "\n   Enter last name: "; cin >> name;
         cout << "   Enter number: ";      cin >> number;
         }
      void putdata()
         {
         cout << "\n   Name: " << name;
         cout << "\n   Number: " << number;
         }
   };
```

(continued on next page)

(continued from previous page)

```
class manager : public employee     // management class
   {
   private:
      char title[LEN];  // "vice-president" etc.
      double dues;      // golf club dues
   public:
      void getdata()
         {
         employee::getdata();
         cout << "   Enter title: ";         cin >> title;
         cout << "   Enter golf club dues: "; cin >> dues;
         }
      void putdata()
         {
         employee::putdata();
         cout << "\n   Title: " << title;
         cout << "\n   Golf club dues: " << dues;
         }
   };
class scientist : public employee      // scientist class
   {
   private:
      int pubs;     // number of publications
   public:
      void getdata()
         {
         employee::getdata();
         cout << "   Enter number of pubs: "; cin >> pubs;
         }
      void putdata()
         {
         employee::putdata();
         cout << "\n   Number of publications: " << pubs;
         }
   };

class laborer : public employee        // laborer class
   {
   };

void main()
   {
   manager m1, m2;
   scientist s1;
   laborer l1;

   cout << endl;
   cout << "\nEnter data for manager 1";    // get data for
   m1.getdata();                            // several employees

   cout << "\nEnter data for manager 2";
   m2.getdata();

   cout << "\nEnter data for scientist 1";
```

```
    s1.getdata();

    cout << "\nEnter data for laborer 1";
    l1.getdata();

    cout << "\nData on manager 1";          // display data for
    m1.putdata();                           // several employees

    cout << "\nData on manager 2";
    m2.putdata();

    cout << "\nData on scientist 1";
    s1.putdata();

    cout << "\nData on laborer 1";
    l1.putdata();
    }
```

The `main()` part of the program declares four objects of different classes: two managers, a scientist, and a laborer. (Of course many more employees of each type could be defined, but the output would become rather large.) It then calls the `getdata()` member functions to obtain information about each employee, and the `putdata()` function to display this information. Here's a sample interaction with EMPLOY. First the user supplies the data.

```
Enter data for manager 1
   Enter last name: Wainsworth
   Enter number: 10
   Enter title: President
   Enter golf club dues: 1000000
Enter data on manager 2
   Enter last name: Bradley
   Enter number: 124
   Enter title: Vice-President
   Enter golf club dues: 500000
Enter data for scientist 1
   Enter last name: Hauptman-Frenglish
   Enter number: 234234
   Enter number of pubs: 999
Enter data for laborer 1
   Enter last name: Jones
   Enter number: 6546544
```

The program then plays it back.

```
Data on manager 1
   Name: Wainsworth
   Number: 10
   Title: President
   Golf club dues: 1000000
Data on manager 2
   Name: Bradley
   Number: 124
   Title: Vice-President
   Golf club dues: 500000
Data on scientist 1
```

(continued on next page)

(continued from previous page)

```
    Name: Hauptman-Frenglish
    Number: 234234
    Number of publications: 999
Data on laborer 1
    Name: Jones
    Number: 6546544
```

A more sophisticated program would use an array or some other more complex way to arrange the data so that a large number of employee objects could be accommodated.

"Abstract" Base Class

Notice that we don't define any objects of the base class `employee`. We use this as a general class whose sole purpose is to act as a base from which other classes are derived.

The `laborer` class operates identically to the `employee` class, since it contains no additional data or functions. It may seem that the `laborer` class is unnecessary, but by making it a separate class we emphasize that all classes are descended from the same source, `employee`. Also, if in the future we decided to modify the `laborer` class, we would not need to change the specifier for `employee`.

Classes used only for deriving other classes, as `employee` is in EMPLOY, are sometimes loosely called *abstract* classes, meaning that no actual instances (objects) of this class are created. However, the term *abstract* has a more precise definition, connected with virtual functions, that we'll look at in Chapter 13.

Constructors and Member Functions

There are no constructors in either the base or derived classes, so the compiler creates objects of the various classes automatically when it encounters definitions like

```
manager m1, m2;
```

with the default constructor for `manager` calling the default constructor for `employee`.

The `getdata()` and `putdata()` functions in `employee` accept a name and number from the user and display a name and number. Functions also called `getdata()` and `putdata()` in the `manager` and `scientist` classes use the functions in `employee`, and also do their own work. In `manager` the `getdata()` function asks the user for a title and the amount of golf club dues, and `putdata()` displays these values. In `scientist` these functions handle the number of publications.

Public and Private Inheritance

C++ provides a wealth of ways to fine-tune access to class members. One such access-control mechanism is the way derived classes are declared. Our examples so far have used publicly declared classes, with specifiers like

```
class manager : public employee
```

which appeared in the EMPLOY example.

What is the effect of the `public` keyword in this statement, and what are the alternatives? Listen up: The keyword `public` specifies that objects of the derived class are able to access public member functions of the base class. The alternative is the keyword `private`. When this keyword is used, objects of the derived class cannot access public member functions of the base class. Since objects can never access `private` or `protected` members of a class, the result is that no member of the base class is accessible to objects of the derived class.

Access Combinations

There are so many possibilities for access that it's instructive to look at an example program that shows what works and what doesn't. Here's the listing for PUBPRIV:

```
// pubpriv.cpp
// tests publicly- and privately-derived classes
#include <iostream.h>

class A                       // base class
   {
   private:
      int privdataA;          // (functions have the same access
   protected:                 // rules as the data shown here)
      int protdataA;
   public:
      int pubdataA;
   };

class B : public A            // publicly-derived class
   {
   public:
      void funct()
         {
         int a;
         a = privdataA;             // error: not accessible
         a = protdataA;             // ok
         a = pubdataA;              // ok
         }
   };

class C : private A           // privately-derived class
   {
   public:
      void funct()
         {
         int a;
         a = privdataA;             // error: not accessible
         a = protdataA;             // ok
         a = pubdataA;              // ok
         }
   };

void main()                   // main()
```

(continued on next page)

(continued from previous page)

```
   int a;

   B objB;
   a = objB.privdataA;   // error: not accessible
   a = objB.protdataA;   // error: not accessible
   a = objB.pubdataA;    // ok                  (A public to B)

   C objC;
   a = objC.privdataA;   // error: not accessible
   a = objC.protdataA;   // error: not accessible
   a = objC.pubdataA;    // error: not accessible (A private to C)
   }
```

The program specifies a base class, `A`, with private, protected, and public data items. Two classes, `B` and `C`, are derived from `A`. `B` is publicly derived and `C` is privately derived.

As we've seen before, functions in the derived classes can access protected and public data in the base class. Objects of the derived classes cannot access private or protected members of the base class.

What's new is the difference between publicly derived and privately derived classes. Objects of the publicly derived class `B` can access public members of the base class `A`, while objects of the privately derived class `C` cannot; they can only access the public members of their own derived class. This is shown in Figure 10-6.

If you don't supply any access specifier when creating a class, `private` is assumed.

Classes and Structures

Remember that access specifiers are the only way to distinguish structures and classes. In structures the default is public; for classes it's private.

```
class X : A          // private is assumed
   { };
struct X : A         // public is assumed
   { };
```

Access Specifiers: When to Use What

How do you decide when to use private as opposed to public inheritance? In most cases a derived class exists to offer an improved—or a more specialized—version of the base class. We've seen examples of such derived classes; for instance the `CountDn` class that adds the decrement operator to the `Counter` class and the `manager` class that is a more specialized version of the `employee` class. In such cases it makes sense for objects of the derived class to access the public functions of the base class if they want to perform a basic operation, and to access functions in the derived class to perform the more specialized operations that the derived class provides. In such cases public derivation is appropriate.

In some situations, however, the derived class is created as a way of completely modifying the operation of the base class, hiding or disguising its original interface. For example, imagine that you have already created a really nice `Array` class that acts like an array but provides protection against out-of-bounds array indexes.

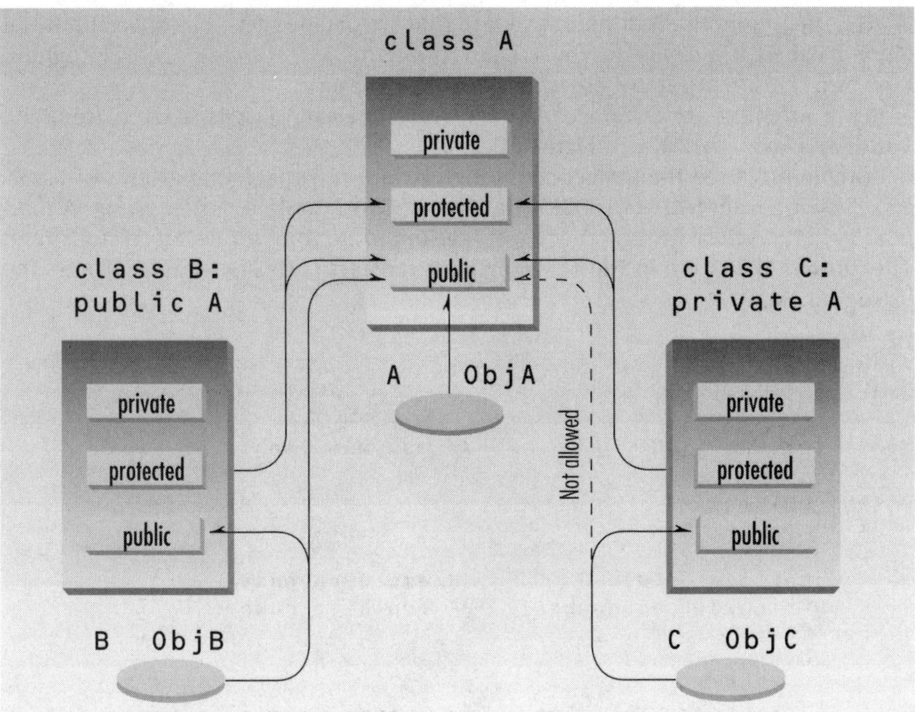

Figure 10-6 Public and Private Derivation

Then suppose you want to use this `Array` class as the basis for a `Stack` class, instead of using a basic array. You might derive `Stack` from `Array`, but you wouldn't want the users of `Stack` objects to treat them as if they were arrays, using the `[]` operator to access them, for example. They should always be treated as if they were stacks, using `push()` and `pop()`. That is, you want to disguise the `Array` class as a `Stack` class. In this situation, private derivation would allow you to conceal all the `Array` class functions from objects of the derived `Stack` class. Users wouldn't even know the array was implemented as a stack.

Levels of Inheritance

Classes can be derived from classes that are themselves derived. Here's a miniprogram that shows the idea:

```
class A
   { };
class B : public A
   { };
class C : public B
   { };
```

Here `B` is derived from `A`, and `C` is derived from `B`. The process can be extended to an arbitrary number of levels—`D` could be derived from `C`, and so on.

As a more concrete example, suppose that we decided to add a special kind of laborer called a *foreman* to the EMPLOY program. We'll create a new program, EMPLOY2, that incorporates objects of class `foreman`.

Since foremen are a kind of laborer, the `foreman` class is derived from the `laborer` class, as shown in Figure 10-7.

Foremen oversee the widget-stamping operation, supervising groups of laborers. They are responsible for the widget production quota for their group. A foreman's ability is measured by the percentage of production quotas successfully met. The `quotas` data item in the `foreman` class represents this percentage. Here's the listing for EMPLOY2:

```
// employ2.cpp
// multiple levels of inheritance
#include <iostream.h>

const int LEN = 80;           // maximum length of names

class employee
   {
   private:
      char name[LEN];          // employee name
      unsigned long number;    // employee number
   public:
      void getdata()
         {
         cout << "\n   Enter last name: "; cin >> name;
```

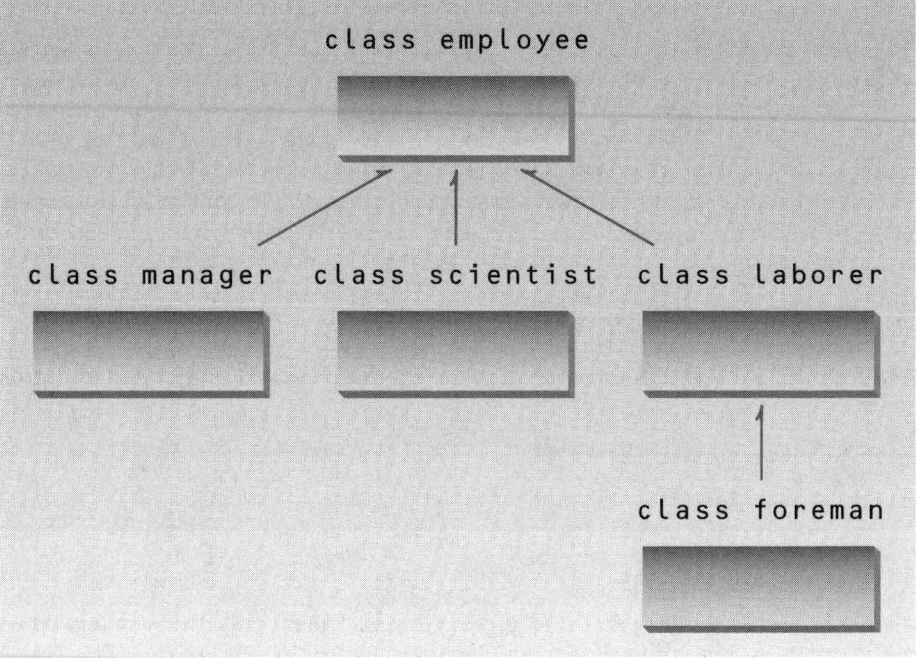

Figure 10-7 Class Hierarchy in EMPLOY2

```
        cout << "   Enter number: ";      cin >> number;
        }
      void putdata()
        {
        cout << "\n   Name: " << name;
        cout << "\n   Number: " << number;
        }
   };

class manager : public employee     // management class
   {
   private:
      char title[LEN];  // "vice-president" etc.
      double dues;      // golf club dues
   public:
      void getdata()
         {
         employee::getdata();
         cout << "   Enter title: ";           cin >> title;
         cout << "   Enter golf club dues: "; cin >> dues;
         }
      void putdata()
         {
         employee::putdata();
         cout << "\n   Title: " << title;
         cout << "\n   Golf club dues: " << dues;
         }
   };
class scientist : public employee      // scientist class
   {
   private:
      int pubs;     // number of publications
   public:
      void getdata()
         {
         employee::getdata();
         cout << "   Enter number of pubs: "; cin >> pubs;
         }
      void putdata()
         {
         employee::putdata();
         cout << "\n   Number of publications: " << pubs;
         }
   };

class laborer : public employee        // laborer class
   {
   };

class foreman : public laborer         // foreman class
   {
   private:
      float quotas;    // percent of quotas met successfully
   public:
```

(continued on next page)

(continued from previous page)

```
      void getdata()
         {
         laborer::getdata();
         cout << "   Enter quotas: "; cin >> quotas;
         }
      void putdata()
         {
         laborer::putdata();
         cout << "\n   Quotas: " << quotas;
         }
   };
void main()
   {
   laborer l1;
   foreman f1;

   cout << endl;
   cout << "\nEnter data for laborer 1";
   l1.getdata();
   cout << "\nEnter data for foreman 1";
   f1.getdata();

   cout << endl;
   cout << "\nData on laborer 1";
   l1.putdata();
   cout << "\nData on foreman 1";
   f1.putdata();
   }
```

Notice that a class hierarchy is not the same as an organization chart. An organization chart shows lines of command. A class hierarchy results from generalizing common characteristics. The more general the class, the higher it is on the chart. Thus a laborer is more general than a foreman, who is a specialized kind of laborer, so `laborer` is shown above `foreman` in the class hierarchy.

Multiple Inheritance

A class can be derived from more than one base class. This is called *multiple inheritance*. Figure 10-8 shows how this looks when a class `C` is derived from base classes `A` and `B`.

The syntax for multiple inheritance is similar to that for single inheritance. In the situation shown in Figure 10-8, the relationship is expressed like this:

```
class A                              // base class A
   {
   };
class B                              // base class B
   {
   };
class C : public A, public B         // C is derived from A and B
   {
   };
```

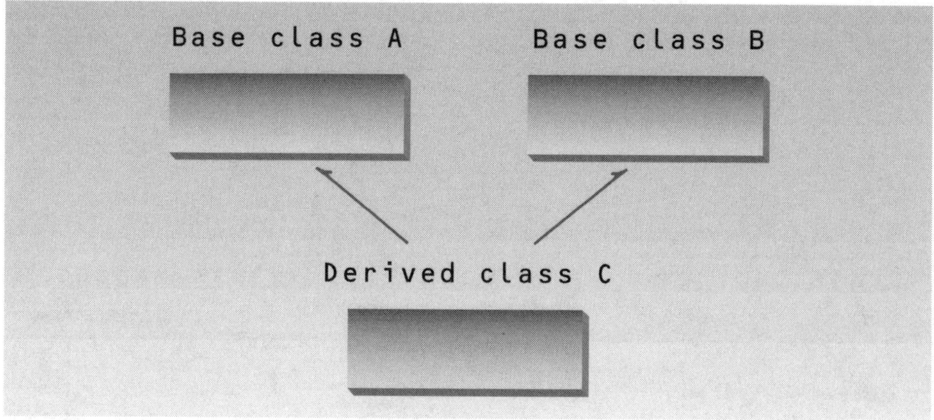

Figure 10-8 Multiple Inheritance

The base classes from which `C` is derived are listed following the colon in `C`'s specification; they are separated by commas.

Member Functions in Multiple Inheritance

As an example of multiple inheritance, suppose that we needed to record the educational experience of some of the employees in the EMPLOY program. Let's also suppose that, perhaps in a different project, we had already developed a class called `student` that models students with different educational backgrounds. We decide that instead of modifying the `employee` class to incorporate educational data, we will add this data by multiple inheritance from the `student` class.

The `student` class stores the name of the school or university last attended and the highest degree received. Both these data items are stored as strings. Two member functions, `getedu()` and `putedu()`, ask the user for this information and display it.

Educational information is not relevant to every class of employee. Let's suppose, somewhat undemocratically, that we don't need to record the educational experience of laborers; it's only relevant for managers and scientists. We therefore modify `manager` and `scientist` so that they inherit from both the `employee` and `student` classes, as shown in Figure 10-9.

Here's a miniprogram that shows these relationships (but leaves out everything else):

```
class student
   { };
class employee
   { };
class manager : private employee, private student
   { };
class scientist : private employee, private student
   { };
class laborer : public employee
   { };
```

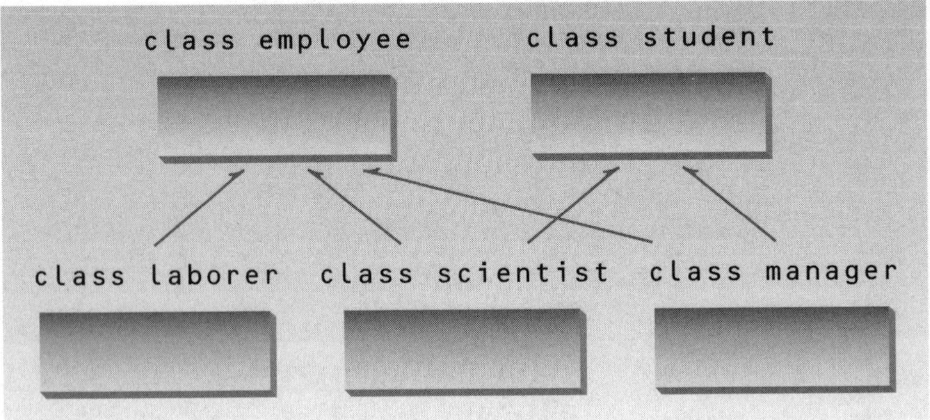

Figure 10-9 Class Hierarchy in EMPMULT

And here, featuring considerably more detail, is the listing for EMPMULT:

```
// empmult.cpp
// multiple inheritance with employees and education
#include <iostream.h>

const int LEN = 80;              // maximum length of names

class student                    // educational background
   {
   private:
      char school[LEN];   // name of school or university
      char degree[LEN];   // highest degree earned
   public:
      void getedu()
         {
         cout << "   Enter name of school or university: ";
         cin >> school;
         cout << "   Enter highest degree earned \n";
         cout << "   (Highschool, Bachelor's, Master's, PhD): ";
         cin >> degree;
         }
      void putedu()
         {
         cout << "\n   School or university: " << school;
         cout << "\n   Highest degree earned: " << degree;
         }
   };
class employee
   {
   private:
      char name[LEN];             // employee name
      unsigned long number;       // employee number
   public:
      void getdata()
```

```
        {
        cout << "\n   Enter last name: "; cin >> name;
        cout << "   Enter number: ";      cin >> number;
        }
     void putdata()
        {
        cout << "\n   Name: " << name;
        cout << "\n   Number: " << number;
        }
  };
class manager : private employee, private student  // management
  {
  private:
     char title[LEN];  // "vice-president" etc.
     double dues;      // golf club dues
  public:
     void getdata()
        {
        employee::getdata();
        cout << "   Enter title: ";          cin >> title;
        cout << "   Enter golf club dues: "; cin >> dues;
        student::getedu();
        }
     void putdata()
        {
        employee::putdata();
        cout << "\n   Title: " << title;
        cout << "\n   Golf club dues: " << dues;
        student::putedu();
        }
  };
class scientist : private employee, private student  // scientist
  {
  private:
     int pubs;     // number of publications
  public:
     void getdata()
        {
        employee::getdata();
        cout << "   Enter number of pubs: "; cin >> pubs;
        student::getedu();
        }
     void putdata()
        {
        employee::putdata();
        cout << "\n   Number of publications: " << pubs;
        student::putedu();
        }
  };

class laborer : public  employee        // laborer
  {
  };
```

(continued on next page)

(continued from previous page)

```
void main()
   {
   manager m1;
   scientist s1, s2;
   laborer l1;

   cout << endl;
   cout << "\nEnter data for manager 1";    // get data for
   m1.getdata();                            // several employees
   cout << "\nEnter data for scientist 1";
   s1.getdata();

   cout << "\nEnter data for scientist 2";
   s2.getdata();

   cout << "\nEnter data for laborer 1";
   l1.getdata();

   cout << "\nData on manager 1";           // display data for
   m1.putdata();                            // several employees

   cout << "\nData on scientist 1";
   s1.putdata();

   cout << "\nData on scientist 2";
   s2.putdata();

   cout << "\nData on laborer 1";
   l1.putdata();
   }
```

The `getdata()` and `putdata()` functions in the `manager` and `scientist` classes incorporate calls to functions in the `student` class, such as

```
student::getedu();
```

and

```
student::putedu();
```

These routines are accessible in `manager` and `scientist` because these classes are descended from `student`.

Here's some sample interaction with EMPMULT:

```
Enter data for manager 1
   Enter last name: Bradley
   Enter number: 12
   Enter title: Vice-President
   Enter golf club dues: 100000
   Enter name of school or university: Yale
   Enter highest degree earned
   (Highschool, Bachelor's, Master's, PhD): Bachelor's

Enter data for scientist 1
   Enter last name: Twilling
   Enter number: 764
```

```
    Enter number of pubs: 99
    Enter name of school or university: MIT
    Enter highest degree earned
    (Highschool, Bachelor's, Master's, PhD): PhD

Enter data for scientist 2
    Enter last name: Yang
    Enter number: 845
    Enter number of pubs: 101
    Enter name of school or university: Stanford
    Enter highest degree earned
    (Highschool, Bachelor's, Master's, PhD): Master's

Enter data for laborer 1
    Enter last name: Jones
    Enter number: 48323
```

As we saw in the EMPLOY and EMPLOY2 examples, the program then displays this information in roughly the same form.

`private` Derivation in EMPMULT

The `manager` and `scientist` classes in EMPMULT are privately derived from the `employee` and `student` classes. There is no need to use public derivation because objects of `manager` and `scientist` never call routines in the `employee` and `student` base classes. However, the `laborer` class must be publicly derived from `employer`, since it has no member functions of its own and relies on those in `employee`.

Constructors in Multiple Inheritance

EMPMULT has no constructors. Let's look at an example that does use constructors, and see how they're handled in multiple inheritance.

Imagine that we're writing a program for building contractors, and that this program models lumber-supply items. It uses a class that represents a quantity of lumber of a certain type: 100 8-foot-long construction grade 2x4s, for example.

The class should store various kinds of data about each such lumber item. We need to know the length (3'-6" or whatever) and we need to store the number of such pieces of lumber and their unit cost.

We also need to store a description of the lumber we're talking about. This has two parts. The first is the nominal dimensions of the cross-section of the lumber. This is given in inches. For instance, lumber 2 inches by 4 inches (for you metrickers, about 5 cm by 10 cm) is called a *two-by-four*. This is usually written *2x4*. (The actual dimensions are smaller than these nominal dimensions, but that doesn't matter here.) We also need to know the grade of lumber—rough-cut, construction grade, surfaced-four-sides, and so on. We find it convenient to create a `Type` class to hold this data. This class incorporates member data for the nominal dimensions and the grade of the lumber, both expressed as strings, such as *2x6* and *construction*. Member functions get this information from the user and display it.

We'll use the `Distance` class from previous examples to store the length. Finally we create a `Lumber` class that inherits both the `Type` and `Distance` classes. Here's the listing for ENGLMULT:

```
// englmult.cpp
// multiple inheritance with English Distances
#include <iostream.h>
#include <string.h>          // for strcpy()

const int LEN = 40;          // maximum length of strings
class Type                   // type of lumber
   {
   private:
      char dimensions[LEN];
      char grade[LEN];
   public:
      Type()                          // constructor (no args)
         { strcpy(dimensions, "N/A"); strcpy(grade, "N/A"); }

      Type(char di[], char gr[])  // constructor (two args)
         { strcpy(dimensions, di); strcpy(grade, gr); }

      void gettype()                  // get type from user
         {
         cout << "   Enter nominal dimensions (2x4 etc.): ";
         cin >> dimensions;
         cout << "   Enter grade (rough, const, etc.): ";
         cin >> grade;
         }
      void showtype()                 // display type
         {
         cout << "\n   Dimensions: " << dimensions;
         cout << "\n   Grade: " << grade;
         }
   };

class Distance                        // English Distance class
   {
   private:
      int feet;
      float inches;
   public:
      Distance()                      // constructor (no args)
         { feet = 0; inches = 0.0; }
      Distance(int ft, float in)  // constructor (two args)
         { feet = ft; inches = in; }
      void getdist()                  // get length from user
         {
         cout << "   Enter feet: ";  cin >> feet;
         cout << "   Enter inches: ";  cin >> inches;
         }
      void showdist()                 // display distance
         { cout  << feet << "\'-" << inches << '\"'; }
   };

class Lumber : public Type, public Distance
   {
   private:
```

```
      int quantity;                         // number of pieces
      float price;                          // price of each piece
   public:
      Lumber() : Type(), Distance()         // constructor (no args)
         { quantity = 0; price = 0.0; }
                                            // constructor (6 args)
      Lumber( char di[], char gr[],         // args for Type
              int ft, float in,             // args for Distance
              int qu, float prc ) :         // our own args
              Type(di, gr),                 // call Type constructor
              Distance(ft, in)              // call Distance constr
         {
         quantity = qu; price = prc;        // use our own args
         }
      void getlumber()
         {
         Type::gettype();
         Distance::getdist();
         cout << "   Enter quantity: "; cin >> quantity;
         cout << "   Enter price per piece: "; cin >> price;
         }
      void showlumber()
         {
         Type::showtype();
         cout << "\n   Length: ";
         Distance::showdist();
         cout << "\n   Price for " << quantity
              << " pieces: $" << price * quantity;
         }
   };

void main()
   {
   Lumber siding;                        // constructor (no args)

   cout << "\nSiding data:\n";
   siding.getlumber();                   // get siding from user

                                         // constructor (6 args)
   Lumber studs( "2x4", "const", 8, 0.0, 200, 4.45 );

                                         // display lumber data
   cout << "\nSiding";  siding.showlumber();
   cout << "\nStuds";     studs.showlumber();
   }
```

The major new feature in this program is the use of constructors in the derived class `Lumber`. These constructors call the appropriate constructors in `Type` and `Distance`.

No-Argument Constructor

The no-argument constructor in `Type` looks like this:

```
Type()
   { strcpy(dimensions, "N/A"); strcpy(grade, "N/A"); }
```

This constructor fills in "N/A" (not available) for the `dimensions` and `grade` variables so the user will be made aware if an attempt is made to display data for an uninitialized lumber object.

You're already familiar with the no-argument constructor in the `Distance` class:

```
Distance()
   { feet = 0; inches = 0.0; }
```

The no-argument constructor in `Lumber` calls both these constructors.

```
Lumber() : Type(), Distance()
```

The names of the base-class constructors follow the colon and are separated by commas. When the `Lumber()` constructor is invoked, these base-class constructors—`Type()` and `Distance()`—will be executed.

Multi-Argument Constructor

The situation is more complex when constructors with arguments are used. Here is the two-argument constructor for `Type`:

```
Type(char di[], char gr[])
   { strcpy(dimensions, di); strcpy(grade, gr); }
```

This constructor copies string arguments to the `dimensions` and `grade` member data items.

Here's the constructor for `Distance`, which is again familiar from previous programs:

```
Distance(int ft, float in)
   { feet = ft; inches = in; }
```

The constructor for `Lumber` calls both these constructors, so it must supply values for their arguments. In addition it has two arguments of its own: the quantity of lumber and the unit price. This constructor has six arguments. It then makes two calls to the two constructors, each of which takes two arguments. Here's what it looks like:

```
Lumber( char di[], char gr[],        <------- args for Type class
        int ft, float in,            <------- args for Distance class
        int qu, float prc ) :        <------- args for this class
        Type(di, gr),                <------- call Type constructor
        Distance(ft, in);            <------- call Distance constructor
   {
   quantity = qu; price = prc;       <------- set our own data
   }
```

As before, a colon signals the start of the list of constructors to be called, with the members of the list separated by commas. The first four arguments passed to `Lumber` are passed on to `Type()` and `Distance()`. The last two arguments are used to initialize the `quantity` and `price` members of `Lumber` in the body of the function.

Ambiguity in Multiple Inheritance

Odd sorts of problems may surface in certain situations involving multiple inheritance. Here's a common one. Two base classes have functions with the same name, while a class derived from both base classes has no function with this name. How do objects of the derived class access the correct base class function? The name of the function alone is insufficient, since the compiler can't figure out which of the two functions is meant.

Here's an example, AMBIGU, that demonstrates the situation:

```
// ambigu.cpp
// demonstrates ambiguity in multiple inheritance
#include <iostream.h>

class A
   {
   public:
      void show()   { cout << "\nClass A"; }
   };
class B
   {
   public:
      void show()   { cout << "\nClass B"; }
   };
class C : public A, public B
   {
   };

void main()
   {
   C objC;               // object of class C
   objC.show();          // ambiguous--will not compile
   objC.A::show();       // ok
   objC.B::show();       // ok
   }
```

The problem is resolved using the scope-resolution operator to specify the class in which the function lies. Thus

```
objC.A::show();
```

refers to the version of `show()` that's in the `A` class, while

```
objC.B::show();
```

refers to the function in the `B` class.

The scope-resolution operator resolves the ambiguity and keeps the compiler happy.

Containership: Classes Within Classes

In inheritance, if a class `B` is derived from a class `A`, we can say that "`B` is a kind of `A`." This is because `B` has all the characteristics of `A`, and in addition some of its own. It's like saying that a starling is a kind of bird: A starling has the characteristics shared by all birds (wings, feathers, and so on) but has some distinctive characteristics of its own (such as dark iridescent plumage). For this reason inheritance is sometimes called a "kind of" relationship.

There's another kind of relationship, called a "has a" relationship, or *containership*. We say that a starling has a tail, meaning that each starling includes an instance of a tail. In object-oriented programming the "has a" relationship occurs when one object is contained in another. Here's a case where an object of class A is contained in a class B:

```
class A
   {
   };
class B
   {
   A objA;    // define objA as an object of class A
   };
```

In some situations inheritance and containership relationships can serve similar purposes. For example, we can rewrite the EMPMULT program to use containership instead of inheritance. In EMPMULT the `manager` and `scientist` classes are derived from the `employee` and `student` classes using the inheritance relationship. In our new program, EMPCONT, the `manager` and `scientist` classes contain instances of the `employee` and `student` classes, as shown in Figure 10-10.

The following miniprogram shows these relationships in a different way:

```
class student
   {};
class employee
   {};
class manager
   {
   student stu;      // stu is an object of class student
   employee emp;     // emp is an object of class employee
   };
class scientist
   {
   student stu;      // stu is an object of class student
   employee emp;     // emp is an object of class employee
   };
class laborer
```

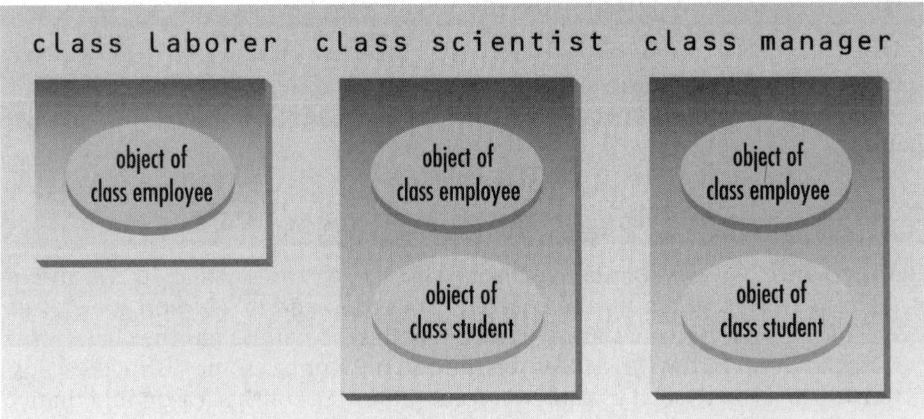

Figure 10-10 Class Hierarchy in EMPCONT

```
   {
   employee emp;    // emp is an object of class employee
   };
```

Here's the full-scale listing for EMPCONT:

```
// empcont.cpp
// containership with employees and education
#include <iostream.h>

const int LEN = 80;               // maximum length of names

class student                     // educational background
   {
   private:
      char school[LEN];  // name of school or university
      char degree[LEN];  // highest degree earned
   public:
      void getedu()
         {
         cout << "   Enter name of school or university: ";
         cin >> school;
         cout << "   Enter highest degree earned \n";
         cout << "   (Highschool, Bachelor's, Master's, PhD): ";
         cin >> degree;
         }
      void putedu()
         {
         cout << "\n   School or university: " << school;
         cout << "\n   Highest degree earned: " << degree;
         }
   };

class employee
   {
   private:
      char name[LEN];             // employee name
      unsigned long number;       // employee number
   public:
      void getdata()
         {
         cout << "\n   Enter last name: "; cin >> name;
         cout << "   Enter number: ";      cin >> number;
         }
      void putdata()
         {
         cout << "\n   Name: " << name;
         cout << "\n   Number: " << number;
         }
   };
class manager                  // management
   {
   private:
```

(continued on next page)

(continued from previous page)

```
      char title[LEN];  // "vice-president" etc.
      double dues;      // golf club dues
      employee emp;     // object of class employee
      student stu;      // object of class student
   public:
      void getdata()
         {
         emp.getdata();
         cout << "   Enter title: ";          cin >> title;
         cout << "   Enter golf club dues: "; cin >> dues;
         stu.getedu();
         }
      void putdata()
         {
         emp.putdata();
         cout << "\n   Title: " << title;
         cout << "\n   Golf club dues: " << dues;
         stu.putedu();
         }
   };
class scientist          // scientist
   {
   private:
      int pubs;          // number of publications
      employee emp;      // object of class employee
      student stu;       // object of class student
   public:
      void getdata()
         {
         emp.getdata();
         cout << "   Enter number of pubs: "; cin >> pubs;
         stu.getedu();
         }
      void putdata()
         {
         emp.putdata();
         cout << "\n   Number of publications: " << pubs;
         stu.putedu();
         }
   };

class laborer         // laborer
   {
   private:
      employee emp;  // object of class employee
   public:
      void getdata()
         { emp.getdata(); }
      void putdata()
         { emp.putdata(); }
   };

void main()
   {
```

```
manager m1;
scientist s1, s2;
laborer l1;

cout << endl;
cout << "\nEnter data for manager 1";       // get data for
m1.getdata();                               // several employees

cout << "\nEnter data for scientist 1";
s1.getdata();

cout << "\nEnter data for scientist 2";
s2.getdata();

cout << "\nEnter data for laborer 1";
l1.getdata();

cout << "\nData on manager 1";              // display data for
m1.putdata();                               // several employees

cout << "\nData on scientist 1";
s1.putdata();

cout << "\nData on scientist 2";
s2.putdata();

cout << "\nData on laborer 1";
l1.putdata();
}
```

The `student` and `employee` classes are the same in EMPCONT as they were in EMPMULT, but they are used in a different way by the `manager` and `scientist` classes.

Containership is clearly useful with classes that act like a data type, as does the `Distance` class, for example. Then an object of that type can be used in a class in almost the same way a variable would be. In other situations you will need to examine the problem carefully and perhaps try different approaches to see what makes sense. Often the inheritance relationship is simpler to implement and offers a clearer conceptual framework.

Inheritance and Program Development

The program-development process, as practiced for decades by programmers everywhere, is being fundamentally altered by object-oriented programming. This is due not only to the use of classes in OOP but to inheritance as well. Let's see how this comes about.

Programmer A creates a class. Perhaps it's something like the `Distance` class, with a complete set of member functions for arithmetic operations on a user-defined data type.

Programmer B likes the `Distance` class but thinks it could be improved by using signed distances. The solution is to create a new class, like `DistSign` in the ENGLEN example, that is derived from `Distance` but incorporates the extensions necessary to implement signed distances.

Programmers C and D then write applications that use the `DistSign` class.

Programmer B may not have access to the source code for the `Distance` member functions, and programmers C and D may not have access to the source code for `DistSign`. Yet, because of the software reusability feature of C++, B can modify and extend the work of A, and C and D can make use of the work of B (and A).

Notice that the distinction between software tool developers and application writers is becoming blurred. Programmer A creates a general-purpose programming tool, the `Distance` class. Programmer B creates a specialized version of this class, the `DistSign` class. Programmers C and D create applications. A is a tool developer, and C and D are applications developers. B is somewhere in between. In any case OOP is making the programming scene more flexible and at the same time more complex.

In Chapter 15, on larger programs, we'll see how a class can be divided into a client-accessible part and a part that is distributed only in object form, so it can be used by other programmers without the distribution of source code.

Summary

A class, called the derived class, can inherit the features of another class, called the base class. The derived class can add other features of its own, so it becomes a specialized version of the base class. Inheritance provides a powerful way to extend the capabilities of existing classes, and to design programs using hierarchical relationships.

Accessibility of base class members from derived classes and from objects of derived classes is an important issue. Data or functions in the base class that are prefaced by the keyword `protected` can be accessed from derived classes but not by objects of derived classes. Classes may be publicly or privately derived from base classes. Objects of a publicly derived class can access public members of the base class, while objects of a privately derived class cannot.

A class can be derived from more than one base class. This is called multiple inheritance. A class can also be contained within another class.

Inheritance permits the reusability of software: Derived classes can extend the capabilities of base classes with no need to modify—or even access the source code of—the base class. This leads to new flexibility in the software development process, and to a wider range of roles for software developers.

Questions

Answers to questions can be found in Appendix D.

1. Inheritance is a way to
   - **a.** make general classes into more specific classes.
   - **b.** pass arguments to objects of classes.
   - **c.** add features to existing classes without rewriting them.
   - **d.** improve data hiding and encapsulation.

2. A "child" class is said to be _________ from a base class.

3. Advantages of inheritance include
   a. providing class growth through natural selection.
   b. facilitating class libraries.
   c. avoiding the rewriting of code.
   d. providing a useful conceptual framework.

4. Write the first line of the specifier for a class `Bosworth` that is publicly derived from a class `Alphonso`.

5. True or false: Adding a derived class to a base class requires fundamental changes to the base class.

6. To be accessed from a member function of the derived class, data or functions in the base class must be `public` or _________.

7. If a base class contains a member function `basefunc()`, and a derived class does not contain a function with this name, can an object of the derived class access `basefunc()`?

8. Assume the classes mentioned in Question 4, and that class `Alphonso` contains a member function called `alfunc()`. Write a statement that allows object `BosworthObj` of class `Bosworth` to access `alfunc()`.

9. True or false: If no constructors are specified for a derived class, objects of the derived class will use the constructors in the base class.

10. If a base class and a derived class each include a member function with the same name, which member function will be called by an object of the derived class, assuming the scope-resolution operator is not used?

11. Write a declarator for a no-argument constructor of the derived class `Bosworth` of Question 4 that calls a no-argument constructor in the base class `Alphonso`.

12. The scope-resolution operator usually
    a. limits the visibility of variables to a certain function.
    b. tells what base class a class is derived from.
    c. specifies a particular class.
    d. resolves ambiguities.

13. True or false: It is sometimes useful to specify a class from which no objects will ever be created.

14. Assume there is a class `Derv` that is derived from a base class `Base`. Write the declarator for a derived-class constructor that takes one argument and passes this argument along to the constructor in the base class.

15. Assume a class `Derv` that is privately derived from class `Base`. An object of class `Derv` located in `main()` can access
    a. public members of `Derv`.
    b. protected members of `Derv`.
    c. private members of `Derv`.
    d. public members of `Base`.
    e. protected members of `Base`.
    f. private members of `Base`.

16. True or false: A class `D` can be derived from a class `C`, which is derived from a class `B`, which is derived from a class `A`.

17. A class hierarchy
    a. shows the same relationships as an organization chart.
    b. describes "has a" relationships.
    c. describes "is a kind of" relationships.
    d. shows the same relationships as a family tree.

18. Write the first line of a specifier for a class `Tire` that is derived from class `Wheel` and from class `Rubber`.

19. Assume a class `Derv` derived from a base class `Base`. Both classes contain a member function `func()` that takes no arguments. Write a statement to go in a member function of `Derv` that calls `func()` in the base class.

20. True or false: It is illegal to make objects of one class members of another class.

Exercises

Answers to starred exercises can be found in Appendix D.

1.* Imagine a publishing company that markets both book and audiocassette versions of its works. Create a class `publication` that stores the title (a string) and price (type `float`) of a publication. From this class derive two classes: `book`, which adds a page count (type `int`); and `tape`, which adds a playing time in minutes (type `float`). Each of these three classes should have a `getdata()` function to get its data from the user at the keyboard, and a `putdata()` function to display its data.

Write a `main()` program to test the `book` and `tape` classes by creating instances of them, asking the user to fill in data with `getdata()`, and then displaying the data with `putdata()`.

2.* Recall the STRCONV example from Chapter 9. The `String` class in this example has a flaw: It does not protect itself if its objects are initialized to have too many characters. (The SZ constant has the value 80.) For example, the definition

```
String s = "This string will surely exceed the width of the \
screen, which is what the SZ constant represents.";
```

will cause the `str` array in `s` to overflow, with unpredictable consequences, such as crashing the system. (The `'\'` character in this statement permits a long string to wrap over two lines in the source file, while the compiler sees an unbroken string.)

With `String` as a base class, derive a class `Pstring` (for "protected string") that prevents buffer overflow when too long a string constant is used in a definition. A new constructor in the derived class should copy only SZ–1 characters into `str` if the string constant is longer, but copy the entire constant if it's shorter. Write a `main()` program to test different lengths of strings.

3.* Start with the `publication`, `book`, and `tape` classes of Exercise 1. Add a base class `sales` that holds an array of three `floats` so that it can record the dollar sales of a particular publication for the last three months. Include a `getdata()` function to get three sales amounts from the user, and a `putdata()` function to display the sales figures. Alter the `book` and `tape` classes so they are derived from both `publication` and `sales`. An object of class `book` or `tape` should input and output sales data along with its other data. Write a `main()` function to create a `book` object and a `tape` object and exercise their input/output capabilities.

4. Assume that the publisher in Exercises 1 and 3 decides to add a third way to distribute books: on computer disk, for those who like to do their reading on their laptop. Add a `disk` class that, like `book` and `tape`, is derived from `publication`. The `disk` class should incorporate the same member functions as the other classes. The data item unique to this class is the disk size: either 3-1/2 inches or 5-1/4 inches. You can use an `enum` Boolean type to store this item, but the complete size should be displayed. The user could select the appropriate size by typing 3 or 5.

5. Derive a class called `employee2` from the `employee` class in the EMPLOY program in this chapter. This new class should add a type `double` data item

called compensation, and also an enum type called period to indicate whether the employee is paid hourly, weekly, or monthly. For simplicity you can change the manager, scientist, and laborer classes so they are derived from employee2 instead of employee. However, note that in many circumstances it might be more in the spirit of OOP to create a separate base class called compensation and three new classes manager2, scientist2, and laborer2, and use multiple inheritance to derive these three classes from the original manager, scientist, and laborer classes and from compensation. This way none of the original classes needs to be modified.

6. Start with the ARROVER3 program in Chapter 9. Keep the safearay class the same as in that program, and, using inheritance, derive the capability for the user to specify both the upper and lower bounds of the array in a constructor. This is similar to Exercise 9 in Chapter 9, except that inheritance is used to derive a new class (you can call it safehilo) instead of modifying the original class.

7. Start with the COUNTEN2 program in this chapter. It can increment or decrement a counter, but only using prefix notation. Using inheritance, add the ability to use postfix notation for both incrementing and decrementing. (See Chapter 9 for a description of postfix notation.)

8. Operators in some computer languages, such as BASIC, allow you to select parts of an existing string and assign them to other strings. Using inheritance, add this capability to the Pstring class of Exercise 2. In the derived class, Pstring2, incorporate three new functions: left(), mid(), and right().

```
s2.left(s1, n)     // s2 is assigned the leftmost n characters
                   //    from s1
s2.mid(s1, s, n)   // s2 is assigned the middle n characters
                   //    from s1, starting at character number s
                   //    (leftmost character is 0)
s2.right(s1, n)    // s2 is assigned the rightmost n characters
                   //    from s1
```

You can use for loops to copy the appropriate parts of s1, character by character, to a temporary Pstring2 object, which is then returned. For extra credit, have these functions return by reference, so they can be used on the left side of the equal sign to change parts of an existing string.

9. Start with the publication, book, and tape classes of Exercise 1. Suppose you want to add the date of publication for both books and tapes. From the publication class, derive a new class called publication2 that includes this member data. Then change book and tape so they are derived from publication2 instead of publication. Make all the necessary changes in

member functions so the user can input and output dates along with the other data. For the dates, you can use the `date` class from Exercise 5 in Chapter 7, which stores a date as three `int`s, for month, day, and year.

10. There is only one kind of manager in the EMPMULT program in this chapter. Any serious company has executives as well as managers. From the `manager` class derive a class called `executive`. (We'll assume an executive is a high-end kind of manager.) The additional data in the `executive` class will be the size of the employee's yearly bonus and the number of shares of company stock held in his or her stock-option plan. Add the appropriate member functions so these data items can be input and displayed along with the other `manager` data.

11. Various situations require that pairs of numbers be treated as a unit. For example, each screen coordinate has an x (horizontal) component and a y (vertical) component. Represent such a pair of numbers as a structure called `pair` that comprises two `int` member variables.

Now, assume you want to be able to store `pair` variables on a stack. That is, you want to be able to place a pair (which contains two integers) onto a stack using a single call to a `push()` function, with a structure of type `pair` as an argument; and retrieve a pair using a single call to a `pop()` function, which will return a structure of type `pair`. Start with the `Stack2` class in the STAKEN program in this chapter, and from it derive a new class called `pairStack`. This new class need contain only two members: the overloaded `push()` and `pop()` functions. The `pairStack::push()` function will need to make two calls to `Stack2::push()` to store the two integers in its pair, and the `pairStack::pop()` function will need to make two calls to `Stack2::pop()` (although not necessarily in the same order).

12. Amazing as it may seem, the old British pounds-shillings-pence money notation (£9.19.11, see Exercise 10 in Chapter 5) isn't the whole story. A penny was further divided into halfpennies and farthings, with a farthing being worth 1/4 of a penny. There was a halfpenny coin, a farthing coin, and a halffarthing coin. Fortunately all this can be expressed numerically in eighths of a penny:

1/8 penny is a halffarthing
1/4 penny is a farthing
3/8 penny is a farthing and a half
1/2 penny is a halfpenny (pronounced ha'penny)
5/8 penny is a halfpenny plus a halffarthing
3/4 penny is a halfpenny plus a farthing
7/8 penny is a halfpenny plus a farthing and a half

Let's assume we want to add to the `sterling` class the ability to handle such fractional pennies. The I/O format can be something like `£1.1.1-1/4` or `£9.19.11-7/8`, where the hyphen separates the fraction from the pennies.

Derive a new class called `sterfrac` from `sterling`. It should be able to perform the four arithmetic operations on sterling quantities that include eighths of a penny. Its only member data is an `int` indicating the number of eighths; you can call it `eighths`. You'll need to overload many of the functions in `sterling` to handle the eighths. The user should be able to type any fraction in lowest terms, and the display should also show fractions in lowest terms. It's not necessary to use the full-scale `fraction` class (see Exercise 11 in Chapter 7), but you could try that for extra credit.

11

Borland C++ Graphics

TEXT-MODE GRAPHICS

SETTING UP FOR GRAPHICS MODE

SHAPES, LINES, COLOR, AND PATTERN

GRAPHICS SHAPES AS C++ OBJECTS

TEXT IN GRAPHICS MODE

11

Borland C++ and Turbo C++ include an extensive collection of graphics-oriented library functions for use in DOS programs. These functions open up an exciting new world: With them you can place almost any sort of image on the screen. Graphics and object-oriented programming work together particularly well because specific images, such as polygons or text boxes, can be represented by objects. Graphics provide a visual way to see objects in action.

Borland C++ graphics functions ("Borland" in this context means both Borland and Turbo) fall into two categories: those that work in text mode and those that work in graphics mode. The text-mode functions, which we'll look at first, are concerned with placing text and IBM graphics characters on the screen with more flexibility than is possible with the normal C++ display functions. You can use text-mode functions even if you have a text-only (nongraphics) display.

The graphics-mode functions, which we look at in the second part of the chapter, require a graphics monitor and adapter card, such as EGA or VGA. See the description of the `initgraph()` function in the Borland (or Turbo) C++ documentation for a complete list of supported graphics adapters. Graphics-mode functions allow you to draw dots, lines, and shapes (like circles and rectangles), add color to lines and areas, and perform many other graphics-related activities.

The emphasis in this chapter is on how graphics images can be implemented as C++ objects. No major new object-oriented topics are introduced, so this chapter gives you a chance to reinforce the concepts you've learned already, including objects, classes, and inheritance. (Even in the unlikely event that your computer does not have a graphics display, you should read this chapter, as graphics provide an intuitive, visual demonstration of object-oriented programming.)

We do not cover all the Borland C++ graphics functions. Our aim is to show the most important functions and how they work in the object-oriented environment. However, we show the general approach to a variety of situations, so you can probably figure out the remaining graphics functions on your own. (The books *C Programming Using Turbo C++* and *Turbo C++ Bible*, listed in Appendix E, contain more details on Borland and Turbo C++ graphics functions.)

The library functions discussed in this chapter don't work in EasyWin programs. They require a full-scale DOS screen, not a window. Thus, if you're using Borland C++ to create the example programs, you'll need to use the Application target type and the Standard DOS platform. This was described in Chapter 2. There's no problem in Turbo C++, since it only builds DOS programs. In Borland C++ you'll find many of the graphics functions described in the Borland C++ *DOS Reference*; a few others are in the *Library Reference*.

Unlike most of the Borland C++ library functions mentioned in this book, the graphics library functions described in this chapter work only in the MS-DOS environment. They are not portable to other platforms such as Unix, or even to other compilers besides Borland C++ and Turbo C++.

Text-Mode Graphics

In a *text mode* (sometimes called a *console mode*) display, the screen is divided into character positions, typically 80 columns by 25 rows (although there can also be 40x25, 80x43, and other arrangements). The video output operations we've seen so far, such as `cout <<`, are text-mode functions. However, Borland C++ adds an additional text-mode function to facilitate writing text to *windows*. A window in this context is a rectangular area on the screen that confines the text written to it.

Windows are useful in programs that use a Graphical User Interface (GUI) display in DOS text mode. The Turbo C++ IDE environment is an example of this kind of display, and you are probably familiar with other DOS programs that use windows. In this section we'll examine text-mode windows and various ways to manipulate them.

There are two approaches to text-mode graphics. First, in the spirit of OOP, Borland provides the `constream` class to help you create and use windows. Second, you can use stand-alone library functions that aren't related to a class (but that can be used in classes of our own devising). We'll look at these two approaches in turn.

The `constream` Class

The `constream` class gives you a simple object-oriented way to make use of windows in text mode. This class is derived from the I/O stream class `ostream`. We don't cover I/O streams until Chapter 14, but `constream` is more applicable to graphics than to I/O, so it makes sense to discuss it here.

A `constream` object represents a text window. There's no visible border around this window; it's simply an area in which text is confined. Thus you can't see where the window is until you start writing in it. Member functions and manipulators of `constream` allow you to set the size of the window, write text to it, change its color, move the cursor within it, and so on.

To use the `constream` class you must include the CONSTREA.H header file, which declares the class and its member functions.

Unlike graphics mode, which requires special functions to initialize the graphics system, text mode needs no preparation before use, since you're already in it when you're at the DOS prompt. You can start right in using `constream` objects.

Here's an example that makes use of `constream`. This program creates two `constream` windows and uses the `window()` member function to specify their sizes. It then writes text into the first window, writes text to a second window, and finally writes different text into the first window. Here's the listing for CONWIN:

```
// conwin.cpp
// uses the constream class
#include <constrea.h>     // for constream class

void main()
   {
   clrscr();                // clear entire screen

   char s1[] = "The disk drive is jammed\n\
or on fire, or the CPU\n\
is flooded.  Correct the\n\
situation and try again.\n\
Press Enter to continue: ";

   char s2[] = "This is a string that will wrap at the right \
```

```
edge of the window, probably breaking words inappropriately \
in the process.";

   char s3[] = "Everything is under control\n\
now, and we are carrying\n\
out our mission. You have\n\
nothing to worry about.";

   constream w1, w2;               // make two windows

   w1.window(25, 6, 55, 18);       // window 1, middle of screen
   w2.window(1, 1, 25, 10);        // window 2, upper left corner

   w1 << s1;                       // output text to window 1
   getch();                        // wait for keypress
   w1.clrscr();                    // clear window 1 only

   w2 << setclr(BLUE) << s2;       // output blue text to window 2
   getch();                        // wait for keypress
   w2.clrscr();                    // clear window 2 only

   w1 << s3;                       // output new text to window 1
   getch();                        // wait for keypress
   }
```

Figures 11-1 and 11-2 show the two windows with the first two messages in them. Notice how the words in the second message do indeed break inappropriately at the edge of the window. Objects of the `constream` class confine text to the window, but they don't know anything about words.

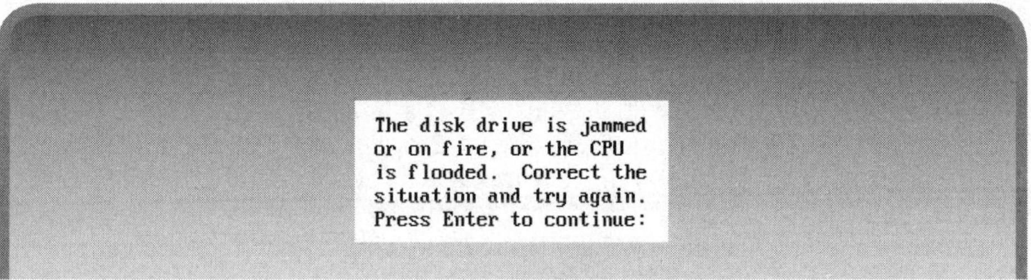

Figure 11-1 Output of WINDOW, Part 1

This is a string that wil
l wrap at the right edge
of the window, probably b
reaking words inappropria
tely in the process.

Figure 11-2 Output of WINDOW, Part 2

The `window()` Member Function

A key member function for `constream` objects is `window()`. This function takes four integer arguments that determine the left, top, right, and bottom coordinates of the window. On an 80x25 display, the columns run from 1 to 80, and the rows from 1 to 25. Text written by other member functions will appear inside the area specified by these coordinates, starting at the upper-left corner of the window. Text too long for the width of the window is automatically wrapped at the right edge. Text that goes beyond the bottom of the window causes the contents of the window to scroll upward. (Actually, writing a character at the right-most position in the bottom line causes it to scroll.)

The Overloaded << Operator

One of the surprising features of the `constream` class is that you can use the `<<` operator to display text in the window. As we'll see in Chapter 14, this is because `constream` is derived from `ostream`. However, at this point all you need to know is that it works. You can use `<<` to display all the usual data types: numbers, characters, and strings.

Other `constream` Functions

We use another `constream` function, `clrscr()`, to clear the window before writing text to it. Note that, when used as a member function, `clrscr()` clears only the window, not the entire screen.

There is only one other commonly used member function, `textmode()`. It's used to alter the graphics mode. These `constream` member functions are shown in Table 11-1.

We also use an ordinary library function, `getch()`, to pause the program while the user reads the text in the window.

Manipulators

The `constream` class contains a number of manipulators for use with the `<<` operator. In CONWIN we've used one of them, `setclr`, to change the color of the text that appears in the second window. Table 11-2 shows some of the manipulators.

The colors that are available in text mode are shown in Table 11-3. Only the first are available for setting the text background.

The `constream` class makes it easy to create text-mode windows for use in DOS user interfaces. We'll show how to use it to make text-mode windows with lined borders in the last example in this section.

Function	Purpose
`clrscr()`	Clear window
`window()`	Set size of window
`textmode()`	Set graphics mode

Table 11-1 Some `constream` Member Functions

Manipulator	Purpose
`setclr(int)`	Set text color (see Table 11-3)
`setbk(int)`	Set text background (see Table 11-3)
`setcrsrtype(int)`	Set cursor type (`_NOCURSOR`, `_SOLIDCURSOR`, `_NORMALCURSOR`)
`clreol`	Clear to end of line
`highvideo`	High intensity text
`normvideo`	Normal intensity text
`delline`	Delete text line
`insline`	Insert text line

Table 11-2 Some `constream` Manipulators

Color number	Color constant	Color number	Color constant
0	BLACK	8	DARKGRAY
1	BLUE	9	LIGHTBLUE
2	GREEN	10	LIGHTGREEN
3	CYAN	11	LIGHTCYAN
4	RED	12	LIGHTRED
5	MAGENTA	13	LIGHTMAGENTA
6	BROWN	14	YELLOW
7	LIGHTGRAY	15	WHITE
		128	BLINK

Table 11-3 Text-Mode Colors

Stand-Alone Text-Mode Functions

The functionality of the member functions of `constream` can also be obtained using stand-alone functions. This allows you to create text-mode graphics without using `constream` objects. In our next example we create almost the same screen display, using almost the same `main()` as in CONWIN. However, we've defined our own window class instead of using `constream`, and used stand-alone text-mode functions in the member functions of this class. Here's the listing for HOMEWIN:

```
// homewin.cpp
// home-made text window class
#include <conio.h>       // for window(), cputs()

class textwin            // text window class
   {
   private:
      int left, top, right, bottom;      // window dimensions
   public:
                                         // set window size
      void setsize(int l, int t, int r, int b)
         {
         left=l; top=t; right=r; bottom=b;
         }
      void erase()                       // erase the window
         {
         window(left, top, right, bottom);
         clrscr();
         }
      void drawtext(char* str)           // draw text in window
         {
         window(left, top, right, bottom);
         cputs(str);
         }
      void color(int c)                  // change text color
        {
        textcolor(c);
        }
   };

void main()
   {

   char s1[] = "Keep an eye out at all times\n\r\
for stragglers from Major\n\r\
Higsby's brigade.";

   char s2[] = "We can't be too careful.\n\r\
You remember what happened to\n\r\
those poor chaps at Khartoum.";

   char s3[] = "As dusk approaches we\n\r\
may hear to the south\n\r\
the sound of elephants.";

   textwin a, b;                // define two text windows

   clrscr();                    // clear entire screen

   a.setsize(25, 6, 55, 18);    // window in middle of screen
   a.drawtext(s1);              // draw text in it
   getch();                     // wait for keypress
   a.erase();                   // erase window

   b.setsize(1, 1, 30, 10);     // window in upper left corner
```

```
b.color(BLUE);                  // set color to blue
b.drawtext(s2);                 // draw text in it
getch();                        // wait for keypress
b.erase();                      // erase window

a.color(WHITE);                 // restore color
a.drawtext(s3);                 // draw new text in first window
getch();                        // wait for keypress
}
```

Here we create a class called `textwin`, which has some (actually a small part) of the functionality of the `constream` class. Our homemade member function `setsize()` sets the size, as `window()` does in `constream`; `erase()` mimics `clrscr()`; `drawtext()` replaces the overloaded `<<` operator; and `color()` replaces the `setclr` manipulator.

The output of HOMEWIN looks similar to that of CONWIN (see Figures 11-1 and 11-2), except that the text is different.

Within the member functions of our `textwin` class, we've used some stand-alone Borland text-mode graphics library functions, which we'll now discuss. Note that we'll be talking about two kinds of functions: these stand-alone library functions, like `window()` and `cputs()` on the one hand; and member functions of classes we create ourselves, like `drawtext()` and `color()` on the other. We will try to clarify which kind of function we mean by describing it as either a *library function* or a *member function* when it is introduced, but you should be aware of the possibility of confusion.

The stand-alone text-mode library functions require the header file CONIO.H.

The `window()` Function

The `window()` function specifies the size of a text window. Since it isn't a member function, there can only be one window active on the screen at a time. You specify the window's coordinates with `window()`, and all text-mode functions that follow, like `cputs()`, apply to that window. If you want to write text somewhere else, you must use `window()` again to specify a new window.

The default setting for the text window is the entire screen; this is the window you're writing to before you use `window()`.

The `cputs()` Function

The usual approach to text output, using `cout` and the `<<` operator, does not work within a text window (unless you use `constream`). Most C++ functions don't recognize the existence of text windows; they assume they have the entire screen to work with. To work within a text window you must use library functions specifically created for that purpose. One of the most useful is the function `cputs()`, which writes a string of text to a window. (The letter `'c'` stands for *console*, meaning the screen.) We use this function to display the text from the `textwin` class.

A peculiarity of `cputs()` is that it does not translate a newline character (`'\n'`) into the carriage-return-plus-linefeed combination. We must do this manually, by inserting both a linefeed (represented by the `'\n'` character) and a separate carriage return (represented by `'\r'`) wherever we want to start a new line. This combination is used to terminate each line in `s1`, `s2`, and `s3`.

The `clrscr()` Function

The `clrscr()` library function erases the text window. It is used twice in HOMEWIN. The first time is in `main()`, where—since the `window()` function has not yet been invoked to change the text window from its default setting—`clrscr()` erases the entire screen. It's also used in the `textwin::erase()` member function to erase the contents of the window.

The `main()` part of HOMEWIN defines three strings and then creates two window objects of type `textwin`. The first window, in the middle of the screen, displays the first string. Then, after the user presses a key, the second window displays the second string.

The `textcolor()` Function

The color to be used for text output is set by our member function `color()`. This function simply calls the library function `textcolor()`. All subsequent text output will be in this color until it's changed. The possible values for the argument to `textcolor()` were shown in Table 11-3.

Other stand-alone graphics functions, which we don't use in this program, can be used to change the appearance of text written to the screen. Many of them are similar to `constream` member functions. For instance, you can set the text background color with the `textbackground()` library function. This function accepts only the first eight colors in Table 11-3. The function `highvideo()` turns on high-intensity text, and `normvideo()` restores the original intensity.

A Class Within a Class

Let's rewrite the `textwin` class from HOMEWIN so that, in addition to displaying text, it also outlines its text windows with a rectangle. This will give them a more "window-like" appearance. We'll do this with graphics characters that represent vertical and horizontal line segments and corners. Since the window created by this class is enclosed by lines, we'll name its class `textbox`.

Our strategy in this program is to embed a `constream` object in our `textbox` class. This way we'll be able to use the convenient `constream` member functions within our own `textbox` member functions.

Here's the listing for CONBOXES:

```
// conboxes.cpp
// text boxes as objects
// each text box is based on a constream window

#include <constrea.h>     // for constream class
#include <string.h>       // for strcpy()

const int LEFT = 25;      // default window dimensions
const int TOP = 6;
const int RIGHT = 55;
const int BOTTOM = 18;

class textbox             // text window class
   {
   private:
```

```
      int left, top, right, bottom;       // box dimensions
      constream w;                        // a constream window
      int color;                          // text color
   public:
      textbox()                           // no-arg constructor
         {                                // default size
         left=LEFT; top=TOP; right=RIGHT; bottom=BOTTOM;
         color = WHITE;                   // default color
         }
                                          // 5-arg constructor
      textbox(int l, int t, int r, int b, int c=WHITE)
         {                                // size from arguments
         left=l; top=t; right=r; bottom=b;
         color=c;                         // color from arg
         }
      void erase()                        // erase the box
         { w.clrscr(); }
      void drawtext(char*);               // display the box
   };

void textbox::drawtext(char* str)         // display box with text
   {
   w.window(left, top, right, bottom+1); // frame window
   w.clrscr();                           // erase window
   w << setclr(color);                   // set window color
   int width = right - left + 1;
   int height = bottom - top + 1;
   for(int j=1; j<=width; j++)           // draw horiz lines
      {
      w << setxy(j, 1) << char(205);        // top
      w << setxy(j, height) << char(205);   // bottom
      }

   for(j=1; j<=height; j++)              // draw vertical lines
      {
      w << setxy(1, j) << char(186);        // left
      w << setxy(width, j) << char(186);    // right
      }
                                         // draw corners
   w << setxy(1, 1) << char(201);           // upper left
   w << setxy(width, 1) << char(187);       // upper right
   w << setxy(1, height) << char(200);      // lower left
   w << setxy(width, height) << char(188);  // lower right
                                         // reframe window
   w.window(left+2, top+1, right-2, bottom-3);
   w << str;                             // display text

   w.window(left, top, right, bottom+1); // reframe window
   w << setxy(3, height-1);              // go to last line
   w << "Press any key to continue: ";   // display prompt
   getch();                              // wait for keypress
   }

void main()
```

(continued on next page)

(continued from previous page)

```
   {
   clrscr();                          // clear screen

   textbox bx1;                       // box, no-arg constructor
   textbox bx2(1, 1, 31, 8, YELLOW);  // box, 5-arg constructor

                                      // text for box 1
   char s1[] = "\"The time,\" said the\n\
Duchess, \"is surely ripe;\n\
make haste, lest seconds\n\
spoil.\"";
                                      // text for box 2
   char s2[] = "Should you continue\n\
along the present path you\n\
risk investigation\n\
for felonious chicanery.";

   bx1.drawtext(s1);                  // output text in box 1
   bx1.erase();                       // erase box 1
   bx2.drawtext(s2);                  // output text in box 2
   bx2.erase();                       // erase box 2
   bx2.drawtext("Thank you");         // output new text in box 2
   }
```

The `textbox` class in this program has two constructors. One uses no arguments and creates a text box with standard dimensions in the middle of the screen. The other sets the text box to dimensions chosen by the user. The text is added to the text box by a separate member function, `drawtext()`, which also displays the text box. The `erase()` member function erases the text box.

The `setxy()` Manipulator

The `setxy()`manipulator from the `constream` class positions the cursor within a text window. Since text is written starting at the cursor position, this allows us to place text where we want it. The `setxy()` manipulator takes two integer parameters: the x and y coordinates where the cursor should go. The coordinate system is that of the window, not the screen, so 1,1 is the upper-left corner of the window. We use this function numerous times in the `drawtext()` member function to position the various graphics characters that make up the box's outline.

Figures 11-3, 11-4, and 11-5 show three stages in the output of CONBOXES. Each new screen display is drawn when the user presses a key.

Figure 11-3 shows box `bx1`, Figure 11-4 shows box `bx2` with its first string, and Figure 11-5 shows the same box with its second string. Box `bx1` is displayed in white, while `bx2` is yellow.

Windows Within Windows

The `drawtext()` member function in CONBOXES uses the `window()` function to create several windows that are in the same location but have slightly different sizes. Early in `drawtext()` the statement

```
w.window(left, top, right, bottom+1);
```

sets up what we call the *frame* window: the rectangle where the lines forming the

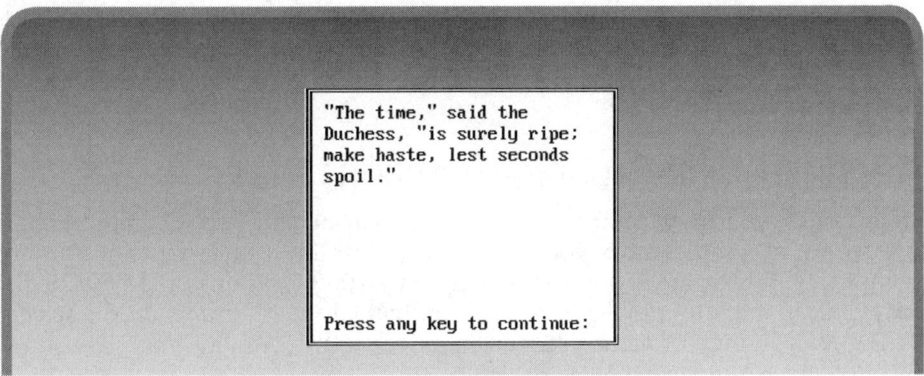

Figure 11-3 Output of CONBOXES, Part 1

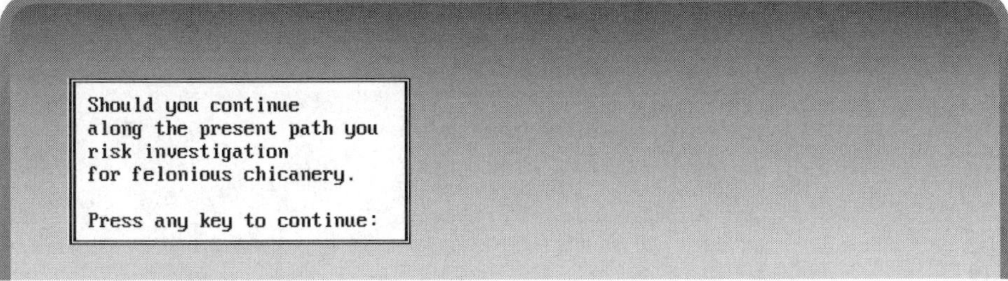

Figure 11-4 Output of CONBOXES, Part 2

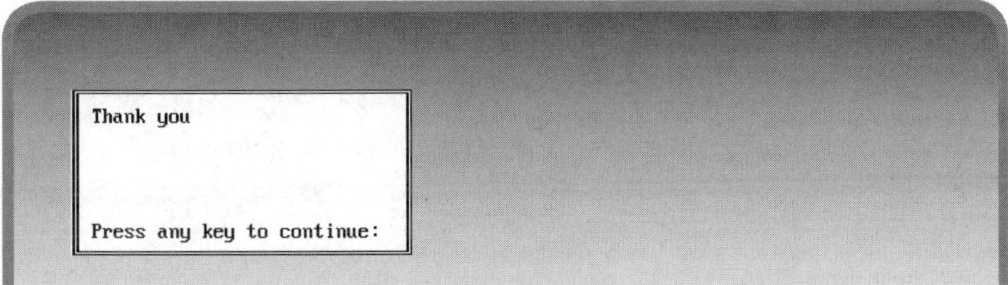

Figure 11-5 Output of CONBOXES, Part 3

outline of the window will be drawn. The bottom of this outline is one line lower than the dimensions specified in `textbox` because we want to be able to display the lower-right corner character without causing the entire window contents to scroll upward.

After the outline is drawn, the statement

```
w.window(left+2, top+1, right-2, bottom-3);
```

specifies the rectangle where the text will actually be drawn. The dimensions are smaller than those in the `textwin` object because we want to keep the text inside the outline, with a 1-space separation on the left and right edges. The bottom spacing allows room for the line *Press Enter to Continue:*, which is always placed at the bottom of the window. Figure 11-6 shows the relation of the various windows and dimension systems.

Graphics-Mode Graphics Functions

In text mode you are restricted, as we've seen, to displaying text (or graphics characters), but in graphics mode you can display points, lines, and shapes of arbitrary complexity. In text mode you can address only 2000 locations (in an 80x25 display), but in graphics mode you address individual *pixels*, or dots on the screen. This gives you much finer resolution: In a 640x480 VGA mode you can address 307,200 pixels (somewhat fewer for EGA).

Like the text-mode graphics functions, graphics-mode functions require a DOS target, not an EasyWin program. In Borland C++ they also (this is important) require you to check the box marked *BGI* in the *Standard Libraries* part of the *New Project* box when you're creating your program's project. BGI is the Borland Graphics Interface

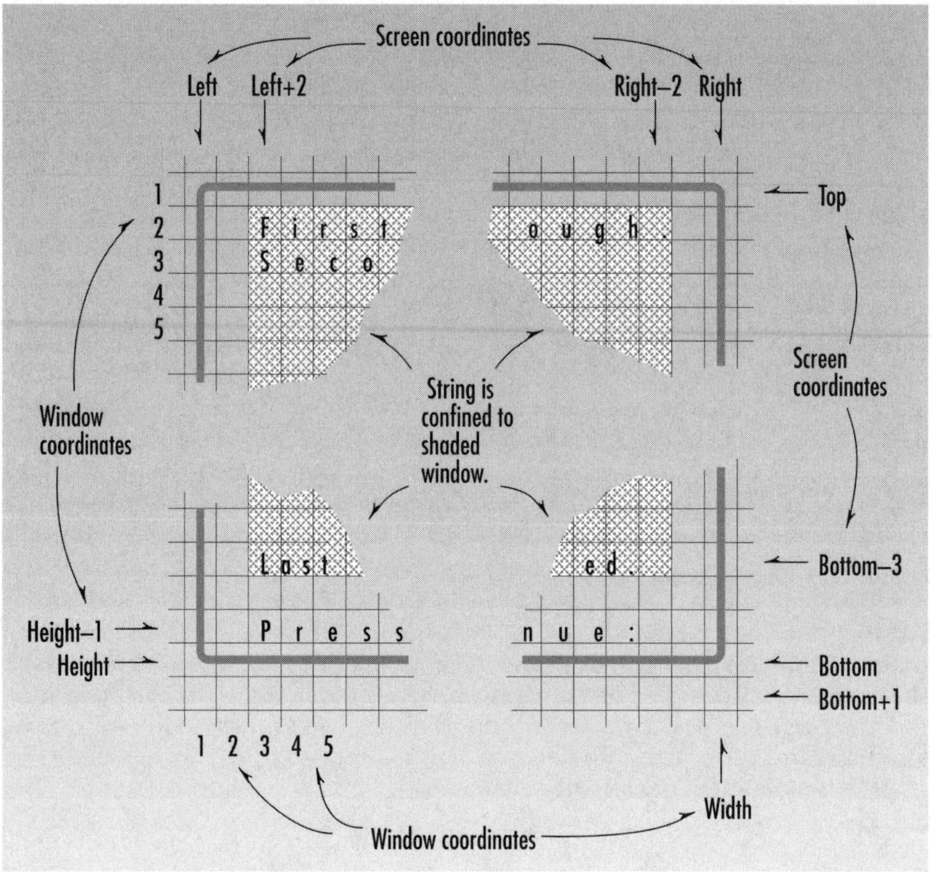

Figure 11-6 Windows in CONBOXES

library, and checking the box causes a library of graphics routines to be linked automatically with your program. If you don't check this box, the linker won't recognize any of the graphics functions. In Turbo C++, select *Linker* from the *Options* menu, then select *Libraries* from the submenu. In the resulting window, click on the *Graphics Library* checkbox, and then on *OK*.

The graphics program itself must perform some preliminary work to set the appropriate graphics mode. Let's look at a simple program that uses a class `ball` to model circles displayed on the screen.

The `ball` class stores the coordinates of the center of the circle. The member function `set()` sets these coordinates from arguments passed to it. Another member function, `draw()`, draws the ball. All `ball` objects have the same radius, as specified by the external variable RAD.

Here's the listing for EZBALL:

```
// ezball.cpp
// stationary ball class
#include <graphics.h>          // for graphics functions
#include <conio.h>             // for getch()

const int RAD = 75;

class ball                     // ball class
   {
   private:
      int xCo, yCo;            // coordinates of center
   public:
      ball()                   // no-argument constructor
         { xCo=0; yCo=0; }
      void set(int x, int y)   // set position
         { xCo=x; yCo=y; }
      void draw()              // draw the ball
         { circle(xCo, yCo, RAD); }
   };
void main()
   {
   int driver, mode;
   driver = DETECT;            // set to best graphics mode
   initgraph(&driver, &mode, "\\bc45\\bgi");

   ball b1;              // create three balls
   ball b2;
   ball b3;

   b1.set(320, 150);     // position them
   b2.set(255, 150);
   b3.set(385, 150);

   b1.draw();            // draw them
   b2.draw();
   b3.draw();

   getch();              // wait for keypress
   closegraph();         // close graphics system
   }
```

There are several new graphics functions in this program, so we'll describe the role each one plays.

The `initgraph()` Function

The `initgraph()` library function must be executed before any other graphics-mode functions can be used. It switches your computer's display system into the appropriate graphics mode. This function—like all the graphics-mode functions—requires the GRAPHICS.H header file.

There are two ways to handle the choice of display mode. You can specify it yourself, or you can let the system select it. In the examples in this chapter we'll let the system select the best mode. This is the most versatile approach, since programs written this way will run on systems with different graphics displays. However, we'll first explain how to specify a particular mode.

The Graphics Driver

To specify the mode, you need to choose appropriate values for the parameters to `initgraph()`. The first argument to `initgraph()` specifies the graphics *driver* to be used. This is the software routine that interfaces with the display adapter. The most common choices are shown in Table 11-4.

The constants in Table 11-4 represent numerical values and are defined in the GRAPHICS.H file. (Other possibilities are shown in the description of `initgraph()` in the Borland C++ or Turbo C++ documentation.) Ordinarily you choose the constant for the system you're using: `EGA` if you have an EGA display, and so on. However, because the PC's display adapters are backward compatible, you can also select a less powerful mode; if you have a VGA display you can select EGA or CGA mode, for example. This is useful if you want to test a program with other display modes.

The Graphics Mode

The second parameter to `initgraph()` specifies the particular mode. Each adapter can use several possible modes. Table 11-5 shows the choices for CGA, EGA, and VGA.

A *palette* is a set of colors. CGA has four palettes, each representing a different set of four colors. EGA and VGA don't use palettes for `initgraph()`. The normal mode choice for EGA is EGAHI, which gives the highest resolution. In VGA the normal choice is VGAHI.

Display driver	Constant for `initgraph()`
CGA	CGA
EGA	EGA
VGA	VGA

Table 11-4 Display Driver Constants

Driver selected	Mode constant	Display mode
CGA	CGAC0	320x200, 4 color, palette 0
	CGAC1	320x200, 4 color, palette 1
	CGAC2	320x200, 4 color, palette 2
	CGAC3	320x200, 4 color, palette 3
	CGAHI	640x200, 2 color
EGA	EGALO	640x200, 16 color
	EGAHI	640x350, 16 color
VGA	VGALO	640x200, 16 color
	VGAMED	640x350, 16 color
	VGAHI	640x480, 16 color

Table 11-5 Graphics Mode Constants

As an example, here are the statements you would use to initialize VGAHI mode:

```
int driver = VGA;                                    // VGA driver
int mode = VGAHI;                                    // VGA hi-res mode
initgraph(&driver, &mode, "\\BC45\\BGI");
```

Let the System Decide

If you let the system decide what graphics mode to use, it will check your adapter and choose the driver and mode that give the highest resolution. This is called *auto-detect*. To do this, set the driver argument to the constant `DETECT`. You don't need to specify a mode argument. The example programs show how this is done.

The *Address of* Operator: &

You may have noticed that instead of placing the constants like `EGA` and `EGAHI` directly into the function call, we place them in the variables `driver` and `mode`, and then use the names of these variables in `initgraph()`, preceded by a `&` symbol, as in `&driver`. What does this do?

It turns out that in C++ the `&` symbol means *address of*, so we are actually telling `initgraph()` the addresses where the constants are stored, rather than telling it the constants themselves. This is similar to (but by no means the same as) passing arguments by reference. Understanding addresses is one of the keys to understanding pointers, which we'll cover in Chapter 12. For the moment, don't worry about this syntax. Just set up the constants as shown in the examples, and everything should work properly.

The Path

The third argument to `initgraph()` is the path to the graphics driver. This argument must be specified whether you use auto-detect or specify a mode yourself.

The drivers are supplied as part of Borland C++ or Turbo C++, and are installed in a specific directory. In Borland C++ 4.0 this is normally \BC45\BGI\. In Turbo C++ it's the \TC\BGI\ directory. In older versions of Borland C++ it was \BORLANDC\BGI\ or \BC4\BGI.

The drivers all have the .BGI extension (for Borland Graphics Interface). For CGA the driver is called CGA.BGI, and for EGA and VGA it's EGAVGA.BGI. You need the path to the driver but you don't need the driver name. Here's how to specify this argument in Borland C++ 4.0:

```
"\\bc4\\bgi"
```

Either upper- or lowercase can be used. If the drivers are installed elsewhere, then you'll need to modify this pathname accordingly.

The pathname is a string, and must be surrounded by quotes in the call to `initgraph()`. Notice that, since the backslash `\` is an escape character in C++ strings, you must double it to give it its normal value: `\\`. Forgetting to do this creates a particularly hard-to-diagnose programming bug.

Creating Stand-Alone Programs

The approach described here, using `initgraph()` to specify the path to the directory that contains the .BGI files, requires the existence of such a directory in the system. Thus programs written with this approach won't run in a system that doesn't already have Borland (or Turbo) C++ installed in it. To create a stand-alone program you need a different approach. This is described in Appendix C.

The `circle()` Function

In `main()` we use `initgraph()` to initialize the graphics system. Then we create three objects of class `ball`, set their locations with the `set()` member function, and display the objects with `draw()`. The `draw()` member function uses the Borland C++ library function `circle()` to actually draw a circle.

The `circle()` library function takes three integer parameters: the x and y coordinates of the center of the circle, and the radius of the circle. We use a fixed radius, `RAD`, for all objects of class `ball`. The x and y coordinates are taken from the private data in `ball`, so the call to `circle()` looks like this:

```
circle(xCo, yCo, RAD);
```

The three invocations of the `ball` constructor in `main()` establish three overlapping balls with centers on the same horizontal line. Figure 11-7 shows the output of EZBALL.

The `closegraph()` Function

When you exit from a graphics program you should restore the system to the video mode that was previously in use—probably a text mode. If you don't, you may experience undesirable effects, such as the loss of the cursor or off-size characters, as the operating system tries to write text in a graphics mode.

To restore the previous mode, and to release whatever memory the graphics system was using, execute the `closegraph()` library function just before exiting your program.

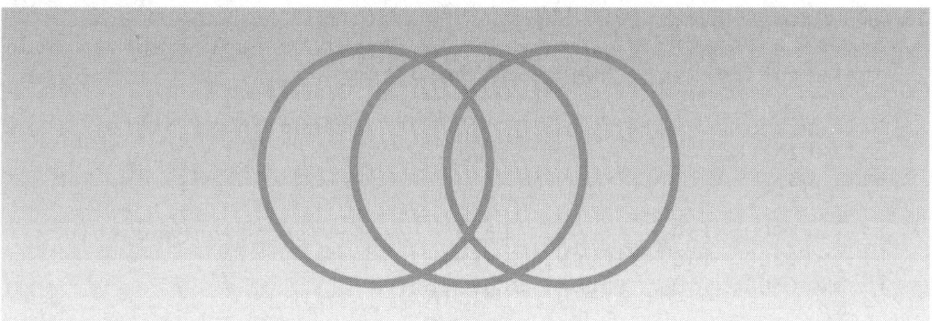

Figure 11-7 Output of EZBALL

Colors

If you have a color display you can draw lines, circles, and so on in different colors. You can also fill enclosed areas with color. Our next program, COLORBAL, is a variation of the EZBALL program that demonstrates the use of color. Here's the listing:

```
// colorbal.cpp
// adds colors to ball class
#include <graphics.h>             // for graphics functions
#include <conio.h>                // for getch()

const int RAD = 75;

class ball                        // ball class
   {
   private:
      int xCo, yCo;               // coordinates of center
      int linecolor;              // color of outline
      int fillcolor;              // color of interior
   public:
      ball()                      // no-arg constructor
         { xCo=0; yCo=0; linecolor=WHITE; fillcolor=WHITE; }
      void set(int x, int y, int lc, int fc)     // set data
         { xCo=x; yCo=y; linecolor=lc; fillcolor=fc; }
      void draw()                 // draw the ball
         {
         setcolor(linecolor);                        // line color
         setlinestyle(SOLID_LINE, 0, THICK_WIDTH); // line width
         circle(xCo, yCo, RAD);                      // draw circle
         setfillstyle(SOLID_FILL, fillcolor);    // set fill color
         floodfill(xCo, yCo, linecolor);         // fill circle
         }
   };

void main()
   {
   int driver, mode;
```

(continued on next page)

(continued from previous page)
```
   driver = DETECT;                        // set to best graphics mode
   initgraph(&driver, &mode, "\\bc45\\bgi");

   ball b1;                                // create three balls
   ball b2;
   ball b3;

   b1.set(100, 150, YELLOW, RED);          // set position and colors
   b2.set(200, 150, YELLOW, GREEN);
   b3.set(300, 150, YELLOW, BLUE);

   b1.draw();                              // draw them
   b2.draw();
   b3.draw();

   getch();                                // wait for keypress
   closegraph();                           // close graphics system
   }
```

Don't forget to modify the pathname in `initgraph()` to correspond to the location of the .BGI files in your particular version of the compiler.

The `ball` class in this program now features a four-argument `set()` function. The first two arguments are the center of the circle as before. The third argument specifies the color of the circle's outline, and the fourth specifies the color used to fill the interior of the circle. Figure 11-8 shows the effect. Unfortunately, we can't show the figure in color; instead different kinds of shading are used to indicate the colors.

The changes to this program lie mostly in the `draw()` member function. Here it is:

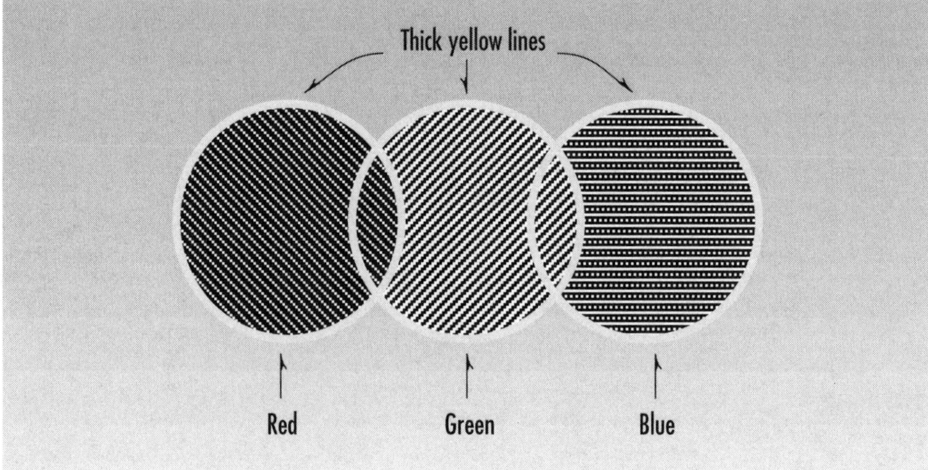

Figure 11-8 Output of COLORBALL

```
void draw()
   {
   setcolor(linecolor);
   setlinestyle(SOLID_LINE, 0, THICK_WIDTH);
   circle(xCo, yCo, RAD);
   setfillstyle(SOLID_FILL, fillcolor);
   floodfill(xCo, yCo, linecolor);
   }
```

Let's examine the new Borland C++ graphics functions used in the `draw()` member function, and see how they generate colors. Note that this program is written for EGA and VGA displays. If you're using CGA or another display adapter, you may need to make some adjustments or use different colors to achieve an equivalent output. See the Borland or Turbo C++ documentation for detailed descriptions of the individual library functions.

The `setcolor()` Function

The `setcolor()` library function sets the color used for drawing lines. The word *lines* here means not only straight lines but also the *outlines* of shapes such as circles and rectangles. The interior of shapes is not affected by `setcolor()`.

In EGA and VGA modes there are 16 colors available to `setcolor()`. These are the same colors that are available for the `textcolor()` library function and are listed in Table 11-3. In the `draw()` member function, the `setcolor()` library function uses the `linecolor` member data as its single argument. In `main()` all three balls have their outlines set to YELLOW by the `set()` member function.

The `setlinestyle()` Function

We use the `setlinestyle()` library function to specify thick lines for the circle outlines. The first argument to this function specifies a *style*. This can be one of the constants shown in Table 11-6.

Unfortunately these styles apply only to straight lines, not to circles, so in our program it doesn't matter what we put as the first argument. The second argument specifies a user-defined style if the first argument is set to `USERBIT_LINE`. We'll

Value	Constant	Effect
0	SOLID_LINE	Solid line
1	DOTTED_LINE	Dotted line
2	CENTER_LINE	Dot-dash line
3	DASHED_LINE	Dashed line
4	USERBIT_LINE	User-defined line

Table 11-6 Line Styles

ignore this possibility, so we set this argument to 0. The third argument has two possible values, as shown in Table 11-7.

By using THICK_WIDTH we cause wider lines to be drawn for our circle outlines.

The `setfillstyle()` Function

Now let's see how to fill the interior of a shape with a specific color. There are two parts to this. First we set the color to be filled, using the `setfillstyle()` library function. This function takes two arguments. The first argument is a pattern, shown in Table 11-8.

The second argument to `setfillstyle()` is the color. This can be one of the same color constants used for the `setcolor()` library function shown in Table 11-3. We use SOLID_FILL for the pattern, and the color from the `fillcolor`

Value	Constant	Effect
0	NORM_WIDTH	Line 1 pixel wide (default)
3	THICK_WIDTH	Line 3 pixels wide

Table 11-7 Line Widths

Value	Constant	Effect
0	EMPTY_FILL	Background color
1	SOLID_FILL	Solid color
2	LINE_FILL	Horizontal lines
3	LTSLASH_FILL	SW-NE light lines
4	SLASH_FILL	SW-NE heavy lines
5	BKSLASH_FILL	NW-SE heavy lines
6	LTBKSLASH_FILL	NW-SE light lines
7	HATCH_FILL	Light cross hatch
8	XHATCH_FILL	Heavy cross hatch
9	INTERLEAVE_FILL	Interleave
10	WIDE_DOT_FILL	Wide-spaced dots
11	CLOSE_DOT_FILL	Close-spaced dots
12	USER_FILL	User-defined

Table 11-8 Pattern Constants

member data in `ball`. In `main()` we choose three different colors for the three balls: `RED`, `GREEN`, and `BLUE`.

The `floodfill()` Function

The `floodfill()` library function fills in the color in the interior of the circle. This function starts the fill at a particular x, y location inside the object. This location is specified by the first two arguments. The fill, in the color and pattern specified by `setfillstyle()`, expands outward from this point until it reaches a boundary. The color of this boundary is specified in the third parameter to `floodfill()`. Remember that this argument is the boundary color, not the fill color.

Notice in Figure 11-8 that, since the red ball is drawn and filled first, it is the only one completely filled with a color. The fill for the other two balls stops at the edge of the previously drawn circle. The fill will always stop at the specified boundary color.

You may find that with a CGA display the `floodfill()` library function does not work perfectly. The colors tend to escape from their boundaries and engulf the entire screen. This appears to be a bug in the function.

Rectangles and Lines

The next program is very similar to COLORBAL, except that it models rectangles rather than circles. Each rectangle represented by the `rect` class is filled with color, with a diagonal line across it. Here's the listing for RECTLINE:

```
// rectline.cpp
// rectangle and line
#include <graphics.h>          // for graphics functions
#include <conio.h>             // for getch()
const int W = 75;              // 1/2 width of rectangle

class rect                     // rect class
   {
   private:
      int xCo, yCo;            // coordinates of center
      int linecolor;           // color of outline
      int fillcolor;           // color of interior
   public:
      rect()                   // no-arg constructor
         { xCo=0; yCo=0; linecolor=WHITE; fillcolor=WHITE; }
      void set(int x, int y, int lc, int fc)  // set data
         { xCo=x; yCo=y; linecolor=lc; fillcolor=fc; }
      void draw()              // draw the rectangle
         {
         setcolor(linecolor);                     // line color
         setlinestyle(SOLID_LINE, 0, THICK_WIDTH); // line width
         rectangle(xCo-W, yCo-W, xCo+W, yCo+W); // draw rectangle
         setfillstyle(SOLID_FILL, fillcolor);   // set fill color
         floodfill(xCo, yCo, linecolor);        // fill rectangle
```

(continued on next page)

(continued from previous page)

```
         line(xCo-W, yCo+W, xCo+W, yCo-W);      // draw diagonal
         }
   };

void main()
   {
   int driver, mode;
   driver = DETECT;                      // set to best graphics mode
   initgraph(&driver, &mode, "\\bc45\\bgi");

   rect r1;                              // create three rects
   rect r2;
   rect r3;

   r1.set(80, 150, YELLOW, RED);    // set position and colors
   r2.set(250, 150, YELLOW, GREEN);
   r3.set(420, 150, YELLOW, BLUE);

   r1.draw();                            // draw them
   r2.draw();
   r3.draw();

   getch();                              // wait for keypress
   closegraph();                         // close graphics system
   }
```

Figure 11-9 shows the output of this program. The new library functions used in RECTLINE are `rectangle()` and `line()`.

The `rectangle()` Function

The `rectangle()` library function draws the outline of a rectangle. You specify the edges of the rectangle with four integers, like this:

```
rectangle(left, top, right, bottom);
```

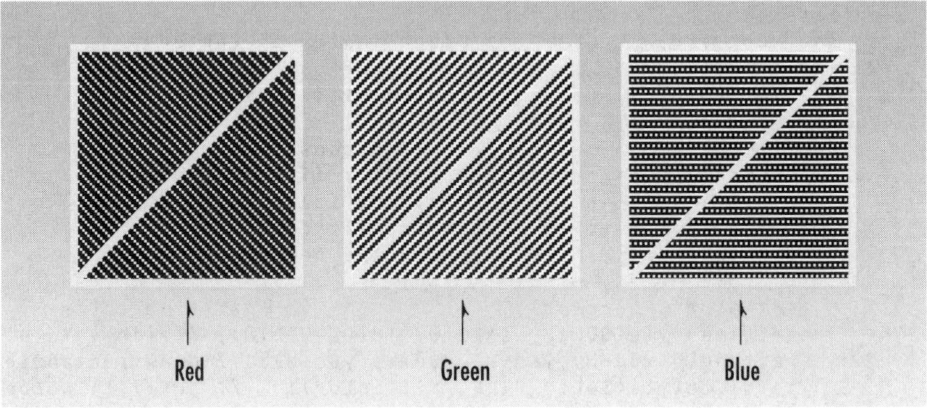

Figure 11-9 Output of RECTLINE

The `line()` Function

The `line()` library function draws a line from one point to another. The first two arguments to the function specify the x and y coordinates of the line's starting point, and the last two arguments specify the end point:

```
line(x1, y1, x2, y2);
```

The line can be given a style and thickness with the `setlinestyle()` function described previously.

Polygons and Inheritance

The next example uses inheritance to tie together the circular and rectangular shapes generated in the COLORBAL and RECTLINE examples and a new triangle shape. This program also introduces a new graphics library function, `fillpoly()`, which it uses to create the triangle. Here's the listing for MULTSHAP:

```
// multshap.cpp
// balls, rects, and polygons
#include <graphics.h>          // for graphics functions
#include <conio.h>             // for getch()

const int W = 75;              // size of images

class shape                    // base class
   {
   protected:
      int xCo, yCo;            // coordinates of center
      int linecolor;           // color of outline
      int fillcolor;           // color of interior
   public:
      shape()                  // no-arg constructor
         { xCo=0; yCo=0; linecolor=WHITE; fillcolor=WHITE; }
      void set(int x, int y, int lc, int fc)  // set data
         { xCo=x; yCo=y; linecolor=lc; fillcolor=fc; }
      void draw()
         {
         setcolor(linecolor);                        // line color
         setlinestyle(SOLID_LINE, 0, THICK_WIDTH); // line width
         setfillstyle(SOLID_FILL, fillcolor);    // set fill color
         }
   };

class ball : public shape
   {
   public:
      ball() : shape()         // no-arg constr
         { }
      void set(int x, int y, int lc, int fc)    // set data
          { shape::set(x, y, lc, fc); }
      void draw()              // draw the ball
```

(continued on next page)

(continued from previous page)

```
         {
         shape::draw();                               // set colors
         circle(xCo, yCo, W);                         // draw circle
         floodfill(xCo, yCo, linecolor);              // fill circle
         }
   };

class rect : public shape
   {
   public:
      rect() : shape()          // no-arg constr
         { }
      void set(int x, int y, int lc, int fc)    // set data
           { shape::set(x, y, lc, fc); }
      void draw()               // draw the rectangle
         {
         shape::draw();                               // set colors
         rectangle(xCo-W, yCo-W, xCo+W, yCo+W); // draw rectangle
         floodfill(xCo, yCo, linecolor);              // fill rectangle
         line(xCo-W, yCo+W, xCo+W, yCo-W);            // draw diagonal
         }
   };

class tria : public shape
   {
   public:
      tria() : shape()          // no-arg constr
         { }
      void set(int x, int y, int lc, int fc)    // set data
           { shape::set(x, y, lc, fc); }
      void draw()               // draw the triangle
         {
         int triarray[] = { xCo,   yCo-W,        // top
                            xCo+W, yCo+W,        // bottom right
                            xCo-W, yCo+W };      // bottom left
         shape::draw();                          // set colors
         fillpoly(3, triarray);                  // draw triangle
         }
   };

void main()
   {
   int driver, mode;
   driver = DETECT;                     // set to best graphics mode
   initgraph(&driver, &mode, "\\bc45\\bgi");

   ball b1;                             // create ball
   rect r2;                             // create rectangle
   tria t3;                             // create triangle

   b1.set(80, 150, YELLOW, RED);     // set position and colors
   r2.set(250, 150, YELLOW, GREEN);
   t3.set(420, 150, YELLOW, BLUE);
```

```
    b1.draw();                         // draw them
    r2.draw();
    t3.draw();

    getch();                           // wait for keypress
    closegraph();                      // close graphics system
    }
```

The shape Class

If you look at the ball class in the COLORBAL example, and at the rect class from RECTLINE, you will see that they have many similarities. They both store the coordinates of the center of the shape and the colors of the shape's outline and interior. They both have a set() member function that supplies values for these data members, and a draw() function that draws the shape, although of course the draw functions do different things.

In designing a C++ program, we look for common elements of classes. Such common elements are candidates for a base class, from which the other classes will be derived. In MULTSHAP we create a base class shape, from which revised ball and rect classes are descended. The shape class contains the common elements of ball and rect, which we saw in previous examples.

Polygons

We've added another class to MULTSHAP, the tria class, which models a triangle. This new class is also derived from shape. A triangle is the simplest example of a polygon—a number of straight-line segments that outline a closed shape. The triangle polygon in MULTSHAP is created using a library function called fillpoly(). This is a somewhat more complex graphics function than those we've seen before. Before it can be used, an array must be created that contains the points that define the polygon. For a polygon with four points, such an array might look like this:

```
int polyarray[] = { x1, y1,  x2, y2,  x3, y3,  x4, y4 };
```

This array could represent the corners of a square, a parallelogram, or any other closed figure made of four line segments. This is shown in Figure 11-10.

The fillpoly() library function takes two arguments. The first is the number of points specified in the array (not the number of integers!). The second is the address of the array. (Remember that the name of an array, with no brackets, is its address.) Here's a call that uses the array just shown:

```
fillpoly(4, polyarray);
```

The function draws a line from the first point specified to the second point, from the second point to the third, and from the third to the fourth. This creates three of the four line segments for our four-sided figure. Very cleverly, fillpoly() then completes the figure by drawing the fourth line segment from the fourth point back to the first. You don't need to specify the first point again at the end of the sequence to make it do this; it's automatic. After that the function fills the figure using the color and pattern set with the setfillstyle() library function.

Another Borland C++ library function, drawpoly(), can be used to draw a polygon without filling it.

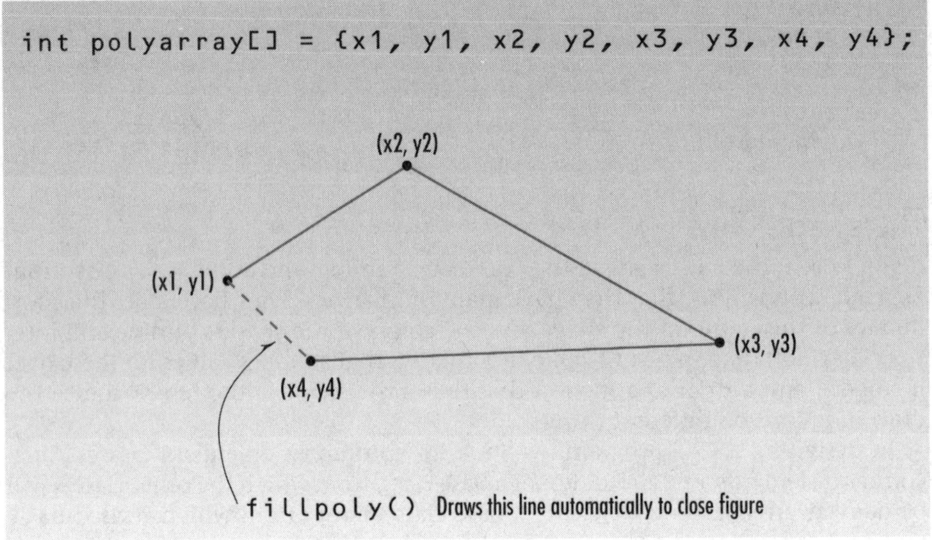

Figure 11-10 Array for `fillpoly()`

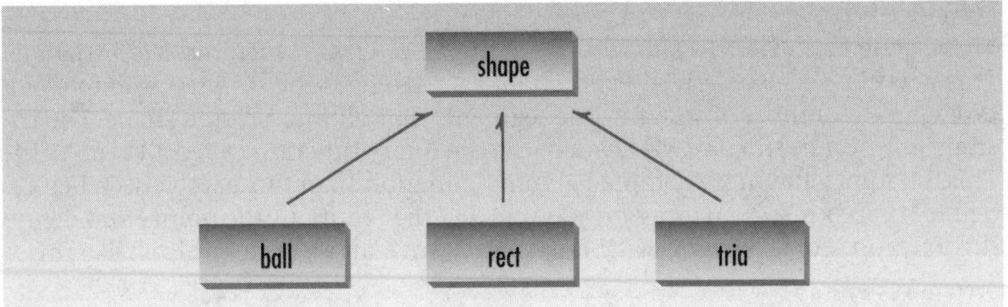

Figure 11-11 Class Hierarchy in MULTSHAP

Program Design

We created the `shape` class by extracting the common parts of the `ball`, `rect`, and `tria` classes. However, `shape` can also be understood as a generalization of balls, rectangles, and triangles. One of the important mental processes engaged in by humans is that of creating a general category from specific cases. We do this naturally; any 6-year-old could tell you that circles, squares, and triangles are all shapes. The C++ inheritance mechanism gives us a way to model this kind of abstraction in a computer language.

The `shape` class concentrates all the features of shapes into one place. As a result, the `ball`, `rect`, and `tria` classes are simpler than before. When we look at them we can see immediately what is unique about them, since the only code and data in them are what is needed to make them different from the generic `shape`. Figure 11-11 shows the class hierarchy in MULTSHAP.

The `main()` part of MULTSHAP creates and displays three objects—a red ball, a green rectangle, and a blue triangle. The result is shown in Figure 11-12.

Sound and Motion

Here's a program that uses the approach shown in previous examples to model a slot machine, where colored shapes appear in a window, as if slot-machine wheels were turning. This is shown in Figure 11-13. This program also uses Borland C++ library functions to generate sound.

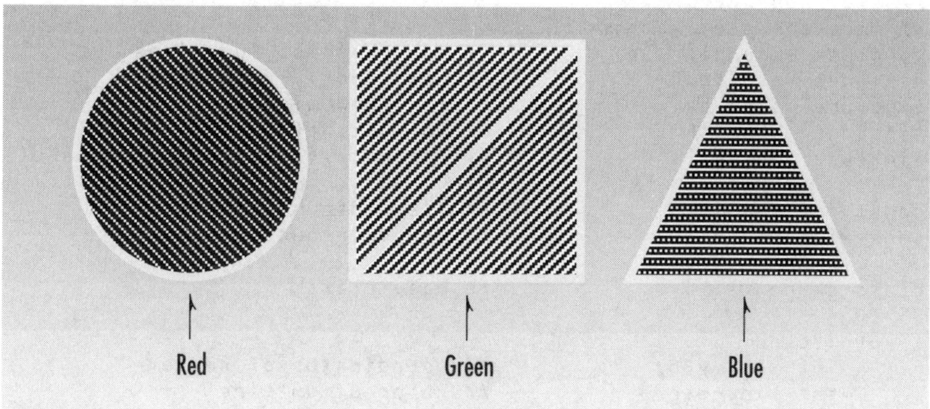

Figure 11-12 Output of MULTSHAP

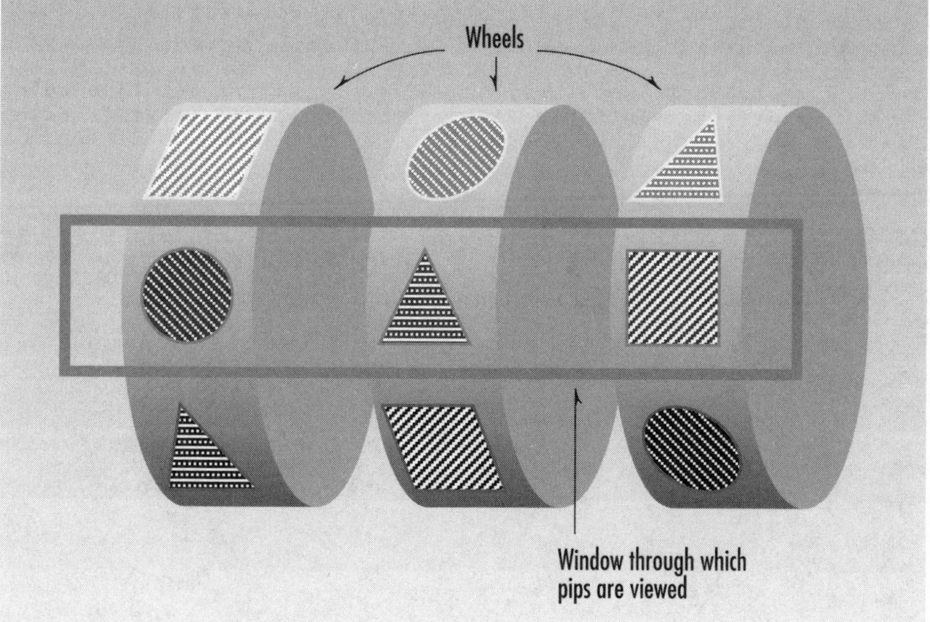

Figure 11-13 A Slot Machine

When you first start the program, three square windows appear on the screen. One of four different shapes appears randomly in each window: a red circle (representing a cherry), a blue circle (representing a grape), a square, and a pyramid. Each time the shapes appear, a clicking sound is heard. Gradually the shapes appear more and more slowly, as if the slot-machine wheels were slowing down. Finally they stop, and the program sounds a two-tone signal. If three cherries are displayed, you win. Figure 11-14 shows a typical display.

Here's the listing for SLOT:

```
// slot.cpp
// models a slot machine
#include <graphics.h>            // for graphics functions
#include <stdlib.h>              // for rand(), randomize()
#include <time.h>                // for randomize()
#include <conio.h>               // for getche()
#include <dos.h>                 // for delay(), sound(), nosound()

const int W = 15;                // 1/2 width of images
const int MAR = 10;              // margin around images

class shape                      // base class
   {
   protected:
      int xCo, yCo;              // coordinates of center
      int linecolor;             // color of outline
      int fillcolor;             // color of interior
   public:
      shape()                    // no-arg constructor
         { xCo=0; yCo=0; linecolor=WHITE; fillcolor=WHITE; }
      void set(int x, int y, int lc, int fc)
         { xCo=x; yCo=y; linecolor=lc; fillcolor=fc; }
      void draw()
         {
         setcolor(linecolor);                     // set line color
         setfillstyle(SOLID_FILL, fillcolor);     // set fill color
         }
   };
```

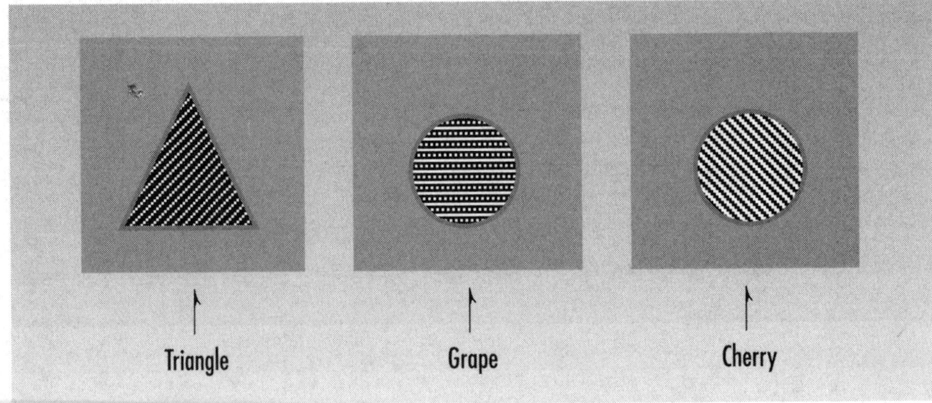

Figure 11-14 Output of SLOT

```
class ball : public shape
   {
   public:
      ball() : shape()         // no-arg constructor
         { }
      void set(int x, int y, int lc, int fc)    // set data
         { shape::set(x, y, lc, fc); }
      void draw()              // draw the ball
         {
         shape::draw();                         // set colors
         circle(xCo, yCo, W);                   // draw circle
         floodfill(xCo, yCo, linecolor);        // fill circle
         }
   };

class rect : public shape
   {
   public:
      rect() : shape()         // no-arg constructor
         { }
      void set(int x, int y, int lc, int fc)    // set data
         { shape::set(x, y, lc, fc); }
      void draw()              // draw the rectangle
         {
         shape::draw();                         // set colors
         rectangle(xCo-W, yCo-W, xCo+W, yCo+W); // draw rectangle
         floodfill(xCo, yCo, linecolor);        // fill rectangle
         line(xCo-W, yCo+W, xCo+W, yCo-W);      // draw diagonal
         }
   };

class tria : public shape
   {
   public:
      tria() : shape()         // no-arg constructor
         { }
      void set(int x, int y, int lc, int fc)    // set data
         { shape::set(x, y, lc, fc); }
      void draw()              // draw the triangle
         {
         int triarray[] = { xCo,   yCo-W,      // top
                            xCo+W, yCo+W,      // bottom right
                            xCo-W, yCo+W };    // bottom left
         shape::draw();                        // set colors
         fillpoly(3, triarray);                // draw triangle
         }

   };
class noshape : public shape
   {
   public:
      void erase()             // erase old shape
         {
         int border[] =                   // rectangle to erase
```

(continued on next page)

(continued from previous page)

```
                 { xCo-W-MAR, yCo-W-MAR,     // upper-left
                   xCo+W+MAR, yCo-W-MAR,     // upper-right
                   xCo+W+MAR, yCo+W+MAR,     // bottom-right
                   xCo-W-MAR, yCo+W+MAR };   // bottom-left
         setfillstyle(SOLID_FILL, DARKGRAY); // background color
         fillpoly(4, border);                // fill it
         }
   };

class Cherry : public ball, public noshape
   {
   public:
      Cherry() : ball()                     // no-arg constructor
         { }
      void set(int x, int y)                // set data
         {
         ball::set(x, y, WHITE, RED);
         noshape::set(x, y, WHITE, RED);
         }
      void draw()                           // draw a cherry
         { erase(); ball::draw(); }
   };

class Grape : public ball, public noshape
   {
   public:
      Grape() : ball()                      // no-arg constructor
         { }
      void set(int x, int y)                // set data
         {
         ball::set(x, y, WHITE, BLUE);
         noshape::set(x, y, WHITE, BLUE);
         }
      void draw()                           // draw a grape
         { erase(); ball::draw(); }
   };

class Square : public rect, public noshape
   {
   public:
      Square() : rect()                     // no-arg constructor
         { }
      void set(int x, int y)                // set data
         {
         rect::set(x, y, WHITE, CYAN);
         noshape::set(x, y, WHITE, CYAN);
         }
      void draw()                           // draw a square
         { erase(); rect::draw(); }

   };
class Pyramid : public tria, public noshape
```

```
   {
   public:
      Pyramid() : tria()                    // no-arg constructor
         { }
      void set(int x, int y)                // set data
         {
         tria::set(x, y, WHITE, GREEN);
         noshape::set(x, y, WHITE, GREEN);
         }
      void draw()                           // draw a pyramid
         { erase(); tria::draw(); }
   };

class Wheel
   {
   private:
      Cherry ch;   // make one pip of each kind
      Grape gr;
      Square sq;
      Pyramid py;
      int xCo, yCo;                //wheel position
   public:
      Wheel()                      // no-arg constructor
         { xCo=0; yCo=0; }
      void set(int x, int y)
         {
         xCo=x; yCo=y;             // set our position
         ch.set(xCo, yCo);         // set four pips to
         gr.set(xCo, yCo);         //    our position
         sq.set(xCo, yCo);
         py.set(xCo, yCo);
         }
      void draw();                 // draw a random pip
   };

void Wheel::draw()                 // draw a random pip
   {
   switch( random(4) )             // random number from 0 to 3
      {
      case 0 : ch.draw(); break;  // draw one of the pips
      case 1 : gr.draw(); break;  // selected randomly
      case 2 : sq.draw(); break;
      case 3 : py.draw(); break;
      }
   }

void main()
   {
   const int NUMBER = 60;         // number of times to cycle
   int driver, mode;
   driver = DETECT;               // set to best graphics mode
   initgraph(&driver, &mode, "\\bc4\\bgi");
   randomize();                   // seed random number generator
```

(continued on next page)

(continued from previous page)

```
   Wheel w1;                          // make three wheels
   Wheel w2;
   Wheel w3;
   w1.set(100, 100);                  // position in horizontal row
   w2.set(160, 100);
   w3.set(220, 100);

   for(int j=0; j<NUMBER; j++)    // spin the wheels
      {
      w1.draw();                      // draw each wheel
      w2.draw();
      w3.draw();
      sound(100); delay(20); nosound();   // click
      delay( j*j/20 );                // delay gets longer and longer
      }
   sound(400); delay(400);            // two tones to signal done
   sound(500); delay(800); nosound();
   getche();                          // wait for keypress
   closegraph();                      // close graphics system
   }
```

This is a more complicated program, so we'll examine the overall organization first and then discuss some new functions.

Class Hierarchy in SLOT

The SLOT program uses the classes from previous programs in this chapter: `shape`, `ball`, `rect`, and `tria`. Our goal is to use these classes with as little modification as possible. This reflects the situation where you have purchased a library of commercial classes, or where you simply want to make use of existing code with a minimum of effort.

SLOT creates four new classes that are shapes with particular colors: `Cherry`, derived from `ball` and colored red; `Grape`, derived from `ball` and colored blue; `Square`, derived from `rect` and colored cyan (greenish blue); and `Pyramid`, derived from `tria` and colored green. The `set()` member functions in these new derived classes simply call the `set()` functions in their base classes but with these specific colors (the line color is always white).

In addition, the class `noshape` is introduced to erase shapes. We need to erase each shape before drawing a new one on top of it. Otherwise, the corners of the triangle would still be sticking out when you draw a circle over it. The `noshape` class contains a single member function, `erase()`, which erases the area on the screen occupied by the shape.

The classes `Cherry`, `Grape`, `Square`, and `Pyramid` are derived not only from `ball` and similar classes but also, through multiple inheritance, from `noshape`. This gives them the capability to erase themselves. Because `noshape` needs a place to store coordinates, just as the other shapes do, it is derived from the `shape` class, although it is not exactly a shape in the same sense the other classes are.

Finally a class `Wheel` represents one wheel of a slot machine.

Figure 11-15 shows the relationship of the different classes in SLOT.

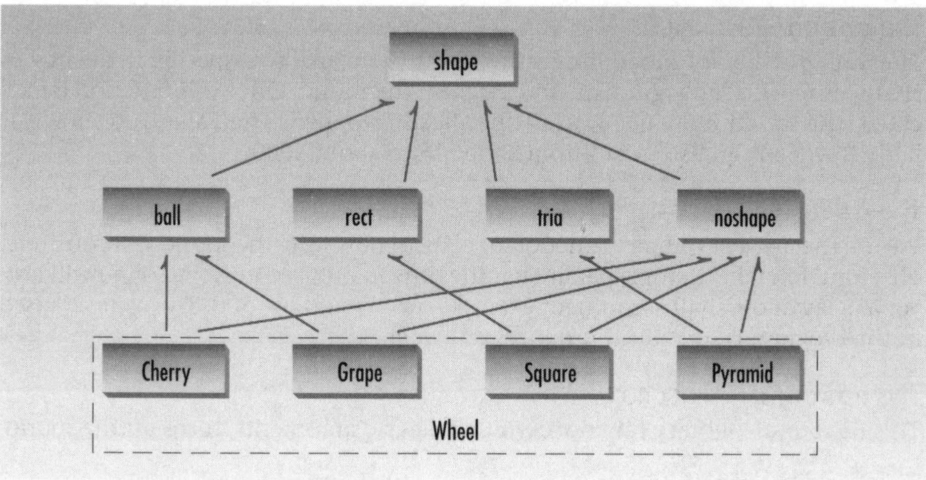

Figure 11-15 Class Hierarchy in SLOT

Each `wheel` object contains (but is not derived from) one each of the four kinds of pips. This is shown by the dotted line in Figure 11-15.

Operation of SLOT

The `main()` function creates three objects of type `Wheel`. Using the `set()` member function, it positions them in a row in the upper-left of the screen. Then, in a `for` loop, it repeatedly draws and redraws the wheels.

The `Wheel` class creates the four different kinds of pips, `Cherry`, `Grape`, `Square`, and `Pyramid` in its `private` section; they're called `ch`, `gr`, `sq`, and `py`. The `set()` member function in `Wheel` specifies the wheel's position and sets all the pips to the same position. A `draw()` member function draws a border around the pip's location and then draws one of the pips, selecting which pip to draw based on a random number. Thus, the image drawn by each wheel changes randomly from one pip to another each time that wheel's `draw()` function is called.

Each time all three wheels are redrawn, the program generates a clicking sound and then delays for a fixed amount of time. The delay grows longer each time through the loop. This gives the illusion that the wheels are rotating—rapidly at first, and then slower and slower, until they stop.

The Sound Generation Functions

Sound generation in C++ requires three steps: (1) turning the sound on, (2) delaying for an appropriate amount of time, and (3) turning the sound off again. To make the click after redrawing the wheels, the following line is used:

```
sound(100); delay(20); nosound();
```

All three of the Borland C++ library functions in this line require the DOS.H header file.

The `sound()` Function

The `sound()` library function sets the sound generator to a specific frequency in Hertz, supplied as an argument, and turns on the sound. Once this function is executed, the sound remains on until specifically stopped. The value 100 shown is fairly low; you can use values from about 15 to about 3000.

The `delay()` Function

We use the `delay()` library function to control how long the sound will continue. This function takes a single parameter: the time in milliseconds the sound will last. For a delay of one-half second, for example, you would use 500. The value 20 used in the program is so short it produces only a click.

The `nosound()` Function

This `nosound()` library function, which takes no arguments, turns off the sound.

Thinking About Classes

The SLOT program shows some of the organizational power of object-oriented programming. Starting with simple classes, we use inheritance to create more complex classes. Multiple inheritance gives even more flexibility.

The relationships among the different parts of the program are—once you get used to them, anyway—more intuitive than those in a traditional procedural program. In C++ these relationships are among classes, while in a procedural program they are among functions. Classes are often better than functions at modeling objects in the real world (or on the screen), and inheritance corresponds, more closely than functions, to something we do every day: create a more general concept from a number of specific instances.

Simulating Moving Objects

OOP lends itself nicely to modeling real-world objects that move in physical space, such as cars and planets. When connected with a graphics display, a whole world of object-oriented animation opens up to the C++ programmer.

As a simple example, let's make a class of molecules that can bounce around inside a closed container. Such simulations (in a rather more complex form) can be used by scientists to model chemical reactions or explore the pressure of gases. (Science phobes can think of the molecules as billiard balls on a table.) Instance variables of the `molecule` class include the position of each molecule (in screen coordinates measured in pixels), the speed of the molecule (in pixels per time period), and the molecule's color. To avoid complicated mathematics, we'll restrict the directions the molecules can go to eight, which we can think of as north, northeast, east, southeast, south, southwest, west, and northwest. There is a vertical and a horizontal component of each direction. Horizontal can be specified as right, left, or stopped, and vertical can be down, up, or stopped. Combining these components in all possible ways provides the eight directions.

Member functions of `molecule` erase the molecule at its old position, calculate the new position, and draw the molecule at the new position. This is how the animation effect—an object moving on the screen—is achieved, by continually erasing and redrawing the object. Here's the listing for MOLECULE:

```
// molecule.cpp
// moving balls reflect on edges of screen
#include <graphics.h>            // for graphics functions
#include <conio.h>               // for getch()

const int RAD = 5;               // radius of molecules
const int MAX = 6;               // maximum speed of molecules
const int DIST = (RAD+MAX);      // reflection distance

const int LEFT   =   0;          // screen coordinates
const int TOP    =   0;
const int RIGHT  = 639;          // standard VGA screen
const int BOTTOM = 479;

enum hdir {hSTOP=0, hRIGHT, hLEFT}; // horizontal direction
enum vdir {vSTOP=0, vDOWN, vUP};    // vertical direction

class molecule                   // molecule class
   {
   private:
      int xCo, yCo;        // coordinates of center
      int oldx, oldy;      // previous coordinates
      int speed;           // speed: pixels per unit time
      hdir horz;           // horiz direction: stop, right, left
      vdir vert;           // vert direction: stop, down, up
      COLORS color;        // color
   public:
                           // constructor
      molecule(int x, int y, int s, hdir h, vdir v, COLORS c)
         { xCo=x; yCo=y; speed=s; horz=h; vert=v; color=c; }
      void erase();        // erase old position
      void calculate();    // calculate new position
      void draw();         // draw new position
   };

void molecule::erase()   // erase molecule in old position
   {
   setcolor(DARKGRAY);                   // draw gray circle
   circle(oldx, oldy, RAD);
   setfillstyle(SOLID_FILL, BLACK);      // fill with black
   floodfill(oldx, oldy, DARKGRAY);
   setcolor(BLACK);                      // erase gray circle
   circle(oldx, oldy, RAD);
   }
                         // find molecule's new position
void molecule::calculate()
   {
   oldx = xCo;           // remember old location
   oldy = yCo;
   switch(horz)          // move left or right
      {
      case hSTOP:   /* no move */  break;
      case hRIGHT: xCo += speed;  break;
      case hLEFT:  xCo -= speed;  break;
      }
```

(continued on next page)

(continued from previous page)

```
   if(xCo<=LEFT+DIST)         // if at left edge,
      horz = hRIGHT;          // go right
   else if(xCo>=RIGHT-DIST)   // if at right edge,
      horz = hLEFT;           // go left

   switch(vert)         // move up or down
      {
      case vSTOP: /* no move */  break;
      case vDOWN: yCo += speed;  break;
      case vUP:   yCo -= speed;  break;
      }
   if(yCo<=TOP+DIST)          // if at top edge,
      vert = vDOWN;           // go down
   else if(yCo>=BOTTOM-DIST) // if at bottom edge,
      vert = vUP;             // go up
   }

void molecule::draw()   // draw molecule in new position
   {
   setcolor(color);
   circle(xCo, yCo, RAD);
   setfillstyle(SOLID_FILL, color);
   floodfill(xCo, yCo, color);
   }

void main()
   {
   int driver, mode;
   driver = DETECT;              // set to best graphics mode
   initgraph(&driver, &mode, "\\bc45\\bgi");

                                 // create some molecules
   molecule m1(100, 120, 2, hRIGHT, vUP,    BLUE);
   molecule m2(150, 220, 2, hLEFT,  vUP,    GREEN);
   molecule m3(200, 140, 3, hRIGHT, vDOWN, CYAN);
   molecule m4(250, 240, 3, hLEFT,  vDOWN, RED);
   molecule m5(300, 160, 3, hRIGHT, vUP,    MAGENTA);
   molecule m6(350, 260, 4, hLEFT,  vUP,    LIGHTGREEN);
   molecule m7(150, 350, 4, hLEFT,  vSTOP, LIGHTGRAY);
   molecule m8(150, 350, 4, hSTOP,  vUP,    BROWN);

                                 // outline screen
   rectangle(LEFT, TOP, RIGHT, BOTTOM);
   while( !kbhit() )             // quit on keypress
      {                          // move molecules around
      m1.calculate(); m1.erase(); m1.draw();
      m2.calculate(); m2.erase(); m2.draw();
      m3.calculate(); m3.erase(); m3.draw();
      m4.calculate(); m4.erase(); m4.draw();
      m5.calculate(); m5.erase(); m5.draw();
      m6.calculate(); m6.erase(); m6.draw();
      m7.calculate(); m7.erase(); m7.draw();
      m8.calculate(); m8.erase(); m8.draw();
      }
   closegraph();                 // close graphics system
   }
```

In this example we create eight molecules and set them in motion. Figure 11-16 shows the screen with the molecules bouncing around; unfortunately the figure can't show the motion.

As usual in animation, the effect of motion is created by moving the molecule in small discrete steps that are repeated very quickly. If you have a slow computer you may find the molecules go too slowly. You can speed things up by removing some of the molecules. Removing half should double the speed of those remaining. If you have a very fast machine the molecules may go too fast. Try inserting a `delay()` function in the while loop in `main()`.

As we noted, a molecule's direction has two components: x and y. To calculate its new position, we either add or subtract the speed to the x position, depending on the angle. If the direction is stopped we do nothing. We do the same for the y position. If either of these operations brings the molecule to the edge of the screen, we change the appropriate component of the direction, so that the molecule appears to bounce off the wall. If it hits the top of the box, for example, we change the y direction from up to down, but we leave the x direction alone.

To draw the molecule we draw the outline of a circle in the molecule's color and fill it with the same color. To erase it we draw over it with a dark gray circle, then fill the circle with black and erase it. (Note that you shouldn't use any dark gray molecules, since they will confuse the erase function.) All three member functions must be called for each molecule, in the correct order: `calculate()` the new position, `erase()` the old position, and `draw()` the new position.

Figure 11-16 Output of the MOLECULE Program

Note that `COLORS` is defined as a synonym for `int` in GRAPHICS.H, so you can use it as a data type when defining variables that will hold color values.

In this program the molecules pass right through each other. Could they bounce when they run into each other, instead of ignoring each other's existence? We'll explore this in an exercise.

Text in Graphics Mode

Creating text is far more flexible in graphics mode than it is in character mode. You can use different fonts (character designs), change the size and proportions of the characters, print vertically as well as horizontally, and, in general, exercise far more control over the appearance of the finished text.

Our example program demonstrates these capabilities, and also uses objects to represent graphics strings. These strings are somewhat similar to the string objects seen in previous examples, except that they include a variety of graphics characteristics.

A Graphics String Class

The example, GRAST (GRAphics STring), uses a single class of type `Gstring`. This class contains private data that specifies the graphical characteristics of the string. This includes the contents of the string, its starting point, the font in which it's displayed, its direction (vertical or horizontal), the character size and color, how the text is justified (positioned relative to its starting point), and the proportions of the characters (tall and thin, short and wide, and so on).

All these characteristics have default values, set by a no-argument constructor when an object of class `Gstring` is defined. The values can be modified using member functions. You modify only as many values as you need to. The simplest is to use all the defaults and specify only the string itself.

Here's the listing for GRAST:

```
// grast.cpp
// string class for graphics modes
#include <graphics.h>         // for graphics functions
#include <conio.h>            // for getch()
#include <string.h>           // for strcpy()

class Gstring                 // graphics string class
   {
   protected:
      char str[80];           // string to store text
      int xCo, yCo;           // coordinates of text
      int font;               // DEFAULT_FONT, TRIPLEX_FONT, etc.
      int direction;          // HORIZ_DIR or VERT_DIR
      int size;               // 1, 2, 3, etc.
      int color;              // BLUE, RED, etc.
      int horzjustify;        // LEFT_TEXT, etc.
      int vertjustify;        // BOTTOM_TEXT, etc.
      int multx, divx;        // horizontal scale factors
      int multy, divy;        // vertical scale factors
   public:
      Gstring()               // no-arg constructor
```

```
      {                     // set to default values
      str[0] = '\0';                  // empty string
      xCo = 0; yCo = 0;               // position
      font = DEFAULT_FONT;            // font
      direction = HORIZ_DIR;          // horizontal or vertical
      size = 4;                       // character size
      color = WHITE;                  // character color
      horzjustify = LEFT_TEXT;        // horizontal positioning
      vertjustify = TOP_TEXT;         // vertical positioning
      multx = 1; divx = 1;            // horizontal scale factors
      multy = 1; divy = 1;            // vertical scale factors
      }
   void DrawText()                    // draw the text
      {
      moveto(xCo, yCo);
      settextstyle(font, direction, size);
      setcolor(color);
      settextjustify(horzjustify, vertjustify);
      setusercharsize(multx, divx, multy, divy);
      outtext(str);
      }
   void SetText(char s[])     // set text string
      { strcpy(str, s); }
   void SetPosition(int x, int y)  // set position
      { xCo=x; yCo=y; }
   void SetFont(int f)        // set font
      { font = f; }
   void SetDirection(int d) // set direction
      { direction = d; }
   void SetSize(int s)        // set size
      { size = s; }
   void SetColor(int c)       // set color
      { color = c; }
   void SetHJust(int hj)      // set horizontal justification
      { horzjustify = hj; }
   void SetVJust(int vj)      // set vertical justification
      { vertjustify = vj; }
   void SetHorzSize(int m, int d)  // set horiz proportions
      { size=0; multx=m; divx=d; };
   void SetVertSize(int m, int d)  // set vertical proportions
      { size=0; multy=m; divy=d; };
   };
void main()
   {
   int driver, mode;
   driver = DETECT;                        // use best graphics mode
   initgraph(&driver, &mode, "\\bc45\\bgi");
   Gstring s1, s2, s3, s4, s5, s6;       // make some strings

   s1.SetText("Default everything");    // all defaults

   s2.SetText("Gothic Font");            // gothic font
   s2.SetFont(GOTHIC_FONT);
   s2.SetPosition(0, 75);
```

(continued on next page)

(continued from previous page)

```
   s3.SetText("Vertical Sans Serif");  // vertical
   s3.SetFont(SANS_SERIF_FONT);
   s3.SetPosition(600, 0);
   s3.SetDirection(VERT_DIR);

   s4.SetText("Centered Triplex");     // centered
   s4.SetFont(TRIPLEX_FONT);
   s4.SetPosition(300, 150);
   s4.SetHJust(CENTER_TEXT);

   s5.SetText("Centered Sans Serif");  // centered
   s5.SetFont(SANS_SERIF_FONT);
   s5.SetSize(6);
   s5.SetPosition(300, 225);
   s5.SetHJust(CENTER_TEXT);

   s6.SetText("Tall and narrow Triplex");  // change proportions
   s6.SetFont(TRIPLEX_FONT);
   s6.SetPosition(0, 300);
   s6.SetHorzSize(2, 3);               // two-thirds as wide
   s6.SetVertSize(4, 1);               // four times as high

   s1.DrawText();                      // display all
   s2.DrawText();                      // the Gstrings
   s3.DrawText();
   s4.DrawText();
   s5.DrawText();
   s6.DrawText();

   getch();                            // wait for keypress
   closegraph();                       // close graphics system
   }
```

In the `main()` function we create six objects of class `Gstring` (for Graphics string). The first string is printed with all the defaults set. The second uses a Gothic font instead of the default font. The third is displayed vertically, and the fourth and fifth are centered about their starting points. In the sixth, the proportions of the characters are changed.

When the characteristics of the six graphics strings have been specified, they are all displayed. Figure 11-17 shows the result.

Borland C++ Graphics Text Functions

The `DrawText()` member function in `Gstring` displays the text. This function uses a variety of Borland C++ library functions to change the characteristics of the text to be displayed. Let's examine these library functions.

The `moveto()` Function

Borland C++ uses an imaginary point on the screen called the *current position*, or CP, to act as the starting point for text display. The library function `moveto()` sets the location of the CP, using two `int` arguments to indicate the x and y coordinates.

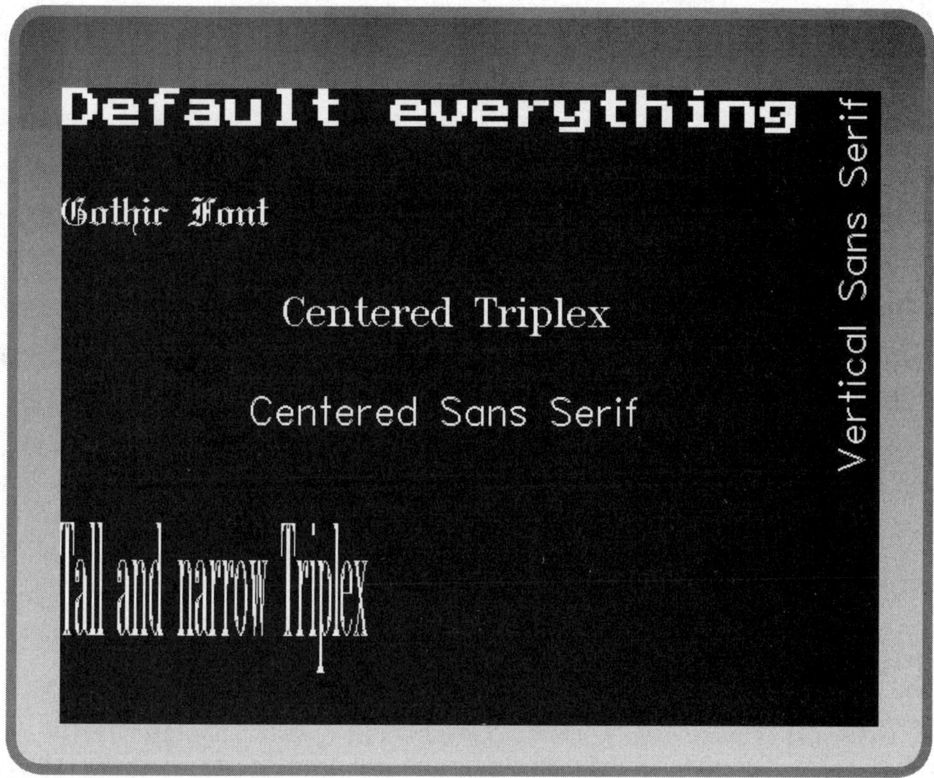

Figure 11-17 Output of GRAST

Text is normally displayed with the CP in the upper-left corner (although this can be modified, as we'll see in a moment).

The `settextstyle()` Function

The `settextstyle()` library function modifies three different characteristics of the text: the font, the direction, and the character size. These are specified as three integer arguments.

The current versions of Borland C++ and Turbo C++ have five possible fonts, which can be specified by constants defined in GRAPHICS.H. These constants are shown in Table 11-9.

To use these fonts you must ensure that appropriate font files are available in the directory specified in the path argument to `initgraph()`. This path is normally \BC45\BGI in Borland C++ and \TC\BGI in Turbo C++. The files all have the .CHR (for *character*) extension. TRIP.CHR contains descriptions of the Triplex font, SANS.CHR describes the Sans Serif font, and so on.

We noted earlier that the .BGI files you use must be in your system, in a directory specified in the `initigraph()` function. The same is true of the .CHR files needed to use text in graphics. To create a stand-alone program that will run without these external directories, see Appendix C.

Constant	Type of font
DEFAULT_FONT	Bit-mapped font, "computer look"
TRIPLEX_FONT	Serif font, like Times Roman
SMALL_FONT	Best for small text
SANS_SERIF_FONT	Sans serif font, like Helvetica
GOTHIC_FONT	Old English style
SCRIPT_FONT	Handwriting style
SIMPLEX_FONT	Narrow strokes
TRIPLEX_SCR_FONT	Italicized triplex
COMPLEX_FONT	More sophisticated serif font
EUROPEAN_FONT	Stylized letters, narrow strokes
BOLD_FONT	Double outlines

Table 11-9 Font Constants

The second argument to `settextstyle` has one of two values: HORIZ_DIR or VERT_DIR. Vertically oriented text runs from the bottom of the screen up, rather than from left to right.

The third argument specifies the character size. A value of 1 gives the smallest characters; 2 gives characters twice as big; 3 makes them three times as big; and so on.

The `settextjustify()` Function

The `settextjustify()` library function specifies where the text will be displayed relative to the CP. There are two arguments—one specifying the horizontal position and the other the vertical position, as shown in Tables 11-10 and 11-11.

As we noted, the default is for the CP to be in the upper-left corner. Figure 11-18 shows the possibilities.

The `setusercharsize()` Function

The `setusercharsize()` library function changes the proportions of the characters by independently changing their width and height. For this function to be effective, the size argument to `settextstyle()` must be set to 0. This automatically gives the fonts a size of 4. The `setusercharsize()` library function then modifies this size.

This function takes four arguments. The first two represent the numerator and denominator of a fraction that modifies the width. The normal width of the character is multiplied by the fraction. Thus if the first two arguments are 5 and 2, the new character width will be 5/2 times 4, or 10. The third and fourth arguments operate similarly on the character height.

Constant	Position
LEFT_TEXT	CP to left of text (default)
CENTER_TEXT	CP in horizontal center of text
RIGHT_TEXT	CP to right of text

Table 11-10 Horizontal Text Position

Constant	Position
TOP_TEXT	CP on top of text (default)
CENTER_TEXT	CP in vertical center of text
BOTTOM_TEXT	CP on bottom of text

Table 11-11 Vertical Text Position

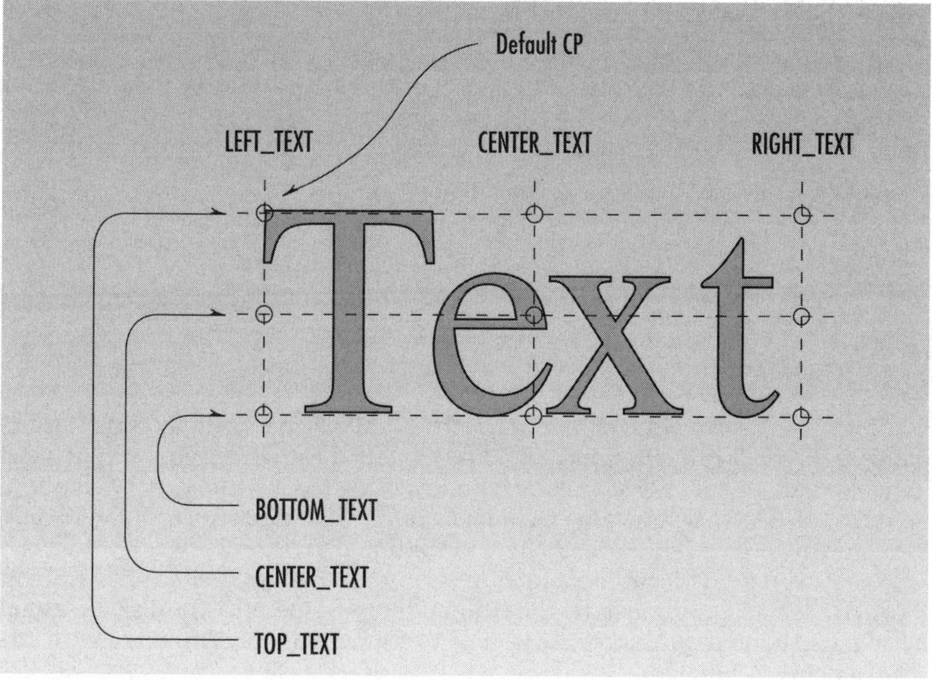

Figure 11-18 Justification

The `outtext()` Function

Graphics text is displayed with the `outtext()` library function. This function takes as its single argument the string to be displayed.

Redefining a Function Set

Notice that the effect of using the `Gstring` class is to redefine the set of functions used to specify the text characteristics. For instance, Borland C++ uses a single library function, `settextstyle()`, to specify the font, direction, and size, while the `Gstring` class uses three separate member functions—`SetFont()`, `SetDirection()`, and `SetSize()`. Which approach you use is a matter of taste, but it's nice to know you can redefine an existing set of functions if you don't like their syntax.

Extending the `Gstring` Class

The `Gstring` class could be extended to include such features as overloading the `+` operator to perform concatenation (described in Chapter 9). This and similar additions could provide a powerful and versatile class for use in graphics programs.

Using `cout` with Graphics

If you don't want to get involved with the complexities of fonts, styles, and sizes that we've described for graphics-mode text functions, you can fall back on ordinary character-based output with `cout`. This works in graphics mode, and although the text appears rather crude in the graphics environment, it does provide a quick and dirty way to generate text output.

You can use `gotoxy()` to position the text cursor on the graphics screen, just as you do on the text screen. Then you can output the text in the usual way:

```
gotoxy(1, 10);          // position cursor at column 1, line 10
cout << "speed=" << speed;
```

This approach is sometimes helpful in debugging, when you want to check the values of variables but don't want to go to the trouble of using `outtext()` or the debugger.

Summary

Borland C++ has two kinds of functions loosely called graphics functions. The first kind works only with text displays and is concerned with displaying text in a rectangular area of the screen called a window. The key function in this mode is `window()`, which defines the rectangular area. You can also use `constream` objects, which produce a similar effect as the functions.

The second kind of graphics function requires a graphics display such as CGA, EGA, or VGA. Programs that use these functions must initialize the display system to a graphics mode using the `initgraph()` function, and terminate with the `closegraph()` function.

Library functions can write lines, circles, squares, and polygons to the screen, use different line widths, and fill shapes with color. Text in a variety of fonts can be displayed, and its size, color, positioning, and aspect ratio can be manipulated.

Graphics objects on the screen can have a close relationship with C++ objects in the program. This simplifies the conceptualization of a program and allows the generalization of common characteristics into a base class.

Questions

Answers to questions can be found in Appendix D.

1. Using Borland C++ library functions you can
    a. color any closed figure.
    b. draw lines and circles.
    c. write text in a variety of fonts and sizes.
    d. make sounds of different pitches.
2. The key function that confines character-mode text inside a window on the screen is __________.
3. True or false: A program that uses text-mode functions like `cputs()` must start with the `initgraph()` function.
4. Write the code to initialize the graphics system to a VGA adapter in VGAHI mode.
5. With a VGA adapter, in text mode, you can display up to __________ colors.
6. True or false: A graphics program must ordinarily run in the Borland C++ (or Turbo C++) development environment.
7. The pathname supplied to `initgraph()` must
    a. be used unless auto-detect is specified.
    b. be surrounded by quotes.
    c. specify the desired .BGI file.
    d. use double backslashes to separate directories.
8. Write a statement that draws a circle centered at (99, 44), with a radius of 13.
9. True or false: The `setcolor()` function determines what color will be displayed by the `rect()` function.
10. Write the code necessary to draw a line from (2, 7) to (5, 11).
11. The `setfillstyle` function is used to specify
    a. the width of a line.
    b. the color of a polygon.
    c. the pattern of a square.
    d. the position of a circle.

12. Write a statement that will cause all straight lines to be written in dot-dash, dot-dash style with normal width.

13. In graphics programs, C++ objects correspond nicely to

    a. relationships.
    b. shapes.
    c. functions.
    d. programs.

14. Write the code to draw a triangle with points (0, 10), (5, 0), (10, 10).

15. A base class will often

    a. model more specific objects than its derived classes.
    b. correspond to something in the real world.
    c. behave badly when the chips are down.
    d. be a generalized version of its derived classes.

16. Write the code to create a two-second beep at 1000 Hertz.

17. The random-number generator should be seeded so that it doesn't always ________.

18. In the SLOT program, multiple inheritance is used to add to an object the ability to itself.

19. To display text in the gothic font, you would use

    a. `drawtext()`.
    b. `cputs()`.
    c. `outtext()`.
    d. `cout`.

20. The point on a graphics screen where the next pixel will be drawn is called the ________.

Exercises

Answers to starred exercises can be found in Appendix D.

1.* Modify the `ball` class in the EZBALL program in this chapter so that the size of the ball is an instance variable rather than a constant. You can call this data member `rad`. Change the `set()` member function to accept a value for the radius, and the `draw()` function so that it uses `rad` to draw a circle with any radius. Change the `main()` program so that each ball object is set to a different radius as well as to a different position.

2.* Modify the `shape` class from the MULTSHAP program in this chapter so that the size of an object is variable rather than constant. Use both `width` and `height` as member data items so that the shape as well as the size of the shape can be specified.

Change the `set()` function to accept the width and height as arguments, along with the position. Modify the `set()` member function in the `ball` and `rect` classes so that it passes the width and height values along to `shape::set()`. (You can delete the `tria` class.) Modify the `draw()` member functions in `ball` and `rect` so that they use the width and height data (one or the other is enough for `ball`).

Modify the `main()` program to draw a car, using a rectangle for the lower part of the car, another rectangle for the windows area, and two `ball` objects for the wheels.

3.* To the program in Exercise 2, add a class called `car` that models the car image that was created from four separate objects in `main()`. The `car` class should make cars the same size and color but allow different positions. In `main()` create three `car` objects, set them to different positions with `set()`, and display them with `draw()`.

4. Add a `hexa` class, derived from the `shape` class, to the MULTSHAP program in this chapter. The `hexa` class uses `fillpoly()` to draw hexagons, which should be `2*W` high and `2*W` wide, with six equal (or approximately equal) sides. Modify `main()` to create and draw a hexagon, as well as one example of the three other shapes.

5. Create a class of rectangles. (They should not be derived from `shape` or anything else.) We'll use these rectangles later, as bars in an exercise about bar charts. Call the class `nubar`. Its instance data should specify the location of the lower-left corner of the bar, the bar's width and height, and its color. A constructor should allow all this data to be specified for each bar, and a `display()` function should display the bar.

Bar-chart bars look nice with a three-dimensional effect. An easy way to do this is to draw a second rectangle, in a lighter variation of the same color, just behind the first but offset a few pixels up and to the right. The main foreground rectangle is then drawn on top of this lighter-colored rectangle covering all of it but a little of its top and right edges. This gives the appearance of an illuminated edge to the foreground bar. Take advantage of the fact that, in BGI graphics, the colors with values from 0 to 7 are the same colors, but darker than, the colors with values 8 to

15. Thus 1 is blue, while 9 is light blue; 2 is green, while 10 is light green; and so on up to 7 and 15, which are light gray and white. The values 0 and 8 aren't so useful because 0 is black, which is usually the background color. So restrict yourself to color values from 1 to 7, and draw the background rectangle with a color value 8 higher than the foreground.

Write a `main()` function that draws a number of bars in different colors and sizes at different locations on the screen. Note that Borland provides functions called `bar()` and `bar3d()` for making bar-chart bars, but you can make bars that look better than theirs. Also, if you create your own bar class, you can customize it however you want.

6. It is possible to read the nonalphanumeric keyboard keys, such as the arrow keys and function keys, using something called *extended keyboard codes.* To do this you read a character in the usual way, and, if it's 0, then you know another character follows whose value is not an ASCII code but an extended code. Here's a fragment of a program that will read extended codes until a normal character is typed, and act on the arrow (cursor) keys:

```
const char LEFT_ARROW  = 75;  // extended codes for arrow keys
const char RIGHT_ARROW = 77;
const char UP_ARROW    = 72;
const char DOWN_ARROW  = 80;

while( getch()==0 )            // read the 0; if not 0 then quit
   {
   switch( getch() )           // read the extended code
      {
      case L_ARROW:   /* do something */ break;
      case R_ARROW:   /* do something */ break;
      case U_ARROW:   /* do something */ break;
      case D_ARROW:   /* do something */ break;
      default: break;
      }
   }
```

Use inheritance to augment the `textbox` class from the CONBOXES program in this chapter so that the user can move a box around the screen using the cursor control keys. The derived class can be called `mbox`. When an arrow key is pressed, a new member function of `mbox`, call it `move()`, will need to erase the previous box, change the appropriate box coordinates (`left` and `right`, or `up` and `down`, as appropriate), and then redraw the box. In `main()`, create some boxes of class `mbox`. The `move()` function should be called for each box as soon as the box is drawn. This function will allow the user to move the box until a nonarrow key is pressed, at which time the function returns and `main()` can draw the next box or terminate the program.

7. Start with the MULTSHAP program of this chapter, and derive classes that create three-dimensional versions of the three shapes. You can call them `ball3d`, `rect3d`, and `tria3d`; and derive them from `ball`, `rect`, and `tria`, respectively. In the derived classes, first draw the same shape offset a few pixels up and to the right, in a lighter color, as discussed in Exercise 5. Then draw the original shape on top of the background shape.

   It's easier to fill the shapes if the outline around the background shape is not the same color as the outline around the foreground shape. Also, you may want to modify the `shape` class to draw an outline 1 pixel wide instead of 3; a thinner outline looks better for 3-D shapes. Finally, ask yourself what is the easiest and most OOP-like way to create the background shape from within the derived class member functions.

8. Traffic engineers like to create computer models of automobiles on highways so they can improve the design of roads and the timing of traffic lights. As a first step in this process, imagine that three or four eastbound lanes of a freeway run across your screen from left to right, with the curb lane on the bottom and the fast lane on top. Create a class called `car` (no relation to the `car` class in Exercise 3). Objects of the `car` class will be moving along these lanes, with faster cars in the higher lanes. There can be several cars in each lane, but in this example they should all go at the same speed, so there is no need to pass. Cars drive off the right edge of the screen, and "wrap around," reappearing on the left. They can be represented by simple rectangles, each one a different color.

   Use instance data to record miles (horizontal position on the screen, in pixels), speed (position change in pixels per unit time), lane (vertical position on the screen), and the car's color. A constructor can initialize this data. You can use three member functions: one to erase the car's old position, one to calculate the new position (adding the speed to the x position, and wrapping the car back to the left if it goes off the right edge), and one to draw the car in the new position. (See the MOLECULE program in this chapter for one approach to animation.)

   In `main()` you can draw some lane-divider lines (in dashed white, for realism), create some cars, and then, in a loop, continually erase, calculate, and redraw each one. Exit from the loop if the user presses a key. If the display is too fast, you can put a `delay()` function in the loop. If it is too slow, you can reduce the number of cars or their size.

9. Using the `molecule` class from the MOLECULE program in this chapter, derive another class that will allow molecules to bounce when they hit each other. To make this (comparatively) simple, each molecule should use a single call to the

getpixel() function to sample the screen color directly under its own center. If this color is neither black nor the same color as itself, it knows it's on top of another molecule. When this happens, it should reverse both its x and y directions. Or if the molecule is not moving in a particular direction (x or y), it should remain stopped in that direction and only reverse the other one. This gives the visual effect of the molecule bouncing off other molecules.

We should not reverse direction instantly when we sense the other molecule. Why? Because we want to ensure the other molecule has time to sense our presence before we move away, since it needs to bounce too. So we must wait at least one time tick before reversing. Also, as soon as another molecule is detected, we should stop looking for other molecules, and not resume looking until we're sure we're clear of the one we're bouncing off of. Otherwise, we'll reverse our direction a second time while we're still overlapped, and we'll keep reversing direction and never move away from the other molecule. The solution to these problems is to install an instance variable that acts as a timer. We start the timer when we detect another molecule, and wait until it's reached 2 before reversing direction. Then, as long as the timer continues to run, we look at the color under our center and wait for it to return to black or our own color before we reset the timer and resume searching for other molecules.

The following program fragment gives some idea what the overloaded calculate() function for the derived class might look like. Of course, there are many ways to achieve the same functionality; you're welcome to improve on this version.

```
void molecu2::calculate()
   {
   int bkgnd = getpixel(xCo, yCo);    // read background color
   if(timer==0)
      {
      // if a different (colored) molecule under us, start timer
      if( bkgnd!=color && bkgnd!=BLACK)
         timer = 1;
      }
   else if(timer==2)      // wait for it to see us too
      {
      switch(horz)        // change horizontal direction
         {
         case hSTOP:  /* stopped */  break;
         case hRIGHT: horz=hLEFT;    break;
         case hLEFT:  horz=hRIGHT;   break;
         }
      switch(vert)        // change vertical direction
         {
         case vSTOP: /* stopped */  break;
         case vDOWN: vert=vUP;      break;
```

```
         case vUP:    vert=vDOWN;     break;
         }
      ++timer;              // keep counting
      }
                            // when we're disengaged,
   else if( timer>0 && (bkgnd==BLACK || bkgnd==color) )
      timer = 0;            // turn off timer
   else                     // otherwise,
      ++timer;              // keep timer running
   molecule::calculate(); // always calculate our new position
   }
```

It's easier to see what's happening when molecules bounce off each other if you make them fairly large (a radius of, say, 20 pixels). Also, debugging the bounce algorithm is easier if there are only two molecules on the screen at once. You can slow things down by putting `getch()` statements wherever you want to pause the action.

10. Let's see if we can make the cars in Exercise 8 stop at traffic lights. Imagine the cars are running on a multilane road, with, as before, the faster lanes on top. This road has several traffic lights. Red lights are represented by red rectangles that appear lying across all lanes of the road (as if the cross street had turned red). When the light turns red, the rectangle appears; when it turns green, the rectangle vanishes. The cars can sense the rectangles using a `getpixel()` probe ahead of them. (You may need two probes at, say, one car-length ahead and two car-lengths ahead, to avoid smashing into the light.) When a car senses a red light ahead, it slows down by subtracting an increment (2 or 3) from its speed every time period. When the light turns green and it no longer senses the rectangle, the car accelerates by adding an increment (1 or 2) to its speed each time period until it has reached its "ideal" or normal cruising speed. You'll need to modify the `car` class from Exercise 8 to include not only the actual speed, but this "ideal" speed. Cars use the same mechanism to sense other cars stopped ahead of them as they do to sense the traffic lights.

The traffic lights don't all need to turn on and off at the same time. By arranging for lights further downstream to cycle later, it's possible for cars that travel at a certain speed to make all the lights, without even slowing down.

Create a class called `light` to model the traffic lights. Objects of this class act like timers. A `tick()` member function in each light is called each time `main()` cycles through its loop. Instance data in `light` includes how long the light stays green, how long it stays red, and when to start its cycle compared with the other lights. A timer variable is continually incremented, so the light knows when to turn on and off. Another instance variable specifies the location of the light in miles (pixels) along the road. When it's time for the light to turn red, the `tick()` function draws the red rectangle, and when it's time to turn green, it erases the rectangle, which lets the cars start up again.

For extra credit, give your highway two or three lanes in each direction, and see if you can time the lights so that cars going at a certain speed can hit all green lights in both directions at the same time. You'll need to add an instance variable to specify direction (left or right), and rewrite the `calculate()` function in `car`, or overload it.

11. Start with the `nubar` class from Exercise 5. To it, add a `barchart` class. Each object of this class is a complete bar chart, consisting of a white rectangular border to delimit the outside of the chart and an arbitrary number of bars. Arguments to a constructor of class `barchart` are the position of the chart on the screen, the number of bars, the width of the bars, and the address of an `int` array holding the heights of the bars. A `display()` function should display the complete chart.

If you make the data in the `nubar` class public, then it will be easy to access it from member functions in `barchart`. This isn't an approved approach, since it defeats data hiding, but in subsequent chapters we'll see how to overcome this problem.

12. The bouncing mechanism in Exercise 9 in this chapter doesn't work perfectly for large molecules in that they squish too far into each other before bouncing back. It would be nice if the molecules sensed each other's presence when their edges first touched, rather than when the center of one met the other's edge.

We can achieve this effect by installing sensors all around the periphery of each molecule. Modify the derived class in Exercise 7 to incorporate eight sensors instead of one, one for each of the compass points north, northeast, east, southeast, south, southwest, west, and northwest.

The sensors should be located beyond their own molecule, so they don't need to check for its color, only for black. The NE, SE, SW, and NW sensors are located at the corners of a square into which the molecule just fits. In the following program fragment, `RADP` is `(RAD+RAD/3)`. This locates the N, E, S, and W sensors an appropriate distance out from the middle of the edges of the molecule so all eight sensors form an approximate circle.

```
void molecu2::calculate()
   {
   int p1, p2, p3, p4, p5, p6, p7, p8;

   if(timer==0)
```

```
    {
    // read each sensor
    p1 = getpixel(xCo,        yCo-RADP);  //  N
    p2 = getpixel(xCo+RAD,    yCo-RAD);   //  NE
    p3 = getpixel(xCo+RADP, yCo);         //  E
    p4 = getpixel(xCo+RAD,    yCo+RAD);   //  SE
    p5 = getpixel(xCo,        yCo+RADP);  //  S
    p6 = getpixel(xCo-RAD,    yCo+RAD);   //  SW
    p7 = getpixel(xCo-RADP, yCo);         //  W
    p8 = getpixel(xCo-RAD,    yCo-RAD);   //  NW

    // start timer and temporarily store new directions
    if(p1!=BLACK)      // N
       { timer=1; newh=horz; newv=vDOWN; }
    if(p2!=BLACK)      // NE
       { timer=1; newh=hLEFT; newv=vDOWN; }
    if(p3!=BLACK)      // E
       { timer=1; newh=hLEFT; newv=vert; }
    if(p4!=BLACK)      // SE
       { timer=1; newh=hLEFT; newv=vUP; }
    if( p5!=BLACK)     // S
       { timer=1; newh=horz; newv=vUP; }
    if(p6!=BLACK)      // SW
       { timer=1; newh=hRIGHT; newv=vUP; }
    if( p7!=BLACK)     // W
       { timer=1; newh=hRIGHT; newv=vert; }
    if(p8!=BLACK)      // NW
       { timer=1; newh=hRIGHT; newv=vDOWN; }
    }
 else if(timer==MAX)      // wait for it to see us too
    {
    horz = newh;          // change our direction
    vert = newv;
    ++timer;              // keep counting
    }
 else if(timer==3*MAX)    // when we're disengaged,
    timer = 0;            // turn off timer
 else                     // otherwise,
    ++timer;              // keep timer running

 molecule::calculate();   // calculate new position
 }
```

It's complicated to use the sensors to tell when we've moved away from the other molecule, so we use the timer instead.

When using multiple sensors, it simplifies the programming to restrict all the molecules to a speed of 1 or 2 pixels per time period, and have them all move at the same speed. Thus `MAX` might be 2 in the program fragment above.

13. Start with the `barchart` class from Exercise 11. Derive another class from `barchart` (call it `capchart`) that will add labels on the vertical and horizontal axes of the chart. It should place text labels just under each bar (they could be months of the year like "Jan" or sales districts like "East"), and numbers up the side of the graph that indicate the height of the bar in pixels (or some other quantity, like dollars, if you prefer). It's also nice to add tick marks alongside the numbers, so the viewer can more accurately see what height each number refers to. One of the arguments to the `capchart` constructor should be the address of an array containing the text labels for the horizontal axis. The `display()` function can figure out for itself what numbers to use, based on the height of the bars.

14. So far our traffic simulations have kept the cars in just one lane. How about passing? From the `car` class of Exercise 8, derive a class called `passcar`. It will need instance variables specifying the "ideal" speed and lane for the car. That is, the speed and lane the car will use if nothing is ahead of it. If there is an obstruction ahead, the car will check to its left (using a `getpixel()` sensor), and, if it is safe to pass, it will move to the lane to its left and pass the car in front. When the pass is completed, it will move back to its own lane. Cars don't need to change their speed to pass, since the car in front is going slower.

As you know from real-world experience, passing requires some care. Once a car has established that there is an obstruction (a slower car) in front, it should check for other cars, not only directly to its left, but also behind and to its left (perhaps at several different distances behind) and even a little ahead and to its left, where there might be a slower-moving car. Only then should it pull out to pass. It should perform similar checking before moving back to the right, into its own lane, when the pass is completed. You may want a timer to ensure that a car completes a lane-change maneuver before it thinks about starting another one.

Cars should be able to move left more than one lane to pass. If a car can't pass because of cars to its left, it should (of course) slow down before running into the car ahead. Passing on the right is not a good idea.

12

Pointers

ADDRESS CONSTANTS AND VARIABLES

POINTERS AND ARRAYS

POINTERS AND FUNCTION ARGUMENTS

POINTERS AND STRINGS

MEMORY MANAGEMENT WITH `new` AND `delete`

POINTERS AND OBJECTS

LINKED LISTS

12

Pointers are the hobgoblin of C++ (and C) programming; seldom has such a simple idea inspired so much perplexity for so many. But fear not. In this chapter we will try to demystify pointers and show practical uses for them in C++ programming.

What are pointers for? Here are some common uses:

- Accessing array elements
- Passing arguments to a function when the function needs to modify the original argument
- Passing arrays and strings to functions
- Obtaining memory from the system
- Creating data structures such as linked lists

Pointers are much more commonly used in C++ (and C) than in many other languages (such as BASIC and Pascal). Is this emphasis on pointers really necessary? You can do a lot without them, as their absence from the preceding chapters demonstrates. Some operations that use pointers in C++ can be carried out in other ways. For example, array elements can be accessed with array notation rather than pointer notation (we'll see the difference soon), and a function can modify arguments passed by reference, as well as those passed by pointer.

However, in some situations pointers provide an essential tool for increasing the power of C++. A notable example is the creation of data structures such as linked lists and binary trees. In fact, several key features of C++, such as virtual functions and the `this` pointer (discussed in Chapter 13), require the use of pointers. So, although you can do a lot of programming in C++ without using pointers, you will find them essential to obtaining the most from the language.

In this chapter we'll introduce pointers gradually, starting with fundamental concepts and working up to complex pointer applications.

If you already know C, you can probably skim over the first half of the chapter. However, you should read the sections in the second half on the `new` and `delete` operators, accessing member functions using pointers, arrays of pointers to objects, and linked-list objects.

Addresses and Pointers

The ideas behind pointers are not complicated. Here's the first key concept: Every byte in the computer's memory has an *address*. Addresses are numbers, just as they are for houses on a street. The numbers start at 0 and go up from there—1, 2, 3, and so on. If you have 640K of memory, the highest address is 655,359; for 1 MB of memory, it is 1,048,575.

Your program, when it is loaded into memory, occupies a certain range of these addresses. That means that every variable and every function in your program starts at a particular address. Figure 12-1 shows how this looks.

The Address of Operator &

You can find out the address occupied by a variable by using the *address of* operator &. Here's a short program, VARADDR, that demonstrates how to do this:

```
// varaddr.cpp
// addresses of variables
#include <iostream.h>

void main()
   {
   int var1 = 11;              // define and initialize
   int var2 = 22;              // three variables
   int var3 = 33;

   cout << endl << &var1       // print out the addresses
        << endl << &var2       // of these variables
        << endl << &var3;
   }
```

This simple program defines three integer variables and initializes them to the values 11, 22, and 33. It then prints out the addresses of these variables.

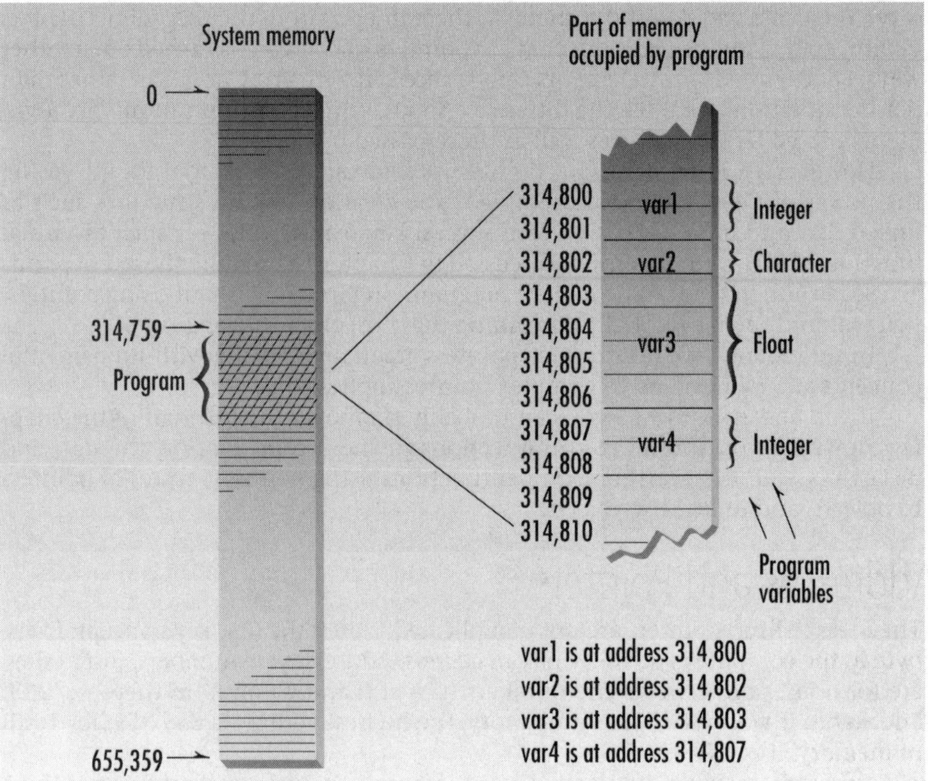

Figure 12-1 Memory Addresses

The actual addresses occupied by the variables in a program depend on many factors, such as the computer the program is running on, the size of the operating system, and whether any other programs are currently in memory. For these reasons you probably won't get the same addresses we did when you run this program. Here's the output on our machine:

```
0x8f4ffff4   <------- address of var1
0x8f4ffff2   <------- address of var2
0x8f4ffff0   <------- address of var3
```

Remember that the *address* of a variable is not at all the same as its *contents*. The contents of the three variables are 11, 22, and 33. Figure 12-2 shows the three variables in memory.

The << insertion operator interprets the addresses in hexadecimal arithmetic, as indicated by the prefix `0x` before each number. This is the usual way to show memory addresses. If you aren't familiar with the hexadecimal number system, don't worry. All you really need to know is that each variable starts at a unique address. However, you might note in the output above that each address differs from the next by exactly 2 bytes. That's because integers occupy 2 bytes of memory. If we had used variables of type `char`, they would have adjacent addresses, since a `char` occupies 1 byte; and if we had used type `double`, the addresses would have differed by 8 bytes.

The addresses appear in descending order because automatic variables are stored on the stack, which grows downward in memory. If we had used external variables,

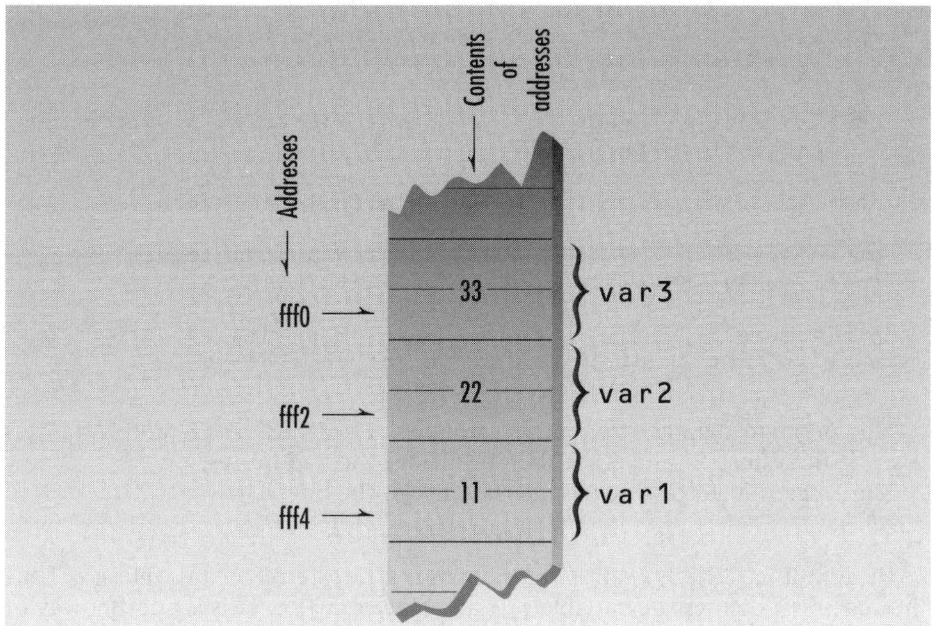

Figure 12-2 Addresses and Contents of Variables

they would have ascending addresses, since external variables are stored on the heap, which grows upward. Again, you don't need to worry too much about these considerations, since the compiler keeps track of the details for you.

Don't confuse the address of operator `&`, which precedes a variable name in a variable declaration, with the reference operator `&`, which follows the type name in a function prototype or definition. (References were discussed in Chapter 6.)

Pointer Variables

Addresses by themselves are rather limited. It's nice to know that we can find out where things are in memory, as we did in VARADDR, but printing out address values is not all that useful. The potential for increasing our programming power requires an additional idea: *variables that hold address values*. We've seen variable types that store characters, integers, floating-point numbers, and so on. Addresses are stored similarly. A variable that holds an address value is called a *pointer variable*, or simply a *pointer*.

What is the data type of pointer variables? It's not the same as the variable whose address is being stored; a pointer to `int` is not type `int`. You might think a pointer data type would be called something like `pointer` or `ptr`. However, things are slightly more complicated. The next program, PTRVAR, shows the syntax for pointer variables.

```
// ptrvar.cpp
// pointers (address variables)
#include <iostream.h>

void main()
   {
   int var1 = 11;                  // two integer variables
   int var2 = 22;

   cout << endl << &var1           // print addresses of variables
        << endl << &var2;

   int* ptr;                       // pointer to integers

   ptr = &var1;                    // pointer points to var1
   cout << endl << ptr;            // print pointer value

   ptr = &var2;                    // pointer points to var2
   cout << endl << ptr;            // print pointer value
   }
```

This program defines two integer variables, `var1` and `var2`, and initializes them to the values 11 and 22. It then prints out their addresses.

The program next defines a *pointer variable* in the line

```
int* ptr;
```

To the uninitiated this is a rather bizarre syntax. The asterisk means *pointer to*. Thus the statement defines the variable `ptr` as a *pointer to* `int`. This is another way of saying that this variable can hold the addresses of integer variables.

What's wrong with the idea of a general-purpose pointer type that holds pointers to any data type? If we called it type `pointer` we could write declarations like

```
pointer ptr;
```

The problem is that the compiler needs to know what kind of variable the pointer points to. (We'll see why when we talk about pointers and arrays.) The syntax used in C++ allows pointers to any type to be declared.

```
char* cptr;           // pointer to char
int* iptr;            // pointer to int
float* fptr;          // pointer to float
Distance* distptr;    // pointer to user-defined Distance class
```

and so on.

Syntax Quibbles

We should note that it is common to write pointer definitions with the asterisk closer to the variable name than to the type.

```
char *charptr;
```

It doesn't matter to the compiler, but placing the asterisk next to the type helps emphasize that the asterisk is part of the variable type (pointer to `char`), not part of the name itself.

If you define more than one pointer of the same type on one line, you need only insert the type-pointed-to once, but you need to place an asterisk before each variable name.

```
char* ptr1, * ptr2, * ptr3;  // three variables of type char*
```

Or you can use the asterisk-next-to-the-name approach.

```
char *ptr1, *ptr2, *ptr3;  // three variables of type char*
```

Pointers Must Have a Value

An address like 0x8f4ffff4 can be thought of as a *pointer constant*. A pointer like `ptr` can be thought of as a *pointer variable*. Just as the integer variable `var1` can be assigned the constant value 11, so can the pointer variable `ptr` be assigned the constant value 0x8f4ffff4.

When we first define a variable, it holds no value (unless we initialize it at the same time). It may hold a garbage value, but this has no meaning. In the case of pointers, a garbage value is the address of something in memory, but probably not of something that we want. So before a pointer is used, a specific address must be placed in it. In the PTRVAR program, `ptr` is first assigned the address of `var1` in the line

```
ptr = &var1; <——— put address of var1 in ptr
```

Following this the program prints out the value contained in `ptr`, which should be the same address printed for `&var1`. The same pointer variable `ptr` is then assigned the address of `var2`, and this value is printed out. Figure 12-3 shows the operation of the PTRVAR program. Here's the output of PTRVAR:

```
0x8f51fff4    <——— address of var1
0x8f51fff2    <——— address of var2
0x8f51fff4    <——— ptr set to address of var1
0x8f51fff2    <——— ptr set to address of var2
```

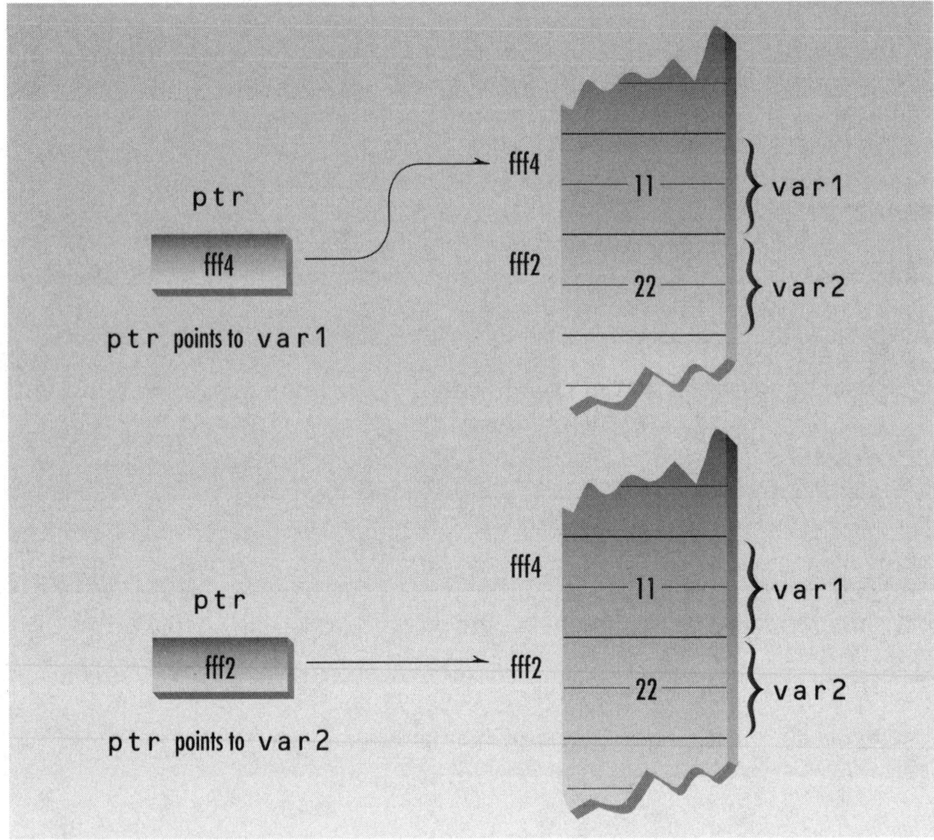

Figure 12-3 Changing Values in `ptr`

To summarize: A pointer can hold the address of any variable of the correct type; it's a receptacle awaiting an address. However, it must be given *some* value, otherwise it will point to an address we don't want it to point to, such as into our program code or the operating system. Rogue pointer values can result in system crashes and are difficult to debug, since the compiler gives no warning. The moral: Make sure you give every pointer variable a valid address value before using it.

Accessing the Variable Pointed To

Suppose that we don't know the name of a variable but we do know its address. Can we access the contents of the variable? (It may seem like mismanagement to lose track of variable names, but we'll soon see that there are many variables whose names we don't know.)

There is a special syntax to access the value of a variable using its address instead of its name. Here's an example program, PTRACC, that shows how it's done:

```
// ptracc.cpp
// accessing the variable pointed to
#include <iostream.h>

void main()
   {
   int var1 = 11;                // two integer variables
   int var2 = 22;

   int* ptr;                     // pointer to integers

   ptr = &var1;                  // pointer points to var1
   cout << endl << *ptr;         // print contents of pointer (11)

   ptr = &var2;                  // pointer points to var2
   cout << endl << *ptr;         // print contents of pointer (22)
   }
```

This program is very similar to PTRVAR, except that instead of printing the address values in `ptr`, we print the integer value stored at the address that's stored in `ptr`. Here's the output:

```
11
22
```

The expression that accesses the variables `var1` and `var2` is `*ptr`, which occurs in each of the two `cout` statements.

When an asterisk is used in front of a variable name, as it is in the `*ptr` expression, it is called the *indirection operator*. It means *the value of the variable pointed to by*. Thus the expression `*ptr` represents the value of the variable pointed to by `ptr`. When `ptr` is set to the address of `var1`, the expression `*ptr` has the value 11, since `var1` is 11. When `ptr` is changed to the address of `var2`, the expression `*ptr` acquires the value 22, since `var2` is 22. The indirection operator is sometimes called the *contents of* operator, which is another way to say the same thing. Figure 12-4 shows how this looks.

You can use a pointer not only to display a variable's value, but also to perform any operation you would perform on the variable directly. Here's a program, PTRTO, that uses a pointer to assign a value to a variable, and then to assign that value to another variable:

```
// ptrto.cpp
// other access using pointers
#include <iostream.h>

void main()
   {
   int var1, var2;              // two integer variables
   int* ptr;                    // pointer to integers
   ptr = &var1;                 // set pointer to address of var1
   *ptr = 37;                   // same as var1=37
   var2 = *ptr;                 // same as var2=var1

   cout << endl << var2;        // verify var2 is 37
   }
```

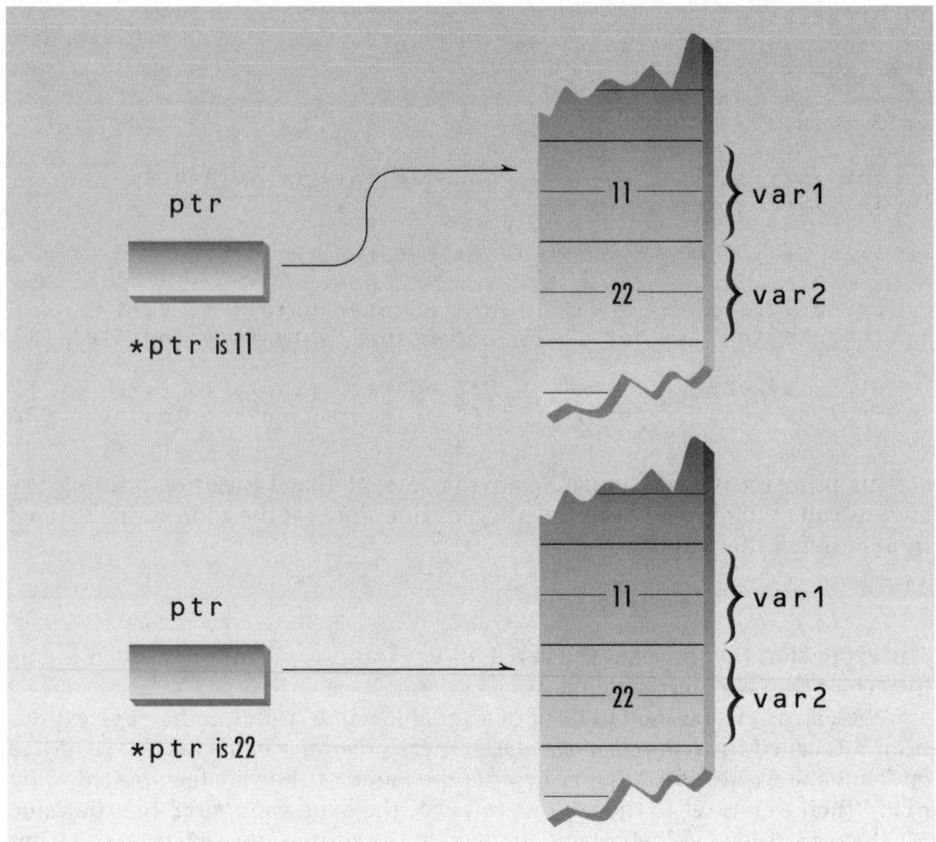

Figure 12-4 Access via Pointer

Remember that the asterisk used as the indirection operator has a different meaning than the asterisk used to declare pointer variables. The indirection operator precedes the variable and means *value of the variable pointed to by*. The asterisk used in a declaration means *pointer to*.

```
int* ptr;      // declaration:
*ptr = 37;     // indirection:
```

Using the indirection operator to access the value stored in an address is called *indirect addressing*, or sometimes *dereferencing*, the pointer.

Here's a capsule summary of what we've learned so far:

```
int v;          // defines variable v of type int
int* p;         // defines p as a pointer to int
p = &v;         // assigns address of variable v to pointer p
v = 3;          // assigns 3 to v
*p = 3;         // also assigns 3 to v
```

The last two statements show the difference between normal or direct addressing, where we refer to a variable by name, and pointer or indirect addressing, where we refer to the same variable using its address.

These two approaches are vaguely analogous to delivering a letter to a friend. If you drive to the friend's house and stick the letter in the mailslot, that's direct addressing. You can also write the address on the envelope and put the letter in a public mailbox. The mail personnel will read the address and see that the letter gets to the right place. That's indirect addressing.

In the example programs we've shown so far in this chapter, there's really no advantage to using the pointer expression to access variables, since we can access them directly. Pointers come into their own when you can't access a variable directly, as we'll see.

Pointer to void

Before we go on to see pointers at work, we should note one peculiarity of pointer data types. Ordinarily, the address that you put in a pointer must be the same type as the pointer. You can't assign the address of a `float` variable to a pointer to `int`, for example. However, there is an exception to this. There is a sort of general-purpose pointer that can point to any data type. This is called a pointer to `void`, and is defined like this:

```
void* ptr;   // ptr can point to any data type
```

Such pointers have certain specialized uses, such as passing pointers to functions that operate independently of the data type pointed to.

The next example uses a pointer to `void` and also shows that, if you don't use `void`, you must be careful to assign pointers an address of the same type as the pointer. Here's the listing for PTRVOID:

```
// ptrvoid.cpp
// pointers to type void
#include <iostream.h>

void main()
   {
   int intvar;                      // integer variable
   float flovar;                    // float variable

   int* ptrint;                     // define pointer to int
   float* ptrflo;                   // define pointer to float
   void* ptrvoid;                   // define pointer to void

   ptrint = &intvar;                // ok, int* to int*
// ptrint = &flovar;                // error, float* to int*
// ptrflo = &intvar;                // error, int* to float*
   ptrflo = &flovar;                // ok, float* to float*

   ptrvoid = &intvar;               // ok, int* to void*
   ptrvoid = &flovar;               // ok, float* to void*
   }
```

You can assign the address of `intvar` to `ptrint` because they are both type `int*`, but you can't assign the address of `flovar` to `ptrint` because the first is type `float*` and the second is type `int*`. However, `ptrvoid` can be given any pointer value, such as `int*`, because it is a pointer to `void`.

Pointers and Arrays

There is a close association between pointers and arrays. We saw in Chapter 8 how array elements are accessed. The following program, ARRNOTE, provides a review.

```
// arrnote.cpp
// array accessed with array notation
#include <iostream.h>

void main()
   {
   int intarray[5] = { 31, 54, 77, 52, 93 };  // array

   for(int j=0; j<5; j++)                     // for each element
      cout << endl << intarray[j];            // print value
   }
```

The `cout` statement prints each array element in turn. For instance, when `j` is 3, the expression `intarray[j]` takes on the value `intarray[3]` and accesses the fourth array element, the integer 52. Here's the output of ARRNOTE:

```
31
54
77
52
93
```

Surprisingly, array elements can be accessed using pointer notation as well as array notation. The next example, PTRNOTE, is similar to ARRNOTE except that it uses pointer notation.

```
// ptrnote.cpp
// array accessed with pointer notation
#include <iostream.h>

void main()
   {
   int intarray[5] = { 31, 54, 77, 52, 93 };  // array

   for(int j=0; j<5; j++)                     // for each element,
      cout << endl << *(intarray+j);          // print value
   }
```

The expression `*(intarray+j)` in PTRNOTE has exactly the same effect as `intarray[j]` in ARRNOTE, and the output of the programs is identical. But how do we interpret the expression `*(intarray+j)`? Suppose `j` is 3, so the expression is equivalent to `*(intarray+3)`. We want this to represent the contents of the fourth element of the array (52). Remember that the name of an array is its address. The expression `intarray+j` is thus an address with something added to it. You might expect that `intarray+3` would cause 3 bytes to be added to `intarray`. But that doesn't produce the result we want: `intarray` is an array of integers, and 3 bytes into this array is the middle of the second element, which is not very useful. We want to obtain the fourth *integer* in the array, not the fourth byte, as shown in Figure 12-5.

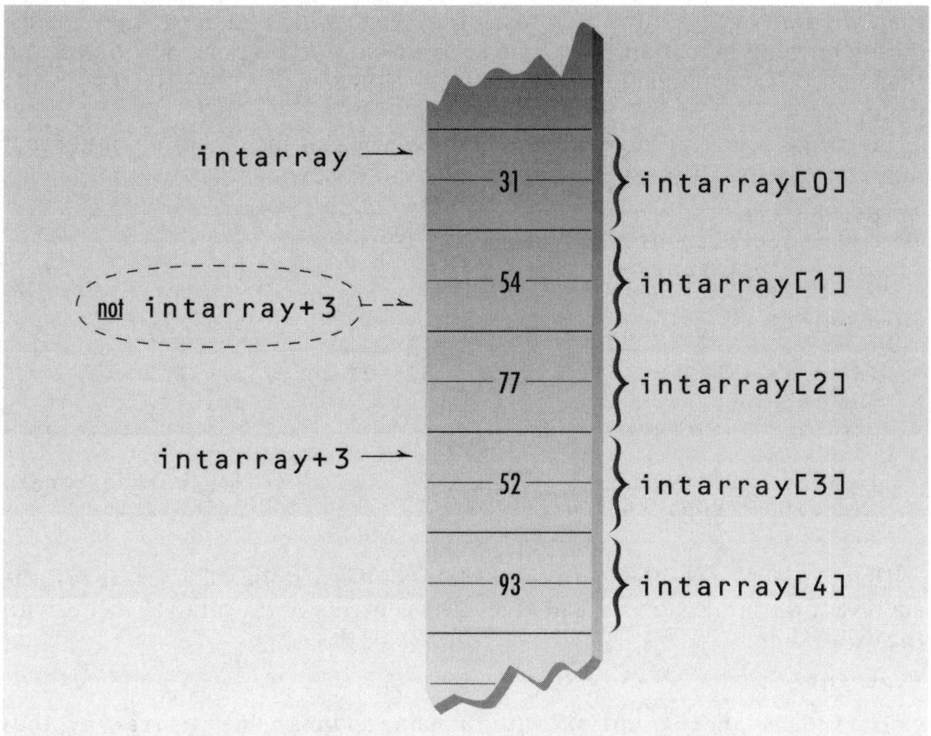

Figure 12-5 Counting by Integers

The C++ compiler is smart enough to take the size of the data into account when it performs arithmetic on data addresses. It knows that `intarray` is an array of type `int` because it was declared that way. So when it sees the expression `intarray+3`, it interprets it as the address of the fourth *integer* in `intarray`, not the fourth byte.

But we want the *value* of this fourth array element, not the *address*. To take the value, we use the indirection operator `*`. The resulting expression, when `j` is 3, is `*(intarray+3)`, which is the contents of the fourth array element, or 52.

Now we see why a pointer declaration must include the type of the variable pointed to. The compiler needs to know whether a pointer is a pointer to `int` or a pointer to `double` so that it can perform the correct arithmetic to access elements of the array. It multiplies the index value by 2 in the case of type `int`, but by 8 in the case of `double`.

Pointer Constants and Pointer Variables

Suppose that, instead of adding `j` to `intarray` to step through the array addresses, you wanted to use the increment operator. Could you write `*(intarray++)`?

The answer is no, and the reason is that you can't increment a constant (or indeed change it in any way). The expression `intarray` is the address where the system has chosen to place your array, and it will stay at this address until the program terminates. `intarray` is a constant. You can't say `intarray++` any more than you can say 7++. (In a multitasking system, variable addresses may change during program execution. An active program may be swapped out to disk and then reloaded at a different memory location. However, this process is invisible to your program.)

But while you can't increment an address, you can increment a pointer that holds an address. The next example, PTRINC, shows how:

```
// ptrinc.cpp
// array accessed with pointer
#include <iostream.h>

void main()
   {
   int intarray[] = { 31, 54, 77, 52, 93 }; // array
   int* ptrint;                             // pointer to int
   ptrint = intarray;                       // points to intarray

   for(int j=0; j<5; j++)                   // for each element,
      cout << endl << *(ptrint++);          // print value
   }
```

Here we define a pointer to `int`—`ptrint`—and give it the value `intarray`, the address of the array. Now we can access the contents of the array elements with the expression

```
*(ptrint++)
```

The variable `ptrint` starts off with the same address value as `intarray`, thus allowing the first array element, `intarray[0]`, which has the value 31, to be accessed as before. But, because `ptrint` is a variable and not a constant, it can be incremented. After it is incremented, it points to the second array element, `intarray[1]`. The expression `*(ptrint++)` then represents the contents of the second array element, or 54. The loop causes the expression to access each array element in turn. The output of PTRINC is the same as that for PTRNOTE.

Pointers and Functions

In Chapter 6 we noted that there are three ways to pass arguments to a function: by value, by reference, and by pointer. If the function is intended to modify variables in the calling program, then these variables cannot be passed by value, since the function obtains only a copy of the variable. However, either a reference argument or a pointer can be used in this situation.

Passing Simple Variables

We'll first review how arguments are passed by reference, and then compare this to passing pointer arguments. The PASSREF program shows passing by reference.

```
// passref.cpp
// arguments passed by reference
#include <iostream.h>

void main()
```

```
    {
    void centimize(double&);      // prototype

    double var = 10.0;            // var has value of 10 inches
    cout << endl << "var=" << var << " inches";

    centimize(var);               // change var to centimeters
    cout << endl << "var=" << var << " centimeters";
    }

void centimize(double& v)
    {
    v *= 2.54;                    // v is the same as var
    }
```

Here we want to convert a variable `var` in `main()` from inches to centimeters. We pass the variable by reference to the function `centimize()`. (Remember that the `&` following the data type `double` in the prototype for this function indicates that the argument is passed by reference.) The `centimize()` function multiplies the original variable by 2.54. Notice how the function refers to the variable. It simply uses the argument name `v`; `v` and `var` are different names for the same thing.

Once it has converted `var` to centimeters, `main()` displays the result. Here's the output of PASSREF:

```
var=25.4 centimeters
```

The next example, PASSPTR, shows an equivalent situation when pointers are used:

```
// passptr.cpp
// arguments passed by pointer
#include <iostream.h>

void main()
    {
    void centimize(double*);      // prototype

    double var = 10.0;            // var has value of 10 inches
    cout << endl << "var=" << var << " inches";

    centimize(&var);              // change var to centimeters
    cout << endl << "var=" << var << " centimeters";
    }

void centimize(double* ptrd)
    {
    *ptrd *= 2.54;                // *ptrd is the same as var
    }
```

The output of PASSPTR is the same as that of PASSREF.

The function `centimize()` is declared as taking an argument that is a pointer to `double`:

```
void centimize(double*)    // argument is pointer to double
```

When `main()` calls the function it supplies the address of the variable as the argument:

```
centimize(&var);
```

Remember that this is not the variable itself, as it is in passing by reference, but the variable's address.

Because the `centimize()` function is passed an address, it must use the indirection operator, `*ptrd`, to access the value stored at this address:

```
*ptrd *= 2.54;   // multiply the contents of ptrd by 2.54
```

Of course this is the same as

```
*ptrd = *ptrd * 2.54;   // multiply the contents of ptrd by 2.54
```

where the stand-alone asterisk means multiplication. (This operator really gets around.)

Since `ptrd` contains the address of `var`, anything done to `*ptrd` is actually done to `var`. Figure 12-6 shows how changing `*ptrd` in the function changes `var` in the calling program.

Passing a pointer as an argument to a function is in some ways similar to passing a reference. They both permit the variable in the calling program to be modified by the function. However, the mechanism is different. A reference is an alias for the original variable, while a pointer is the address of the variable.

Passing Arrays

We've seen numerous examples, starting in Chapter 8, of arrays passed as arguments to functions, and their elements being accessed by the function. Until this chapter, since we had not yet learned about pointers, this was done using array

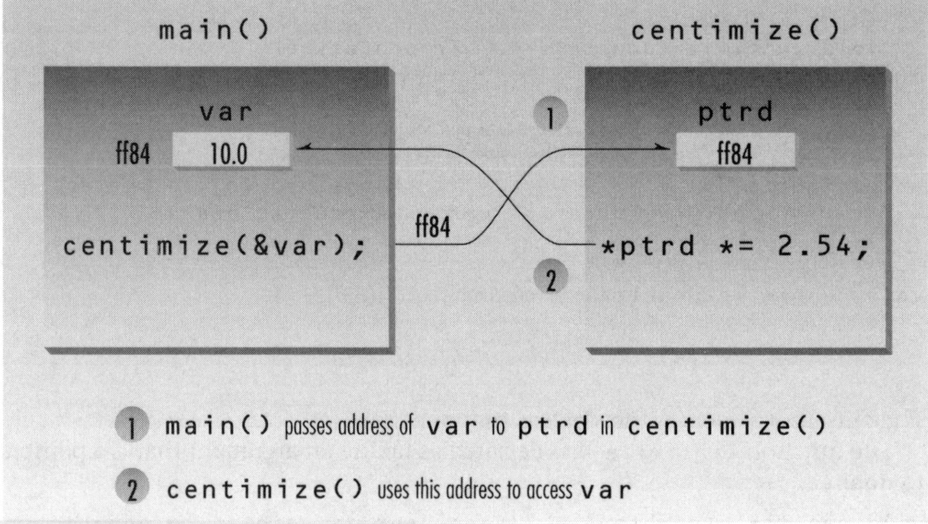

Figure 12-6 Pointer Passed to Function

notation. However, it's more common to use pointer notation instead of array notation when arrays are passed to functions. The PASSARR program shows how this looks:

```
// passarr.cpp
// array passed by pointer
#include <iostream.h>

const int MAX = 5;              // number of array elements

void main()
   {
   void centimize(double*);    // prototype

   double varray[MAX] = { 10.0, 43.1, 95.9, 59.7, 87.3 };

   centimize(varray);           // change elements of varray to cm

   for(int j=0; j<MAX; j++)    // display new array values

      cout << endl << "varray[" << j << "]="
           << varray[j] << " centimeters";
   }

void centimize(double* ptrd)
   {
   for(int j=0; j<MAX; j++)
      *ptrd++ *= 2.54;          // ptrd points to elements of varray
   }
```

The prototype for the function is the same as in PASSPTR; the function's single argument is a pointer to `double`. In array notation this is written as

```
void centimize(double[]);
```

That is, `double*` is equivalent here to `double[]`, although the pointer syntax is more commonly used.

Since the name of an array is the array's address, there is no need for the address operator `&` when the function is called:

```
centimize(varray);  // pass array address
```

In `centimize()` this array address is placed in the variable `ptrd`. To point to each element of the array in turn, we need only increment `ptrd`:

```
*ptrd++ *= 2.54;
```

Figure 12-7 shows how the array is accessed. Here's the output of PASSARR:

```
varray[0]=25.4 centimeters
varray[1]=109.474 centimeters
varray[2]=243.586 centimeters
varray[3]=151.638 centimeters
varray[4]=221.742 centimeters
```

Here's a syntax question: How do we know that the expression `*ptrd++` increments the pointer and not the pointer contents? In other words, does the compiler interpret it as `*(ptrd++)`, which is what we want, or as `(*ptrd)++`? It turns out that `*` (when used as the indirection operator) and `++` have the same precedence.

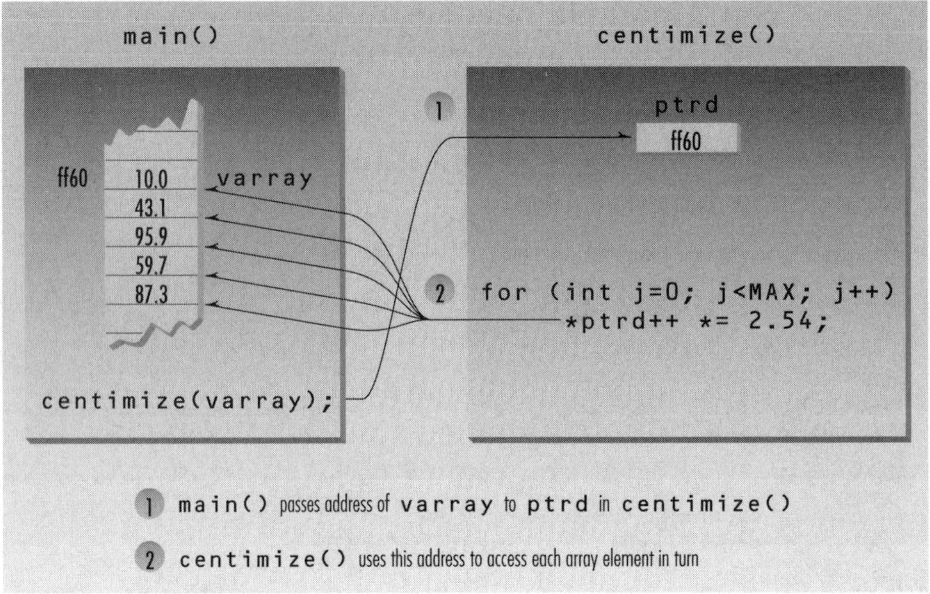

Figure 12-7 Accessing Array from Function

However, operators of the same precedence are distinguished in a second way: by *associativity*. Associativity is concerned with whether the compiler performs operations starting with an operator on the right or an operator on the left. If a group of operators has right associativity, the compiler performs the operation on the right side of the expression first, then works its way to the left. The unary operators like `*` and `++` do have right associativity, so the expression is interpreted as `*(ptrd++)`, which increments the pointer, not what it points to. That is, the pointer is incremented first and the indirection operator applied to the result.

Sorting Array Elements

As a further example of using pointers to access array elements, let's see how to sort the contents of an array. We'll use two program examples—the first to lay the groundwork, and the second, an expansion of the first, to demonstrate the sorting process.

Ordering with Pointers

The first program is similar to the REFORDER program in Chapter 6, except that it uses pointers instead of references. It orders two numbers passed to it as arguments, exchanging them if the second is smaller than the first. Here's the listing for PTRORDER:

```
// ptrorder.cpp
// orders two arguments using pointers
#include <iostream.h>

void main()
```

```
    {
    void order(int*, int*);          // prototype

    int n1=99, n2=11;                // one pair ordered, one not
    int n3=22, n4=88;

    order(&n1, &n2);                 // order each pair of numbers
    order(&n3, &n4);

    cout << endl << "n1=" << n1;     // print out all numbers
    cout << endl << "n2=" << n2;
    cout << endl << "n3=" << n3;
    cout << endl << "n4=" << n4;
    }

void order(int* numb1, int* numb2)  // orders two numbers
    {
    if(*numb1 > *numb2)              // if 1st larger than 2nd,
       {
       int temp = *numb1;            // swap them
       *numb1 = *numb2;
       *numb2 = temp;
       }
    }
```

The function `order()` works the same as it did in REFORDER, except that it is passed the *addresses* of the numbers to be ordered, and it accesses the numbers using pointers. That is, `*numb1` accesses the number in `main()` passed as the first argument, and `*numb2` accesses the second.

Here's the output from PTRORDER:

```
n1=11  <——— this and
n2=99  <——— this are swapped, since they weren't in order
n3=22  <——— this
n4=88  <——— and this are not swapped, since they were in order
```

We'll use the `order()` function from PTRORDER in our next example program, PTRSORT, which sorts an array of integers.

```
// ptrsort.cpp
// sorts an array using pointers
#include <iostream.h>

void main()
   {
   void bsort(int*, int);           // prototype
   const int N = 10;                // array size
                                    // test array
   int arr[N] = { 37, 84, 62, 91, 11, 65, 57, 28, 19, 49 };

   bsort(arr, N);                   // sort the array

   for(int j=0; j<N; j++)           // print out sorted array
      cout << arr[j] << " ";
   }
```

(continued on next page)

(continued from previous page)

```
void bsort(int* ptr, int n)
   {
   void order(int*, int*);         // prototype
   int j, k;                       // indexes to array

   for(j=0; j<n-1; j++)            // outer loop
      for(k=j+1; k<n; k++)         // inner loop starts at outer
         order(ptr+j, ptr+k);      // order the pointer contents
   }

void order(int* numb1, int* numb2)   // orders two numbers
   {
   if(*numb1 > *numb2)                // if 1st larger than 2nd,
      {
      int temp = *numb1;              // swap them
      *numb1 = *numb2;
      *numb2 = temp;
      }
   }
```

The array `arr` of integers in `main()` is initialized to unsorted values. The address of the array, and the number of elements, are passed to the `bsort()` function. This sorts the array, and the sorted values are then printed. Here's the output of the PTRSORT:

```
11 19 28 37 49 57 62 65 84 91
```

The Bubble Sort

The `bsort()` function sorts the array using a variation of the *bubble sort*. This is a simple (although notoriously slow) approach to sorting. Here's how it works, assuming we want to arrange the numbers in the array in ascending order. First the first element of the array (`arr[0]`) is compared in turn with each of the other elements (starting with the second). If it's greater than any of them, the two are swapped. When this is done we know that at least the first element is in order; it's now the smallest element. Next the second element is compared in turn with all the other elements, starting with the third, and again swapped if it's bigger. When we're done we know that the second element has the second-smallest value. This process is continued for all the elements until the next-to-the-last, at which time the array is assumed to be ordered. Figure 12-8 shows the bubble sort in action (with fewer items than in PTRSORT).

In PTRSORT, the number in the first position, 37, is compared with each element in turn, and swapped with 11. The number in the second position, which starts off as 84, is compared with each element. It's swapped with 62; then 62 (which is now in the second position) is swapped with 37, 37 is swapped with 28, and 28 is swapped with 19. The number in the third position, which is 84 again, is swapped with 62, 62 is swapped with 57, 57 with 37, and 37 with 28. The process continues until the array is sorted.

The `bsort()` function in PTRSORT consists of two nested loops, each of which controls a pointer. The outer loop uses the loop variable `j`, and the inner one uses `k`. The expressions `ptr+j` and `ptr+k` point to various elements of the array, as

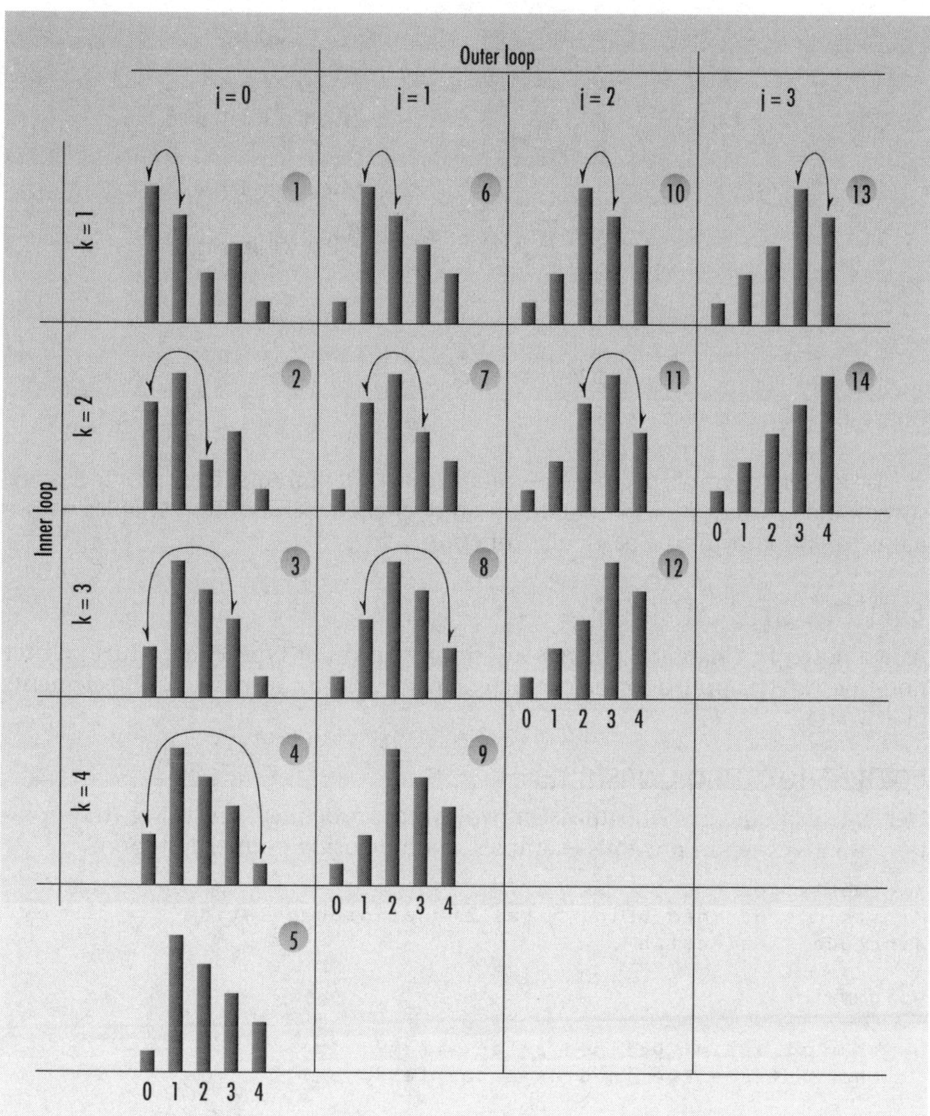

Figure 12-8 Operation of the Bubble Sort

determined by the loop variables. The expression `ptr+j` moves down the array, starting at the first element (the top) and stepping down integer by integer until one short of the last element (the bottom). For each position taken by `ptr+j` in the outer loop, the expression `ptr+k` in the inner loop starts pointing one below `ptr+j` and moves down to the bottom of the array. Each time through the inner loop, the elements pointed to by `ptr+j` and `ptr+k` are compared, using the `order()` function, and if the first is greater than the second, they're swapped. Figure 12-9 shows this process.

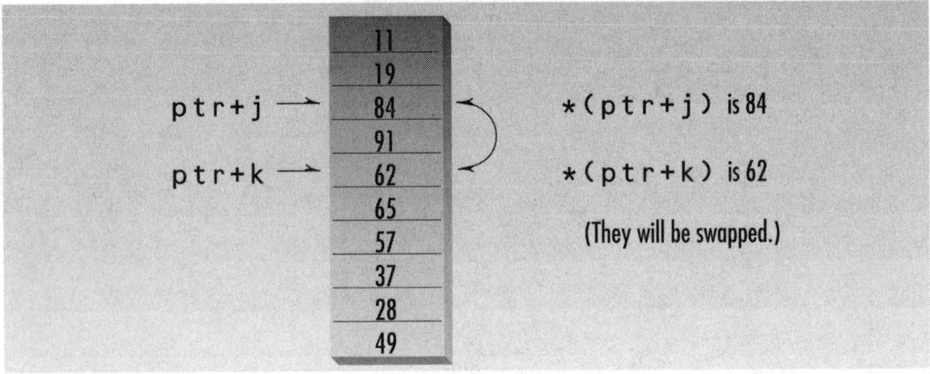

Figure 12-9 Operation of PTRSORT

The PTRSORT example begins to reveal the power of pointers. They provide a consistent and efficient way to operate on array elements and other variables whose names aren't known to a particular function.

Pointers and Strings

As we noted in Chapter 8, strings are simply arrays of type `char`. Thus pointer notation can be applied to the characters in strings, just as it can to the elements of any array.

Pointers to String Constants

Here's an example, TWOSTR, in which two strings are defined, one using array notation as we've seen in previous examples, and one using pointer notation:

```
// twostr.cpp
// strings defined using array and pointer notation
#include <iostream.h>

void main()
   {
   char str1[] = "Defined as an array";
   char* str2 = "Defined as a pointer";

   cout << endl << str1;     // display both strings
   cout << endl << str2;

// str1++;                   // can't do this; str1 is a constant
   str2++;                   // this is OK, str2 is a pointer

   cout << endl << str2;     // now str2 starts "efined..."
   }
```

In many ways these two types of definition are equivalent. You can print out both strings as the example shows, use them as function arguments, and so on. But there is a subtle difference: `str1` is an address—that is, a pointer constant—while `str2` is a pointer variable. So `str2` can be changed, while `str1` cannot, as demonstrated in the program. Figure 12-10 shows how these two kinds of strings look in memory.

We can increment `str2`, since it is a pointer, but once we do, it no longer points to the first character in the string. Here's the output of TWOSTR:

```
Defined as an array
Defined as a pointer
efined as a pointer   ←——— following str2++
```

A string defined as a pointer is considerably more flexible than one defined as an array. The following examples will make use of this flexibility.

Strings As Function Arguments

Here's an example that shows a string used as a function argument. The function simply prints the string, by accessing each character in turn. Here's the listing for PTRSTR:

```
// ptrstr.cpp
// displays a string with pointer notation
#include <iostream.h>

void main()
   {
   void dispstr(char*);        // prototype

   char str[] = "Idle people have the least leisure.";
```

(continued on next page)

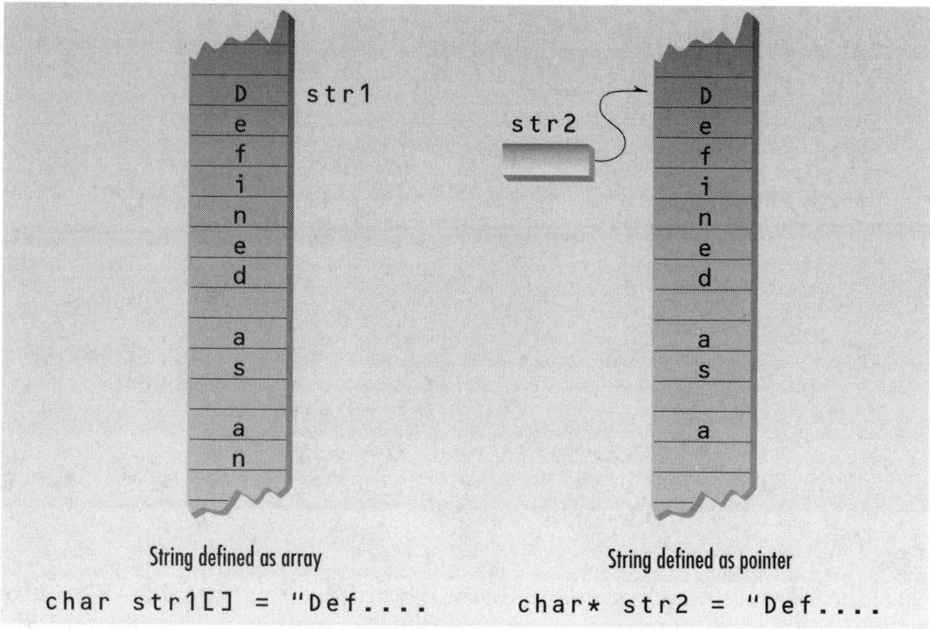

Figure 12-10 Strings As Arrays and Pointers

(continued from previous page)
```
   dispstr(str);                  // display the string
   }

void dispstr(char* ps)
   {
   cout << endl;                  // start on new line
   while( *ps )                   // until null character,
      cout << *ps++;              // print characters
   }
```

The array address `str` is used as the argument in the call to function `dispstr()`. This address is a constant, but since it is passed by value, a copy of it is created in `dispstr()`. This copy is a pointer, `ps`. A pointer can be changed, so the function increments `ps` to display the string. The expression `*ps++` returns the successive characters of the string. The loop cycles until it finds the null character (`'\0'`) at the end of the string. Since this has the value 0, which represents *false*, the `while` loop terminates at this point.

Copying a String Using Pointers

We've seen examples of pointers used to obtain values from an array. Pointers can also be used to insert values into an array. The next example, COPYSTR, demonstrates a function that copies one string to another:

```
// copystr.cpp
// copies one string to another with pointers
#include <iostream.h>

void main()
   {
   void copystr(char*, char*);   // prototype

   char* str1 = "Self-conquest is the greatest victory.";
   char str2[80];                // empty string

   copystr(str2, str1);          // copy str1 to str2
   cout << endl << str2;         // display str2
   }

void copystr(char* dest, char* src)
   {
   while( *src )                 // until null character,
      *dest++ = *src++;          // copy chars from src to dest
   *dest = '\0';                 // terminate dest
   }
```

Here the `main()` part of the program calls the function `copystr()` to copy `str1` to `str2`. In this function the expression

```
*dest++ = *src++;
```

takes the value at the address pointed to by `src` and places it in the address pointed to by `dest`. Both pointers are then incremented, so the next time through the loop the next character will be transferred. The loop terminates when a null character is found in `src`; at this point a null is inserted in `dest` and the function returns. Figure 12-11 shows how the pointers move through the strings.

Library String Functions

Many of the library functions we have already used for strings have string arguments that are specified using pointer notation. As an example we can look at the description of `strcpy()` in the Borland or Turbo C++ documentation (or in the STRING.H header file). This function copies one string to another; we can compare it with our homemade `copystr()` function in the COPYSTR example. Here's the syntax for the `strcpy()` library function:

```
char* strcpy(char* dest, const char* src);
```

This function takes two arguments of type `char*`. What is the effect of the `const` modifier in the second argument? It indicates that `strcpy()` cannot change the characters pointed to by `src`. (It does not imply that the `src` pointer itself cannot be modified. To do that the argument declaration would be `char * const src`.)

The `strcpy()` function also returns a pointer to `char`; this is the address of the `dest` string. In other respects this function works very much like our homemade `copystr()` function.

Arrays of Pointers to Strings

Just as there are arrays of variables of type `int` or type `float`, there can also be arrays of pointers. A common use for this construction is an array of pointers to strings.

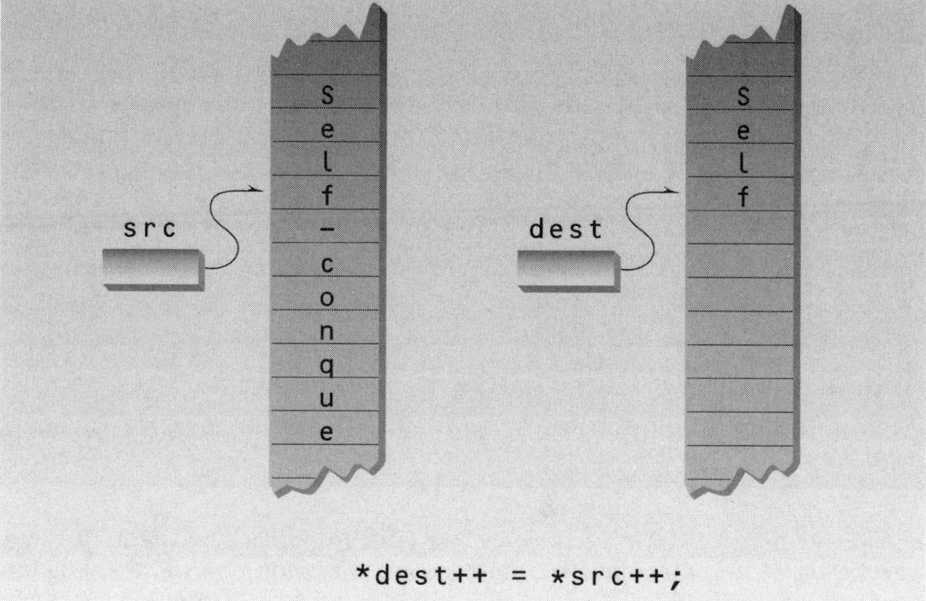

Figure 12-11 Operation of COPYSTR

In Chapter 8 the STRARAY program demonstrated an array of strings. As we noted, there is a disadvantage to using an array of strings, in that the subarrays that hold the strings must all be the same length, so space is wasted when strings are shorter than the length of the subarrays (see Figure 8-10 in Chapter 8).

Let's see how to use pointers to solve this problem. We will modify STRARAY to create an array of pointers to strings, rather than an array of strings. Here's the listing for PTRTOSTR:

```
// ptrtostr.cpp
// an array of pointers to strings
#include <iostream.h>
const int DAYS = 7;              // number of pointers in array

void main()
   {                             // array of pointers to char
   char* arrptrs[DAYS] = { "Sunday", "Monday", "Tuesday",
                           "Wednesday", "Thursday",
                           "Friday", "Saturday"  };

   for(int j=0; j<DAYS; j++)     // display every string
      cout << arrptrs[j] << endl;
   }
```

The output of this program is the same as that for STRARAY:

```
Sunday
Monday
Tuesday
Wednesday
Thursday
Friday
Saturday
```

When strings are not part of an array, C++ places them contiguously in memory, so there is no wasted space. However, to find the strings, there must be an array that holds pointers to them. A string is itself an array of type `char`, so an array of pointers to strings is an array of pointers to `char`. That is the meaning of the definition of `arrptrs` in PTRTOSTR. Now recall that a string is always represented by a single address: the address of the first character in the string. It is these addresses that are stored in the array. Figure 12-12 shows how this looks.

Memory Management: `new` and `delete`

We've seen many examples where arrays are used to set aside memory. The statement

```
int arr1[100];
```

reserves memory for 100 integers. Arrays are a useful approach to data storage, but they have a serious drawback: We must know at the time we write the program how big the array will be. We can't wait until the program is running to specify the array size. The following approach won't work:

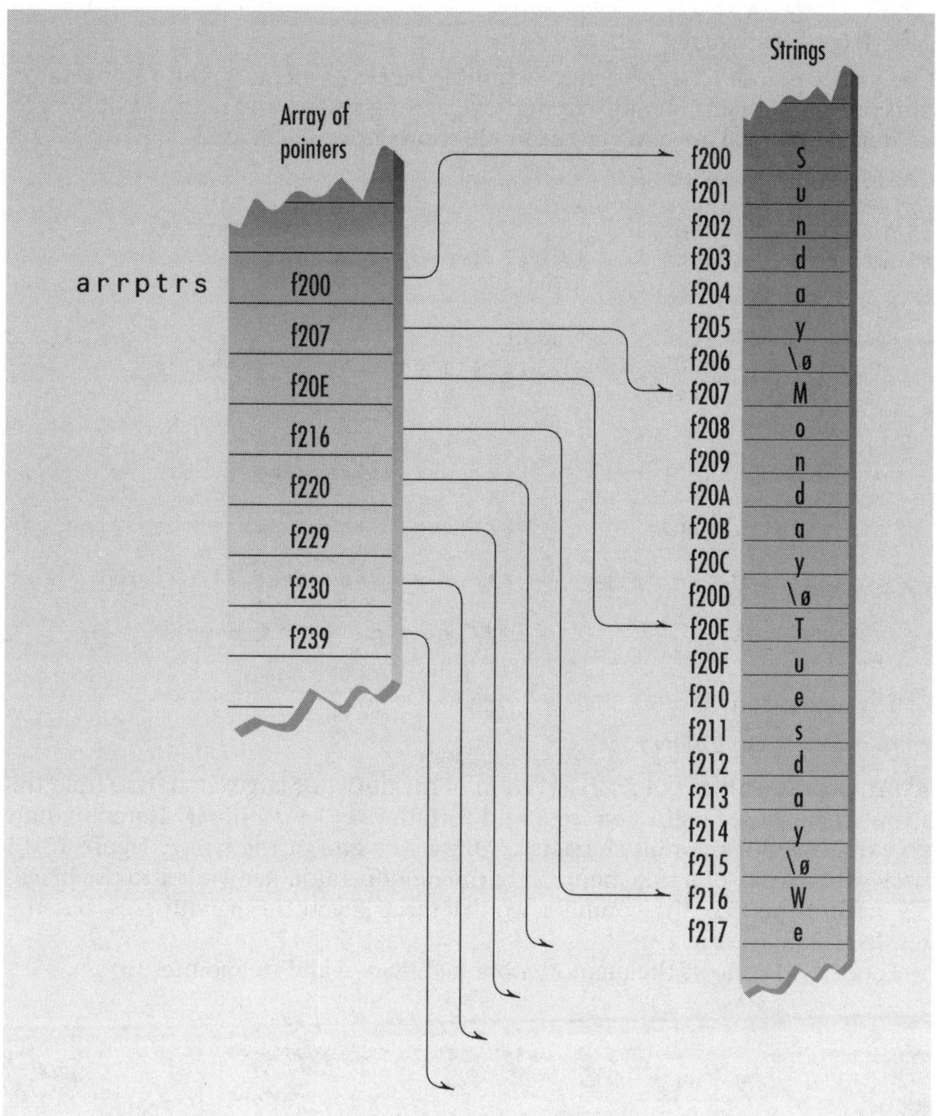

Figure 12-12 Array of Pointers to Strings

```
cin >> size;        // get size from user
int arr[size];      // error; array size must be a constant
```

The compiler requires the array size to be a constant.

But in many situations we don't know how much memory we need until run-time. We might want to store a string that was typed in by the user, for example. In this situation we can define an array sized to hold the largest string we expect, but this wastes memory.

The new Operator

C++ provides another approach to obtaining blocks of memory: the new operator. This operator obtains memory from the operating system and returns a pointer to its starting point. The NEWINTRO example shows how new is used:

```
// newintro.cpp
// introduces operator new
#include <iostream.h>
#include <string.h>         // for strcpy()

void main()
   {
   char* str = "Idle hands are the devil's workshop.";
   int len = strlen(str);        // get length of str

   char* ptr;                    // make a pointer to char
   ptr = new char[len+1];        // set aside memory: string + '\0'

   strcpy(ptr, str);             // copy str to new memory area ptr

   cout << endl << "ptr=" << ptr;  // show that str is now in ptr

   delete[] ptr;                 // release ptr's memory
   }
```

The expression

```
ptr = new char[len+1];
```

returns a pointer that points to a section of memory just large enough to hold the string str, whose length len we found with the strlen() library function, plus an extra byte for the null character '\0' at the end of the string. Figure 12-13 shows the syntax of a statement using the new operator. Remember to use brackets around the size; the compiler won't object if you use parentheses, but the results will be incorrect.

Figure 12-14 shows the memory obtained by new and the pointer to it.

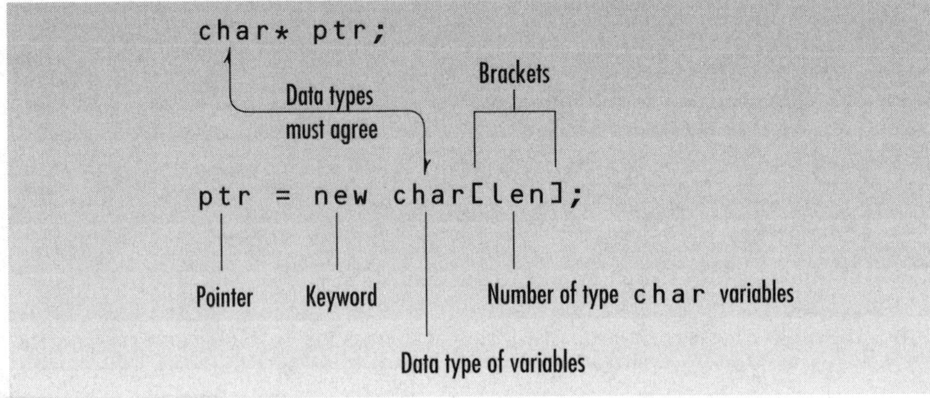

Figure 12-13 Syntax of new Operator

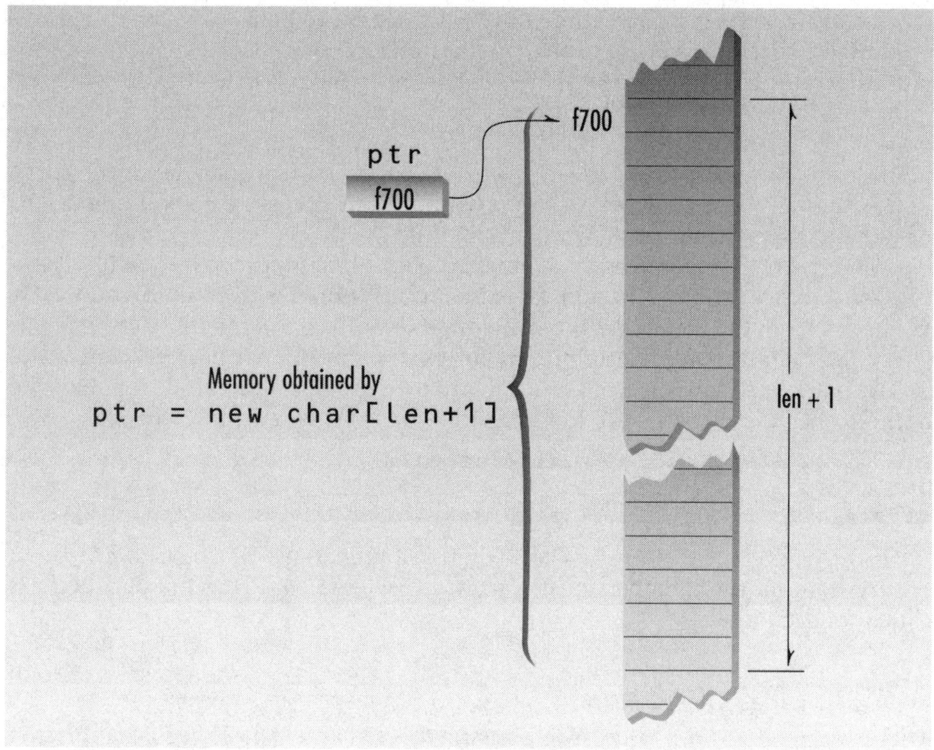

Figure 12-14 Memory Obtained by `new` Operator

In NEWINTRO we use `strcpy()` to copy string `str` to the newly created memory area pointed to by `ptr`. Since we made this area equal in size to the length of `str`, the string fits exactly. The output of NEWINTRO is:

```
ptr=Idle hands are the devil's workshop.
```

C programmers will recognize that `new` plays a role similar to the `malloc()` family of library functions. The `new` approach is superior in that it returns a pointer to the appropriate data type, while `malloc()`'s pointer must be cast to the appropriate type. There are other advantages as well.

C programmers may wonder if there is a C++ equivalent to `realloc()`, for changing the size of memory that has already been reallocated. Sorry, there's no `renew` in C++. You'll need to fall back on the ploy of creating a larger (or smaller) space with `new`, and copying your data from the old area to the new one.

The `delete` Operator

If your program reserves many chunks of memory using `new`, eventually all the available memory will be reserved and the system will crash. To ensure safe and efficient use of memory, the `new` operator is matched by a corresponding `delete` operator that returns memory to the operating system. In NEWINTRO the statement

```
delete[] ptr;
```

returns to the system whatever memory was pointed to by `ptr`.

Actually, there is no need for this operator in NEWINTRO, since memory is automatically returned (at least using the small memory model) when the program terminates. However, suppose you use `new` in a function. If the function uses a local variable as a pointer to this memory, then when the function terminates, the pointer will be destroyed but the memory will be left as an orphan, taking up space that is inaccessible to the rest of the program. Thus it is always good practice to `delete` memory when you're through with it.

Deleting the memory doesn't delete the pointer that points to it (`str` in NEWINTRO), and doesn't change the address value in the pointer. However, this address is no longer valid; the memory it points to may be changed to something entirely different. Be careful that you don't use pointers to memory that has been `deleted`.

The brackets following delete indicate that we're deleting an array. If you create a single object with `new`, you don't need the brackets when you delete it.

```
ptr = new SomeClass;   // allocate a single object
. . .
delete ptr;            // no brackets following delete
```

However, don't forget the brackets when deleting arrays of objects. Using them ensures that all the members of the array are deleted, and that the destructor is called for each one.

A String Class Using `new`

The `new` operator often appears in constructors. As an example, we'll modify the `String` class, last seen in examples such as STRPLUS in Chapter 9. You may recall that a potential defect of that class was that all `String` objects occupied the same fixed amount of memory. A string shorter than this fixed length wasted memory, and a longer string—if one were mistakenly generated—could crash the system by extending beyond the end of the array. Our next example uses `new` to obtain exactly the right amount of memory. Here's the listing for NEWSTR:

```
// newstr.cpp
// using new to get memory for strings
#include <iostream.h>
#include <string.h>         // for strcpy(), etc

class String                // user-defined string type
   {
   private:
      char* str;                         // pointer to string
   public:
      String(char* s)                    // constructor, one arg
         {
         int length = strlen(s);         // length of string argument
         str = new char[length+1];       // get memory
         strcpy(str, s);                 // copy argument to it
         }
      ~String()                          // destructor
         {
         delete[] str;                   // release memory
         }
```

```
      void display()                    // display the String
         {
         cout << str;
         }
   };

void main()
   {                                   // uses 1-arg constructor
   String s1 = "Who knows nothing doubts nothing.";

   cout << endl << "s1=";              // display string
   s1.display();
   }
```

The `String` class has only one data item: a pointer to `char`, called `str`. This pointer will point to the string held by the `String` object. There is no array within the object to hold the string. The string is stored elsewhere; only the pointer to it is a member of `String`.

Constructor in NEWSTR

The constructor in this example takes a normal string as its argument. It obtains space in memory for this string with `new`; `str` points to the newly obtained memory. The constructor then uses `strcpy()` to copy the string into this new space.

Destructor in NEWSTR

We haven't seen many destructors in our examples so far, but now that we're allocating memory with `new`, destructors become increasingly important. If we allocate memory when we create an object, it's reasonable to deallocate the memory when the object is no longer needed. As you may recall from Chapter 7, a destructor is a routine that is called automatically when an object is destroyed. The destructor in NEWSTR looks like this:

```
~String()
   {
   delete[] str;
   }
```

This destructor gives back to the system the memory obtained when the object was created. Objects (like other variables) are typically destroyed when the function in which they were defined terminates. This destructor ensures that memory obtained by the `String` object will be returned to the system, and not left in limbo, when the object is destroyed.

We should note a potential glitch in using destructors as shown in NEWSTR. If you copy one `String` object to another, say with a statement like `s2 = s1`, you're really only copying the pointer to the actual (`char*`) string. Both objects now point to the same string in memory. But if you now delete one string, the destructor will delete the `char*` string, leaving the other object with an invalid pointer. This can be subtle, because objects can be deleted in nonobvious ways, such as when a function, in which a local object has been created, returns. In Chapter 13 we'll see how to make a smarter destructor, which counts how many `String` objects are pointing to a string.

Pointers to Objects

Pointers can point to objects as well as to simple data types. We've seen many examples of objects defined and given a name, in statements like

```
Distance dist;
```

where an object called `dist` is defined to be of the `Distance` class.

Sometimes, however, we don't know, at the time that we write the program, how many objects we want to create. When this is the case we can use `new` to create objects while the program is running. As we've seen, `new` returns a pointer to an unnamed object. Let's look at a short example program, ENGLPTR, that compares the two approaches to creating objects.

```
// englptr.cpp
// accessing member functions by pointer
#include <iostream.h>

class Distance                         // English Distance class
   {
   private:
      int feet;
      float inches;
   public:
      void getdist()                   // get length from user
         {
         cout << "\nEnter feet: ";  cin >> feet;
         cout << "Enter inches: ";  cin >> inches;
         }
      void showdist()                  // display distance
         { cout << feet << "\'-" << inches << '\"'; }
   };

void main()
   {
   Distance dist;              // define a named Distance object
   dist.getdist();             // access object members
   dist.showdist();            //    with dot operator

   Distance* distptr;          // pointer to Distance
   distptr = new Distance;     // points to new Distance object
   distptr->getdist();         // access object members
   distptr->showdist();        //    with -> operator
   }
```

This program uses a variation of the English `Distance` class seen in previous chapters. The `main()` function defines `dist`, uses the `Distance` member function `getdist()` to get a distance from the user, and then uses `showdist()` to display it.

Referring to Members

ENGLPTR then creates another object of type `Distance` using the `new` operator, and returns a pointer to it called `distptr`.

The question is, how do we refer to the member functions in the object pointed to by `distptr`? You might guess that we would use the dot (`.`) membership-access operator, as in

```
distptr.getdist();    // won't work; distptr is not a variable
```

but this won't work. The dot operator requires the identifier on its left to be a variable. Since `distptr` is a pointer to a variable, we need another syntax. One approach is to *dereference* (get the contents of the variable pointed to by) the pointer:

```
(*distptr).getdist();   // ok but inelegant
```

However, this is slightly cumbersome because of the parentheses. A more concise approach is furnished by the membership-access operator `->`, which consists of a hyphen and a greater-than sign:

```
distptr->getdist();    // better approach
```

As you can see in ENGLPTR, the `->` operator works with pointers to objects in just the same way that the `.` operator works with objects. Here's the output of the program:

```
Enter feet: 10   ←——— this object uses the dot operator

Enter inches: 6.25
10'-6.25"

Enter feet: 6    ←——— this object uses the -> operator
Enter inches: 4.75
6'-4.75"
```

Another Approach to `new`

You may come across another—less common—approach to using `new` to obtain memory for objects.

Since `new` can return a pointer to an area of memory that holds an object, we should be able to refer to the original object by dereferencing the pointer. The ENGLREF example shows how this is done.

```
// englref.cpp
// defererencing pointer returned by new
#include <iostream.h>

class Distance                          // English Distance class
   {
   private:
      int feet;
      float inches;
   public:
      void getdist()                    // get length from user
         {
         cout << "\nEnter feet: ";  cin >> feet;
         cout << "Enter inches: ";  cin >> inches;
         }
      void showdist()                   // display distance
```

(continued on next page)

(continued from previous page)

```
         { cout << feet << "\'-" << inches << '\"'; }
   };

void main()
   {
   Distance& dist = *(new Distance);   // create Distance object
                                       // alias is "dist"
   dist.getdist();                     // access object members
   dist.showdist();                    //    with dot operator
   }
```

The expression

```
new Distance
```

returns a pointer to a memory area large enough for a `Distance` object, so we can refer to the original object as

```
*(new Distance)
```

This is the object pointed to by the pointer. Using a reference, we define `dist` to be an object of type `Distance`, and we set it equal to `*(new Distance)`. Now we can refer to members of `dist` using the dot membership operator, rather than `->`.

This approach is less common than using pointers to objects obtained with `new`, or simply declaring an object, but it works in a similar way.

An Array of Pointers to Objects

A common programming construction is an array of pointers to objects. This arrangement allows easy access to a group of objects, and is more flexible than placing the objects themselves in an array. (For instance, in the PERSORT example in this chapter we'll see how a group of objects can be sorted by sorting an array of pointers to them, rather than sorting the objects themselves.)

Our next example, PTROBJS, creates an array of pointers to the `person` class. Here's the listing:

```
// ptrobjs.cpp
// array of pointers to objects
#include <iostream.h>

class person                           // class of persons
   {
   protected:
      char name[40];                   // person's name
   public:
      void setName(void)               // set the name
         {
         cout << "Enter name: ";
         cin >> name;
         }
      void printName(void)             // get the name
         {
         cout << "\n   Name is: "
              << name;
         }
   };
```

```
void main(void)
   {
   person* persPtr[100];      // array of pointers to persons
   int n = 0;                 // number of persons in array
   char choice;

   do                                  // put persons in array
      {
      persPtr[n] = new person;         // make new object
      persPtr[n]->setName();           // set person's name
      n++;                             // count new person
      cout << "Enter another (y/n)? "; // enter another
      cin >> choice;                   // person?
      }
   while( choice=='y' );               // quit on 'n'

   for(int j=0; j<n; j++)              // print names of
      {                                // all persons
      cout << "\nPerson number " << j+1;
      persPtr[j]->printName();
      }
   }  // end main()
```

The class `person` has a single data item, `name`, which holds a string representing a person's name. Two member functions, `setName()` and `printName()`, allow the name to be set and displayed.

Program Operation

The `main()` function defines an array, `persPtr`, of 100 pointers to type `person`. In a `do` loop it then asks the user to enter a name. With this name it creates a `person` object using `new`, and stores a pointer to this object in the array `persPtr`. To demonstrate how easy it is to access the objects using the pointers, it then prints out the `name` data for each `person` object.

Here's a sample interaction with the program:

```
Enter name: Stroustrup   <------- user enters names
Enter another (y/n)? y
Enter name: Ritchie
Enter another (y/n)? y
Enter name: Kernighan
Enter another (y/n)? n
Person number 1          <------- program displays all names stored
   Name is: Stroustrup
Person number 2
   Name is: Ritchie
Person number 3
   Name is: Kernighan
```

Accessing Member Functions

We need to access the member functions `setName()` and `printName()` in the `person` objects pointed to by the pointers in the array `persPtr`. Each of the elements of the array `persPtr` is specified in array notation to be `persPtr[j]` (or equivalently by pointer notation to be `*(persPtr+j)`). The elements are pointers to objects of type `person`. To access a member of an object using a pointer, we use the `->` operator. Putting this all together, we have the following syntax for `getname()`:

```
persPtr[j]->getName()
```

This executes the `getname()` function in the `person` object pointed to by element `j` of the `persPtr` array. (It's a good thing we don't have to program using English syntax.)

A Linked List Example

Our next example shows a simple linked list. What is a linked list? It's another way to store data. You've seen numerous examples of data stored in arrays. Another data structure is an array of pointers to data members, as in the PTRTOSTRS and PTROBJS examples. Both the array and the array of pointers suffer from the necessity to declare a fixed-size array before running the program.

A Chain of Pointers

The linked list provides a more flexible storage system in that it doesn't use arrays at all. Instead, space for each data item is obtained as needed with `new`, and each item is connected, or *linked*, to the next data item using a pointer. The individual items don't need to be located contiguously in memory the way array elements are; they can be scattered anywhere.

In our example the entire linked list is an object of class `linklist`. The individual data items, or links, are represented by structures of type `link`. Each such structure contains an integer—representing the object's single data item—and a pointer to the next link. The list itself stores a pointer to the link at the head of the list. This arrangement is shown in Figure 12-15.

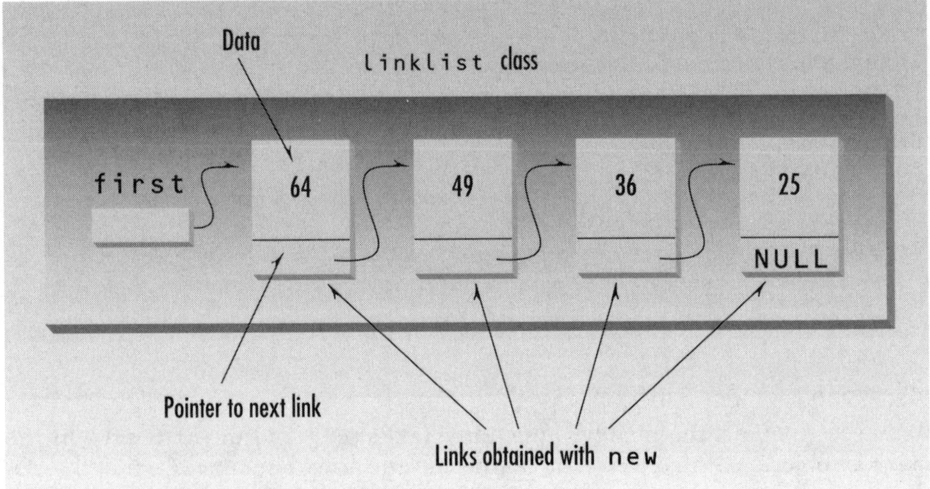

Figure 12-15 A Linked List

Here's the listing for LINKLIST:

```
// linklist.cpp
// linked list
#include <iostream.h>

struct link                                 // one element of list
   {
   int data;                                // data item
   link* next;                              // pointer to next link
   };

class linklist                              // a list of links
   {
   private:
      link* first;                          // pointer to first link
   public:
      linklist()                            // no-argument constructor
         { first = NULL; }                  // no first link
      void additem(int d);                  // add data item (one link)
      void display();                       // display all links
   };

void linklist::additem(int d)               // add data item
   {
   link* newlink = new link;                // make a new link
   newlink->data = d;                       // give it data
   newlink->next = first;                   // it points to next link
   first = newlink;                         // now first points to this
   }

void linklist::display()                    // display all links
   {
   link* current = first;                   // set ptr to first link
   while( current != NULL )                 // quit on last link
      {
      cout << endl << current->data;        // print data
      current = current->next;              // move to next link
      }
   }

void main()
   {
   linklist li;          // make linked list

   li.additem(25);       // add four items to list
   li.additem(36);
   li.additem(49);
   li.additem(64);

   li.display();         // display entire list
   }
```

The `linklist` class has only one member data item: the pointer to the start of the list. When the list is first created, the constructor initializes this pointer, `first`, to `NULL`. The `NULL` constant is defined in the MEM.H header file (which is `#included` in the IOSTREAM.H file) to be 0. This value serves as a signal that a pointer does not hold a valid address. In our program a link whose `next` member has a value of `NULL` is assumed to be at the end of the list.

Adding an Item to the List

The `additem()` member function adds an item to the linked list. A new link is inserted at the beginning of the list. (We could write the `additem()` function to insert items at the end of the list, but that is a little more complex to program.) Let's look at the steps involved in inserting a new link.

First, a new structure of type `link` is created by the line

```
link* newlink = new link;
```

This creates memory for the new `link` structure with `new` and saves the pointer to it in the `newlink` variable.

Next we want to set the members of the newly created structure to appropriate values. A structure is just like a class in that, when it is referred to by pointer rather than by name, its members are accessed using the `->` member-access operator. The following two lines set the `data` variable to the value passed as an argument to `additem()`, and the `next` pointer to point to whatever address was in `first`, which holds the pointer to the start of the list.

```
newlink->data = d;
newlink->next = first;
```

Finally, we want the `first` variable to point to the new link:

```
first = newlink;
```

The effect is to uncouple the connection between `first` and the old first link, insert the new link, and move the old first link into the second position. Figure 12-16 shows this process.

Displaying the List Contents

Once the list is created it's easy to step through all the members, displaying them (or performing other operations). All we need to do is follow from one `next` pointer to another until we find a `next` that is `NULL`, signaling the end of the list. In the function `display()`, the line

```
cout << endl << current->data;
```

prints the value of the data, and

```
current = current->next;
```

moves us along from one link to another, until

```
current != NULL
```

in the `while` expression becomes false. Here's the output of LINKLIST:

```
64
49
36
25
```

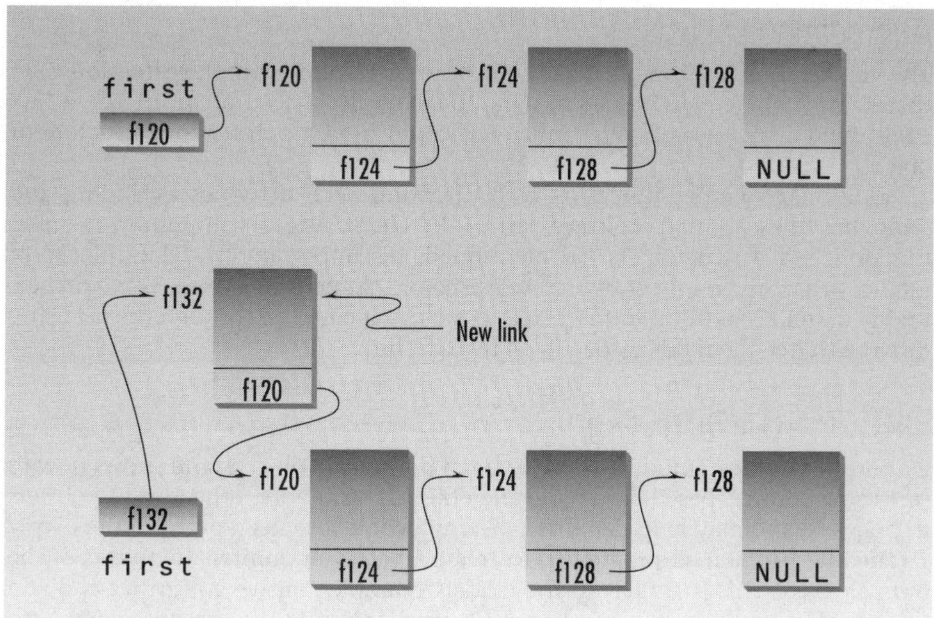

Figure 12-16 Adding to a Linked List

Linked lists are perhaps the most commonly used data storage arrangements after arrays. As we noted, they avoid the wasting of memory space engendered by arrays. The disadvantage is that finding a particular item on a linked list requires following the chain of links from the head of the list until the desired link is reached. This can be time consuming. An array element, on the other hand, can be accessed quickly, provided its index is known in advance. We'll have more to say about linked lists and other data-storage techniques in Chapter 17.

Self-Containing Classes

We should note a possible pitfall in the use of self-referential classes and structures. The `link` structure in LINKLIST contained a pointer to the same kind of structure. You can do the same with classes:

```
class sampleclass
   {
   sampleclass* ptr;   // this is fine
   };
```

However, while a class can contain a *pointer* to an object of its own type, it cannot contain an *object* of its own type:

```
class sampleclass
   {
   sampleclass obj;   // can't do this
   };
```

This is true of structures as well as classes.

Augmenting LINKLIST

The general organization of LINKLIST can serve for a more complex situation than that shown. There could be more data in each link. Instead of an integer, a link could hold a number of data items or it could hold a pointer to a structure or object.

Additional member functions could perform such activities as adding and removing links from an arbitrary part of the chain. Another important member function is a destructor. As we mentioned, it's important to delete blocks of memory that are no longer in use. A destructor that performs this task would be a highly desirable addition to the `linklist` class. It could go through the list using `delete` to free the memory occupied by each link.

Pointers to Pointers

Our next example demonstrates an array of pointers to objects, and shows how to sort these pointers based on data in the object. This involves the idea of pointers to pointers, and may help demonstrate why people lose sleep over pointers.

The idea in the next program is to create an array of pointers to objects of the `person` class. This is similar to the PTROBJS example, but we go further and add variations of the `order()` and `bsort()` functions from the PTRSORT example so that we can sort a group of `person` objects based on the alphabetical order of their names. Here's the listing for PERSORT:

```
// persort.cpp
// sorts person objects using array of pointers
#include <iostream.h>
#include <string.h>                   // for strcmp()

class person                          // class of persons
   {
   protected:
      char name[40];                  // person's name
   public:
      void setName(void)              // set the name
         { cout << "Enter name: "; cin >> name; }
      void printName(void)            // display the name
         { cout << endl << name; }
      char* getName()                 // return the name
         { return name; }
   };

void main(void)
   {
   void bsort(person**, int);         // prototype
   person* persPtr[100];              // array of pointers to persons
   int n = 0;                         // number of persons in array
   char choice;                       // input char

   do                                 // put persons in array
      {
      persPtr[n] = new person;        // make new object
```

```
      persPtr[n]->setName();        // set person's name
      n++;                          // count new person
      cout << "Enter another (y/n)? "; // enter another
      cin >> choice;                //    person?
      }
   while( choice=='y' );            // quit on 'n'

   cout << "\nUnsorted list:";
   for(int j=0; j<n; j++)           // print unsorted list
      { persPtr[j]->printName(); }

   bsort(persPtr, n);               // sort pointers
   cout << "\nSorted list:";
   for(j=0; j<n; j++)               // print sorted list
      { persPtr[j]->printName(); }
   }  // end main()

void bsort(person** pp, int n)      // sort pointers to persons
   {
   void order(person**, person**);  // prototype
   int j, k;                        // indexes to array

   for(j=0; j<n-1; j++)             // outer loop
      for(k=j+1; k<n; k++)          // inner loop starts at outer
         order(pp+j, pp+k);         // order the pointer contents
   }

void order(person** pp1, person** pp2)  // orders two pointers
   {                                    // if 1st larger than 2nd,
   if( strcmp((*pp1)->getName(), (*pp2)->getName()) > 0)
      {
      person* tempptr = *pp1;           // swap the pointers
      *pp1 = *pp2;
      *pp2 = tempptr;
      }
   }
```

When the program is first executed it asks for a name. When the user gives it one, it creates an object of type `person` and sets the `name` data in this object to the name entered by the user. The program also stores a pointer to the object in the `persPtr` array.

When the user types `n` to indicate that no more names will be entered, the program calls the `bsort()` function to sort the `person` objects based on their `name` member variables. Here's some sample interaction with the program:

```
Enter name: Washington
Enter another (y/n)? y
Enter name: Adams
Enter another (y/n)? y
Enter name: Jefferson
Enter another (y/n)? y
Enter name: Madison
Enter another (y/n)? n
```

(continued on next page)

(continued from previous page)

```
Unsorted list:
Washington
Adams
Jefferson
Madison

Sorted list:
Adams
Jefferson
Madison
Washington
```

Sorting Pointers

Actually, when we sort `person` objects, we don't move the objects themselves; we move the pointers to the objects. This eliminates the need to shuffle the objects around in memory, which can be very time consuming if the objects are large. The process is shown in Figure 12-17.

To facilitate the sorting activity we've added a `getName()` member function to the `person` class, so we can access the names from `order()` to decide when to swap pointers.

The `person**` Data Type

You will notice that the first argument to the `bsort()` function, and both arguments to `order()`, have the type `person**`. What do the two asterisks mean? These arguments are used to pass the address of the array `persPtr`, or—in the case of `order()`—the addresses of elements of the array. If this were an array of type `person`, then the address of the array would be type `person*`. However, the array is of type *pointers* to `person`, or `person*`, so its address is type `person**`. The address of a pointer is a pointer to a pointer. Figure 12-18 shows how this looks.

Compare this program with PTRSORT, which sorted an array of type `int`. You'll find that the data types passed to functions in PERSORT all have one more asterisk than they did in PTRSORT, because the array is an array of pointers.

Since the `persPtr` array contains pointers, the construction

```
persPtr[j]->printName()
```

executes the `printName()` function in the object pointed to by element `j` of `persPtr`.

Comparing Strings

The `order()` function in PERSORT has been modified to order two strings lexigraphically—that is, by putting them in alphabetical order. To do this it compares the strings using the C++ library function `strcmp()`. This function takes the two strings `s1` and `s2` as arguments, as in `strcmp(s1, s2)`, and returns one of the following values.

Value	**Condition**
<0	s1 comes before s2
0	s1 is the same as s2
>0	s1 comes after s2

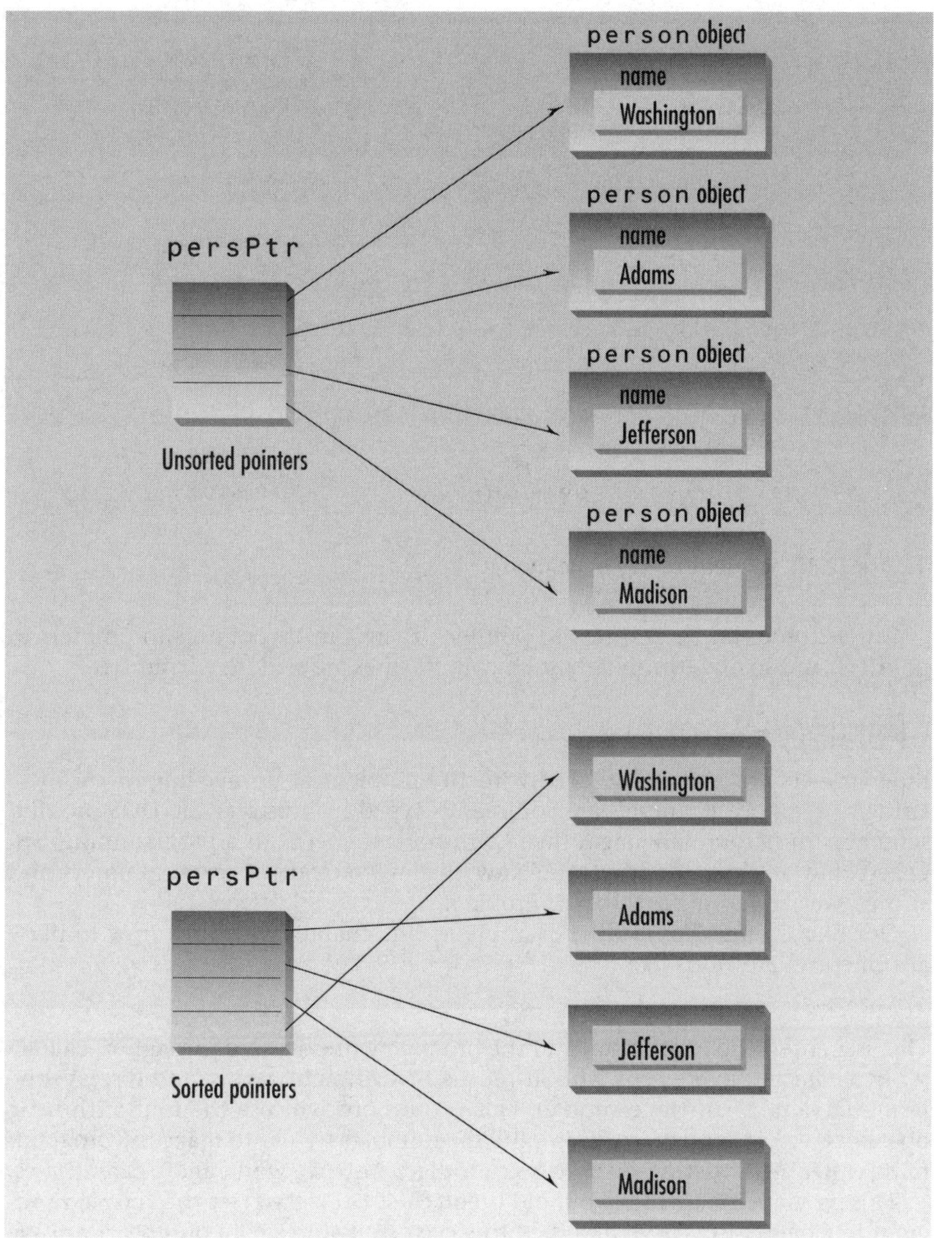

Figure 12-17 Sorting an Array of Pointers

The strings are accessed using the syntax

```
(*pp1)->getname()
```

The argument `pp1` is a pointer to a pointer, and we want the name pointed to by the pointer it points to. The member-access operator `->` dereferences one level, but we need to dereference another level, hence the asterisk preceding `pp1`.

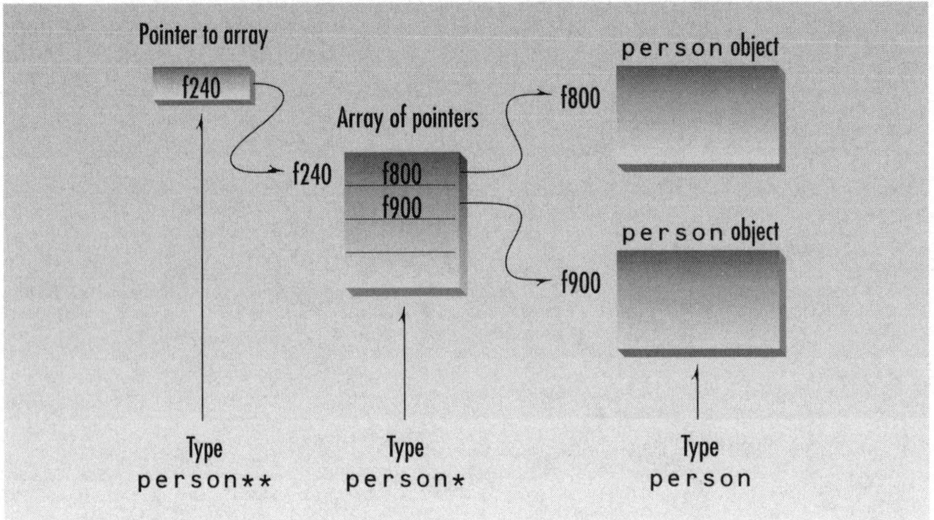

Figure 12-18 Pointer to Array of Pointers

Just as there can be pointers to pointers, there can be pointers to pointers to pointers, and so on. Fortunately such complexities are seldom encountered.

A Parsing Example

Programmers are frequently faced with the problem of unravelling or *parsing* a string of symbols. Examples are commands typed by a user at the DOS prompt, sentences in natural languages (like English), statements in a programming language, and algebraic expressions. Now that we've learned about pointers and strings, we can handle this sort of problem.

Our final (somewhat longer) example in this chapter will show how to parse arithmetic expressions like

```
6/3+2*3-1
```

The user enters the expression, and the program works its way through it, character by character, figures out what it means in arithmetic terms, and displays the resulting value (7 in the example). Our expressions will use the four arithmetic operators: `+`, `-`, `*`, and `/`. We'll simplify the numbers we use to make the programming easier by restricting them to a single digit. Also, we won't allow parentheses.

This program makes use of our old friend the `Stack` class (see the STAKARAY program in Chapter 8). We've modified this class so it stores data of type `char`. We use the stack to store both numbers and operators (both as characters). The stack is a useful storage mechanism because, when parsing expressions, we frequently need to access the last item stored, and a stack is a last-in-first-out (LIFO) container.

Besides the `Stack` class, we'll use a class called `express` (short for "expression"), representing an entire arithmetic expression. Member functions for this class allow us to initialize an object with an expression in the form of a string (entered by the user), parse the expression, and return the resulting arithmetic value.

Parsing Arithmetic Expressions

Here's how we parse an arithmetic expression. We start at the left, and look at each character in turn. It can be either a "number" (always a single digit; a character between '0' and '9'), or an operator (the characters '+', '-', '*', and '/').

If the character is a number, we always push it onto the stack. We also push the first operator we encounter. The trick is how we handle subsequent operators. Note that we can't execute the *current* operator, because we haven't yet read the number that follows it. Finding an operator is merely the signal that we can execute the *previous* operator, which is stored on the stack. That is, if the sequence 2+3 is on the stack, then we wait until we find another operator before carrying out the addition.

Thus whenever we find that the current character is an operator (except the first), we pop the previous number (3 in the example above) and the previous operator (+) off the stack, placing them in the variables `lastval` and `lastop`. Finally we pop the first number (2) and carry out the arithmetic operation on the two numbers (obtaining 5). Can we always execute the previous operator? No. Remember that * and / have a higher precedence than + and -. In the expression 3+4/2, we can't execute the + until we've done the division. So when we get to the / in this expression, we must put the 2 and the + back on the stack until we've carried out the division.

On the other hand, if the current operator is a + or -, we know we can always execute the previous operator. That is, when we see the + in the expression 4-5+6, we know it's all right to execute the -, and when we see the - in 6/2-3 , we know it's OK to do the division. Table 12-1 shows the four possibilities.

The `parse()` member function carries out this process of going through the input expression and performing those operations it can. However, there is more work to do. The stack still contains either a single number or several sequences of number-operator-number. Working down through the stack, we can execute these sequences. Finally, a single number is left on the stack; this is the value of the original expression. The `solve()` member function carries out this task, working its way down through the stack until only a single number is left. In general, `parse()` puts things on the stack, and `solve()` takes them off.

Previous operator	Current operator	Example	Action
+ or -	* or /	3+4/	Push previous operator and previous number (+, 4)
* or /	* or /	9/3*	Execute previous operator, push result (3)
+ or -	+ or -	6+3+	Execute previous operator, push result (9)
* or /	+ or -	8/2-	Execute previous operator, push result (4)

Table 12-1 Operators and Parsing Actions

The PARSE Program

Some typical interaction with PARSE might look like this:

```
Enter an arithmetic expression
of the form 2+3*4/3-2.
No number may have more than one digit.
Don't use any spaces or parentheses.
Expression: 9+6/3

The numerical value is: 11
Do another (Enter y or n)?
```

Note that it's all right if the *results* of arithmetic operations contain more than one digit. They are limited only by the numerical size of type char, from –128 to +127. Only the input string is limited to numbers from 0 to 9.

Here's the listing for the program:

```
// parse.cpp
// evaluates arithmetic expressions composed of 1-digit numbers

#include <iostream.h>
#include <string.h>                  // for strlen(), etc
#include <process.h>                 // for exit()

const int LEN = 80;    // length of expressions, in characters
const int MAX = 40;    // size of stack

class Stack
   {
   private:
      char st[MAX];                  // stack: array of chars
      int top;                       // number of top of stack
   public:
      Stack()                        // constructor
         { top = 0; }
      void push(char var)            // put char on stack
         { st[++top] = var; }
      char pop()                     // take char off stack
         { return st[top--]; }
      int gettop()                   // get top of stack
         { return top; }
   };

class express                        // arith expression class
   {
   private:
      Stack s;                       // stack for analysis
      char* pStr;                    // pointer to input string
      int len;                       // length of input string
   public:
      express(char* ptr)             // constructor
         {
         pStr = ptr;                 // set pointer to string
```

```
         len = strlen(pStr);          // set length
         }
      void parse();                   // parse the input string
      int solve();                    // evaluate the stack
   };

void express::parse()                 // add items to stack
   {
   char ch;                           // char from input string
   char lastval;                      // last value
   char lastop;                       // last operator

   for(int j=0; j<len; j++)           // for each input character
      {
      ch = pStr[j];                   // get next character

      if(ch>='0' && ch<='9')          // if it's a digit,
         s.push(ch-'0');              // save numerical value
                                      // if it's operator
      else if(ch=='+' || ch=='-' || ch=='*' || ch=='/')
         {
         if(s.gettop()==1)            // if it's first operator
            s.push(ch);               // put on stack
         else                         // not first operator
            {
            lastval = s.pop();        // get previous digit
            lastop = s.pop();         // get previous operator
            // if this is * or / AND last operator was + or -
            if( (ch=='*' || ch=='/') &&
                (lastop=='+' || lastop=='-') )
               {
               s.push(lastop);        // restore last two pops
               s.push(lastval);
               }
            else                      // in all other cases
               {
               switch(lastop)         // do last operation
                  {                   // push result on stack
                  case '+': s.push(s.pop() + lastval); break;
                  case '-': s.push(s.pop() - lastval); break;
                  case '*': s.push(s.pop() * lastval); break;
                  case '/': s.push(s.pop() / lastval); break;
                  default:  cout << "\nUnknown oper"; exit(1);
                  }  // end switch
               }  // end else, in all other cases
            s.push(ch);               // put current op on stack
            }  // end else, not first operator
         }  // end else if, it's an operator
      else                            // not a known character
         { cout << "\nUnknown input character"; exit(1); }
      }  // end for
   }  // end parse()

int express::solve()                  // remove items from stack
```

(continued on next page)

(continued from previous page)

```
   {
   char lastval;                          // previous value

   while(s.gettop() > 1)
      {
      lastval = s.pop();                  // get previous value
      switch( s.pop() )                   // get previous operator
         {                                // do operation, push answer
         case '+': s.push(s.pop() + lastval); break;
         case '-': s.push(s.pop() - lastval); break;
         case '*': s.push(s.pop() * lastval); break;
         case '/': s.push(s.pop() / lastval); break;
         default:  cout << "\nUnknown operator"; exit(1);
         }  // end switch
      }  // end while
   return int( s.pop() );                 // last item on stack is ans
   }  // end solve()

void main()
   {
   char ans;                              // 'y' or 'n'
   char string[LEN];                      // input string from user

   do
      {
      cout << "\nEnter an arithmetic expression"
              "\nof the form 2+3*4/3-2."
              "\nNo number may have more than one digit."
              "\nDon't use any spaces or parentheses."
              "\nExpression: ";
      cin >> string;                         // input from user
      express* eptr = new express(string);   // make expression
      eptr->parse();                         // parse it
      cout << "\nThe numerical value is: "
           << eptr->solve();                 // solve it
      delete eptr;                           // delete expression
      cout << "\nDo another (Enter y or n)? ";
      cin >> ans;
      } while(ans == 'y');
   }
```

This is a longish program, but it shows how a previously designed class, `Stack`, can come in handy in a new situation; it demonstrates the use of pointers in a variety of ways; and it shows how useful it can be to treat a string as an array of characters.

Debugging Pointers

Pointers can be the source of mysterious and catastrophic program bugs. The most common problem is that the programmer has failed to place a valid address in a pointer variable. When this happens the pointer can end up pointing anywhere in memory. It could be pointing to the program code, or to the operating system. If the programmer then inserts a value into memory using the pointer, the value will write over the program or operating instructions, and the computer will crash or evince other uncharming behavior.

A particular version of this scenario takes place when the pointer points to address 0, which is called `NULL`. This happens, for example, if the pointer variable is defined as an external variable, since external variables are automatically initialized to 0. Instance variables in classes are considered external, so they are also initialized to 0. Here's a miniprogram that demonstrates the situation:

```
int* intptr;            // external variable, initialized to 0
void main()
   {                    // failure to put valid address in intptr
   *intptr = 37;        // attempts to put 37 in address at 0
   }                    // result is "Null pointer assignment"
```

When `intptr` is defined, it is given the value 0, since it is external. The single program statement will attempt to insert the value 37 into the address at 0.

Fortunately, however, the runtime error-checking unit, built into the program by the compiler, is waiting for attempts to access address 0, and will display an infamous error message: *Null pointer assignment*. If you find this message on the screen after running your program, you can guess that you have failed to properly initialize a pointer.

In a complex program it may be difficult to figure out where in the listing the null pointer assignment takes place. One way to localize the problem is to set a *Watch* window on the contents of the 0 address and single-step through the program, waiting for any change in the value pointed to by 0. When it changes you've found the offending program statement. However, you can't just put `*0` in the *Watch* window. Here's the expression you need: `*(char *)0, 4M`. The `0` must be cast to a pointer-to-`char`. The `4M` tells the debugger to display 4 bytes of memory. These 4 bytes are normally 0, so when they change to something else, you've found the problem.

Summary

This has been a whirlwind tour through the land of pointers. There is far more to learn about pointers, but the topics we've covered here will provide a basis for the examples in the balance of the book and for further study of pointers.

We've learned that everything in the computer's memory has an address, and that addresses are *pointer constants*. We can find the addresses of variables using the address of operator `&`.

Pointers are variables that hold address values. Pointers are defined using an asterisk (`*`) to mean *pointer to*. A data type is always included in pointer definitions, since the compiler must know what is being pointed to, so that it can perform arithmetic correctly on the pointer. We access the thing pointed to using the asterisk in a different way, as the indirection operator, meaning *contents of the variable pointed to by*.

Array elements can be accessed using array notation with brackets or pointer notation with an asterisk. Like other addresses, the address of an array is a constant, but it can be assigned to a variable, which can be incremented and changed in other ways.

When the address of a variable is passed to a function, the function can work with the original variable. (This is not true when arguments are passed by value.) In this respect passing by pointer offers the same benefits as passing by reference, although pointer arguments must be *dereferenced* or accessed using the indirection operator. However, pointers offer more flexibility in some cases.

A string constant can be defined as an array or as a pointer. The pointer approach may be more flexible, but there is a danger that the pointer value will be corrupted. Strings, being arrays of type `char`, are commonly passed to functions and accessed using pointers.

The `new` operator obtains a specified amount of memory from the system and returns a pointer to the memory. This operator is used to create variables and data structures during program execution. The `delete` operator releases memory obtained with `new`.

When a pointer points to an object, members of the object's class can be accessed using the access operator `->`. The same syntax is used to access structure members.

Classes and structures may contain data members that are pointers to their own type. This permits the creation of complex data structures like linked lists.

There can be pointers to pointers. These variables are defined using the double asterisk: `int** pptr`.

Questions

Answers to questions can be found in Appendix D.

1. Write a statement that displays the address of the variable `testvar`.
2. The contents of two pointers that point to adjacent variables of type `float` differ by _________.
3. A pointer is
   a. the address of a variable.
   b. an indication of the variable to be accessed next.
   c. a variable for storing addresses.
   d. the data type of an address variable.
4. Write expressions for the following:
   a. The address of `var`
   b. The contents of the variable pointed to by `var`
   c. The variable `var` used as a reference argument
   d. The data type pointer-to-`char`
5. An address is a _________, while a pointer is a _________.
6. Write a definition for a variable of type pointer to `float`.
7. One way pointers are useful is to refer to a memory address that has no _________.

8. If a pointer `testptr` points to a variable `testvar`, write a statement that represents the contents of `testvar` but does not use its name.

9. An asterisk placed after a data type means ________. An asterisk placed in front of a variable name means ________.

10. The expression `*test` can be said to
    a. be a pointer to `test`.
    b. refer to the contents of `test`.
    c. dereference `test`.
    d. refer to the value of the variable pointed to by `test`.

11. Is the following code correct?

```
int intvar = 333;
int* intptr;
cout << *intptr;
```

12. A pointer to `void` can hold pointers to ________.

13. What is the difference between `intarr[3]` and `*(intarr+3)`?

14. Write some code that uses pointer notation to display every value in the array `intarr`, which has 77 elements.

15. If `intarr` is an array of integers, why is the expression `intarr++` not legal?

16. Of the three ways to pass arguments to functions, only passing by ________ and passing by ________ allow the function to modify the argument in the calling program.

17. The type of variable a pointer points to must be part of the pointer's definition so that
    a. data types don't get mixed up when arithmetic is performed on them.
    b. pointers can be added to one another to access structure members.
    c. no one's religious conviction will be offended.
    d. the compiler can perform arithmetic correctly to access array elements.

18. Using pointer notation, write a prototype (declaration) for a function called `func()` that returns type `void` and takes a single argument that is an array of type `char`.

19. Using pointer notation, write some code that will transfer 80 characters from the string `s1` to the string `s2`.

20. The first element in a string is
    a. the name of the string.
    b. the first character in the string.
    c. the length of the string.
    d. the name of the array holding the string.

21. Using pointer notation, write the prototype for a function called `revstr()` that returns a string value and takes one argument that represents a string.

22. Write a definition for an array `numptrs` of pointers to the strings `One`, `Two`, and `Three`.

23. The `new` operator
    - a. returns a pointer to a variable.
    - b. creates a variable called `new`.
    - c. obtains memory for a new variable.
    - d. tells how much memory is available.

24. Using `new` may result in less _________ memory than using an array.

25. The `delete` operator returns _________ to the operating system.

26. Given a pointer `p` that points to an object of type `upperclass`, write an expression that executes the `exclu()` member function in this object.

27. Given an object with index number 7 in array `objarr`, write an expression that executes the `exclu()` member function in this object.

28. In a linked list
    - a. each link contains a pointer to the next link.
    - b. an array of pointers point to the links.
    - c. each link contains data or a pointer to data.
    - d. the links are stored in an array.

29. Write a definition for an array `arr` of 8 pointers that point to variables of type `float`.

30. If you wanted to sort many large objects or structures, it would be most efficient to
    - a. place them in an array and sort the array.
    - b. place pointers to them in an array and sort the array.
    - c. place them in a linked list and sort the linked list.
    - d. place references to them in an array and sort the array.

Exercises

Answers to starred exercises can be found in Appendix D.

1.* Write a program that reads a group of numbers from the user and places them in an array of type `float`. Once the numbers are stored in the array, the program should average them and print the result. Use pointer notation wherever possible.

2.* Start with the `String` class from the NEWSTR example in this chapter. Add a member function called `upit()` that converts the string to all uppercase. You can use the `toupper()` library function, which takes a single character as an argument and returns a character that has been converted (if necessary) to uppercase. This function uses the CTYPE.H header file. Write some code in `main()` to test `upit()`.

3.* Start with an array of pointers to strings representing the days of the week, as found in the PTRTOSTR program in this chapter. Provide functions to sort the strings into alphabetical order, using variations of the `bsort()` and `order()` functions from the PTRSORT program in this chapter. Sort the pointers to the strings, not the actual strings.

4.* Add a destructor to the LINKLIST program. It should delete all the links when a `linklist` object is destroyed. It can do this by following along the chain, deleting each link as it goes. You can test the destructor by having it display a message each time it deletes a link; it should delete the same number of links that was added to the list. (A destructor is called automatically by the system for any existing objects when the program exits.)

5. Suppose you have a `main()` with three local arrays, all the same size and type (say `float`). The first two are already initialized to values. Write a function called `addarrays()` that accepts the addresses of the three arrays as arguments; adds the contents of the first two arrays together, element by element; and places the results in the third array before returning. A fourth argument to this function can carry the size of the arrays. Use pointer notation throughout; the only place you need brackets is in defining the arrays.

6. Make your own version of the library function `strcmp(s1, s2)`, which compares two strings and returns –1 if `s1` comes first alphabetically, 0 if `s1` and `s2` are the same, and 1 if `s2` comes first alphabetically. Call your function `compstr()`. It should take two strings as arguments and return an `int`. Write a `main()` program to test the function with different combinations of strings. Use pointer notation throughout.

7. Modify the `person` class in the PERSORT program in this chapter so that it includes not only a name, but also a `salary` item of type `float` representing the person's salary. You'll need to change the `setName()` and `printName()` member functions to `setData()` and `printData()`, and include in them the ability to set and display the salary as well as the name. You'll also need a `getSalary()` function. Using pointer notation, write a `salsort()` function that sorts the pointers in the `persPtr` array by salary rather than by name. Try doing all the sorting in `salsort()`, rather than calling another function as PERSORT does. If you do this, don't forget that `->` takes precedence over `*`, so you'll need to say

```
if( (*(pp+j))->getSalary() > (*(pp+k))->getSalary() )
    { // swap the pointers }
```

8. Revise the `additem()` member function from the LINKLIST program so that it adds the item at the end of the list, rather than the beginning. This will cause the first item inserted to be the first item displayed, so the output of the program will be

```
25
36
49
64
```

To add the item you'll need to follow the chain of pointers to the end of the list, then change the last link to point to the new link.

9. Start with the program from Exercise 8 in Chapter 11, which created a number of cars moving on a freeway. Modify it so that, instead of declaring a number of individual car objects, you declare an array of pointers to cars, and use `new` in a loop to create the cars. The pointers to the cars are stored in the array. The member functions that erase and draw the cars and calculate their positions are then accessed using these pointers. You can generate the characteristics of each car automatically within the loop. For example, the statement

```
int lane = j/2 + 1;
```

generates lane numbers 1, 1, 2, 2, 3, 3 for the first first six cars, as `j` (the loop variable) goes from 0 to 5. Similar statements can generate appropriate sequences for miles, speed, and color. The output should be the same as that of the earlier program.

10. Let's say that you need to store 100 integers so that they're easily accessible. However, let's further assume that there's a problem: The memory in your computer is so fragmented that the largest array that you can use holds only 10 integers. (Such problems actually arise, although usually with larger memory objects.) You can solve this problem by defining 10 separate `int` arrays of 10 integers each, and an array of 10 pointers to these arrays. The `int` arrays can have names like `a0`, `a1`, `a2`, and so on. The address of each of these arrays can be stored in the pointer array of type `int*`, which can have a name like `ap` (for array of pointers). You can then access individual integers using expressions like `ap[j][k]`, where `j` steps through the pointers in `ap` and `k` steps through individual integers in each array. This looks like you're accessing a two-dimensional array, but it's really a group of one-dimensional arrays.

   Fill such a group of arrays with test data (say the numbers 0, 10, 20, and so on up to 990). Then display the data to make sure it's correct.

11. As presented, Exercise 10 is rather inelegant because each of the 10 `int` arrays is declared in a different program statement, using a different name. Each of their addresses must also be obtained using a separate statement. You can simplify

things by using `new`, which allows you to allocate the arrays in a loop and assign pointers to them at the same time:

```
for(j=0; j<NUMARRAYS; j++)           // allocate NUMARRAYS arrays
   *(ap+j) = new int[MAXSIZE];       // each MAXSIZE ints long
```

Rewrite the program in Exercise 10 to use this approach. You can access the elements of the individual arrays using the same expression mentioned in Exercise 10, or you can use pointer notation: `*(*(ap+j)+k)`. The two notations are equivalent.

12. Create a class that allows you to treat the 10 separate arrays in Exercise 11 as a single one-dimensional array, using array notation with a single index. That is, statements in `main()` can access their elements using expressions like `a[j]`, even though the class member functions must access the data using the two-step approach. Overload the subscript operator `[]` (see Chapter 9) to achieve this result. Fill the arrays with test data and then display it. Although array notation is used in `main()` to access "array" elements, you should use only pointer notation for all the operations within the class member functions.

13. One theory of cosmology holds that matter is continuously being created throughout space. To model this, start with the MOLECULE program in Chapter 11. Arrange for it to add a new molecule every so often, in random places, as the other ones are flying around. For example, you might add a new molecule, using statements within the `while` loop, every 50 time ticks. The speed should be the same for all molecules, but the directions should be random. To create random directions you can use statements like

```
hdir hd = hdir(random(3));   // random horizontal direction
```

since variables of type `hdir` can have values of 0, 1, or 2. Use a similar statement for the vertical direction. However, you should avoid motionless molecules where both the x and y directions are stopped. The color can cycle through all the colors, except that dark gray (or whatever color is used as the erase delimiter) should be avoided.

You'll need an array of pointers to molecules so you can reference the molecules after you create them.

```
pmo[n++] = new molecule(x, y, sp, hd, vd, c);  // create molecule
```

Using these pointers, you can call the various member functions for the molecules. You can also delete all the molecules before exiting from the program.

You'll find, not surprisingly, that as you add more and more molecules, their apparent speed on the screen gets slower and slower. To compensate for this, you can increase the speed of all the molecules whenever there are enough new ones to make it worthwhile. If you start with a speed of 3 for example, you might increase it by 1 every time 10 new molecules are created. Unfortunately, as written, the `molecule` class won't allow you to access the speed after a molecule is created. To fix this, add a `setspeed()` member function to `molecule`, either directly or by inheritance. Then every so often, by going through the array of pointers to molecules, you can set new speeds for all the molecules. Of course, as the speeds get higher and higher, the motion of the molecules appears more and more jerky. This limits the number of molecules you can create, especially on slower computers.

14. Pointers are complicated, so let's see if we can make their operation more understandable (or possibly more impenetrable) by simulating their operation with a class.

To clarify the operation of our homemade pointers, we'll model the computer's memory using arrays. This way, since array access is well understood, you can see what's really going on when we access memory with pointers.

We'd like to use a single array of type `char` to store all types of variables. This is what a computer memory really is: an array of bytes (which are the same size as type `char`), each of which has an address (or, in array-talk, an index). However, C++ won't ordinarily let us store a `float` or an `int` in an array of type `char`. (We could use unions, but that's another story.) So we'll simulate memory by using a separate array for each data type we want to store. In this exercise we'll confine ourselves to one numerical type, `float`, so we'll need an array of this type; call it `fmemory`. However, pointer values (addresses) are also stored in memory, so we'll need another array to store them. Since we're using array indexes to model addresses, and indexes for all but the largest arrays can be stored in type `int`, we'll create an array of this type, call it `pmemory`, to hold these "pointers."

An index to `fmemory` , call it `fmem_top`, points to the next available place where a `float` value can be stored. There's a similar index to `pmemory`, call it `pmem_top`. Don't worry about running out of "memory." We'll assume these arrays are big enough so that each time we store something we can simply insert it at the next index number in the array. Other than this, we won't worry about memory management.

Create a class called `Float`. We'll use it to model numbers of type `float` that are stored in `fmemory` instead of real memory. The only instance data in `Float` is its own "address"; that is, the index where its `float` value is stored in `fmemory`. Call this instance variable `addr`. Class `Float` also needs two member functions. The first is a one-argument constructor to initialize the `Float` with a `float` value. This constructor stores the `float` value in the element of `fmemory` pointed to by `fmem_top`, and stores the value of `fmem_top` in `addr`. This is similar to how the compiler and linker arrange to store an ordinary variable in real memory. The second member function is the overloaded `&` operator. It simply returns the pointer (really the index, type `int`) value in `addr`.

Create a second class called `ptrFloat`. The instance data in this class holds the address (index) in `pmemory` where some other address (index) is stored. A member function initializes this "pointer" with an `int` index value. The second member function is the overloaded `*` (indirection, or "contents of") operator. Its operation is a tad more complicated. It obtains the address from `pmemory`, where its data, which is also an address, is stored. It then uses this new address as an index into `fmemory` to obtain the float value pointed to by its address data.

```
float& ptrFloat::operator*()
   {
   return fmemory[ pmemory[addr] ];
   }
```

In this way it models the operation of the indirection operator (`*`). Notice that you need to return by reference from this function so that you can use `*` on the left side of the equal sign.

The two classes `Float` and `ptrFloat` are similar, but `Float` stores `float`s in an array representing memory, and `ptrFloat` stores `int`s (representing memory pointers, but really array index values) in a different array that also represents memory.

Here's a typical use of these classes, from a sample `main()`:

```
Float var1 = 1.234;           // define and initialize two Floats
Float var2 = 5.678;

ptrFloat ptr1 = &var1;        // define two pointers-to-Floats,
ptrFloat ptr2 = &var2;        // initialize to addresses of Floats

cout << " *ptr1=" << *ptr1;   // get values of Floats indirectly
cout << " *ptr2=" << *ptr2;   // and display them

*ptr1 = 7.123;                // assign new values to variables
*ptr2 = 8.456;                // pointed to by ptr1 and ptr2

cout << " *ptr1=" << *ptr1;   // get new values indirectly
cout << " *ptr2=" << *ptr2;   // and display them
```

Notice that, aside from the different names for the variable types, this looks just the same as operations on real variables. Here's the output from the program:

```
*ptr1=1.234
*ptr2=2.678

*ptr1=7.123
*ptr2=8.456
```

This may seem like a roundabout way to implement pointers, but by revealing the inner workings of the pointer and address operator, we have provided a different perspective on their true nature.

13

Virtual Functions and Other Subtleties

VIRTUAL FUNCTIONS

FRIEND FUNCTIONS

STATIC FUNCTIONS

OVERLOADED ASSIGNMENT OPERATOR

OVERLOADED COPY CONSTRUCTOR

THE `this` POINTER

FINDING AN OBJECT'S CLASS WITH `typeid()`

13

Now that we understand something about pointers, we can delve into more advanced C++ topics. This chapter covers a rather loosely related collection of such subjects: virtual functions, friend functions, static functions, the overloaded = operator, the overloaded copy constructor, and the `this` pointer. These are advanced features; they are not necessary for every C++ program. However, they are widely used, and are essential in some situations. Studying them also casts light on the inner workings of C++.

Virtual Functions

Virtual means *existing in effect but not in reality*. A virtual function, then, is one that does not really exist but nevertheless appears real to some parts of a program.

Why are virtual functions needed? Suppose you have a number of objects of different classes but you want to put them all on a list and perform a particular operation on them using the same function call. For example, suppose a graphics program includes several different shapes: a triangle, a ball, a square, and so on, as in the MULTSHAP program in Chapter 11. Each of these classes has a member function `draw()` that causes the object to be drawn on the screen.

Now suppose you plan to make a picture by grouping a number of these elements together, and you want to draw the picture in a convenient way. One approach is to create an array that holds pointers to all the different objects in the picture. The array might be defined like this:

```
shape* ptrarr[100];   // array of 100 pointers to shapes
```

If you insert pointers to all the shapes into this array, you can then draw an entire picture using a simple loop:

```
for(int j=0; j<N; j++)
   ptrarr[j]->draw();
```

This is an amazing capability: Completely different functions are executed by the same function call. If the pointer in `ptrarr` points to a ball, the function that draws a ball is called; if it points to a triangle, the triangle-drawing function is drawn. This is an important example of *polymorphism*, or giving different meanings to the same thing.

However, for this polymorphic approach to work, several conditions must be met. First, all the different classes of shapes, such as balls and triangles, must be derived from a single base class (called `shape` in MULTSHAP). Second, the `draw()` function must be declared to be `virtual` in the base class.

This is all rather abstract, so let's start with some short programs that show parts of the situation, and put everything together later.

Normal Member Functions Accessed with Pointers

Our first example shows what happens when a base class and derived classes all have functions with the same name, and you access these functions using pointers but without using virtual functions. Here's the listing for NOTVIRT:

```
// notvirt.cpp
// normal functions accessed from pointer
#include <iostream.h>

class Base                                  // base class
   {
   public:
      void show()                           // normal function
         { cout << "\nBase"; }
   };
class Derv1 : public Base                   // derived class 1
   {
   public:
      void show()
         { cout << "\nDerv1"; }
   };
class Derv2 : public Base                   // derived class 2
   {
   public:
      void show()
         { cout << "\nDerv2"; }
   };
void main()
   {
   Derv1 dv1;                // object of derived class 1
   Derv2 dv2;                // object of derived class 2
   Base* ptr;                // pointer to base class

   ptr = &dv1;               // put address of dv1 in pointer
   ptr->show();              // execute show()

   ptr = &dv2;               // put address of dv2 in pointer
   ptr->show();              // execute show()
   }
```

The `Derv1` and `Derv2` classes are derived from class `Base`. Each of these three classes has a member function `show()`. In `main()` we create objects of class `Derv1` and `Derv2`, and a pointer to class `Base`. Then we put the address of a derived class object in the base class pointer in the line

```
ptr = &dv1;  // derived class address in base class pointer
```

But wait—how can we get away with this? Doesn't the compiler complain that we're assigning an address of one type (`Derv1`) to a pointer of another (`Base`)? On the contrary, the compiler is perfectly happy, because type checking has been relaxed in this situation, for reasons that will become apparent soon. The rule is that pointers to objects of a derived class are type-compatible with pointers to objects of the base class.

Now the question is, when you execute the line

```
ptr->show();
```

what function is called? Is it `Base::show()` or `Derv1::show()`? Again, in the last two lines of NOTVIRT we put the address of an object of class `Derv2` in the pointer, and again execute

```
ptr->show();
```

Which of the show() functions is called here? The output from the program answers these questions:

```
Base
Base
```

As you can see, the function in the base class is always executed. The compiler ignores the *contents* of the pointer ptr and chooses the member function that matches the *type* of the pointer, as shown in Figure 13-1.

Sometimes this is what we want, but it doesn't solve the problem posed at the beginning of this section: accessing objects of different classes using the same statement.

Virtual Member Functions Accessed with Pointers

Let's make a single change in our program: We'll place the keyword virtual in front of the declarator for the show() function in the base class. Here's the listing for the resulting program, VIRT:

```
// virt.cpp
// virtual functions accessed from pointer
#include <iostream.h>
```

(continued on next page)

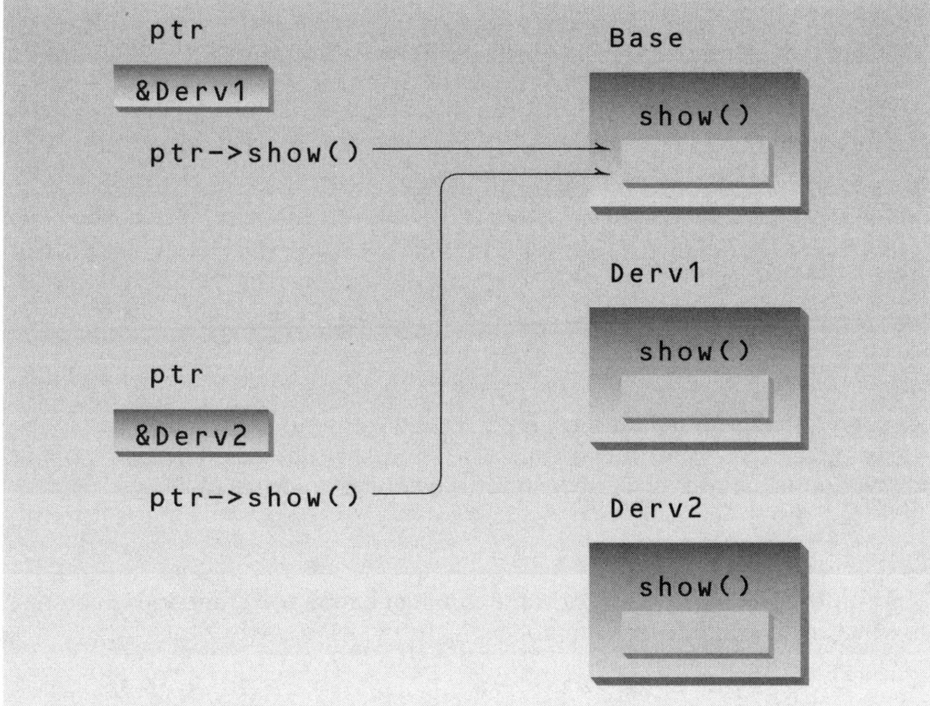

Figure 13-1 Nonvirtual Pointer Access

(continued from previous page)
```
class Base                              // base class
   {
   public:
      virtual void show()               // virtual function
         { cout << "\nBase"; }
   };
class Derv1 : public Base               // derived class 1
   {
   public:
      void show()
         { cout << "\nDerv1"; }
   };
class Derv2 : public Base               // derived class 2
   {
   public:
      void show()
         { cout << "\nDerv2"; }
   };
void main()
   {
   Derv1 dv1;               // object of derived class 1
   Derv2 dv2;               // object of derived class 2
   Base* ptr;               // pointer to base class
   ptr = &dv1;              // put address of dv1 in pointer
   ptr->show();             // execute show()

   ptr = &dv2;              // put address of dv2 in pointer
   ptr->show();             // execute show()
   }
```

The output of this program is

```
Derv1
Derv2
```

Now, as you can see, the member functions of the derived classes, not the base class, are executed. We change the contents of `ptr` from the address of `Derv1` to that of `Derv2`, and the particular instance of `show()` that is executed also changes. So the same function call,

```
ptr->show();
```

executes different functions, depending on the contents of `ptr`. The rule is that the compiler selects the function based on the *contents* of the pointer `ptr`, not on the *type* of the pointer, as in NOTVIRT. This is shown in Figure 13-2.

Late Binding

The astute reader may wonder how the compiler knows what function to compile. In NOTVIRT the compiler has no problem with the expression

```
ptr->show();
```

It always compiles a call to the `show()` function in the base class. But in VIRT the compiler doesn't know what class the contents of `ptr` may contain. It could be the

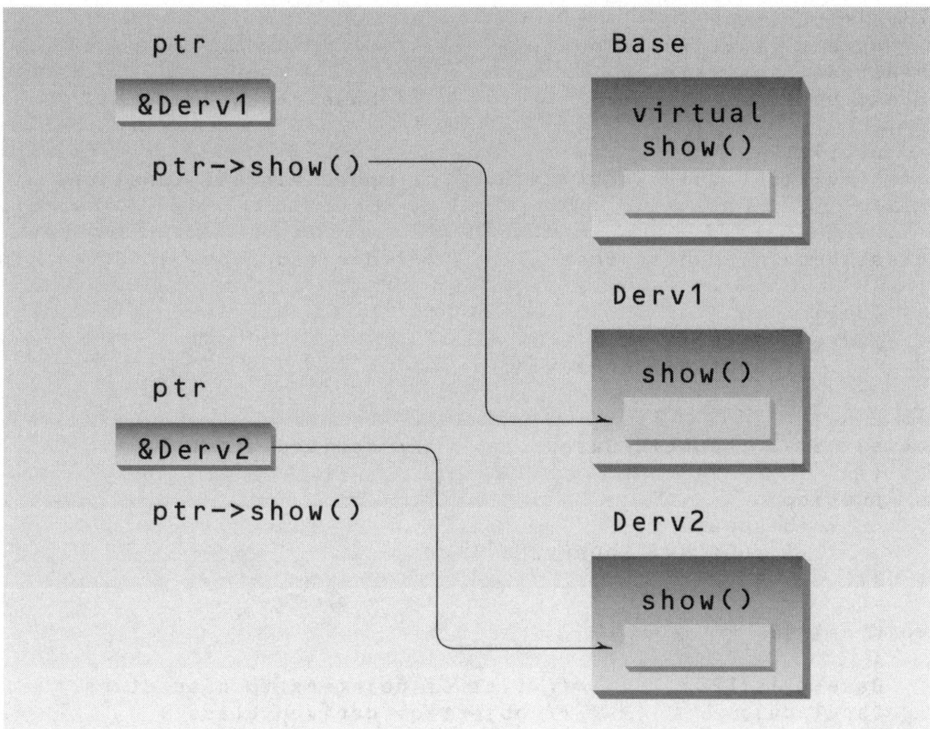

Figure 13-2 Virtual Pointer Access

address of an object of the `Derv1` class or of the `Derv2` class. Which version of `draw()` does the compiler call? In fact the compiler doesn't know what to do, so it arranges for the decision to be deferred until the program is running. At runtime, when it is known what class is pointed to by `ptr`, the appropriate version of `draw` will be called. This is called *late binding* or *dynamic binding*. (Choosing functions in the normal way, during compilation, is called *early binding*, or *static binding*.) Late binding requires some overhead but provides increased power and flexibility.

We'll put these ideas to use in a moment, but first let's consider a refinement to the idea of virtual functions.

Pure Virtual Functions

A *pure* virtual function is a virtual function with no body (another OOP sentence that sounds as if it describes an esoteric religious concept). You may have noticed in the VIRT program that `Base::show()` is never executed. This is a common situation. There is no need for the base-class version of the particular function; we only use the versions of the function in the derived classes. When this is true, the body of the virtual function in the base class can be removed, and the notation `=0` added to the function declaration, as shown in the VIRTPURE example.

```
// virtpure.cpp
// pure virtual function
#include <iostream.h>
class Base                              // base class
   {
   public:
      virtual void show() = 0;          // pure virtual function
   };

class Derv1 : public Base               // derived class 1
   {
   public:
      void show()
         { cout << "\nDerv1"; }
   };

class Derv2 : public Base               // derived class 2
   {
   public:
      void show()
         { cout << "\nDerv2"; }
   };

void main()
   {
   Base* list[2];             // list of pointers to base class
   Derv1 dv1;                 // object of derived class 1
   Derv2 dv2;                 // object of derived class 2

   list[0] = &dv1;            // put address of dv1 in list

   list[1] = &dv2;            // put address of dv2 in list

   list[0]->show();           // execute show() in both objects
   list[1]->show();
   }
```

Now the virtual function is declared as

```
virtual void show() = 0;  // pure virtual function
```

The equal sign here has nothing to do with assignment; the value 0 is not assigned to anything. The `=0` syntax is simply how we tell the compiler that a function will be pure—that is, have no body.

You might wonder, if we can remove the body of the virtual `show()` function in the base class, why we can't remove the function altogether. That would be even cleaner, but it doesn't work. Without a function `show()` in the base class, statements like

```
list[0]->show();
```

would not be valid, because the pointers in the `list[]` array must point to members of class `Base`.

As you can see, we've made another, unrelated, change in VIRTPURE: The addresses of the member functions are stored in an array of pointers, and accessed using array elements. This works in just the same way as using a single pointer. The output of VIRTPURE is the same as VIRT:

```
Derv1
Derv2
```

Virtual Functions and the `person` Class

Now that we understand some of the mechanics of virtual functions, let's look at a situation where it makes sense to use them. Our example is an extension of the PTROBJ and PERSORT examples from Chapter 12. It uses the same `person` class, but adds two derived classes, `student` and `professor`. These derived classes each contain a function called `isOutstanding()`. This function makes it easy for the school administrators to create a list of outstanding students and professors for the venerable Awards Day ceremony. Here's the listing for VIRTPERS:

```
// virtpers.cpp
// virtual functions with person class
#include <iostream.h>
enum boolean { false, true };

class person                                // person class
   {
   protected:
      char name[40];
   public:
      void setName()
         { cout << "   Enter name: "; cin >> name; }
      void printName()
         { cout << "Name is: " << name << endl; }
      boolean virtual isOutstanding() = 0;  // pure virtual func
   };

class student : public person               // student class
   {
   private:
      float gpa;                            // grade point average
   public:
      void setGpa()                         // set GPA
         { cout << "   Enter student's GPA: "; cin >> gpa; }
      boolean isOutstanding()
         { return (gpa > 3.5) ? true : false; }
   };

class professor : public person             // professor class
   {
   private:
      int numPubs;                 // number of papers published
   public:
      void setNumPubs()            // set number of papers published
         {
         cout << "   Enter number of professor's publications: ";
```

(continued on next page)

(continued from previous page)

```
         cin >> numPubs;
         }
      boolean isOutstanding()
         { return (numPubs > 100) ? true : false; }
   };

void main(void)
   {
   person* persPtr[100];      // list of pointers to persons
   student* stuPtr;           // pointer to student
   professor* proPtr;         // pointer to professor
   int n = 0;                 // number of persons on list
   char choice;

   do
      {
      cout << "Enter student or professor (s/p): ";
      cin >> choice;
      if(choice=='s')                    // it's a student
         {
         stuPtr = new student;           // make new student
         stuPtr->setName();              // set student name
         stuPtr->setGpa();               // set GPA
         persPtr[n++] = stuPtr;          // put pointer in list
         }
      else                               // it's a professor
         {
         proPtr = new professor;         // make new professor
         proPtr->setName();              // set professor name
         proPtr->setNumPubs();           // set number of pubs
         persPtr[n++] = proPtr;          // put pointer in list
         }
      cout << "   Enter another (y/n)? ";  // do another person?
      cin >> choice;
      }  while( choice=='y' );           // cycle until not 'y'

   for(int j=0; j<n; j++)                // print names of all
      {                                  // persons, and
      persPtr[j]->printName();           // say if outstanding
      if( persPtr[j]->isOutstanding()==true )
         cout << "   This person is outstanding\n";
      }
   }  // end main()
```

The `student` and `professor` Classes

The `student` and `professor` classes add new data items to the base class. The `student` class contains a variable `gpa` of type `float`, which represents the student's grade point average (GPA). The `professor` class contains a variable `numPubs` of type `int`, which represents the number of scholarly publications the professor has published. A student with a GPA of over 3.5, and a professor who has published more than 100 publications, are considered outstanding. (We'll refrain from comment on the desirability of these criteria for judging educational excellence.)

The isOutstanding() Function

The isOutstanding() function is declared as a pure virtual function in person. In the student class this function returns a Boolean true if the student's GPA is greater than 3.5, and false otherwise. In professor it returns true if the professor's numPubs variable is greater than 100.

The main() Program

In main() we first let the user enter a number of student and teacher names. For students, the program also asks for the GPA, and for professors it asks for the number of publications. When the user is finished, the program prints out the names of all the students and professors, noting those that are outstanding. Here's some sample interaction:

```
Enter student or professor (s/p): s
   Enter name: Timmy
   Enter student's GPA: 1.2
   Enter another (y/n)? y
Enter student or professor (s/p): s
   Enter name: Brenda
   Enter student's GPA: 3.9
   Enter another (y/n)? y
Enter student or professor (s/p): s
   Enter name: Sandy
   Enter student's GPA: 2.4
   Enter another (y/n)? y
Enter student or professor (s/p): p
   Enter name: Shipley
   Enter number of professor's publications: 714
   Enter another (y/n)? y
Enter student or professor (s/p): p
   Enter name: Wainright
   Enter number of professor's publications: 13
   Enter another (y/n)? n

Name is: Timmy
Name is: Brenda
   This person is outstanding
Name is: Sandy
Name is: Shipley
   This person is outstanding
Name is: Wainright
```

Virtual Functions in a Graphics Example

Let's try another example of virtual functions, this one a graphics example derived from the MULTSHAP program in Chapter 11. As we noted at the beginning of this section, you may want to draw a number of shapes using the same statement. The VIRTSHAP program does this.

```
// virtshap.cpp
// virtual functions with shapes
#include <graphics.h>          // for graphics functions
#include <conio.h>             // for getche()
```

(continued on next page)

(continued from previous page)

```
const int W = 50;                // size of images

class shape                      // base class
   {
   protected:
      int xCo, yCo;              // coordinates of center
      int linecolor;             // color of outline
      int fillcolor;             // color of interior
   public:
      shape()                    // no-arg constructor
         { xCo=0; yCo=0; linecolor=WHITE; fillcolor=WHITE; }
      void set(int x, int y, int lc, int fc)  // set data
         { xCo=x; yCo=y; linecolor=lc; fillcolor=fc; }
      void colorize()            // set colors
         {
         setcolor(linecolor);                         // line color
         setlinestyle(SOLID_LINE, 0, THICK_WIDTH); // line width
         setfillstyle(SOLID_FILL, fillcolor);    // set fill color
         }
      virtual void draw() = 0;      // pure virtual draw function
   };

class ball : public shape
   {
   public:
      ball() : shape()           // no-arg constr
         { }
      void set(int x, int y, int lc, int fc)    // set data
          { shape::set(x, y, lc, fc); }
      void draw()                // draw the ball
         {
         shape::colorize();                        // set colors
         circle(xCo, yCo, W);                      // draw circle
         floodfill(xCo, yCo, linecolor);           // fill circle
         }
   };

class rect : public shape
   {
   public:
      rect() : shape()           // no-arg constr
         { }
      void set(int x, int y, int lc, int fc)    // set data
          { shape::set(x, y, lc, fc); }
      void draw()                // draw the rectangle
         {
         shape::colorize();                        // set colors
         rectangle(xCo-W, yCo-W, xCo+W, yCo+W); // draw rectangle
         floodfill(xCo, yCo, linecolor);           // fill rectangle
         moveto(xCo-W, yCo+W);                     // draw diagonal
         lineto(xCo+W, yCo-W);                     //    line
         }
   };
```

```
class tria : public shape
   {
   public:
      tria() : shape()            // no-arg constr
         { }
      void set(int x, int y, int lc, int fc)    // set data
          { shape::set(x, y, lc, fc); }
      void draw()                 // draw the triangle
         {
         shape::colorize();                         // set colors
         int triarray[] = { xCo,    yCo-W,          // top
                            xCo+W, yCo+W,           // bottom right
                            xCo-W, yCo+W };         // bottom left
         fillpoly(3, triarray);                     // draw triangle
         }
   };

void main()
   {
   int driver, mode;
   driver = DETECT;               // set to best graphics mode
   initgraph(&driver, &mode, "\\tc\\bgi");

   shape* ptrarr[3];              // array of pointers to shapes

   ball b1;                       // define three shapes
   rect r1;
   tria t1;
                                  // set values in shapes
   b1.set(100, 100, WHITE, BLUE);
   r1.set(100, 200, WHITE, RED);
   t1.set(100, 300, WHITE, GREEN);

   ptrarr[0] = &b1;               // put addresses in array
   ptrarr[1] = &r1;
   ptrarr[2] = &t1;

   for(int j=0; j<3; j++)         // draw all shapes
      ptrarr[j]->draw();

   getche();                      // wait for keypress
   closegraph();                  // close graphics system
   }
```

The class specifiers in VIRTSHAP are similar to those in MULTSHAP, except that the `draw()` function in the `shape` class has been made into a pure virtual function.

In `main()`, we set up an array, `ptrarr`, of pointers to shapes. Next we create three objects, one of each class, and place their addresses in an array. Now it's easy to draw all three shapes. The statement

```
ptrarr[j]->draw();
```

does this as the loop variable `j` changes.

This is a powerful approach to combining graphics elements, especially when a large number of objects need to be grouped together and drawn as a unit.

Abstract Classes

An *abstract class* is often defined as one that will not be used to create any objects, but exists only to act as a base class of other classes. Ellis and Stroustrup (see Appendix E) tighten up this definition by requiring that, to be called abstract, a class must contain at least one pure virtual function. This ensures that you can never create an object of the class; the compiler won't permit it. Both the `Shape` class in VIRTSHAP and the `person` class in VIRTPERS meet this criterion.

Virtual Base Classes

Before leaving the subject of virtual programming elements, we should mention *virtual base classes*.

Consider the situation shown in Figure 13-3, with a base class, `Parent`; two derived classes, `Child1` and `Child2`; and a fourth class, `Grandchild`, derived from both `Child1` and `Child2`.

In this arrangement a problem can arise if a member function in the `Grandchild` class wants to access data or functions in the `Parent` class. The NORMBASE program shows what happens.

```
// normbase.cpp
// ambiguous reference to base class

class Parent
   {
   protected:
      int basedata;
   };
class Child1  : public Parent
   { };
class Child2  : public Parent
   { };
class Grandchild  : public Child1, public Child2
   {
   public:
      int getdata()
        { return basedata; }    // ERROR: ambiguous
   };
```

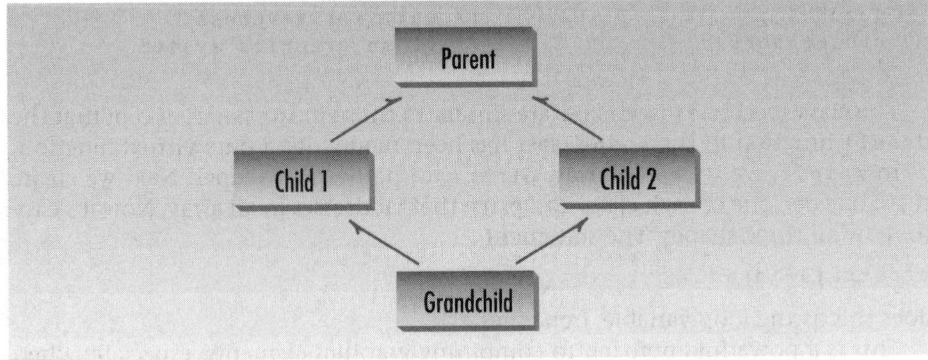

Figure 13-3 Virtual Base Class

A compiler error occurs when the `getdata()` member function in `Grandchild` attempts to access `basedata` in `Parent`. Why? When the `Child1` and `Child2` classes are derived from `Parent`, each inherits a copy of `Parent`; this copy is called a *subobject*. Each of the two subobjects contains its own copy of `Parent`'s data, including `basedata`. Now, when `Grandchild` refers to `basedata`, which of the two copies will it access? The situation is ambiguous, and that's what the compiler reports.

To eliminate the ambiguity, we make `Child1` and `Child2` into virtual base classes, as shown by the example VIRTBASE.

```
// virtbase.cpp
// virtual base classes

class Parent
   {
   protected:
      int basedata;
   };
class Child1 : virtual public Parent    // shares copy of Parent
   { };
class Child2 : virtual public Parent    // shares copy of Parent
   { };
class Grandchild : public Child1, public Child2
   {
   public:
      int getdata()
        { return basedata; }      // OK: only one copy of Parent
   };
```

The use of the keyword `virtual` in these two classes causes them to share a single common *subobject* of their base class `Parent`. Since there is only one copy of `basedata`, there is no ambiguity when it is referred to in `Grandchild`.

Friend Functions

The concepts of encapsulation and data hiding dictate that nonmember functions should not be able to access an object's private or protected data. The policy is, if you're not a member, you can't get in. However, there are situations where such rigid discrimination leads to considerable inconvenience.

Friends As Bridges

Imagine that you want a function to operate on objects of two different classes. Perhaps the function will take objects of the two classes as arguments, and operate on their private data. If the two classes are inherited from the same base class, then you may be able to put the function in the base class. But what if the classes are unrelated?

In this situation there's nothing like a `friend` function. Here's a simple example, FRIEND, that shows how `friend` functions can act as a bridge between two classes:

```
// friend.cpp
// friend functions
#include <iostream.h>

class beta;                 // needed for frifunc declaration

class alpha
   {
   private:
      int data;
   public:
      alpha()  { data = 3; }                 // no-arg constructor
      friend int frifunc(alpha, beta);      // friend function
   };

class beta
   {
   private:
      int data;
   public:
      beta()  { data = 7; }                  // no-arg constructor
      friend int frifunc(alpha, beta);      // friend function
   };

int frifunc(alpha a, beta b)                // function definition
   {
   return( a.data + b.data );
   }

void main()
   {
   alpha aa;
   beta bb;
   cout << frifunc(aa, bb);                 // call the function
   }
```

In this program, the two classes are `alpha` and `beta`. The constructors in these classes initialize their single data items to fixed values (3 in `alpha` and 7 in `beta`).

We want the function `frifunc()` to have access to both these private data members, so we make it a `friend` function. It's declared with the `friend` keyword in both classes:

```
friend int frifunc(alpha, beta);
```

This declaration can be placed anywhere in the class; it doesn't matter if it goes in the `public` or the `private` section.

An object of each class is passed as an argument to the function `frifunc()`, and it accesses the private `data` member of both classes through these arguments. The function doesn't do much: It adds the data items and returns the sum. The `main()` program calls this function and prints the result.

A minor point: Remember that a class can't be referred to until it has been declared. Class `beta` is referred to in the declaration of the function `frifunc()` in class `alpha`, so `beta` must be declared before `alpha`. Hence the declaration

```
class beta;
```

at the beginning of the program.

Breaching the Walls

We should note that `friend` functions are controversial. During the development of C++, arguments raged over the desirability of including this feature. On the one hand, it adds flexibility to the language; on the other, it is not in keeping with the philosophy that only member functions can access a class's private data.

How serious is the breach of data integrity when `friend` functions are used? A `friend` function must be declared as such within the class whose data it will access. Thus a programmer who does not have access to the source code for the class cannot make a function into a `friend`. In this respect the integrity of the class is still protected. Even so, `friend` functions are conceptually messy, and potentially lead to a spaghetti-code situation if numerous `friends` muddy the clear boundaries between classes. For this reason `friend` functions should be used sparingly. If you find yourself using many `friends`, you may need to rethink the design of the program.

English Distance Example

However, sometimes `friend` functions are too convenient to avoid. One example is when `friends` are used to increase the versatility of overloaded operators. The following program shows a limitation in the use of such operators when friends are not used. This example is a variation on the ENGLPLUS and ENGLCONV programs in Chapter 9. It's called NOFRI.

```
// nofri.cpp
// limitation to overloaded + operator
#include <iostream.h>

class Distance                        // English Distance class
   {
   private:
      int feet;
      float inches;
   public:
      Distance()                      // constructor (no args)
         { feet = 0; inches = 0.0; }
      Distance( float fltfeet )       // constructor (one arg)
         {                            // convert float to Distance
         feet = int(fltfeet);               // feet is integer part
         inches = 12*(fltfeet-feet);        // inches is what's left
         }
      Distance(int ft, float in)      // constructor (two args)
         { feet = ft; inches = in; }
      void showdist()                 // display distance
         { cout << feet << "\'-" << inches << '\"'; }
      Distance operator + (Distance);
   };
```

(continued on next page)

(continued from previous page)

```
                                          // add this distance to d2
Distance Distance::operator + (Distance d2)    // return the sum
   {
   int f = feet + d2.feet;                // add the feet
   float i = inches + d2.inches;          // add the inches
   if(i >= 12.0)                          // if total exceeds 12.0,
      { i -= 12.0; f++;  }                // less 12 inches, plus 1 foot
   return Distance(f,i);                  // return new Distance with sum
   }

void main()
   {
   Distance d1 = 2.5;                       // constructor converts
   Distance d2 = 1.25;                      // meters to Distance
   Distance d3;
   cout << "\nd1 = "; d1.showdist();
   cout << "\nd2 = "; d2.showdist();

   d3 = d1 + 10.0;                          // distance + float: ok
   cout << "\nd3 = "; d3.showdist();
// d3 = 10.0 + d1;                          // float + Distance: ERROR
// cout << "\nd3 = "; d3.showdist();
   }
```

In this program, the + operator is overloaded to add two objects of type `Distance`. Also, there is a one-argument constructor that converts a value of type `float`, representing feet and decimal fractions of feet, into a `Distance` value. (That is, it converts 10.25' into 10'-3".)

When such a constructor exists, you can make statements like this in `main()`:

```
d3 = d1 + 10.0;
```

The overloaded + is looking for objects of type `Distance` both on its left and on its right, but if the argument on the right is type `float`, the compiler will use the one-argument constructor to convert this `float` to a `Distance` value, and then carry out the addition.

Here is what appears to be a subtle variation on this statement:

```
d3 = 10.0 + d1;
```

Does this work? No, because the object of which the overloaded + operator is a member must be the variable to the left of the operator. When we place a variable of a different type there, or a constant, then the compiler uses the + operator that adds that type (`float` in this case), not the one that adds `Distance` objects. Unfortunately this operator does not know how to convert `float` to `Distance`, so it can't handle this situation. Here's the output from NOFRI:

```
d1 = 2'-6"
d2 = 1'-3"
d3 = 12'-6"
```

The second addition won't compile, so these statements are commented out. We could get around this problem by casting the number to type `Distance`:

```
d3 = Distance(10, 0) + d1;
```

but this is nonintuitive and inelegant. How can we write natural-looking statements that have nonmember data types to the left of the operator? As you may have guessed, a `friend` can help you out of this dilemma. The FRENGL program shows how.

```
// frengl.cpp
// friend overloaded + operator
#include <iostream.h>

class Distance                          // English Distance class
   {
   private:
      int feet;
      float inches;
   public:
      Distance()                        // constructor (no args)
         { feet = 0; inches = 0.0; }
      Distance( float fltfeet )         // constructor (one arg)
         {                              // convert float to Distance
         feet = int(fltfeet);              // feet is integer part
         inches = 12*(fltfeet-feet);       // inches is what's left
         }
      Distance(int ft, float in)        // constructor (two args)
         { feet = ft; inches = in; }
      void showdist()                   // display distance
         { cout << feet << "\'-" << inches << '\"'; }
      friend Distance operator + (Distance, Distance);  // friend
   };
                                        // add D1 to d2
Distance operator + (Distance d1, Distance d2)
   {
   int f = d1.feet + d2.feet;              // add the feet
   float i = d1.inches + d2.inches;        // add the inches
   if(i >= 12.0)                        // if inches exceeds 12.0,
      { i -= 12.0; f++;  }              // less 12 inches, plus 1 foot
   return Distance(f,i);                // return new Distance with sum
   }

void main()
   {
   Distance d1 = 2.5;                      // constructor converts
   Distance d2 = 1.25;                     // float-feet to Distance
   Distance d3;
   cout << "\nd1 = "; d1.showdist();
   cout << "\nd2 = "; d2.showdist();

   d3 = d1 + 10.0;                         // distance + float: ok
   cout << "\nd3 = "; d3.showdist();
   d3 = 10.0 + d1;                         // float + Distance: ok
   cout << "\nd3 = "; d3.showdist();
   }
```

The overloaded + operator is made into a `friend`:

```
friend Distance operator + (Distance, Distance);
```

Notice that, while the overloaded + operator took one argument as a member function, it takes two as a `friend` function. In a member function, one of the objects on which the + operates is the object of which it was a member, and the second is an argument. In a `friend`, both objects must be arguments.

The only change to the body of the overloaded + function is that the variables `feet` and `inches`, used in NOFRI for direct access to the object's data, have been replaced in FRENGL by `d1.feet` and `d1.inches`, since this object is supplied as an argument.

Remember that, to make a function a friend, only the function declaration within the class is preceded by the keyword `friend`. The class definition is written normally, as are calls to the function.

`friends` for Functional Notation

Sometimes a `friend` allows a more obvious syntax for calling a function than does a member function. For example, suppose we want a function that will square (multiply by itself) an object of the English `Distance` class and return the result in square feet, as a type `float`. The MISQ example shows how this might be done with a member function.

```
// misq.cpp
// member square() function for Distance
#include <iostream.h>

class Distance                          // English Distance class
   {
   private:
      int feet;
      float inches;
   public:
      Distance()                        // constructor (no args)
         { feet = 0; inches = 0.0; }
      Distance(int ft, float in)        // constructor (two args)
         { feet = ft; inches = in; }
      void showdist()                   // display distance
         { cout << feet << "\'-" << inches << '\"'; }

      float square();                   // member function
   };

float Distance::square()                // return square of
   {                                    // this Distance
   float fltfeet = feet + inches/12;       // convert to float
   float feetsqrd = fltfeet * fltfeet;     // find the square
   return feetsqrd;                     // return square feet
   }

void main()
   {
   Distance dist(3, 6.0);               // two-arg constructor (3'-6")
   float sqft;
```

```
   sqft = dist.square();            // return square of dist
                                    // display distance and square
   cout << "\nDistance = "; dist.showdist();
   cout << "\nSquare = " << sqft << " square feet";
   }
```

The `main()` part of the program creates a `Distance` value, squares it, and prints out the result. The output shows the original distance and the square:

```
Distance = 3'-6"
Square = 12.25 square feet
```

In `main()` we use the statement

```
sqft = dist.square();
```

to find the square of `dist` and assign it to `sqft`. This works all right, but if we want to work with `Distance` objects using the same syntax that we use with ordinary numbers, we would probably prefer a functional notation:

```
sqft = square(dist);
```

We can achieve this effect by making `square()` a `friend` of the `Distance` class, as shown in FRISQ:

```
// frisq.cpp
// friend square() function for Distance
#include <iostream.h>

class Distance                        // English Distance class
   {
   private:
      int feet;
      float inches;
   public:
      Distance()                      // constructor (no args)
         { feet = 0; inches = 0.0; }
      Distance(int ft, float in)      // constructor (two args)
         { feet = ft; inches = in; }
      void showdist()                 // display distance
         { cout << feet << "\'-" << inches << '\"'; }

      friend float square(Distance);  // friend function
   };

float square(Distance d)              // return square of
   {                                  // this Distance
   float fltfeet = d.feet + d.inches/12;  // convert to float
   float feetsqrd = fltfeet * fltfeet;    // find the square
   return feetsqrd;                   // return square feet
   }

void main()
   {
   Distance dist(3, 6.0);             // two-arg constructor (3'-6")
   float sqft;
```

(continued on next page)

(continued from previous page)
```
   sqft = square(dist);             // return square of dist
                                    // display distance and square
   cout << "\nDistance = "; dist.showdist();
   cout << "\nSquare = " << sqft << " square feet";
   }
```

Where `square()`, as a member function in MISQ, takes no arguments, it takes one as a `friend` in FRISQ. In general, the `friend` version of a function requires one more argument than when the function is a member. The `square()` function in FRISQ is similar to that in MISQ, but it refers to the data in the source `Distance` object as `d.feet` and `d.inches`, instead of as `feet` and `inches`.

`friend` Classes

The member functions of a class can all be made friends at the same time when you make the entire class a friend. The program FRICLASS shows how this looks.

```
// friclass.cpp
// friend classes
#include <iostream.h>

class alpha
   {
   private:
      int data1;
   public:
      alpha()  { data1 = 99; }
      friend class beta;            // beta is a friend class
   };

class beta
   {                                // all member functions can
   public:                          // access private alpha data
      void func1(alpha a)  { cout << "\ndata1=" << a.data1; }
      void func2(alpha a)  { cout << "\ndata1=" << a.data1; }
      void func3(alpha a)  { cout << "\ndata1=" << a.data1; }
   };

void main()
   {
   alpha a;
   beta b;

   b.func1(a);
   b.func2(a);
   b.func3(a);
   }
```

In class `alpha` the entire class `beta` is proclaimed a friend. Now all the member functions of `beta` can access the private data of `alpha` (in this program the single data item `data1`).

Note that in the `friend` declaration we specify that `beta` is a class using the `class` keyword:

```
friend class beta;
```

We could also have declared `beta` to be a class before the `alpha` class specifier, as in previous examples.

```
class beta;
```

and then, within `alpha`, referred to `beta` without the `class` keyword:

```
friend beta;
```

Static Functions

In the STATIC example in Chapter 7 we introduced `static` member data. As you may recall, a static data member is not duplicated for each object; rather a single data item is shared by all objects of a class. The STATIC example showed a class that kept track of how many objects of itself there were. Let's extend this concept by showing how functions as well as data may be `static`. Besides showing static functions, our example will model a class that provides an ID number for each of its objects. This allows you to query an object to find out which object it is—a capability that is sometimes useful in debugging a program, among other situations. The program also casts some light on the operation of destructors. Here's the listing for STATFUNC:

```
// statfunc.cpp
// static functions and ID numbers for objects
#include <iostream.h>

class gamma
   {
   private:
      static int total;          // total objects of this class
                                 //    (declaration only)
      int id;                    // ID number of this object
   public:
      gamma()                    // no-argument constructor
         {
         total++;                // add another object
         id = total;             // id equals current total
         }
      ~gamma()                   // destructor
         {
         total--;
         cout << "\nDestroying ID number " << id;
         }
      static void showtotal()    // static function
         {
         cout << "\nTotal is " << total;
         }
      void showid()              // non-static function
         {
         cout << "\nID number is " << id;
         }
   };

int gamma::total = 0;            // definition of total
```

(continued on next page)

(continued from previous page)
```
void main()
   {
   cout << endl << endl;
   gamma g1;
   gamma::showtotal();

   gamma g2, g3;
   gamma::showtotal();

   g1.showid();
   g2.showid();
   g3.showid();
   cout << "\n----------end of program----------";
   }
```

Accessing `static` Functions

In this program there is a static data member, `total`, in the class `gamma`. This data keeps track of how many objects of the class there are. It is incremented by the constructor and decremented by the destructor.

Suppose we want to access `total` from outside the class. We construct a function, `showtotal()`, that prints the `total`'s value. But how do we access this function?

When a data member is declared `static`, there is only one such data value for the entire class, no matter how many objects of the class are created. In fact, there may be no such objects at all, but we still want to be able to learn this fact. We could create a dummy object to use in calling a member function, as in

```
gamma dummyObj;          // make an object so we can call function
dummyObj.showtotal();    // call function
```

But this is rather inelegant. We shouldn't need to refer to a specific object when we're doing something that relates to the entire class. It's more reasonable to use the name of the class itself with the scope-resolution operator.

```
gamma::showtotal();    // more reasonable
```

However, this won't work if `showtotal()` is a normal member function; an object and the dot member-access operator are required in such cases. To access `showtotal()` using only the class name, we must declare it to be a `static` member function. This is what we do in STATFUNC. Now the function can be accessed using only the class name. Here's the output:

```
Total is 1
Total is 3
ID number is 1
ID number is 2
ID number is 3
----------end of program--------
Destroying ID number 3
Destroying ID number 2
Destroying ID number 1
```

We define one object, `g1`, and then print out the value of `total`, which is 1. Then we define two more objects, `g2` and `g3`, and again print out the total, which is now 3.

Numbering the Objects

We've placed another function in `gamma()` to print out the ID number of individual members. This ID number is set equal to `total` when an object is created, so each object has a unique number. The `showid()` function prints out the ID of its object. We call it three times in `main()`, in the statements

```
g1.showid();
g2.showid();
g3.showid();
```

As the output shows, each object has a unique number. The `g1` object is numbered 1, `g2` is 2, and `g3` is 3.

Investigating Destructors

Now that we know how to number objects, we can investigate an interesting fact about destructors. STATFUNC prints an *end of program* message in its last statement, but it's not done yet, as the output shows. The three objects created in the program must be destroyed before the program terminates, so that memory is not left in an inaccessible state. The compiler takes care of this by invoking the destructor.

We can see that this happens by inserting in the destructor a statement that prints a message. Since we've numbered the objects, we can also find out the order in which the objects are destroyed. As the output shows, the last object created, `g3`, is destroyed first. One can infer from this last-in-first-out approach that local objects are stored on the stack.

Simulations: A Horse Race

Static members come in handy in programs that simulate physical processes such as assembly lines, air-traffic control, and games. As an example we'll show a horse-racing game. In this game a number of horses appear on the screen, and, starting from the left, race to a finish line on the right. Each horse's speed is created randomly, so there is no way to figure out in advance which one will win. The program uses character graphics, so the horses are easily (although somewhat crudely) displayed. You'll need to compile it as a DOS program, since it uses the DOS-only function `delay()` to slow it down so you can see the horses move.

When our program, HORSE, is started, it asks the user to supply the race's distance and the number of horses that will run in it. The classic unit of distance for horse racing (at least in English-speaking countries) is the furlong, which is 1/8 of a mile. Typical races are 6, 8, 10, or 12 furlongs. You can enter from 1 to 10 horses. The program draws vertical lines corresponding to each furlong, along with start and finish lines. Each horse is represented by a rectangle with a number in the middle. Figure 13-4 shows the screen with a race in progress.

Designing the Horse Race

How do we approach an OOP design for our horse race? Our first question might be, is there a group of similar entities that we're trying to model? The answer is yes, the horses. So it seems reasonable to make each horse an object. There will be a class called `horse`, which will contain data specific to each horse, such as its

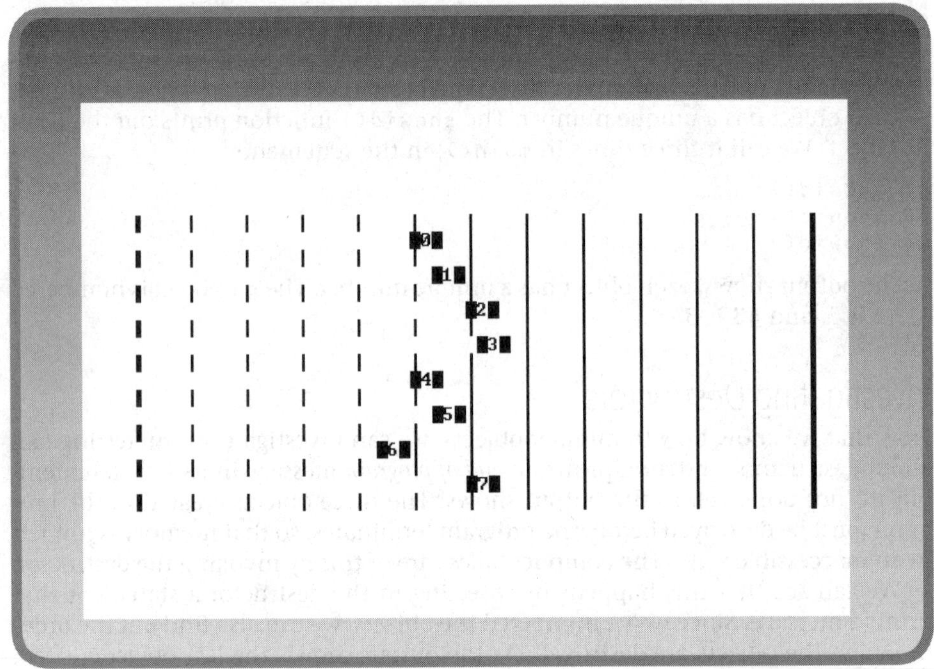

Figure 13-4 Output of the HORSE program

number and the distance it has run so far (which is used to display the horse in the correct screen position).

However, there is also data that applies to all the horses, such as the track length, the elapsed time (starting from 0:00 at the start of the race), and the total number of horses. We can say that this data applies to the entire race track. What do we do with this track-related (as opposed to horse-related) data? One possibility is to make a class called, say, `track`, and install this data in it. An array of horse objects could then be a member of the `track` class. However, this doesn't work very well because simply making objects of one class members of another class doesn't do much to simplify communication between them. Each class's private data is still inaccessible to the other, so it would be hard, for example, for the horses to find out how long the course was. What about using inheritance to make the horses descendants of the track? This doesn't make much sense either, because the horses aren't a "kind of" race track; they're a completely different thing.

Static Data to the Rescue

The best approach is to make all track-related data static, so it can be accessed by all the horses and so we can access it without using a specific horse object. In addition to the track-related items we've already mentioned, we're going to use `new` to obtain memory for all the horse objects, since we don't know in advance how many horses the user will specify. It will be handy to make the pointer returned by `new` into a static variable, since this memory is common to all the horses, although each one occupies a different space in it. Each horse can then be accessed through the same pointer (plus an index). As each horse is created, its constructor uses a temporary count of how many horses have been created so far, so that each horse can number itself sequentially. All these data items should be static, since they apply to the class of horses in general.

The `horse` constructor operates on each horse individually, so it's convenient to have another function, which we call `init_track()`, to initialize the various static (track-oriented) data. This should be a static function, since it's called only once, for the entire class, not in connection with a particular horse.

Here's the listing for HORSE:

```
// horse.cpp
// models a horse race

#include <iostream.h>
#include <dos.h>                        // for delay()
#include <conio.h>                      // for kbhit()
#include <stdlib.h>                     // for random()
#include <time.h>                       // for randomize()

const int CPF = 5;                      // screen columns per furlong

class horse
   {
   private:
      // track characteristics (declarations only)
      static horse* hptr;               // pointer to horse memory
      static int total;                 // total number of horses
      static int count;                 // horses created so far
      static int track_length;          // track length in furlongs
      static float elapsed_time;        // time since start of race

      // horse characteristics
      int horse_number;                 // this horse's number
      float finish_time;                // this horse's finish time
      float distance_run;               // distance since start
   public:
      static void init_track(float l, int t); // initialize track
      static void create_horses()       // create horses
         {
         hptr = new horse[total];       // get memory for all horses
         }
      static void track_tick();         // time tick for entire track
      horse()                           // constructor for each horse
         {
         horse_number = count++;        // set our horse's number
         distance_run = 0.0;            // haven't moved yet
         }
      void horse_tick();                // time tick for one horse
   };

horse* horse::hptr;                     // define static (track) vars
```

(continued on next page)

(continued from previous page)

```
int horse::total;
int horse::count = 0;
int horse::track_length;
float horse::elapsed_time = 0.0;

void horse::init_track(float l, int t)  // static (track) function
   {
   total = t;                           // set number of horses
   track_length = l;                    // set track length
   randomize();                         // initialize random numbers
   clrscr();                            // clear screen
                                        // display track

   for(int f=0; f<=track_length; f++)     // for each furlong
      for(int r=1; r<=total*2 + 1; r++)  // for each screen row
         {
         gotoxy(f*CPF + 5, r);
         if(f==0 || f==track_length)
            cout << '\xDE';             // draw start or finish line
         else
            cout << '\xB3';             // draw furlong marker
         }
   }

void horse::track_tick()                // static (track) function
   {
   elapsed_time += 1.75;                // update time

   for(int j=0; j<total; j++)           // for each horse,
      (hptr+j)->horse_tick();           // update horse
   }

void horse::horse_tick()                // for each horse
   {                                    // display horse & number
   gotoxy( 1 + int(distance_run * CPF), 2 + horse_number*2 );
   cout << " \xDB" << horse_number << "\xDB";
   if(distance_run < track_length + 1.0/CPF)  // until finish,
      {
      if( random(3) % 3 )               // skip about 1 of 3 ticks
         distance_run += 0.2;           // advance 0.2 furlongs
      finish_time = elapsed_time;       // update finish time
      }
   else
      {                                 // display finish time
      int mins = int(finish_time)/60;
      int secs = int(finish_time) - mins*60;
      cout << " Time=" << mins << ":" << secs;
      }
   }

void main()
   {
   float length;
   int total;
```

```
   cout << "\nEnter track length (furlongs): ";
   cin >> length;
   cout << "\nEnter number of horses (1 to 10): ";
   cin >> total;
                                  // initialize track
   horse::init_track(length, total);
   horse::create_horses();        // create horses
   while( !kbhit() )              // exit on keypress
      {
      horse::track_tick();        // move and display all horses
      delay(500);                 // wait 1/2 second
      }
   }
```

Keeping Time

Simulation programs usually involve an activity taking place over a period of time. To model the passage of time, such programs typically energize themselves at fixed intervals. In the HORSE program, the `main()` program uses a `while` loop to repeatedly call a static `horse` function, `tick_track()`; the time tick sent to the track as a whole. The `tick_track()` function then makes a series of calls, one for each horse, to a nonstatic function: `horse_tick()` (which should not be confused with the insect that carries equine fever). This function then redraws the horses in their new position.

Assignment and Copy Initialization

The C++ compiler is always busy on your behalf, doing things you can't be bothered to do. If you take charge, it will defer to your judgment; otherwise it will do things its own way. Two important examples of this process are the assignment operator and the copy constructor.

You've used the assignment operator many times, probably without thinking too much about it. Suppose `a1` and `a2` are objects. Unless you tell the compiler otherwise, the statement

```
a2 = a1;        // set a2 to the value of a1
```

will cause the compiler to copy the data from `a1`, member by member, into `a2`. This is the default action of the assignment operator, =.

You're also familiar with initializing variables. Initializing an object with another object, as in

```
alpha a2(a1);   // initialize a2 to the value of a1
```

causes a similar action. The compiler creates a new object, `a2`, and copies the data from `a1`, member by member, into `a2`. This is the default action of the copy constructor.

Both these default activities are provided, free of charge, by the compiler. If member-by-member copying is what you want, you need take no further action. However, if you want assignment or initialization to do something more complex, then you can override the default functions. We'll discuss the techniques for overloading the assignment operator and the copy constructor separately, and then put them together in an example that gives a `String` class a more efficient way to manage memory.

Overloading the Assignment Operator

Let's look at a short example that demonstrates the technique of overloading the assignment operator. Here's the listing for ASSIGN:

```
// assign.cpp
// overloads assignment operator (=)
#include <iostream.h>

class alpha
   {
   private:
      int data;
   public:
      alpha()                           // no-arg constructor
         { }
      alpha(int d)                      // one-arg constructor
         { data = d; }
      void display()                    // display data
         { cout << data; }
      alpha operator = (alpha& a)   // overloaded = operator
         {
         data = a.data;                 // not done automatically
         cout << "\nAssignment operator invoked";
         return alpha(data);            // return copy of this alpha
         }
   };

void main()
   {
   alpha a1(37);
   alpha a2;

   a2 = a1;                             // invoke overloaded =
   cout << "\na2="; a2.display();   // display a2

   alpha a3 = a2;                       // does NOT invoke =
   cout << "\na3="; a3.display();   // display a3
   }
```

The `alpha` class is very simple; it contains only one data member. Constructors initialize the data, and a member function can print out its value. The new aspect of ASSIGN is the function `operator=()`, which overloads the = operator.

In `main()`, we define `a1` and give it the value 37, and define `a2` but give it no value. Then we use the assignment operator to set `a2` to the value of `a1`:

```
a2 = a1;    // assignment statement
```

This causes our overloaded `operator=()` function to be invoked. Here's the output from ASSIGN:

```
Assignment operator invoked
a2=37
a3=37
```

Initialization Is Not Assignment

In the last two lines of ASSIGN we initialize the object `a3` to the value `a2`, and display it. Don't be confused by the syntax here. The equal sign in

```
alpha a3 = a2;    // copy initialization, not an assignment
```

is not an assignment but an initialization, with the same effect as

```
alpha a3(a2);     // alternative form of copy initialization
```

This is why the the assignment operator is executed only once, as shown by the single invocation of the line

```
Assignment operator invoked
```

in the output of ASSIGN.

Taking Responsibility

When you overload the = operator you assume responsibility for doing whatever the default assignment operator did. Often this involves copying the member data from one object to another. The `alpha` class in ASSIGN has only one data item, `data`, so the `operator=()` function copies its value with the statement

```
data = a.data;
```

The function also prints the *Assignment operator invoked* message so that we can tell when it executes.

Passing by Reference

Notice that the argument to `operator=()` is passed by reference. It is not absolutely necessary to do this, but it's usually a good idea. Why? As you know, an argument passed by value generates a copy of itself in the function to which it is passed. The argument passed to the `operator=()` function is no exception. If such objects are large, the copies can waste a lot of memory. Values passed by reference don't generate copies, and thus help to conserve memory.

Also, there are certain situations in which you want to keep track of the number of objects (as in the STATFUNC example, where we assigned numbers to the objects). If the compiler is generating extra objects every time you use the assignment operator, you may wind up with more objects than you expected. Passing by reference helps avoid such spurious object creation.

Returning a Value

As we've seen, a function can return information to the calling program by value or by reference. When an object is returned by value, a new object is created and returned to the calling program. In the calling program the value of this object can be assigned to a new object, or it can be used in other ways. When an object is returned by reference, no new object is created. A reference to the original object in the function is all that's returned to the calling program.

The `operator=()` function in ASSIGN returns a value by creating a temporary `alpha` object and initializing it using the one-argument constructor in the statement

```
return alpha(data);
```

The value returned is a copy of, but not the same object as, the object of which the overloaded = operator is a member. Returning a value makes it possible to chain = operators:

```
a3 = a2 = a1;
```

However, returning by value has the same disadvantages as passing an argument by value: It creates an extra copy that wastes memory and can cause confusion. Can we return this value with a reference, using the declarator shown here for the overloaded = operator?

```
alpha& operator = (alpha& a)   // bad idea in this case
```

Unfortunately we can't use reference returns on variables that are local to a function. Remember that local (`automatic`) variables—that is, those created within a function (and not designated `static`)—are destroyed when the function returns. A return by reference returns only the address of the data being returned, and, for local data, this address points to data within the function. When the function is terminated and this data is destroyed, the pointer is left with a meaningless value. (We'll see one way to solve this problem when we talk about the `this` pointer later in this chapter.)

Not Inherited

The assignment operator is unique among operators in that it is not inherited. If you overload the assignment operator in a base class, you can't use this same function in any derived classes.

The Copy Constructor

As we discussed, you can define and at the same time initialize an object to the value of another object with two kinds of statements:

```
alpha a3(a2);       // copy initialization
alpha a3 = a2;      // copy initialization, alternate syntax
```

Both styles of definition invoke a *copy constructor:* a constructor that copies its argument into a new object. The default copy constructor, which is provided automatically by the compiler for every object, performs a member-by-member copy. This is similar to what the assignment operator does; the difference is that the copy constructor also creates a new object.

Like the assignment operator, the copy constructor can be overloaded by the user. The XOFXREF example shows how it's done.

```
// xofxref.cpp
// copy constructor: X(X&)
#include <iostream.h>

class alpha
   {
   private:
      int data;
   public:
      alpha()                         // no-arg constructor
         { }
```

```
      alpha(int d)                    // one-arg constructor
         { data = d; }
      alpha(alpha& a)                 // overloaded copy constructor
         {
         data = a.data;
         cout << "\nCopy constructor invoked";
         }
      void display()                  // display
         { cout << data; }
      void operator = (alpha& a) // overloaded = operator
         {
         data = a.data;
         cout << "\nAssignment operator invoked";
         }
   };

void main()
   {
   alpha a1(37);
   alpha a2;

   a2 = a1;                          // invoke overloaded =
   cout << "\na2="; a2.display();   // display a2

   alpha a3(a1);                     // invoke copy constructor
// alpha a3 = a1;                    // equivalent definition of a3
   cout << "\na3="; a3.display();   // display a3
   }
```

This program overloads both the assignment operator and the copy constructor. The overloaded assignment operator is similar to that in the ASSIGN example. The copy constructor takes one argument: an object of type `alpha`, passed by reference. Here's its declarator:

```
alpha(alpha&)
```

This declarator has the form `X(X&)` (pronounced "X of X ref"), which is often used as a shorthand name for copy constructors. Here's the output of XOFXREF:

```
Assignment operator invoked
a2=37
Copy constructor invoked
a3=37
```

The statement

```
a2 = a1;
```

invokes the assignment operator, while

```
alpha a3(a1);
```

invokes the copy constructor. The equivalent statement

```
alpha a3 = a1;
```

could also be used to invoke the copy constructor.

We've seen that the copy constructor may be invoked when an object is defined. It is also invoked when arguments are passed by value to functions and when values are returned from functions. Let's mention these situations briefly.

Function Arguments

The copy constructor is invoked when an object is passed by value to a function. It creates the copy that the function operates on. Thus if the function

```
void func(alpha);
```

was declared in XOFXREF, and this function was called by the statement

```
func(a1);
```

then the copy constructor would be invoked to create a copy of the `a1` object for use by `func()`. (Of course, the copy constructor is not invoked if the argument is passed by reference or if a pointer to it is passed. In these cases no copy is created; the function operates on the original variable.)

Function Return Values

The copy constructor also creates a temporary object when a value is returned from a function. Suppose there were a function like this in XOFXREF:

```
alpha func();
```

and this function was called by the statement

```
a2 = func();
```

then the copy constructor would be invoked to create a copy of the value returned by `func()`, and this value would be assigned (invoking the assignment operator) to `a2`.

Why Not an `X(X)` Constructor?

Do we need to use a reference in the argument to the copy constructor? Could we pass by value instead? No, the compiler complains that it is *out of memory* if we try to compile

```
alpha(alpha a)
```

Why? Because when an argument is passed by value, a copy of it is constructed. What makes the copy? The copy constructor. But this *is* the copy constructor, so it calls itself. In fact it calls itself over and over until the compiler runs out of memory. So, in the copy constructor, the argument must be passed by reference, which creates no copies.

Don't Let It Copy Member by Member

When you overload the assignment operator, you almost always want to overload the copy constructor as well (and vice versa). You don't want your custom copying routine used in some situations, and the default member-by-member scheme used in others. Even if you don't think you'll use one or the other, you may find the compiler using them in nonobvious situations, such as passing an argument to a function by value, and returning from a function by value.

Watch Out for Destructors

The situations referred to above, passing arguments to a function by value and returning by value, cause the destructor to be called as well, when the temporary objects created by the function are destroyed when the function returns. This can cause considerable consternation if you're not expecting it. The moral is, when working with objects that require more than member-by-member copying, to pass and return by reference—not by value—whenever possible.

How to Prohibit Copying

We've discussed how to customize the copying of objects using the assignment operator and the copy constructor. Sometimes, however, you may want to prohibit the copying of an object using these operations. For example, it might be essential that each member of a class be created with a unique value for some member, which is provided as an argument to the constructor. If an object is copied, the copy would be given the same value. To avoid copying, overload the assignment operator and the copy constructor as private members.

```
class alpha
   {
   private:
      alpha& operator = (alpha&);  // private assignment operator
      alpha(alpha&);               // private copy constructor
   };
```

As soon as you attempt a copying operation, such as

```
alpha a1, a2;
a1 = a2;          // assignment
alpha a3(a1);     // copy constructor
```

the compiler will tell you that the function is not accessible. You don't need to define the functions, since they will never be called.

A Memory-Efficient String Class

The ASSIGN and XOFXREF examples don't really need to have overloaded assignment operators and copy constructors. They use straightforward classes with only one data item, so the default assignment operator and copy constructor would work just as well. Let's look at an example where it is essential for the user to overload these operators.

Defects with the `String` Class

We've seen various versions of the `String` class in previous chapters. However, these versions are not very sophisticated. It would be nice to overload the = operator so that we could assign the value of one `String` object to another with the statement

```
s2 = s1;
```

If we overload the = operator, the question arises how we will handle the actual string (the array of type `char`), which is the principal data item in the `String` class.

One possibility is for each `String` object to have a place to store a string. If we assign one `String` object to another (from `s1` into `s2` in the previous statement), we simply copy the string from the source into the destination object. The problem with this is that the same string now exists in two (or more) places in memory. This is not very efficient, especially if the strings are long. Figure 13-5 shows how this looks.

Instead of having each `String` object contain its own string, we could arrange for it to contain only a *pointer* to a string. Now, if we assign one `String` object to another, we need only copy the pointer from one object to another; both pointers will point to the same string. This is efficient, since only a single copy of the string itself needs to be stored in memory. Figure 13-6 shows how this looks.

However, if we use this system we need to be careful when we destroy a `String`

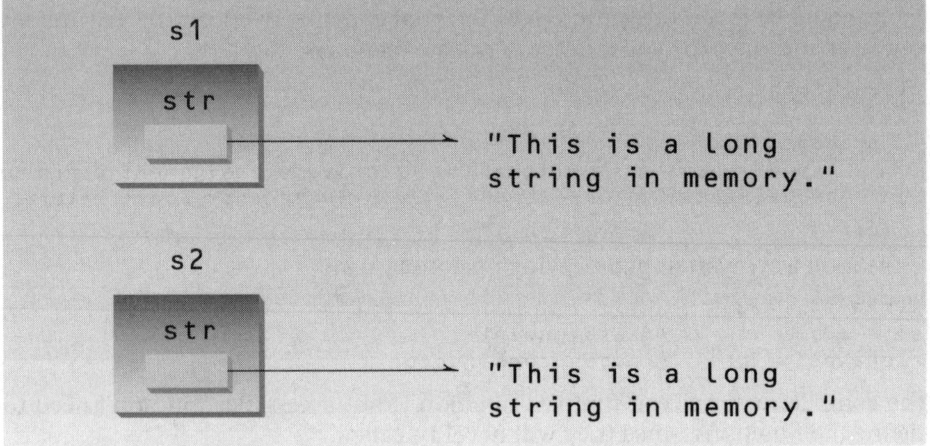

Figure 13-5 Replicating Strings

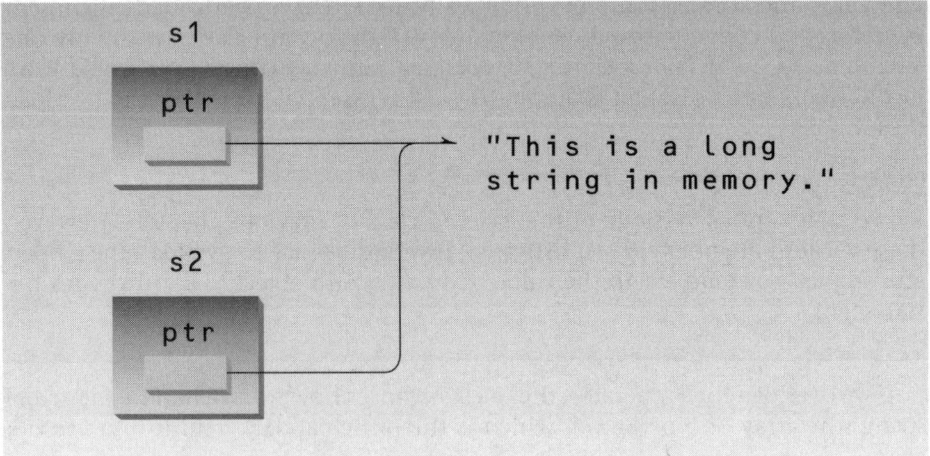

Figure 13-6 Replicating Pointers to Strings

object. If a String's destructor uses delete to free the memory occupied by the string, and if there are several objects with pointers pointing to the string, then these other objects will be left with pointers pointing to memory that may no longer hold the string they think it does; they become dangling pointers.

To use pointers to strings in String objects, we need a way to keep track of how many String objects point to a particular string, so that we can avoid deleteing the string until the last String that points to it is itself deleted. Our next example, STRIMEM, does just this.

A String-Counter Class

Suppose we have several String objects pointing to the same string and we want to keep a count of how many Strings point to the string. Where will we store this count?

It would be cumbersome for every String object to maintain a count of how many of its fellow Strings were pointing to a particular string, so we don't want to use a member variable in String for the count. Could we use a static variable? This is a possibility; we could create a static array and use it to store a list of string addresses and counts. However, this requires considerable overhead. It's more efficient to create a new class to store the count. Each object of this class, which we call strCount, contains a count and also a pointer to the string itself. Each String object contains a pointer to the appropriate strCount object. Figure 13-7 shows how this looks.

To ensure that String objects have access to strCount objects, we make String a friend of strCount. Here's the listing for STRIMEM:

```
// strimem.cpp
// memory-saving String class

// overloaded assignment and copy constructor
#include <iostream.h>
#include <conio.h>                    // for getch()
#include <string.h>                   // for strcpy(), etc

class strCount                        // keep track of number
   {                                  // of unique strings
   private:
      int count;                      // number of instances
      char* str;                      // pointer to string
      friend class String;            // make ourselves available
   public:
      strCount(char* s)               // one-arg constructor
         {
         int length = strlen(s);  // length of string argument
         str = new char[length+1];  // get memory for string
         strcpy(str, s);              // copy argument to it
         count=1;                     // start count at 1
         }
      ~strCount()                     // destructor
         {
         delete[] str;                // delete the string
         }
   };
```

(continued on next page)

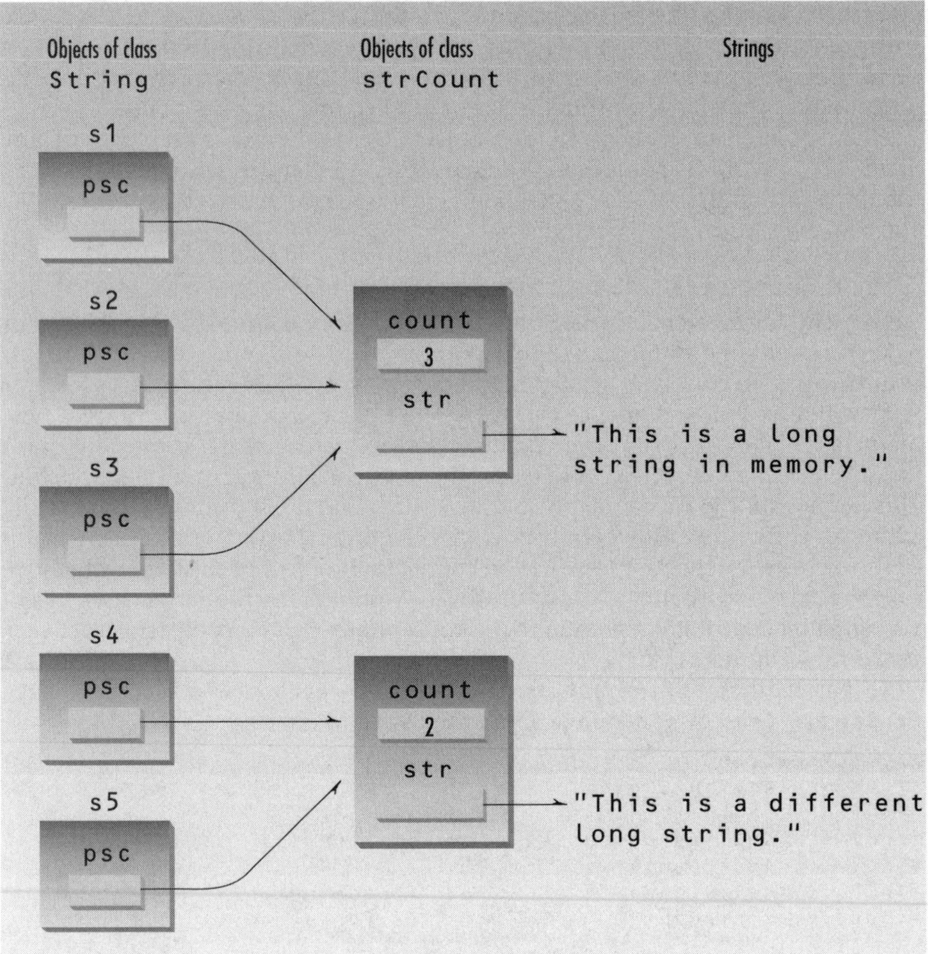

Figure 13-7 `String` and `strCount` Classes

(continued from previous page)

```
class String                          // String class
   {
   private:
      strCount* psc;                  // pointer to strCount
   public:
      String()                        // no-arg constructor
         {
         psc = new strCount("NULL");
         }
      String(char* s)                 // 1-arg constructor
         {
         psc = new strCount(s);
         }
      String(String& S)               // copy constructor
```

```
         {
         psc = S.psc;
         (psc->count)++;
         }
      ~String()                       // destructor
         {
         if(psc->count==1)            // if this is last instance,
            delete psc;               //    release strCount
         else                         //    if not last instance
            (psc->count)--;           //    decrement count
         }
      void display()                  // display the String
         {
         cout << psc->str;                    // print string
         cout << " (addr=" << psc << ")";     // print address
         }
      void operator = (String& S)  // assign the string
         {
         if(psc->count==1)            // if this is last instance,
            delete psc;               //    release strCount
         else                         //    if not last instance
            (psc->count)--;           //    decrement count
         psc = S.psc;                 // use argument's strCount
         (psc->count)++;              // increment count
         }
   };

void main()
   {
   String s3 = "When the fox preaches, look to your geese.";
   cout << "\ns3="; s3.display();     // display s3

   String s1;                         // define String
   s1 = s3;                           // assign it another String
   cout << "\ns1="; s1.display();     // display it

   String s2(s3);                     // initialize with String
   cout << "\ns2="; s2.display();     // display it
   getch();                           // wait for keypress
   }
```

In the `main()` part of STRIMEM we define a `String` object, `s3`, to contain the proverb "When the fox preaches, look to your geese." We define another `String` `s1` and set it equal to `s3`; then we define `s2` and initialize it to `s3`. Setting `s1` equal to `s3` invokes the overloaded assignment operator; initializing `s2` to `s3` invokes the overloaded copy constructor. We print out all three strings, and also the address of the `strCount` object pointed to by each object's `psc` pointer, to show that these objects are all the same. Here's the output from STRIMEM:

```
s3=When the fox preaches, look to your geese. (addr=0x8f510e00)
s1=When the fox preaches, look to your geese. (addr=0x8f510e00)
s2=When the fox preaches, look to your geese. (addr=0x8f510e00)
```

The other duties of the `String` class are divided between the `String` and `strCount` classes. Let's see what they do.

The strCount Class

The strCount class contains the pointer to the actual string and the count of how many String class objects point to this string. Its single constructor takes a pointer to a string as an argument and creates a new memory area for the string. It copies the string into this area and sets the count to 1, since just one String points to it when it is created. The destructor in strCount frees the memory used by the string. (We use delete[] with brackets because a string is an array.)

The String Class

The String class uses three constructors. If a new string is being created, as in the zero- and one-argument constructors, a new strCount object is created to hold the string, and the psc pointer is set to point to this object. If an existing String object is being copied, as in the copy constructor and the overloaded assignment operator, then the pointer psc is set to point to the old strCount object, and the count in this object is incremented. The overloaded assignment operator, as well as the destructor, must also delete the old strCount object pointed to by psc if the count is 1. (We don't need brackets on delete because we're deleting only a single strCountobject.) Figure 13-8 shows the action of the overloaded assignment operator, and Figure 13-9 shows the copy constructor.

(See also the section "Equal to Itself?" at the end of this chapter.)

The this Pointer

The member functions of every object have access to a sort of magic pointer named this, which points to the object itself. Thus any member function can find out the address of the object of which it is a member. Here's a short example, WHERE, that shows the mechanism:

```
// where.cpp
// the this pointer
#include <iostream.h>

class where
   {
   private:
      char charray[10];    // occupies 10 bytes
   public:
      void reveal()
         { cout << "\nMy object's address is " << this; }
   };

void main()
   {
   where w1, w2, w3;     // make three objects
   w1.reveal();          // see where they are
   w2.reveal();
   w3.reveal();
   }
```

The main() program in this example creates three objects of type where. It then asks each object to print its address, using the reveal() member function. This function prints out the value of the this pointer. Here's the output:

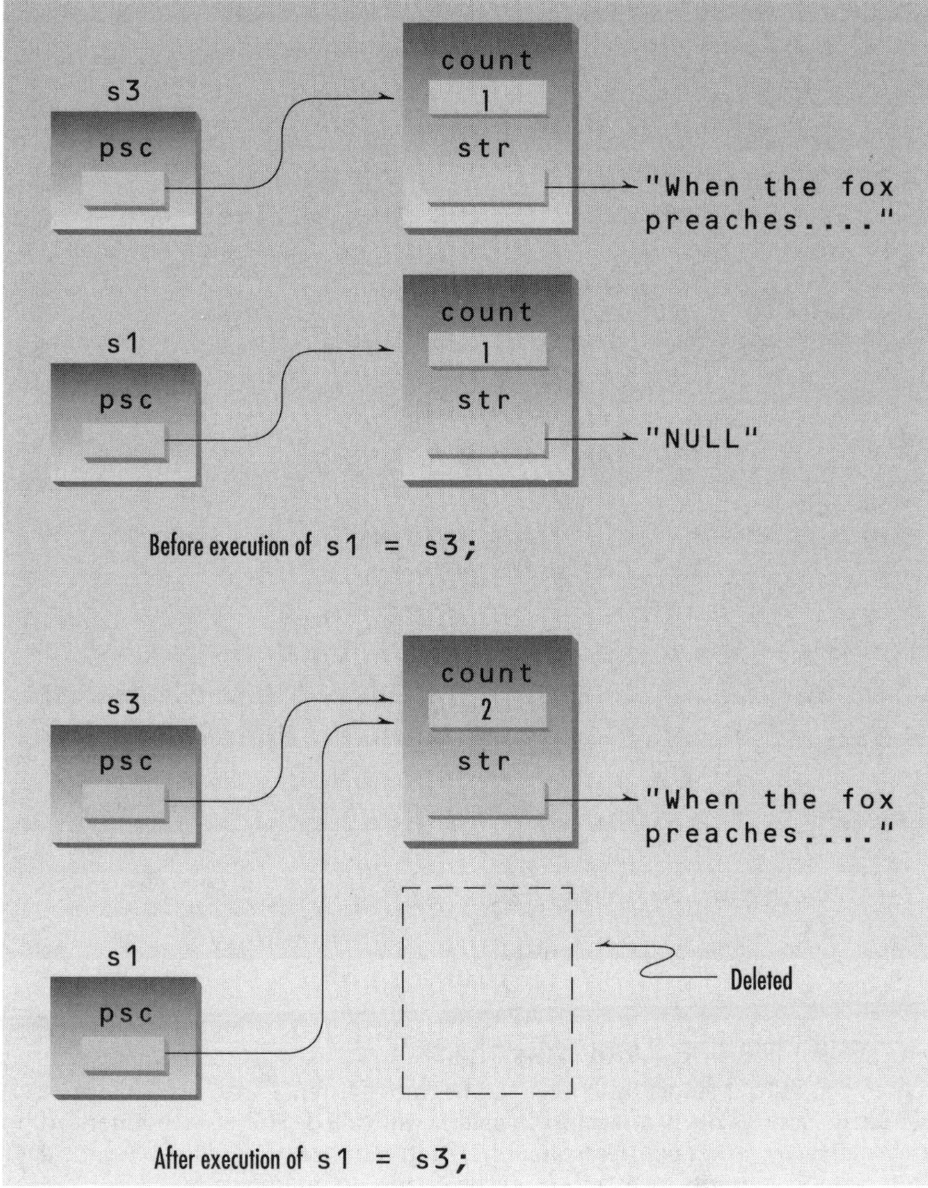

Figure 13-8 Assignment Operator in STRIMEM

```
My object's address is 0x8f4effec
My object's address is 0x8f4effe2
My object's address is 0x8f4effd8
```

Since the data in each object consists of an array of 10 bytes, the objects are spaced 10 bytes apart in memory. (EC minus E2 is 10 decimal, as is E2 minus D8.)

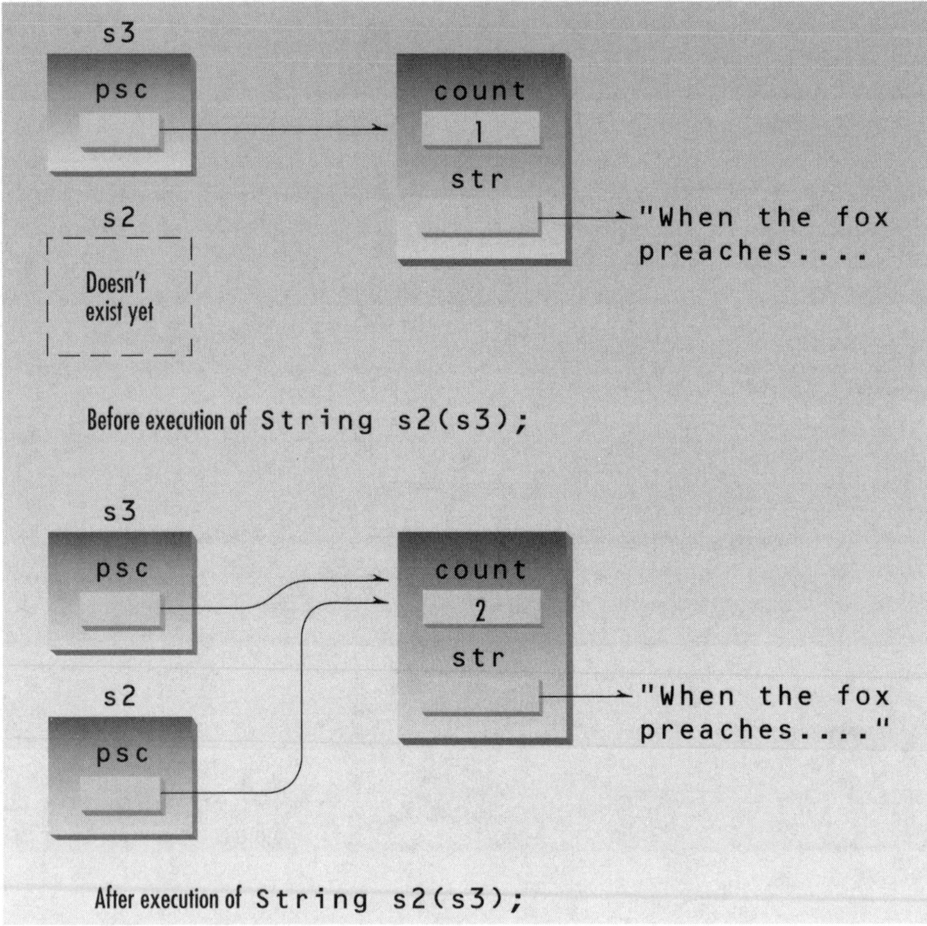

Figure 13-9 Copy Constructor in STRIMEM

Accessing Member Data with `this`

When you call a member function, it comes into existence with the value of `this` set to the address of the object for which it was called. The `this` pointer can be treated like any other pointer to an object, and can thus be used to access the data in the object it points to, as shown in the DOTHIS program:

```
// dothis.cpp
// the this pointer referring to data
#include <iostream.h>

class what
   {
   private:
      int alpha;
   public:
      void tester()
```

```
         {
         this->alpha = 11;      // same as alpha = 11;
         cout << this->alpha;   // same as cout << alpha;
         }
   };

void main()
   {
   what w;
   w.tester();
   }
```

This program simply prints out the value 11. Notice that the `tester()` member function accesses the variable `alpha` as

```
this->alpha
```

This is exactly the same as referring to `alpha` directly. This syntax works, but there is no reason for it except to show that `this` does indeed point to the object.

Using `this` for Returning Values

A more practical use for `this` is in returning values from member functions and overloaded operators.

Recall that in the ASSIGN program we could not return an object by reference, because the object was local to the function returning it and thus was destroyed when the function returned. We need a more permanent object if we're going to return it by reference. The object of which a function is a member is more permanent than its individual member functions. An object's member functions are created and destroyed every time they're called, but the object itself endures until it is destroyed by some outside agency (for example, when it is `deleted`). Thus returning by reference the object of which a function is a member is a better bet than returning a temporary object created in a member function. The `this` pointer makes this easy.

Here's the listing for ASSIGN2, in which the `operator=()` function returns by reference the object that invoked it:

```
// assign2.cpp
// returns contents of the this pointer
#include <iostream.h>

class alpha
   {
   private:
      int data;
   public:
      alpha()                        // no-arg constructor
         { }
      alpha(int d)                   // one-arg constructor
         { data = d; }
      void display()                 // display data
         { cout << data; }
      alpha& operator = (alpha& a) // overloaded = operator
```

(continued on next page)

(continued from previous page)

```
         {
         data = a.data;             // not done automatically
         cout << "\nAssignment operator invoked";
         return *this;              // return copy of this alpha
         }
   };

void main()
   {
   alpha a1(37);
   alpha a2, a3;

   a3 = a2 = a1;                              // invoke overloaded =
   cout << "\na2="; a2.display();   // display a2

   cout << "\na3="; a3.display();   // display a3
   }
```

In this program we can use the declaration

```
alpha& operator = (alpha& a)
```

which returns by reference, instead of

```
alpha operator = (alpha& a)
```

which returns by value. The last statement in this function is

```
return *this;
```

Since `this` is a pointer to the object of which the function is a member, `*this` is that object itself, and the statement returns it by reference. Here's the output of ASSIGN2:

```
Assignment operator invoked
Assignment operator invoked
a2=37
a3=37
```

Each time the equal sign is encountered in

```
a3 = a2 = a1;
```

the overloaded `operator=()` function is called, which prints the messages. The three objects all end up with the same value.

You usually want to return by reference from overloaded assignment operators, using `*this`, to avoid the creation of extra objects.

Revised STRIMEM Program

Using the `this` pointer we can revise the `operator=()` function in STRIMEM to return a value by reference, thus making possible multiple assignment operators for `String` objects, such as

```
s1 = s2 = s3;
```

At the same time, we can avoid the creation of spurious objects, such as those that are created when objects are returned by value. Here's the listing for STRIMEM2:

```
// strimem2.cpp
// memory-saving String class
// the this pointer in overloaded assignment
#include <iostream.h>
#include <string.h>                 // for strcpy(), etc
#include <conio.h>                  // for getch()

class strCount                      // keep track of number
   {                                // of unique strings
   private:
      int count;                    // number of instances
      char* str;                    // pointer to string
      friend class String;          // make ourselves available
   public:
      strCount(char* s)             // one-arg constructor
         {
         int length = strlen(s);  // length of string argument
         str = new char[length+1];  // get memory for string
         strcpy(str, s);            // copy argument to it
         count=1;                   // start count at 1
         }
      ~strCount()                   // destructor
         {
         delete[] str;              // delete the string
         }
   };

class String                        // String class
   {
   private:
      strCount* psc;                // pointer to strCount
   public:
      String()                      // no-arg constructor
         {
         psc = new strCount("NULL");
         }
      String(char* s)               // 1-arg constructor
         {
         psc = new strCount(s);
         }
      String(String& S)             // copy constructor
         {
         cout << "\nCOPY CONSTRUCTOR";
         psc = S.psc;
         (psc->count)++;
         }
      ~String()                     // destructor
         {
         if(psc->count==1)          // if we are its last user,
            delete psc;             //    delete our strCount
         else                       //    otherwise,
            (psc->count)--;         //    decrement its count
         }
```

(continued on next page)

(continued from previous page)

```
    void display()                    // display the String
       {
       cout << psc->str;                       // print string
       cout << " (addr=" << psc << ")";  // print address
       }
    String& operator = (String& S)  // assign the string
       {
       cout << "\nASSIGNMENT";
       if(psc->count==1)              // if we are its last user,
          delete psc;                 //    delete our strCount
       else                           //    otherwise,
          (psc->count)--;             //    decrement its count
       psc = S.psc;                   // use argument's strCount
       (psc->count)++;                // increment count
       return *this;                  // return this object
       }
 };

void main()
   {
   String s3 = "When the fox preaches, look to your geese.";
   cout << "\ns3="; s3.display();    // display s3

   String s1, s2;                     // define Strings
   s1 = s2 = s3;                      // assign them
   cout << "\ns1="; s1.display();    // display it
   cout << "\ns2="; s2.display();    // display it
   getch();                           // wait for keypress
   }
```

Now the declarator for the = operator is

```
String& operator = (String& S)  // return by reference
```

And, as in ASSIGN2, this function returns a pointer to `this`. Here's the output:

```
s3=When the fox preaches, look to your geese. (addr=0x8f640d3a)
ASSIGNMENT
ASSIGNMENT
s1=When the fox preaches, look to your geese. (addr=0x8f640d3a)
s2=When the fox preaches, look to your geese. (addr=0x8f640d3a)
```

The output shows that, following the assignment statement, all three `String` objects point to the same `strCount` object.

We should note that the `this` pointer is not available in static member functions, since they are not associated with a particular object.

Finding an Object's Class

Sometimes you need to find the class of an object. You may wonder how you could lose track of an object's class. However, imagine that you have an array of pointers to objects, and these pointers may point to objects of several different derived classes, as in the VIRTPERS program in this chapter. How do you know what kind of object a pointer points to?

We know we can use such a pointer to call a virtual function for the object, and the appropriate function will be called, depending on the type of object. The virtual function mechanism knows what kind of object the pointer points to. However, this information is not immediately available to the programmer.

Fortunately, recent versions of Borland C++ (later than Borland C++ 4.5 and Turbo C++ for Windows 4.5) include a special function, `typeid()`, that allows you to find the type (or class, which is the same thing) of an object. This is called *Run Time Type Identification*, or RTTI. Earlier Turbo C++ versions don't have this capability. Our example program, TYPEID, shows how `typeid()` works.

```
// typeid.cpp
// demonstrates typeid() function
#include <iostream.h>
#include <typeinfo.h>        // for typeid()

class ClassA
   { };

class ClassB
   { };

void main()
   {
   ClassA ObjA;
   ClassB ObjB;

   if( typeid(ObjA) == typeid(ClassA) )
      cout << "\nObjA is an object of ClassA";
   else
      cout << "\nObjA is not a member of ClassA";

   if( typeid(ObjB) == typeid(ClassA) )
      cout << "\nObjB is an object of ClassA";
   else
      cout << "\nObjB is not an object of ClassA";
   }
```

Here's the output from the program:

```
ObjA is an object of ClassA
ObjB is not an object of ClassA
```

You'll need to include the TYPINFO.H header file. You can use either an object name or a class name as an operand to `typeid()`, so it's easy to see if an object is from a particular class. The return value from `typeid()` is a pointer that is difficult to use except for comparison purposes, as with the == and != operators. However, this is usually all you need. It also works with basic types like `int` and `float`.

In the EMPL_IO example in Chapter 14 we'll see an example where `typeid()` comes in handy for finding the size of objects before writing them to a file.

Equal to Itself?

When overloading the = operator, you might want to consider the possibility that the user will set an object equal to itself, like this:

```
s1 = s1;
```

There's no reason for the user to do this, but—as you know—somewhere, some time, a user will do it anyway. In the `String` class this causes problems by confusing the `count` member of the `strCount`. The solution is to check explicitly for such an assignment. In the `String` class, at the very beginning of the `operator=()` member function, insert the lines

```
if( s.psc == psc )     // if argument is the same as us,
   return;             // don't do anything
```

We left this out for simplicity, but in a serious program it's a good idea to insert similar code in any class in which you overload the = operator.

Summary

Virtual functions provide a way for a program to decide, when it is running, what function to call. Ordinarily such decisions are made at compile time. Virtual functions make possible greater flexibility in performing the same kind of action on different kinds of objects. In particular, they allow the use of functions called from an array of type pointer-to-base that actually holds pointers to a variety of derived types. Typically a function is declared virtual in the base class, and other functions with the same name are declared in derived classes. A pure virtual function has no body in the base class.

A `friend` function can access a class's private data, even though it is not a member function of the class. This is useful when one function must have access to two or more unrelated classes and when an overloaded operator must use, on its left side, a value of a class other than the one of which it is a member. `friends` are also used to facilitate functional notation.

A `static` function is one that operates on the class in general, rather than on objects of the class. In particular it can operate on static variables. It can be called with the class name and scope-resolution operator.

The assignment operator = can be overloaded. This is necessary when it must do more than merely copy one object's contents into another. The copy constructor, which creates copies during initialization, and also when arguments are passed and returned by value, can also be overloaded. This is necessary when the copy constructor must do more than simply copy an object.

The `this` pointer is predefined in member functions to point to the object of which the function is a member. The `this` pointer is useful in returning the object of which the function is a member.

Questions

Answers to questions can be found in Appendix D.

1. Virtual functions allow you to

   a. create an array of type pointer-to-base class that can hold pointers to derived classes.

b. create functions that have no body.
c. group objects of different classes so they can all be accessed by the same function code.
d. use the same function call to execute member functions of objects from different classes.

2. True or false: A pointer to a base class can point to objects of a derived class.

3. If there is a pointer `p` to objects of a base class, and it contains the address of an object of a derived class, and both classes contain a nonvirtual member function, `ding()`, then the statement `p->ding();` will cause the version of `ding()` in the ________ class to be executed.

4. Write a declarator for a virtual function called `dang()` that returns type `void` and takes one argument of type `int`.

5. Deciding—*after* a program starts to execute—what function will be executed by a particular function call statement, is called ________.

6. If there is a pointer, `p`, to objects of a base class, and it contains the address of an object of a derived class, and both classes contain a virtual member function, `ding()`, then the statement `p->ding();` will cause the version of `ding()` in the ________ class to be executed.

7. Write the declaration for a pure virtual function called `aragorn` that returns no value and takes no arguments.

8. A pure virtual function is a virtual function that
   a. has no body.
   b. returns nothing.
   c. is used in a base class.
   d. takes no arguments.

9. Write the definition of an array called `parr` of 10 pointers to objects of class `dong`.

10. A virtual base class is useful when
    a. different functions in base and derived classes have the same name.
    b. there are multiple paths from one derived class to another.
    c. the identification of a function in a base class is ambiguous.
    d. it makes sense to use a base class with no body.

11. True or false: A `friend` function can access a class's private data without being a member of the class.

12. A `friend` function can be used to

    a. avoid arguments between classes.
    b. allow access to classes whose source code is unavailable.
    c. allow one class to access an unrelated class.
    d. increase the versatility of an overloaded operator.

13. Write the declaration for a friend function called `harry()` that returns type `void` and takes one argument of class `george`.

14. The keyword `friend` appears in

    a. the class allowing access to another class.
    b. the class desiring access to another class.
    c. the private section of a class.
    d. the public section of a class.

15. Write a declaration that, in the class in which it appears, will make every member of the class `harry` a `friend` function.

16. A static function

    a. should be called when an object is destroyed.
    b. is closely connected to an individual object of a class.
    c. can be called using the class name and function name.
    d is used when a dummy object must be created.

17. Explain what the default assignment operator = does when applied to objects.

18. Write a declaration for an overloaded assignment operator in class `zeta`.

19. An assignment operator might be overloaded to

    a. help keep track of the number of identical objects.
    b. assign a separate ID number to each object.
    c. ensure that all member data is copied exactly.
    d. signal when assignment takes place.

20. True or false: The user must always define the operation of the copy constructor.

21. The operation of the assignment operator and that of the copy constructor are

    a. similar, except that the copy constructor creates a new object.
    b. similar, except that the assignment operator copies member data.
    c. different, except that they both create a new object.
    d. different, except that they both copy member data.

22. Write the declaration of a copy constructor for a class called `Bertha`.

23. True or false: A copy constructor could be defined to copy only part of an object's data.

24. The lifetime of a variable that is defined as
    a. automatic if a member function coincides with the lifetime of the function.
    b. external coincides with the lifetime of a class.
    c. nonstatic member data of an object coincides with the lifetime of the object.
    d. static in a member function coincides with the lifetime of the function.

25. True or false: There is no problem with returning the value of a variable defined as automatic within a member function so long as it is returned by value.

26. Explain the difference in operation between these two statements.

```
person p1(p0);
person p1 = p0;
```

27. A copy constructor is invoked when
    a. a function returns by value.
    b. an argument is passed by value.
    c. a function returns by reference.
    d. an argument is passed by reference.

28. What does the `this` pointer point to?

29. If, within a class, `da` is a member variable, will the statement `this.da=37;` assign 37 to `da`?

30. Write a statement that a member function can use to return the entire object of which it is a member, without creating any temporary objects.

Exercises

Answers to starred exercises can be found in Appendix D.

1.* Imagine the same publishing company described in Exercise 1 in Chapter 10 that markets both book and audiocassette versions of its works. As in that exercise, create a class called `publication` that stores the title (a string) and price (type `float`) of a publication. From this class derive two classes: `book`, which adds a page count (type `int`); and `tape`, which adds a playing time in minutes (type `float`). Each of the three classes should have a `getdata()` function to get its data from the user at the keyboard, and a `putdata()` function to display the data.

    Write a `main()` program that creates an array of pointers to `publication`. This is similar to the VIRTPERS example in this chapter. In a loop, ask the user for data about a particular book or tape, and use `new` to create an object of type `book` or `tape` to hold the data. Put the pointer to the object in the array. When the user has finished entering the data for all books and tapes, display the resulting data for all the books and tapes entered, using a `for` loop and a single statement such as

```
pubarr[j]->putdata();
```

to display the data from each object in the array.

2.* In the `Distance` class, as shown in the FRENGL and FRISQ examples in this chapter, create an overloaded * operator so that two distances can be multiplied together. Make it a `friend` function so that you can use such expressions as

```
dist1 = 7.5 * dist2;
```

You'll need a one-argument constructor to convert floating-point values into `Distance` values. Write a `main()` program to test this operator in several ways.

3.* As we saw earlier, it's possible to make a class that acts like an array. The CLARRAY example shown here is a complete program that shows one way to create your own array class:

```
// clarray.cpp
// creates array class
#include <iostream.h>

class Array                             // models a normal C++ array
   {
   private:
      int* ptr;                         // pointer to Array contents
      int size;                         // size of Array
   public:
      Array(int s)                      // one-argument constructor
         {
         size = s;                      // argument is size of Array
         ptr = new int[s];              // make space for Array
         }
      ~Array()                          // destructor
         { delete[] ptr; }
      int& operator [] (int j)          // overloaded subscript operator
         { return *(ptr+j); }
   };

void main()
   {
   const int ASIZE = 10;                // size of array
   Array arr(ASIZE);                    // make an array

   for(int j=0; j<ASIZE; j++)           // fill it with squares
      arr[j] = j*j;

   for(j=0; j<ASIZE; j++)               // display its contents
      cout << arr[j] << "  ";
   }
```

The output of this program is

```
0  1  4  9  16  25  36  49  64  81
```

Starting with CLARRAY, add an overloaded assignment operator and an overloaded copy constructor to the `Array` class. Then add statements such as

```
Array arr2(arr1);
```

and

```
arr3 = arr1;
```

to the `main()` program to test whether these overloaded operators work.

4. Start with the program of Exercise 1 in this chapter, and add a Boolean member function called `isOversize()` to the `book` and `tape` classes. Let's say that a book with more than 800 pages, or a tape with a playing time longer than 90 minutes (which would require two cassettes), is considered oversize. You can access these function from `main()` and display the string "Oversize" for oversize books and tapes when you display their other data. If `book` and `tape` objects are to be accessed using pointers to them that are stored in an array of type `publication`, what do you need to add to the `publication` base class? Can you instantiate members of this base class?

5. Start with the program of Exercise 8 in Chapter 9, which overloaded five arithmetic operators for money strings. Add the two operators that couldn't be overloaded in that exercise. These operations,

```
long double * bMoney   // number times money
long double / bMoney   // number divided by money
```

require `friend` functions, since an object appears on the right side of the operator while a numerical constant appears on the left. Make sure that the `main()` program allows the user to enter two money strings and a floating-point value, and then carries out all seven arithmetic operations on appropriate pairs of these values.

6. As in the previous exercise, start with the program of Exercise 8 in Chapter 9. This time, add a function that rounds a `bMoney` value to the nearest dollar. It should be used like this:

```
mo2 = round(mo1);
```

As you know, amounts of $0.49 and less are rounded down, while those $0.50 and above are rounded up. A library function called `modfl()` is useful here. It separates a type `long double` variable into a fractional part and an integer part.

If the fractional part is less than 0.50, return the integer part as is; otherwise add 1.0. In `main()`, test the function by sending it a sequence of `bMoney` amounts that go from less than 49 cents to more than 50 cents.

7. Remember the PARSE program from Chapter 12? It would be nice to improve this program so it could evaluate expressions with real numbers, say type `float`, instead of single-digit numbers. For example,

```
3.14159 / 2.0 + 75.25 * 3.333 + 6.02
```

As a first step toward this goal, you need to develop a stack that can hold both operators (type `char`) and numbers (type `float`). But how can you store two different types on a stack, which is basically an array? After all, type `char` and type `float` aren't even the same size. Could you store pointers to different types? They're the same size, but the compiler still won't allow you to store type `char*` and type `float*` in the same array. The only way two different types of pointers can be stored in the same array is if they are derived from the same base class. So we can encapsulate a `char` in one class and a `float` in another, and arrange for both classes to be derived from a base class. Then we can store both kinds of pointers in an array of pointers to the base class. The base class doesn't need to have any data of its own; it can be an abstract class from which no objects will be instantiated.

Constructors can store the values into the derived classes in the usual way, but you'll need to use pure virtual functions to get the values back out again. Here's a possible scenario:

```
class Token                          // abstract base class
   {
   public:
      virtual float getNumber()=0;     // pure virtual functions
      virtual char getOperator()=0;
   };
class Operator : public Token
   {
   private:
      char oper;                     // operators +, -, *, /
   public:
      Operator(char);                // constructor sets value
      char getOperator();            // gets value
      float getNumber();             // dummy function
   };
class Number : public Token
   {
   private:
      float fnum;                    // the number
   public:
      Number(float);                 // constructor sets value
```

```
      float getNumber();          // gets value
      char getOperator();         // dummy function
   };

Token* atoken[100];               // holds types Operator* and Number*
```

Base-class virtual functions need to be instantiated in all derived classes, or the classes themselves become abstract. Thus the `Operand` class needs a `getNumber()` function, even though it doesn't store a number, and the the `Number` class needs `getOperand()`, even though it doesn't store an operand.

Expand this framework into a working program by adding a `Stack` class that holds `Token` objects, and a `main()` that pushes and pops various operators (such as `+` and `*`) and floating-point numbers (1.123) on and off the stack.

8. Let's put a little twist into the HORSE example in this chapter by making a class of extra-competitive horses. We'll assume that any horse that's ahead by the halfway point in the race starts to feel its oats and becomes almost unbeatable. From the horse class, derive a class called `comhorse` (for competitive horse). Overload the `horse_tick()` function in this class so that each horse can check if it's the front-runner and if there's another horse close behind it (say 0.1 furlong). If there is, it should speed up a bit. Perhaps not enough to win every time, but enough to give it a decided advantage.

How does each horse know where the other horses are? It must access the pointer to the memory that holds them, `hptr`, which was obtained by the `create_horses()` function. Be careful, however. You want to create comhorses, not horses. So the `comhorse` class will need to overload `hptr` and the `create_horses()` function. With this arrangement you can find out where a horse is by using an expression like `(hptr+j)->distance_run`. For example, here's a code fragment that figures out which horse is farthest ahead:

```
for(int j = 0; j<total; j++)   // check every horse
   {
   if( (hptr+j) != this &&     // (except us)
                               // if it's the farthest so far
     (hptr+j)->distance_run > farthest_distance )
      {                        // remember farthest distance
      farthest_distance = (hptr+j)->distance_run;
      pfarthest = hptr+j;      // remember the horse
      }
   }
```

You can continue on to check if your horse is ahead of the (otherwise) leading horse, and if it's by a small margin. If so, accelerate a bit.

9. Exercise 4 in Chapter 12 involved adding an overloaded destructor to the `linklist` class. Suppose we fill an object of such a destructor-enhanced class with data, and then assign the entire class with a statement such as

```
list2 = list1;
```

using the default assignment operator. Now, suppose we later delete the `list1` object. Can we still use `list2` to access the same data? No, because when `list1` was deleted, its destructor deleted all its links. The only data actually contained in a `linklist` object is a pointer to the first link. Once the links are gone, the pointer in `list2` becomes invalid, and attempts to access the list lead to meaningless values or a program crash.

One way to fix this is to overload the assignment operator so that it copies all the data links, as well as the `linklist` object itself. You'll need to follow along the chain, copying each link in turn. As we noted earlier, you should overload the copy constructor as well. To make it possible to delete `linklist` objects in `main()`, you may want to create them using pointers and `new`. That makes it easier to test the new routines. Don't worry if the copy process reverses the order of the data.

Notice that copying all the data is not very efficient in terms of memory usage. Contrast this approach with that used in the STRIMEM example in Chapter 12, which used only one set of data for all objects, and kept track of how many objects pointed to this data.

10. Start with the CONBOXES program in Chapter 11. Write some classes that allow the user to choose from three kinds of boxes. First, the Text box from the original program that displays text and uses a *Press any key to continue* prompt. Second, a YesNo box that asks a yes-or-no question, displays a *Type y or n* prompt, and returns 0 for 'n' and 1 for 'y' to the calling program. Third, a Get Integer box that asks a question that can be answered with an integer, displays a rectangle into which the integer can be typed, and returns the integer. Use a base class with a pure virtual function so no objects of the class can be created. A function in this class can draw the window and the text, but functions in the derived classes will need to supply the prompt and await the user's input.

In `main()` arrange to have pointers to some of the boxes placed on a list, and the boxes drawn one after the other from a single statement in a loop, using their pointers.

11. Start with the CARSPASS program from Exercise 14 in Chapter 11. Modify the derived class, `passcar`, which provides the capability for passing, so that instead of sensing other cars by using the `getpixel()` function, it queries the other cars'

positions by asking them directly. It can read data from the other cars if there is an array of pointers to the other cars provided as (say) a static variable.

For example, the following function might be called to test if another car is so close ahead that our car needs to reduce speed:

```
boolean passcar::car_ahead()            // is there a car ahead?
   {
   for(int j=0; j<NUMCARS; j++)         // check every car
      if( aptrCar[j] != this &&         // except ourselves
          aptrCar[j]->lane == lane &&   // if it's in our lane,
                                        // and within two lengths
          abs(aptrCar[j]->miles - miles) < 2*LCAR &&
          miles < aptrCar[j]->miles )   // and we're behind it
         return TRUE;                   // there is a car ahead
   return FALSE;                        // no car ahead
   }
```

This assumes that, as each car is created, you put the pointer to it in the array `aptrCar[]`. Similar routines can check if there are cars to the left (when passing) and to the right (when returning to our own lane after a pass) by modifying the question about lanes.

12. Carry out the modification, discussed in Exercise 7, to the PARSE program of Chapter 12. That is, make it possible to parse expressions containing floating-point numbers. Combine the classes from Exercise 7 with the algorithms from PARSE. You'll need to operate on pointers to tokens instead of characters. This involves statements of the kind

```
Number* ptrN = new Number(ans);
s.push(ptrN);
```

and

```
Operator* ptrO = new Operator(ch);
s.push(ptrO);
```

14

Streams and Files

THE STREAM CLASS HIERARCHY

`ios` AND ERROR-HANDLING

OBJECTS AND DISK FILES

OVERLOADING << AND >>

COMMAND-LINE ARGUMENTS

PRINTER OUTPUT

14

This chapter focuses on the C++ stream classes. We'll start off with a look at the hierarchy in which these classes are arranged, and we'll summarize their important features. The largest part of this chapter is devoted to showing how to perform file-related activities using C++ streams. We'll show how to read and write data to files in a variety of ways, how to handle errors, and how files and OOP are related. Later in the chapter we'll examine several other features of C++ that are related to files, including in-memory text formatting, redirection, command-line arguments, overloading the insertion and extraction operators, and sending data to the printer.

Stream Classes

A *stream* is a general name given to a flow of data. In C++ a stream is represented by an object of a particular class. So far we've used the `cin` and `cout` streams, but there are others, most notably those for reading and writing to disk files. Different streams are used to represent different kinds of data flow. For example, the `ifstream` class represents input disk files.

Advantages of Streams

C programmers may wonder what advantages there are to using the stream classes for I/O, instead of traditional C functions such as `printf()` and `scanf()`, and—for files—`fprintf()`, `fscanf()`, and so on.

One reason is simplicity. If you've ever used a `%d` formatting character when you should have used a `%f` in `printf()`, you'll appreciate this. There are no such formatting characters in streams, since each object already knows how to display itself. This removes a major source of errors.

Second, you can overload existing operators and functions, such as the insertion (<<) and extraction (>>) operators, to work with classes that you create. This makes your own classes work in the same way as the built-in types, which again makes programming easier and more error free (not to mention more aesthetically satisfying).

Some stodgy old C programmers persist in using the `printf()` approach in C++, but we don't recommend this.

You may wonder if stream I/O is important if you plan to program in an environment with a Graphics User Interface such as Windows, where direct text output to the screen is not used. Do you still need to know about C++ streams? Yes, because they are the best way to write data to files, and also to format data in memory for later use in dialog boxes and other GUI elements.

The Stream Class Hierarchy

The stream classes are arranged in a rather complex hierarchy. Figure 14-1 shows the arrangement of the most important of these classes.

We've already made extensive use of some stream classes. The extraction operator `>>` is a member of the `istream` class, and the insertion operator `<<` is a

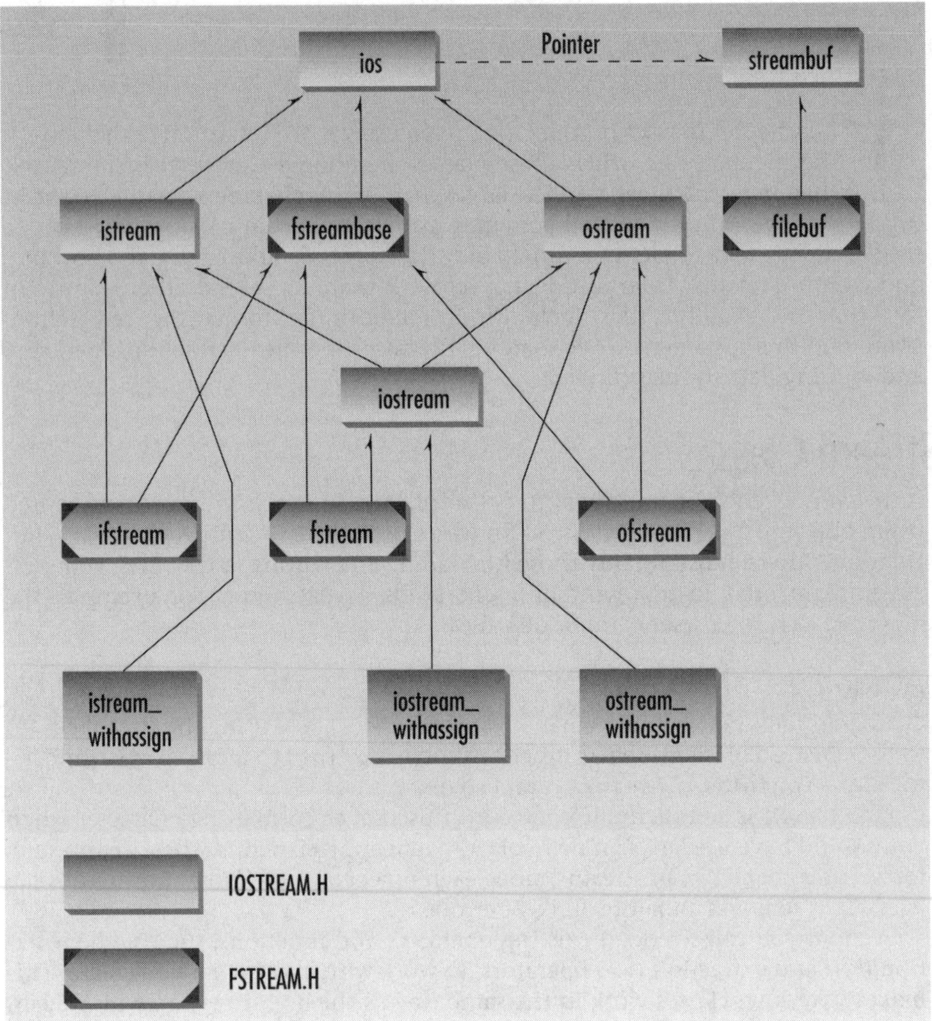

Figure 14-1 Stream Class Hierarchy

member of the `ostream` class. Both of these classes are derived from the `ios` class. The `cout` object, representing the standard output stream, which is usually directed to the video display, is a predefined object of the `ostream_withassign` class, which is derived from the `ostream` class. Similarly `cin` is an object of the `istream_withassign` class, which is derived from `istream`.

The classes used for input and output to the video display and keyboard are declared in the header file IOSTREAM.H, which we routinely included in our examples in previous chapters. The classes used specifically for disk file I/O are declared in the file FSTREAM.H. Figure 14-1 shows which classes are in which of these two header files. (Also, some manipulators are declared in IOMANIP.H, and in-memory classes are declared in STRSTREA.H.) You may find it educational to print out these header files and trace the relationships among the various classes. They're in your compiler's INCLUDE subdirectory. Many questions about streams can be answered by studying their class and constant declarations.

As you can see from Figure 14-1, the `ios` class is the base class for the hierarchy. It contains many constants and member functions common to input and output operations of all kinds. Some of these, such as the `showpoint` and `fixed` formatting flags, we've seen already. The `ios` class also contains a pointer to the `streambuf` class, which contains the actual memory buffer into which data is read or written, and the low-level routines for handling this data. Ordinarily you don't need to worry about the `streambuf` class, which is referenced automatically by other classes.

The `istream` and `ostream` classes are derived from `ios` and are dedicated to input and output, respectively. The `istream` class contains such functions as `get()`, `getline()`, `read()`, and the overloaded extraction (>>) operators, while `ostream` contains `put()` and `write()`, and the overloaded insertion (<<) operators.

The `iostream` class is derived from both `istream` and `ostream` by multiple inheritance. Classes derived from it can be used with devices, such as disk files, that may be opened for both input and output at the same time. Three classes—`istream_withassign`, `ostream_withassign`, and `iostream_withassign`—are inherited from `istream`, `ostream`, and `iostream`, respectively. They add assignment operators to these classes, so that `cin`, `cout`, and so on can be assigned to other streams. We'll see what this means when we talk about redirection.

The following summary of stream classes may seem rather abstract. You may want to skim it now, and return to it later when you need to know how to perform a particular stream-related activity.

The `ios` Class

The `ios` class is the granddaddy of all the stream classes, and contains the majority of the features you need to operate C++ streams. The three most important features are the formatting flags, the error-status bits, and the file operation mode. We'll look at formatting flags and error-status bits next. We'll save the file operations mode for later, when we talk about disk files.

Formatting Flags

Formatting flags are a set of `enum` definitions in `ios`. They act as on/off switches that specify choices for various aspects of input and output format and operation. We won't provide a detailed discussion of each flag, since we've already seen some of them in use, and others are more or less self-explanatory. Some we'll discuss later in this chapter. Table 14-1 is a complete list of the formatting flags.

There are several ways to set the formatting flags, and different ones can be set in different ways. Since they are members of the `ios` class, you must usually precede them with the name `ios` and the scope-resolution operator (for example, `ios::skipws`). All the flags can be set using the `setf()` and `unsetf()` `ios` member functions. For example,

```
cout.setf(ios::left);     // left justify output text
cout >> "This text is left-justified";
cout.unsetf(ios::left);  // return to default (right justified)
```

Flag	Meaning
`skipws`	Skip (ignore) whitespace on input
`left`	Left adjust output `[12.34       ]`
`right`	Right adjust output `[       12.34]`
`internal`	Use padding between sign or base indicator and number `[+      12.34]`
`dec`	Convert to decimal
`oct`	Convert to octal
`hex`	Convert to hexadecimal
`showbase`	Use base indicator on output (`0` for octal, `0x` for hex)
`showpoint`	Show decimal point on output
`uppercase`	Use uppercase `X`, `E`, and hex output letters (`ABCDEF`); the default is lowercase
`showpos`	Display + before positive integers
`scientific`	Use exponential format on floating-point output `[9.1234E2]`
`fixed`	Use fixed format on floating-point output `[912.34]`
`unitbuf`	Flush all streams after insertion
`stdio`	Flush `stdout`, `stderror` after insertion

Table 14-1 `ios` Formatting Flags

Many formatting flags can be set using manipulators, so let's look at them now.

Manipulators

Manipulators are formatting instructions inserted directly into a stream. We've seen examples before, such as the manipulator `endl`, which sends a newline to the stream and flushes it:

```
cout << "To each his own." << endl;
```

We've also used the `setiosflags()` manipulator (see the SALEMON program in Chapter 8):

```
cout << setiosflags(ios::fixed)       // use fixed decimal point
     << setiosflags(ios::showpoint)   // always show decimal point
     << var;
```

As these examples demonstrate, manipulators come in two flavors: those that take an argument and those that don't. Table 14-2 summarizes the no-argument manipulators.

Manipulator	Purpose
`ws`	Turn on whitespace skipping on input
`dec`	Convert to decimal
`oct`	Convert to octal
`hex`	Convert to hexadecimal
`endl`	Insert newline and flush the output stream
`ends`	Insert null character to terminate an output string
`flush`	Flush the output stream
`lock`	Lock file handle
`unlock`	Unlock file handle

Table 14-2 No-Argument `ios` Manipulators

You insert these manipulators directly into the stream. For example, to output `var` in hexadecimal format, you can say

```
cout << hex << var;
```

Table 14-3 summarizes the manipulators that take arguments. You need the IOMANIP.H header file for these functions.

Functions

The `ios` class contains a number of functions that you can use to set the formatting flags and perform other tasks. Table 14-4 shows most of these functions, except those that deal with errors, which we'll examine separately.

These functions are called for specific stream objects using the normal dot operator. For example, to set the field width to 14, you can say

```
cout.width(14);
```

Manipulator	Argument	Purpose
`setw()`	field width (`int`)	Set field width for output
`setfill()`	fill character (`int`)	Set fill character for output (default is a space)
`setprecision()`	precision (`int`)	Set precision (number of digits displayed)
`setiosflags()`	formatting flags (`long`)	Set specified flags
`resetiosflags()`	formatting flags (`long`)	Clear specified flags

Table 14-3 `ios` Manipulators with Arguments

Function	Purpose
`ch = fill();`	Return the fill character (fills unused part of field; default is space)
`fill(ch);`	Set the fill character
`p = precision()`	Get the precision (number of digits displayed for floating-point)
`precision(p);`	Set the precision
`w = width();`	Get the current field width (in characters)
`width(w);`	Set the current field width
`setf(flags);`	Set specified formatting flags (for example, `ios::left`)
`unsetf(flags);`	Unset specified formatting flags
`setf(flags, field);`	First clear field, then set flags

Table 14-4 `ios` Functions

The following statement sets the fill character to an asterisk (as for check printing):

```
cout.fill('*');
```

You can use several functions to manipulate the `ios` formatting flags directly. For example, to set left justification, use

```
cout.setf(ios::left);
```

To restore right justification, use

```
cout.unsetf(ios::left);
```

A two-argument version of `setf()` uses the second argument to reset all the flags of a particular type or *field*. Then the flag specified in the first argument is set. This makes it easier to reset the relevant flags before setting a new one. Table 14-5 shows the arrangement.

For example,

```
cout.setf(ios::left, ios::adjustfield);
```

clears all the flags dealing with text justification and then sets the `left` flag for left-justified output.

First argument: flags to set	Second argument: field to clear
`dec, oct, hex`	`basefield`
`left, right, internal`	`adjustfield`
`scientific, fixed`	`floatfield`

Table 14-5 Two-Argument Version of `setf()`

By using the techniques shown here with the formatting flags, you can usually figure out a way to format I/O not only for the keyboard and display, but, as we'll see later in this chapter, for files as well.

The `istream` Class

The `istream` class, which is derived from `ios`, performs input-specific activities, or *extraction*. It's easy to confuse extraction and the related output activity, *insertion*. Figure 14-2 emphasizes the difference.

Table 14-6 lists the functions you'll most commonly use from the `istream` class.

You've seen some of these functions, such as `get()`, before. Most of them operate on the `cin` object, representing the keyboard, as well as disk files. However, the last four deal specifically with disk files.

The `ostream` Class

The `ostream` class handles output or insertion activities. Table 14-7 shows the most commonly used member functions of this class. The last four functions in this table deal specifically with disk files.

The `iostream` and the `_withassign` Classes

The `iostream` class, which is derived from both `istream` and `ostream`, acts only as a base class from which other classes, specifically `iostream_withassign`, can be derived. It has no functions of its own (except constructors and destructors). Classes derived from `iostream` can perform both input and output.

There are three `_withassign` classes:

- `istream_withassign`, derived from `istream`
- `ostream_withassign`, derived from `ostream`
- `iostream_withassign`, derived from `iostream`

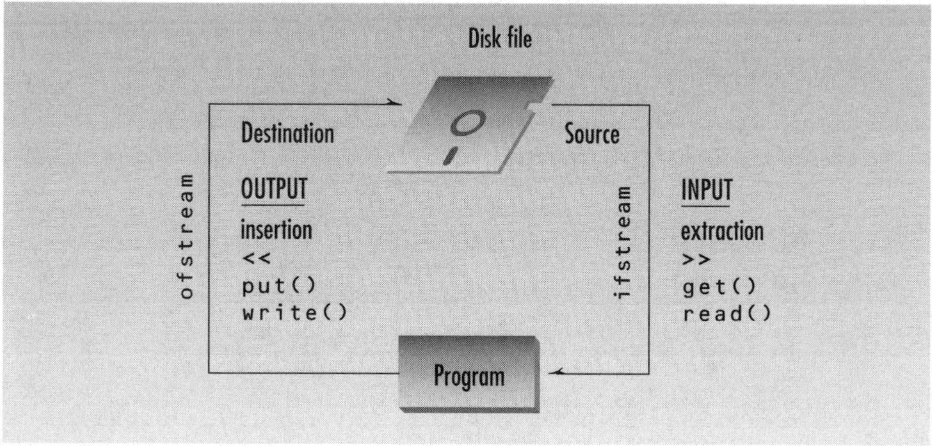

Figure 14-2 File Input and Output

Function	Purpose
`>>`	Formatted extraction for all basic (and overloaded) types
`get(ch);`	Extract one character into `ch`
`get(str)`	Extract characters into array `str`, until `'0'`
`get(str, MAX)`	Extract up to `MAX` characters into array
`get(str, DELIM)`	Extract characters into array `str` until specified delimiter (typically `'\n'`). Leave delimiting char in stream
`get(str, MAX, DELIM)`	Extract characters into array `str` until `MAX` characters or the DELIM character. Leave delimiting char in stream
`getline(str, MAX, DELIM)`	Extract characters into array `str`, until `MAX` characters or the DELIM character. Extract delimiting character
`putback(ch)`	Insert last character read, back into input stream
`ignore(MAX, DELIM)`	Extract and discard up to `MAX` characters until (and including) the specified delimiter (typically `'\n'`)
`peek(ch)`	Read one character, leave it in stream
`count = gcount()`	Return number of characters read by a (immediately preceding) call to `get()`, `getline()`, or `read()`
`read(str, MAX)`	For files. Extract up to `MAX` characters into `str`, until EOF
`seekg()`	Set distance (in bytes) of file pointer from start of file
`seekg(pos, seek_dir)`	Set distance (in bytes) of file pointer from specified place in file. `seek_dir` can be `ios::beg`, `ios::cur`, `ios::end`
`pos = tellg(pos)`	Return position (in bytes) of file pointer from start of file

Table 14-6 `istream` Functions

Function	Purpose
<<	Formatted insertion for all basic (and overloaded) types
`put(ch)`	Insert character `ch` into stream
`flush()`	Flush buffer contents and insert newline
`write(str, SIZE)`	Insert `SIZE` characters from array `str` into file
`seekp(position)`	Set distance in bytes of file pointer from start of file
`seekp(position, seek_dir)`	Set distance in bytes of file pointer, from specified place in file. `seek_dir` can be `ios::beg`, `ios::cur`, or `ios::end`
`pos = tellp()`	Return position of file pointer, in bytes

Table 14-7 `ostream` Functions

These `_withassign` classes are much like those they're derived from except that they include overloaded assignment operators so their objects can be copied.

Why do we need separate copyable and uncopyable stream classes? In general, it's not a good idea to copy stream class objects. The reason is that each such object is associated with a particular `streambuf` object, which includes an area in memory to hold the object's actual data. If you copy the stream object, it causes confusion if you also copy the `streambuf` object. However, in a few cases it's important to be able to copy a stream object, as in the case of redirection of the predefined objects `cout` and `cin`. (We'll discuss redirection later in this chapter.)

Accordingly, the `istream`, `ostream`, and `iostream` classes are made uncopyable (by making their overloaded copy constructors and assignment operators private), while the `_withassign` classes derived from them can be copied.

Predefined Stream Objects

We've already made extensive use of two predefined stream objects that are derived from the `_withassign` classes: `cin` and `cout`. These are normally connected to the keyboard and display, respectively. The two other predefined objects are `cerr` and `clog`.

- `cin`, an object of `istream_withassign`, normally used for keyboard input
- `cout`, an object of `ostream_withassign`, normally used for screen display
- `cerr`, an object of `ostream_withassign`, for error messages
- `clog`, an object of `ostream_withassign`, for log messages

The `cerr` object is often used for error messages and program diagnostics. Output sent to `cerr` is displayed immediately, rather than being buffered, as `cout` is. Also, it cannot be redirected (more on this later). For these reasons you have a better chance of seeing a final output message from `cerr` if your program dies prematurely. Another object, `clog`, is similar to `cerr` in that it is not redirected, but its output is buffered, while `cerr`'s is not.

Stream Errors

So far in this book we've mostly used a rather straightforward approach to input and output, using statements of the form

```
cout << "Good morning";
```

and

```
cin >> var;
```

However, as you may have discovered, this approach assumes that nothing will go wrong during the I/O process. This isn't always the case, especially on input. What happens if a user enters the string "nine" instead of the integer 9, or pushes (ENTER) without entering anything? Or what happens if there's a hardware failure? In this section we'll explore such problems. Many of the techniques we'll see here are applicable to file I/O as well.

Error-Status Bits

The stream error-status bits are an `ios enum` member that reports errors that occurred in an input or output operation. They're summarized in Table 14-8. Figure 14-3 shows how these bits look. Various `ios` functions can be used to read (and even set) these error bits, as shown in Table 14-9.

Inputting Numbers

Let's see how to handle errors when inputting numbers. This approach applies to both numbers read from the keyboard and from disk, as we'll see later. The idea is to check the value of `goodbit`, signal an error if it's not true, and give the user another chance to enter the correct input.

Name	Meaning
`goodbit`	No errors (no bits set, value = 0)
`eofbit`	Reached end of file
`failbit`	Operation failed (user error, premature EOF)
`badbit`	Invalid operation (no associated streambuf)
`hardfail`	Unrecoverable error

Table 14-8 Error-Status Bits

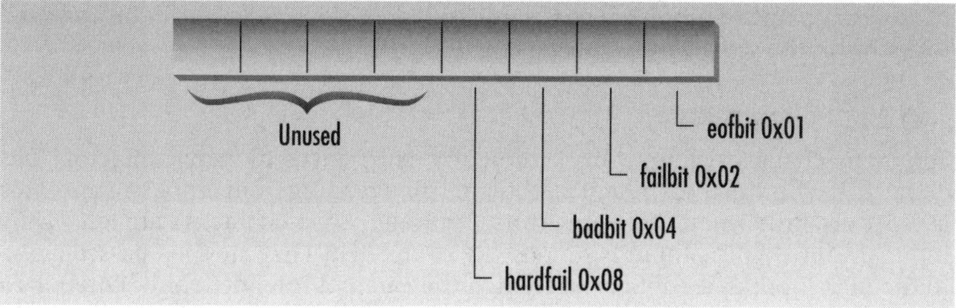

Figure 14-3 Stream Status Bits

Function	Purpose
`int = eof();`	Returns true if EOF bit set
`int = fail();`	Returns true if failbit or badbit or hardfail bit set
`int = bad();`	Returns true if badbit or hardfail bit set
`int = good();`	Returns true if everything OK; no bits set
`clear(int=0);`	With no argument, clears all error bits; otherwise sets specified bits, as in `clear(ios::failbit)`

Table 14-9 Functions for Error Bits

```
while(1)                                // cycle until input OK
   {
   cout << "\nEnter an integer: ";
   cin >> i;
   if( cin.good() )                     // if no errors
      {
      cin.ignore(10, '\n');             // remove newline
      break;                            // exit loop
      }
   cin.clear();                         // clear the error bits
   cout << "Incorrect input";
   cin.ignore(10, '\n');                // remove newline
   }
cout << "integer is " << i;             // error-free integer
```

The most common error this scheme detects when reading keyboard input is the user typing nondigits (like "nine" instead of 9). This causes the `failbit` to be set. However, it also detects system-related failures that are more common with disk files.

Floating-point numbers (`float`, `double`, and `long double`) can be analyzed for errors in the same way as integers.

Too Many Characters

Too many characters sounds like a difficulty experienced by movie directors, but extra characters can also present a problem when reading from input streams. This is especially true when there are errors. Typically, extra characters are left in the input stream after the input is supposedly completed. They are then passed along to the next input operation, even though they are not intended for it. Often it's a newline that remains behind, but sometimes other characters are left over as well. To get rid of these extraneous characters the `ignore(MAX, DELIM)` member function of `istream` is used. It reads and throws away up to `MAX` characters, including the specified delimiter character. In our example, the line

```
cin.ignore(10, '\n');
```

causes `cin` to read up to 10 characters, including the `'\n'`, and remove them from the input.

No-Input Input

Whitespace characters, such as tab space and `'\n'`, are normally ignored (skipped) when inputting numbers. This can have some undesirable side effects. For example, users, prompted to enter a number, may simply press the (ENTER) key without typing any digits. (Perhaps they think that this will enter 0, or perhaps they are simply confused.) In the code shown above, as well as the simple statement

```
cin >> i;
```

pressing (ENTER) causes the cursor to drop down to the next line, while the stream continues to wait for the number. What's wrong with the cursor dropping to the next line? First, inexperienced users, seeing no acknowledgement when they press (ENTER), may assume the computer is broken. Second, pressing (ENTER) repeatedly normally causes the cursor to drop lower and lower until the entire screen begins to scroll upward. This is all right in teletype-style interaction, where the program and the user simply type at each other. However, in text-based graphics programs (such as the CONBOXES program in Chapter 11 or the ELEV program in Chapter 15), scrolling the screen disarranges and eventually obliterates the display.

Thus it's important to be able to tell the input stream *not* to ignore whitespace. This is handled by clearing the `skipws` flag:

```
cout << "\nEnter an integer: ";
cin.unsetf(ios::skipws);          // don't ignore whitespace
cin >> i;
if( cin.good() )
   {
   // no error
   }
// error
```

Now if the user types (ENTER) without any digits, the `failbit` will be set and an error generated. The program can then tell the user what to do, or reposition the cursor so the screen does not scroll.

Inputting Strings and Characters

The user can't really make any mistakes inputting strings and characters, since all input, even numbers, can be interpreted as a string. However, if coming from a disk file, characters and strings should still be checked for errors, in case an EOF or something worse is encountered. Unlike the situation with numbers, you often do want to ignore whitespace when inputting strings and characters.

Error-Free Distances

Let's look at a program in which user input to the English `Distance` class is checked for errors. This program simply accepts `Distance` values in feet and inches from the user and displays them. However, if the user commits an entry error, the program rejects the input with an appropriate explanation to the user, and prompts for new input.

The program is very simple except that the member function `getdist()` has been expanded to handle errors. Parts of this new code follow the approach of the fragment shown above. However, we've also added some statements to ensure that the user does not enter a floating-point number for feet. This is important because, while the feet value is an integer, the inches value is floating-point, and the user could easily become confused.

Ordinarily, if it's expecting an integer, the extraction operator simply terminates when it sees a decimal point, without signalling an error. We want to know about such an error, so we read the feet value as a string instead of an `int`. We then examine the string with a homemade function `isint()`, which returns true if the string proves to be an `int`. To pass the `int` test, it must contain only digits, and they must evaluate to a number between –32,768 and 32,767 (the range of type `int`). If the string passes the `int` test, we convert it to an actual `int` with the library function `atoi()`.

The inches value is a floating-point number. We want to check its range, which should be 0 or greater and less than 12.0. We also check it for `ios` error bits. Most commonly, the `failbit` will be set because the user typed nondigits instead of a number. Here's the listing for ENGLERR:

```
// englerr.cpp
// input checking with English Distance class
#include <iostream.h>
#include <string.h>                    // for strchr()
#include <stdlib.h>                    // for atoi()

int isint(char*);                      // prototype
const int IGN = 10;                    // characters to ignore

class Distance                         // English Distance class
   {
   private:
      int feet;
      float inches;
   public:
      Distance()                       // constructor (no args)
         { feet = 0; inches = 0.0; }
```

(continued on next page)

(continued from previous page)

```
      Distance(int ft, float in)  // constructor (two args)
         { feet = ft; inches = in; }
      void showdist()              // display distance
         { cout << feet << "\'-" << inches << '\"'; }
      void getdist();              // get length from user
   };

void Distance::getdist()           // get length from user
   {
   char instr[80];                 // for input string

   while(1)                        // cycle until feet are right
      {
      cout << "\n\nEnter feet: ";
      cin.unsetf(ios::skipws);     // do not skip whitespace
      cin >> instr;                // get feet as a string
      if( isint(instr) )           // is it an integer?
         {                         // yes
         cin.ignore(IGN, '\n');    // eat chars, including newline
         feet = atoi(instr);       // convert to integer
         break;                    // break out of 'while'
         }                         // no, not an integer
      cin.ignore(IGN, '\n');       // eat chars, including newline
      cout << "Feet must be an integer\n";  // start again
      }  // end while feet

   while(1)                        // cycle until inches are right
      {
      cout << "Enter inches: ";
      cin.unsetf(ios::skipws);     // do not skip whitespace
      cin >> inches;               // get inches (type float)
      if(inches>=12.0 || inches<0.0)
         {
         cout << "Inches must be between 0.0 and 11.99\n";
         cin.clear(ios::failbit); // "artificially" set fail bit
         }
      if( cin.good() )             // check for cin failure
         {                         // (most commonly a non-digit)
         cin.ignore(IGN, '\n');    // eat the newline
         break;                    // input is OK, exit 'while'
         }
      cin.clear();                 // error; clear the error state
      cin.ignore(IGN, '\n');       // eat chars, including newline
      cout << "Incorrect inches input\n";  // start again
      }  // end while inches
   }

int isint(char* str)               // return true if the string
   {                               //    represents type int
   int slen = strlen(str);         // get length
   if( slen==0 || slen > 5)        // if no input, or too long
      return 0;                    // not an int
   for(int j=0; j<slen; j++)       // check each character
                                   // if not digit or minus
```

```
      if( (str[j] < '0' || str[j] > '9') && str[j] != '-' )
         return 0;                    // string is not an int
   long n = atol(str);                // convert to long int
   if( n<-32768L || n>32767L )        // is it out of int range?
      return 0;                       // if so, not an int
   return 1;                          // it is an int
   }

void main()
   {
   Distance d;                        // make a Distance object
   char ans;
   do
      {
      d.getdist();                    // get its value from user
      cout << "\nDistance = ";
      d.showdist();                   // display it
      cout << "\nDo another (y/n)? ";
      cin >> ans;
      cin.ignore(IGN, '\n');          // eat chars, including newline
      } while(ans != 'n');            // cycle until 'n'
   }
```

We've used another dodge here: setting an error-state flag manually. We do this because we want to ensure that the inches value is greater than 0 but less than 12.0. If it isn't, we turn on the `failbit` with the statement

```
cin.clear(ios::failbit);  // set failbit
```

When the program checks for errors with `cin.good()`, it will find the `failbit` set and signal that the input is incorrect.

Disk File I/O with Streams

Most programs need to save data to disk files and read it back in. Working with disk files requires another set of classes: `ifstream` for input, `fstream` for both input and output, and `ofstream` for output. Objects of these classes can be associated with disk files, and we can use their member functions to read and write to the files.

Referring back to Figure 14-1, you can see that `ifstream` is derived from `istream`, `fstream` is derived from `iostream`, and `ofstream` is derived from `ostream`. These ancestor classes are in turn derived from `ios`. Thus the file-oriented classes derive many of their member functions from more general classes. The file-oriented classes are also derived, by multiple inheritance, from the `fstreambase` class. This class contains an object of class `filebuf`, which is a file-oriented buffer and its associated member functions, derived from the more general `streambuf` class. You don't usually need to worry about these buffer classes.

The `ifstream`, `ofstream`, and `fstream` classes are declared in the FSTREAM.H file. This file includes the IOSTREAM.H header file, so there is no need to include it explicitly; FSTREAM.H takes care of all stream I/O.

C programmers will note that the approach to disk I/O used in C++ is quite different from that in C. The old C functions, such as `fread()` and `fwrite()`, will still work in C++, but they are not so well suited to the object-oriented environment. The new C++ approach is considerably cleaner and easier to implement. (Incidentally, be careful about mixing the old C functions with C++ streams. They don't always work together gracefully, although there are ways to make them cooperate.)

Formatted File I/O

In formatted I/O, numbers are stored on disk as a series of characters. Thus 6.02, rather than being stored as a 4-byte type `float` or an 8-byte type `double`, is stored as the characters `'6'`, `'.'`, `'0'`, and `'2'`. This can be inefficient for numbers with many digits, but it's appropriate in many situations and easy to implement. Characters and strings are stored more or less normally.

Writing Data

The following program writes a character, an integer, a type double, and two strings to a disk file. There is no output to the screen. Here's the listing for FORMATO:

```
// formato.cpp
// writes formatted output to a file, using <<

#include <fstream.h>                  // for file I/O

void main()
   {
   char ch = 'x';                     // character
   int j = 77;                        // integer
   double d = 6.02;                   // floating point
   char str1[] = "Kafka";             // strings
   char str2[] = "Proust";            // (no embedded spaces)

   ofstream outfile("fdata.txt"); // create ofstream object

   outfile << ch                      // insert (write) data
           << j
           << ' '                     // needs space between numbers
           << d
           << str1
           << ' '                     // needs space between strings
           << str2;
   }
```

Here we define an object called `outfile` to be a member of the `ofstream` class At the same time, we initialize it to the file FDATA.TXT. This initialization sets aside various resources for the file, and accesses or *opens* the file of that name on the disk. If the file doesn't exist, it is created. If it does exist, it is truncated and the new data replaces the old. The `outfile` object acts much as `cout` did in previous programs, so we can use the insertion operator (`<<`) to output variables of any basic type to the file. This works because the insertion operator is appropriately overloaded in `ostream`, from which `ofstream` is derived.

When the program terminates, the `outfile` object goes out of scope. This calls its destructor, which closes the file, so we don't need to close the file explicitly.

There are several potential formatting glitches. First, you must separate numbers (such as 77 and 6.02) with nonnumeric characters. Since numbers are stored as a sequence of characters, rather than as a fixed-length field, this is the only way the extraction operator will know, when the data is read back from the file, where one number stops and the next one begins. Second, strings must be separated with whitespace for the same reason. This implies that strings cannot contain imbedded blanks. In this example we use the space character (`' '`) for both kinds of delimiters. Characters need no delimiters, since they have a fixed length.

You can verify that FORMATO has indeed written the data by examining the FDATA.TXT file with the WORDPAD accessory or the DOS command TYPE.

Reading Data

We can read the file generated by FERMATO by using an `ifstream` object, initialized to the name of the file. The file is automatically opened when the object is created. We can then read from it using the extraction (`>>`) operator.

Here's the listing for the FORMATI program, which reads the data back in from the FDATA.TXT file:

```
// formati.cpp
// reads formatted output from a file, using >>

#include <fstream.h>
const int MAX = 80;

void main()
   {
   char ch;
   int j;
   double d;
   char str1[MAX];
   char str2[MAX];

   ifstream infile("fdata.txt");      // create ifstream object
                                      // extract (read) data from it
   infile >> ch >> j >> d >> str1 >> str2;

   cout << ch << endl                 // display the data
        << j << endl
        << d << endl
        << str1 << endl
        << str2 << endl;
   }
```

Here the `ifstream` object, which we name `infile`, acts much the way `cin` did in previous programs. Provided that we have formatted the data correctly when inserting it into the file, there's no trouble extracting it, storing it in the appropriate variables, and displaying their contents. The program's output looks like this:

```
x
77
6.02
Kafka
Proust
```

Of course the numbers are converted back to their binary representations for storage in the program. That is, the 77 is stored in the variable `j` as a type `int`, not as two characters; and the 6.02 is stored as a `double`.

Strings with Embedded Blanks

The technique of our last examples won't work with strings containing embedded blanks. To handle such strings, you need to write a specific delimiter character after each one, and use the `getline()` function, rather than the extraction operator, to read them in. Our next program, OLINE, outputs some strings with blanks embedded in them.

```
// oline.cpp
// file output with strings
#include <fstream.h>                    // for file functions

void main()
   {
   ofstream outfile("TEST.TXT");        // create file for output
                                        // send text to file
   outfile << "I fear thee, ancient Mariner!\n";
   outfile << "I fear thy skinny hand\n";
   outfile << "And thou art long, and lank, and brown,\n";
   outfile << "As is the ribbed sea sand.\n";
   }
```

When you run the program, the lines of text (from Samuel Taylor Coleridge's *The Rime of the Ancient Mariner*) are written to a file. Each one is specifically terminated with a newline (`'\n'`) character.

To extract the strings from the file, we create an `ifstream` and read from it one line at a time using the `getline()` function, which is a member of `istream`. This function reads characters, including whitespace, until it encounters the `'\n'` character, and places the resulting string in the buffer supplied as an argument. The maximum size of the buffer is given as the second argument. The contents of the buffer is displayed after each line.

```
// iline.cpp
// file input with strings
#include <fstream.h>                    // for file functions

void main()
   {
   const int MAX = 80;                  // size of buffer
   char buffer[MAX];                    // character buffer
   ifstream infile("TEST.TXT");         // create file for input
   while( infile )                      // until end-of-file
      {
      infile.getline(buffer, MAX);      // read a line of text
      cout << buffer;                   // display it
      }
   }
```

The output of ILINE to the screen is the same as the data written to the TEST.TXT file by OLINE: the four-line Coleridge stanza. The program has no way of knowing in advance how many strings are in the file, so it continues to read one string at a time until it encounters an end-of-file. Incidentally, don't use this program to read random text files. It requires all the text lines to terminate with the `'\n'` character, and if you encounter a file in which this is not the case, the program will hang.

Detecting End-of-File

As we have seen, objects derived from `ios` contain error-status bits that can be checked to determine the results of operations. When we read a file little by little, as we do here, we will eventually encounter an end-of-file (EOF) condition. The EOF is a signal sent to the program from the hardware when there is no more data to read. In ILINE we could have checked for this in the line

```
while( !infile.eof() )    // until eof encountered
```

However, checking specifically for an `eofbit` means that we won't detect the other error bits, such as the `failbit` and `badbit`, which may also occur, although more rarely. To do this, we can change our loop condition:

```
while( infile.good() )    // until any error encountered
```

You can also test the stream directly. Any stream object, such as `infile`, has a value that can be tested for the usual error conditions, including EOF. If any such condition is true, the object returns a zero value. If everything is going well, the object returns a nonzero value. This value is actually a pointer, but the "address" returned has no significance except to be tested for a zero or nonzero value. Thus we can rewrite our `while` loop again:

```
while( infile )           // until any error encountered
```

This is certainly simple, but it may not be quite so clear to the uninitiated what it does.

Character I/O

The `put()` and `get()` functions, which are members of `ostream` and `istream`, respectively, can be used to output and input single characters. Here's a program, OCHAR, that outputs a string, one character at a time:

```
// ochar.cpp
// file output with characters
#include <fstream.h>                    // for file functions
#include <string.h>                     // for strlen()

void main()
   {
   char str[] = "Time is a great teacher, but unfortunately "
                "it kills all its pupils.  Berlioz";

   ofstream outfile("TEST.TXT");        // create file for output
   for(int j=0; j<strlen(str); j++)     // for each character,
      outfile.put(str[j]);              // write it to file
   }
```

In this program an `ofstream` object is created as it was in OLINE. The length of the string is found using the `strlen()` function, and the characters are output using `put()` in a `for` loop. The aphorism by Hector Berlioz (a 19th-century composer of operas and program music) is written to the file TEST.TXT. We can read this file back in and display it using the ICHAR program.

```
// ichar.cpp
// file input with characters
#include <fstream.h>                    // for file functions

void main()
   {
   char ch;                             // character to read
   ifstream infile("TEST.TXT");         // create file for input
   while( infile )                      // read until EOF
      {
      infile.get(ch);                   // read character
      cout << ch;                       // display it
      }
   }
```

This program uses the `get()` function and continues reading until the EOF is reached. Each character read from the file is displayed using `cout`, so the entire aphorism appears on the screen.

Another approach to reading characters from a file is the `rdbuf()` function, a member of the `ios` class. This function returns a pointer to the `streambuf` (or `filebuf`) object associated with the stream object. This object contains a buffer that holds the characters read from the stream, so you can use the pointer to it as a data object in its own right. Here's the listing for ICHAR2:

```
// ichar2.cpp
// file input with characters
#include <fstream.h>                    // for file functions

void main()
   {
   ifstream infile("TEST.TXT");         // create file for input

   cout << infile.rdbuf();              // send its buffer to cout
   }
```

This program has the same effect as ICHAR. It also takes the prize for the shortest file-oriented program. Note that this function knows that it should return when it encounters an EOF.

Binary I/O

You can write a few numbers to disk using formatted I/O, but if you're storing a large amount of numerical data it's more efficient to use binary I/O, in which numbers are stored as they are in the computer's RAM memory, rather than as strings of characters. In binary I/O an integer is always stored in 2 bytes, whereas its text version might be "12345", requiring 5 bytes. Similarly, a `float` is always stored in 4 bytes, while its formatted version might be "6.02314e13", requiring 10 bytes.

Our next example shows how an array of integers is written to disk and then read back into memory, using binary format. We use two new functions: `write()`, a member of `ofstream`; and `read()`, a member of `ifstream`. These functions think about data in terms of bytes (type `char`). They don't care how the data is formatted, they simply transfer a buffer full of bytes from and to a disk file. The parameters to `write()` and `read()` are the address of the data buffer and its length. The address must be cast to type `char`, and the length is the length in bytes (characters), *not* the the number of data items in the buffer. Here's the listing for BINIO:

```
// binio.cpp
// binary input and output with integers

#include <fstream.h>                         // for file streams

const int MAX = 100;                         // number of ints
int buff[MAX];                               // buffer for integers

void main()
   {
   for(int j=0; j<MAX; j++)                  // fill buffer with data
      buff[j] = j;                           // (0, 1, 2, ...)
                                             // create output stream
   ofstream os("edata.dat", ios::binary);
                                             // write to it
   os.write( (char*)buff, MAX*sizeof(int) );
   os.close();                               // must close it

   for(j=0; j<MAX; j++)                      // erase buffer
      buff[j] = 0;
                                             // create input stream
   ifstream is("edata.dat", ios::binary);
                                             // read from it
   is.read( (char*)buff, MAX*sizeof(int) );

   for(j=0; j<MAX; j++)                      // check data
      if( buff[j] != j )
         { cerr << "\nData is incorrect"; return; }
   cout << "\nData is correct";
   }
```

You must use the `ios::binary` argument in the second parameter to `write()` and `read()` when working with binary data. This is because the default, text mode, takes some liberties with the data. For example, in text mode the `'\n'` character is expanded into two bytes—a carriage-return and a linefeed—before being stored to disk. This makes a formatted text file more readable by DOS-based utilities like TYPE, but it causes confusion when it is applied to binary data, since every byte that happens to have the ASCII value 10 is translated into 2 bytes. The `ios::binary` argument is an example of a *mode bit*. We'll say more about this when we discuss the `open()` function later in this chapter.

Closing Files

So far in our example programs there has been no need to close streams explicitly, since they are closed automatically when they go out of scope; this invokes their destructors and closes the associated file. However, in BINIO, since both the output stream `os` and the input stream `is` are associated with the same file, EDATA.DAT, the first stream must be closed before the second is opened. We use the `close()` member function for this.

Object I/O

Since C++ is an object-oriented language, it's reasonable to wonder how objects can be written to and read from disk. The next examples show the process. The `person` class, used in several previous examples (for example, the VIRTPERS program in Chapter 13), supplies the objects.

Writing an Object to Disk

When writing an object we generally want to use binary mode. This writes the same bit configuration to disk that was stored in memory, and ensures that numerical data contained in objects is handled properly. Here's the listing for OPERS, which asks the user for information about an object of class `person`, and then writes this object to the disk file PERSON.DAT:

```
// opers.cpp
// saves person object to disk
#include <fstream.h>                 // for file streams

class person                         // class of persons
   {
   protected:
      char name[40];                 // person's name
      int age;                       // person's age
   public:
      void getData(void)             // get person's data
         {
         cout << "Enter name: "; cin >> name;
         cout << "Enter age: "; cin >> age;
         }
   };

void main(void)
   {
   person pers;                      // create a person
   pers.getData();                   // get data for person
                                     // create ofstream object
   ofstream outfile("PERSON.DAT", ios::binary);
   outfile.write( (char*)&pers, sizeof(pers) );  // write to it
   }
```

The `getData()` member function of `person` is called to prompt the user for information, which it places in the `pers` object. Here's some sample interaction:

```
Enter name: Coleridge
Enter age: 62
```

The contents of the `pers` object are then written to disk, using the `write()` function. We use the `sizeof` operator to find the length of the `pers` object.

Reading an Object from Disk

Reading an object back from the PERSON.DAT file requires the `read()` member function. Here's the listing for IPERS:

```
// ipers.cpp
// reads person object from disk
#include <fstream.h>                  // for file streams

class person                          // class of persons
   {
   protected:
      char name[40];                  // person's name
      int age;                        // person's age
   public:
      void showData(void)             // display person's data
         {
         cout << "\n   Name: " << name;
         cout << "\n   Age: " << age;
         }
   };

void main(void)
   {
   person pers;                       // create person variable
   ifstream infile("PERSON.DAT", ios::binary); // create stream
   infile.read( (char*)&pers, sizeof(pers) );  // read stream
   pers.showData();                            // display person
   }
```

The output from IPERS reflects whatever data the OPERS program placed in the PERSON.DAT file:

```
Name: Coleridge
Age: 62
```

Compatible Data Structures

To work correctly, programs that read and write objects to files, as do OPERS and IPERS, must be talking about the same class of objects. Objects of class `person` in these programs are exactly 42 bytes long, with the first 40 being occupied with a string representing the person's name, and the last 2 containing an `int` representing the person's age. If two programs thought the name field was a different length, for example, neither could accurately read a file generated by the other.

Notice, however, that while the `person` classes in OPERS and IPERS have the same data, they may have different member functions. The first includes the single function `getData()`, while the second has only `showData()`. It doesn't matter what member functions you use, since they are not written to disk along with the object's data. The data must have the same format, but inconsistencies in the member functions have no effect. However, this is true only in simple classes that don't use virtual functions.

If you read and write objects of derived classes to a file, you must be even more careful. Objects of derived classes include a mysterious number placed just before the object's data in memory. This number helps identify the object's class when virtual functions are used. When you write an object to disk, this number is written along with the object's other data. If you change a class's member functions, this number changes as well. If you write an object of one class to a file, and then read it back into an object of a class that has identical data but a different member function, you'll encounter big trouble if you try to use virtual functions on the object. The moral: Make sure a class that reads an object is *identical* to the class that wrote it.

I/O with Multiple Objects

The OPERS and IPERS programs wrote and read only one object at a time. Our next example opens a file and writes as many objects as the user wants. Then it reads and displays the entire contents of the file. Here's the listing for DISKFUN:

```
// diskfun.cpp
// reads and writes several objects to disk
#include <fstream.h>                  // for file streams

class person                          // class of persons
   {
   protected:
      char name[40];                  // person's name
      int age;                        // person's age
   public:
      void getData(void)              // get person's data
         {
         cout << "\n   Enter name: "; cin >> name;
         cout << "   Enter age: "; cin >> age;
         }
      void showData(void)            // display person's data
         {
         cout << "\n   Name: " << name;
         cout << "\n   Age: " << age;
         }
   };

void main(void)
   {
   char ch;
   person pers;                       // create person object
   fstream file;                      // create input/output file
                                      // open for append
   file.open("PERSON.DAT", ios::app | ios::out
                                    | ios::in | ios::binary );

   do                                 // data from user to file
      {
      cout << "\nEnter person's data:";
      pers.getData();                 // get one person's data
```

```
                                       // write to file
      file.write( (char*)&pers, sizeof(pers) );
      cout << "Enter another person (y/n)? ";
      cin >> ch;
      }
   while(ch=='y');                     // quit on 'n'

   file.seekg(0);                      // reset to start of file
                                       // read first person
   file.read( (char*)&pers, sizeof(pers) );
   while( !file.eof() )                // quit on EOF
      {
      cout << "\nPerson:";             // display person
      pers.showData();
      file.read( (char*)&pers, sizeof(pers) );  // read another
      }                                         // person
   }
```

Here's some sample interaction with DISKFUN. The output shown assumes that the program has been run before and that two `person` objects have already been written to the file.

```
Enter person's data:
   Enter name: McKinley
   Enter age: 22
Enter another person (y/n)? n

Person:
   Name: Whitney
   Age: 20
Person:
   Name: Rainier
   Age: 21
Person:
   Name: McKinley
   Age: 22
```

Here one additional object is added to the file, and the entire contents, consisting of three objects, is then displayed.

The `fstream` Class

So far in this chapter the file objects we created were for either input or output. In DISKFUN we want to create a file that can be used for both input and output. This requires an object of the `fstream` class, which is derived from `iostream`, which is derived from both `istream` and `ostream` so it can handle both input and output.

The `open()` Function

In previous examples we created a file object and initialized it in the same statement:

```
ofstream outfile("TEST.TXT");
```

In DISKFUN we use a different approach: We create the file in one statement and open it in another, using the `open()` function, which is a member of the `fstream`

Mode bit	Result
`in`	Open for reading (default for `ifstream`)
`out`	Open for writing (default for `ofstream`)
`ate`	Start reading or writing at end of file (`AT End`)
`app`	Start writing at end of file (`APPend`)
`trunc`	Truncate file to zero length if it exists (`TRUNCate`)
`nocreate`	Error when opening if file does not already exist
`noreplace`	Error when opening for output if file already exists, unless `ate` or `app` is set
`binary`	Open file in binary (not text) mode

Table 14-10 Mode Bits for `open()` Function

class. This is a useful approach in situations where the open may fail. You can create a stream object once, and then try repeatedly to open it, without the overhead of creating a new stream object each time.

The Mode Bits

We've seen the mode bit `ios::binary` before. In the `open()` function we include several new mode bits. The mode bits, defined in `ios`, specify various aspects of how a stream object will be opened. Table 14-10 shows the possibilities.

In DISKFUN we use `app` because we want to preserve whatever was in the file before. That is, we can write to the file, terminate the program, and start up the program again, and whatever we write to the file will be added following the existing contents. We use `in` and `out` because we want to perform both input and output on the file, and we use `binary` because we're writing binary objects. The vertical bars between the flags cause the bits representing these flags to be ORed together into a single integer, so that several flags can apply simultaneously.

We write one `person` object at a time to the file, using the `write()` function. When we've finished writing, we want to read the entire file. Before doing this we must reset the file's current position. We do this with the `seekg()` function, which we'll examine in the next section. It ensures we'll start reading at the beginning of the file. Then, in a `while` loop, we repeatedly read a `person` object from the file and display it on the screen.

This continues until we've read all the `person` objects—a state that we discover using the `eof()` function, which returns the state of the `ios::eofbit`.

File Pointers

Each file object has associated with it two integer values called the *get pointer* and the *put pointer*. These are also called the *current get position* and the *current put position*, or—if it's clear which one is meant—simply the *current position*. These values specify the byte number in the file where writing or reading will take place. (The term *pointer* in this context should not be confused with normal C++ pointers used as address variables.)

Often you want to start reading an existing file at the beginning and continue until the end. When writing, you may want to start at the beginning, deleting any existing contents, or at the end, in which case you can open the file with the `ios::app` mode specifier. These are the default actions, so no manipulation of the file pointers is necessary. However, there are times when you must take control of the file pointers yourself so that you can read from and write to an arbitrary location in the file. The `seekg()` and `tellg()` functions allow you to set and examine the get pointer, and the `seekp()` and `tellp()` functions perform these same actions on the put pointer.

Specifying the Position

We saw an example of positioning the get pointer in the DISKFUN program, where the `seekg()` function set it to the beginning of the file so that reading would start there. This form of `seekg()` takes one argument, which represents the absolute position in the file. The start of the file is byte 0, so that's what we used in DISKFUN. Figure 14-4 shows how this looks.

Specifying the Offset

The `seekg()` function can be used in two ways. We've seen the first, where the single argument represents the position from the start of the file. You can also use it with two arguments, where the first argument represents an offset from a particular location in the file, and the second specifies the location from which the offset is measured. There are three possibilities for the second argument: `beg` is the beginning of the file, `cur` is the current pointer position, and `end` is the end of the file. The statement

```
seekp(-10, ios::end);
```

for example, will set the put pointer to 10 bytes before the end of the file. Figure 14-5 shows how this looks.

Here's an example that uses the two-argument version of `seekg()` to find a particular `person` object in the PERSON.DAT file already created with DISKFUN, and to display the data for that particular person. Here's the listing for SEEKG:

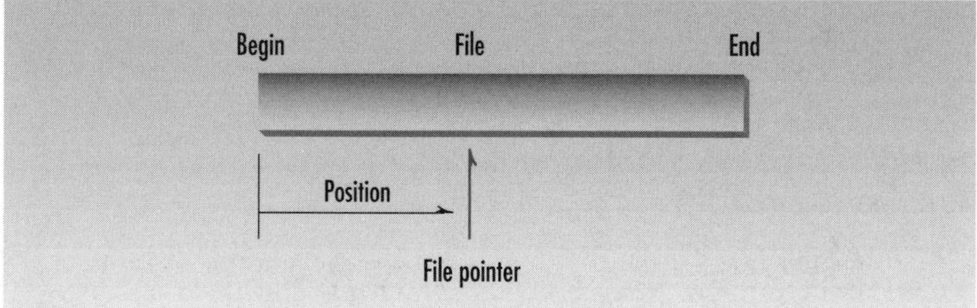

Figure 14-4 The `seekg()` Function with One Argument

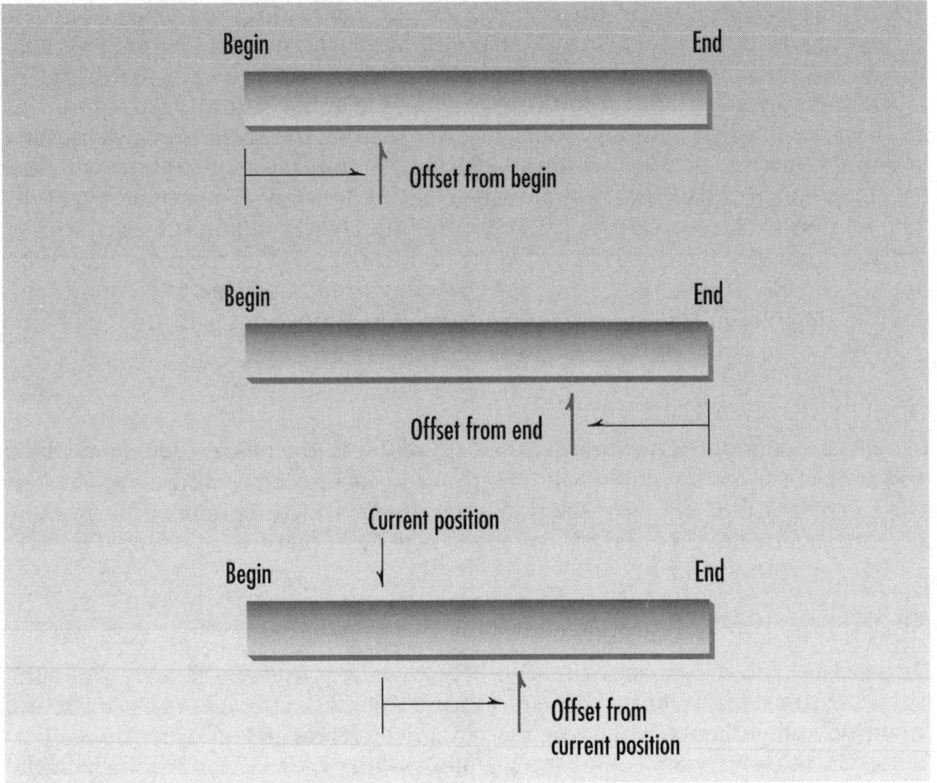

Figure 14-5 The `seekg()` Function with Two Arguments

```
// seekg.cpp
// seeks particular person in file
#include <fstream.h>                  // for file streams
class person                          // class of persons
   {
   protected:
      char name[40];                  // person's name
      int age;                        // person's age
   public:
      void showData(void)             // display person's data
         {
         cout << "\n   Name: " << name;
         cout << "\n   Age: " << age;
         }
   };

void main(void)
   {
   person pers;                       // create person object
   ifstream infile;                   // create input file
   infile.open("PERSON.DAT", ios::binary); // open file
```

```
infile.seekg(0, ios::end);       // go to 0 bytes from end
int endposition = infile.tellg();        // find where we are
int n = endposition / sizeof(person);    // number of persons
cout << "\nThere are " << n << " persons in file";

cout << "\nEnter person number: ";
cin >> n;
int position = (n-1) * sizeof(person);   // number times size
infile.seekg(position);          // bytes from begin
                                 // read one person
infile.read( (char*)&pers, sizeof(pers) );
pers.showData();                 // display the person
}
```

Here's the output from the program, assuming that the PERSON.DAT file is the same as that just accessed in the DISKFUN example:

```
There are 3 persons in file
Enter person number: 2

   Name: Rainier
   Age: 21
```

For the user, we number the items starting at 1, although the program starts numbering at 0; so person 2 is the second person of the three in the file.

The `tellg()` Function

The first thing the program does is figure out how many persons are in the file. It does this by positioning the get pointer at the end of the file with the statement

```
infile.seekg(0, ios::end);
```

The `tellg()` function returns the current position of the get pointer. The program uses this function to return the pointer position at the end of the file; this is the length of the file in bytes. Next, the program calculates how many `person` objects there are in the file by dividing by the size of a `person`; it then displays the result.

In the output shown, the user specifies the second object in the file, and the program calculates how many bytes into the file this is, using `seekg()`. It then uses `read()` to read one `person`'s worth of data starting from that point. Finally, it displays the data with `showData()`.

Error Handling in File I/O

In the file-related examples so far we have not concerned ourselves with error situations. In particular, we have assumed that the files we opened for reading already existed, and that those opened for writing could be created or appended to. We've also assumed that there were no failures during reading or writing. In a real program it is important to verify such assumptions and take appropriate action if they turn out to be incorrect. A file that you think exists may not, or a filename that you assume you can use for a new file may already apply to an existing file. Or, there may be no more room on the disk, a diskette drive door may be open, and so on.

Reacting to Errors

Our next program shows how such errors are most conveniently handled. All disk operations are checked after they are performed. If an error has occurred, a message is printed and the program terminates. We've used the technique, discussed earlier, of checking the return value from the object itself to determine its error status. The program opens an output stream object, writes an entire array of integers to it with a single call to `write()`, and closes the object. Then it opens an input stream object and reads the array of integers with a call to `read()`.

```
// rewerr.cpp
// handles errors during input and output

#include <fstream.h>        // for file streams
#include <process.h>        // for exit()

const int MAX = 1000;
int buff[MAX];

void main()
   {
   for(int j=0; j<MAX; j++)                 // fill buffer with data
      buff[j] = j;

   ofstream os;                             // create output stream
                                            // open it
   os.open("a:edata.dat", ios::trunc | ios::binary);
   if(!os)
      { cerr << "\nCould not open output file"; exit(1); }

   cout << "\nWriting...";                  // write buffer to it
   os.write( (char*)buff, MAX*sizeof(int) );
   if(!os)
      { cerr << "\nCould not write to file"; exit(1); }
   os.close();                              // must close it

   for(j=0; j<MAX; j++)                     // clear buffer
      buff[j] = 0;

   ifstream is;                             // create input stream
   is.open("a:edata.dat", ios::binary);
   if(!is)
      { cerr << "\nCould not open input file"; exit(1); }

   cout << "\nReading...";                  // read file
   is.read( (char*)buff, MAX*sizeof(int) );
   if(!is)
      { cerr << "\nCould not read from file"; exit(1); }

   for(j=0; j<MAX; j++)                     // check data
      if( buff[j] != j )
         { cerr << "\nData is incorrect"; exit(1); }
   cout << "\nData is correct";
   }
```

Analyzing Errors

In the REWERR example we determined whether an error occurred in an I/O operation by examining the return value of the entire stream object.

```
if(!is)
   // error occurred
```

Here `is` returns a pointer value if everything went well, but 0 if it didn't. This is the shotgun approach to errors: No matter what the error is, it's detected in the same way and the same action is taken. However, it's also possible, using the `ios` error-status bits, to find out more specific information about a file I/O error. We've already seen some of these status bits at work in screen and keyboard I/O. Our next example, FERRORS, shows how they can be used in file I/O.

```
// ferrors.cpp
// checks for errors opening file
#include <fstream.h>            // for file functions

void main()
   {
   ifstream file;
   file.open("GROUP.DAT", ios::nocreate);

   if( !file )
      cout << "\nCan't open GROUP.DAT";
   else
      cout << "\nFile opened successfully.";
   cout << "\nfile = " << file;
   cout << "\nError state = " << file.rdstate();
   cout << "\ngood() = " << file.good();
   cout << "\neof() = " << file.eof();
   cout << "\nfail() = " << file.fail();
   cout << "\nbad() = " << file.bad();
   file.close();
   }
```

This program first checks the value of the object `file`. If its value is zero, then probably the file could not be opened because it didn't exist. Here's the output from FERRORS when that's the case:

```
Can't open GROUP.DAT
file = 0x1c730000
Error state = 4
good() = 0
eof() = 0
fail() = 4
bad() = 4
```

The error state returned by `rdstate()` is 4. This is the bit that indicates that the file doesn't exist; it's set to 1. The other bits are all set to 0. The `good()` function returns 1 (true) only when no bits are set, so it returns 0 (false). We're not at EOF, so `eof()` returns 0. The `fail()` and `bad()` functions return nonzero, since an error occurred.

In a serious program some or all of these functions should be used after every I/O operation to ensure that things went as expected.

File I/O with Member Functions

So far we've let the `main()` function handle the details of file I/O. When you use more sophisticated classes it's natural to include file I/O operations as member functions of the class. In this section we'll show two programs that do this. The first uses ordinary member functions in which each object is responsible for reading and writing itself to a file. The second shows how static member functions can read and write all the objects of a class at once.

Objects That Read and Write Themselves

Sometimes it makes sense to let each member of a class read and write itself to a file. This is a simple approach, and works well if there aren't many objects to be read or written at once. In this example we add member functions—`diskOut()` and `diskIn()`—to the `person` class. These functions allow a `person` object to write itself to disk and read itself back in.

We've made some simplifying assumptions. First, all objects of the class will be stored in the same file, called PERSON.DAT. Second, new objects are always appended to the end of the file. An argument to the `diskIn()` function allows us to read the data for any person in the file. To prevent an attempt to read data beyond the end of the file, we include a static member function, `diskCount()`, that returns the number of persons stored in the file. Here's the listing for REWOBJ:

```
// rewobj.cpp
// person objects do disk I/O
#include <fstream.h>                  // for file streams

class person                          // class of persons
   {
   protected:
      char name[40];                  // person's name
      int age;                        // person's age
   public:
      void getData(void)              // get person's data
         {
         cout << "\n   Enter name: "; cin >> name;
         cout << "   Enter age: "; cin >> age;
         }
      void showData(void)             // display person's data
         {
         cout << "\n   Name: " << name;
         cout << "\n   Age: " << age;
         }
      void diskIn(int);               // read from file
      void diskOut();                 // write to file
      static int diskCount();         // return number of
                                      //    persons in file
   };

void person::diskIn(int pn)           // read person number pn
   {                                  // from file
   ifstream infile;                           // make stream
   infile.open("PERSON.DAT", ios::binary);    // open it
```

```
   infile.seekg( pn*sizeof(person) );          // move file ptr
   infile.read( (char*)this, sizeof(*this) ); // read one person
   }

void person::diskOut()                 // write person to end of file
   {
   ofstream outfile;                   // make stream
                                       // open it
   outfile.open("PERSON.DAT", ios::app | ios::binary);
   outfile.write( (char*)this, sizeof(*this) ); // write to it
   }

int person::diskCount()                // return number of persons
   {                                   // in file
   ifstream infile;
   infile.open("PERSON.DAT", ios::binary);
   infile.seekg(0, ios::end);     // go to 0 bytes from end
                                       // calculate number of persons
   return infile.tellg() / sizeof(person);
   }

void main(void)
   {
   person p;                           // make an empty person
   char ch;

   do                                  // save persons to disk
      {
      cout << "\nEnter data for person:";
      p.getData();                     // get data
      p.diskOut();                     // write to disk
      cout << "Do another (y/n)? ";
      cin >> ch;
      }
   while(ch=='y');                     // until user enters 'n'

   int n = person::diskCount();   // how many persons in file?
   cout << "\nThere are " << n << " persons in file";
   for(int j=0; j<n; j++)              // for each one,
      {
      cout << "\nPerson #" << j;
      p.diskIn(j);                     // read person from disk
      p.showData();                    // display person
      }
   }
```

There shouldn't be too many surprises here; you've seen most of the elements of this program before. It operates in the same way as the DISKFUN program. Notice, however, that all the details of disk operation are invisible to `main()`, having been hidden away in the `person` class.

We don't know in advance where the data is that we're going to read and write, since each object is in a different place in memory. However, the `this` pointer always tells us where we are when we're in a member function. In the `read()` and `write()` stream functions, the address of the object to be read or written is `this` and its size is `sizeof(*this)`.

Here's some output, assuming there were already two persons in the file when the program was started:

```
Enter data for person:
   Enter name: Acheson
   Enter age: 63
Enter another (y/n)? y

Enter data for person:
   Enter name: Dulles
   Enter age: 72
Enter another (y/n)? n

Person #1
   Name: Stimson
   Age: 45
Person #2
   Name: Hull
   Age: 58
Person #3
   Name: Acheson
   Age: 63
Person #4
   Name: Dulles
   Age: 72
```

If you want the user to be able to specify the filename used by the class, instead of hardwiring it into the member functions as we do here, you could create a static member variable (say `char fileName[]`) and a static function to set it. Or, you might want to give each object the name of the file it was associated with, using a nonstatic function.

Classes That Read and Write Themselves

Let's assume you have many objects in memory, and you want to write them all to a file. It's not efficient to have a member function for each object open the file, write one object to it, and then close it, as in the REWOBJ example. It's much faster—and the more objects there are the truer this is—to open the file once, write all the objects to it, and then close it.

Static Functions

One way to write many objects at once is to use a static member function, which applies to the class as a whole rather than to each object. This function can write all the objects at once. How will such a function know where all the objects are? It can access an array of pointers to the objects, which can be stored as static data. As each object is created, a pointer to it is stored in this array. A static data member also keeps track of how many objects have been created. The static write function can open the file; then in a loop go through the array, writing each object in turn; and finally close the file.

Size of Derived Objects

To make things really interesting, let's make a further assumption: that the objects stored in memory are different sizes. Why would this be true? This situation typically arises when several classes are derived from a base class. For example, consider the EMPLOY program in Chapter 10. Here we have an **employee** class that acts as a base class for the **manager**, **scientist**, and **laborer** classes. Objects of these three derived classes are different sizes, since they contain different amounts of data. Specifically, in addition to the name and employee number, which apply to all employees, there are a title and golf-club dues for the manager and the number of publications for the scientist.

We would like to write the data from a list containing all three types of derived objects (**manager**, **scientist**, and **laborer**) using a simple loop and the **write()** member function of **ofstream**. But to use this function we need to know how large the object is, since that's its second argument.

Suppose we have an array of pointers (call it **arrap[]**) to objects of type **employee**. These pointers can point to objects of the three derived classes. (See the VIRTPERS program in Chapter 13 for an example of an array of pointers to objects of derived classes.) We know that if we're using virtual functions we can make statements like

```
arrap[j]->putdata();
```

The version of the **putdata()** function that matches the object pointed to by the pointer will be used, rather than the function in the base class. But can we also use the **sizeof()** function to return the size of a pointer argument? That is, can we say

```
ouf.write( (char*)arrap[j], sizeof(*arrap[j]) );    // no good
```

No, because **sizeof()** isn't a virtual function. It doesn't know that it needs to consider the type of object pointed to, rather than the type of the pointer. It will always return the size of a base class object.

Using the **typeid()** Function

How can we find the size of an object, if all we have is a pointer to it? One answer to this is the **typeid()** function, introduced in Chapter 13. We can use this function to find the class of an object, and use this class name in **sizeof()**. Our next example shows how this works. Once we know the size of the object, we can use it in the **write()** function to write the object to disk.

We've added a simple user interface to the EMPLOY program, and made the member-specific functions virtual so we can use an array of pointers to objects. We've also incorporated some of the error-detection techniques discussed in the last section.

This is a rather ambitious program, but it demonstrates many of the techniques that could be used in a full-scale database application. It also shows the real power of OOP. How else could you use a single statement to write objects of different sizes to a file? Here's the listing for EMPL_IO:

```
// empl_io.cpp
// performs file I/O on employee objects
// handles different sized objects

#include <fstream.h>              // for file-stream functios
#include <conio.h>                // for getche()
#include <process.h>              // for exit()
```

(continued on next page)

(continued from previous page)

```
#include <typeinfo.h>              // for typeid()

const int LEN = 32;                // maximum length of last names
const int MAXEM = 100;             // maximum number of employees

enum employee_type {tmanager, tscientist, tlaborer};

class employee                     // employee class
   {
   private:
      char name[LEN];              // employee name
      unsigned long number;        // employee number
      static int n;                // current number of employees
      static employee* arrap[];  // array of ptrs to emps
   public:
      virtual void getdata()
         {
         cout << "\n   Enter last name: "; cin >> name;
         cout << "   Enter number: ";      cin >> number;
         }
      virtual void putdata()
         {
         cout << "\n   Name: " << name;
         cout << "\n   Number: " << number;
         }
      virtual employee_type get_type();  // get type
      static void add();           // add an employee
      static void display();  // display all employees
      static void read();          // read from disk file
      static void write();         // write to disk file
   };

// static variables
int employee::n;                   // current number of employees
employee* employee::arrap[MAXEM];  // array of ptrs to emps

// manager class
class manager : public employee
   {
   private:
      char title[LEN];             // "vice-president" etc.
      double dues;                 // golf club dues
   public:
      void getdata()
         {
         employee::getdata();
         cout << "   Enter title: ";          cin >> title;
         cout << "   Enter golf club dues: "; cin >> dues;
         }
      void putdata()
         {
         employee::putdata();
         cout << "\n   Title: " << title;
         cout << "\n   Golf club dues: " << dues;
         }
   };
```

```
// scientist class
class scientist : public employee
   {
   private:
      int pubs;                  // number of publications
   public:
      void getdata()
         {
         employee::getdata();
         cout << "   Enter number of pubs: "; cin >> pubs;
         }
      void putdata()
         {
         employee::putdata();
         cout << "\n   Number of publications: " << pubs;
         }
   };

// laborer class
class laborer : public employee
   {
   };

// add employee to list in memory
void employee::add()
   {
   cout << "\n'm' to add a manager"
           "\n's' to add a scientist"
           "\n'l' to add a laborer"
           "\nType selection: ";
   switch( getche() )
      {                          // create specified employee type
      case 'm': arrap[n] = new manager;   break;
      case 's': arrap[n] = new scientist; break;
      case 'l': arrap[n] = new laborer;   break;
      default: cout << "\nUnknown employee type"; return;
      }
   arrap[n++]->getdata();     // get employee data from user
   }

// display all employees
void employee::display()
   {
   for(int j=0; j<n; j++)
      {
      cout << '\n' << (j+1);  // display number
      switch( arrap[j]->get_type() )    // display type
         {
         case tmanager:    cout << ". Type: Manager";   break;
         case tscientist:  cout << ". Type: Scientist"; break;
         case tlaborer:    cout << ". Type: Laborer";   break;
         default: cout << ". Unknown type"; return;
         }
      arrap[j]->putdata();    // display employee data
      }
```

(continued on next page)

(continued from previous page)

```
   }
// return the type of this object
employee_type employee::get_type()
   {
   if( typeid(*this) == typeid(manager) )
      return tmanager;
   else if( typeid(*this)==typeid(scientist) )
      return tscientist;
   else if( typeid(*this)==typeid(laborer) )
      return tlaborer;
   else
      { cout << "\nBad employee type"; exit(1); }
   return tmanager;
   }

// write all current memory objects file
void employee::write()
   {
   int size;
   cout << "\nWriting " << n << " employees.";
   ofstream ouf;                  // open ofstream in binary
   employee_type etype;           // type of each employee object

   ouf.open("EMPLOY.DAT", ios::trunc | ios::binary);
   if(!ouf)
      { cout << "\nCan't open file"; return; }
   for(int j=0; j<n; j++)         // for every employee object
      {                           // get it's type
      etype = arrap[j]->get_type();
                                  // write type to file
      ouf.write( (char*)&etype, sizeof(etype) );
      switch(etype)               // find its size
         {
         case tmanager:   size=sizeof(manager); break;
         case tscientist: size=sizeof(scientist); break;
         case tlaborer:   size=sizeof(laborer); break;
         }                        // write employee object to file
      ouf.write( (char*)(arrap[j]), size );
      if(!ouf)
         { cout << "\nCan't write to file"; return; }
      }
   }

// read data for all employees from file into memory
void employee::read()
   {
   int size;                      // size of employee object
   employee_type etype;           // type of employee
   ifstream inf;                  // open ifstream in binary
   inf.open("EMPLOY.DAT", ios::binary);
   if(!inf)
      { cout << "\nCan't open file"; return; }
   n = 0;                         // no employees in memory yet
   while(1)
```

```
      {                          // read type of next employee
      inf.read( (char*)&etype, sizeof(etype) );
      if( inf.eof() )            // quit loop on eof
         break;
      if(!inf)                   // error reading type
         { cout << "\nCan't read type from file"; return; }
      switch(etype)
         {                       // make new employee
         case tmanager:          // of correct type
            arrap[n] = new manager;
            size=sizeof(manager);
            break;
         case tscientist:
            arrap[n] = new scientist;
            size=sizeof(scientist);
            break;
         case tlaborer:
            arrap[n] = new laborer;
            size=sizeof(laborer);
            break;
         default: cout << "\nUnknown type in file"; return;
         }                       // read data from file into it
      inf.read( (char*)arrap[n], size  );
      if(!inf)                   // error but not eof
         { cout << "\nCan't read data from file"; return; }
      n++;                       // count employee
      }  // end while
   cout << "\nReading " << n << " employees";
   }
void main()
   {
   while(1)
      {
      cout << "\n'a' -- add data for an employee"
              "\n'd' -- display data for all employees"
              "\n'w' -- write all employee data to file"
              "\n'r' -- read all employee data from file"
              "\n'x' -- exit"
              "\nType selection: ";
      switch( getche() )
         {
         case 'a':               // add an employee to list
            employee::add();
            break;
         case 'd':               // display all employees
            employee::display();
            break;
         case 'w':               // write employees to file
            employee::write();
            break;
         case 'r':               // read all employees from file
            employee::read();
            break;
         case 'x':               // exit program
```

(continued on next page)

(continued from previous page)

```
            return;
        default: cout << "\nUnknown command";
        }
    }  // end while
}
```

Code Number for Object Type

We know how to find the class of an object that's in memory, but how do we know the class of the object whose data we're about to read from the disk? There's no magic function to help us with this one. When we write an object's data to disk, we need to write a code number (the `enum` variable `employee_type`) directly to the disk just before the object's data. Then when we are about to read an object back from the file to memory, we read this value and create a new object of the type indicated. Finally we copy the data from the file into this new object.

No Homemade Objects, Please

Incidentally, you might be tempted to read an object's data into just any place, say into an array of type `char`, and then set a pointer-to-object to point to this area, perhaps with a cast to make it kosher.

```
char someArray[MAX];
aClass* aPtr_to_Obj;
aPtr_to_Obj = (aClass*)someArray;   // don't do this
```

However, this does not create an object, and attempts to use the pointer as if it pointed to an object will lead to trouble. There are only two legitimate ways to create an object. You can define it explicitly at compile time:

```
aClass anObj;
```

or you can create it with `new` at runtime, and assign its location to a pointer:

```
aPtr_to_Obj = new aClass;
```

When you create an object properly its constructor is invoked. This is necessary even if you have not defined a constructor and are using the default constructor. An object is more than an area of memory with data in it; it is also a set of member functions, some of which you don't even see.

Interaction with EMPL_IO

Here's some sample interaction with the program, in which we create a manager, a scientist, and a laborer in memory, write them to disk, read them back in, and display them. (For simplicity, multiword names and titles are not allowed; say VicePresident, not Vice President.)

```
'a' -- add data for an employee
'd' -- display data for all employees
'w' -- write all employee data to file
'r' -- read all employee data from file
'x' -- exit
Type selection: a
'm' to add a manager
's' to add a scientist
```

```
'l' to add a laborer
Type selection: m
   Enter last name: Johnson
   Enter number: 1111
   Enter title: President
   Enter golf club dues: 20000

'a' -- add data for an employee
'd' -- display data for all employees
'w' -- write all employee data to file
'r' -- read all employee data from file
'x' -- exit
Type selection: a
'm' to add a manager
's' to add a scientist
'l' to add a laborer
Type selection: s
   Enter last name: Faraday
   Enter number: 2222
   Enter number of pubs: 99

'a' -- add data for an employee
'd' -- display data for all employees
'w' -- write all employee data to file
'r' -- read all employee data from file
'x' -- exit
Type selection: a
'm' to add a manager
's' to add a scientist
'l' to add a laborer
Type selection: l
   Enter last name: Smith
   Enter number: 3333

'a' -- add data for an employee
'd' -- display data for all employees
'w' -- write all employee data to file
'r' -- read all employee data from file
'x' -- exit
Type selection: w
Writing 3 employees

'a' -- add data for an employee
'd' -- display data for all employees
'w' -- write all employee data to file
'r' -- read all employee data from file
'x' -- exit
Type selection: r
Reading 3 employees

'a' -- add data for an employee
'd' -- display data for all employees
'w' -- write all employee data to file
'r' -- read all employee data from file
```

(continued on next page)

(continued from previous page)
```
'x' -- exit
Type selection: d
1. Type: Manager
   Name: Johnson
   Title: President
   Golf club dues: 20000
2. Type: Scientist
   Name: Faraday
   Number: 2222
   Number of publications: 99
3. Type: Laborer
   Name: Smith
   Number: 3333
```

Of course you can also exit the program after writing the data to disk. When you start it up again, you can read the file back in and all the data will reappear.

It would be easy to add functions to this program to delete an employee, retrieve data for a single employee from the file, search the file for employees with particular characteristics, and so forth.

Overloading the Extraction and Insertion Operators

Let's move on to another stream-related topic: overloading the extraction and insertion operators. This is a powerful feature of C++. It lets you treat I/O for user-defined data types in the same way as basic types like `int` and `double`. For example, if you have an object of class `crawdad` called `cd1`, you can display it with the statement

```
cout << "\ncd1=" << cd1;
```

just as if it were a basic data type.

We can overload the extraction and insertion operators so they work with the display and keyboard (`cout` and `cin`) alone. With a little more care, we can also overload them so they work with disk files as well. We'll look at examples of both these situations.

Overloading for `cout` and `cin`

Here's an example, ENGLIO, that overloads the insertion and extraction operators for the `Distance` class so they work with `cout` and `cin`.

```
// englio.cpp
// overloaded << and >> operators
#include <iostream.h>

class Distance                              // English Distance class
   {
   private:
      int feet;
      float inches;
   public:
      Distance()                            // constructor (no args)
         { feet = 0; inches = 0.0; }
```

```
      Distance(int ft, float in)           // constructor (two args)
         { feet = ft; inches = in; }
      friend istream& operator >> (istream& s, Distance& d);
      friend ostream& operator << (ostream& s, Distance& d);
   };

istream& operator >> (istream& s, Distance& d)  // get Distance
   {                                            // from user
   cout << "\nEnter feet: ";  s >> d.feet;      // using
   cout << "Enter inches: ";  s >> d.inches;    // overloaded
   return s;                                    // >> operator
   }

ostream& operator << (ostream& s, Distance& d)  // display
   {                                            // Distance
   s << d.feet << "\'-" << d.inches << '\"';    // using
   return s;                                    // overloaded
   }                                            // << operator

void main()
   {
   Distance dist1, dist2;            // define Distances
   cout << "\nEnter two Distance values:";
   cin >> dist1 >> dist2;            // get values from user

   Distance dist3(11, 6.25);         // define, initialize dist3

                                     // display distances
   cout << "\ndist1 = " << dist1 << "\ndist2 = " << dist2;
   cout << "\ndist3 = " << dist3;
   }
```

This program asks for two distance values from the user, and then prints out these values and another value that was initialized in the program. Here's a sample interaction:

```
Enter feet: 10
Enter inches: 3.5

Enter feet: 12
Enter inches: 6

dist1 = 10'-3.5"
dist2 = 12'-6"
dist3 = 11'-6.25"
```

Notice how convenient and natural it is to treat `Distance` objects like any other data type, using statements like

```
cin >> dist1 >> dist2;
```

and

```
cout << "\ndist1=" << dist1 << "\ndist2=" << dist2;
```

The << and >> operators are overloaded in similar ways. They return, by reference, an object of `istream` (for >>) or `ostream` (for <<). These return values permits chaining. The operators take two arguments, both passed by reference. The first argument for >> is an object of `istream` (such as `cin`). For << it's an object of `ostream` (such as `cout`). The second argument is an object of the class to be displayed, `Distance` in this example. The >> operator takes input from the stream specified in the first argument and puts it in the member data of the object specified by the second argument. The << operator removes the data from the object specified by the second argument and sends it into the stream specified by the first argument.

The `operator<<()` and `operator>>()` functions must be `friends` of the `Distance` class, since the `istream` and `ostream` objects appear on the left side of the operator. (See the discussion of `friend` functions in Chapter 13.)

You can overload the insertion and extraction operators for other classes by following these same steps.

Overloading for Files

Our next example shows how we might overload the << and >> operators in the `Distance` class so they work with file I/O as well as with `cout` and `cin`.

```
// englio2.cpp
// overloaded << and >> operators can work with files
#include <fstream.h>

class Distance                                // English Distance class
   {
   private:
      int feet;
      float inches;
   public:
      Distance()                              // constructor (no args)
         { feet = 0; inches = 0.0; }
      Distance(int ft, float in)              // constructor (two args)
         { feet = ft; inches = in; }
      friend istream& operator >> (istream& s, Distance& d);
      friend ostream& operator << (ostream& s, Distance& d);
   };

istream& operator >> (istream& s, Distance& d)   // get Distance
   {                                             // from file or
   char dummy;  // for ('), (-), and (")         // keyboard
                                                 // with
   s >> d.feet >> dummy >> dummy >> d.inches >> dummy;
   return s;                                     // overloaded
   }                                             // >> operator

ostream& operator << (ostream& s, Distance& d)   // send Distance
   {                                             // to file or
   s << d.feet << "\'-" << d.inches << '\"';     // screen with
   return s;                                     // overloaded
```

```
   }                                              // << operator

void main()
   {
   char ch;
   Distance dist1;
   ofstream ofile;                           // create and open
   ofile.open("DIST.DAT");                   // output stream

   do
      {
      cout << "\nEnter Distance: ";
      cin >> dist1;                          // get distance from user
      ofile << dist1;                        // write it to output str
      cout << "Do another (y/n)? ";
      cin >> ch;
      }
   while(ch != 'n');
   ofile.close();                            // close output stream

   ifstream ifile;                           // create and open
   ifile.open("DIST.DAT");                   // input stream

   cout << "\nContents of disk file is:";
   while(1)
      {
      ifile >> dist1;                        // read dist from stream
      if( ifile.eof() )                      // quit on EOF
         break;
      cout << "\nDistance = " << dist1;  // display distance
      }
   }
```

We've made minimal changes to the overloaded operators themselves. The `>>` operator no longer prompts for input, since it doesn't make sense to prompt a file. We assume the user knows exactly how to enter a feet-and-inches value, including the various punctuation marks. The `<<` operator is unchanged. The program asks for input from the user, writing each `Distance` value to the file as it's obtained. When the user is finished with input, the program then reads and displays all the values from the file. Here's some sample interaction:

```
Enter Distance: 3'-4.5"
Do another (y/n)? yes

Enter Distance: 7'-11.25"
Do another (y/n)? yes

Enter Distance: 11'-6"
Do another (y/n)? no

Contents of disk file is:
Distance = 3'-4.5"
Distance = 7'-11.25"
Distance = 11'-6"
```

The distances are stored character by character to the file. In this example the contents of the file would be

```
3'-4.5"7'-11.25"11'-6
```

If the user fails to enter the distances with the correct punctuation, they won't be written to the file correctly and the file won't be readable for the << operator. In a real program error checking the input is essential.

Memory As a Stream Object

You can treat a section of memory as a stream object, inserting data into it just as you would a file. This is useful when you need to format your output in a particular way (such as displaying exactly two digits to the right of the decimal point), but you also need to use a text-output function that requires a string as input. This is common when calling output functions in a GUI environment such as Windows, since these functions often require a string as an argument. (C programmers will remember using the `sprintf()` function for this purpose.)

A family of stream classes implements such in-memory formatting. For output to memory there is `ostrstream`, which is derived from (among other classes) `ostream`. For input from memory there is `istrstream`, derived from `istream`; and for memory objects that do both input and output there is `strstream`, derived from `iostream`.

Most commonly you will want to use `ostrstream`. Our next example shows how this works. You start with a data buffer in memory. Then you create an `ostrstream` object, using the memory buffer and its size as arguments to the stream's constructor. Now you can output formatted text to the memory buffer as if it were a stream object. Here's the listing for OSTRSTR:

```
// ostrstr.cpp
// writes formatted data into memory

#include <strstrea.h>                   // for ostrstream class
#include <iomanip.h>                    // for setiosflags()
const int SIZE = 80;                    // size of memory buffer

void main()
   {
   char ch = 'x';                       // test data
   int j = 77;
   double d = 67890.12345;
   char str1[] = "Kafka";
   char str2[] = "Freud";

   char membuff[SIZE];                  // buffer in memory
   ostrstream omem(membuff, SIZE);      // create stream object

   omem << "ch=" << ch << endl          // insert formatted data
        << "j=" << j << endl            // into object
        << setiosflags(ios::fixed)      // format with decimal point
        << setprecision(2)              // two digits to right of pt
        << "d=" << d << endl
        << "str1=" << str1 << endl
        << "str2=" << str2 << endl
```

```
        << ends;                          // end the buffer with '\0'

    cout << membuff;                      // display the memory buffer
    }
```

When you run the program, `membuff` will be filled with the formatted text:

```
ch=x\nj=77\nd=67890.12\nstr1=Kafka\nstr2=Freud\n\0
```

We can format floating-point numbers using the usual methods. Here we specify a fixed decimal format (rather than exponential) with `ios::fixed`, and two digits to the right of the decimal point. The manipulator `ends` inserts a `'\0'` character at the end of the string to provide an EOF. Displaying this buffer in the usual way with `cout` produces the program's output:

```
ch=x
j=77
d=67890.12
str1=Kafka
str2=Freud
```

In this example the program displays the contents of the buffer only to show what it looks like. Ordinarily you would have a more sophisticated use for this formatted data. We make use of this technique in the CALC program in Chapter 15 to format the text display for a calculator.

Redirection

The programs in this section should be executed from a DOS box in Windows or from DOS itself. You need to see a DOS prompt when invoking the program so you can enter additional information besides the program name.

In DOS it's possible to read and write to files using only the objects `cout` and `cin`. These predefined objects normally represent the display and the keyboard, but they can be redirected by the user to represent disk files. Redirection is a technique, originally imported from Unix into DOS, that allows the user additional flexibility in the way programs are used. Redirection is supplied by DOS, not by C++; but C++ supports it, so it's interesting to see how to use it. As an example, consider the program REDIR.

```
// redir.cpp
// demonstrates redirection
// syntax: redir <source >destination
#include <iostream.h>
#include <iomanip.h>                          // for resetiosflags()

void main()
   {
   char ch;
   while( !cin.eof() )                        // quit on EOF
      {
      cin >> resetiosflags(ios::skipws)       // keep whitespace
          >> ch;                              // read from std input
      cout << ch;                             // send to std output
      }
   }
```

Before exploring how this program can be used for redirection, we should note that we must reset the skipws flag when getting input from cin. This is necessary because cin normally skips over whitespace, which includes spaces, newlines, and EOFs. We want to read all these characters.

Using REDIR

When invoked in the usual way at the command line, REDIR simply echoes whatever the user types, each time ENTER is pressed. Here's some sample interaction (from a poem by the 16th-century poet Ben Jonson):

```
C>redir
Truth is the trial of itself,      <------ entered by user
Truth is the trial of itself,      <------ echoed by program
And needs no other touch;
And needs no other touch;
And purer than the purest gold,
And purer than the purest gold,
Refine it ne'er so much.
Refine it ne'er so much.
^Z
```

The user enters the CTRL-Z combination (or the F6 function key) to terminate the program. This character is interpreted as an EOF.

Using redirection gives the program additional capabilities. It can take input from the keyboard and write it to a disk file, display text from a disk file on the screen, or copy one file to another.

Redirecting Output

To redirect a program's output from the screen to a file, you use the > operator. This is a DOS operator; it has nothing to do with C++ comparison or overloading. Here's how to invoke REDIR to take keyboard input and redirect it to a file called SAMPLE.TXT:

```
C>redir >sample.txt
If you would avoid suspicion,                <------ entered by user
don't lace your shoes in a melon field.      <------ entered by user
^Z                                           <------ entered by user
```

The text you type will be written to SAMPLE.TXT. You can check this file with the DOS command TYPE to be sure it contains this text.

Redirecting Input

To redirect a program's input so that it comes from a file and not the keyboard, you use the < operator. Here's how to invoke REDIR to take data from the file SAMPLE.TXT and use it as input to the program, which then displays it:

```
C>redir <sample.txt
If you would avoid suspicion,                <------ displayed by program
don't lace your shoes in a melon field.      <------ displayed by program
```

Redirecting Input and Output

Both input and output can be redirected at the same time. As an example, here's how to use REDIR to copy one file to another:

```
C>redir <src.txt >dest.txt
```

Nothing is displayed, but you will find that SRC.TXT has been copied to DEST.TXT. Note that this only works for text files, not binary files.

If you want to display a particular message on the screen even when the output of your program has been redirected to a file, you can use the `cerr` object. Insert this line into the `while` loop in REDIR:

```
cerr << ch;
```

Now try copying one file to another. Each character `ch` will be sent to the screen by `cerr`, even though the output to `cout` is going to a file.

Redirection and the _withassign Classes

The need to support redirection explains the `_withassign` classes discussed earlier. Redirection is carried out by setting the `cout` or `cin` stream object equal to another stream object: namely, one associated with the filename provided on the command line. But to set `cin` and `cout` equal to other objects, they must be derived from a class that supports the assignment operation. Most stream classes don't, but the three `_withassign` classes, from which `cout` and `cin` are derived, do.

Command-Line Arguments

Unless you are a Windows-only user, you are probably familiar with command-line arguments, used when invoking a program from DOS. They are typically used to pass the name of a data file to an application. For example, you can invoke a word processor application and the document it will work on at the same time:

```
C>wordproc afile.doc
```

Here `afile.doc` is a command-line argument. How can we get a C++ program to read the command-line arguments? Here's an example, COMLINE, that reads and displays as many command-line arguments as you care to type (they're separated by spaces):

```
// comline.cpp
// demonstrates command-line arguments
#include <iostream.h>

void main(int argc, char* argv[] )
   {
   cout << "\nargc = " << argc;

   for(int j=0; j<argc; j++)
      cout << "\nArgument " << j << " = " << argv[j];
   }
```

And here's a sample interaction with the program:

```
C>comline uno dos tres

argc = 4
Argument 0 = C:\CPP\CHAP14\COMLINE.EXE
Argument 1 = uno
Argument 2 = dos
Argument 3 = tres
```

To read command-line arguments, the `main()` function (don't forget it's a function!) must itself be given two arguments. The first, `argc` (for *argument count*), represents the total number of command-line arguments. The first command-line argument is always the pathname of the current program. The remaining command-line arguments are those typed by the user; they are delimited by the space character. In the example above they are *uno*, *dos*, and *tres*.

The system stores the command-line arguments as strings in memory, and creates an array of pointers to these strings. In the example the array is called `argv` (for *argument values*). Individual strings are accessed through the appropriate pointer, so the first string (the pathname) is `argv[0]`, the second (`uno` in this example) is `argv[1]`, and so on. COMLINE accesses the arguments in turn and prints them out in a `for` loop that uses `argc`, the number of command-line arguments, as its upper limit.

You don't need to use the particular names `argc` and `argv` as arguments to `main()`, but they are so common that any other names would cause consternation to everyone but the compiler.

Here's a program that uses a command-line argument for something useful. It displays the contents of a text file whose name is supplied by the user on the command line. Thus it imitates the DOS command TYPE. Here's the listing for OTYPE:

```
// otype.cpp
// imitates TYPE command
#include <fstream.h>              // for file functions
#include <process.h>              // for exit()

void main(int argc, char* argv[] )
   {
   if( argc != 2 )
      {
      cerr << "\nFormat: otype filename";
      exit(-1);
      }
   char ch;                         // character to read
   ifstream infile;                 // create file for input
   infile.open( argv[1] );          // open file
   if( !infile )                    // check for errors
      {
      cerr << "\nCan't open " << argv[1];
      exit(-1);
      }
   while( infile.get(ch) != 0 )     // read a character
      cout << ch;                   // display the character
   }
```

This program first checks to see if the user has entered the correct number of command-line arguments. Remember that the pathname of OTYPE.EXE itself is always the first command-line argument. The second argument is the name of the file to be displayed, which the user should have entered when invoking the program:

```
C>otype ichar.cpp
```

Thus the total number of command-line arguments should equal 2. If it doesn't, the user probably doesn't understand how to use the program, and the program sends an error message via `cerr` to clarify matters.

If the number of arguments is correct, the program tries to open the file whose name is the second command-line argument (`argv[1]`). Again, if the file can't be opened, the program signals an error. Finally, in a `while` loop, the program reads the file character by character and writes it to the screen.

A value of 0 for the character signals an EOF. This is another way to check for EOF. You can also use the value of the file object itself, as we've done before:

```
while( infile )
   {
   infile.get(ch);
   cout << ch;
   }
```

You could also replace this entire `while` loop with the statement

```
cout << infile.rdbuf();
```

as we saw earlier in the ICHAR2 program.

Printer Output

In DOS it's fairly easy to send data to the printer. DOS predefines a number of special filenames for hardware devices. These make it possible to treat the devices as if they were files. Table 14-11 shows these predefined names.

In most systems the printer is connected to the first parallel port, so the filename for the printer should be `prn` or `lpt1`. (You can substitute the appropriate name if your system is configured differently.)

The following program, EZPRINT, sends a string and a number to the printer, using formatted output with the insertion operator.

```
// ezprint.cpp
// demonstrates simple output to printer

#include <fstream.h>                  // for file streams

void main(void)
   {
   char* s1 = "\nToday's winning number is ";
   int   n1 = 17982;

   ofstream outfile;                  // make a file
   outfile.open("PRN");               // open it for printer
   outfile << s1 << n1 << endl;       // send data to printer
   outfile << '\x0D';                 // formfeed for page eject
   }
```

Name	Device
con	Console (keyboard and screen)
aux or com1	First serial port
com2	Second serial port
prn or lpt1	First parallel printer
lpt2	Second parallel printer
lpt3	Third parallel printer
nul	Dummy (nonexistent) device

Table 14-11 Hardware Device Names

You can send any amount of formatted output to the printer this way. The `'\x0D'` character causes the page to eject from the printer.

This technique only works for DOS programs, so you must use a DOS target when you create EZPRINT with Borland C++, not an EasyWin target. Sending output to the printer in Windows is beyond the scope of this book.

The next example, OPRINT, prints the contents of a disk file, specified on the command line, to the printer. It uses the character-by-character approach to this data transfer.

```
// oprint.cpp
// imitates print command
#include <fstream.h>              // for file functions
#include <process.h>              // for exit()

void main(int argc, char* argv[] )
   {
   if( argc != 2 )
      {
      cerr << "\nFormat: oprint filename";
      exit(-1);
      }
   char ch;                          // character to read
   ifstream infile;                  // create file for input
   infile.open( argv[1] );           // open file
   if( !infile )                     // check for errors
      {
      cerr << "\nCan't open " << argv[1];
      exit(-1);
      }
   ofstream outfile;                 // make file
   outfile.open("PRN");              // open it for printer
   while( infile.get(ch) != 0 )      // read a character
      outfile.put(ch);               // write character to printer
   }
```

You can use this program to print any text file, such as any of your .CPP source files. It acts much the same as the DOS PRINT command. Like the OTYPE example, this program checks for the correct number of command-line arguments, and for a successful opening of the specified file.

Summary

In this chapter we briefly examined the hierarchy of stream classes and showed how to handle various kinds of I/O errors. Then we saw how to perform file I/O in a variety of ways. Files in C++ are associated with objects of various classes, typically `ofstream` for output, `ifstream` for input, and `fstream` for both input and output. Member functions of these or base classes are used to perform I/O operations. Such functions as `<<`, `put()`, and `write()` are used for output, while `>>`, `get()`, and `read()` are used for input.

The `read()` and `write()` functions work in binary mode, so that entire objects can be saved to disk no matter what sort of data they contain. Single objects can be stored, as can arrays or other data structures of many objects. File I/O can be handled by member functions. This can be the responsibility of individual objects, or the class itself can handle I/O using static member functions.

A check for error conditions should be made after each file operation. The file object itself takes on a value of 0 if an error occurred. Also, several member functions can be used to determine specific kinds of errors. The extraction operator `>>` and the insertion operator `<<` can be overloaded so that they work with programmer-defined data types. Memory can be considered a stream, and data sent to it as if it were a file.

Redirection provides an easily programmed (although not entirely user-friendly) approach to file I/0, using input and output to `cin` and `cout`. Sending output to the printer involves outputting to a file usually called PRN.

Questions

Answers to questions can be found in Appendix D.

1. A C++ stream is
   a. the flow of control through a function.
   b. a flow of data from one place to another.
   c. associated with a particular class.
   d. a file.
2. The base class for most stream classes is the _________ class.
3. Name three stream classes commonly used for disk I/O.
4. Write a statement that will create an object called `salefile` of the `ofstream` class and associate it with a file called SALES.JUN.

5. True or false: Some streams work with input, and some with output.

6. Write an `if` statement that checks if an `ifstream` object called `foobar` has reached the end of file or has encountered an error.

7. We can output text to an object of class `ofstream` using the insertion operator << because

   a. the `ofstream` class is a stream.
   b. the insertion operator works with all classes.
   c. we are actually outputting to `cout`.
   d. the insertion operator is overloaded in `ofstream`.

8. Write a statement that writes a single character to an object called `fileOut`, which is of class `ofstream`.

9. To write data that contains variables of type `float` to an object of type `ofstream`, you should use

   a. the insertion operator.
   b. `seekg()`.
   c. `write()`.
   d. `put()`.

10. Write a statement that will read the contents of an `ifstream` object called `ifile` into an array called `buff`.

11. Mode bits such as `app` and `ate`

    a. are defined in the `ios` class.
    b. can specify if a file is open for reading or writing.
    c. work with the `put()` and `get()` functions.
    d. specify ways of opening a file.

12. Define what *current position* means when applied to files.

13. True or false: A file pointer always contains the address of the file.

14. Write a statement that moves the current position 13 bytes backward in a stream object called `f1`.

15. The statement

```
f1.write( (char*)&obj1, sizeof(obj1) );
```

    a. writes the member functions of `obj1` to `f1`.
    b. writes the data in `obj1` to `f1`.
    c. writes the member functions and the data of `obj1` to `f1`.
    d. writes the address of `obj1` to `f1`.

16. Redirection redirects
    a. a stream from a file to the screen.
    b. a file from a device to a stream.
    c. a device from the screen to a file.
    d. the screen from a device to a stream.
17. Used with `cin`, what does the `skipws` flag accomplish?
18. Write a declarator for `main()` that will enable command-line arguments.
19. The printer can be accessed using the predefined filename ________.
20. Write the declarator for the overloaded `>>` operator that takes output from an object of class `istream` and displays it as the contents of an object of class `Sample`.

Exercises

Answers to starred exercises can be found in Appendix D.

1.* Start with the `Distance` class from the ENGLCON example in Chapter 7. Using a loop similar to that in the DISKFUN example in this chapter, get a number of `Distance` values from the user, and write them to a disk file. Append them to existing values in the file, if any. When the user signals that no more values will be input, read the file and display all the values.

2.* Write a program that emulates the DOS COPY command. That is, it should copy the contents of a character file (such as any .CPP file) to another file. Invoke the program with two command-line arguments—the source file and the destination file—like this:

```
C>ocopy srcfile.cpp destfile.cpp
```

In the program, check that the user has typed the correct number of command-line arguments, and that the files specified can be opened. Improve on the DOS TYPE command by having the program signal an error if the destination file already exists. This will prevent inadvertently writing over a valuable file. (Hint: Use the `noreplace` flag.)

3.* Write a program that returns the size in bytes of a program entered on the command line:

```
C>filesize program.ext
```

4. In a loop, prompt the user to enter *name data* consisting of a first name, middle initial, last name, and employee number (type `unsigned long`). Then, using

formatted I/O with the insertion (<<) operator, write these four data items to an `ofstream` object. Don't forget that strings must be terminated with a space or other whitespace character. When the user indicates that no more name data will be entered, close the `ofstream` object, open an `ifstream` object, read and display all the data in the file, and terminate the program.

5. Create a `time` class that includes integer member values for `hours`, `minutes`, and `seconds`. Make a member function `get_time()` that gets a time value from the user, and a function `put_time()` that displays a time in 12:59:59 format. Add error checking to the `get_time()` function to minimize user mistakes. This function should request hours, minutes, and seconds separately, and check each one for `ios` error status flags and the correct range. Hours should be between 0 and 23, and minutes and seconds between 0 and 59. Don't input these values as strings and then convert them; read them directly as integers. This implies that you won't be able to screen out entries with superfluous decimal points, as does the ENGL_IO program in this chapter, but we'll assume that's not important.

   In `main()`, use a loop to repeatedly get a `time` value from the user with `get_time()` and then display it with `put_time()`, like this:

```
Enter hours: 11
Enter minutes: 59
Enter seconds: 59
time = 11:59:59

Do another (y/n)? y
Enter hours: 25
Hours must be between 0 and 23
Enter hours: 1
Enter minutes: 10
Enter seconds: five
Incorrect seconds input
Enter seconds: 5
time = 1:10:05
```

6. Make a class called `name` from the data in Exercise 4 (first name, middle initial, last name, employee number). Create member functions for this class that read and write an object's data to a disk file, using `ofstream`, and read it back using `ifstream`. Use formatted data with the << and >> operators. The read and write member functions should be self-contained: They should include statements to open the appropriate stream and read or write a record.

   The write function can simply append its data to the end of the file. The read function will need a way to select which record it's going to read. One way to do this is to call it with a parameter representing the record number. Once it knows which record it should read, how does the read function find the record? You might think you could use the `seekg()` function, but that isn't much help because in formatted I/O the records are all different lengths (depending on the number of characters in the strings and the number of digits in the integer). So you'll need to actually read records until you've skipped forward to the one you want.

In `main()`, call these member functions to emulate the action in Exercise 5. That is, the user enters data for a number of objects that are written to a file as they are entered. The program then displays all this data by reading it from the file.

7. Another approach to adding file stream I/O to an object is to make the file stream itself a static member of the object. Why do that? Well, it's often conceptually easier to think of the stream as being related to the class as a whole than to the individual objects of the class. Also, it's more efficient to open a stream only once, then read and write objects to it as needed. For example, once the file is opened, then each time the read function is called it can return the data for the next object in the file. The file pointer will progress automatically through the file because the file is not closed between reads.

Rewrite the program in Exercises 4 and 6 to use an `fstream` object as a static data item of the `name` class. Keep the same functionality as in those exercises. Write a static function to open this stream, and another static function to reset the file pointer to the beginning of the file. You can use this reset function when you're done writing and want to read all the records back from the file.

8. Starting with the LINKLIST program in Chapter 12, create a program that gives the user four options, which can be selected by pressing a key.

- Add a link to the list in memory (the user supplies the data, which is one integer)
- Display the data from all the links in memory
- Write the data for all the links to a disk file (creating or truncating the file as necessary)
- Read all the data back from the file, and construct a new linked list in which to store it

The first two options can use the member functions already implemented in LINKLIST. You'll need to write functions to read to, and write from, the disk file. You can use the same file for all reads and writes. The file should store only the data; there's no sense in its storing the contents of pointers, which will probably not be relevant when the list is read back in.

9. Start with Exercise 7 in Chapter 9, and overload the the insertion (<<) and extraction (>>) operators for the `frac` class in the four-function calculator. Note that you can chain the operators, so asking for a fraction, an operator, and a fraction should require only one statement:

```
cin >> frac1 >> op >> frac2;
```

10. Add error checking to the extraction (>>) operator of the `frac` class in Exercise 9 in this chapter. With error checking it's probably better to prompt for the first fraction, then for the operator, and then for the second fraction, rather than using a single statement as shown in Exercise 9. This makes the format more comprehensible when it is interspersed with error messages.

```
Enter first fraction: 5/0
Denominator cannot be 0
   Enter fraction again: 5/1
Enter operator (+, -, *, /): +
Enter second fraction: one third
Input error
   Enter fraction again: 1/3
Answer is --------------------- 16/3
Do another (y/n)?
```

As implied in this sample interaction, you should check for `ios` error bits and also for a denominator of 0. If there's an error, prompt the user to enter the fraction again.

11. Start with the `bMoney` class, last seen in Exercise 5 in Chapter 13. Overload the insertion (<<) and extraction (>>) operators to perform I/O on `bMoney` quantities. Perform some sample I/O in `main()`.

12. To the EMPL_IO program in this chapter add the ability to search through all the employee objects in a disk file, looking for one with a specified employee number. If it finds a match, it should display the data for the employee. The user can invoke this `find()` function by typing the f character. The function should then prompt for the employee number. Ask yourself if the function should be static, virtual, or something else. This search and display operation should not interfere with the data in memory. Note: Don't try to read a file generated with the EMPL_IO program. The classes are not the same because of the `find()` member function in the new program, and disaster will result if their data is mixed, as discussed in this chapter.

15

Larger Programs

REASONS FOR MULTIFILE PROGRAMS

PUBLIC AND PRIVATE COMPONENTS

CREATING MULTIFILE PROGRAMS

PROGRAM: GUI WINDOWS AS OBJECTS

PROGRAM: A CLASS OF VERY LARGE NUMBERS

PROGRAM: SIMULATING HIGH-RISE ELEVATORS

PROGRAM: MODELING A WATER SYSTEM

15

In previous chapters we've seen how the various parts of a C++ program—such as class declarations, member functions, and a `main()` function—are combined. However, the programs in those chapters all consisted of a single file. Now let's look at program organization from a more global perspective, involving multiple files.

Besides demonstrating multifile programs, this chapter will introduce some longer and more ambitious applications. Our aim in these programs is not that you necessarily understand every detail of their operation, but that you acquire a general understanding of how the elements of larger programs relate to one another. These programs also show how classes can be used in more realistic applications than the short examples we've seen so far. On the other hand, they are not so long that it takes all spring to wade through them.

Reasons for Multifile Programs

There are several reasons for using multifile programs. These include the use of class libraries, the organization of programmers working on a project, and the conceptual design of a program. Let's reflect briefly on these issues.

Class Libraries

In traditional procedure-oriented languages it has long been customary for software vendors to furnish libraries of functions. Other programmers then combine these libraries with their own custom-written routines to create an application for the end-user.

Libraries provide ready-made functions for a wide variety of fields. For instance, a vendor might supply a library of functions for handling statistics calculations or for advanced memory management. Libraries that provide the functions necessary to create a graphics user interface (GUI) for DOS programs are popular.

Since C++ is organized around classes rather than functions, it's not surprising that libraries for C++ programs consist of classes. What may be surprising is how superior a class library is to an old-fashioned function library. Because classes encapsulate both data and functions, and because they more closely model objects in real life, the interface between a class library and the application that makes use of it can be much cleaner than that provided by a function library.

For these reasons class libraries assume a more important role in C++ programming than function libraries do in traditional programming. A class library can take over a greater portion of the programming burden. An applications programmer, if the right class library is available, may find that only a minimal amount of programming is necessary to create a final product. Also, as more and more class libraries are created, the chances of finding one that solves your particular programming problem continues to increase.

A class library often includes two components: public and private. Let's see what the difference is.

Public Components

To use a class library, the applications programmer needs to access various declarations, including class declarations. These declarations can be thought of as the public part of the library and are usually furnished in source-code form as a header file, with the .H extension. This file is typically combined with the client's source code using an `#include` statement.

The declarations in such a header file need to be public for several reasons. First, it's a convenience to the client to see the actual definitions rather than to have to read a description of them. More importantly, the client's program will need to declare objects based on these classes and call on member functions from these objects. Only by declaring the classes in the source file is this possible.

Private Components

On the other hand, the inner workings of the member functions of the various classes don't need to be known by the client. The developers of the class library, like any other software developer, don't want to release source code if they can help it, since it might be illegally modified or pirated. Member functions—except for short inline functions—are therefore usually distributed in object form, as .OBJ files or as library (.LIB) files.

Figure 15-1 shows how the various files are related in a multifile system.

In this chapter we'll show several larger programs organized according to these principles. The first provides a set of classes of visual screen elements, such as buttons and output windows. An application then uses these classes to create a four-function pocket calculator. The second program introduces a class of very large numbers. By "very large," we mean numbers with an almost unlimited number of digits. Such numbers are important in various kinds of mathematics, such as calculating *pi* to thousands of digits. The third example simulates an elevator system in a high-rise building, using a class for the elevators. The final program provides classes that allow you to create your own water-distribution system. You can connect valves, tanks, pipes, and similar components to model water systems such as the cooling system in a nuclear reactor.

Organization and Conceptualization

Programs may be broken down into multiple files for reasons other than the accommodation of class libraries. As in other programming languages, such as C, a common situation involves a project with several programmers (or teams of programmers). Confining each programmer's responsibility to a separate file helps organize the project and define more cleanly the interface among different parts of the program.

It is also often the case that a program is divided into separate files according to functionality: One file can handle the code involved in a graphics display, for example, while another file handles mathematical analysis, and a third handles disk I/O. In large programs a single file may simply become too large to handle conveniently.

Figure 15-1 Files in Multifile Application

The techniques used for working with multifile programs are similar, whatever the reasons for dividing the program. Let's see how Borland C++ and Turbo C++ handle program development with multiple files.

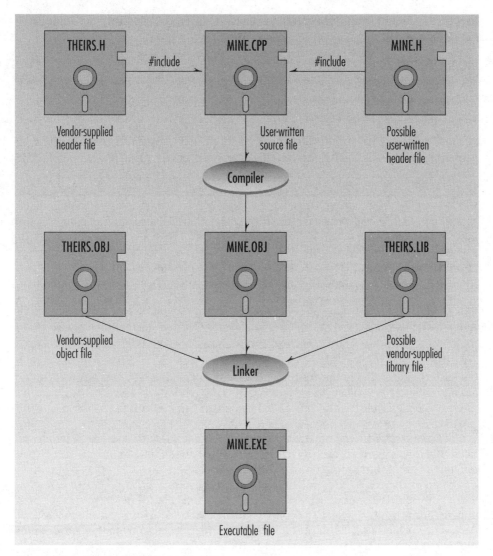

How to Create a Multifile Program

Suppose that you have purchased a prewritten class file called THEIRS.OBJ. (A library file with the .LIB extension is dealt with in much the same way.) It probably comes with a header file, say THEIRS.H. You have also written your own program to use the classes in the library; your source file is called MINE.CPP. Now you want to combine these component files—THEIRS.OBJ, THEIRS.H, and MINE.CPP—into a single executable program.

Header Files

The header file THEIRS.H is easily incorporated into your own source file, MINE.CPP, with an `#include` statement:

```
#include "THEIRS.H"
```

Quotes rather than angle brackets around the filename tell the compiler to look first for the file in the current directory, rather than in the default include directory.

Directory

Make sure all the component files, THEIRS.OBJ, THEIRS.H, and MINE.CPP, are in the same directory. In fact, you will probably want to create a separate directory for the project, to avoid confusion. (This isn't strictly necessary, but it's the simplest approach.) In Borland C++ you create the project file MINE.IDE in this directory in the usual way, as described in Chapter 2. In Turbo C++, change to this directory and call up Turbo C++ by typing `tc` at the DOS prompt. You don't have to open any of the component files when you call up Borland C++ or Turbo C++; a blank screen is all you need.

Multiple Files in Borland C++

It's easy to add a file to an existing project in Borland C++. Let's assume you've already created a project called MINE, and that you started it up with the file MINE.CPP, as described in Chapter 2. Now you want to add the THEIRS.OBJ file to the project.

In the *Project* window you should see a MINE.EXE icon, with a MINE.CPP icon connected below it. This indicates that the project will generate MINE.EXE as the executable file, and that MINE.CPP is needed as a source file.

To add THEIRS.OBJ to the project, click the right mouse button on the MINE.EXE. From the resulting menu, select *Add Node*. A dialog box, *Add to Project List*, will appear. From the list, select the file you want to add, in this example THEIRS.OBJ. (In later examples in this chapter it will be another .CPP file.) Note that header files like THEIRS.H don't need to appear in the project window.

That's all there is to it. You'll see from the *Project* window that MINE.EXE is now dependent on two files: MINE.CPP and THEIRS.OBJ. You can now compile, link, and run the project in the usual way, by selecting *Run* from the *Debug* menu.

Multiple Files in Turbo C++

Using multiple files in Turbo C++ requires more complex steps than in Borland C++. The reason is that Borland C++ assumes in all cases that you're using a project, while in Turbo C++ you don't need a project for programs with a single source file; only for multiple files.

Open a Project

Select *Open Project* from the *Project* menu. A window called *Load Project File* will appear. This window has a text field at the top, also called *Load Project File*. Into this field type the name of the project file you want to create. You should give this file the same name you want to use for your final executable program, but with the extension .PRJ instead of .EXE. Thus if you want your executable file to be called MINE.EXE, type **MINE.PRJ** into the *Load Project File* field. (You may have to backspace to delete existing text before typing.) Then press (ENTER) or select *OK*. The *Load Project File* window will vanish, and another window, called *Project: MINE* (or whatever name you chose), will appear at the bottom of the screen.

Enter Component Filenames

You want to enter the names of your component files into this new *Project* window. To do this, press the (INS) key (or select *Add Item...* from the *Project* menu). A third window, called *Add Item to Project List*, will be displayed. This window has a text field called *Name* at the top. Into this field type the name of one of your component files—for instance, THEIRS.OBJ. Press (ENTER) or click on the *Add* button. You'll see the name you typed added to the *Project* window at the bottom of the screen. Now type the name of the next file, MINE.CPP, into the *Name* field (backspacing over existing text first, if necessary). This name will also appear in the *Project* window. You can now click on *Cancel* to make the *Add Item...* window go away. That's it. You've created the project file.

Create Executable File

To create the executable file, first make sure the *Project* window is active. (You may have other files open on the screen.) Then select *Make EXE file* from the *Compile* menu. At this point the MINE.CPP file will be compiled (unless it has already been compiled and is up to date). Then the resulting MINE.OBJ file will be linked with THEIRS.OBJ, creating the executable file MINE.EXE.

To execute MINE.EXE, select *Run* from the Run menu (or press (CTRL)-(F9)). If you exit Turbo C++, you'll see MINE.EXE in your directory, where it can be executed as a stand-alone program. You'll also see the MINE.PRJ project file.

Automatic Compilation

Note that the project file stores the dates your files were last changed. This makes it possible for Turbo C++ to know which files need to be compiled and which don't. Thus if a source file was compiled before the executable file was created, there's no need to compile it again before relinking it. But if it has been changed since the last relinking, then Turbo C++ will cause it to be recompiled before linking its OBJ file. This automation means that as a programmer you can ignore the issue of what needs to be compiled and what doesn't, and that you can trust Turbo C++ to do the right thing when you select *Make EXE file*.

You can always compile a source file directly, using *Compile to OBJ* from the *Compile* menu. Each source file should compile correctly on its own. You'll probably want to do this while you're developing a set of classes or an application program that uses them. When all the source files compile correctly, you can start using the project feature to link them together and handle future changes.

Automatic Project Files

In Turbo C++ you may be surprised to find that a project file for one program is automatically loaded, when in fact you want to start writing a completely different program. Why does this happen? If there is exactly one project file in a directory, Turbo C++ will load it automatically whenever you start it up. This may be what you want, since a directory often holds only one multifile program. But if you want to start another project in the same directory, you may have trouble. To avoid this problem, you can create a dummy (empty) .PRJ file, since if there is more than one, Turbo C++ won't automatically open any of them.

Automatic Directories

You should be aware that each project has its own default LIB and INCLUDE directories. In Borland C++ you can see what these are by selecting *Project...* from the *Options* menu and clicking on *Directories*. (Select *Directories* from the *Options* menu in Turbo C++.) When you begin a project, the IDE may be confused about what directories you want to use. If you get compiler error messages like *Unable to open include file XXX.H* or linker messages like *Unable to open file XXX.LIB*, then your default directories may be incorrectly set. Change them by typing in the correct pathnames in the fields provided.

In Borland C++, the examples in this chapter all use \BC4\INCLUDE as the include directory and \BC45\LIB as the library directory. These are set automatically, so there should be no problem. (In Turbo C++, it's \TC\INCLUDE and \TC\LIB.) However, as we'll see in the next chapter, things can get more complicated.

A Pocket Calculator: The CALC Program

Now that we know how to compile multifile programs, let's look at our first example based on this approach. Suppose you plan to write a program that models a four-function pocket calculator, placing a picture of the calculator on the screen. However, you don't want to go to the trouble of programming the visual elements, such as push buttons and output display windows. Fortunately, you know where to obtain a set of classes designed to model the elements of screen calculators. You use these ready-made classes to model the visual elements, and write the interface and math routines yourself. In this example we'll show these two major parts of the program, and how they fit together.

The complete program puts a four-function calculator on the screen. The calculator can be used to perform arithmetic in the same way as a handheld calculator. The program requires an EGA or VGA graphics adapter. Figure 15-2 shows how it looks on the screen.

Using the Calculator

The buttons on the calculator appear to push in when activated, as they do in Microsoft Windows and other GUI applications. This is an optical illusion, achieved by changing the shading around the edge of the button.

Different kinds of buttons are colored differently to emphasize their functions. Digits have a black background, arithmetic operators are blue, and the clear button is red.

To use the calculator, the user types the digits of the first number, then an arithmetic operator (/, *, -, or +), then a second number, and then the equal sign (=). The answer is displayed. You can chain to another calculation: The answer

Figure 15-2 Output of CALC Program

automatically becomes the first operand, so you can press another arithmetic operator and key in another number to get the next answer. You can use a decimal point in the numbers you input, but not exponential notation or negative signs. The output has a fixed decimal place with two digits on its right. The equal sign and the plus sign are on the same button on the screen, and you can use either the (=) key or the (+) key for either operation; the program distinguishes them by context, as on many pocket calculators.

To exit the program, press the (ESC) key.

Ideally a calculator screen-display would have its buttons activated by a mouse. However, Turbo C++ does not provide library functions for the mouse, and writing our own would make the program excessively complex. We simulate the action of a mouse using the keyboard keys: When you type a digit, for instance, the corresponding button on the screen appears to push in. A clicking noise accompanies the "push" and "pop" of the button.

Files in the CALC Program

The CALC program consists of three files. First there is the header file, CALC.H, containing the class declarations. Next is CALC.CPP, which contains the member functions. We present this file in source form so you can read it, but if you had actually purchased it from a class library vendor it would probably be in object form, as a .LIB or .OBJ file. Finally there is CALC_APP.CPP, the file that we write ourselves.

To build this program, make sure these three files are in the same directory. In Borland C++, make sure you use a DOS target, not EasyWin. Because CALC uses `delay()` and other DOS-only functions, it won't run in Windows. Use an Application target type (rather than an EasyWin) on a DOS Standard platform. (See Chapter 2 for a description of DOS projects.) Create a project called CALC_APP.PRJ. Add the files CALC.CPP and CALC_APP.CPP to the project file. When you're finished, you can compile and run the program as described at the beginning of this chapter.

Let's look first at CALC.H and CALC.CPP, the programs supplied by our mythical class vendor. First the public part of the package:

```
// calc.h
// header file for calc.cpp
#include <string.h>       // for strcpy()
#include <graphics.h>     // for graphics functions
#include <conio.h>        // for getche()
#include <dos.h>          // for delay(), sound(), etc.
#include <strstrea.h>     // for ostrstream class
#include <iomanip.h>      // for setiosflags()
#include <math.h>         // for atof()

class Window;                              // (needed for SCREEN)
Window* const SCREEN = (Window*)0;         // ultimate owner

enum buttonstatus { unpushed, pushed };
enum boolean { false, true };

class Window                     // parent class
   {
   protected:
      Window* ptrOwner;              // address of owner of this window
      int left, top, right, bot;     // outside edges of rectangle
      int delta;                     // distance between borders
      int deltacolor;                // color between borders
      int centercolor;               // color within inside border

   public:                           // constructor: initialize window
      Window(Window* ptro, int l, int t, int r, int b,
               int dc, int cc);
      void Display(void);            // display the window
   };

class Border : public Window     // border
   {
   public:
      Border(Window* ptro, int l, int t, int r, int b,
               int dc=BLUE, int cc=DARKGRAY)
              : Window(ptro, l, t, r, b, dc, cc)
         { }
   };

class Button : public Window     // push button
   {
   private:
      char text[20];                     // characters on button
      buttonstatus bstatus;              // pushed or unpushed
   public:
      Button(Window* ptro, int l, int t, int r, int b,
               int cc=BLACK, char* tx="")
              : Window(ptro, l, t, r, b, BLACK, cc)
            { strcpy(text, tx);  bstatus = unpushed; }
```

```
      void Click(void);              // click the button
      void Display(void);            // display the button
   };

class Output : public Window    // output window
   {
   private:
      char text[80];
   public:
      Output(Window* ptro, int l, int t, int r, int b,
             int dc=BLUE, int cc=WHITE)
            : Window(ptro, l, t, r, b, dc, cc)
         { }
      void Text(char *);     // display text sent as string
      void Number(double);   // display number
   };
```

Here's the private file, CALC.CPP, which contains the actual member functions for the `Window` class and its descendants:

```
// calc.cpp
// member functions for calc
#include "calc.h"               // calc header file

                                // constructor: initialize window
Window::Window(Window* ptro, int l, int t, int r, int b,
       int dc, int cc)
   {                                 // set private data
   ptrOwner=ptro; left=l; top=t; right=r; bot=b;
   deltacolor=dc; centercolor=cc;
                                     // calculate delta
   delta = ((right-left)+(bot-top))/150 + 3;
   if( ptrOwner != SCREEN )          // if there is an owner,
      {                              // our coordinates
      left  += ptrOwner->left;       // start at owner's
      right += ptrOwner->left;       // upper left corner
      top   += ptrOwner->top;
      bot   += ptrOwner->top;
      }
   }

void Window::Display(void)    // display the window
   {
   setcolor(WHITE);

   int p[10];                          // draw outer rectangle and
   p[0]=left;  p[1]=top;               // fill it
   p[2]=right; p[3]=top;               // use fillpoly to clear
   p[4]=right; p[5]=bot;               // existing pattern
   p[6]=left;  p[7]=bot;               // (floodfill won't do this)
   p[8]=left;  p[9]=top;
   setfillstyle(SOLID_FILL, deltacolor);
   fillpoly(5, p);
                                       // draw inner rectangle
   rectangle(left+delta+1, top+delta,
```

(continued on next page)

(continued from previous page)

```
                right-delta-1, bot-delta);
                                    // and fill it
   setfillstyle(SOLID_FILL, centercolor);
   floodfill(left+(right-left)/2, top+delta+1, WHITE );
   }

void Button::Click(void)       // click the button
   {
   bstatus = pushed;                         // push it
   Button::Display();                        // display it
   sound(500); delay(10); nosound();         // in beep
   delay(250);                               // wait 1/4 sec
   bstatus = unpushed;                       // unpush it
   Button::Display();                        // display it
   sound(400); delay(10); nosound();         // out beep
   }

void Button::Display(void)     // display the button
   {
   Window::Display();                        // display basic button
                                             // charcter on button
   moveto(left+(right-left)/2+1, top+(bot-top)/2);
   settextjustify(CENTER_TEXT, CENTER_TEXT);
   settextstyle(SANS_SERIF_FONT, HORIZ_DIR, USER_CHAR_SIZE );
   setusercharsize(5, 8, 2, 3);              // 5/8 width, 2/3 height
   setcolor(WHITE);                          // always white on black
   outtext(text);                            // write the character

   moveto(left, top);                        // upper left diagonal
   lineto(left+delta, top+delta);
   moveto(right, top);                       // upper right diagonal
   lineto(right-delta, top+delta);
   moveto(left, bot);                        // lower left diagonal
   lineto(left+delta, bot-delta);
   moveto(right, bot);                       // lower right diagonal
   lineto(right-delta, bot-delta);

   setfillstyle(SOLID_FILL, LIGHTGRAY); // illuminated edge color
   if(bstatus==unpushed)
      {                                      // shade top and left
      floodfill(left+(right-left)/2, top+1, WHITE);  // top
      floodfill(left+1, top+(bot-top)/2, WHITE);     // left
      }
   else  // pushed
      {                                      // shade bot and right
      floodfill(left+(right-left)/2, bot-1, WHITE);  // bot
      floodfill(right-1, top+(bot-top)/2, WHITE);    // right
      }
   }

void Output::Text(char *ptrstring)  // display text
   {
   Display();                           // clear output window
   moveto(right-delta, top+(bot-top)/2);
```

```
   settextjustify(RIGHT_TEXT, CENTER_TEXT);
   settextstyle(SANS_SERIF_FONT, HORIZ_DIR, USER_CHAR_SIZE );
   setusercharsize(5, 8, 1, 1);      // 5/8 width, 1/1 height
   setcolor(BLACK);                  // black text
   outtext(ptrstring);               // insert the text
   }

void Output::Number(double d)       // display number
   {
   char buffer[80];                  // set up text buffer
   ostrstream omem(buffer, 80);      // memory stream object
   omem << setiosflags(ios::fixed)   // format 123.00
        << setprecision(2)           // two digits to right of pt
        << setw(16)                  // field width 16
        << d;
   Output::Text(buffer);             // display string
   }
```

Class Declarations

The CALC.H file contains the declarations of the functions. CALC.CPP contains the member functions themselves. Note that CALC.CPP `#includes` CALC.H. Every file that works with the classes declared in CALC.H must `#include` this file.

The image of the calculator has a border, an output window to display the results, and 16 buttons. These three kinds of visual objects—border, output window, and buttons—have common features. They all occupy a certain position on the screen, and they all have a certain size. We make the further assumption that all these objects are created from two rectangles: an outer edge and an inner edge close to it. The space between these edges can be colored differently than the space within the inner rectangle, creating a picture-frame effect.

Since the image elements have common features, it's natural to put these features into a base class and use derived classes for borders, output windows, and buttons.

The Base Class `Window`

In CALC.H we first declare a base class called `Window` that has the characteristics described above. Its private data includes the left, top, right, and bottom coordinates of the outside edge of the window. A variable, `delta`, specifies the distance in pixels between the inside and outside edges. The variables `deltacolor` and `centercolor` hold the color of the space between the edges and the color of the inner rectangle, respectively.

Window Owners

In a visual image like a calculator, the graphics elements have a fixed visual relationship to one another; the "1" button is next to the "2" button, and so forth. Ordinarily we want to position one graphics element at a particular location on the screen, and then position other graphics elements *relative to the first.* This makes it easy to move an entire image, consisting of many elements, by changing only one set of coordinates. In our calculator, we want to position the border relative to the screen, and then position the buttons and the output window relative to this border. However, we might want to position a second border relative to the first (to provide visual separation for a group of buttons, for instance). Thus when we create a window—whether it is a border, a button, or an output window—we want to tell it what other window it should position itself relative to. We'll call this other window its `owner`. (We could have used the term *parent*, as is done in Microsoft Windows and OS/2 Presentation Manager programming, but this could be confused with the C++ concept of inheritance.)

When we create a window we'll send it a pointer to its owner so it can access the owner's coordinates and position itself relative to them. This is the variable `ptrOwner` in the declaration of the `Window` class.

Windows can own windows that own other windows. But the ultimate owner—the root of the ownership tree—is assumed to be the screen itself. In CALC.H we define the variable `SCREEN` to be a null (0) pointer. When a window detects that the pointer to its parent has a null value, it assumes that it should position itself relative to the screen, not to another window, so it treats the coordinates passed to it as absolute coordinates. Figure 15-3 shows the ownership relationship.

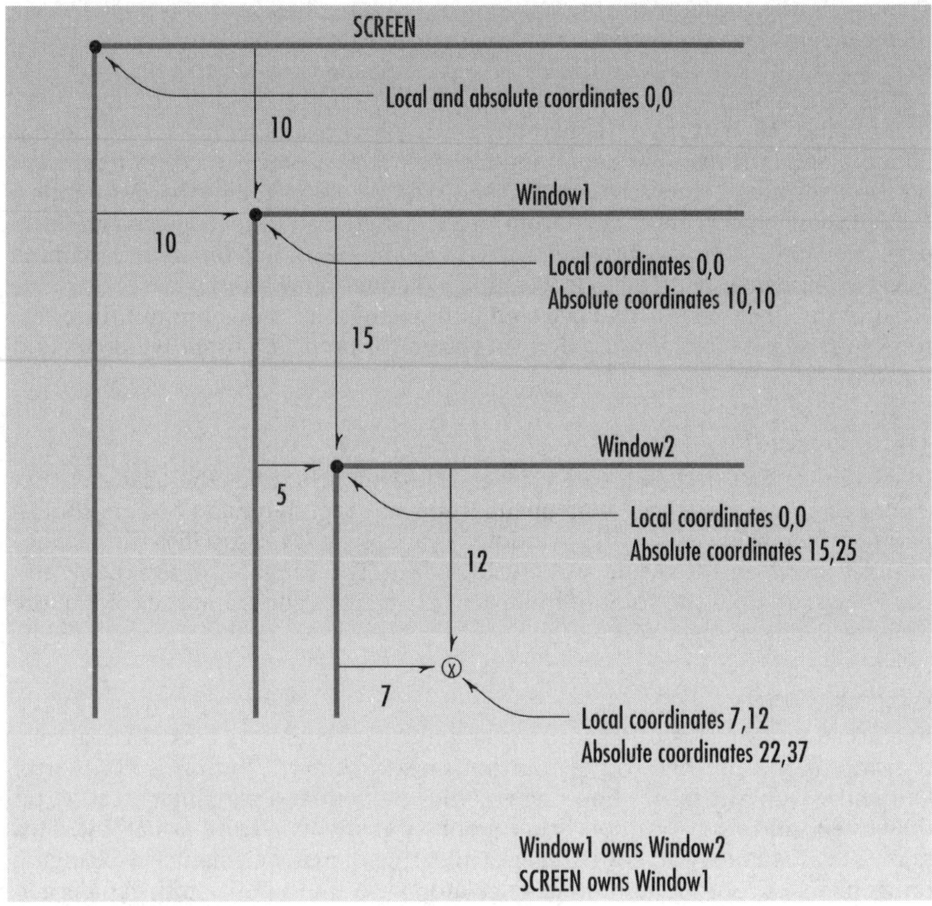

Figure 15-3 Window Ownership

Window Member Functions

The member functions for the `Window` class are declared in CALC.H, but are defined in CALC.CPP. There are only two of these functions. The first is the constructor `Window()`. This function calculates the coordinates of the window, using the coordinates of the owner and the relative coordinates passed from the window definition, and then copies them into the window's protected data space. The constructor also copies the color arguments from the definition, and calculates `delta`, the distance between the inner and outer rectangles, based on the size of the window. The relationship of `delta` to the window is shown in Figure 15-4.

The value of `delta` is larger for larger windows but never smaller than 3 pixels. (The constant 150 in its definition was chosen by trial and error.)

The second member function, `Display()`, displays the window. This involves drawing and filling two rectangles. The outer rectangle must obliterate whatever is underneath, so we use the `fillpoly()` library function. For the inner rectangle we can use the `floodfill()` function, which is somewhat easier to set up.

The `Border` Class

The `Border` class is very simple, being almost identical to the `Window` class. It simply adds some optional colors so you can declare a standard border without worrying about what colors to use. We could have dispensed with the `Border` class entirely, but it's conceptually cleaner to avoid creating objects of the base

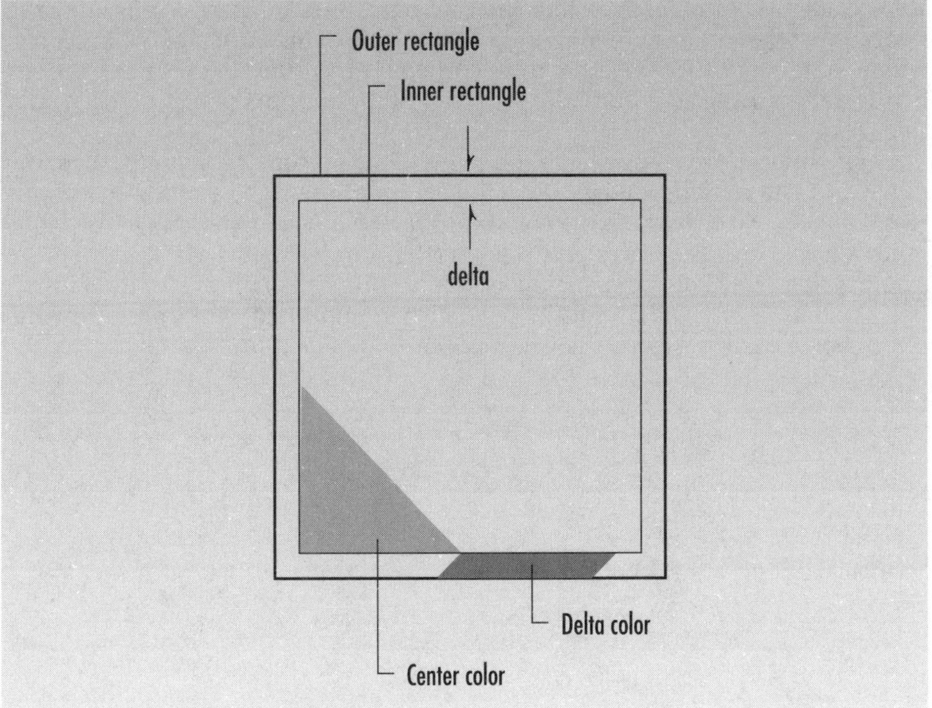

Figure 15-4 `Window` and `delta`

class and instead use it as an abstract class from which usable (or *instance*) classes are derived.

The `Button` Class

The `Button` class adds two items of data to a window: the status of the button (whether it is pushed in or not) and the text that will appear in the center of the button. We use an `enum` to specify two possible values for the type `buttonstatus`: `unpushed` and `pushed`. A button's text is printed in the center of the button, and is usually very short, although you could specify larger buttons that accommodate longer text.

The `Button` class adds three member functions, declared in CALC.H and defined in CALC.CPP. They are `Click()`, `Display()`, and the constructor `Button()`, which is similar to that in `Border`.

The `Click()` function depresses the button for a quarter of a second. (This is a little long if you're a fast typist, but it gives you time to see the button sink in and pop out.) It does this by changing the button status to `pushed`, displaying it, then changing the status back to `unpushed` and displaying it again. A clicking sound is added to accentuate the action.

The `Display()` function in the `Button` class first calls the `Display()` function in `Window` to draw the underlying rectangles. Note that the scope-resolution operator (`::`) must be used to distinguish which `Display()` we want. Next `Display()` draws the button's text. Finally, it shades the button's edges—the space between the button's inner and outer rectangles.

To shade the button's edges, four short diagonal lines are drawn connecting the upper-left corner of the outer rectangle with the upper-left corner of the inner rectangle, and similarly for the other three corners. This creates four separate sections between the rectangles, around the periphery of the button: upper, lower, left, and right.

What happens next depends on the status of the button. If it is not pushed, the upper and left sections are colored light gray, and the right and lower sections remain black. If it is pushed, the coloring is reversed: The upper and left sections remain black, and the lower and right sections are colored light gray. The eye assumes that light falls from the upper left, so this scheme provides the illusion that the button protrudes from the screen when unpushed, and sinks below the screen when pushed. Figure 15-5 shows a button.

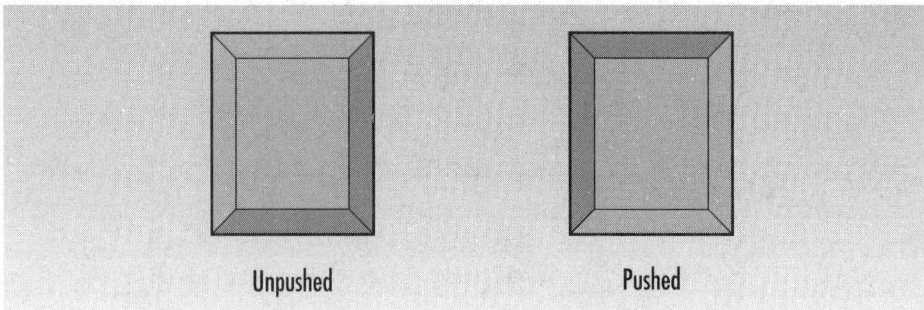

Figure 15-5 A Push Button

The Output Window

The `Output` class creates the window in which the numerical results of calculations are displayed. This class adds one additional data item to `Window`: the text to be displayed in the output window. There are two member functions. `Text()` displays output provided by a string argument to the function, and `Number()` displays output taken from a numerical argument. `Number()` converts the floating-point number to a string using the `sprintf()` library function, and then calls `Text()` to display the string.

The CALC_APP.CPP File

The CALC_APP.CPP file contains the code that uses the various classes to create the calculator. This code also interacts with the keyboard and performs the arithmetic requested by the user of the program. This is all handled in one function—`main()`. As written, the program specifies an EGA graphics adapter, but you can change it to specify VGA if you wish. The image of the calculator will be somewhat smaller, but it will work the same way.

```
// calc_app.cpp
// four-function calculator with 15 digits
// uses calc.cpp

#include "calc.h"                        // header file for calc.app

main()
   {
   int driver, mode;
   driver = EGA;                         // set graphics driver
   mode = EGAHI;                         // and graphics mode
   initgraph(&driver, &mode, "\\bc4\\bgi");

   // this section defines the various objects
                                         // border and output windows
   Border border1(SCREEN,  240, 30, 480, 330);
   Output output1(&border1, 20, 20, 220,  60, BLUE, WHITE);
                                         // buttons
   Button button0(&border1, 30, 230, 65, 265, BLACK, "0");
   Button button1(&border1, 30, 180, 65, 215, BLACK, "1");
   Button button2(&border1, 78, 180, 113, 215, BLACK, "2");
   Button button3(&border1, 127, 180, 162, 215, BLACK, "3");
   Button button4(&border1, 30, 130, 65, 165, BLACK, "4");
   Button button5(&border1, 78, 130, 113, 165, BLACK, "5");
   Button button6(&border1, 127, 130, 162, 165, BLACK, "6");
   Button button7(&border1, 30, 80, 65, 115, BLACK, "7");
   Button button8(&border1, 78, 80, 113, 115, BLACK, "8");
   Button button9(&border1, 127, 80, 162, 115, BLACK, "9");
   Button buttonDiv(&border1, 175, 80, 210, 115, BLUE, "/");
   Button buttonMul(&border1, 175, 130, 210, 165, BLUE, "*");
   Button buttonSub(&border1, 175, 180, 210, 215, BLUE, "-");
   Button buttonDot(&border1, 78, 230, 113, 265, BLACK, ".");
   Button buttonClr(&border1, 127, 230, 162, 265, RED, "clr");
```

(continued on next page)

(continued from previous page)

```
   Button buttonAdd(&border1, 175, 230, 210, 265, BLUE, "+=");

   // this section displays the various objects

   border1.Display();                // border and output windows
   output1.Display();
                                     // buttons
   button7.Display();    button8.Display();  button9.Display();
   button4.Display();    button5.Display();  button6.Display();
   button1.Display();    button2.Display();  button3.Display();
   buttonSub.Display();  buttonDiv.Display();
   buttonMul.Display();  buttonAdd.Display();
   button0.Display();  buttonDot.Display();  buttonClr.Display();
   output1.Number(0.0);              // display 0.0

   // this section handles the keyboard and activates display

   const char ESC=27;                // Escape key
   char dstring[80];                 // string for display
   char tempbuf[80];                 // temp string holder
   int numchars = 0;                 // number of chars in dstring
   char ch;                          // character read from keyboard
   char oper;                        // operator: /, *, -, +
   boolean isfirst = true;           // first (not second) operator
   boolean chain = false;            // chaining to next number
   double number1, number2;          // first and second numbers
   double answer;                    // answer to arithmetic

   while( (ch=getch()) != ESC )      // quit program on Escape key
      {                              // is it a digit (or dot)
      if( (ch>='0' && ch<='9') || ch=='.' )
         {
         switch(ch)
            {                        // click the button
            case '0': button0.Click(); break;
            case '1': button1.Click(); break;
            case '2': button2.Click(); break;
            case '3': button3.Click(); break;
            case '4': button4.Click(); break;
            case '5': button5.Click(); break;
            case '6': button6.Click(); break;
            case '7': button7.Click(); break;
            case '8': button8.Click(); break;
            case '9': button9.Click(); break;
            case '.': buttonDot.Click(); break;
            }  // end switch
         dstring[numchars++] = ch;  // put char in buffer
         dstring[numchars] = '\0';  // put 0 at end of string
         if( atof( dstring) > 99999999999.99 ||  // if too big
                 numchars > 11 )                  // or too long
            {                        // beep
            delay(100); sound(200); delay(300); nosound();
            dstring[--numchars] = '\0';  // delete last char
            }
```

```
      output1.Text(dstring);      // send it to output window
      }  // end if (it's a digit)

                                  // if it's a valid math operator
   else if( ch=='/' || ch=='*' || ch=='-' || ch=='+' ||
            ch=='=')
      {
      strcpy(tempbuf,dstring);    // save the input string
      numchars = 0;               // empty input buffer
      dstring[numchars] = '\0';
      output1.Text(dstring);      // display empty buffer
      if( isfirst )               // if first operator
         {                        // 1st time, n1 = answer
         number1 = (chain) ? answer : atof(tempbuf);
         isfirst = false;         // next op will be second
         switch(ch)               // store the operator
            {
            case '/':  buttonDiv.Click();  oper='/';  break;
            case '*':  buttonMul.Click();  oper='*';  break;
            case '-':  buttonSub.Click();  oper='-';  break;
            case '+':                 // + and = do same thing
            case '=':  buttonAdd.Click();  oper='+';  break;
            }  // end switch (ch)
         }  // end if (first number)
      else                          // second operator
         {                          //    (should be '=')
         buttonAdd.Click();         // assume it was '='
         number2 = atof(tempbuf);   // get second number
         switch(oper)               // do the action
            {
            case '/':  answer = number1 / number2;  break;
            case '*':  answer = number1 * number2;  break;
            case '-':  answer = number1 - number2;  break;
            case '+':  answer = number1 + number2;  break;
            }
         if(answer > 99999999999.99)  // if answer too big
            output1.Text("Overflow");   // to display
         else                         // otherwise
            {                         // answer ok
            output1.Number(answer); // display the answer
            number1 = answer;
            }                         // set up to chain to
         isfirst = true;              // another 2nd operator
         chain = true;                // and another 2nd number
         } // end else (second operator)
      }  // end else if (operator)
   else if( ch=='C' || ch=='c' )    // if it's Clear
      {
      buttonClr.Click();              // click the button
      isfirst = true;                 // next number is first
      chain = false;                  // not chaining
      numchars = 0;                   // empty input buffer
      dstring[numchars] = '\0';
      output1.Number(0.0);            // display 0.0
```

(continued on next page)

(continued from previous page)

```
         }  // end else if (clear)
      else                                  // it's a bad character
         {                                  // beep
         delay(100); sound(200); delay(300); nosound();
         }  // end else (bad character)
      }  // end while
   closegraph();                // shut down graphics system
   }  // end main()
```

Note that CALC_APP.CPP, like CALC.CPP, must `#include` the header file CALC.H so that it can access the various class declarations.

In `main()` we first define all the visual elements of the calculator, then display them using each one's `Display()` function. (We could have made these display routines into a family of virtual functions, but in this particular application there was no need to do so. In a more general situation, virtual functions would provide added flexibility.)

The complicated part of `main()` involves handling the keyboard input. This is done in a large `while` loop. At the top of the loop the character is read by the `getche()` function. Pressing (ESC) terminates the loop and the program. The body of the loop is a series of `if` and `else...if` constructions that decipher the character typed.

Digits

If the character is a digit or the decimal point, the appropriate button is clicked and the digit is added to the end of a character buffer called `dstring`. The `'\0'` character is then added in the position following the character to terminate the string. If the buffer is too full or the number too big, an error beep is generated and the offending digit is removed from the buffer (by writing over it with `'\0'`). The resulting buffer contents are displayed using the `Output.Text()` function.

Operators

If the character is an arithmetic operator, the string in `dstring` is saved temporarily, and `dstring` is emptied and the empty buffer displayed.

What we do next depends on whether this is the first arithmetic operator or the second. A Boolean flag variable, `isfirst`, keeps track of this state. If this flag is `true`, we know we are dealing with the first operator, which should be `\`, `*`, `-` or `+`. We save the number from `dstring` in `number1`, then click the button corresponding to the operator and save the operator for later use. (We'll ignore the possibility of chaining for the moment.)

If we've just read the second operator, it must be the = operator, so we click the `+=` button, store the number in `number2`, and—using the previously stored operator—perform the corresponding arithmetic operation on `number1` and `number2`. The result is stored in `answer`. If it isn't too big, we display it; otherwise we display the word *Overflow*.

Clear Button

If the character is 'C' or 'c', we click the `Clr` button and clear the `dstring` buffer in preparation for starting over. We respond to any other keyboard character with an error beep but no other change.

Chaining

Often the user wants to retain the result of an operation and use it as the first operand of a second operation. This is mediated by a `chain` flag variable, which is set to `true` if we've already completed one operation. When this is the case the value to be inserted in `number1` is taken from `answer` rather than from the user, before the indicated arithmetic is carried out.

Not a Stand-Alone File

Note that, as written, CALC.EXE is not a stand-alone program; the \BC45\BGI or \TC\BGI directory specified in `initgraph()` must be available to the program. This directory contains the files EGAVGA.BGI (the graphics driver for EGA and VGA) and SANS.CHR (the font file for the sans serif font). We describe the procedure for creating a stand-alone graphics program in Appendix C.

Not the Windows Approach

In Windows and OS/2 Presentation Manager, window-type objects like buttons are supplied with the operating system. The operating system also informs your program when the mouse is clicked on certain objects. For these reasons, writing a program like CALC is easier in Windows or PM than writing your own visual interface, as we've shown here.

A Very Long Number Class

Sometimes even the basic data type `unsigned long` does not provide enough precision for certain integer arithmetic operations. `unsigned long` is the largest integer type in Borland C++, holding integers up to 4,294,967,295, or about ten digits. This is about the same number of digits a pocket calculator can handle. But if you need to work with numbers containing more significant digits than this, you have a problem.

Our next example shows a way to solve this problem. It provides a class that holds numbers up to 200 digits long. If you want to make even longer numbers, you can change a single constant in the program. Need 1000-digit numbers? No problem.

Since it doesn't use any fancy graphics or other DOS-only functions, you can create this program as an EasyWin program in Borland C++.

Numbers As Strings

The `verylong` class stores numbers as strings of digits. This explains its large capacity; the basic types in C++ can handle long strings, since they are simply arrays. By representing numbers as strings we can make them as long as we want. There are two data members in `verylong`: a `char` array to hold the string of digits, and an `int` to tell how long the string is. (This length data isn't strictly necessary, but it saves using `strlen()` to find the string length over and over.) The digits in the string are stored in reverse order, with the least significant digit stored first, at `vlstr[0]`. This simplifies various operations on the string. Figure 15-6 shows a number stored as a string.

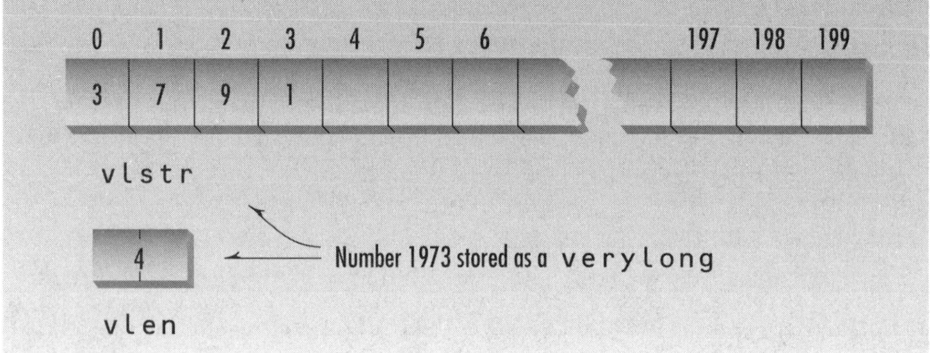

Figure 15-6 A `verylong` Number

We've provided user-accessible routines for addition and multiplication of `verylong` numbers. (We leave it as an exercise for the reader to write subtraction and division routines.)

The Class Specifier

Here's the header file for VERYLONG. It shows the specifiers for the `verylong` class.

```
// verylong.h
// class specifier for very long integer type
#include <iostream.h>
#include <string.h>          // for strlen(), etc.
#include <stdlib.h>          // for ltoa()

const int SZ = 200;          // maximum digits in verylongs

class verylong
   {
   private:
      char vlstr[SZ];        // verylong number as a string
      int vlen;              // length of verylong string
      verylong multdigit(int);          // prototypes for
      verylong mult10(verylong);        // private functions
   public:
      verylong()                        // no-arg constructor
         { vlstr[0]='\0'; vlen=0; }
      verylong(char s[SZ])              // one-arg constructor
         { strcpy(vlstr, s); vlen=strlen(s); }    // for string
      verylong(unsigned long n)         // one-arg constructor
         {                                        // for long int
         ltoa(n, vlstr, 10);            // convert to string
         strrev(vlstr);                 // reverse it
         vlen=strlen(vlstr);            // find length
         }
      void putvl();                     // display verylong
      void getvl();                     // get verylong from user
      verylong operator + (verylong);   // add verylongs
      verylong operator * (verylong);   // multiply verylongs
   };
```

In addition to the data members, there are two private-member functions in class `verylong`. One multiplies a `verylong` number by a single digit, and one multiplies a `verylong` number by 10. These routines are used internally by the multiplication routine.

There are three constructors. One sets the `verylong` to 0 by inserting a terminating null at the beginning of the array and setting the length to 0. The second initializes it to a string (which is in reverse order), and the third initializes it to a `long int` value.

The `putvl()` member function displays a `verylong`, and the `getvl` gets a `verylong` value from the user. You can type as many digits as you like, up to 200. Note that there is no error checking in this routine; if you type a nondigit the results will be inaccurate.

Two overloaded operators, `+` and `*`, perform addition and multiplication. You can use expressions like

```
alpha = beta * gamma + delta;
```

to do `verylong` arithmetic.

The Member Functions

Here's VERYLONG.CPP, the file that holds the member function definitions:

```
// verylong.cpp
// implements very long integer type
#include "verylong.h"          // header file for verylong

void verylong::putvl()                    // display verylong
   {
   char temp[SZ];
   strcpy(temp,vlstr);                    // make copy
   cout << strrev(temp);                  // reverse the copy
   }                                      // and display it

void verylong::getvl()                    // get verylong from user
   {
   cin >> vlstr;                          // get string from user
   vlen = strlen(vlstr);                  // find its length
   strrev(vlstr);                         // reverse it
   }

verylong verylong::operator + (verylong v)  // add verylongs
   {
   char temp[SZ];
                                          // find longest number
   int maxlen = (vlen > v.vlen) ? vlen : v.vlen;
   int carry = 0;                         // set to 1 if sum >= 10
   for(int j = 0; j<maxlen; j++)          // for each position
      {
      int d1 = (j > vlen-1)   ? 0 : vlstr[j]-'0';    // get digit
      int d2 = (j > v.vlen-1) ? 0 : v.vlstr[j]-'0'; // get digit
      int digitsum = d1 + d2 + carry;               // add digits
      if( digitsum >= 10 )                // if there's a carry,
         { digitsum -= 10; carry=1; }     // decrease sum by 10,
```

(continued on next page)

(continued from previous page)

```
      else                                  // set carry to 1
         carry = 0;                         // otherwise carry is 0
      temp[j] = digitsum+'0';               // insert char in string
      }
   if(carry==1)                             // if carry at end,
      temp[j++] = '1';                      // last digit is 1
   temp[j] = '\0';                          // terminate string
   return verylong(temp);                   // return temp verylong
   }

verylong verylong::operator * (verylong v)  // multiply verylongs
   {
   verylong pprod;                          // product of one digit
   verylong tempsum;                        // running total
   for(int j=0; j<v.vlen; j++)              // for each digit in arg
      {
      int digit = v.vlstr[j]-'0';           // get the digit
      pprod = multdigit(digit);             // multiply this by digit
      for(int k=0; k<j; k++)                // multiply result by
         pprod = mult10(pprod);             //    power of 10
      tempsum = tempsum + pprod;            // add product to total
      }
   return tempsum;                          // return total of prods
   }

verylong verylong::mult10(verylong v)       // multiply argument by 10
   {
   char temp[SZ];
   for(int j=v.vlen-1; j>=0; j--)           // move digits one
      temp[j+1] = v.vlstr[j];               //    position higher
   temp[0] = '0';                           // put zero on low end
   temp[v.vlen+1] = '\0';                   // terminate string
   return verylong(temp);                   // return result
   }

verylong verylong::multdigit(int d2)        // multiply this verylong
   {                                        // by digit in argument
   char temp[SZ];
   int carry = 0;
   for(int j = 0; j<vlen; j++)              // for each position
      {                                     // in this verylong
      int d1 = vlstr[j]-'0';                // get digit from this
      int digitprod = d1 * d2;              // multiply by that digit
      digitprod += carry;                   // add old carry
      if( digitprod >= 10 )                 // if there's a new carry,
         {
         carry = digitprod/10;              // carry is high digit
         digitprod -= carry*10;             // result is low digit
         }
      else
         carry = 0;                         // otherwise carry is 0
      temp[j] = digitprod+'0';              // insert char in string
      }
```

```
if(carry != 0)                           // if carry at end,
   temp[j++] = carry+'0';                // it's last digit
temp[j] = '\0';                          // terminate string
return verylong(temp);                   // return verylong
}
```

The putvl() and getvl() functions are fairly straightforward. They use the strrev() library function to reverse the string, so it is stored in reverse order but input is displayed normally.

The operator+() function adds two verylongs and leaves the result in a third verylong. It does this by considering their digits one at a time. It adds digit 0 from both numbers, storing a carry if necessary. Then it adds the digits in position 1, adding the carry if necessary. It continues until it has added all the digits in the larger of the two numbers. If the numbers are different lengths, the nonexistent digits in the shorter number are set to 0 before being added. Figure 15-7 shows the process.

Multiplication uses the operator*() function. This function performs multiplication by multiplying the multiplicand (the top number when you write it by hand) by each separate digit in the multiplier (the bottom number). It calls the

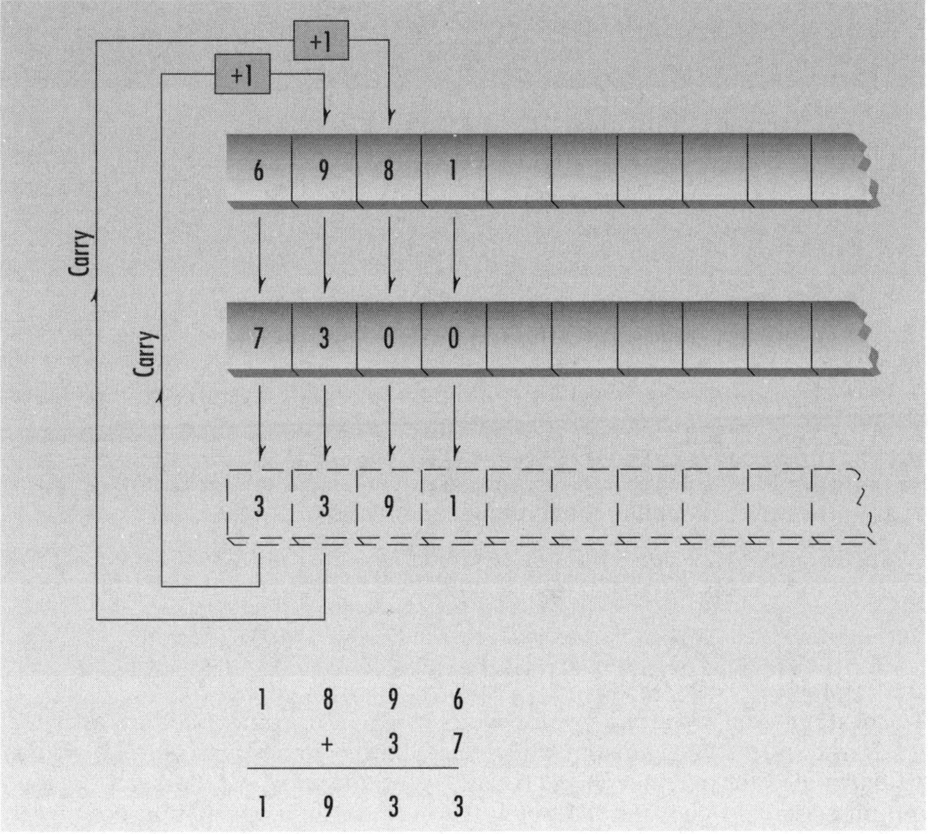

Figure 15-7 Adding verylong Numbers

`multdigit()` routine to this. The results are then multiplied by 10 an appropriate number of times to shift the result to match the position of the digit, using the `mult10()` function. The results of these separate calculations are then added together using the `operator+()` function.

The Application Program

To test the `verylong` class we use a variation of the FACTOR program from Chapter 4 to calculate the factorial of a number entered by the user. Here's the listing for VL_APP.CPP:

```
// vl_app.cpp
// calculates factorials of larger numbers using verylong class
#include "verylong.h"                  // verylong header file
void main()
   {
   unsigned long numb, j;
   verylong fact=1;                    // initialize verylong

   cout << "\n\nEnter number: ";
   cin >> numb;                        // input a long int
   for(j=numb; j>0; j--)               // factorial is numb *
      fact = fact * j;                 //    numb-1 * numb-2 *
   cout << "Factoral is ";             //    numb-3 and so on
   fact.putvl();                       // display factorial
   }
```

In this program `fact` is a `verylong` variable. The other variables, `numb` and `j`, don't need to be `verylong`s because they don't get so big. To calculate the factorial of 200, for example, `numb` and `j` require only three digits, while `fact` requires 158.

Notice how, in the expression

```
fact = fact * j;
```

the `long` variable `j` is automatically converted to `verylong`, using the one-argument constructor, before the multiplication is carried out.

Here's the output when we ask the program to find the factorial of 100:

```
Enter number: 100
Factorial is 93326215443944152681699238856266700490715968264381621
468592963895217599993229915608941463976156518286253697920827223
758251185210916864000000000000000000000000
```

Try *that* using type `long` variables! Surprisingly, the routines are fairly fast; this program executes in a fraction of a second.

A High-Rise Elevator Simulation

The next time you're waiting for an elevator in a high-rise office building, ask yourself how the elevators figure out where to go. In the old days, of course, there was a human elevator operator on each car. ("Good morning, Mr. Burberry," "Good morning, Carl.") Riders needed to tell the operator their destination floor when getting on ("Seventeen, please."). A panel of signal lights lit up inside the car to show which floors were requesting service up or down. Operators decided which way to go and where to stop on the basis of these verbal requests and their observation of the signal lights.

Nowadays enough intelligence is built into elevator systems to permit the cars to operate on their own. In our next example we use C++ classes to model an elevator system.

What are the components of such a system? In a typical building there are a number of similar elevators. On each floor there are up and down buttons. Note that there is usually only one such pair of buttons per floor; when you push a button you don't know which elevator will stop for you. Within the elevator there is a larger number of buttons: one for each floor. After entering the elevator, riders push a button to indicate their destination. Our simulation program will model all these components.

Running the ELEV Program

When you start up the ELEV program you'll see four elevators sitting at the bottom of the screen, and a list of numbers on the left, starting at 1 on the bottom of the screen and continuing up to 20 at the top. The elevators are initially on the ground (first) floor. This is shown in Figure 15-8.

Making a Floor Request

If you press any key, text at the bottom of the screen prompts

```
Enter the floor you're on:
```

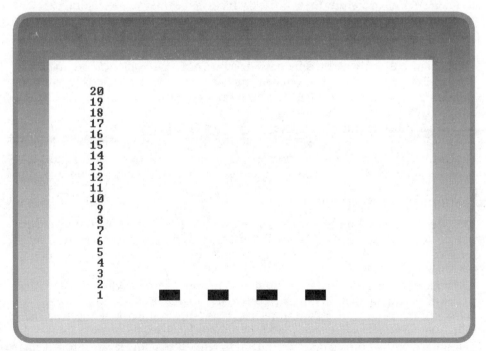

Figure 15-8 The ELEV Program Initial Screen

You can enter any floor number. If you've just arrived for work on the ground floor, you'll enter 1. If you're leaving a higher floor to go out to lunch, you'll enter your floor's number. The next prompt is

```
Enter direction you want to go (u or d):
```

If you're on the first floor you must go up, and if you're on the 20th floor you must go down. For intermediate floors you can go either way. When you've completed your floor request, a triangle will appear next to the appropriate floor number on the left. It will point either up or down, depending on the direction you requested. As more requests are made, triangles will appear beside additional floor numbers.

If there is an elevator car already at a floor where a request has been made, the door will open immediately. You'll see a happy-face character materialize outside the car, then move into the open door. If there is no car on the floor making the request, one will move up or down toward the floor and open its door once it reaches the floor.

Entering Destinations

Once a car arrives at a floor and the happy-face passenger is inside, a prompt appears on the bottom of the screen, something like,

```
Car 1 has stopped at floor 1
Enter destination floors (0 when finished)
Destination 1: 13
```

Here the passenger has entered 13. However, the happy face can represent more than one passenger getting on at once. Each passenger may request a different destination, so the program allows multiple destinations to be entered. Enter as many numbers as you want (at least 1, but no more than 20) and enter 0 when you're done.

The destinations requested by passengers within a particular car are indicated by small rectangles displayed outside the car, just to its left, opposite the floor number requested. Each car has its own set of destinations (unlike floor requests, which are shared by all the cars).

You can make as many floor requests as you like. The system will remember the requests, along with the destinations selected from within each car, and attempt to service them all. All four cars may be in motion at the same time. Figure 15-9 shows a situation with multiple floor requests and multiple destinations.

Designing the System

The elevator cars are all roughly the same, so it seems reasonable to make them objects of a single class. The class will contain data specific to each car: its present location, the direction it's going, the destination floor numbers requested by its occupants, and so on.

However, there is also data that applies to the building as a whole. As described in the HORSE example in Chapter 13, data that is shared by all the objects of a class should be made static. In this example there are three static data items. First there is an array of *floor requests*. This is a list of floors where people, waiting for the elevator, have pushed the up or down button to request that an elevator stop at their floor. Any elevator may respond to such a floor request, so each one needs to know

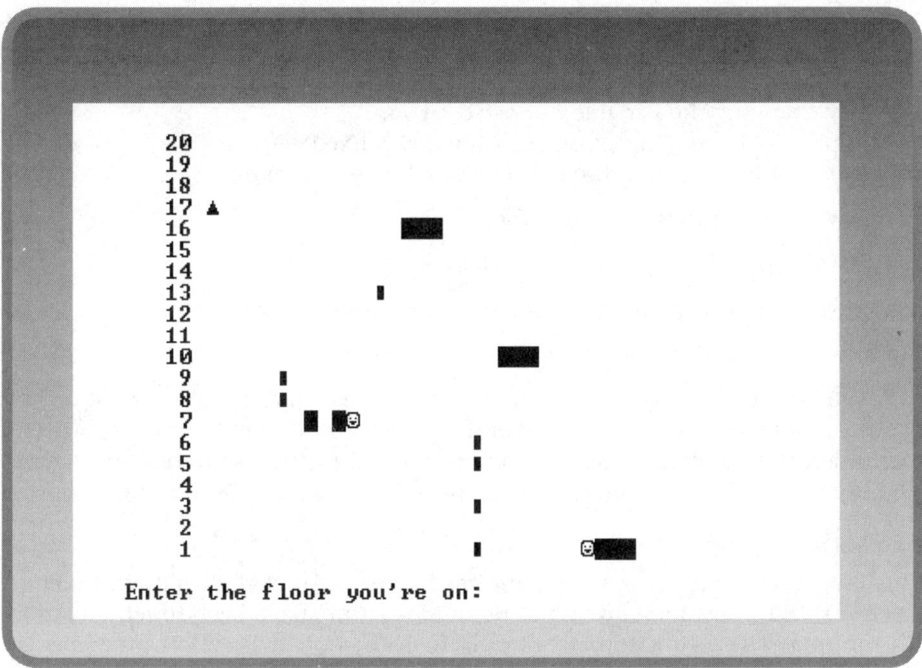

Figure 15-9 Elevators in Action

about them. We use an N-by-2 Boolean array, where N is the number of floors and the 2 allows separate array elements for up and down for each floor. All the elevators can look at this array when they're trying to figure out where to go next.

Besides knowing about the floor requests, each elevator car must also be aware of where the other elevators are. If we're on the first floor, there's no point in rushing up to the 15th floor to answer a request if there's already another car available on the 10th floor. The closest car should head toward the request. To make it easy for each car to find out about the others, the second static data item is an array of pointers to elevators. Each elevator car stores its memory address on this list when it's first created, so the other cars can find it.

The third static item is the number of cars created so far. This allows each car to number itself when it's created.

Managing Time

As in the HORSE program in Chapter 13, the `main()` program calls a static member function at fixed intervals to put things into motion. This function is called `master_tick()`. It in turn calls a function for each elevator car, called `car_tick1()`. This function, among other things, displays each car on the screen and calls another function to decide what the car should do next. The choices are to go up, to go down, to stop, to load a passenger, or to unload a passenger.

Each car must then be moved to its new position. However, things get slightly complicated here. Because each car must figure out where the other ones are before it can decide what to do, all the cars must go through the decision process before any of them moves. To make sure this happens, we use two time ticks for each car. Thus after `car_tick1()` has been called to decide where each car will go, another function, `car_tick2()`, is called to actually move each car. It causes the cars to move by changing the variable `current_floor`.

The process of loading passengers follows a fixed sequence of steps, during which the car is stopped at the desired floor. The program draws, in order

1. Car with closed door, no happy face.
2. Car with open door, happy face on left.
3. Car with happy face in open door, get destinations from user.
4. Car with closed door, no happy face.

A similar sequence applies to unloading. These sequences are carried out by starting a timer (an integer variable) and letting it count down from 3 to 0, decrementing it with each time tick. A `case` statement in the `car_display()` function then draws the appropriate version of the car for each stage of the process.

Can't Use EasyWin

This program, like the HORSE program in Chapter 13, uses the C library function `delay()`. It also uses `sound()` and `nosound()` to make a beep to let you know it's running. These functions work only in DOS, not in EasyWin programs, so you'll need to use that target when creating a project in Borland C++.

Listings for ELEV

We've divided the program into four files. Two of these files, ELEV.H and ELEV.CPP, might be created by a vendor supplying elevator-design software. This software would then be purchased by an engineering company interested in designing an elevator system for a particular building. (This program is not certified by the National Elevator Board, so don't try it with real elevators.) The engineering company would then write another pair of files, ELEV_APP.H and ELEV_APP.CPP. The ELEV_APP.H file specifies the characteristics of the high-rise building. It needs to be a separate file because these characteristics must be known by the elevator class member functions, and the easiest way to do this is to include ELEV_APP.H in the ELEV.H file. The ELEV_APP.CPP file initializes the elevators and then calls elevator functions at fixed intervals to simulate the passage of time.

Class Specifier

The ELEV.H file contains the specification for the `elevator` class. Some of its members, such as `num_cars` and `car_number`, play the same roles as similar variables in the HORSE program in Chapter 13. The array of pointers to elevators, `car_list[]`, allows each elevator to query all the others about their location and direction. Here's the listing:

```
// elev.h
// header file for elevators -- contains class declarations

#include "elev_app.h"                    // provided by client
#include <iostream.h>
```

```
#include <iomanip.h>                    // for setw()
#include <dos.h>                        // for delay()
#include <conio.h>                      // for screen output
#include <stdlib.h>                     // for itoa()
#include <process.h>                    // for exit()

enum direction { UP, DN, STOP };
enum boolean { FALSE, TRUE };
const int LOAD_TIME =    3;   // loading/unloading time (ticks)
const int SPACING =      7;   // visual spacing between cars
const int BUF_LENGTH =  80;   // length of utility string buffer

////////////////////////////////////////////////////////////////
class elevator
   {
   private:
      // data shared by all elevator cars
      static elevator* car_list[NUM_CARS];  // ptrs to cars
      static int num_cars;              // cars created so far
                                        // array of up/down buttons
      static boolean floor_request[2][NUM_FLOORS];
      // data specific to each car
      int car_number;                   // our number (0 to n-1)
      int current_floor;                // where are we? (0 to n-1)
      int old_floor;                    // where were we? (0 to n-1)
      direction current_dir;            // which way are we going?
      boolean destination[NUM_FLOORS];   // selected by occupants
      int loading_timer;                // non-zero if loading
      int unloading_timer;              // non-zero if unloading
      // functions for specific cars
      void car_tick1();                 // time tick 1 for each car
      void car_tick2();                 // time tick 2 for each car
      void car_display();               // display elevator
      void dests_display();             // display elevator requests
      void decide();                    // decide what to do
      void move();                      // move the car
      void get_destinations();          // get destinations
      // functions for data shared by all cars
      static void show_floor_reqs(); // show floor requests

   public:
      // functions for data of specific cars
      elevator();                       // constructor
      // functions for data shared by all cars
      static void init();               // initialize static data
      static void master_tick();        // send ticks to all cars
      static void get_floor_reqs();  // get floor requests
   };
```

Member Functions

The ELEV.CPP file contains the definitions of the `elevator` member functions and static data. Static functions initialize the system, provide a master time tick, display the floor requests, and get floor requests from the user. Normal (nonstatic) functions initialize individual cars (with the constructor), provide two time ticks for each car, display it, display its destinations, decide what to do, move the car to a new floor, and get destinations from the user. Here's the listing:

```
// elev.cpp
// contains class data and member function definitions

#include "elev.h"      // include class declarations

////////////////////////////////////////////////////////////////////
// static data definitions
////////////////////////////////////////////////////////////////////
elevator* elevator::car_list[NUM_CARS];  // list of ptrs to cars
int elevator::num_cars = 0;             // elevs created to date
                                        // array of up/down buttons
boolean elevator::floor_request[2][NUM_FLOORS]; // [0]=UP, [1]=DN

////////////////////////////////////////////////////////////////////
// static function definitions
////////////////////////////////////////////////////////////////////

void elevator::init()                   // initialize static data
   {
   char ustring[BUF_LENGTH];            // string for floor numbers

   clrscr();                            // clear screen
   for(int j=0; j<NUM_FLOORS; j++)      // for each floor
      {
      gotoxy(3, NUM_FLOORS-j);          // put floor number
      itoa(j+1, ustring, 10);           // on screen
      cout << setw(3) << ustring;
      floor_request[UP][j] = FALSE;     // no floor requests yet
      floor_request[DN][j] = FALSE;
      }
   }

void elevator::master_tick(void)        // master time tick
   {
   show_floor_reqs();                   // display floor requests
   for(int j=0; j<NUM_CARS; j++)        // for each elevator
      car_list[j]->car_tick1();         // send it time tick 1
   for(j=0; j<NUM_CARS; j++)            // for each elevator
      car_list[j]->car_tick2();         // send it time tick 2
   }

void elevator::show_floor_reqs()        // display floor requests
   {
   for(int j=0; j<NUM_FLOORS; j++)
      {
      gotoxy(SPACING, NUM_FLOORS-j);
      if(floor_request[UP][j]==TRUE)
         cout << '\x1E';                // up arrow
      else
         cout << ' ';
      gotoxy(SPACING+3, NUM_FLOORS-j);
```

```
      if(floor_request[DN][j]==TRUE)
         cout << '\x1F';               // down arrow
      else
         cout << ' ';
      }
   }
// get_floor_reqs() -- get floor requests from user outside car
void elevator::get_floor_reqs()
   {
   char ch;                       // utility char for input
   char ustring[BUF_LENGTH];      // utility string for input
   int iFloor;                    // floor from which request made
   char chDirection;              // 'u' or 'd' for up or down

   if( !kbhit() )                 // wait for keypress
      return;
   gotoxy(1,23);                  // bottom of screen
   ch = getch();
   if(ch=='\x1B')                 // if escape key, end program
      exit(0);
   gotoxy(1,22);                  // bottom of screen
   cout << "Enter the floor you're on: ";
   cin.get(ustring, BUF_LENGTH);  // (avoid multiple linefeeds)
   cin.get(ch);                   // eat the newline
   iFloor = atoi(ustring);
   cout << "Enter direction you want to go (u or d): ";
   cin.get(chDirection);          // (avoid multiple linefeeds)
   cin.get(ch);                   // eat the newline

   if(chDirection=='u' || chDirection=='U')
      floor_request[UP][iFloor-1] = TRUE;  // up floor request
   if(chDirection=='d' || chDirection=='D')
      floor_request[DN][iFloor-1] = TRUE;  // down floor request
   gotoxy(1,22); clreol();                 // clear old text
   gotoxy(1,23); clreol();
   gotoxy(1,24); clreol();
   }

////////////////////////////////////////////////////////////////
// non-static function definitions
////////////////////////////////////////////////////////////////

elevator::elevator()                    // constructor
   {
   car_list[num_cars] = this;           // put our address on list
   car_number = num_cars++;             // set our number
   current_floor = 0;                   // start at 0 (user's 1)
   old_floor = 0;                       // remember previous floor
   current_dir = STOP;                  // stationary at start
   for(int j=0; j<NUM_FLOORS; j++)      // occupants have not pushed
      destination[j] = FALSE;           //    any buttons yet
   loading_timer = 0;                   // not loading yet
   unloading_timer = 0;                 // not unloading yet
   }
```

(continued on next page)

(continued from previous page)

```
void elevator::car_tick1()              // tick 1 for each car
   {
   car_display();                        // display elevator box
   dests_display();                      // display destinations
   if(loading_timer)                     // count down load time
      --loading_timer;
   if(unloading_timer)                   // count down unload time
      --unloading_timer;
   decide();                             // decide what to do
   }
// all cars must decide before any of them move
void elevator::car_tick2()              // tick 2 for each car
   {
   move();                               // move car if appropriate
   }

void elevator::car_display()            // display elevator image
   {
   gotoxy(SPACING+(car_number+1)*SPACING, NUM_FLOORS-old_floor);
   cout << "    ";                       // erase old position
   gotoxy(SPACING-1+(car_number+1)*SPACING,
                                          NUM_FLOORS-current_floor);
   switch(loading_timer)
      {
      case 3:
         cout << "\x01\xDB \xDB ";       // draw car with open door
         break;                          // happy face on left
      case 2:
         cout << " \xDB\x01\xDB ";       // happy face in open door
         get_destinations();             // get destinations
         break;
      case 1:
         cout << " \xDB\xDB\xDB ";       // draw with closed door
         break;                          // no happy face
      case 0:
         cout << " \xDB\xDB\xDB ";       // draw with closed door, no
         break;                          // happy face (default)
      }
   gotoxy(SPACING+(car_number+1)*SPACING,
                                       NUM_FLOORS-current_floor);
   switch(unloading_timer)
      {
      case 3:
         cout << "\xDB\x01\xDB ";        // draw car with open door
         break;                          // happy face in car
      case 2:
         cout << "\xDB \xDB\x01";        // draw car with open door
         break;                          // happy face on right
      case 1:
         cout << "\xDB\xDB\xDB ";        // draw with closed door
         break;                          // no happy face
      case 0:
         cout << "\xDB\xDB\xDB ";        // draw with closed door, no
         break;                          // happy face (default)
```

```
      }
   old_floor = current_floor;          // remember old floor
   }

void elevator::dests_display()         // display destinations
   {                                   //    selected by buttons
   for(int j=0; j<NUM_FLOORS; j++)     //    inside the car
      {
      gotoxy(SPACING-2+(car_number+1)*SPACING, NUM_FLOORS-j);
      if( destination[j] == TRUE )
         cout << '\xFE';               // small box
      else
         cout << ' ';                  // blank
      }
   }

void elevator::decide()                   // decide what to do
   {
   // flags indicate if destinations or requests above/below us
   boolean destins_above, destins_below;     // destinations
   boolean requests_above, requests_below;   // requests
   // floor number of closest request above us and below us
   int nearest_higher_req = 0;
   int nearest_lower_req = 0;
   // flags indicate if there is another car, going in the same
   // direction, between us and the nearest floor request (FR)
   boolean car_between_up, car_between_dn;
   // flags indicate if there is another car, going in the
   // opposite direction, on the opposite side of the nearest FR
   boolean car_opposite_up, car_opposite_dn;
   // floor and direction of other car (not us)
   int ofloor;                                   // floor
   direction odir;                               // direction

   // ensure we don't go too high or too low
   if( (current_floor==NUM_FLOORS-1 && current_dir==UP)
      || (current_floor==0 && current_dir==DN) )
      current_dir = STOP;

   // if there's a destination on this floor, unload passengers
   if( destination[current_floor]==TRUE )
      {
      destination[current_floor] = FALSE;  // erase destination
      if( !unloading_timer)                // unload
         unloading_timer = LOAD_TIME;
      return;
      }
   // if there's an UP floor request on this floor,
   // and if we're going up or stopped, load passengers
   if( (floor_request[UP][current_floor] && current_dir != DN) )
      {
      current_dir = UP;  // (in case it was STOP)
      // remove floor request for direction we're going
      floor_request[current_dir][current_floor] = FALSE;
```

(continued on next page)

(continued from previous page)

```
      if( !loading_timer)                        // load
         loading_timer = LOAD_TIME;
      return;
      }
   // if there's a down floor request on this floor,
   // and if we're going down or stopped, load passengers
   if( (floor_request[DN][current_floor] && current_dir != UP) )
      {
      current_dir = DN;  // (in case it was STOP)
      // remove floor request for direction we're going
      floor_request[current_dir][current_floor] = FALSE;
      if( !loading_timer)                        // load passengers
         loading_timer = LOAD_TIME;
      return;
      }
   // check if there are other destinations or requests
   // record distance to nearest request
   destins_above = destins_below = FALSE;
   requests_above = requests_below = FALSE;
   for(int j=current_floor+1; j<NUM_FLOORS; j++)
      {                                         // check floors above
      if( destination[j] )                      // if destinations
         destins_above = TRUE;                  // set flag
      if( floor_request[UP][j] || floor_request[DN][j] )
         {                                      // if requests
         requests_above = TRUE;                 // set flag
         if( !nearest_higher_req )              // if not set before
            nearest_higher_req = j;             //    set nearest req
         }
      }
   for(j=current_floor-1; j>=0; j--)            // check floors below
      {
      if(destination[j] )                       // if destinations
         destins_below = TRUE;                  // set flag
      if( floor_request[UP][j] || floor_request[DN][j] )
         {                                      // if requests
         requests_below = TRUE;                 // set flag
         if( !nearest_lower_req )               // if not set before
            nearest_lower_req = j;              //    set nearest req
         }
      }
   // if no requests or destinations above or below, stop
   if( !destins_above && !requests_above &&
       !destins_below && !requests_below)
       {
       current_dir = STOP;
       return;
       }
   // if destinations and we're stopped, or already going the
   // right way, go toward destinations
   if( destins_above && (current_dir==STOP || current_dir==UP) )
      {
      current_dir = UP;
```

```
      return;
      }
   if( destins_below && (current_dir==STOP || current_dir==DN) )
      {
      current_dir = DN;
      return;
      }
   // find out if there are other cars, (a) going in the same
   // direction, between us and the nearest floor request;
   // or (b) going in the opposite direction, on the other
   // side of the floor request
   car_between_up = car_between_dn = FALSE;
   car_opposite_up = car_opposite_dn = FALSE;

   for(j=0; j<NUM_CARS; j++)                  // check each car
      {
      if(j != car_number)                     // if it's not us
         {                                    // get its floor
         ofloor = car_list[j]->current_floor;    // and
         odir = car_list[j]->current_dir; // direction

         // if it's going up and there are requests above us
         if( (odir==UP || odir==STOP) && requests_above )
            // if it's above us and below the nearest request
            if( (ofloor > current_floor
                 && ofloor <= nearest_higher_req)
            // or on same floor as us but is lower car number
               || (ofloor==current_floor && j < car_number) )
                car_between_up = TRUE;
         // if it's going down and there are requests below us
         if( (odir==DN || odir==STOP) && requests_below )
            // if it's below us and above the nearest request
            if( (ofloor < current_floor
                 && ofloor >= nearest_lower_req)
                // or on same floor as us but is lower car number
                || (ofloor==current_floor && j < car_number) )
                car_between_dn = TRUE;
         // if it's going up and there are requests below us
         if( (odir==UP || odir==STOP) && requests_below )
            // it's below request and closer to it than we are
            if(nearest_lower_req >= ofloor
               && nearest_lower_req - ofloor
                  < current_floor - nearest_lower_req)
               car_opposite_up = TRUE;
         // if it's going down and there are requests above us
         if( (odir==DN || odir==STOP) && requests_above )
            // it's above request and closer to it than we are
            if(ofloor >= nearest_higher_req
               && ofloor - nearest_higher_req
                  < nearest_higher_req - current_floor)
               car_opposite_dn = TRUE;
         }  // end if(not us)
      }  // end for(each car)
```

(continued on next page)

(continued from previous page)

```
   // if we're going up or stopped, and there is an FR above us,
   // and there are no other cars going up between us and the FR,
   // or above the FR going down and closer than we are,
   // then go up
   if( (current_dir==UP || current_dir==STOP)
       && requests_above && !car_between_up && !car_opposite_dn )
      {
      current_dir = UP;
      return;
      }

   // if we're going down or stopped, and there is an FR below
   // us, and there are no other cars going down between us and
   // the FR, or below the FR going up and closer than we are,
   // then go down
   if( (current_dir==DN || current_dir==STOP)
       && requests_below && !car_between_dn && !car_opposite_up )
      {
      current_dir = DN;
      return;
      }
   // if nothing else happening, stop
   current_dir = STOP;
   }

void elevator::move()
   {                                // if loading or unloading,
   if(loading_timer || unloading_timer)  // don't move
      return;
   if(current_dir==UP)          // if going up, go up
      current_floor++;
   else if(current_dir==DN)     // if going down, go down
      current_floor--;
   }

void elevator::get_destinations()      // stop, get destinations
   {
   char ch;                            // utility char for input
   char ustring[BUF_LENGTH];           // utility buffer for input
   int dest_floor;                     // destination floor

   gotoxy(1, 22);
   cout << "Car " << (car_number+1)
        << " has stopped at floor " << (current_floor+1)
        << "\nEnter destination floors (0 when finished)";
   for(int j=1; j<NUM_FLOORS; j++)     // get floor requests
      {                                // maximum; usually fewer
      gotoxy(1, 24);
      cout << "Destination " << j << ": ";
      cin.get(ustring, BUF_LENGTH);    // (avoid multiple LFs)
      cin.get(ch);                     // eat the newline
      dest_floor = atoi(ustring);
      gotoxy(1,24); clreol();          // clear old input line
      if(dest_floor==0)                // no more requests
```

```
        {
        gotoxy(1,22); clreol();      // clear bottom three lines
        gotoxy(1,23); clreol();
        gotoxy(1,24); clreol();
        return;
        }
     --dest_floor;                   // start at 0, not 1
     if(dest_floor==current_floor)   // chose this very floor
        { --j; continue; }           //    so forget it
     // if we're stopped, first choice made sets direction
     if(j==1 && current_dir==STOP)
        current_dir = (dest_floor < current_floor) ? DN : UP;
     destination[dest_floor] = TRUE; // record selection
     dests_display();                // display destinations
     }
  }
```

Application

The next two files, ELEV_APP.H and ELEV_APP.CPP, are created by someone with a particular building in mind. They want to customize the software for their building. ELEV_APP.H does this by defining two constants that specify the number of floors and the number of elevators the building will have. Here's its listing:

```
// elev_app.h
// provides constants to specify building characteristics

const int NUM_FLOORS =  20;    // number of floors
const int NUM_CARS =     4;    // number of elevator cars
```

ELEV_APP.CPP initializes the static data in the `elevator` class and creates a number of elevator objects, using `new`. (An array could also be used.) Then, in a loop, it calls the static functions `master_tick()` and `get_floor_requests()` over and over. The `delay()` library function slows things down to a human-oriented speed, and the `sound()` function provides a ticking noise to indicate that time is passing. When the user is answering a prompt, time (the program's time, as opposed to the user's time) stops. This is indicated by the absence of the ticking sound. Here's the listing:

```
// elev_app.cpp
// client-supplied file

#include "elev.h"                     // for class declarations

void main(void)
   {
   elevator::init();                  // initialize static data
   new elevator[NUM_CARS];            // create elevators
   while(TRUE)
      {
      elevator::master_tick();     // send time tick to all cars
      sound(200); delay(30); nosound();  // beep
      delay(1000);                    // pause
      elevator::get_floor_reqs(); // get floor requests from user
      }
   }
```

Elevator Strategy

Building the necessary intelligence into the elevator cars is not trivial. It's handled in the `decide()` function, which consists of a series of rules. These rules are arranged in order of priority. If any one applies, then the appropriate action is carried out; the following rules are not queried. Here is a slightly simplified version:

1. If the elevator is about to crash into the bottom of the shaft, or through the roof, then stop.
2. If this is a destination floor, then unload the passengers.
3. If there is an up floor request on this floor, and we are going up, then load the passengers.
4. Is there is a down floor request on this floor, and we are going down, then load the passengers.
5. If there are no destinations or requests above or below, then stop.
6. If there are destinations above us, then go up.
7. If there are destinations below us, then go down.
8. If we're stopped or going up, and there is a floor request above us, and there are no other cars going up between us and the request, or above it and going down and closer than we are, then go up.
9. If we're stopped or going down, and there is a floor request below us, and there are no other cars going down between us and the request, or below it and going up and closer than we are, then go down.
10. If no other rules apply, stop.

Rules 8 and 9 are rather complicated. They attempt to keep two or more cars from rushing to answer the same floor request. However, the results are not perfect. In some situations cars are slow to answer requests because they are afraid another car is on its way, when in fact the other car is answering a different floor request. The program's strategy could be improved by allowing the `decide()` function to distinguish between up and down requests when it checks whether there are requests above or below the current car. However, this would further complicate `decide()`, which is already long enough. We'll leave such refinements to the reader.

A Water-Distribution System

Have you ever wondered how your house is supplied with water? Or how the cooling system in a nuclear reactor operates? Or how the Alaska Pipeline was designed? The next application can help you answer these questions. It models a liquid-distribution system consisting of pipes, valves, tanks, and other components. This example shows how easy it is to create a set of classes for a specialized situation. A similar approach could be used in other process-control applications, such as the hydraulic systems used to operate aircraft. The general approach is even applicable to electrical distribution systems, or economic systems that track the flow of money.

Figure 15-10 shows a water-distribution system for a small community built on a hillside. This water system is modeled in the PIPES program.

As in the previous program, we break this program into three files. PIPES.H contains the class declarations, and PIPES.CPP contains the definitions of the member functions. These files can be assumed to be provided by a vendor of class libraries. The PIPE_APP.CPP file is the one we write ourselves to specify a water system with a particular arrangement of tanks, valves, and pipes.

In Borland C++, you can create this application as an EasyWin program.

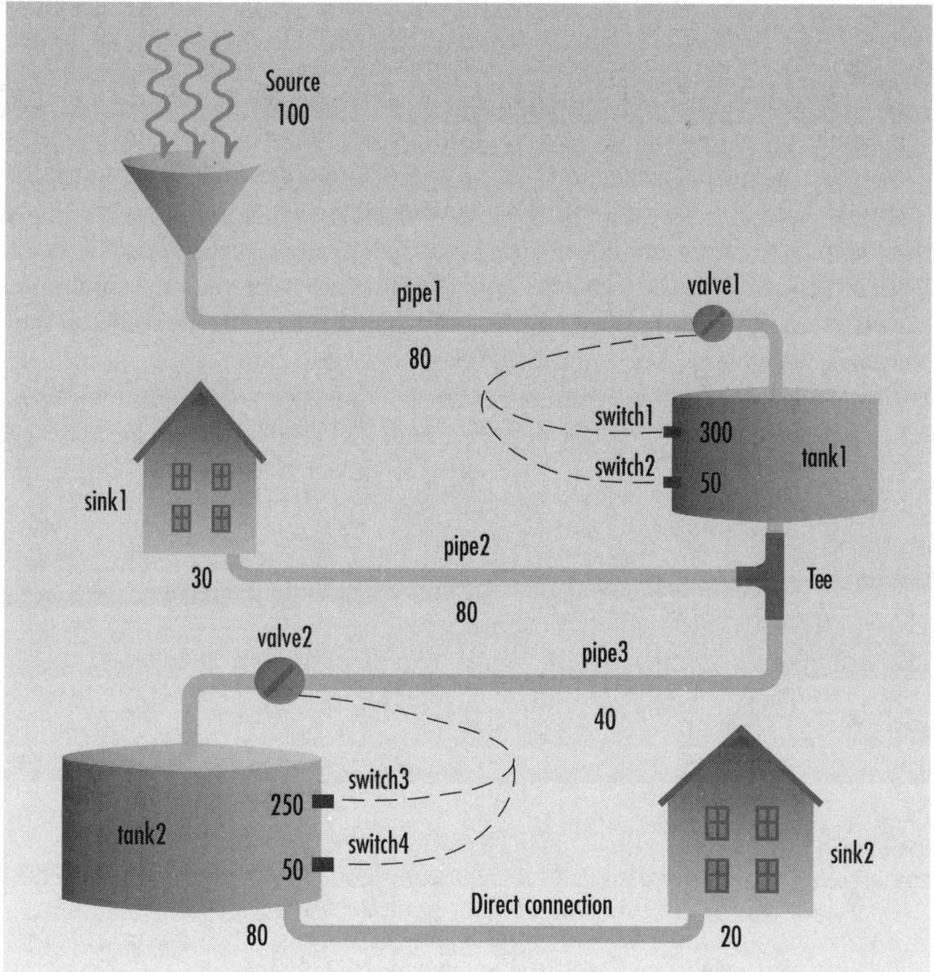

Figure 15-10 A Typical Water System

Components of a Water System

In this application we find that physical objects in the real world—objects we can see and touch—correspond closely with objects in the program. Let's see what these objects are.

- A *source* supplies water to the system. In the real world it might correspond to a spring, well, or reservoir. The water from the source is assumed to be always available but cannot be supplied faster than a certain fixed rate.
- A *sink* is a user of water. It represents a house, factory, or farm, or a group of such water consumers. A sink absorbs water from the system at a fixed rate.
- A *pipe* carries water over a distance. A pipe has a characteristic resistance that limits the amount of water that can flow through it. The water flowing into a pipe equals the water flowing out.
- A *tank* stores water. It also decouples the input/output flows: The rate at which water flows into the tank can be different from the rate at which it flows out. For example, if the input flow is greater than the output, the contents of the tank increases. A tank has a characteristic maximum output flow rate, determined (in this model, at least) by the size of the outlet in the tank.
- To keep a tank from overflowing, and to make sure it doesn't run out of water, we can associate *switches* with the tank. A switch turns on when the amount of water in the tank reaches a certain quantity. Switches are usually used to actuate a valve, which in turn controls the level of water in the tank.
- A *valve* regulates the flow of water. It can be on, causing no resistance to the flow, or off, which stops the flow entirely. A valve is assumed to be operated by some sort of servo-mechanism, and is typically controlled by switches associated with a tank.

Flow, Pressure, and Back Pressure

Every component in the system has three important aspects: flow, pressure, and back pressure. When we connect one component to another, we're connecting these three aspects.

Flow

The bottom-line characteristic of components in the water system is *flow*. This is the amount of water passing through the component per unit time. It's usually what we're interested in measuring when we model a system.

Often the flow into a component is the same as the flow out. This is true of pipes and of valves. However, as noted above, it is not true of tanks.

Pressure

Flow isn't the whole story. For example, when a valve is turned off, the flow both into it and out of it stops, but water may still be *trying* to flow through the valve. This potential for flow is *pressure*. A source or a tank provides water at a certain pressure. If the rest of the system permits, this pressure will cause a proportional flow: The greater the pressure, the greater the flow. But if a valve is turned off, the flow will stop, regardless of what the pressure is. Pressure, like flow, is transmitted downstream from one component to another.

A tank decouples pressure as well as flow. The pressure downstream from a tank is determined by the tank, not by the upstream pressure.

Back Pressure

In opposition to pressure is *back pressure*. This is caused by the resistance to flow of some components. A small-diameter pipe, for instance, will slow the flow of water, so that no matter how much pressure is supplied, the flow will still be small. This back pressure will slow the flow not only into the component causing the back pressure, but into all components upstream.

Back pressure goes the opposite way from flow and pressure. It's transmitted from the downstream component to the upstream component. Tanks decouple back pressure as they do pressure and flow.

Component Input and Output

Sometimes the flow, pressure, or back pressure are the same on both ends of a component. The flow into one end of a pipe, for example, is the same as the flow out the other end (we assume no leaks). However, these characteristics can also be different on the upstream and downstream sides. When a valve is turned off, the pressure on its downstream side becomes zero, no matter what the pressure on the upstream side is. The flow into a tank may be different from the flow out; the difference between input and output flow is reflected in changes to the contents of the tank. The output pressure of a pipe may be less than the input pressure because of the pipe's resistance.

Thus each component, at any given instant, can be characterized by six values. There are three inputs: pressure (from the upstream component), back pressure (from downstream), and flow (from upstream). There are also three outputs: pressure (on the downstream component), back pressure (on the upstream component), and flow (to the downstream component). This situation is shown in Figure 15-11.

The outputs of a component are calculated from its inputs, and also from the internal characteristics and state of the component, such as the resistance of a pipe or whether a valve is open or closed. A member function of each component, called `Tick()` because it occurs at fixed time intervals, is used to calculate the components' output based on their input and internal characteristics. If the input pressure to a pipe is increased, for example, the flow will increase correspondingly (unless the back pressure caused by the pipe's resistance and other components beyond it in the line is too high).

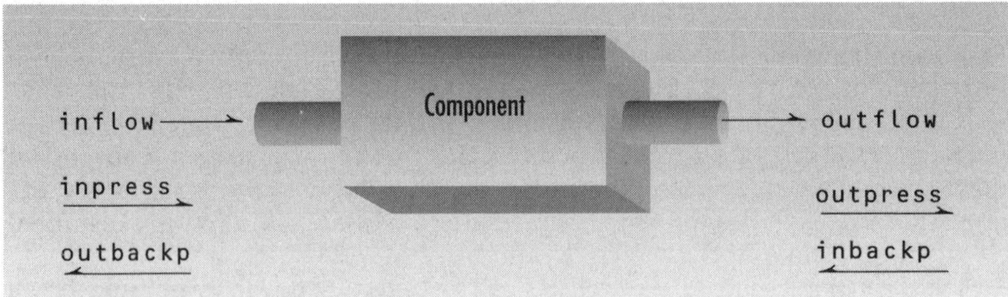

Figure 15-11 A Component's Characteristics

Making Connections

To create a water system we need to connect the various components together. It should be possible to connect any component to any other component so that water flows from one to another. (Switches are not connected in this way, since they don't carry water.) Besides flow, both pressure and back pressure must be connected, since they are also transmitted from component to component.

Thus, making a connection means setting the output pressure and output flow from the upstream object to the input pressure and input flow of the downstream object, and setting the output back pressure from the downstream object to the input back pressure of the upstream object. This is shown in Figure 15-12.

Simplifying Assumptions

To avoid complex mathematics we've made some simplifying assumptions.

What we call back pressure in the program should probably be called something like *ease of flow*. The values we use for this characteristic are *proportional* to the resulting flow, being small if only a small amount can flow, and large when the flow can be large. Real back pressure would be the reciprocal of the resulting flow, but this would unduly complicate the program.

Both pressure and back pressure are assumed to be measured in the same units as flow. To calculate the flow, we examine the pressure pushing water into the system, and the back pressure resisting its flow. The resulting flow is the smallest of these two numbers. Thus if a source provides 100 gallons/minute, and a pipe has a resistance of 60 gallons/minute, which causes a back pressure of 60 gallons/minute, the flow will be 60 gallons/minute.

These assumptions don't model exactly the real world of hydraulic flow, in which flow is determined by complex formulas relating pressure and back pressure, but they do provide a good first approximation.

We assume the output pressure of a tank is a constant. In reality it would depend on the contents of the tank. However, for tanks considerably higher in elevation than the sink, this is a reasonable approximation.

There is also an unavoidable built-in kind of imperfection in our approach to this problem. The physical system we are modeling is an analog system that changes continuously with time. But our model is "digital": It samples the state of the components at discrete "ticks," or time intervals. Thus when something

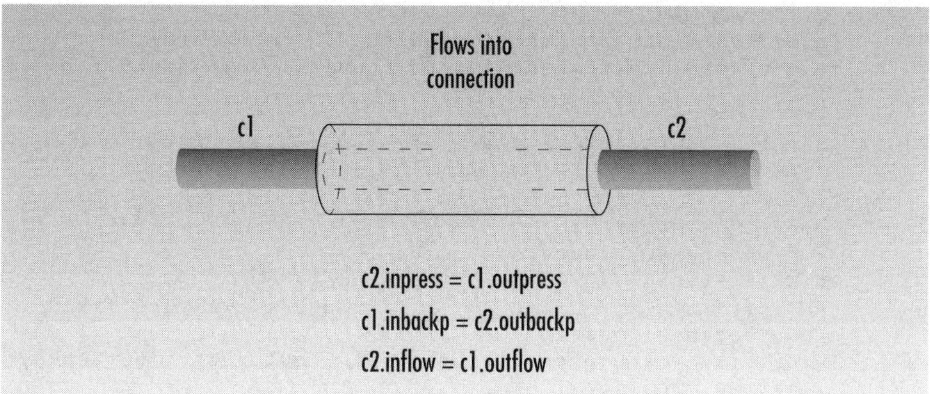

Figure 15-12 Connection Between Components

changes, like a valve opening, it may take several loop cycles for the resulting pressure and flow changes to propagate throughout the system. These transients can be ignored in analyzing the system's behavior.

Program Design

Our goal in this program is to create a family of classes that make it easy to model different water-distribution systems. In this application it's easy to see what the classes should represent. We create a class for each kind of component—a valve class, a tank class, a pipe class, and so on. Once these classes are established, the programmer can then connect components as necessary to model a specific system.

Here are the listings for the PIPES.H and PIPES.CPP files. We assume these files are supplied by a class software vendor.

```
// pipes.h
// header file for pipes

const int infinity = 32767;  // infinite back pressure
enum offon { off, on };      // status of valves and switches
class Tank;                  // for using Tank in Switch

class Component              // components (Pipe, Valve, etc.)
   {
   protected:
      int inpress, outpress;    // pressures in and out
      int inbackp, outbackp;    // back pressures in and out
      int inflow, outflow;      // flow in and out
   public:
      Component(void)
         { inpress = outpress = inbackp = outbackp =
           inflow = outflow = 0; }
      int Flow(void)
         { return inflow; }
```

(continued on next page)

(continued from previous page)

```
        friend void operator >= (Component&, Component&);
        friend void Tee(Component&, Component&, Component&);
    };

class Source : public Component    // flow begins here
    {
    public:
        Source(int outp)
            { outpress = inpress = outp; }
        void Tick(void)                // update
            {                             // output pressure fixed
            outbackp = inbackp;
            outflow = (outpress < outbackp) ? outpress : outbackp;
            inflow = outflow;
            }
    };

class Sink : public Component      // flow ends here
    {
    public:
        Sink(int obp)                  // initialize backpressure
            { outbackp = inbackp = obp; }
        void Tick(void)                // update
            {                          // output back pressure fixed
            outpress = inpress;
            outflow = (outbackp < outpress) ? outbackp : outpress;
            inflow = outflow;
            }
    };

class Pipe : public Component      // connects other components,
    {                                  // has resistance to flow
    private:
        int resist;
    public:
        Pipe(int r)        // initialize
            { inbackp = resist = r; }
        void Tick(void);  // update
    };

class Valve : public Component     // turns flow on or off
    {
    private:
        offon status;                  // on (open) or off (closed)
    public:
        Valve(offon s)
            { status = s; }
        offon& Status(void)
            { return status; }
        void Tick(void);
    };

class Tank : public Component      // stores water
    {
```

```
   private:
      int contents;                    // water in tank (gals)
      int maxoutpress;                 // max output pressure
   public:
      Tank(int mop)                    // initialize to empty tank
           { maxoutpress = mop; contents = 0; }
      int Contents(void)               // get contents
           { return(contents); }
      void Tick(void);
   };

class Switch                           // activated by tank level
   {                                   // can operate valves
   private:
      offon status;    // 'on' if contents > triggercap
      int cap;         // capacity where switch turns on
      Tank* tankptr;   // pointer to owner tank
   public:
      Switch(Tank *tptr, int tcap)   // initialize
         { tankptr = tptr; cap = tcap; status = off; }
      int Status(void)                 // get status
         { return(status); }
      void Tick(void)                  // update status
         { status = (tankptr->Contents() > cap) ? on : off; }
   };

// pipes.cpp
// function definitions for pipes

#include "pipes.h"                 // needed for class definitions

                                   // "flows into" operator: c1 >= c2
void operator >= (Component& c1, Component& c2)
   {
   c2.inpress = c1.outpress;
   c1.inbackp = c2.outbackp;
   c2.inflow =  c1.outflow;
   }
                                 // "tee" divides flow into two
void Tee(Component& src, Component& c1, Component& c2)
   {
                                 // avoid division by 0
   if( (c1.outbackp==0 && c2.outbackp==0) ||
       (c1.outbackp==0 && c2.outbackp==0) )
      {
      c1.inpress = c2.inpress = 0;
      src.inbackp = 0;
      c1.inflow = c2.inflow = 0;
      return;
      }                          // proportion for each output
   float f1 = (float)c1.outbackp / (c1.outbackp + c2.outbackp);
   float f2 = (float)c2.outbackp / (c1.outbackp + c2.outbackp);
                                 // pressures for two outputs
   c1.inpress = src.outpress * f1;
```

(continued on next page)

(continued from previous page)

```
   c2.inpress = src.outpress * f2;
                                  // back pressure for single input
   src.inbackp = c1.outbackp + c2.outbackp;
                                     // flow for two outputs
   c1.inflow = src.outflow * f1;
   c2.inflow = src.outflow * f2;
   }

void Pipe::Tick(void)                 // update pipes
   {
   outpress = (inpress < resist) ? inpress : resist;
   outbackp = (inbackp < resist) ? inbackp : resist;

   // outflow is the lesser of outpress, outbackp, and resist
   if(outpress < outbackp && outpress < resist)
      outflow = outpress;
   else if(outbackp < outpress && outbackp < resist)
      outflow = outbackp;
   else
      outflow = resist;
   }

void Valve::Tick(void)                // update valves
   {
   if(status==on)                     // if valve open
      {
      outpress = inpress;
      outbackp = inbackp;
      outflow = (outpress < outbackp) ? outpress : outbackp;
      }
   else                               // if valve closed
      {
      outpress = 0;
      outbackp = 0;
      outflow = 0;
      }
   }

void Tank::Tick(void)                 // update tanks
   {
   outbackp = infinity;               // will take all the flow
                                      // you can give it
   if( contents > 0 )                 // if not empty
      {
      outpress = (maxoutpress<inbackp) ? maxoutpress : inbackp;
      outflow = outpress;
      }
   else                               // if empty
      {
      outpress = 0;                   // no out pressure,
      outflow = 0;                    // no flow
      }
   contents += inflow - outflow;      // always true
   }
```

Programming the Connections

A key part of program usability is a simple, intuitive way of describing connections in the program. We could use a function, such as

```
Connect(valve1, tank1);
```

However, this can be confusing: Is the upstream component the right argument or the left?

A better approach is to overload an operator to represent connections between components. We'll choose the greater-than-or-equal-to operator, >=, which provides a visual indication of flow direction from left to right. We can call it the *flows into* operator. A program statement establishing a connection would look like this:

```
valve1 >= tank1;
```

meaning that water from valve1 *flows into* tank1.

Base and Derived Classes

When designing our program we look first for similarities among the various objects. The common attributes can be placed in a base class, while the individual features that distinguish the components can be placed in derived classes.

The Component Base Class

In this application we note that all the objects (except switches) have water flowing through them and can be connected to each other. We will therefore create a base class that permits connections. We'll call it Component.

```
class Component                    // components (Pipe, Valve, etc.)
   {
   protected:
      int inpress, outpress;      // pressures in and out
      int inbackp, outbackp;      // back pressures in and out
      int inflow, outflow;        // flow in and out
   public:
      Component(void)
         { inpress = outpress = inbackp = outbackp =
           inflow = outflow = 0; }
      int Flow(void)
           { return inflow; }
      friend void operator >= (Component&, Component&);
      friend void Tee(Component&, Component&, Component&);
   };
```

A component has pressure, back pressure, and flow. These all have two values: input to the component, and output from it. For input we have the flow into the object from upstream, the pressure exerted by objects on its upstream side, and the back pressure exerted by objects on the downstream side. For output there is the flow out of the object, the pressure it transmits to the downstream object, and the back pressure it transmits to the upstream object. These values are all stored in objects of the Component class. A constructor for this class initializes all the data items to 0, and another member function returns the flow, which is, for most components, what we want to measure to see how the system is working.

The *Flows Into* Operator

The *flows into* operator, `>=`, connects an upstream component with a downstream component. Three inputs (the downstream object's pressure and flow and the upstream object's back pressure) are set equal to three outputs (the upstream object's pressure and flow and the downstream object's back pressure).

```
// "flows into" operator: c1 >= c2
void operator >= (Component& c1, Component& c2)
   {
   c2.inpress = c1.outpress;
   c1.inbackp = c2.outbackp;
   c2.inflow =  c1.outflow;
   }
```

The `>=` operator is defined as a `friend` of the `Component` class. It could also be defined as a member class, but another kind of connection, the `Tee()` function, must be a `friend`, so we'll make `>=` a `friend` for consistency. Both arguments to `>=` are passed by reference, since the original arguments must both be modified.

Since the `>=` operator applies to objects of the base class `Component`, it works on objects of the derived classes, such as tanks, valves, and pipes. This saves you from having to write a separate function to handle each kind of connection, such as

```
friend void operator >= (Pipe&, Valve&);
friend void operator >= (Valve&, Tank&);
friend void operator >= (Tank&, Sink&);
```

and so on *ad infinitum*.

Derived Classes

The classes that model the physical objects in the system are derived from the base class `Component`. These are `Source`, `Sink`, `Pipe`, `Valve`, and `Tank`. Each has specific characteristics. A source has a fixed input pressure. A sink has a fixed back pressure. A pipe has a fixed internal resistance; its output back pressure can never be greater than a fixed value. A valve has a status of type `offon`, `off`, or `on` (defined in an `enum` statement). A tank has contents—how full it is. A valve's status and a tank's contents change as the program runs.

Variables that will be constant throughout the program, such as the resistance of a pipe or the output pressure of a tank, are initialized when the object is first created.

As we noted, all these derived classes, and the `switch` class as well, include member functions called `Tick()`. This function is called for each object in the system—once each time period—to update the internal state of the object and to calculate the three outputs (pressure, back pressure, and flow) from the three inputs.

The `Tee()` Function

The `Tee()` function divides a single input flow into two output flows. The proportion of flow going into each downstream component is proportional to the back pressure of each component. A pipe with a lot of resistance will get a smaller proportion of the flow than one with low resistance. (See the listing for this function.)

`Tee()` is called with three arguments: the source component and the two downstream components, in order:

```
Tee(input, output1, output2);
```

It would be nice to use a more intuitive operator than a function with three parameters to connect three components. For instance,

```
input >= output1 + output2;
```

Unfortunately there is no ternary operator (one that takes three arguments) that can be overloaded in C++.

The `switch` Class

The `switch` class has a special relationship to the `Tank` class. Each tank is typically associated with two switches. One switch is set to turn on when the tank level is a certain minimum value (when the tank is almost empty). The other turns on when the level is above a certain maximum value (when the tank is full). This maximum determines the capacity of the tank.

Let's define the relationship between switches and tanks by saying that a switch is "owned" by a tank. When a switch is defined, it's given two values. One is the address of the tank that owns it. The other is the contents level at which it will turn on. The `Tick()` member function in `switch` uses the address of its owner tank to access the tank contents directly. This is how it figures out whether to turn itself on or off.

Switches are typically used to control a valve that regulates the flow of water into a tank. When the tank is full, the valve turns off; when it's nearing empty, the valve turns on again.

The PIPE_APP.CPP File

The `main()` part of the program would be written by an application programmer to model a specific water system. Here's the listing for PIPE_APP.CPP. This file contains only one function: `main()`.

```
// pipe_app.cpp
// models a water supply system

#include "pipes.h"          // for pipes header file
#include <iostream.h>       // for cout, etc.
#include <iomanip.h>        // for setw
#include <conio.h>          // for kbhit()

main()
   {
   Source src(100);              // source(maximum capacity)
   Pipe pipe1(80);               // pipe(resistance)
   Valve valve1(on);             // valve(initially on)

   Tank tank1(60);               // tank1(maximum outflow)
   Switch switch1(&tank1, 300);  // tank1 high switch
   Switch switch2(&tank1, 50);   // tank1 low switch
```

(continued on next page)

(continued from previous page)

```
   Pipe pipe2(80);                    // pipe
   Sink sink1(30);                    // sink(maximum capacity)
   Pipe pipe3(40);                    // pipe
   Valve valve2(on);                  // valve

   Tank tank2(80);                    // tank2
   Switch switch3(&tank2, 250);       // tank2 high switch
   Switch switch4(&tank2, 50);        // tank2 low switch

   Sink sink2(20);                    // sink

   while( !kbhit() )                  // quit on keypress
      {                               // make connections
      src >= pipe1;                   //    source flows into pipe1
      pipe1 >= valve1;                //    pipe1 flows into valve1
      valve1 >= tank1;                //    valve1 flows into tank1
      Tee(tank1, pipe2, pipe3);       //    output of tank1 splits
      pipe2 >= sink1;                 //    pipe2 flows into sink1
      pipe3 >= valve2;                //    pipe3 flows into valve2
      valve2 >= tank2;                //    valve2 flows into tank2
      tank2 >= sink2;                 //    tank2 flows into sink2

      src.Tick();                     // update all components
      pipe1.Tick();                   //    and switches
      valve1.Tick();
      tank1.Tick();
      switch1.Tick();
      switch2.Tick();
      pipe2.Tick();
      sink1.Tick();
      pipe3.Tick();
      valve2.Tick();
      tank2.Tick();
      switch3.Tick();
      switch4.Tick();
      sink2.Tick();
                                      // if tank1 gets too high
      if( valve1.Status()==on && switch1.Status()==on )
         valve1.Status() = off;
                                      // if tank1 gets too low
      if( valve1.Status()==off && switch2.Status()==off )
         valve1.Status() = on;
                                      // if tank2 gets too high
      if( valve2.Status()==on && switch3.Status()==on )
         valve2.Status() = off;
                                      // if tank2 gets too low
      if( valve2.Status()==off && switch4.Status()==off )
         valve2.Status() = on;
                                      // output
      cout << "  Src=" << setw(2) << src.Flow();
      cout << "  P1=" << setw(2) << pipe1.Flow();
      if( valve1.Status()==off )
         cout << "  V1=off";
      else
```

```
         cout << "   V1=on ";
      cout << "   T1=" << setw(3) << tank1.Contents();
      cout << "   P2=" << setw(2) << pipe2.Flow();
      cout << "   Snk1=" << setw(2) << sink1.Flow();
      cout << "   P3=" << setw(2) << pipe3.Flow();
      if( valve2.Status()==off )
         cout << "   V2=off";
      else
         cout << "   V2=on ";
      cout << "   T2=" << setw(3) << tank2.Contents();
      cout << "   Snk2=" << setw(2) << sink2.Flow();
      cout << "\n";
      }
   }
```

Declaring the Components

In `main()` the various components—pipes, valves, tanks, and so on—are first declared. At this time their fixed characteristics are initialized: A pipe is given a fixed resistance, and a tank's contents are initialized to empty.

Connecting and Updating

The bulk of the work in `main()` is carried out in a loop. Each time through the loop represents one time period, or tick of the clock. Pressing any key causes an exit from the loop and terminates the program.

The first business in the loop is to connect the various components. The source `src` is connected to `pipe1`, `pipe1` is connected to `valve1`, and so on. The resulting system is shown in Figure 15-10.

Once the connections are made, the internal states of all the components are updated by calling their `Tick()` functions.

Valves are opened and closed in `if` statements, based on the previous state of the valves and on switches. The goal is to keep the contents of the tank between the upper switch and the lower switch by opening and closing the valve as appropriate. When the tank contents reach the high switch, this switch is turned on, and the `if` statement causes the valve to close. When the contents drop below the bottom switch, turning it off, the valve is opened.

Output

To see what's happening in the system, we use `cout` statements to print out the flow of various components, the capacity of the tanks, and the status of the valves as they change with time. Figure 15-13 shows some sample output.

Notice in this figure that some values occasionally fall below zero. This is due to the digital nature of the simulation, mentioned earlier. Such transients can be ignored.

The goal of most water systems is to supply a continuous flow of water to the various sources. The output of PIPES shows that there are some problems in the system modeled. The flow to `sink1` alternates between 25 and 30 gallons/minute, depending on whether `tank2` is filling or not. The water-system client would probably prefer that the supply was constant. Even worse, `sink2` experiences periods of no flow at all. It would seem that some components of the system need to be resized to eliminate these defects.

```
Src=80  P1=80  V1=on    T1=300  P2=30  Snk1=30  P3= 0  V2=off  T2=172  Snk2=20
Src=80  P1=80  V1=off   T1=350  P2=30  Snk1=30  P3= 0  V2=off  T2=152  Snk2=20
Src=80  P1=80  V1=off   T1=400  P2=30  Snk1=30  P3= 0  V2=off  T2=132  Snk2=20
Src=80  P1=80  V1=off   T1=370  P2=30  Snk1=30  P3= 0  V2=off  T2=112  Snk2=20
Src= 0  P1=80  V1=off   T1=340  P2=30  Snk1=30  P3= 0  V2=off  T2= 92  Snk2=20
Src= 0  P1= 0  V1=off   T1=310  P2=30  Snk1=30  P3= 0  V2=off  T2= 72  Snk2=20
Src= 0  P1= 0  V1=off   T1=280  P2=30  Snk1=30  P3= 0  V2=off  T2= 52  Snk2=20
Src= 0  P1= 0  V1=off   T1=250  P2=30  Snk1=30  P3= 0  V2=on   T2= 32  Snk2=20
Src= 0  P1= 0  V1=off   T1=220  P2=30  Snk1=30  P3= 0  V2=on   T2= 12  Snk2=20
Src= 0  P1= 0  V1=off   T1=190  P2=30  Snk1=30  P3= 0  V2=on   T2= -8  Snk2=20
Src= 0  P1= 0  V1=off   T1=130  P2=12  Snk1=30  P3=17  V2=on   T2= -8  Snk2=20
Src= 0  P1= 0  V1=off   T1= 70  P2=25  Snk1=12  P3=34  V2=on   T2= -8  Snk2= 0
Src= 0  P1= 0  V1=on    T1= 10  P2=25  Snk1=25  P3=34  V2=on   T2=  9  Snk2= 0
Src= 0  P1= 0  V1=on    T1=-50  P2=25  Snk1=25  P3=34  V2=on   T2= 23  Snk2= 0
Src= 0  P1= 0  V1=on    T1= 30  P2=25  Snk1=25  P3=34  V2=on   T2= 37  Snk2=20
Src=80  P1= 0  V1=on    T1= 50  P2= 0  Snk1=25  P3= 0  V2=on   T2= 51  Snk2=20
Src=80  P1=80  V1=on    T1= 70  P2=25  Snk1= 0  P3=34  V2=on   T2= 65  Snk2=20
Src=80  P1=80  V1=on    T1= 90  P2=25  Snk1=25  P3=34  V2=on   T2= 45  Snk2=20
Src=80  P1=80  V1=on    T1=110  P2=25  Snk1=25  P3=34  V2=on   T2= 59  Snk2=20
Src=80  P1=80  V1=on    T1=130  P2=25  Snk1=25  P3=34  V2=on   T2= 73  Snk2=20
Src=80  P1=80  V1=on    T1=150  P2=25  Snk1=25  P3=34  V2=on   T2= 87  Snk2=20
Src=80  P1=80  V1=on    T1=170  P2=25  Snk1=25  P3=34  V2=on   T2=101  Snk2=20
Src=80  P1=80  V1=on    T1=190  P2=25  Snk1=25  P3=34  V2=on   T2=115  Snk2=20

C:\WORK\PIPES>
```

Figure 15-13 Output of PIPES Program

Of course, `cout` provides a very unsophisticated output system. It would be easy to provide a graphic output, where pictures of the components appear on the screen. A `Display()` function built into each component would draw a picture of that component. Pictures would be connected as they are in the program—valve to tank, tank to pipe, and so on. The user could watch tanks fill and empty and valves open and close. Numbers beside pipes could display the flow within. This would make it easier to interpret the system's operation. It would also make the program larger and more complicated, which is why it is not implemented here.

Summary

Vendor-provided object libraries are often distributed as a public component containing class declarations in an .H header file, and a private component containing member function definitions in an .OBJ object file or .LIB library file.

The Turbo C++ project feature can be used to combine several source or object files into a single executable file. This permits files provided by one vendor to be combined with user-written files to create a final application. The project feature simplifies keeping track of what files need to be compiled. It compiles any source file that has been modified since the last linking, and links the resulting object files.

Questions

Answers to questions can be found in Appendix D.

1. Breaking a program into several files is desirable because
   - **a.** some files don't need to be recompiled each time.
   - **b.** a program can be divided functionally.
   - **c.** files can be marketed in object form.
   - **d.** each programmer can work on a separate file.
2. An .H file is attached to a .CPP file using the ________.
3. An .OBJ file is attached to a .CPP file using ________.
4. A *project* file
   - **a.** examines the contents of the files in the project.
   - **b.** examines the dates of the files in the project.
   - **c.** contains instructions for compiling and linking.
   - **d.** contains definitions for C++ variables.
5. A group of related classes, supplied as a separate product, is often called a ________.
6. True or false: A header file may need to be accessed by more than one source file in a project.
7. The so-called private files of a class library
   - **a.** require a password.
   - **b.** can be accessed by `friend` functions.
   - **c.** help prevent code from being pirated.
   - **d.** contain object code.
8. True or false: Class libraries can be more powerful than function libraries.
9. To create a project file, you must
   - **a.** close all other project files in your directory.
   - **b.** put all the relevant filenames into a project file.
   - **c.** put the dates of the relevant files into a project file.
   - **d.** start by selecting *Open Project* from the *Project* menu.
10. The public files in a class library usually contain
    - **a.** constant definitions.
    - **b.** member function definitions.
    - **c.** class declarations.
    - **d.** variable definitions.

Projects

Unfortunately, we don't have room in this book for exercises that involve the kind of larger programs discussed in this chapter. However, here are some suggestions for projects you may wish to pursue on your own.

1. Using the `Window` and related classes from the CALC example, write a new `main()` program that models a hexadecimal calculator. Or, create a scientific calculator with trigonometric (sine, cosine, and tangent), exponential, and similar function keys.

2. Create member functions to perform subtraction and division for the `verylong` class in the VERYLONG example. These should overload the - and / operators. Warning: There's some work involved here. When you include subtraction, you must assume that any `verylong` can be negative as well as positive. This complicates the addition and multiplication routines, which must do different things depending on the signs of the numbers.

   To see one way to perform division, do a long-division example by hand and write down every step. Then incorporate these steps into a division member function. You'll find that you need some comparisons, so you'll need to write a comparison routine, among other things.

3. Modify the ELEV program to be more efficient in the way it handles requests. As an example of its current nonoptimal behavior, start the program and make a down request on floor 20. Then make a down request on floor 10. Car 1 will immediately head up to 20, but car 2, which should head up to 10, waits until car 1 has passed 10 before starting. Modify `decide()` so this doesn't happen.

4. Add a `pump` class to the PIPES example, so you can model water systems that don't rely on gravity. Create a water system that incorporates such a class. (Hint: A pump should derive its input from a tank.)

5. Create a class library that models something you're interested in. Create a `main()` or "client" program to test it. Market your class library and become rich and famous.

16

Templates and Exceptions

FUNCTION TEMPLATES

CLASS TEMPLATES

EXCEPTIONS

MULTIPLE EXCEPTIONS

EXCEPTIONS WITH ARGUMENTS

BUILT-IN EXCEPTIONS

16

This chapter introduces two comparatively new arrivals on the C++ programming scene. Templates make it possible to use one function or class to handle many different data types. Exceptions provide a convenient, uniform way to handle errors that occur within classes. These features were not part of the original specification for C++. They were introduced as "Experimental" topics in Ellis and Stroustrup (1990, see Appendix E) and have since been incorporated into the draft ANSI/ISO C++ standard. Currently Borland C++ implements both templates and exceptions, while Turbo C++ implements only templates.

Templates and exceptions are not essential features of OOP. However, both these advanced features help programmers to construct more robust, error-free programs.

The template concept can be used in two different ways: with functions and with classes. We'll look at function templates first, then go on to class templates, and finally to exceptions.

Function Templates

Suppose you want to write a function that returns the absolute value of two numbers. (As you no doubt remember from high school algebra, the absolute value of a number is its value without regard to its sign: The absolute value of 3 is 3, and the absolute value of –3 is also 3.) Ordinarily this function would be written for a particular data type:

```
int abs(int n)                 // absolute value of ints
   {
   return (n<0) ? -n : n;     // if n is negative, return -n
   }
```

Here the function is defined to take an argument of type `int` and to return a value of this same type. But now suppose you want to find the absolute value of a type `long`. You will need to write a completely new function:

```
long abs(long n)               // absolute value of longs
   {
   return (n<0) ? -n : n;
   }
```

And again, for type `float`:

```
float abs(float n)              // absolute value of floats
   {
   return (n<0) ? -n : n;
   }
```

The body of the function is written the same way in each case, but they are completely different functions because they handle arguments of different types. It's true that in C++ these functions can all be overloaded to have the same name, but you must nevertheless write a separate definition for each one. (In the C language, which does not support overloading, functions for different types can't even have the same name. In the C function library this leads to families of similarly named functions, such as `abs()`, `fabs()`, `fabsl()`, `labs()`, `cabs()`, and so on.)

Rewriting the same function body over and over for different types is time consuming and wastes space in the listing. Also, if you find you've made an error in one such function, you'll need to remember to correct it in each function body. Failing to do this correctly is a good way to introduce inconsistencies into your program.

It would be nice if there were a way to write such a function just once, and have it work for many different data types. This is exactly what function templates do for you. The idea is shown schematically in Figure 16-1.

A Simple Function Template

Our first example shows how to write our absolute-value function as a template, so that it will work with any basic numerical type. This program defines a template version of `abs()` and then, in `main()`, invokes this function a half-dozen times with different data types to prove that it works. Here's the listing for TEMPABS:

```
// tempabs.cpp
// template used for absolute value function

#include <iostream.h>

template <class T>                     // function template
T abs(T n)
      {
      return (n < 0) ? -n : n;
      }

void main()
      {
      int int1 = 5;
      int int2 = -6;
      long lon1 = 70000L;
      long lon2 = -80000L;
      double dub1 = 9.95;
      double dub2 = -10.15;
                                       // calls instantiate functions
      cout << "\nabs(" << int1 << ")=" << abs(int1);   // abs(int)
      cout << "\nabs(" << int2 << ")=" << abs(int2);   // abs(int)
      cout << "\nabs(" << lon1 << ")=" << abs(lon1);   // abs(long)
      cout << "\nabs(" << lon2 << ")=" << abs(lon2);   // abs(long)
      cout << "\nabs(" << dub1 << ")=" << abs(dub1);   // abs(double)
      cout << "\nabs(" << dub2 << ")=" << abs(dub2);   // abs(double)
      }
```

Here's the output of the program:

```
abs(5)=5
abs(-6)=6
abs(70000)=70000
abs(-80000)=80000
abs(9.95)=9.95
abs(-10.15)=10.15
```

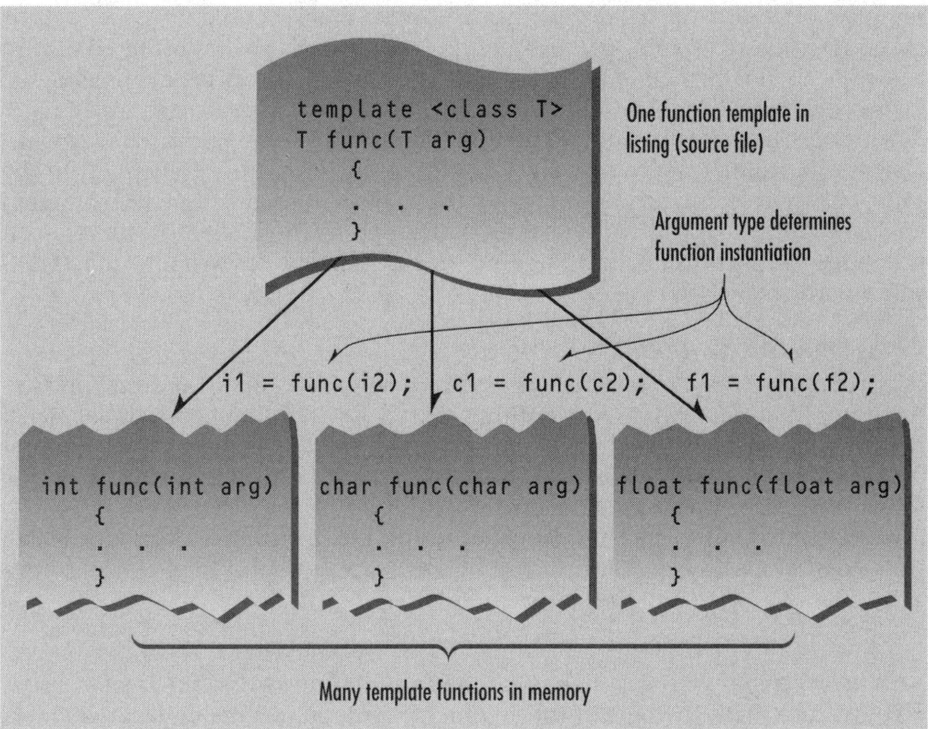

Figure 16-1 A Function Template

As you can see, the `abs()` function now works with all three of the data types (`int`, `long`, and `double`) that we use as arguments. It will work on other basic types as well (`float` and `char`), and it will even work on user-defined data types, provided that the less-than operator (<) is appropriately overloaded.

Here's how we specify the `abs()` function to work with multiple data types:

```
template <class T>          // function template
T abs(T n)
   {
   return (n<0) ? -n : n;
   }
```

This entire syntax, with a first line starting with the keyword `template` and the function definition following, is called a *function template*. How does this new way of writing `abs()` give it such amazing flexibility?

Function Template Syntax

The key innovation in function templates is to represent the data type used by the function not as a specific type such as `int`, but by a name that can stand for *any* type. In the function template above, this name is `T`. (There's nothing magic about this name; it can be anything you want, like `Type`, or `anyType`, or `FooBar`.) The `template` keyword signals the compiler that we're about to define a function template. The keyword `class`, within the angle brackets, might just as well be called *type*. As we've seen, you can define your own data types using classes, so there's really no distinction between types and classes. The variable following the keyword `class` (`T` in this example) is called the *template argument*.

Throughout the definition of the function, whenever a specific data type like `int` would ordinarily be written, we substitute the template argument, `T`. In the `abs()` function this name appears only twice, both in the first line (the function declarator), as the argument type and return type. In more complex functions it may appear numerous times throughout the function body as well (in variable definitions, for example).

What the Compiler Does

What does the compiler do when it sees the `template` keyword and the function definition that follows it? Well, nothing right away. The function template itself doesn't cause the compiler to generate any code. It can't generate code because it doesn't know yet what data type the function will be working with. It simply remembers the template for possible future use.

Code generation doesn't take place until the function is actually called (invoked) by a statement within the program. In TEMPABS this happens in expressions like `abs(int1)` in the statement

```
cout << "\nabs(" << int << ")=" << abs(int1);
```

When the compiler sees such a function call, it knows that the type to use is `int`, because that's the type of the argument `int1`. So it generates a specific version of the `abs()` function for type `int`, substituting `int` wherever it sees the name `T` in the function template. This is called *instantiating* the function template, and each instantiated version of the function is called a *template function*. (That is, a template function is a specific instance of a function template. Isn't English fun?)

The compiler also generates a call to the newly instantiated function, and inserts it into the code where `abs(int1)` is. Similarly, the expression `abs(lon1)` causes the compiler to generate a version of `abs()` that operates on type `long` and a call to this function; while the `abs(dub1)` call generates a function that works on type `double`. Of course, the compiler is smart enough to generate only one version of `abs()` for each data type. Thus, even though there are two calls to the `int` version of the function, the code for this version appears only once in the executable code.

Simplifies the Listing

Notice that the amount of RAM used by the program is the same whether we use the template approach or actually write three separate functions. What we've saved is having to type three separate functions into the source file. This makes the listing shorter and easier to understand. Also, if we want to change the way the function works, we need to make the change in only one place in the listing instead of three.

The Deciding Argument

The compiler decides how to compile the function based entirely on the data type used in the function call's argument (or arguments). The function's return type doesn't enter into this decision. This is similar to the way the compiler decides which of several overloaded functions to call.

Another Kind of Blueprint

We've seen that a function template isn't really a function, since it does not actually cause program code to be placed in memory. Instead it is a pattern, or blueprint, for making many functions. This fits right into the philosophy of OOP. It's similar to the way a class isn't anything concrete (such as program code in memory), but a blueprint for making many similar objects.

Function Templates with Multiple Arguments

Let's look at another example of a function template. This one takes three arguments: two that are template arguments and one of a basic type. The purpose of this function is to search an array for a specific value. The function returns the array index for that value if it finds it, or –1 if it can't find it. The arguments are a pointer to the array, the value to search for, and the size of the array. In `main()` we define four different arrays of different types, and four values to search for. We treat type `char` as a number. Then we call the template function once for each array. Here's the listing for TEMPFIND:

```
// tempfind.cpp
// template used for function that finds number in array

#include <iostream.h>

// function returns index number of item, or -1 if not found
template <class atype>
int find(atype* array, atype value, int size)
   {
   for(int j=0; j<size; j++)
      if(array[j]==value)
         return j;
   return -1;
   }

char chrArr[] =   {1, 3, 5, 9, 11, 13};   // array
char ch = 5;                              // value to find
int intArr[] =    {1, 3, 5, 9, 11, 13};
int in = 6;
long lonArr[] =   {1L, 3L, 5L, 9L, 11L, 13L};
long lo = 11L;
double dubArr[] = {1.0, 3.0, 5.0, 9.0, 11.0, 13.0};
double db = 4.0;

void main()
   {
   cout << "\n 5 in chrArray: index=" << find(chrArr, ch, 6);
   cout << "\n 6 in intArray: index=" << find(intArr, in, 6);
   cout << "\n11 in lonArray: index=" << find(lonArr, lo, 6);
   cout << "\n 4 in dubArray: index=" << find(dubArr, db, 6);
   }
```

Here we name the template argument `atype`. It appears in two of the function's arguments: as the type of a pointer to the array, and as the type of the item to be matched. The third function argument, the array size, is always type `int`; it's not a template argument. Here's the output of the program:

```
 5 in chrArray: index=2
 6 in intArray: index=-1
11 in lonArray: index=4
 4 in dubArray: index=-1
```

The compiler generates four different versions of the function, one for each type used to call it. It finds a 3 at index 2 in the character array, does not find a 4 in the integer array, and so on.

Template Arguments Must Match

When a template function is invoked, all instances of the same template argument must be of the same type. For example, in `find()`, if the array name is of type `int`, the value to search for must also be of type `int`. You can't say

```
int intarray[] = {1, 3, 5, 7};        // int array
float f1 = 5.0;                       // float value
int value = find(intarray, f1, 4);    // uh, oh
```

because the compiler expects all instances of `atype` to be the same type. It can generate a function

```
find(int*, int, int);
```

but it can't generate

```
find(int*, float, int);
```

because the first and second arguments must be the same type.

Syntax Variation

Some programmers put the `template` keyword and the function declarator on the same line:

```
template<class atype> int find(atype* array, atype value, int size)
   {
   // function body
   }
```

Of course the compiler is happy enough with this format, but we find it more forbidding and less clear than the multiline approach.

More Than One Template Argument

You can use more than one template argument in a function template. For example, suppose you like the idea of the `find()` function template, but you aren't sure how large an array it might be applied to. If the array is too large, then type `long` would be necessary for the array size, instead of type `int`. On the other hand, you don't want to use type `long` if you don't need to. You want to select the type of the array size, as well as the type of data stored, when you call the function. To make this possible, you could make the array size into a template argument as well. We'll call it `btype`:

```
template <class atype, class btype>
btype find(atype* array, atype value, btype size)
   {
   for(btype j=0; j<size; j++)     // note use of btype
      if(array[j]==value)
         return j;
   return (btype)-1;
   }
```

Now you can use either type `int` or type `long` (or even a user-defined type) for the size, whichever is appropriate. The compiler will generate different functions based not only on the type of the array and the value to be searched for, but also on the type of the array size.

Note that multiple template arguments can lead to many functions being instantiated from a single template. Two such arguments, if there were six basic types that could reasonably be used for each one, would allow the creation of 36 functions. This can take up a lot of memory if the functions are large. On the other hand, you don't instantiate a version of the function unless you actually call it.

Why Not Macros?

Old-time C programmers may wonder why we don't use macros to create different versions of a function for different data types. For example, the `abs()` function could be defined as

```
#define abs(n) ( (n<0) ? (-n) : (n) )
```

This has a similar effect to the class template in TEMPABS, because it performs a simple text substitution and can thus work with any type. However, as we've noted before, macros aren't much used in C++. There are several problems with them. One is they don't perform any type checking. There may be several arguments to the macro that should be of the same type, but the compiler won't check whether or not they are. Also, the type of the value returned isn't specified, so the compiler can't tell if you're assigning it to an incompatible variable. In any case, macros are confined to functions that can be expressed in a single statement. There are also other, more subtle, problems with macros. On the whole it's best to avoid them.

What Works?

How do you know whether you can instantiate a template function for a particular data type? For example, could you use the `find()` function from TEMPFIND to find a string (type `char*`) in an array of strings? To see if this is possible, check the operators used in the function. If they all work on the data type, then you can probably use it. In `find()`, however, we compare two variables using the equal-equal (`==`) operator. You can't use this operator with strings; you must use the `strcmp()` library function. Thus `find()` won't work on strings. (However, it would work on a user-defined string class in which you overloaded the `==` operator.)

Start with a Normal Function

When you write a template function you're probably better off starting with a normal function that works on a fixed type; `int` or whatever. You can design and debug it without having to worry about template syntax and multiple types. Then, when everything works properly, you can turn the function definition into a template and check that it works for additional types.

Class Templates

The template concept can also be applied to classes. Class templates are generally used for data storage (container) classes. Stacks and linked lists, which we encountered in previous chapters, are examples of data storage classes. However, the examples of these classes that we presented could store data of only a single basic type. The `Stack` class in the STAKARAY program in Chapter 8, for example, could store data only of type `int`. Here's a condensed version of that class.

```
class Stack
   {
   private:
      int st[MAX];          // array of ints
      int top;              // index number of top of stack
   public:
      Stack();              // constructor
      void push(int var);   // takes int as argument
      int pop();            // returns int value
   };
```

If we wanted to store data of type `long` in a stack we would need to define a completely new class:

```
class LongStack
   {
   private:
      long st[MAX];          // array of longs
      int top;               // index number of top of stack
   public:
      LongStack();           // constructor
      void push(long var);   // takes long as argument
      long pop();            // returns long value
   };
```

Similarly we would need to create a new stack class for every data type we wanted to store. It would be nice to be able to write a single class specification that would work for variables of *all* types, instead of a single basic type. As you may have guessed, class templates allow us to do this. We'll create a variation of STAKARAY that uses a class template. Here's the listing for TEMPSTAK:

```
// tempstak.cpp
// implements stack class as a template

#include <iostream.h>
const int MAX = 100;                  // size of array

template <class Type>
class Stack
   {
   private:
      Type st[MAX];                   // stack: array of any type
      int top;                        // number of top of stack
```

```
   public:
      Stack()                      // constructor
         { top = -1; }
      void push(Type var)          // put number on stack
         { st[++top] = var; }
      Type pop()                   // take number off stack
         { return st[top--]; }
   };

void main()
   {
   Stack<float> s1;        // s1 is object of class Stack<float>

   s1.push(1111.1);        // push 3 floats, pop 3 floats
   s1.push(2222.2);
   s1.push(3333.3);
   cout << "1: " << s1.pop() << endl;
   cout << "2: " << s1.pop() << endl;
   cout << "3: " << s1.pop() << endl;

   Stack<long> s2;         // s2 is object of class Stack<long>

   s2.push(123123123L);    // push 3 longs, pop 3 longs
   s2.push(234234234L);
   s2.push(345345345L);
   cout << "1: " << s2.pop() << endl;
   cout << "2: " << s2.pop() << endl;
   cout << "3: " << s2.pop() << endl;
   }
```

Here the the class `Stack` is presented as a template class. The approach is similar to that used in function templates. The `template` keyword signals that the entire class will be a template.

```
template <class Type>
class Stack
   {
   // data and member functions using template argument Type
   };
```

A template argument, named `Type` in this example, is then used (instead of a fixed data type like `int`) everyplace in the class specification where there is a reference to the type of the array `st`. There are three such places: the definition of `st`, the argument type of the `push()` function, and the return type of the `pop()` function.

Class templates differ from function templates in the way they are instantiated. To create an actual function from a function template, you call it using arguments of a specific type. Classes, however, are instantiated by defining an object using the template argument.

```
Stack<float> s1;
```

This creates an object, `s1`, that is a stack that stores numbers of type `float`. The compiler provides space in memory for this object's data, using type `float` wherever the template argument `Type` appears in the class specification. It also provides space for the member functions (if these have not already been placed in memory by another object of type `Stack<float>`). These member functions also operate exclusively on type `float`. Figure 16-2 shows how a class template and definitions of specific objects cause these objects to be placed in memory.

Creating a `Stack` object that stores objects of a different type, as in

```
Stack<long> s2;
```

creates not only a different space for data, but also a new set of member functions that operate on type `long`.

Note that the name of the type of `s1` consists of the class name `Stack` *plus the template argument*: `Stack<float>`. This distinguishes it from other classes that might be created from the same template, such as `Stack<int>` or `Stack<long>`.

We exercise the `s1` and `s2` stacks by pushing and popping three values on each one and displaying each popped value. Here's the output of TEMPSTAK:

```
1: 3333.3        // float stack
2: 2222.2
```

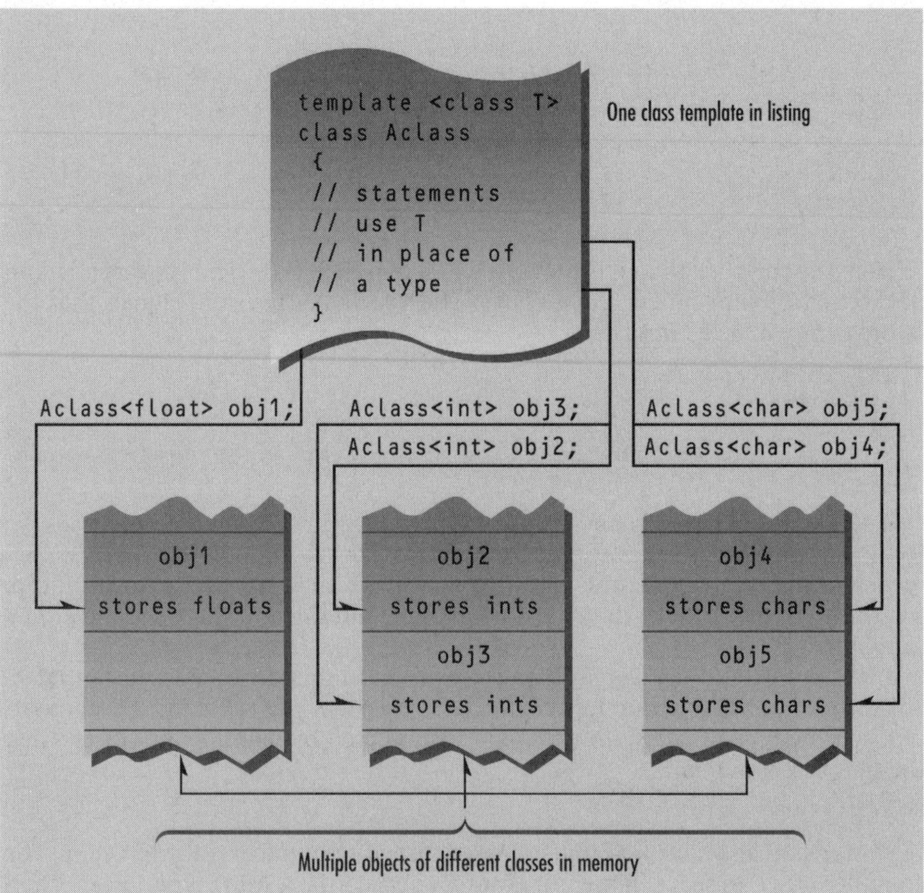

Figure 16-2 A Class Template

```
3: 1111.1
1: 345345345    // long stack
2: 234234234
3: 123123123
```

In this example the template approach gives us two classes for the price of one, and we could instantiate class objects for other numerical types with just a single line of code.

Class Name Depends on Context

In the TEMPSTAK example, the member functions of the class template were all defined within the class. If the member functions are defined externally (outside of the class specification), we need a new syntax. The next program shows how this works. Here's the listing for TEMPSTAK2:

```
// temstak2.cpp
// implements stack class as a template
// member functions are defined outside the class

#include <iostream.h>
const int MAX = 100;

template <class Type>
class Stack
   {
   private:
      Type st[MAX];              // stack: array of any type
      int top;                   // number of top of stack
   public:
      Stack();                   // constructor
      void push(Type var);       // put number on stack
      Type pop();                // take number off stack
   };

template<class Type>
Stack<Type>::Stack()             // constructor
   {
   top = -1;
   }

template<class Type>
void Stack<Type>::push(Type var) // put number on stack
   {
   st[++top] = var;
   }

template<class Type>
Type Stack<Type>::pop()           // take number off stack
   {
   return st[top--];
   }
```

(continued on next page)

(continued from previous page)

```
void main()
   {
   Stack<float> s1;        // s1 is object of class Stack<float>

   s1.push(1111.1);        // push 3 floats, pop 3 floats
   s1.push(2222.2);
   s1.push(3333.3);
   cout << "1: " << s1.pop() << endl;
   cout << "2: " << s1.pop() << endl;
   cout << "3: " << s1.pop() << endl;

   Stack<long> s2;         // s2 is object of class Stack<long>

   s2.push(123123123L);    // push 3 longs, pop 3 longs
   s2.push(234234234L);
   s2.push(345345345L);
   cout << "1: " << s2.pop() << endl;
   cout << "2: " << s2.pop() << endl;
   cout << "3: " << s2.pop() << endl;
   }
```

The expression `template<class Type>` must precede not only the class definition, but each externally defined member function as well. Here's how the `push()` function looks:

```
template<class Type>
void Stack<Type>::push(Type var)
   {
   st[++top] = var;
   }
```

The name `Stack<Type>` is used to identify the class of which `push()` is a member. In a normal nontemplate member function the name `Stack` alone would suffice:

```
void Stack::push(int var)  // Stack() as a non-template function
   {
   st[++top] = var;
   }
```

but for a function template we need the template argument as well: `Stack<Type>`.

Thus we see that the name of the template class is expressed differently in different contexts. Within the class specification, it's simply the name itself: `Stack`. For externally defined member functions, it's the class name plus the template argument name: `Stack<Type>`. When you define actual objects for storing a specific data type, it's the class name plus this specific type: `Stack<float>` (or whatever).

```
class Stack                         // Stack class specifier
   {  };

void Stack<Type>::push(Type var)    // push() definition
   {  }

Stack<float> s1;                    // object of type Stack<float>
```

You must exercise considerable care to use the correct name in the correct context. It's easy to forget to add the `<Type>` or `<float>` to the `Stack`. The compiler hates it when you get it wrong.

Although it's not demonstrated in this example, you must also be careful of the syntax when a member function returns a value of its own class. Suppose we define a class `Int` that provided safety features for integers, as discussed in Exercise 4 in Chapter 9. If you used an external definition for a member function `xfunc()` of this class that returned type `Int`, you would need to use `Int<Type>` for the return type as well as preceding the scope resolution operator:

```
Int<Type> Int<Type>::xfunc(Int arg)
   {   }
```

The class name used as a type of a function argument, on the other hand, doesn't need to include the `<Type>` designation.

A Linked List Class Using Templates

Let's look at another example where templates are used for a data storage class. This is a modification of our LINKLIST program from Chapter 12 (which you are encouraged to reexamine). It requires not only that the `linklist` class itself be made into a template, but that the `link` structure, which actually stores each data item, be made into a template as well. Here's the listing for TEMPLIST:

```
// templist.cpp
// implements linked list as a template

#include <iostream.h>

template<class TYPE>                    // struct link<TYPE>
struct link                             // one element of list
// within this struct definition 'link' means link<TYPE>
   {
   TYPE data;                           // data item
   link* next;                          // pointer to next link
   };

template<class TYPE>                    // class linklist<TYPE>
class linklist                          // a list of links
// within this class definition 'linklist' means linklist<TYPE>
   {
   private:
      link<TYPE>* first;                // pointer to first link
   public:
      linklist()                        // no-argument constructor
         { first = NULL; }              // no first link
      // note: destructor would be nice; not shown for simplicity
      void additem(TYPE d);             // add data item (one link)
      void display();                   // display all links
   };

template<class TYPE>
void linklist<TYPE>::additem(TYPE d)   // add data item
```

(continued on next page)

(continued from previous page)

```
   {
   link<TYPE>* newlink = new link<TYPE>;  // make a new link
   newlink->data = d;                     // give it data
   newlink->next = first;                 // it points to next link
   first = newlink;                       // now first points to this
   }

template<class TYPE>
void linklist<TYPE>::display()            // display all links
   {
   link<TYPE>* current = first;           // set ptr to first link
   while( current != NULL )               // quit on last link
      {
      cout << endl << current->data;      // print data
      current = current->next;            // move to next link
      }
   }

void main()
   {
   linklist<double> ld; // ld is object of class linklist<double>

   ld.additem(151.5);   // add three doubles to list ld
   ld.additem(262.6);
   ld.additem(373.7);
   ld.display();        // display entire list ld

   linklist<char> lch;  // lch is object of class linklist<char>

   lch.additem('a');    // add three chars to list lch
   lch.additem('b');
   lch.additem('c');
   lch.display();       // display entire list lch
   }
```

In `main()` we define two linked lists: one to hold numbers of type `double`, and one to hold characters of type `char`. We then exercise the lists by placing three items on each one with the `additem()` member function, and displaying all the items with the `display()` member function. Here's the output of TEMPLIST:

```
373.7
262.6
151.5
c
b
a
```

Both the `linklist` class and the `link` structure make use of the template argument `TYPE` to stand for any type. (Well, not really *any* type; we'll discuss later what types can actually be stored.) Thus not only `linklist` but also `link` must be templates, preceded by the line

```
template<class TYPE>
```

Notice that it's not just a class that's turned into a template. Any other programming constructs that use a variable data type must also be turned into templates, as the `link` structure is here.

As before, we must pay attention to how the class (and in this program, a structure as well) are named in different parts of the program. Within its own specification we can use the name of the class or structure alone: `linklist` and `link`. In external member functions, we must use the class or structure name and the template argument: `linklist<TYPE>`. When we actually define objects of type `linklist`, we must use the specific data type that the list is to store:

```
linklist<double> ld;  // defines object ld of class linklist<double>
```

Storing User-Defined Data Types

In our programs so far we've used template classes to store basic data types. For example, in the TEMPLIST program we stored numbers of type `double` and type `char` in a linked list. Is it possible to store objects of user-defined types (classes) in these same template classes? The answer is yes, but with a caveat.

Employees in a Linked List

Examine the `employee` class in the EMPLOY program in Chapter 10. (Don't worry about the derived classes.) Could we store objects of type `employee` on the linked list of the TEMPLIST example? As with template functions, we can find out if a template class can operate on objects of a particular class by checking the operations the template class performs on those objects. The `linklist` class uses the overloaded insertion (<<) operator to display the objects it stores:

```
void linklist<TYPE>::display()
   {
   ...
   cout << endl << current->data;  // uses insertion operator (<<)
   ...
   };
```

This is not a problem with basic types, for which the insertion operator is already defined. Unfortunately, however, the `employee` class in the EMPLOY program does not overload this operator. Thus we'll need to modify the `employee` class to include it. Also, to simplify getting employee data from the user, we overload the extraction (>>) operator as well. Data from this operator is placed in a temporary object `emptemp` before being added to the linked list. Here's the listing for TEMLIST2:

```
// temlist2.cpp
// implements linked list as a template
// demonstrates list used with employee class

#include <iostream.h>

//////////////////////////////////////////////////////////////
// the employee class
//////////////////////////////////////////////////////////////
const int LEN = 80;             // maximum length of names
```

(continued on next page)

(continued from previous page)

```
class employee                              // employee class
   {
   private:
      char name[LEN];                       // employee name
      unsigned long number;                 // employee number
   public:
      friend istream& operator >> (istream& s, employee& e);
      friend ostream& operator << (ostream& s, employee& e);
   };

istream& operator >> (istream& s, employee& e)
   {
   cout << "\n   Enter last name: "; cin >> e.name;
   cout << "   Enter number: ";       cin >> e.number;
   return s;
   }
ostream& operator << (ostream& s, employee& e)
   {
   cout << "\n   Name: " << e.name;
   cout << "\n   Number: " << e.number;
   return s;
   }
////////////////////////////////////////////////////////////////
// the linked list template
////////////////////////////////////////////////////////////////
template<class TYPE>                        // struct "link<TYPE>"
struct link                                 // one element of list
   {
   TYPE data;                               // data item
   link* next;                              // pointer to next link
   };

template<class TYPE>                        // class "linklist<TYPE>"
class linklist                              // a list of links
   {
   private:
      link<TYPE>* first;                    // pointer to first link
   public:
      linklist()                            // no-argument constructor
         { first = NULL; }                  // no first link
      void additem(TYPE d);                 // add data item (one link)
      void display();                       // display all links
   };

template<class TYPE>
void linklist<TYPE>::additem(TYPE d)  // add data item
   {
   link<TYPE>* newlink = new link<TYPE>;  // make a new link
   newlink->data = d;                       // give it data
   newlink->next = first;                   // it points to next link
   first = newlink;                         // now first points to this
   }

template<class TYPE>
void linklist<TYPE>::display()              // display all links
```

```
   {
   link<TYPE>* current = first;        // set ptr to first link
   while( current != NULL )            // quit on last link
      {
      cout << endl << current->data;  // display data
      current = current->next;         // move to next link
      }
   }
////////////////////////////////////////////////////////////////////
// main() creates a linked list of employees
////////////////////////////////////////////////////////////////////
void main()
   {                              // lemp is object of
   linklist<employee> lemp;       // class "linklist<employee>"
   employee emptemp;              // temporary employee storage
   char ans;                      // user's response ('y' or 'n')

   do
      {
      cin >> emptemp;             // get employee data from user
      lemp.additem(emptemp);      // add it to linked list 'lemp'
      cout << "\nAdd another (y/n)? ";
      cin >> ans;
      } while(ans != 'n');        // when user is done,
   lemp.display();                // display entire linked list
   }
```

In main() we instantiate a linked list called lemp. Then, in a loop, we ask the user to input data for an employee, and we add that employee object to the list. When the user terminates the loop, we display all the employee data. Here's some sample interaction:

```
   Enter last name: Mendez
   Enter number: 1233
Add another(y/n)? y

   Enter last name: Smith
   Enter number: 2344
Add another(y/n)? y

   Enter last name: Chang
   Enter number: 3455
Add another(y/n)? n

   Name: Chang
   Number: 3455

   Name: Smith
   Number: 2344

   Name: Mendez
   Number: 1233
```

Notice that the linklist class does not need to be modified in any way to store objects of type employee. This is the beauty of template classes: They will work not only with basic types, but with user-defined types as well.

What Can You Store?

You can tell whether you can store variables of a particular type in a data-storage template class by checking the operators in the member functions of that class. For example, is it possible to store a string (type `char*`) in the `linklist` class in the TEMLIST2 program? Member functions in this class use the insertion (`<<`) and extraction (`>>`) operators. These operators work perfectly well with strings, so there's no reason we can't use this class to store strings, as you can verify yourself. But if any operators exist in a storage class's member function that don't operate on a particular data type, then you can't use the class to store that type.

Exceptions

Exceptions, the second major topic in this chapter, provide a systematic, object-oriented approach to handling runtime errors generated by C++ classes. To qualify as an exception, such errors must occur as a result of some action taken within a program, and they must be ones that the program itself can find out about. For example, a constructor in a user-written string class might generate an exception if the application tries to initialize an object with a string that's too long. Similarly, a program can check if a file was opened, or written to, successfully, and generate an exception if it was not.

Not all runtime errors can be handled by the exception mechanism. For instance, some error situations are detected, not by the program, but by the operating system, which then terminates the application. Examples are stack overflow, the user pressing the CTRL-C key combination (sometimes) or a hardware divide-by-zero error.

Why Do We Need Exceptions?

Why do we need a new mechanism to handle errors? Let's look at how the process was handled in the past. In C-language programs, an error is often signalled by returning a particular value from the function in which it occurred. For example, many math functions, like `sin()` and `cos()`, return a special value to indicate an error, and disk-file functions often return NULL or 0 to signal an error. Each time you call one of these functions you check the return value:

```
if( somefunc() == ERROR_RETURN_VALUE )
   // handle the error or call error-handler function
else
   // proceed normally
if( anotherfunc() == NULL )
   // handle the error or call error-handler function
else
   // proceed normally
if( thirdfunc() == 0 )
   // handle the error or call error-handler function
else
   // proceed normally
```

The problem with this approach is that every single call to such a function must be examined by the program. Surrounding each function call with an `if...else` statement, and adding statements to handle the error (or call an error-handler routine), requires a lot of code and makes the listing convoluted and hard to read. Also, it's not practical for some functions to return an error value. For example, imagine a `min()` function that returns the minimum of two values. All possible return values from this function represent valid outcomes. There's no value left to use as an error return.

The problem becomes more complex when classes are used, since errors may take place without a function being explicitly called. For example, suppose an application defines objects of a class:

```
SomeClass obj1, obj2, obj3;
```

How will the application find out if an error occurred in the class constructor? The constructor is called implicitly, so there's no return value to be checked.

Things are complicated even further when an application uses class libraries. A class library and the application that makes use of it are often created by separate people: the class library by a vendor and the application by a programmer who buys the class library. This makes it even harder to arrange for error values to be communicated from a class member function to the program that's calling the function.

The exception mechanism was designed to minimize these difficulties and provide a consistent, easy-to-implement approach to error handling; one that supports the concepts of OOP.

Exception Syntax

Imagine an application that creates and interacts with objects of a certain class. Ordinarily the application's calls to the class member functions cause no problems. Sometimes, however, the application makes a mistake, causing an error to be detected in a member function. This member function then informs the application that an error has occurred. When exceptions are used, this is called *throwing an exception*. In the application we install a separate section of code to handle the error. This code is called an *exception handler* or *catch block*; it *catches* the exceptions thrown by the member function. Any code in the application that uses objects of the class is enclosed in a *try block*. Errors generated in the try block will be caught in the catch block. Code that doesn't interact with the class need not be in a try block. Figure 16-3 shows the arrangement.

The exception mechanism uses three new C++ keywords: `throw`, `catch`, and `try`. Also, we need to create a new kind of entity called an *exception class*. XSYNTAX is not a working program, only a skeleton program to show the syntax.

```
// xsyntax.cpp
// not a working program
class AClass                          // a class
   {
   public:
   class AnError                      // exception class
      {
      };
   void Func()                        // a member function
```

(continued on next page)

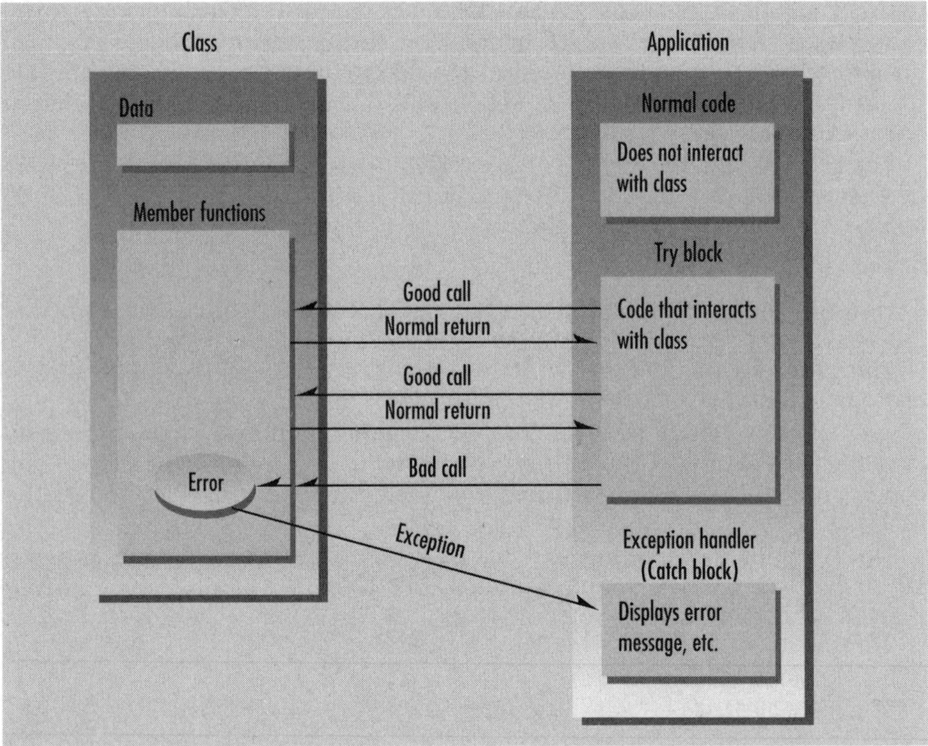

Figure 16-3 The Exception Mechanism

(continued from previous page)

```
      {
      if( /* error condition */ )
         throw AnError();          // throw exception
      }
   };

void main()                        // application
   {
   try                             // try block
      {
      AClass obj1;                 // interact with AClass objects
      obj1.Func();                 // may cause error
      }
   catch(AClass::AnError)          // exception handler
      {                            // (catch block)
      // tell user about error, etc.
      }
   }
```

We start with a class called `AClass`, which represents any class in which errors might occur. An exception class, `AnError`, is specified in the public part of `AClass`. In `AClass`'s member functions we check for errors. If we find one, we throw an exception, using the keyword `throw` followed by the constructor for the error class:

```
throw AnError();  // 'throw' followed by constructor for AnError class
```

In the `main()` part of the program we enclose any statements that interact with `AClass` in a try block. If any of these statements causes an error to be detected in an `AClass` member function, an exception will be thrown and control will go to the catch block that immediately follows the try block.

A Simple Exception Example

Let's look at a working program example that uses exceptions. This example is derived from the STAKARAY program in Chapter 8, which created a stack data structure in which integer data values could be stored. Unfortunately, this earlier example could not detect two common errors. The application program might attempt to push too many objects onto the stack, thus exceeding the capacity of the array, or it might try to pop too many objects off the stack, thus obtaining invalid data. In the XSTAK program we use an exception to handle these two errors.

```
// xstak.cpp
// demonstrates exceptions

#include <iostream.h>
const int MAX = 3;                  // stack holds 3 ints

class Stack
   {
   private:
      int st[MAX];                  // array of integers
      int top;                      // index of top of stack
   public:
      class Range                   // exception class for Stack
         {                          // note: empty class body
         };

      Stack()                       // constructor
         { top = -1; }

      void push(int var)
         {
         if(top >= MAX-1)           // if stack full,
            throw Range();          // throw exception
         st[++top] = var;           // put number on stack
         }
      int pop()
         {
         if(top < 0)                // if stack empty,
            throw Range();          // throw exception
         return st[top--];          // take number off stack
         }
   };
```

(continued on next page)

(continued from previous page)

```
void main()
   {
   Stack s1;
      {

   try
      s1.push(11);
      s1.push(22);
      s1.push(33);
//    s1.push(44);                            // oops: stack full
      cout << "1: " << s1.pop() << endl;
      cout << "2: " << s1.pop() << endl;
      cout << "3: " << s1.pop() << endl;
      cout << "4: " << s1.pop() << endl;  // oops: stack empty
      }
   catch(Stack::Range)                        // exception handler
      {
      cout << "Stack Full or Empty" << endl;
      }

   cout << "Arrive here after catch (or normal exit)" << endl;
   }
```

Note that we've made the stack small so that it's easier to trigger an exception by pushing too many items.

Let's examine the features of this program that deal with exceptions. There are four of them. In the class specification there is an exception class. There are also statements that throw exceptions. In the application (the `main()` part of the program) there is a block of code that may cause exceptions (the try block), and a block of code that handles the exception (the catch block).

Specifying the Exception Class

The program first specifies an exception class within the `Stack` class:

```
class Range
   {   // note: empty class body
   };
```

Here the body of the class is empty, so objects of this class have no data and no member functions. All we really need in this simple example is the class name, `Range`. This name is used to connect a throw statement with a catch block. (The class body need not always be empty, as we'll see later.)

Throwing an Exception

In the `Stack` class an exception occurs if the application tries to pop a value when the stack is empty or tries to push a value when the stack is full. To let the application know that it has made such a mistake when manipulating a `Stack` object, the member functions of the `Stack` class check for these conditions using `if` statements, and throw an exception if they occur. In XSTAK the exception is thrown in two places, both using the statement

```
throw Range();
```

The `Range()` part of this statement invokes the (implicit) constructor for the `Range` class, which creates an object of this class. The `throw` part of the statement transfers program control to the exception handler (which we'll examine in a moment).

The `try` Block

All the statements in `main()` that might cause this exception—that is, statements that manipulate `Stack` objects—are enclosed in braces and preceded by the `try` keyword:

```
try
   {
   // code that operates on objects that might cause an exception
   }
```

This is simply part of the application's normal code; it's what you would need to write even if you weren't using exceptions. Not all the code in the program needs to be in a try block; just the code that interacts with the `Stack` class. Also, there can be many try blocks in your program, so you can access `Stack` objects from different places.

The Exception Handler (Catch Block)

The code that handles the exception is enclosed in braces, preceded by the `catch` keyword, with the exception class name in parentheses. The exception class name must include the class in which it is located: `Stack::Range`:

```
catch(Stack::Range)
   {
   // code that handles the exception
   }
```

This construction is called the *exception handler*. It must immediately follow the try block. In XSTAK the exception handler simply prints an error message to let the user know why the program failed.

Control "falls through" the bottom of the exception handler, so you can continue processing at that point. Or the exception handler may transfer control elsewhere, or (more usually) terminate the program.

Sequence of Events

Let's summarize the sequence of events when an exception occurs.

1. Code is executing normally outside a try block.
2. Control enters the try block.
3. A statement in the try block causes an error in a member function.
4. The member function throws an exception.
5. Control transfers to the exception handler (catch block) following the try block.

That's all there is to it. Notice how clean the resulting code is. Any of the statements in the try block could cause an exception, but we don't need to worry about checking a return value for each one, because the try-throw-catch arrangement handles them all automatically. In this particular example we've deliberately created two statements that cause exceptions. The first,

```
s1.push(44);   // pushes too many items
```

causes an exception if you remove the comment symbol preceding it, and the second,

```
cout << "4: " << s1.pop() << endl;  // pops item from empty stack
```

causes an exception if the first statement is commented out. Try it each way. In both cases the same error message will be displayed:

```
Stack Full or Empty
```

Multiple Exceptions

You can design a class to throw as many exceptions as you want. To show how this works, we'll modify the XSTAK program to throw separate exceptions for attempting to push data on a full stack and attempting to pop data from an empty stack. Here's the listing for XSTAK2:

```
// xstak2.cpp
// demonstrates two exception handlers

#include <iostream.h>
const int MAX = 3;                    // stack holds 3 ints

class Stack
   {
   private:
      int st[MAX];                    // stack: array of integers
      int top;                        // index of top of stack
   public:
      class Full { };                 // exception class
      class Empty { };                // exception class

      Stack()                         // constructor
         { top = -1; }

      void push(int var)              // put number on stack
         {
         if(top >= MAX-1)             // if stack full,
            throw Full();             // throw Full exception
         st[++top] = var;
         }
      int pop()                       // take number off stack
         {
         if(top < 0)                  // if stack empty,
            throw Empty();            // throw Empty exception
         return st[topÑ];
         }
   };

void main()
   {
   Stack s1;
```

```
    try
       {
       s1.push(11);
       s1.push(22);
       s1.push(33);
//     s1.push(44);                            // oops: stack full
       cout << "1: " << s1.pop() << endl;
       cout << "2: " << s1.pop() << endl;
       cout << "3: " << s1.pop() << endl;
       cout << "4: " << s1.pop() << endl;     // oops: stack empty
       }
    catch(Stack::Full)
       {
       cout << "Stack Full" << endl;
       }
    catch(Stack::Empty)
       {
       cout << "Stack Empty" << endl;
       }
    }
```

In XSTAK2 we specify two exception classes:

```
class Full  {  };
class Empty  {  };
```

The statement

```
throw Full();
```

is executed if the application calls `push()` when the stack is already full, and

```
throw Empty();
```

is executed if `pop()` is called when the stack is empty.

A separate catch block is used for each exception:

```
try
   {
   // code that operates on Stack objects
   }
catch(Stack::Full)
   {
   // code to handle Full exception
   }
catch(Stack::Empty)
   {
   // code to handle Empty exception
   }
```

All the catch blocks used with a particular try block must immediately follow the try block. In this case each catch block simply prints a message: *Stack Full* or *Stack Empty*. Only one catch block is activated for a given exception. This group of catch blocks, or *catch ladder*, operates a little like a switch statement, with only the appropriate section of code being executed. When an exception has been handled, control passes to the statement following all the catch blocks. (Unlike a switch statement, you don't need to end each catch block with a `break`. In this way catch blocks act more like functions.)

Exceptions with the Distance Class

Let's look at another example of exceptions, this one applied to the infamous **Distance** class from previous chapters. A **Distance** object has an integer value of feet and a floating-point value for inches. The inches value should always be less than 12.0. A problem with this class in previous examples has been that it couldn't protect itself if the user initialized an object with an inches value of 12.0 or greater. This could lead to trouble when the class tried to perform arithmetic, since the arithmetic routines (such as **operator +()**) assumed **inches** would be less than 12.0. Such impossible values could also be displayed, thus confounding the user with dimensions like 7'-15".

Let's rewrite the **Distance** class to use an exception to handle this error, as shown in XDIST:

```
// xdist.cpp
// exceptions with Distance class
#include <iostream.h>
#include <string.h>                    // for strcpy()

class Distance                         // English Distance class
   {
   private:
      int feet;
      float inches;
   public:
      class InchesEx { };              // exception class

      Distance()                       // constructor (no args)
         { feet = 0; inches = 0.0; }

      Distance(int ft, float in)       // constructor (two args)
         {
         if(in >= 12.0)                // if inches too big,
            throw InchesEx();          // throw exception
         feet = ft;
         inches = in;
         }

      void getdist()                   // get length from user
         {
         cout << "\nEnter feet: ";  cin >> feet;
         cout << "Enter inches: ";  cin >> inches;
         if(inches >= 12.0)            // if inches too big,
            throw InchesEx();          // throw exception
         }

      void showdist()                  // display distance
         { cout << feet << "\'-" << inches << '\"'; }
   };

void main()
   {
   try
      {
```

```
      Distance dist1(17, 3.5);      // 2-arg constructor
      Distance dist2;               // no-arg constructor
      dist2.getdist();              // get distance from user
                                    // display distances
      cout << "\ndist1 = ";  dist1.showdist();
      cout << "\ndist2 = ";  dist2.showdist();
      }
   catch(Distance::InchesEx)        // catch exceptions
      {
      cout << "\nInitialization error: "
              "inches value is too large.";
      }
   }
```

We install an exception class called `InchesEx` in the `Distance` class. Then, whenever the user attempts to initialize the inches data to a value greater than or equal to 12.0, we throw the exception. This happens in two places: in the two-argument constructor, where the programmer may make an error supplying initial values, and in the `getdist()` function, where the user may enter an incorrect value at the *Enter inches* prompt.

In `main()` all interaction with `Distance` objects is enclosed in a try block, and the catch block displays an error message.

In a more sophisticated program, of course, you might want to handle a user error (as opposed to a programmer error) differently. It would be more user friendly to go back to the beginning of the try block and give the user a chance to enter a another distance value.

Exceptions with Arguments

What happens if the application needs more information about what caused an exception? For instance, in the XDIST example, it might help the programmer to know what the bad inches value actually was. Also, if the same exception is thrown by different member functions, as it is in XDIST, it would be nice to know which of the functions was the culprit. Is there a way to pass such information from the member function, where the exception is thrown, to the application that catches it?

This question can be answered by remembering that throwing an exception involves not only transferring control to the handler, but also creating an object of the exception class by calling its constructor. In XDIST, for example, we create an object of type `InchesEx` when we throw the exception with the statement

```
throw InchesEx();
```

If we add data members to the exception class, we can initialize them when we create the object. The exception handler can then retrieve the data from the object when it catches the exception. It's like writing a message on a baseball and throwing it over the fence to your neighbor. We'll modify the XDIST program to do this. Here's the listing for XDIST2:

```
// xdist2.cpp
// exceptions with arguments
#include <iostream.h>
#include <string.h>                   // for strcpy()
```

(continued on next page)

(continued from previous page)

```
class Distance                          // English Distance class
   {
   private:
      float inches;
      int feet;
   public:
      class InchesEx                    // exception class
         {
         public:
            char origin[80];            // for name of routine
            float iValue;               // for faulty inches value

            InchesEx(char* or, float in)  // 2-arg constructor
               {
               strcpy(origin, or);          // store string
               iValue = in;                 // store inches
               }
         };                             // end of exception class

      Distance()                        // no-arg constructor
         { feet = 0; inches = 0.0; }

      Distance(int ft, float in)        // 2-arg constructor
         {
         if(in >= 12.0)
            throw InchesEx("2-arg constructor", in);
         feet = ft;
         inches = in;
         }

      void getdist()                    // get length from user
         {
         cout << "\nEnter feet: ";  cin >> feet;
         cout << "Enter inches: ";  cin >> inches;
         if(inches >= 12.0)
            throw InchesEx("getdist() function", inches);
         }

      void showdist()                   // display distance
         { cout << feet << "\'-" << inches << '\"'; }
   };

void main()
   {
   try
      {
      Distance dist1(17, 3.5);          // 2-arg constructor
      Distance dist2;                   // no-arg constructor
      dist2.getdist();                  // get value
                                        // display distances
      cout << "\ndist1 = ";  dist1.showdist();
      cout << "\ndist2 = ";  dist2.showdist();
      }
   catch(Distance::InchesEx ix)         // exception handler
```

```
      {
      cout << "\nInitialization error in " << ix.origin
           << ".\n   Inches value of " << ix.iValue
           << " is too large.";
      }
   }
```

There are three parts to the operation of passing data when throwing an exception: specifying the data members and a constructor for the exception class, initializing this constructor when we throw an exception, and accessing the object's data when we catch the exception. Let's look at these in turn.

Specifying Data in an Exception Class

It's convenient to make the data in an exception class public so it can be accessed directly by the exception handler. Here's the specification for the new `InchesEx` exception class in XDIST2:

```
class InchesEx                          // exception class
   {
   public:
      char origin[80];                  // for name of routine
      float iValue;                     // for faulty inches value

      InchesEx(char* or, float in)      // 2-arg constructor
         {
         strcpy(origin, or);            // put string in object
         iValue = in;                   // put inches value in object
         }
   };
```

There are public variables for a string, which will hold the name of the member function being called, and a type `float`, for the faulty inches value.

Initializing an Exception Object

How do we initialize the data when we throw an exception? In the two-argument constructor for the `Stack` class we say

```
throw InchesEx("2-arg constructor", in);
```

and in the `getdist()` nmember function for `Stack` it's

```
throw InchesEx("getdist() function", in);
```

When the exception is thrown, the handler will display the string and inches values. The string will tell us which member function is throwing the exception, and the value of `in` will report the faulty inches value detected by the member function. This additional data will make it easier for the programmer or user to figure out what caused the error.

Extracting Data from the Exception Object

How do we extract this data when we catch the exception? The simplest way is to make the data a public part of the exception class, as we've done here. Then in the catch block we can declare `ix` as the name of the exception object we're catching. Using this name we can refer to its data in the usual way, using the dot operator:

```
catch(Distance::InchesEx ix)
   {
   // access 'ix.origin' and 'ix.iValue' directly
   }
```

We can then display the value of `ix.origin` and `ix.iValue`. Here's some interaction with XDIST2, when the user enters too large a value for inches:

```
Enter feet: 7
Enter inches: 13.5

Initialization error in getdist() function.
   Inches value of 13.5 is too large.
```

Similarly, if the programmer changes the definition of `dist1` in `main()` to

```
Distance dist1(17, 22.25);
```

the resulting exception will cause this error message:

```
Initialization error in 2-arg constructor.
   Inches value of 22.25 is too large.
```

Of course we can make whatever use of the exception arguments we want, but they generally carry information that helps us diagnose the error that triggered the exception.

The `xalloc` Class

Borland C++ contains several built-in exception classes. The most commonly used is probably `xalloc`, which is thrown if an error occurs when attempting to allocate memory with `new`. If you set up the appropriate try and catch blocks, you can make use of this class with very little effort on your part. Here's a short example, XALLOC, that shows how it's used:

```
// xalloc.cpp
// demonstrates xalloc class

#include <iostream.h>
#include <except.h>                        // for xalloc class

void main()
   {
   const unsigned int MAX = 60000;     // memory size (chars)
   char* ptr;                          // pointer to memory

   try
      {
      ptr = new char[MAX];             // allocate memry
      // other statements that use 'new'
      }
   catch(xalloc)                       // exception handler
      {
      cout << "\nxalloc exception: can't allocation memory.";
      exit(1);
      }
   for(unsigned int j=0; j<MAX; j++)   // fill memory with data
```

```
      *(ptr+j) = j%128;
   for(j=0; j<MAX; j++)                        // check data
      if(*(ptr+j) != j%128)
         {
         cout << "\nData error";
         exit(1);
         }
   delete[] ptr;                               // release memory
   cout << "\nMemory use is successful.";
   }
```

You'll need to include the EXCEPT.H file, which contains the specification for the `xalloc` class (among others). Then put all the statements that use `new` in a try block. The catch block that follows handles the exception; usually by displaying an error message and terminating the program.

You could do all this yourself by testing the return value from `new` and throwing an exception if it was 0 (indicating the requested memory could not be obtained). However, `xalloc` handles the details for you, which results in a cleaner-looking listing and an easier-to-maintain program.

You can get this program to throw the `xalloc` exception by tinkering with the value of MAX. You can't allocate an entire data segment of 65,536 bytes, so as you increase MAX beyond 60,000 you'll eventually cause the `xalloc` exception to be thrown, which will print the error message and cause the program to terminate:

```
xalloc exception: can't allocate memory
```

The program includes `for` loops to fill the memory with data and verify that it's correct. Note that these statements don't need to be in the try block, since they don't use `new`.

Exception Notes

We've shown only the simplest and most common approach to using exceptions. We won't go into further detail, but we'll conclude with a few thoughts about exception usage.

Destructors Called Automatically

The exception mechanism is surprisingly sophisticated. When an exception is thrown, a destructor is called automatically for any object that was created by the code up to that point in the try block. This is necessary because the application won't know which statement caused the exception, and if it wants to recover from the error, it will (at the very least) need to start over at the top of the try block. The exception mechanism guarantees that the code in the try block will have been "reset," at least as far as the existence of objects is concerned.

Termination Oriented

After you catch an exception, you will probably want to terminate your application. The exception mechanism gives you a chance to indicate the source of the error to the user, and to perform any necessary clean-up chores before terminating. It also makes clean-up easier by executing the destructors for objects created in the try block. This allows you to release system resources, such as memory, that such objects may be using. (In general, DOS programs release system resources automatically when they terminate, but Windows programs may not.)

However, in some cases you may not want to terminate your program. It is also possible to try to recover from the error. Perhaps your program can figure out what caused the error and correct it, or the user can be asked to input different data. When this is the case, the try and catch blocks are typically embedded in a loop, so control can be returned to the beginning of the try block (which the exception mechanism has attempted to restore to its initial state).

If there is no exception handler that matches the exception thrown, the program is unceremoniously terminated by the operating system.

Function Nesting

The statement that causes an exception need not be located directly in the try block; it can also be in a function that is *called* by a statement in the try block. (Or in a function called by a function that is called by a statement in the try block, and so on.) So you only need to install a try block on the program's upper level. Lower-level functions need not be so encumbered, provided they are called directly or indirectly by functions in the try block.

Can't Return to Throw Point

There's no way for an exception handler to return control to the location in the application that caused the exception. Exceptions act more like a `goto` than a function call. Control goes to the exception handler (catch block) and then (unless you do something else), falls through to the code following the catch block.

Summary

Templates allow you to generate a family of functions, or a family of classes, to handle different data types. Whenever you find yourself writing several identical functions that perform the same operation on different data types, you should consider using a function template instead. Similarly, whenever you find yourself writing several different class specifications that differ only in the type of data acted on, you should consider using a class template. You'll save yourself time and the result will be a more robust and more easily maintained program that is also (once you understand templates) easier to understand.

Exceptions are a mechanism for handling C++ errors in a systematic, OOP-oriented way. An exception is typically caused by a faulty statement in a try block that operates on objects of a class. The class member function discovers the error and throws an exception, which is caught by exception-handler code following the try block.

Questions

Answers to questions can be found in Appendix D.

1. A template provides a convenient way to make a family of

a. variables.
b. functions.
c. classes.
d. programs.

2. A template argument is preceded by the keyword ________.

3. True or false: Templates automatically create different versions of a function, depending on user input.

4. Write a template for a function that always returns its argument times 2.

5. A template class

a. is designed to be stored in different containers.
b. works with different data types.
c. generates objects which must all be identical.
d. generates classes with different numbers of member functions.

6. True or false: There can be more than one template argument.

7. Creating an actual function from a template is called ________ the function.

8. Actual code for a template function is generated when

a. the function prototype appears in the source code.
b. the function definition appears in the source code.
c. a call to the function appears in the source code.
d. the function is executed at runtime.

9. The key to the template concept is replacing a ________ with a name that stands for ________.

10. Templates are often used for classes that ________ ________.

11. An exception is an error that is typically caused by

a. the programmer who writes an application's code.
b. the creator of a class who writes the class member functions.
c. the user who enters input values into a program.
d. a malfunction in the operating system that terminates the program.

12. The C++ keywords used with exceptions are ________, ________, and ________.

13. Write a statement that throws an exception using the class `BoundsError`, which has an empty body.

14. True or false: Statements that might cause an exception must be part of a catch block.

15. Exceptions are thrown
    a. from the catch block to the try block.
    b. from a throw statement to the try block.
    c. from the point of the error to a catch block.
    d. from a throw statement to a catch block.
16. Write the specification for an exception class that stores an error number and an error name. Include a constructor.
17. True or false: A statement that throws an exception does not need to be located in a try block.
18. The following are errors for which an exception would typically be thrown.
    a. An excessive amount of data threatens to overflow an array
    b. The user presses CTRL-C to terminate the program
    c. The floating-point processor reports an error
    d. `new` cannot obtain the requested memory
19. Additional information sent when an exception is thrown may be placed in
    a. the `throw` keyword.
    b. the function that caused the error.
    c. the catch block.
    d. an object of the exception class.
20. True or false: A program can continue to operate after an exception has occurred.

Exercises

Answers to starred exercises can be found in Appendix D.

1.* Write a template function that returns the average of all the elements of an array. The arguments to the function should be the array name and the size of the array (type `int`). In `main()`, exercise the function with arrays of type `int`, `long`, `double`, and `char`.

2.* A queue is a data-storage device. It's like a stack, except that, instead of being last-in-first-out, it's first-in-first-out, like the line at a bank teller's window. If you put in 1, 2, 3, you get back 1, 2, 3 in that order.

A stack needs only one index to an array (`top` in the STAKARAY program in Chapter 8). A queue, on the other hand, must keep track of two indexes to an array: one to the tail, where new items are added, and one to the head, where old items are removed. The tail follows the head through the array as items are added and removed. If either the tail or the head reaches the end of the array, it is reset back to the beginning.

Write a class template for a queue class. Assume the programmer using the queue won't make any mistakes, like exceeding the capacity of the queue, or trying to remove an item when the queue is empty. Define several queues of different data types and insert and remove data from them.

3.* Add exceptions to the queue template in Exercise 2. Throw two exceptions: one if the capacity of the queue is exceeded, the other if the program tries to remove an item from an empty queue. One way to handle this is to add a new data member to the queue: a count of the number of items currently in the queue. Increment the count when you insert an item, and decrement it when you remove an item. Throw an exception if this count exceeds the capacity of the queue, or if it becomes less than 0.

    You might try making the `main()` part of this exercise interactive, so the user can put values on a queue and take them off. This makes it easier to exercise the queue. Following an exception, the program should allow the user to recover from a mistake without corrupting the contents of the queue.

4. Create a function called `swap()` that interchanges the values of the two arguments sent to it. (You will probably want to pass these arguments by reference.) Make the function into a template, so it can be used with all numerical data types (`char`, `int`, `float`, and so on). Write a `main()` program to exercise the function with several numerical types.

5. Create a function called `amax()` that returns the value of the largest element in an array. The arguments to the function should be the address of the array and its size. Make this function into a template so it will work with an array of any numerical type. Write a `main()` program that applies this function to arrays of various types.

6. Start with the `safearay` class from the ARROVER3 program in Chapter 9. Make this class into a template, so the safe array can store any kind of data. In `main()`, create safe arrays of at least two different types, and store some data in them.

7. Start with the `frac` class and the four-function fraction calculator of Exercise 7 in Chapter 9. Make the `frac` class into a template so it can be instantiated using different data types for the numerator and denominator. These must be integer types, which pretty much restricts you to `char`, `int`, and `long` (unless you develop an integer type of your own). In `main()`, instantiate a class `frac<int>` and use it for the four-function calculator. Class `frac<int>` will take less memory than `frac<long>` and will operate faster, but won't be able to handle large fractions.

8. Add an exception class to the ARROVER3 program in Chapter 9 so that an out-of-bounds index will trigger the exception. The catch block can print an error message for the user.

9. Modify the exception class in Exercise 8 (adapted from ARROVER3) so that the error message in the catch block reports the value of the index that caused the exception.

10. There are various philosophies about when to use exceptions. Refer to the ENGLERR program from Chapter 14. Should user-input errors be exceptions? For this exercise, let's assume so. Add an exception class to the `Distance` class in that program. (See also the XDIST and XDIST2 examples in this chapter.) Throw an exception in all the places where ENGLERR displayed an error message. Use an argument to the exception constructor to report where the error occurred and the specific cause of the error (inches not a number, inches out of range, and so on). Also, throw an exception when an error is found within the `isint()` function (nothing entered, too many digits, nondigit character, integer out of range). Question: If it throws exceptions, can `isint()` remain an independent function?

    You can insert both the try block and the catch block within the `do` loop so that after an exception you go back to the top of the loop, ready to ask the user for more input.

    You might also want to throw an exception in the two-argument constructor, in case the programmer initializes a `Distance` value with its inches member out of range.

11. Start with the STRPLUS program in Chapter 9. Add an exception class, and throw an exception in the one-argument constructor if the initialization string is too long. Throw another in the overloaded + operator if the result will be too long when two strings are concatenated. Report which of these errors has occurred.

12. Sometimes the easiest way to use exceptions is to create a new class of which an exception class is a member. Try this with a class that uses exceptions to handle file errors. Make a class `dofile` that includes an exception class and member functions to read and write files. A constructor to this class can take the filename as an argument and open a file with that name. You may also want a member function to reset the file pointer to the beginning of the file. Use the REWERR program in Chapter 14 as a model, and write a `main()` program that provides the same functionality, but does so by calling on members of the `dofile` class.

17

The Borland C++ Class Library

ADVANTAGES OF READY-MADE CLASSES

SETTING UP THE CLASS LIBRARY

UTILITY CLASSES: DATES, TIMES, STRINGS

CONTAINER CLASSES: STACKS, ARRAYS, LINKED LISTS, ETC.

STORING YOUR OWN CLASS OBJECTS IN CONTAINERS

17

Borland C++ and Turbo C++ come with an extensive library of prewritten classes. The largest group of such classes that we'll discuss in this chapter is the *container classes*—classes that provide storage for data items or objects. We'll also discuss several utility classes for handling commonly used items such as dates and strings.

There are too many classes and member functions in the Borland class library to cover completely in this chapter. Instead we'll show some example programs to give you the flavor of using the library, and to show how important the concept of library classes can be in C++.

Don't Reinvent the Wheel

In previous chapters we developed examples of utility classes used to hold such quantities as dates and strings. We also created container classes, including stacks, linked lists, and safe arrays. However, these classes were illustrative examples; they featured only a few of many possible member functions. The Borland class library includes fully developed utility classes for dates, times, and strings, and—more importantly—an extensive collection of container classes.

Utility classes greatly simplify the use of such items as times and dates in your programs, since you don't need to develop your own classes. We'll start this chapter by discussing these classes.

Creating data storage structures such as linked lists and stacks is a common programming task. Most substantial programs require several such storage mechanisms, and their creation and debugging can be a major part of a programming effort. In old-fashioned procedural programs it was common to create each data storage structure from the ground up. Each time you needed a linked list, for example, you probably started from scratch to put together the various structures and functions that allowed you to insert and delete elements in the list. Even if you cut and pasted code from previous projects, it probably still needed extensive revision before it would work in the new environment.

As we've seen, one of the major advantages of OOP is the ability to reuse existing classes in your own programs. Borland's container classes are an excellent example. If you need a linked list to hold objects of a class you created, you no longer need to create your own; you can instantiate a Borland class to do the job with a minimum of effort. Using the template approach, the container classes can hold almost any kind of data. Most of this chapter is concerned with these classes.

Developing Programs with the Class Library

In this section we'll describe how to make your compiler work with the Borland class library. We assume that you installed the class library during the compiler installation process, as suggested in Chapter 2. Also, we assume you loaded the library for the Medium or Large memory model. Because the Borland class libraries contain so much code, you'll need these memory models for all but the simplest programs. If you try to use the Small (or Compact) model when your program's code has grown too large, you'll get an error message from the linker such as *_text segment exceeds 64K*.

Older Versions

The Borland class library has evolved rapidly. The original version appeared before templates were implemented in C++, and consequently the container classes required any objects that they held to be derived from a class called `Object`. Borland refers to these early classes as *Object Containers*. They may still be included in your compiler for compatibility with older programs.

The template approach, used in newer versions of the class library, gives the container classes far more flexibility. Containers can now hold objects of almost any type, from basic C++ types to user-defined classes. Borland calls this collection of containers *Borland International Data Structures*, or *BIDS*. This chapter focuses on BIDS, and assumes your compiler includes this version of the container classes. Some early versions of the class library also did not include the `TDate`, `TTime`, and `string` utility classes. We'll assume these classes are available in your system.

Finally, early versions of BIDS prefaced the container class names with `BI_` instead of `T`. For instance, the `TArrayAsVector` class was called `BI_ArrayAsVector` in earlier versions, and `TDate` was called `BI_Date`. If this is the case in your system, you can translate appropriate instances of `T`, as used in this chapter, to `BI_`. Or, better yet, you can obtain a more modern version of the Borland class library.

Preparing Borland C++

It's easy to use the class library In Borland C++. Here's the key: When you create a new project, make sure you click on the *Class Library* box in the *New Project* window.

The files for the class library are distributed in different CLASSLIB subdirectories. Header files, such as ARRAYS.H, LISTIMP.H, and DATE.H, are in the \BC45\INCLUDE\CLASSLIB subdirectory. When you include header files in your program, you'll need to give a partial pathname that includes the CLASSLIB subdirectory:

```
#include <classlib\stacks.h>    // for stack containers
#include <classlib\date.h>      // for TDate class
```

The compiler already knows it should look in \BC45\INCLUDE, so these partial paths are all you need.

Example programs for the class library are in the \BC45\EXAMPLES\CLASSLIB directory.

An anomaly is the CSTRING.H header for for the `string` class, which is not in the CLASSLIB\INCLUDE directory, but in the normal INCLUDE directory.

Preparing Turbo C++

In Turbo C++, all the files for the Borland class library are placed in a single subdirectory, normally called TC\CLASSLIB. This directory contains various subdirectories, including INCLUDE and LIB. (Note that these are not the same as the INCLUDE and LIB directories that are direct descendants of the TC directory.) The Turbo C++ IDE needs to be told where these directories are. The most straightforward approach is to enter their pathnames into the box provided by the *Directories* selection in the Options menu. You need the INCLUDE and LIB directories from both the

\TC\CLASSLIB\ and \TC\. Separate the pathnames with semicolons. That is, in the *Include Directories* field enter

```
C:\TC\CLASSLIB\INCLUDE;C:\TC\INCLUDE
```

and in the *Library Directories* field enter

```
C:\TC\CLASSLIB\LIB;C:\TC\LIB
```

Now when you include header files in your programs, you need specify only the filename:

```
#include <stacks.h>     // for stack containers
#include <date.h>       // for TDate class
```

There is also a directory of example programs under TC\CLASSLIB called EXAMPLES. You will find it informative to study these programs.

Writing a Program with Library Classes

In both Borland C++ and Turbo C++, start up the IDE in the directory where you want to develop your program. Write the source file and give it the .CPP extension (as in MYPROG.CPP). This file should `#include` header files for all the class libraries you intend to use. For instance, if you use the `TDate` class you should include DATE.H, and if you use the `TStackAsArray` class you should include STACKS.H. You can do a DIR of \BC45\INCLUDE\CLASSLIB (or \TC\CLASSLIB\INCLUDE) to see what header files are available. In general the filenames are related in some obvious way to the corresponding class names.

When your source file is complete, you can compile, link, and run your program in the usual way.

Utility Classes

We'll begin with a brief look at three of Borland's utility classes: `TDate` for dates, `TTime` for times, and `string` for strings. These classes provide an easy introduction to the class library, and objects of these classes can also serve as examples of items to be stored in containers.

The `TDate` Class

Handling dates as program variables can raise questions that require extensive programming to solve. What day of the week was March 11, 1938? How many days are there between January 15 and April 15? And if you calculated this, did you remember to include an extra day for leap year? Is 2000 a leap year?

The Borland `TDate` class makes it easy to handle such questions. By using `TDate` variables to hold dates, you have at your disposal a large number of member functions for performing calculations and I/O operations on dates.

In the `TDate` class, a date is stored as a single number of type `unsigned long` called the *Julian number* representing the number of days since—well, since when? Borland's documentation specifies that this number is 2,415,386 when the date is 1/1/1901. Working backward, and assuming a year is 365.2422 days (the astronomical year), brings us to about 4,713 BC as the zero-point for the Julian number. However, for historical reasons, such numbers are not accurate for dates before the establishment of the Gregorian Calendar in 1752.

`TDate` member functions start with this Julian number and calculate such values as the day, month, and year using built-in knowledge about the number of days in each month, the days in a year, when leap years occur, and so on.

Unfortunately for those expecting their programs to work seamlessly in the new millennium, `TDate` thinks of 1/1/01 as being 1/1/1901, not 1/1/2001. To input dates in centuries other than the 20th, you need to enter all four digits of the year.

You'll need the \INCLUDE\CLASSLIB\DATE.H header file for the `TDate` class. You'll also need \INCLUDE\CSTRING.H, since the `TDate` class uses the `string` class.

Our example program demonstrates some member functions applied to objects of the `TDate` class. Here's the listing for DATETEST:

```
// datetest.cpp
// demonstrates the TDate class

#include <cstring.h>
#include <classlib\date.h>
#include <iostream.h>

void main()
   {
   char ch;
   TDate today;
   TDate aday;

   cout << "\nToday is " << today << endl;

   do
      {
      cout << "\nEnter date: ";
      cin >> aday;
      cout << "You entered: " << aday;

      aday.SetPrintOption(TDate::Terse);
      cout << "\nIn Terse style that's " << aday;
      aday.SetPrintOption(TDate::Numbers);
      cout << "\nIn Numbers style it's " << aday;
      aday.SetPrintOption(TDate::Normal);

      cout << "\nDay of year: " << aday.Day();
      cout << "\nDay of month: " << aday.DayOfMonth();
      cout << "\nName of month: " << aday.NameOfMonth();
      cout << "\nName of day: " << aday.NameOfDay();

      cout << (aday.Leap() ? "\nLeap year" : "\nNot leap year");

      if(aday<today)
         cout << "\nThat's " << (today-aday) << " days ago";
      else
         cout << "\nThat's " << (aday-today) << " days from now";

      cout << "\nDay of week: "
           << TDate::DayOfWeek( aday.NameOfDay() );
      cout << "\nIndex of month: "
           << TDate::IndexOfMonth( aday.NameOfMonth() );
```

```
      cout << "\nDo another (y/n)? ";
      cin >> ch;
      }
   while(ch != 'n');
   }
```

The program displays the current date (obtained from the system clock), asks the user to type in a different date, and then displays various aspects of this new date. Here's some sample output:

```
Today is June 15, 1994

Enter date: 12/31/94
You entered: December 31, 1994
In Terse style that's 31-Dec-94
In Numbers style it's 12/31/94
Day of year: 365
Day of month: 31
Name of month: December
Name of day: Saturday
Not leap year
That's 199 days from now
Day of week: 6
Index of month: 12
Do another (y/n)?
```

The no-argument constructor causes the `TDate` variable to be initialized to the date on the system clock (presumably today's date). The (>>) and (<<) operators are overloaded to work with `TDates`. Input can be recognized in several different forms, including `12/31/94` and `December 31, 1994`. `TDates` can also be displayed in several different ways, governed by the `SetPrintOption()` member function. Besides `Normal`, `Terse`, and `Numbers`, shown in the example, you can also use `European` and `EuropeanNumbers`, which reverse the month and day.

The `Day()`, `DayOfMonth()`, `NameOfMonth()`, and `NameOfDay()` member functions return what their names indicate. The `Leap()` function returns 1 if the date is a leap year, 0 otherwise.

All the common arithmetic operators are overloaded to work with `TDates`. We use the (<) operator to compare two dates, and the (-) operator to subtract them.

Static member functions translate the name of the day, supplied as an argument, into the numerical day of the week (Monday is 1, Sunday is 7), and the name of the month into the month number.

You can find descriptions of all the `TDate` member functions and operators in the *Borland C++ Library Reference*, or on online help.

The `TTime` Class

The `TTime` class (do they serve cucumber sandwiches?) is in many ways similar to the `TDate` class. The important data item in this class is an `unsigned long` variable, `Sec`, representing the number of seconds since the beginning of January 1, 1901. The fact that the time includes the date makes it easier for the member functions to compare times that cross date boundaries. Our example program exercises some of the `TTime` member functions. Here's the listing for TIMETEST:

```
// timetest.cpp
// demonstrates the TTime class
#include <classlib\time.h>
#include <iostream.h>

void main()
   {
   TTime now;                                   // create a TTime
   int iyear, ihours, iminutes, iseconds;       // other variables
   char ch;

   cout << "\nThe current date and time is " << now;
   cout << "\n   In Greenwich Mean Time that's "
        << now.HourGMT() << ":" << now.MinuteGMT();
   do
      {
      cout << "\n\nEnter a time (assuming today's date)";
      cout << "\n      hours: "; cin >> ihours;
      cout << "   minutes: "; cin >> iminutes;
      cout << "   seconds: "; cin >> iseconds;

      TTime then(ihours, iminutes, iseconds);   // initialize a TTime

      TTime::PrintDate(0);  // don't print date
      cout << "You entered " << then;
      cout << "\nhour: " << then.Hour();
      cout << "\nminute: " << then.Minute();
      cout << "\nsecond: " << then.Second();
      cout << "\nSeconds since 1/1/1901: " << then.Seconds();

      cout << "\nSeconds between the time you entered and now: ";
      if(then < now)
         cout << ( now.Seconds()-then.Seconds() );
      else
         cout << ( then.Seconds()-now.Seconds() );

      cout << "\n\nEnter a year: ";
      cin >> iyear;
      TTime::PrintDate(1);           // print date along with time
      cout << "Daylight savings time in effect\n   from "
           << TTime::BeginDST(iyear)
           << "\n   to "
           << TTime::EndDST(iyear);
      TTime::PrintDate(0);           // don't print date with time
      cout << "\nDo another (y/n)? ";
      cin >> ch;
      }
   while(ch != 'n');
   }
```

The no-argument constructor creates a `TTime` object initialized to the current time, obtained from the system clock. Our example program prints the current time. The date is normally displayed along with the time, but you can suppress the date using the static `PrintDate()` member function with an argument of 0.

Member functions also obtain the hour and minute of Greenwich Mean Time (GMT). A three-argument constructor initializes a `TTime` object to the specified hours, minutes, and seconds of today's date.

The arithmetic and logical operators are overloaded for `TTime` objects. We use the (<) operator to compare two times, and the (-) operator to subtract them. Static member functions find the dates and hours on which daylight savings time begins and ends in any given year.

Here's some sample output from TIMETEST:

```
The current date and time is June 16, 1994 11:12:53
   In Greenwich Mean Time that's 15:12

Enter a time (assuming today's date):
     hours: 8
   minutes: 30
   seconds: 0
You entered 8:30:00 am
hour: 8
minute: 30
second: 0
Seconds since 1/1/1901: 2949222600
Seconds between the time you entered and now: 9773

Enter a year: 1975
Daylight savings time in effect
   from February 23, 1975 2:00:00 am
   to October 26, 1975 2:00:00 am
Do another (y/n)?
```

Be advised that a time interval in seconds is not the same thing as a `TTime` value. You can't easily convert a seconds quantity (such as the difference between two `TTime` objects), into the equivalent interval in hours, minutes, and seconds, because a `TTime` object represents a time, not a time interval. The arithmetic operators add an interval in seconds to an existing time; they don't add two times.

The `string` Class

Treating strings as arrays of characters, as C and C++ normally do, certainly has an austere sort of elegance. You know you're close to the metal when you must think of a natural-language sentence as an array of type `char`. However, there are disadvantages to this approach. For one thing, you must treat a string variable differently than other variables. The address of a numeric variable might be `&var`, but the address of a string variable is simply `var` because it's an array. Also, with normal `char*` strings you must decide in advance the length of the longest string a variable will hold—you can't change the buffer length dynamically.

Borland's `string` class solves these problems and provides almost everything you would like in a string data type. You can treat string variables almost as you would basic C++ variables. Member functions of `string` provide most of the functionality of the traditional C and C++ string-handling library functions, generally in a more convenient form. The `string` class also saves memory by storing multiple copies of a string in the same place in memory. (We showed a simple way to implement this scheme in the STRIMEM program in Chapter 13.)

Our example program prints a series of sentences. First a template sentence is created by taking two first names entered by the user and inserting them to form, for example, "she told Sandy that she loved Chris". Then the word "only" is inserted at each possible position in the sentence to provide a series of sentences with surprisingly different meanings. Here's the output:

```
Enter a first name: Sandy
Enter another first name: Chris
only she told Sandy that she loved Chris
she only told Sandy that she loved Chris
she told only Sandy that she loved Chris
she told Sandy only that she loved Chris
she told Sandy that only she loved Chris
she told Sandy that she only loved Chris
she told Sandy that she loved only Chris
she told Sandy that she loved Chris only
```

The program that generates this series of sentences makes use of some representative member functions of the `string` class. Here's the listing for STRTEST:

```
// strtest.cpp
// demonstrates the string class
#include <cstring.h>              // for string class
#include <iostream.h>

void main()
   {
   size_t pos;                             // char position in string
   string s1;                              // for complete sentence
   string s2("only ");
   string s3 = "she told ";
   string s4;                              // for first name (X)
   string s5 = " that she loved ";
   string s6;                              // for first name (Y)

   cout << "\nEnter your first name: ";
   cin >> s4;
   cout << "Enter another first name: ";
   cin >> s6;
                        // only she told X that she loved Y
   s1 = s2 + s3 + s4 + s5 + s6;
   cout << s1 << endl;

   pos = 0;
   s1.remove( 0, s2.length() );           // remove "only"
                        // she only told X that she loved Y, etc.
   while( (pos=s1.find(" ", pos)) != NPOS )   // find next space
      {
      pos++;                              // go one space past
      s1.insert(pos, s2);                 // insert "only "
      cout << s1 << endl;                 // display result
      s1.remove( pos, s2.length() );      // remove "only "
      }
   s1 += ' ' + s2;      // she told X that she loved Y only
   cout << s1 << endl;
   }
```

As you can see from the example, you can create `string` objects of zero length, or initialize them with `char*` strings or `string` objects. The << and >> operators are overloaded for `string` objects, which makes I/O easy. The + and += operators are overloaded for concatenation, and the comparison operators allow you to compare two `string` objects alphabetically.

In this program we use the `remove()`, `length()`, `find()`, and `insert()` member functions. The `remove()` function removes a given number of characters from a given position in the `string`; the `length()` function returns the length of a `string`; the `find()` function finds a particular character in a `string`, starting at a given position; and `insert()` inserts another `string` at a given position.

We have shown only a small subset of the available member functions. In general, if you can do something with a library function for a `char*` string, you can find a member function to do the same thing for a `string` object.

Other Utility Classes

The Borland class library includes several other utility classes. There are file classes, persistent stream classes, mathematical classes, diagnostic classes, and classes for handling threads in multithreaded operating systems. Space precludes our coverage of these classes. They are documented in online help, in the *Borland C++ Library Reference*, and in the *Borland C++ Programmer's Guide*.

The Container Classes

The largest group of classes supplied in the Borland class library is the container classes. These classes provide mechanisms for storing data in a variety of ways. They are powerful classes, with the potential of saving significant amounts of programming time and effort.

A Simple Example

Let's introduce the container classes by looking at a simple example program that uses one of these classes, `TStackAsVector`. Here's the listing for STACKINT:

```
// stackint.cpp
// tests the TStackAsVector class with type int
#include <classlib\stacks.h>
#include <iostream.h>

void main()
   {
   TStackAsVector<int> stint; // instantiate a stack for type int

   stint.Push(11);            // push ints onto stack
   stint.Push(12);
   stint.Push(13);

   while( !stint.IsEmpty() )  // pop ints off stack
      cout << stint.Pop() << endl;
   }
```

The container classes are based on templates, so a class must be instantiated to store data of a particular type. (See the discussion of templates in Chapter 16.) Our example program instantiates an object of the `TStackAsVector` class to store data of type `int`. Note how easy this is. We don't need to develop the class ourselves; it's all specified in the \CLASSLIB\STACKS.H header file.

In the program we push three integers (11, 12, and 13) onto the stack, and then pop them off and display them. Here's the output from STACKINT:

```
13
12
11
```

The instantiated object of `TStackAsVector`, called `stint`, knows how to store and operate on variables of type `int`. Three member functions of `TStackAsVector` are used in the program. The `Push()` member function pushes an integer onto the stack, and `Pop()` removes it. The `IsEmpty()` returns 1 when the stack becomes empty, making it easy to construct a `while` loop to remove each item from the stack and display it.

Summary of the Container Classes

Before we show examples of other classes, let's summarize just what container classes are available and how they're related. Borland, somewhat arbitrarily, divides the container classes into two categories: Fundamental Data Structures (FDSs) and Abstract Data Types (ADTs). The idea is that ADTs are derived from FDSs, which are considered to be lower-level constructs. Generally an ADT is more sophisticated and has more member functions than the FDS from which it is derived. However, you can use classes from either category to store data, depending on your needs. The FDS class names end in "Imp", and the ADT class names indicate the FDS from which they are derived following the word "As," as in `TStackAsList`. Tables 17-1 and 17-2 summarize the key classes in these two categories.

Category	Class name	Purpose
Binary tree	TBinarySearchTreeImp	Stores data in hierarchical organization.
Double-linked list	TDoubleListImp	Stores an unknown number of items in a linear chain, without keys or index numbers. Access may begin at either end of chain. Easy to add and delete items. Slow search and access.
Hash table	THashTableImp	Allows fast access to items that can't use an index number but that can use a key derived from their internal data.
Single-linked list	TListImp	Stores an unknown number of items in a linear chain, without keys or index numbers. Access at one end of chain. Easy to add and delete items. Slow search and access.
Vector	TVectorImp	Like an array. Stores and accesses items using index number. Fast access.

Table 17-1 Fundamental Data Structures

Category	Class Name	Purpose
Array	TArrayAsVector	Derived from vector. Useful when each item can be accessed using an index number.
Association	TDDAssociation	Groups a key (like a word) with a value (like a definition). Usually used with a dictionary.
Bag	TBagAsVector	Derived from hash table. The same item may appear more than once.
Deque	TDequeAsVector	A double-ended queue; items can be pushed or popped from either end. Useful when size is known in advance.
	TDequeAsDoubleList	A double-ended queue; items can be pushed or popped from either end. Useful when size is not known in advance.
Dictionary	TDictionaryAsHashTable	Derived from hash table. Usually stores associations. Allows quick access to a data item (like a definition) using a key (like a word).
Queue	TQueueAsVector (or TQueue)	First-in-first-out storage when size is known in advance. Fast access.
	TQueueAsDoubleList	First-in-first-out storage when size is not known in advance. Slower access.
Set	TSetAsVector (or TSet)	Derived from hash table. The same item may appear only once.
Stack	TStackAsVector (or TStack)	Last-in-first-out storage when size is known in advance. Fast access.
	TStackAsList	Last-in-first-out storage when size is not known in advance. Slower access.

Table 17-2 Abstract Data Types

Notice that three kinds of ADTs—deques, queues, and stacks—can be created in two different ways from the underlying FDSs: either as a vector or as a list. The vector implementation is generally faster, but the maximum size must be known in advance. The list implementation is slower but expands and contracts as necessary.

Each of the classes shown in Tables 17-1 and 17-2 potentially represents a family of similar classes. For example, Table 17-3 shows the classes in the `TArrayAsVector` family.

Class Name	Stores object or pointer	Sorted or unsorted	Standard or custom memory management
TArrayAsVector	Object	Unsorted	Standard
TIArrayAsVector	Pointer	Unsorted	Standard
TSArrayAsVector	Object	Sorted	Standard
TISArrayAsVector	Pointer	Sorted	Standard
TMArrayAsVector	Object	Unsorted	Custom
TMIArrayAsVector	Pointer	Unsorted	Custom
TMSArrayAsVector	Object	Sorted	Custom
TMISArrayAsVector	Pointer	Sorted	Custom

Table 17-3 Family of `TArrayAsVector` Classes

Classes with an "I" in their name store pointers to objects, rather than the objects themselves. This may be useful if the container class moves its contents around in memory and if the objects are large, so that rearranging pointers is faster than rearranging the objects themselves.

Classes with an "S" in their name store objects in sorted form. That is, each item is inserted in an appropriate place in the container, rather than at the end. Numbers are stored in ascending order, as you would expect. The sorting criteria for user-defined classes is supplied by overloaded `<` and `==` operators, which the user must define.

Classes with an "M" in their name require you to provide your own memory management class with overloaded `new` and `delete` operators.

The `TVectorImp` class can add a "C" to its name to make it a "counted" class. It maintains an internal count of the number of objects stored, which can be discovered with a `Count()` member function.

The classes in each family generally use the same member functions and are programmed in the same way. Some indirect ("I") classes have a few different member functions than the direct classes.

In the sections that follow we'll introduce additional container classes with simple examples that highlight how each container is used. Later we'll show how you can store objects of your own classes in containers. Finally we'll show a more ambitious example of a container class storing a user-defined class in a more realistic situation.

Stacks

We've already seen an example of the `TStackAsVector` class. The same class can be used to store data of any basic type. Here's an example, STACKFLO, which stores type `float`:

```
// stackflo.cpp
// tests the TStackAsVector class with type float
#include <classlib\stacks.h>
#include <iostream.h>

void main()
   {                              // instantiate stack for type float
   TStackAsVector<float> staflo;

   staflo.Push(11.1);             // push floats onto stack
   staflo.Push(12.2);
   staflo.Push(13.3);

   while( !staflo.IsEmpty() ) // pop floats off stack
      cout << staflo.Pop() << endl;
   }
```

Compare this with the STACKINT example. Notice how few changes need be made to the program to store a different kind of data. Only the instantiation of the template is different.

As we noted, there are two families of stack classes, one based on vectors and one based on lists. Let's look at an example of a stack based on lists. Here's the listing for STAKLIST:

```
// staklist.cpp
// tests the TStackAsList class with type int
#include <classlib\stacks.h>
#include <iostream.h>

void main()
   {
   TStackAsList<int> stint;   // instantiate a stack for type int

   stint.Push(11);            // push ints onto stack
   stint.Push(12);
   stint.Push(13);

   while( !stint.IsEmpty() )  // pop ints off stack
      cout << stint.Pop() << endl;
   }
```

Again, the program remains largely the same; we simply start with a different container class. It's just as easy to change the container in larger and more complex programs. This gives you the opportunity to experiment with different kinds of stacks, to see which works best in your particular situation. Generally ADTs based on vectors operate faster than those based on lists. However, the size of vectors should be known in advance; if a large and unknown number of items must be stored, a list is a better choice.

The key member functions for stack classes are `Push()` and `Pop()`, which store and remove a data item from the stack. Figure 17-1 shows how this looks.

Table 17-4 shows the member function for the `TStackAsVector` class.

More details on these member functions can be found in Borland's *Library Reference*, in online help, or by examining the appropriate header file. We'll examine similar member functions for other classes as we go along.

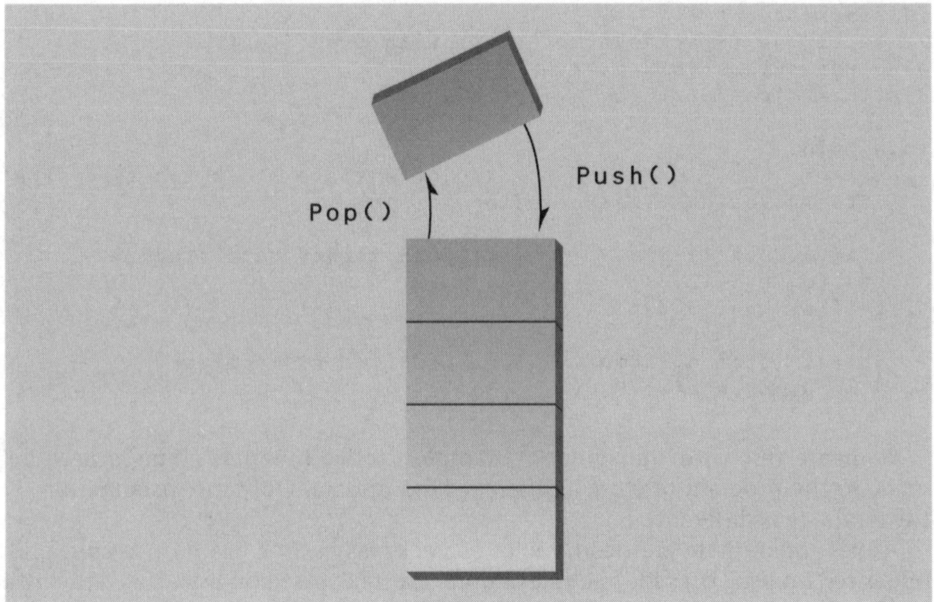

Figure 17-1 A Stack

Arrays

The TArrayAsVector family of classes provides a sophisticated container that operates much like basic C and C++ arrays. Data can be accessed using the traditional [] operator. However there are also many added features. For example, a member function, AddAt(), allows you to insert an item into the middle of an array without writing over existing data. The items above the insertion point are moved up to make room, and the array is automatically expanded.

Our example program shows some of these member functions. Here's the listing for ARRAYFLO:

```
// arrayflo.cpp
// demonstrates TArrayAsVector class
#include <classlib\arrays.h>          // for TArrayAsVector
#include <iostream.h>

void main()
   {
   TArrayAsVector<float> arrflo(10);  // create array of 10 floats

   arrflo.Add(7.1);           // insert at 0
   arrflo.Add(7.2);           // insert at 1
   arrflo.Add(7.3);           // insert at 2
   arrflo.AddAt(7.15, 1);     // insert at 1 (moves 1 and 2)
   arrflo[0] = 7.01;          // overwrite at 0
                                      // display all floats
   for(int j=0; j<arrflo.GetItemsInContainer(); j++)
      cout << arrflo[j] << endl;
   }
```

Member function	Purpose
FirstThat	Returns pointer to first object in stack that satisfies a condition. User supplies function to check for condition.
Flush	Removes all items from stack.
ForEach	Does the same operation to each element in stack. User supplies function to perform operation.
GetItemsInContainer	Returns number items on stack.
IsEmpty	Returns 1 if stack has no elements.
IsFull	Returns 1 if stack is full.
LastThat	Iterates through the stack looking for all the items that satisfy a condition. User supplies function to determine the condition.
Pop	Removes item from top of stack.
Push	Adds item to top of stack.
Top	Returns top item on stack without removing it

Table 17-4 Member Functions for `TStackAsVector`

The `Add()` member function inserts an item at the end of the array. The `AddAt()` function inserts an item at the given index. The `[]` operator, as with ordinary arrays, overwrites an existing element and can also be used to get data from the array. The number of elements in the container can be learned from `GetItemsInContainer()`. Notice that we can't use `IsEmpty()` in a `while` loop as we did in the stack examples, because items are not removed from the array when they are accessed using the `[]` operator. To remove items we could use `Destroy()` or `Detach()`.

Here's the output from the program:

```
7.01
7.15
7.2
7.3
```

Notice how `AddAt()` has moved the 7.2 and 7.3 items to make room for 7.15, and expanded the array. The 7.01, inserted with the `[]` operator, is simply written over 7.1.

In ARRAYFLO we created an array for which we supplied only the upper bound (10). However, you can also supply a lower bound and a parameter called *delta* when you create an array. For example, the statement

```
TArrayAsVector somearray(100, 10, 5);
```

creates an array that has a lower bound of 10, an upper bound of 100, and a delta of 5. If the array needs to be expanded, it will be expanded by delta cells at a time.

That is, it will increase from 100 to 105, then to 110, and so on. If delta is 0, the array cannot be expanded.

The key member functions for array classes are the `[]` operator and the functions `Add()` and `AddAt()`. Figure 17-2 shows how this looks.

Table 17-5 shows the member functions for arrays.

Queues

A queue (pronounced like the letter Q) is somewhat like a stack, but whereas a stack uses the last-in-first-out (LIFO) principle, a queue is first-in-first-out (FIFO). A line at the teller's window in a bank is an example of a queue: The first customer to join the tail of the line is the first customer to reach the head of the line and receive service. It's like a pipe flowing in one direction.

Our example program, QUEINT, shows how this works. Here's the listing:

```
// queint.cpp
// demonstrates TQueueAsVector class
#include <classlib\queues.h>
#include <iostream.h>

void main()
   {
   TQueueAsVector<int> quint;

   quint.Put(101);
   quint.Put(102);
```

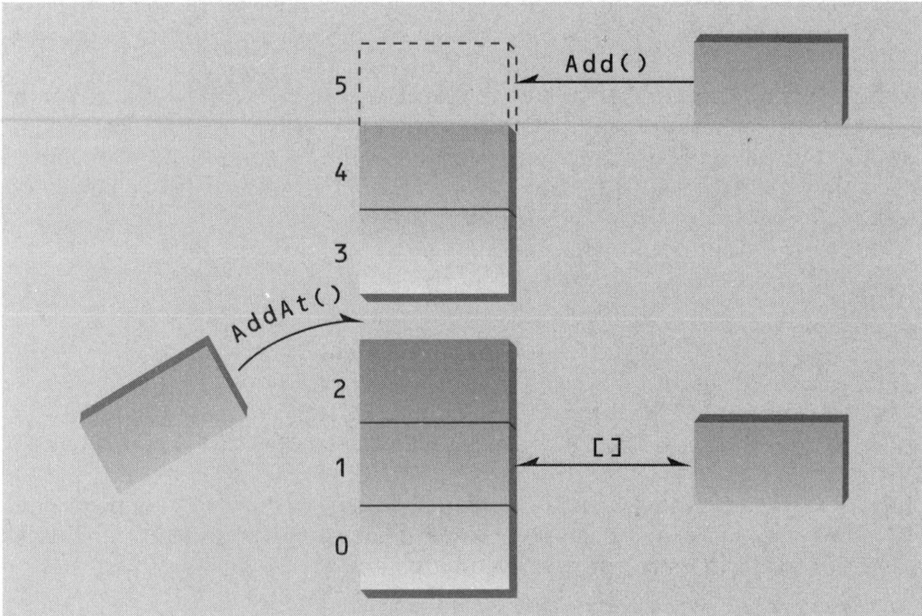

Figure 17-2 An Array

Member function	Purpose
Add	Inserts item in new space at end of array, expands array.
AddAt	Adds item in new space anywhere in array, expands array.
ArraySize	Returns number of cells allocated (not the number of items).
Destroy	Removes item from array and removes the item from memory.
Detach	Removes item but (optionally) does not remove it from memory.
FirstThat	Returns pointer to first object in array that satisfies a condition. User supplies function to check for condition.
Flush	Removes all elements from array.
ForEach	Performs the same operation on each element in array. User supplies function to perform operation.
GetItemsInContainer	Returns number of items in container.
HasMember	Checks if a given item is in the array.
IsEmpty	Returns 1 if array contains no elements.
IsFull	Returns 1 if array is full (the next addition will increase size by delta).
LastThat	Iterates through the array looking for all the items that satisfy a condition. User supplies function to determine the condition.
LowerBound	Returns current lower bound.
UpperBound	Returns current upper bound.

Table 17-5 Member Functions for `TArrayAsVector`

```
    quint.Put(103);

    while( !quint.IsEmpty() )
        cout << quint.Get() << endl;
    }
```

The output from the program shows that items are removed in the same order they were added:

```
101
102
103
```

The basic member functions are `Put()`, which inserts an item at the queue's tail, and `Get()`, which removes an item from its head. This is shown in Figure 17-3.

Table 17-6 shows the member functions for the `TQueueAsVector` class.

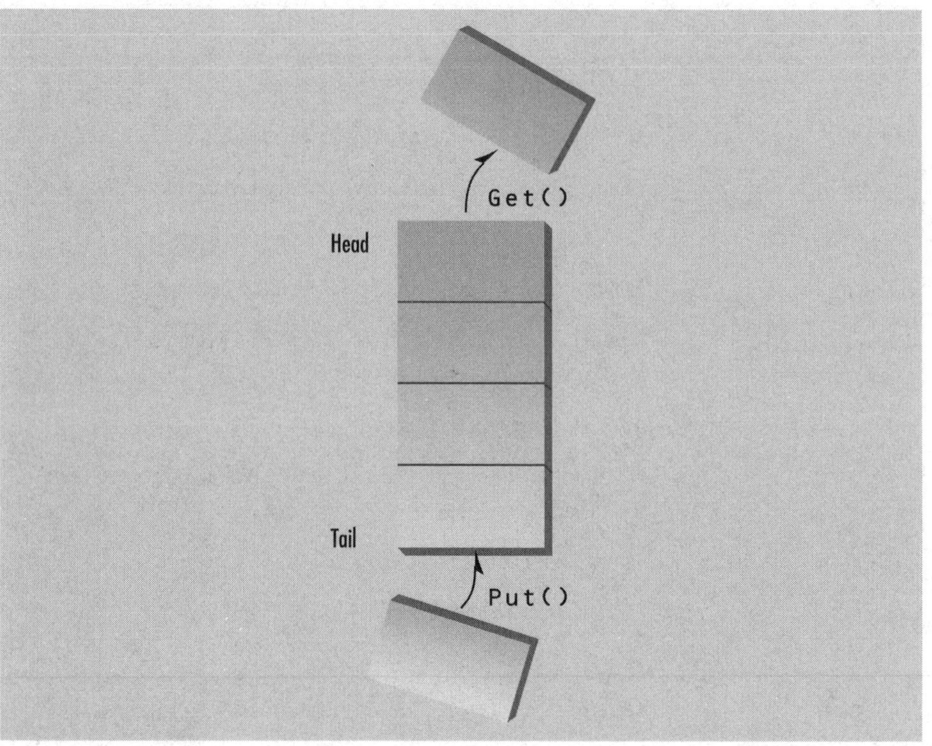

Figure 17-3 A Queue

Member function	Purpose
FirstThat	Returns pointer to first item in queue that satisfies a condition. User supplies function to check for condition.
Flush	Removes all items from queue.
ForEach	Performs the same operation on each item in queue. User supplies function to perform operation.
Get	Removes item from head of queue.
GetItemsInContainer	Returns number of items in queue.
IsEmpty	Returns 1 if queue is empty.
IsFull	Returns 1 if queue is full.
LastThat	Iterates through the queue looking for all the items that satisfy a condition. User supplies function to determine the condition.
Put	Inserts item at tail of queue.

Table 17-6 Member Functions of `TQueueAsVector`

Deques

A deque (pronounced "deck"; the spelling "dequeue" is nonstandard) is a double-ended stack. You can insert items at either end and remove them from either end. There is a loose analogy here with a deck of cards (and possibly a crooked dealer). Our example program inserts three items at each end of a deque, and then removes all six items from the left end, displaying each one, until the deque is empty. Here's the listing for DEQUINT:

```
// dequint.cpp
// demonstrates TDequeAsVector class

#include <classlib\deques.h>
#include <iostream.h>

void main()
   {
   TDequeAsVector<int> dint;

   dint.PutLeft(11);
   dint.PutLeft(12);
   dint.PutLeft(13);
   dint.PutRight(21);
   dint.PutRight(22);
   dint.PutRight(23);

   while( !dint.IsEmpty() )
      cout << dint.GetLeft() << endl;
   }
```

Here's the output:

```
13
12
11
21
22
23
```

The key member functions for deques are `PutLeft()` and `PutRight()` which insert items, and `GetLeft()` and `GetRight()`, which remove items. For iteration purposes, the left end of a deque is considered the head, and the right end is the tail. Figure 17-4 shows how this looks

Table 17-7 shows the member functions for the `TDequeAsVector` class.

Lists

After arrays, lists are probably the most commonly used data storage mechanism. They allow you to store items without using index numbers, and, unlike arrays, you don't need to specify the size of a list in advance. As we've seen in previous examples, a list (which is the same thing as a linked list) is created from a series of pointers. A pointer in each link points to the next link. Thus to find an item in the list you must follow the chain of pointers, examining each item in turn. This makes access to random items slow. However, it's quick to iterate through the list, and fast to add and delete items, since only a few pointers need to be changed.

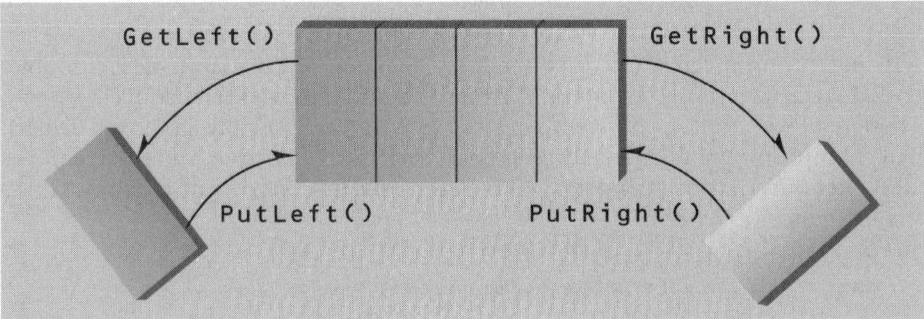

Figure 17-4 A Deque

Member function	Purpose
FirstThat	Returns pointer to first item in deque that satisfies a condition. User supplies function to check for condition.
Flush	Removes all items from deque.
ForEach	Performs the same operation on each item in deque. User supplies function to perform operation.
GetItemsInContainer	Returns number of items in deque.
GetLeft	Removes (pops) item on left end of deque.
GetRight	Removes (pops) item on right end of deque.
IsEmpty	Returns 1 if deque is empty.
IsFull	Returns 1 if deque is full.
LastThat	Iterates through the deque looking for all the items that satisfy a condition. User supplies function to determine the condition.
PeekLeft	Returns item on left end of deque, but doesn't remove it.
PeekRight	Returns item on right end of deque, but doesn't remove it.
PutLeft	Inserts (pushes) item on left end of deque.
PutRight	Inserts (pushes) item on right end of deque.

Table 17-7 Member Functions for `TDequeAsVector`

Our next example demonstrates a list in the form of the `TListImp` class. It also shows how to use the `ForEach()` member function. This function is common to most container classes. Here's the listing for LISTINT:

```
// listint.cpp
// demonstrates TListImp class
// also shows ForEach() member function
#include <classlib\listimp.h>          // for list containers
#include <iostream.h>

void Display(int&, void*);            // prototype

void main()
   {
   TListImp<int> listint;             // list of ints

   listint.Add(101);                  // add ints to list
   listint.Add(102);
   listint.Add(103);

   listint.ForEach(Display, 0);       // display all ints
   cout << endl;

   listint.Detach(102);               // remove an int
   listint.ForEach(Display, 0);       // display remaining ints
   }

void Display(int& i, void*)           // function displays an int
   {                                  // passed as argument
   cout << i << " ";
   }
```

This program stores three items in a `TListImp` container using the `Add()` function. It then displays all the items on the list, deletes an item with `Detach()`, and displays the list again.

Here's the output:

```
103 102 101
103 101
```

The `ForEach()` Member Function

The `ForEach()` function is a miracle of modern engineering. You call it once, and it performs an action on every item in a list (or other container). If there are 100 items, it performs the action 100 times. What is this action that it performs? That's up to you, the programmer. You give `ForEach()` the name of a function, and it calls that function for each (hence the name) item on the list. `ForEach()` passes each separate item as an argument to your function each time it calls it, so you can do whatever you want to the item. `ForEach()` saves you from figuring out how to access each item in a container; the container does it automatically.

In LISTINT we give the function called by `ForEach()` the name `Display()`. We use the variable `Display`, which is the address of the `Display()` function, as the first argument to `ForEach()`. The second argument to `ForEach()` can be used as a pointer to additional data we want to send to our function, but we ignore that possibility in this example.

Our `Display()` function simply displays the value of the item passed to it. Thus a single call to `ForEach()` results in all the integers on the list being displayed.

Whatever function is called by `ForEach()` must always have the same argument types and the same return type. Here's how the prototype should look:

```
void IterFunc(aClass&, void*);
```

The first argument is the type for which the class is instantiated; it can be a class name but it's `int` in the LISTINT example. This argument must be passed by reference. The second argument is a pointer to `void`, which passes the same pointer supplied as the second argument to `ForEach()`. Again, we don't make use of that argument here. Don't forget to install the prototype in your listing.

The `Detach()` Member Function

The `Detach()` member function of `TListImp` searches through the list until it finds an item equal to its argument. If the list holds class objects, this equality is determined by overloading the == operator for the class. In the LISTINT example, which stores integers, it simply looks for an integer of equal value. This item is then deleted from the list, as the second line of the output shows.

Member Function Summary

The key member functions for lists are `Add()` and `Detach()`, as shown in Figure 17-5.

Table 17-8 shows the member functions for the `TListImp` class.

Double Lists

A double list, or doubly linked list, is a list that can be accessed from either end. That is, the chain of pointers can be followed either backward or forward. The double list is similar to a deque, and in fact one of the deque classes is derived from a double list.

Our example program shows a double list and also introduces the powerful `LastThat()` member function. Here's the listing for DLISTINT:

```
// dlistint.cpp
// demonstrates TDoubleListImp class
```

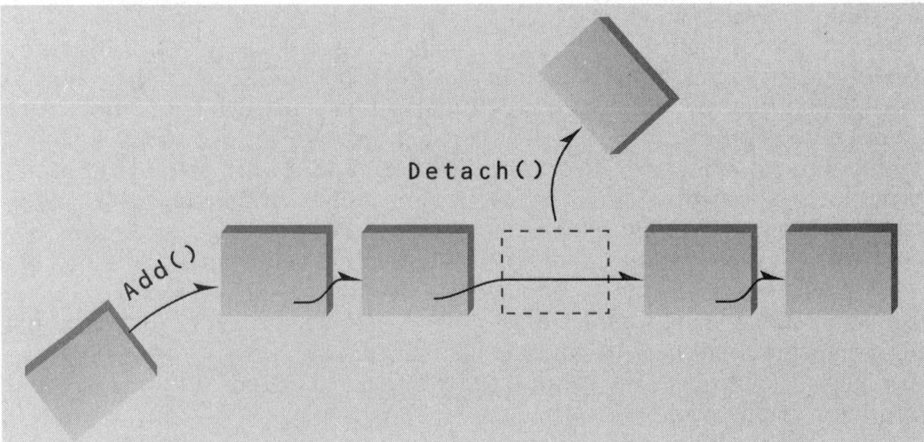

Figure 17-5 A List

Member function	Purpose
Add	Adds item to head of list.
Detach	Removes item from head of list.
FirstThat	Returns pointer to first item in list that satisfies a condition. User supplies function to check for condition.
Flush	Removes all items from list.
ForEach	Performs the same operation on each item in list. User supplies function to perform operation.
IsEmpty	Returns 1 if list contains no items.
LastThat	Iterates through the list looking for all the items that satisfy a condition. User supplies function to determine the condition.
PeekHead	Returns item at head of list but does not remove it.

Table 17-8 Member Functions for `TListImp`

```
// also shows LastThat() function

#include <classlib\dlistimp.h>      // for double list
#include <iostream.h>

void Display(int&, void*);          // prototypes
int FindDisplay(const int&, void*);

void main()
   {
   TDoubleListImp<int> dlistint;    // double list of ints
   int Range;                       // 200 means 200-299, etc.

   dlistint.AddAtHead(101);         // add ints to head of list
   dlistint.AddAtHead(102);
   dlistint.AddAtHead(103);
   dlistint.AddAtTail(201);         // add ints to tail of list
   dlistint.AddAtTail(202);
   dlistint.AddAtTail(203);

   cout << "\nContents of list: ";
   dlistint.ForEach(Display, 0);    // display all ints
   cout << endl;

   cout << "\nEnter start of range (100, 200, etc): ";
   cin >> Range;
   cout << "\nData in range "
```

(continued on next page)

(continued from previous page)

```
         << Range << '-' << (Range+99) << ": ";
   if( !dlistint.LastThat(FindDisplay, (void*)&Range) )
      cout << "No such values";
   }  // end main()

// function displays an int passed as argument
void Display(int& i, void*)
   {
   cout << i << " ";
   }

// function displays int passed as argument, if within range
int FindDisplay(const int& i, void* ptrRange)
   {
   if(i>=(*(int*)ptrRange) && i<(*(int*)ptrRange)+100)
      {                             // if(range <= i < range+100)
      cout << i << " ";             // then display int
      return 1;                     // and return 1
      }                             // otherwise,
   return 0;                        // return 0
   }
```

In this program we instantiate a `TDoubleListImp` object to hold type `int`. We insert three items at the head of the list and three items at the tail, and then display them, using the `ForEach()` function and our homemade `Display()` function, as in the last example. This produces a similar output to the deque class in the DEQUINT example.

The `LastThat()` Member Function

The function `LastThat()` iterates through all the items in a list. In this way it's like the `ForEach()` function. However, `LastThat()` allows you to examine each item on the list to determine if it meets certain conditions. You specify these conditions in a homemade function that you arrange for `LastThat()` to call. `LastThat()` returns the last item found that meets these conditions, or it returns 0 to let you know that no item was found that met the conditions. The name `LastThat` is somewhat misleading, in that this function's power lies in its power to iterate through *all* the items in a container, not just the last one (although it is the last one that it returns).

In the DLISTINT example we ask the user to enter a range number. If the user enters 100, the range is set to 100-199. If the user enters 200, the range is set to 200-299, and so on. We tell `LastThat()` to call our `FindDisplay()` function. This function checks to see if the item passed to it from `LastThat()` is in the specified range. If it is, `FindDisplay()` displays it; if it's not in the range, it doesn't.

We make use of the second argument to `LastThat()` to pass a pointer to the range number, `ptrRange`. This is how `FindDisplay()` knows what condition to check. Here's the output from DLISTINT if the user enters 200 for the range:

```
Contents of list: 103 102 101 201 202 203

Enter start of range (100, 200, etc.): 200

Data in range 200-299: 201, 202, 203
```

Thanks to `LastThat()`, only the data in the specified range is displayed in the last line.

The function called by `LastThat()` must always have the same argument and return types. Here's how its prototype should look:

```
int CondFunc(const aClass&, void*);
```

The arguments are the same as for `ForEach()`, except that the first argument is `const`. This implies that `LastThat()` cannot change the item passed to it. The return type is `int` so that the function can report back to `LastThat()` if this particular object meets the specified condition. If none of the items meet the condition, then `LastThat()` returns 0.

The `FirstThat()` Member Function

The `FirstThat()` member function is not as powerful as as `LastThat()`. Like `LastThat()`, it finds the first item in the list meeting a condition specified in a user-supplied function. However, once it finds this first item, it does not continue to iterate through the entire list. It terminates immediately, returning a pointer to the item. If it finds no item meeting the search conditions, it returns 0.

Other Member Functions

The key member functions for double lists are `AddAtHead()`, `AddAtTail()`, and `Detach()`, as shown in Figure 17-6.

Table 17-9 shows the member functions for the `TDoubleListImp` class.

Dictionaries and Associations

An *association* relates two data items: a *key* and a *value*. A key can be thought of as a short piece of data, like a word, that's easy to search for. A value can be thought of as a more substantial piece of data, like a long string or a record. A *dictionary* contains a number of associations, just as an English language dictionary contains a number of word/definition pairs. The Borland Class library provides a family of

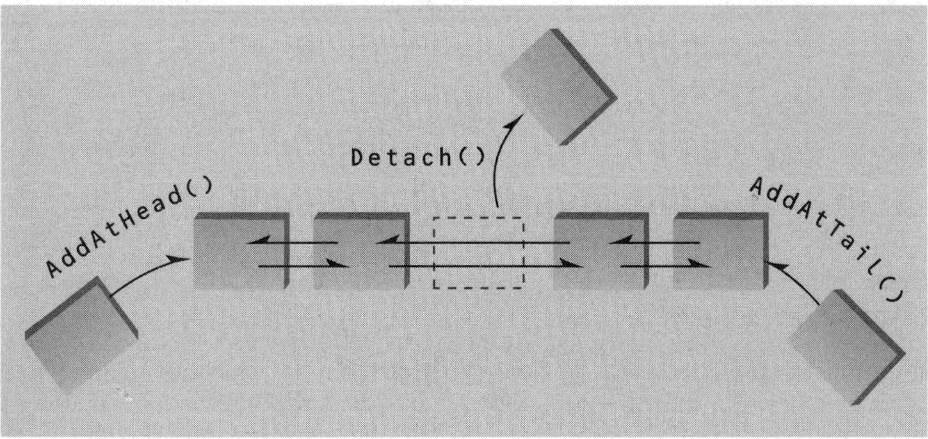

Figure 17-6 A Double List

Member function	Purpose
Add	Inserts item at head of list.
AddAtHead	Inserts item at head of list (same as Add).
AddAtTail	Inserts item at tail of list.
Detach	Removes item from head of list.
FirstThat	Returns pointer to first item in list that satisfies a condition. User supplies function to check for condition.
Flush	Removes all items from list.
ForEach	Performs the same operation on each item in list. User supplies function to perform operation.
IsEmpty	Returns 1 if no items in list.
LastThat	Iterates through the list looking for all the items that satisfy a condition. User supplies function to determine the condition.
PeekHead	Returns item at head of list without removing it.
PeekTail	Returns item at tail of list without removing it.

Table 17-9 Member Functions of `TDoubleListImp`

association classes and a family of dictionary classes. You can combine these to form many kinds of dictionaries.

The family of associations is a little different than the other container class families. In an association both the key and the value can hold either the data item itself or a pointer to it. Table 17-10 shows the members of the association class family.

Members of the `TDDAssociation` family have only four public member functions, as shown in Table 17-11.

Hash Values

The dictionary stores associations according to the hash values, which are derived from keys but are not the same as keys. What is a hash value? In Borland's implementation it's a number of type `unsigned int`. This is true no matter what kind of data the key consists of. How the hash value is derived from the key depends on the type of data used as the key. If the key is a number, the hash value might be the number itself. If the key is a string, the hash value might be the sum of all the characters in the string.

What is the purpose of the hash value? The dictionary uses the hash value to find an association. It does this by transforming the hash value into an index to a table of addresses, called the hash table. The address in the hash table points to where the association is stored. Thus, once the dictionary has calculated the hash code for a key, it can quickly find the corresponding association.

Class name	Key	Value	Standard or custom memory management
TDDAssociation	Direct	Direct	Standard
TDIAssociation	Direct	Indirect	Standard
TIDAssociation	Indirect	Direct	Standard
TIIAssociation	Indirect	Indirect	Standard
TMDDAssociation	Direct	Direct	Custom
TMDIAssociation	Direct	Indirect	Custom
TMIDAssociation	Indirect	Direct	Custom
TMIIAssociation	Indirect	Indirect	Custom

Table 17-10 Family of `TDDAssociation` Classes

Member function	Purpose
HashValue	Returns the hash value for the key.
Key	Returns the key.
Value	Returns the value.
operator ==	Tests equality of keys.

Table 17-11 Member Functions of `TDDAssociation`

All this implies that the key must belong to a class which provides its own function for calculating hash values. In Borland's scheme this function must be named `HashValue()`. Any class that we use as a key must have such a function.

Dictionary of Nautical Terms

Our example program consists of a dictionary in which the user can look up the meaning of nautical terms. The user enters the term, and the program displays its meaning. The keys and values are stored as two separate arrays of strings of type `char*`. We'll use the `TDictionaryAsHashTable` class to store associations of the `TDDAssociation` class. We'll also use members of Borland's `string` class for both the key (the nautical term) and the value (the definition of the term).

Unfortunately the `string` class has no function called `HashValue()`, which, as we've seen, is necessary for keys. No problem—we can use inheritance to derive another class from `string` that does have such a function. We'll call this class `hvString`. Besides `HashValue()`, all it needs are two constructors. It uses the `string` member functions for everything else. Here's the listing for DICT:

```
// dict.cpp
// demonstrates TDictionaryAsHashTable
// and TDDAssociation classes

#include <classlib\dict.h>    // for TDictionaryAsHashTable class
#include <classlib\assoc.h>   // for TDDAssociation class
#include <cstring.h>          // for string class

// need this class because HashValue() is not a member of string
class hvString : public string
   {
   public:
      hvString() : string()
         { }
      hvString(const char* str) : string(str)
         { }
      unsigned HashValue() const
         { return hash(); }
   };

const int ENTRIES = 9;
hvString term[ENTRIES] =
            { "Athwartships",
              "Bight",
              "Chine",
              "Deviation",
              "Eye of the wind",
              "Full and by",
              "Gunwale",
              "To heave to",
              "In irons" };
hvString meaning[ENTRIES] =
            { "At right angles to the boat",
              "A loop in a rope",
              "Transition between a boat's topsides and bottom",
              "Compass error due to metallic objects aboard",
              "The direction exactly upwind",
              "Sailing close-hauled without luffing",
              "Rail where the topsides join the deck",
              "To slow the boat by backwinding the jib",
              "Head to wind and unable to bear off" };

typedef TDDAssociation<hvString, hvString> StrAssoc;

void main()
   {
   hvString::set_case_sensitive(0);  // ignore case
                                     // create dictionary
   TDictionaryAsHashTable<StrAssoc> dictionary(ENTRIES);
   void Display(StrAssoc&, void*);   // prototype
   StrAssoc* ptrSA;                  // pointer to associations
   char buffer[80];                  // for input strings
   hvString hvSearch;                // hvString to search for
   char ch;
```

```
   for(int j=0; j<ENTRIES; j++)      // for every entry,
      {
      StrAssoc sa(term[j], meaning[j]);    // create association
      dictionary.Add(sa);                  // put it in dictionary
      }

   dictionary.ForEach(Display, 0);   // display contents

   do
      {
      cout << "Enter nautical term: ";
      cin.getline(buffer, 80);       // get term from user
      hvString hvSearch(buffer);     // make an hvString
                                     // find term in dictionary
      StrAssoc tempAssoc(hvSearch, 0);     // create association
      ptrSA = dictionary.Find(tempAssoc);  // look for it
      if( ptrSA==0 )
         cout << "Term not found";
      else                           // display, with definition
         cout << ptrSA->Key() << ": " << ptrSA->Value();
      cout << "\nDo another (y/n)? ";
      cin >> ch;
      cin.ignore(80, '\n');          // eat extra chars
      }
   while(ch != 'n');
   }

// function to display term and meaning for one association
void Display(StrAssoc& sa, void*)
   {
   cout << sa.Key() << "\n   " << sa.Value() << endl;
   }
```

The `typedef` keyword

The instantiation of a template with particular data types defines a class, or data type. This type name can be rather unwieldy. In our present program we need to instantiate a class called `TDDAssociation<hvString, hvString>`. We'll have occasion to declare several variables of this type in the program. This is a rather lengthy name to write many times, especially in the midst of other expressions.

Fortunately, C++ contains a feature that lets you give a data type a different name. This feature uses the keyword `typedef`. For example, the statement

```
typedef unsigned char uchar;
```

gives the name `uchar` to the data type `unsigned char`. This means you can declare variables or function arguments using this name just as if it were a real type:

```
uchar ch1, ch2;                       // two unsigned chars
int FindChar(string s, uchar ch); // second arg is unsigned char
```

We use `typedef` in our DICT example to reduce `TDDAssociation <hvString, hvString>` to the somewhat more manageable `StrAssoc`.

Using the Dictionary

We use the `set_case_sensitive()` member function of the string class with a 0 argument so the user doesn't have to worry about case when typing the term to search for. We create a dictionary of type `TDictionaryAsHashTable<StrAssoc>`. Then, for every term-definition pair, we create an association and add the association to the dictionary.

To show that this is possible, the program displays all the terms and definitions by having the `ForEach()` function call a `Display()` function, as we've seen in earlier examples. However, you probably wouldn't want to do this in a real dictionary program with a larger number of entries.

The more useful way to access the dictionary is for the user to enter a term, and for the dictionary to then find the corresponding association using the `Find()` member function. If `Find()` returns 0, no matching key was found. Otherwise, it returns a pointer to the association. The association's `Key()` and `Value()` functions are then used to display the term and its definition. Here's the output if the user requests definitions for a few nautical terms:

```
Enter nautical term: Bight
Bight: a loop in a rope
Do another (y/n)? y
Enter nautical term: EYE OF THE WIND
Eye of the wind: The direction exactly upwind
Do another (y/n)? n
```

The important member functions for a dictionary are `Add()` and `Find()`, as shown in Figure 17-7.

The member functions for `TDictionaryAsHashTable` are shown in Table 17-12.

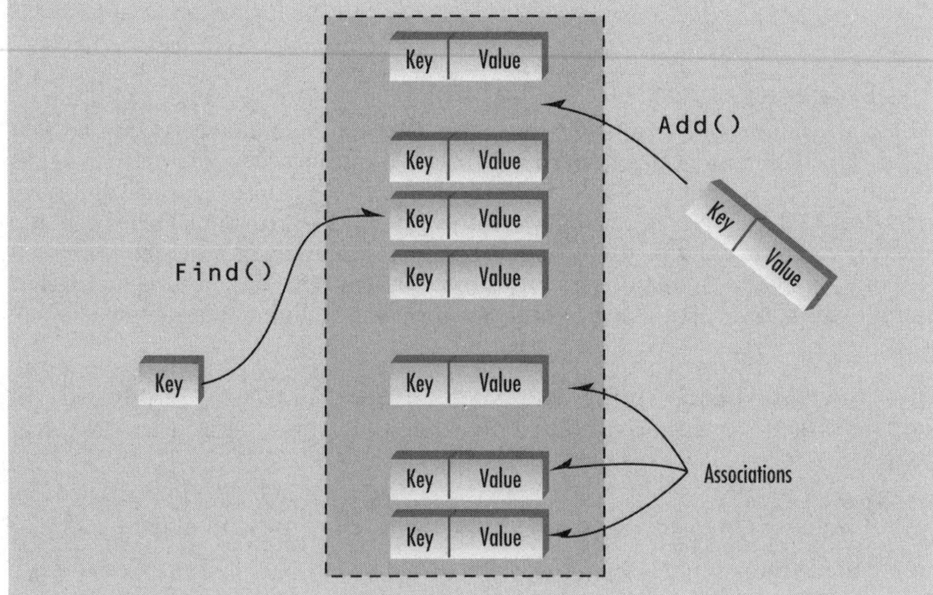

Figure 17-7 A Dictionary

Member function	Purpose
Add	Adds an association (if key not already in dictionary).
Detach	Removes association from dictionary.
Find	Finds an association, using the key.
Flush	Removes all associations from dictionary.
ForEach	Performs the same operation on each association in dictionary. User supplies function to perform operation.
GetItemsInContainer	Returns number of associations in dictionary.
IsEmpty	Returns 1 if no associations in dictionary.

Table 17-12 Member Functions of `TDictionaryAsHashTable`

Sorted Classes

In the unsorted `TArrayAsVector` class, the `Add()` member function simply places each new piece of data at the end of the array. However, other classes in the same family will sort the data automatically when you insert it into the array. For example, if you use the `TSArrayAsVector` class, the `Add()` member function will insert data into the array so that the data is always ordered. This makes quite a lot of extra work for `Add()`, since it must frequently move many array elements in order to insert the new one in the proper place.

Here's the listing for SORTARAY, which shows how a sorted array works:

```
// sortaray.cpp
// demonstrates sorted array with TSArrayAsVector class
#include <classlib\arrays.h>          // for TSArrayAsVector
#include <iostream.h>

void main()
   {
   TSArrayAsVector<float> arrflo(10); // create array of 10 floats

   arrflo.Add(7.2);                   // insert floats
   arrflo.Add(7.4);
   arrflo.Add(7.5);
   arrflo.Add(7.3);
   arrflo.Add(7.1);
                                      // display all floats
   for(int j=0; j<arrflo.GetItemsInContainer(); j++)
      cout << "arrflo[" << j << "]=" << arrflo[j] << endl;
   }
```

The output from this program shows that the data, despite being entered in random order, is stored in sorted form:

```
arrflo[0]=7.1
arrflo[1]=7.2
arrflo[2]=7.3
arrflo[3]=7.4
arrflo[4]=7.5
```

The `AddAt()` function doesn't work in sorted array classes. You can use the `[]` operator to insert data, but it doesn't cause the data to be sorted, it simply replaces the contents of an existing element, as in an unsorted class.

The array, double list, list, and vector families all contain classes—with "S" in their names—that store data automatically in sorted form. In other families, such as associations, deques, dictionaries, hash tables, queues, sets, and stacks, the order of the data is so important that it doesn't make sense to sort it. Sorted classes don't exist in these families.

Indirect Classes

There are classes in almost all the container families that store pointers to items rather than the items themselves. These classes have an "I" (for indirect) in their names.

In our example program we use the `TIArrayAsVector` class to store an array of type `float*` (pointer to `float`). We then use `Add()` to insert, not the values of the floating-point variables themselves, but their addresses, into the array. Here's the listing for INDARAY:

```
// indaray.cpp
// demonstrates indirect array with TIArrayAsVector class
#include <classlib\arrays.h>          // for TIArrayAsVector
#include <iostream.h>

void main()
   {
   float f1 = 7.1;
   float f2 = 7.2;
   float f3 = 7.3;
   float f4 = 7.4;
   float f5 = 7.5;

   TIArrayAsVector<float> arrflo(10); // create array of 10
                                      //    pointers to float
   arrflo.Add(&f1);                   // insert addresses
   arrflo.Add(&f2);                   //    of floats
   arrflo.Add(&f3);
   arrflo.Add(&f4);
   arrflo.Add(&f5);
                                      // display all floats
   for(int j=0; j<arrflo.GetItemsInContainer(); j++)
      cout << "*arrflo[" << j << "]=" << *arrflo[j] << endl;
   }
```

The output from INDARAY looks like this:

```
*arrflo[0]=7.1
*arrflo[1]=7.2
*arrflo[2]=7.3
```

```
*arrflo[3]=7.4
*arrflo[4]=7.5
```

Notice that it's the value of the variable pointed to by the array elements that we want to display, not the elements themselves. We must therefore dereference the elements with the `*` operator to access the original items.

Of course, in container families that allow it, you can combine sorting, indirection, and custom memory management in any combination. For example, the `TMISListImp` class provides a list of sorted pointers using custom memory management.

Storing User-Defined Classes

One of the major advantages of using container classes in C++ is that you can use them to store your own classes. This is easy: Storing class objects in containers is just like storing basic types like `int` and `float`. Our first example stores objects of the `person` class in a container of the `TArrayAsVector` class. Here's the listing for PERSARAY:

```
// persaray.cpp
// demonstrates TArrayAsVector class holding user-defined class

#include <classlib\arrays.h>    // for TArrayAsVector class
#include <cstring.h>            // for string class
#include <iostream.h>

class person                    // person class
   {
   private:
      string name;
      int age;
   public:
      person()                  // no-arg constructor
         { }
      person(char* n, int a)    // two-arg constructor
         { name = n; age = a; }

      void putPerson() const    // display person data
         { cout << "\n   " << name << "\n   " << age; }
                                // overloaded == operator
      int operator == (const person& p) const
         {
         return (p.name==name && p.age==age) ? 1 : 0;
         }
   };

void main()
   {
   TArrayAsVector<person> arrpers(10);   // array for 10 persons

   person p1("Gloria", 18);              // create 4 persons
   person p2("George", 25);
   person p3("Harry", 47);
   person p4("Lynette", 34);
```

(continued on next page)

(continued from previous page)

```
   arrpers.Add(p1);                        // put persons in array
   arrpers.Add(p2);
   arrpers.Add(p3);
   arrpers.Add(p4);
                                           // access persons
   for(int j=0; j<arrpers.GetItemsInContainer(); j++)
      {
      cout << "\nPerson " << (j+1);
      arrpers[j].putPerson();
      }
   }
```

In this program we specify the class `person`. In `main()` we create a `TArrayAsVector<person>` object and four `person` objects. We store the `persons` in the array using the `Add()` member function, and access them with the `[]` operator so we can display them. Here's the output:

```
Person 1
   Gloria
   18
Person 2
   George
   25
Person 3
   Harry
   47
Person 4
   Lynette
   34
```

Required Operators and Functions

The surprise in this program is the overloaded (==) operator in the `person` class. We don't make use of this operator in `main()`, so why do we need it? A container class may require that the class whose objects it is storing possess various operators. The container needs these operators for its own internal use. As do most container classes, `TArrayAsVector` requires its objects to have an overloaded (==) operator.

Borland's *Library Reference* specifies the operators and functions a class must have to be storable in different containers, so we won't detail them here. However, if the compiler reports an error deep within one of the header files used for container classes, the problem may be that you have not provided a necessary operator in your class. For example, if you omit the overloaded (==) operator in the `person` class, the compiler will report something like

```
\BC4\INCLUDE\CLASSLIB\VECTIMP.H 577 Illegal structure operation
```

If you double-click on this error message, you can examine the offending program line in the header file. It often features the missing operator. In this case the line is

```
if( Data[loc] == t )
```

This statement has attempted to apply the (==) operator to an object of the class you're trying to store, but has found no matching operator in the class. When you see this situation, you know you need to rewrite your class to supply the missing operator.

Most container classes require a constructor and a copy constructor, but the default ones will do, so you don't need to supply them explicitly. You don't need any special operators or functions for containers that store pointers (those with "I" in their names) because pointers (along with other basic types) have all the necessary operators built in. However, if the container is sorted (has an "S" in its name), it requires an overloaded (<) operator. This is true even if the sorted container holds pointers, since it is the objects themselves that are sorted, not the pointers to them.

Storing `Person` Objects in `TListImp`

Our next example uses the `TListImp` class as the container, and demonstrates how to apply the `ForEach()` and `LastThat()` member functions to objects of a user-defined class: `person`. Here's the listing for LISTCLAS:

```
// listclas.cpp
// demonstrates TListImp class holding user-defined class

#include <classlib\listimp.h>       // for TListImp class
#include <Cstring.h>                // for string class
#include <iostream.h>

class person                        // person class
   {
   private:
      string name;
      int age;
   public:
      void getPerson()              // get person data from user
         {
         cout << "   Name: ";
         cin >> name;
         cout << "   Age: ";
         cin >> age;
         }
      void putPerson() const        // display person data
         {
         cout << "   " << name << ", " << age;
         }
                                    // compare with a name
      int isSameName(string* MatchName) const
         {
         return name==*MatchName;
         }
                                    // check for equality
      int operator == (person& p) const
         {
         if( this->name==p.name && this->age==p.age )
            return 1;
         return 0;
         }
   };
```

(continued on next page)

(continued from previous page)

```
void Display(person&, void*);        // prototypes
int FindDisplay(const person&, void*);

void main()
   {
   TListImp<person> listpers;        // list of persons
   person tempers;                   // temporary person holder
   string Sname;                     // name to search for
   char ch;

   do
      {
      tempers.getPerson();           // get data for one person
      listpers.Add(tempers);         // store copy of on list
      cout << "Do another (y/n)? ";
      cin >> ch;
      }
   while( ch != 'n');

   cout << "\nPersons on list: ";
   listpers.ForEach(Display, 0);     // display all persons
   cout << endl;

   cout << "\nEnter name to search for: ";
   cin >> Sname;
   cout << "Persons with that name: ";
   if( !listpers.LastThat(FindDisplay, (void*)&Sname) )
      cout << "No such values";
   }  // end main()

// function displays a person passed as argument
void Display(person& pers, void*)
   {
   cout << endl;
   pers.putPerson();
   }

// function displays person passed as argument, if name matches
int FindDisplay(const person& pers, void* ptrName)
   {
   if( pers.isSameName( (string*)ptrName) )
      {                              // if name matches
      cout << endl;
      pers.putPerson();              // display person
      return 1;                      // and return 1
      }                              // otherwise,
   return 0;                         // return 0
   }
```

The program asks the user to enter the data, consisting of the name and age, of a series of `person` objects. It then asks for a name, and returns all persons who have this name. Here's an example of this interaction:

```
   Name: Gretchen
   Age: 23
Do another (y/n)? y
   Name: Mary
   Age: 89
Do another (y/n)? y
   Name: Winslow
   Age: 44
Do another (y/n)? y
   Name: Mary
   Age: 13

Persons on list:
   Mary, 13
   Winslow, 44
   Mary, 89
   Gretche, 23

Enter name to search for: Mary
Persons with that name:
   Mary, 13
   Mary, 89
```

Here two person objects have the same name, so they are both reported by the `LastThat()` function, which calls the `FindDisplay()` function, which in turn calls the `isSameName()` member function of the `person` class to actually determine if there is a match. In a user-defined class, a member function must often be invoked to test if a certain condition is true.

A Scheduling Example

Our final example is a more ambitious program that creates a database for a shipping company, using various Borland library classes. It records information about ship voyages: the port of embarkation (the starting point), the port of debarkation (the ending point), the ship name, and the date and time of departure. The database can be searched for voyages with particular characteristics, such as all voyages that start at New York. All the voyages can be listed, and voyages can also be deleted. Here's the listing for SCHLIST:

```
// schlist.cpp
// database for shipping schedule; uses a sorted list

#include <cstring.h>               // for string class
#include <classlib\date.h>         // for TDate class
#include <classlib\time.h>         // for TTime class
#include <classlib\listimp.h>      // for TSListImp class
#include <iostream.h>              // for stream functions
#include <process.h>               // for exit()

void getstring(string&);           // prototype

class Voyage                       // single port-to-port voyage
```

(continued on next page)

(continued from previous page)

```
{
private:
   string embarkation;        // departure port
   string debarkation;        // arrival port
   string shipname;           // name of vessel
   TDate  emdate;             // departure date
   TTime  emtime;             // departure time
public:
   void putData() const
      {
      emtime.PrintDate(0);  // don't print date with time
      cout << "\nFrom " << embarkation
           << ", To " << debarkation
           << ", on vessel " << shipname << endl
           << "   Departing " << emdate << ", at "
           << emtime.Hour() << ':' << emtime.Minute();
      }
   void getData()
      {
      char dummy;
      int ihours, iminutes;

      cout << "\n   Embarkation port: ";
      getstring(embarkation);
      cout << "   Destination port: ";
      getstring(debarkation);
      cout << "   Ship name: ";
      getstring(shipname);
      cout << "   Departure date: ";
      cin >> emdate;

      cout << "   Departure time (24-hour format, 23:59): ";
      cin >> ihours >> dummy >> iminutes;
      TTime t(emdate, ihours, iminutes);
      emtime = t;
      cin.ignore(100, '\n');
      }

   int isSameDate(TTime* pt) const
      { return (emtime == *pt); }

   int isSameEmbark(string* pstr) const
      { return (embarkation == *pstr); }

   int isSameDebark(string* pstr) const
      { return (debarkation == *pstr); }

   int isSameShip(string* pstr) const
      { return (shipname == *pstr); }
                                             // friends
   friend int operator == (const Voyage&, const Voyage&);
   friend int operator < (const Voyage&, const Voyage&);
};
```

```
int operator == (const Voyage& v1, const Voyage& v2)
   {
   if( v1.embarkation == v2.embarkation &&
       v1.debarkation == v2.debarkation &&
       v1.shipname    == v2.shipname &&
       v1.emdate      == v2.emdate &&
       v1.emtime      == v2.emtime )
     return 1;
   else
     return 0;
   }
                                          // overloaded <
int operator < (const Voyage& v1, const Voyage& v2)
   {
   return (v1.emtime < v2.emtime);
   }

void getstring(string& s)                 // input a string
   {                                      // with embedded
   char buff[80];                         // blanks;
   cin.ignore(100, '\n');                 // convert to
   cin.get(buff, sizeof(buff), '\n');     // string  object
   s = buff;
   }

//////////////////////////////////////////////////////////////
void add_voyage();                        // prototypes
void delete_voyage();
void find_voyage();
void list_voyages();

TSListImp<Voyage> VoyageList;             // create master list
//////////////////////////////////////////////////////////////

void main()                               // get user's choice
   {                                      // and carry it out
   char ch;

   while(1)
      {
      cout << "\n\nEnter a to add a voyage"
                "\n      d to delete a voyage"
                "\n      f to find a voyage"
                "\n      l to list all voyages"
                "\n      x to exit"
                "\nSelection: ";
      cin >> ch;
      switch(ch)
         {
         case 'a': add_voyage();    break;
         case 'd': delete_voyage(); break;
         case 'f': find_voyage();   break;
         case 'l': list_voyages();  break;
```

(continued on next page)

(continued from previous page)

```
            case 'x': exit(0);          break;
            default: cout << "\nNo such command"; break;
            }  // end switch
         }  // end while
      }  // end main

void ShowVoyage(Voyage& voy, void*)            // used by ForEach()
   {
   voy.putData();
   }

int FindDate(const Voyage& voy, void* pt)    // used by FirstThat()
   {
   return voy.isSameDate( (TTime*)pt );
   }

int matchEmbark( const Voyage& voy, void* pstr)
   {
   int i = voy.isSameEmbark( (string*)pstr );
   if( i )
      voy.putData();
   return i;
   }

int matchDebark(const Voyage& voy, void* pstr)
   {
   int i = voy.isSameDebark( (string*)pstr );
   if( i )
      voy.putData();
   return i;
   }

int matchShip(const Voyage& voy, void* pstr)
   {
   int i = voy.isSameShip( (string*)pstr );
   if( i )
      voy.putData();
   return i;
   }

void add_voyage()                             // add a voyage
   {
   Voyage vtemp;

   cout << "\nEnter data for a voyage";
   vtemp.getData();
   if( !VoyageList.Add(vtemp) )
      { cerr << "\nCan't add voyage to list"; }
   }

void list_voyages()                           // list all voyages
   {
   cout << "\nSCHEDULE\n--------";
   if( VoyageList.IsEmpty() )
```

```
      { cout << "\nNo voyages listed"; return; }
   VoyageList.ForEach(ShowVoyage, 0);
   }

void delete_voyage()                          // delete a voyage
   {
   int ihours, iminutes;
   char ch;
   Voyage vtemp;
   Voyage* pVoy;
   TDate vdate;

   cout << "\nEnter date and time of voyage to be deleted";
   cout << "\n   Date (format 12/31/91): ";
   cin >> vdate;
   cout <<  "   Time (24-hour format 23:59): ";
   cin >> ihours >> ch >> iminutes;
   TTime vtime(vdate, ihours, iminutes);
   cin.ignore(100, '\n');
                                              // search for voyage
   pVoy = VoyageList.FirstThat(FindDate, (void*)&vtime);
   if(!pVoy)
      { cout << "No voyage with that time and date."; return; }
   cout << "\nVoyage With This Time and Date:";
   pVoy->putData();
   cout << "\nAre you sure you want to delete it (y/n)? ";
   cin >> ch;
   if(ch=='y')
      VoyageList.Detach(*pVoy);
   }

void find_voyage()                            // find a voyage
   {
   char ch;
   string s;

   cout << "\nEnter e to find embarkation port"
           "\n      d to find debarkation port"
           "\n      s to find name of ship"
           "\nSelection: ";
   cin >> ch;
   switch(ch)
      {
      case 'e':
         cout << "\nEnter embarkation port: ";
         getstring(s);
         if( !VoyageList.LastThat(matchEmbark, (void*)&s) )
            cout << "No match for embarkation " << s;
         break;
      case 'd':
         cout << "\nEnter debarkation port: ";
         getstring(s);
         if( !VoyageList.LastThat(matchDebark, (void*)&s) )
            cout << "No match for debarkation " << s;
```

(continued on next page)

(continued from previous page)

```
            break;
         case 's':
            cout << "\nEnter vessel name: ";
            getstring(s);
            if( !VoyageList.LastThat(matchShip, (void*)&s) )
               cout << "No match for vessel name " << s;
            break;
         default: cout << "\nNo such selection";
         }
   }
```

This program uses a sorted list in the form of the `TSListImp` class. This requires a comparison operator for the class that it stored. We overload this operator to compare two voyages on the basis of their embarkation times. Since these times, from the `TTime` class, include the dates, the voyages are sorted according to date and time (provided the voyages take place after January 1, 1900). When all the voyages are displayed, they appear in this order.

To allow the user to input strings with embedded blanks, we create our own `getstring()` function, which accepts a `char*` string using `cin.get()` and converts it to an object of the utility class `string`.

The user can perform five possible actions. Here's a part of the interaction with the program when the user adds a voyage:

```
Enter a to add a voyage
      d to delete a voyage
      f to find a voyage
      l to list all voyages
      x to exit
Selection: a

Enter data for a voyage
   Embarkation port: New York
   Debarkation port: Southampton
   Ship name: Royal Consort
   Departure date: 12/25/29
   Departure time: (24-hour format, 23:59): 20:40
```

If the user enters `f` to find a voyage, the interaction might look like this (assuming there are many voyages already in the database):

```
Selection: f

Enter e to find embarkation port
      d to find debarkation port
      s to find ship name
Selection: s

Enter vessel name: Flying Dutchman

From Le Havre, to Cape Town, on Vessel Flying Dutchman
   Departing June 23, 1916, at 10:30
From Rio de Janeiro, to Rangoon, on Vessel Flying Dutchman
   Departing November 16, 1917, at 15:45
```

Here's what happens if you want to delete a voyage:

```
Selection: d

Enter date and time of voyage to be deleted
   Date (format 12/31/91): 5/17/38
   Time (24-hour format 23:59): 15:30
Voyage with this time and date:
From Sydney, to Djarkarta, on vessel Pacific Queen
   Departing May 17, 1938, at 15:30
Are you sure you want to delete it (y/n)? y
```

This program demonstrates how the various features of the container classes can be fitted together to produce a potentially useful program. A similar approach can be used to create a custom database for any sort of data.

Summary

The Borland class library provides several utility classes for commonly used data items, including strings, dates, and times. It also provides a wide selection of container classes, which represent programming mechanisms for storing data in various arrangements. This data can be either a basic C++ type, or a user-defined class type. These library classes all relieve the programmer from developing similar classes over and over for each new programming situation.

The following outline summarizes the key container classes, along with the header files necessary for their use, and their public member functions.

Fundamental Data Structures

Binary Tree (BINIMP.H)

TBinarySearchTreeImp (needs `operator<`, `operator==`, constructor)

`Add(), Detach(), Find(), Flush(), ForEach(), GetItemsInContainer(), Parent::IsEmpty`

TIBinarySearchTreeImp

Same as above

Double-Linked List (DLISTIMP.H)

TDoubleListImp (needs copy constructor, `operator==`, constructor)

`Add(), AddAtHead(), AddAtTail(), Detach(), FirstThat(), Flash(), ForEach(), IsEmpty(),⇐`
`LastThat(), PeekHead(), PeekTail()`

TIDoubleListImp

Same as above, plus `DetachAtHead(), DetachatTail(), GetItemsInContainer(), FindPred()`

Hash Table (HASHIMP.H)

THashTableImp (needs copy constructor, `operator=`, `operator==`, constructor)

`Add(), Detach(), Find(), Flush(), ForEach(), GetItemsInContainer(), IsEmpty()`

TIHashTableImp

Same as above

List (LISTIMP.H)

TListImp (needs copy constructor, `operator==`, constructor)

`Add(), Detach(), FirstThat(), Flush(), ForEach(), IsEmpty(), LastThat(), PeekHead()`

TIListImp

`Add(), Detach(), FirstThat(), ForEach(), LastThat(), PeekHead()`

Vector (VECTIMP.H)

TVectorImp (needs copy constructor, `operator==`, constructor)

`FirstThat(), Flush(), ForEach(), GetDelta(), LastThat(), Limit(), Resize(), Top(), ⇐`

`Operator[], Operator=`

TIVectorImp

`FirstThat(), Flush(), ForEach(), GetDelta(), LastThat(), Limit(), Resize(), Top(), Zero(), ⇐`

`Operator[]`

TCVectorImp

`Add(), AddAt(), Count(), Detach(), Find(), GetDelta()`

TICVectorImp

`Add(), Find(), FirstThat(), Flush(), ForEach(), GetDelta(), LastThat(), Limit(), Resize(), ⇐`

`Top(), Zero(), Operator[]`

Abstract Data Types

Array (ARRAYS.H)

TArrayAsVector (needs `operator ==`)

`Add(), AddAt(), ArraySize(), Destroy(), Detach(), FirstThat(), Flush(), ForEach(), ⇐`

`GetItemsInContainer(), HasMember(), IsEmpty(), IsFull(), LastThat(), LowerBound(), ⇐`

`UpperBound(), Operator[]`

TIArrayAsVector

The above plus `Find()`

Association (ASSOC.H)

TDDAssociation, direct key, direct value. (Needs `HashValue(), operator ==`)

`HashValue(), Key(), Value(), Operator==`

TDIAssociation, direct key, indirect value

Same as above

TIDAssociation, indirect key, direct value

Same as above

TIIAssociation, indirect key, indirect value

Same as above

Bag (BAGS.H)

TBagAsVector

`Add(), Detach(), FindMember(), Flush(), ForEach(), GetItemsInContainer(), HasMember(), ⇐`

`IsEmpty(), IsFull()`

TIBagAsVector

The above plus `FirstThat(), LastThat()`

Deque (DEQUES.H)

TDequeAsVector

`FirstThat(), Flush(), ForEach(), GetItemsInContainer(), GetLeft(), GetRight(), IsEmpty(), ⇐`

`IsFull(), LastThat(), PeekLeft(), PeekRight(), PutLeft(), PutRight()`

TIDequeAsVector

Same as above

TDequeAsDoubleList

Same as above

TIDequeAsDoubleList
Same as above

Dictionary (DICT.H; needs copy constructor, `operator =`, `operator ==`, constructor)
TDictionaryAsHashTable
`Add(), Detach(), Find(), Flush(), ForEach(), GetItemsInContainer(), IsEmpty()`
TIDictionaryAsHashTable
Same as above

Queue (QUEUES.H)
TQueueAsVector (needs copy constructor, `operator =`, `operator <`, constructor)
`FirstThat(), Flush(), ForEach(), Get(), GetItemsInContainer(), IsEmpty(), IsFull(),⇐`
`LastThat(), Put()`
TIQueueAsVector
Same as above
TQueueAsDoubleList
Same as above
TQueue: same as TQueueAsVector

Set (SETS.H)
TSetAsVector
Same as TBagAsVector
TISetAsVector
Same as TIBagAsVector
TSet: same as TSetAsVector

Stack (STACKS.H)
TStackAsVector
`FirstThat(), Flush(), ForEach(), GetItemsInContainer(), IsEmpty(), IsFull(), LastThat(),⇐`
`Pop(), Push(), Top()`
TIStackAsVector
Same as above
TStackAsList
Same as above
TIStackAsList
Same as above
TStack: same as TStackAsList

Sorted types (with "S" in the name, such as TSDoubleListImp) require `operator <`.

Questions

Answers to questions can be found in Appendix D.

1. The type of the objects stored in a Borland container class is determined
   a. by an argument to the container class constructor.
   b. when a template for the class is instantiated.
   c. by the type of pointers stored in the container.
   d. by the name of the particular class.

2. In Borland C++, the Borland class library .H files are in the directory ________.

3. True or false: You must tell Borland C++ to add special library files to use Borland class library files.

4. If you're writing a program that uses the TTime and TArrayAsVector classes, you must include the ________ and ________ header files.

5. The string class is useful because

   a it is an example of a container class.
   b. string objects can be placed in containers.
   c. it simplifies some string operations.
   d. TDate and TTime are derived from it.

6. Write a statement that causes an object st of Borland's class string to display itself.

7. To be stored in an object of the TStackAsVector class, objects must

   a. be derived from stack classes.
   b. belong to a container class.
   c. be basic C++ types.
   d. belong to a class that includes an overloaded operator (==) operator.

8. Write a statement that puts an object called obj on a TStackAsVector object called stack1. Write another statement that removes it.

9. Write a while loop that terminates when a TStackAsVector object, called stack1, is empty.

10. True or false: A TDate object is a container.

11. The ForEach() member function

    a. displays each object in a container.
    b. executes the same function for each object in a container.
    c. is called by each stored object to display the object.
    d. is called by each stored object to execute the same function.

12. Write a statement that will put an object called obj1 into an object called array1 of class TArrayAsVector, at position 3, without overwriting the element at that position.

13. True or false: An object of class TListImp can hold objects of only one class at a time.

14. A dictionary must contain ________.

15. The `LastThat()` member function

    a. causes a user-written function to be called for every object in a container.
    b. finds all the objects in a container meeting a certain condition.
    c. must be defined differently for different classes.
    d. alters selected objects in a container.

16. State two differences between an FDS and an ADT.

17. Write an expression that returns the number of objects in the `TDequeAsVector` object `d1`.

18. What member function can you use to search a `TDictionaryAsHashTable` object for an object that has a certain value?

19. True or false: A vector-based stack operates more quickly than a list-based stack.

20. What are the two parts of an association?

Exercises

Answers to starred exercises can be found in Appendix D.

1.* Rewrite the STACKINT program from this chapter to hold `TDate` objects instead of type `int`. Use the three-argument constructor from `TDate` to create three date objects, and push them onto the stack. Then pop them off and display them.

2.* Convert the LISTINT program from this chapter to hold `string` objects instead of type `int`. Add three strings to the list, then display them using `ForEach()`. Remove one of the strings and then display the remaining contents of the list.

3.* Change the STACKINT program from this chapter to use a `for` loop to display the stored items rather than a `while` loop. How do you find out how many items are in the container?

4. Start with the program from Exercise 7 in Chapter 12, which sorted an array of pointers to `person` objects so that the `persons` were arranged according to salary. (The private data for person objects consists of a name, type `char*`, and a salary, type `float`.) Substitute a `TIArrayAsVector` object for the `person*` array. (Note the "I" in the name.) Keep the homemade function that sorts the array's contents by rearranging the pointers.

5. Revise Exercise 4 above to use an array of type `TISArrayAsVector`. (Note the "S".) Will you still need the homemade sorting routine?

6. Push some objects of type `frac` (see Exercise 7, Chapter 9) into a `TStack-AsVector` object. Then pop them off and display them. You can expurgate `frac` to list only those member functions necessary for this program.

7. Start with the TOKEN program from Exercise 7 in Chapter 13. This program uses inheritance to make it possible to store pointers to two different classes on the same stack. Remove the homemade stack from that program and replace it with one instantiated from `TIStackAsVector`. (Note that this container stores pointers.)

8. Modify the DICT program in this chapter to use `TDIAssociation` in its dictionary—that is, an association that groups a key (term) and a pointer to a value (meaning).

9. Convert the SCHLIST program in this chapter to store its `voyage` objects in `TSArrayAsVector` instead of `TSListImp`.

10. Convert the program in Exercise 12 in Chapter 13 to use a `TStackAsVector` object instead of the homemade `Stack` class. Notice that `gettop()` in `Stack` returns the index number, while `Top()` in `TStackAsVector` returns the contents of the first item on the stack without replacing it.

18

Just for Fun

18

This chapter contains several programs that are more complex or idiosyncratic than those we've seen earlier in this book. Nevertheless, they demonstrate some interesting ways that classes can be used in C++ programming. (These programs are also fun to use, even for people who don't know anything about C++.)

There are three programs. The first uses fractals to generate flowers, the second is an OOP version of Conway's Game of Life, and the third is a program that will probably beat (or at least tie) you in tic-tac-toe. The fractal program requires a graphics display, but the other two programs require only a character display, and so will run on any MS-DOS computer.

Fractal Flowers

Fractals are mathematical graphics constructions with the property of self-similarity. This means that a part has the same appearance as the whole, a part of a part has the same appearance as a part, and so on. The best way to understand fractals is to see an example. Our program, TENDRILS, uses fractals to create a flowering plant. Figure 18-1 shows the output of the program.

Every time you run TENDRILS, the output is different. Some plants look fairly regular; others are weird and distorted. You can create an entire jungle of plants, each completely unique.

Fractal Fundamentals

Fractals start with a simple graphics element and duplicate this element at various scales to build up the final image. In TENDRILS the fundamental graphics element is a series of short line segments that form a curved line. Each segment is connected to the next at a slight angle, so the result is a line with a curving shape and a fixed length, which we'll call a *tendril*. This is shown in Figure 18-2.

When fractals are used to imitate natural phenomena such as flowers (or mountains or clouds or similar forms), an element of randomness is commonly introduced into the creation of the fundamental graphics elements so that the image will display natural-looking variations. We introduce randomness by deciding in a random way whether the angle that joins any two segments in a tendril will bend to the left or to the right. We also arrange things so that the angle is more likely to turn to the left than to the right. This generates tendrils that tend to curve leftward, but do so in an irregular way.

A number of tendrils are grouped together to form a cluster. The tendrils in a cluster all start at the same point and radiate from this point at equally spaced angles. However, their random bending soon destroys this initial symmetry.

Here's the listing for TENDRILS:

```
// tendrils.cpp
// draws "biological" forms
#include <graphics.h>          // for graphics functions
```

(continued on next page)

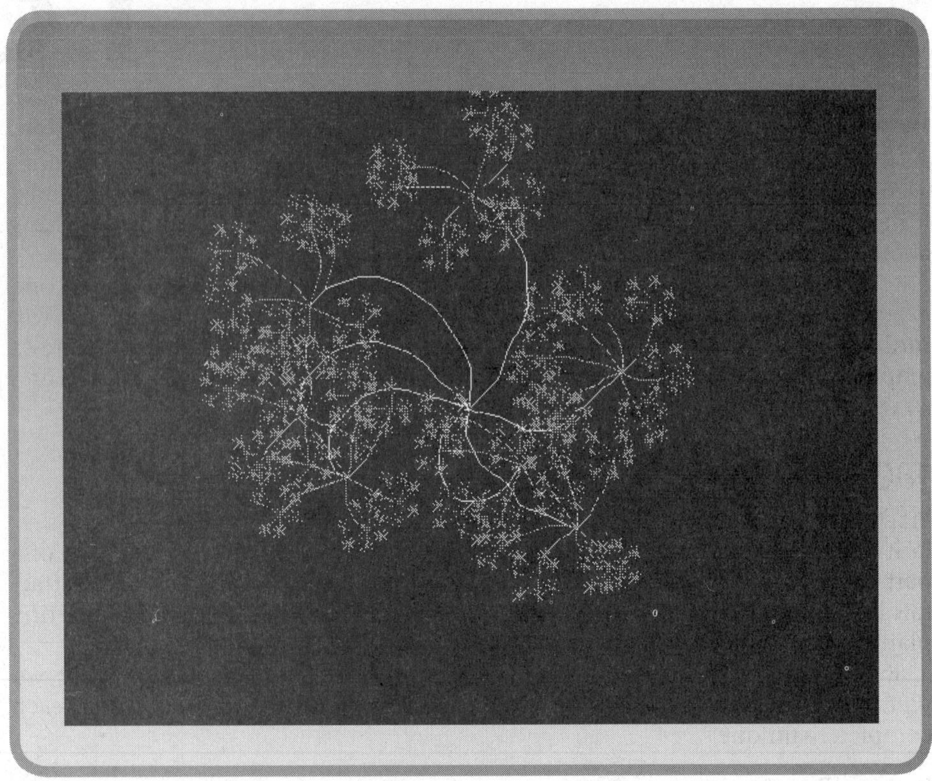

Figure 18-1 Output of TENDRILS Program

(continued from previous page)
```
#include <stdlib.h>              // for randomize(), rand()
#include <time.h>                // for randomize()
#include <math.h>                // for sin(), cos()
#include <conio.h>               // for getch()

const int   X0=320;              // center of screen
const int   Y0=240;
const float PI=3.14159;          // pi
const int   NUME=30;             // numerator of probability
const int   DENOM=100;           // denominator of probability
const int   NUMBER = 7;          // number of tendrils per cluster
const float RAD = 3.0;           // length of straight line segments
const float DELTHETA = 0.1;      // change in theta (radians)
const int   SEGS = 60;           // max line segments per tendril
const int   REDUX = 3;           // how much to divide # of segments
const int   MIN = 1;             // minimum number of line segments

class cluster
   {
   public:
      void display(int size, int x, int y);
   };
```

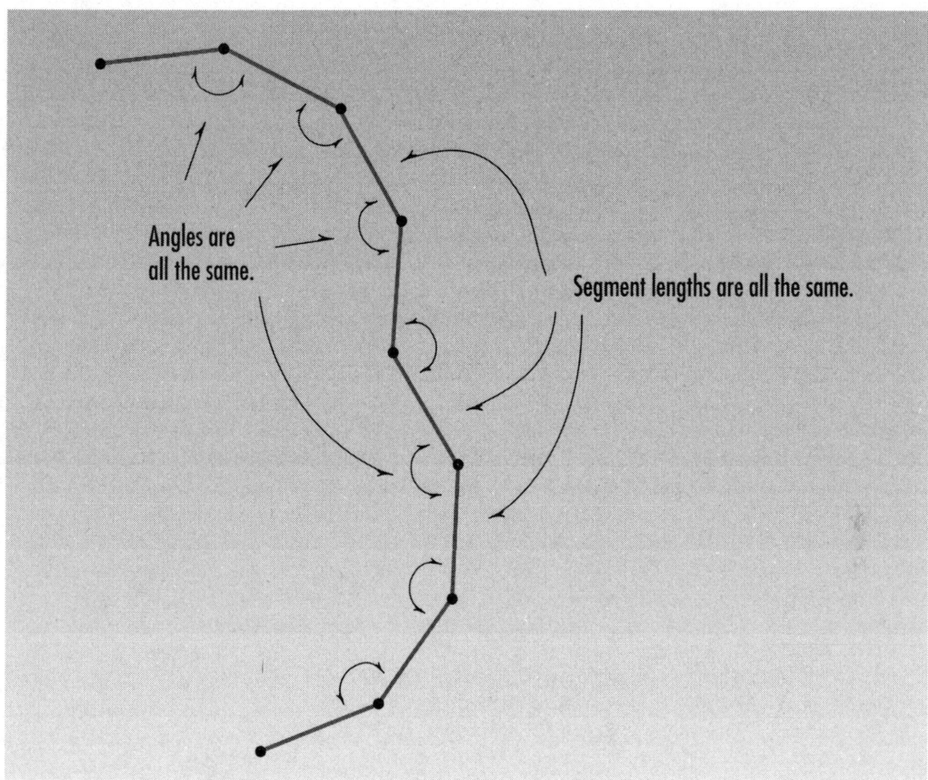

Figure 18-2 Tendril Formed from Line Segments

```
class tendril
   {
   public:
      void display(int size, float theta, int x, int y);
   };

void cluster::display(int size, int x0, int y0)
   {
   if( kbhit() )
      exit(0);
   for(int i=0; i<NUMBER; i++)        // for each tendril
      {
      float theta = i * 2*PI/NUMBER;
      int x=x0, y=y0;
      moveto(x, y);
      tendril t;                      // make a tendril
      t.display(size, theta, x, y);   // display it
      }
   }

void tendril::display(int size, float theta, int x, int y)
   {
```

(continued on next page)

(continued from previous page)

```
   for(int j=0; j<size; j++)
      {                                       // left or right
      int chng = ( random(DENOM)<NUME ) ? -1 : 1;
      theta = theta + chng*DELTHETA;    // new angle
      x = x + RAD*sin(theta);           // x and y of
      y = y + RAD*cos(theta);           //    next point
      if(size < 4) setcolor(RED);
      else if(size < 13) setcolor(GREEN);
      else if(size < 40) setcolor(LIGHTGREEN);
      else setcolor(YELLOW);
      lineto(x, y);                     // draw line
      }
   if( size > MIN )
      {                                 // if tendril long enough
      cluster c;                        // make a new cluster
      int newsize = size / REDUX;       // but smaller than before
      c.display(newsize, x, y);         // display it
      }
   }

void main()
   {
   int driver, mode;
   driver = VGA;         // set graphics driver
   mode = VGAHI;         // and graphics mode
   initgraph(&driver, &mode, "\\tc\\bgi");
   randomize();          // seed random number generator
   int x=X0, y=Y0;       // set origin of cluster
   int size = SEGS;
   cluster c;            // define a cluster
   c.display(size, x, y);   // display the cluster
   getch();              // hold image until keypress
   closegraph();         // reset graphics system
  }
```

There are two classes in TENDRILS. The class `cluster` models a group or cluster of tendrils, and the class `tendril` models a single tendril. Each class has only one member function: `display`. After a `tendril` or `cluster` object draws itself, it is not used again in the program. Since it doesn't need to remember anything, it has no need for any data items; thus there is no private data in either class.

The main program creates a single object of class `cluster` and displays it. This cluster object in turn creates a series of tendril objects, all starting at the same place but at different angles. The cluster object displays each one. Each of these tendril objects, in the course of displaying itself, draws the series of line segments that form its body, and then—at the end of the tendril—creates an object of type `cluster` but with a smaller size. It then tells this cluster to display itself. Figure 18-3 shows how this looks.

Tendrils create clusters, and clusters create tendrils, until the tendrils are too short to be usefully displayed. At this point each tendril creates itself but no cluster, and the program ends. The result is a screen display that looks like some sort of exotic flowering plant.

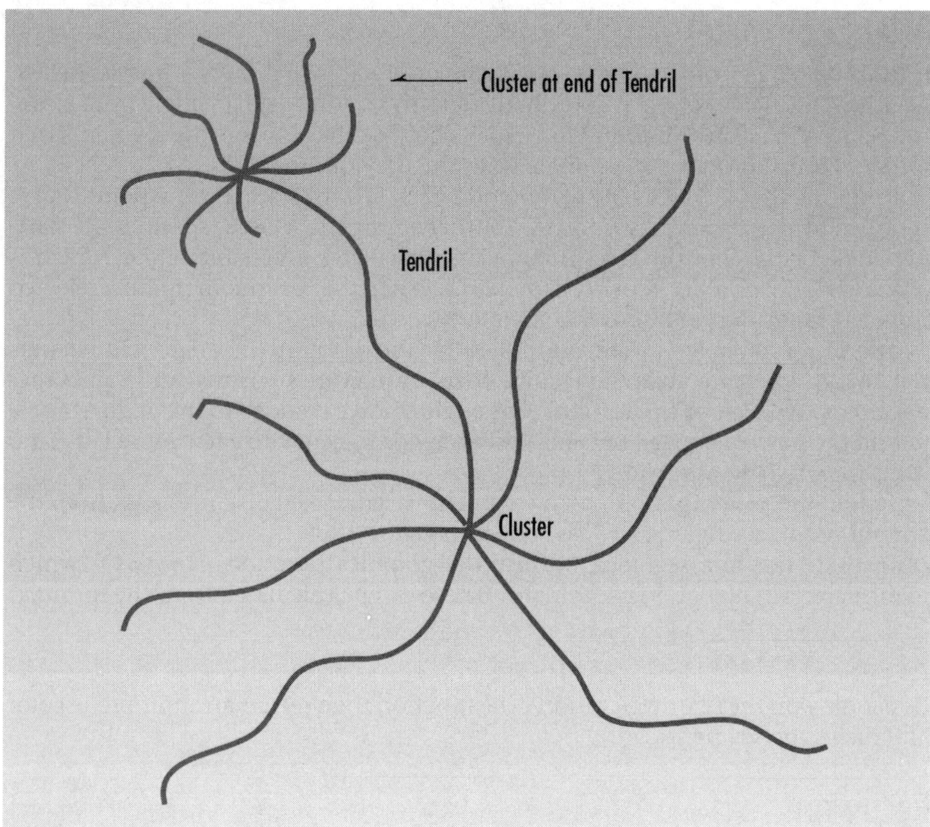

Figure 18-3 Tendril and Cluster

Constants

The program starts with a series of constant definitions. These constants are used to control the appearance of the flowers generated by the program. `NUME` divided by `DENUM` specifies the probability that a segment will bend to the right. `NUMBER` is the number of tendrils in a cluster. `RAD` is the length of a straight line segment. `DELTHETA` is the change in angle between one line segment of a tendril and the next. `SEGS` is the number of line segments per tendril. `REDUX` is the scale factor; each set of clusters is `REDUX` times as small as the previous one. `MIN` is the minimum length of a tendril; when tendrils become this small, their clusters are not created. You can vary the appearance of the flowers by changing these constants.

Clusters

The `cluster::display()` function uses a `for` loop to create `NUMBER` tendrils. It calculates the angle of each tendril (`theta`), creates a tendril, and calls `tendril::display()` to display the tendril—sending it arguments to specify its size, angle, and starting point. The size parameter determines the number of line segments used to create a tendril.

Polar Coordinates

It turns out to be convenient to use polar coordinates to draw the line segments. As noted in Chapter 9, polar coordinates specify a radius and an angle from a central point. This system is useful in TENDRILS because each of the line segments that forms a tendril is drawn at an angle from the previous segment.

In the `tendril::display()` function each tendril starts from a point that is specified by the arguments `x` and `y`. Another argument, `theta`, specifies the starting angle of the tendril. The function first calculates a variable, `chng`, which is given one of two values, 1 or –1, depending on whether a random number selected from the range 0 to `DENUM` is less than `NUME`.

The `chng` variable is then multiplied by the amount the angle will change, `DELTHETA`, to create an angle change that is sometimes positive and sometimes negative (to the left or to the right). The angle change is added to the original angle to find the new angle, `theta`. This process tends to generate a few more left-hand turns than right-hand turns.

To find the endpoint of each line segment we go a fixed distance, `RAD`, from the current point, at angle `theta`, as shown in Figure 18-4.

To draw the line segment, we use the graphics function `lineto()`, which requires rectangular (x, y) coordinates. These can be calculated from the formulas

```
x = x + RAD*sin(theta);
y = y + RAD*cos(theta);
```

Depending on the size of the tendril, the function then selects an appropriate color and draws the segment.

Recursion

When all the line segments that constitute the tendril have been drawn, `tendril::display()` then creates a cluster, using a size `REDUX` times as small as its own size.

Since a `tendril` object is created by a `cluster` object, and a `cluster` object is created by a `tendril` object, the program is *recursive*. This nesting of one object within another, like Chinese boxes, must terminate at some point, or the program

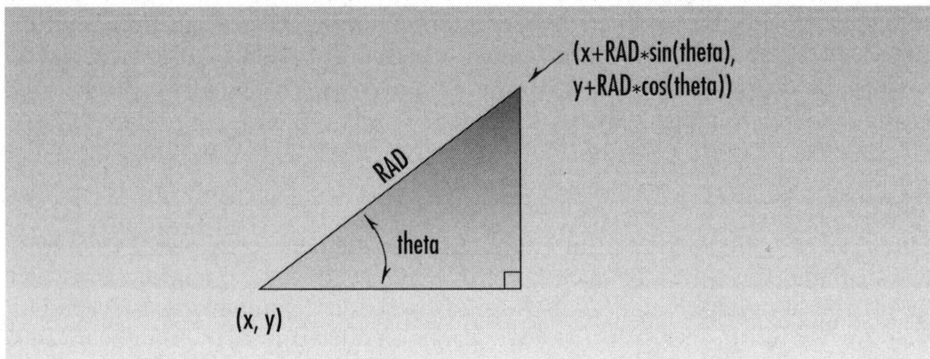

Figure 18-4 Line Segment in Polar Coordinates

will run forever, generating ever more microscopic tendrils. This terminating point is determined by the `if` statement in `tendril::display()`, which decides whether to create a cluster based on the current tendril size. If the size is smaller than the `MIN` constant, the recursion stops.

The TENDRILS program could easily be written without classes, as a series of nested `for` loops. Using classes, however, makes clearer the association between the parts of the program (class `tendril` and class `cluster`) and the specific graphics elements they display.

You can cause radical alterations in the appearance of the flowers generated by the TENDRILS program by altering the constants at the start of the program. For example, by causing all the tendrils to branch upward in each cluster, you can create shapes that look like trees rather than flowers. Fine tuning of the constants will reveal different kinds of trees, from poplars to evergreens.

For more on fractals read *Computers, Pattern, Chaos and Beauty*, by Clifford A. Pickover (listed in Appendix E), which sowed the seeds of the TENDRILS program.

Conway's Game of Life

The Game of Life is an old favorite, invented by Cambridge mathematician John Conway in the 1970s. Life simulates a microbe colony. The cells are displayed on the computer screen as squares in a two-dimensional array. Each cell lives and dies according to a few simple rules.

Our C++ program LIFE models this game. This program (unlike most versions of Life) runs on a character display; you don't need a graphics monitor. The display routine in this program uses a somewhat unusual approach to displaying the cells. To make the cells square instead of oblong, and to increase the number of cells, we put two cells in each character position, one over the other, as shown in Figure 18-5. An 80x25-character screen can thus display an array of 80x50 cells—enough for most Life demonstrations.

Rules of LIFE

A cell can be either alive (displayed as a white square) or dead (a dark or empty square). Each cell has eight potential neighbors: cells above and below it, to its left

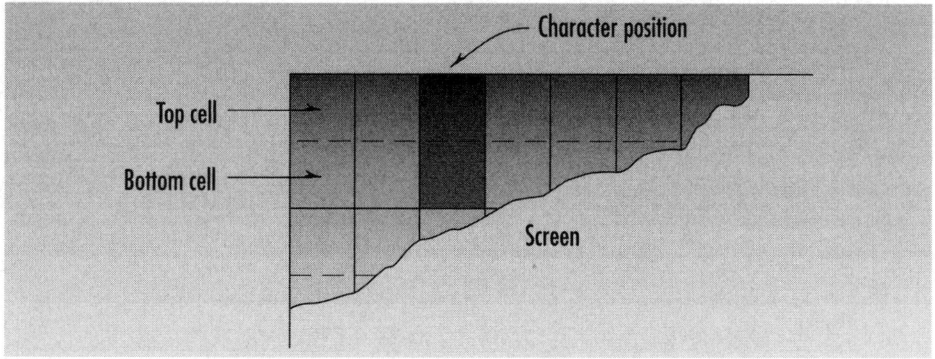

Figure 18-5 Two Cells in Each Character

and right, and the four diagonal cells. If an empty (dead) cell has exactly three neighbors, it becomes alive (is born). If a living cell has either two or three neighbors, it continues to live. But if a living cell has fewer than two neighbors, it dies (presumably from loneliness); if it has more than three neighbors it also dies (from overcrowding).

The program calculates the fate of all the cells and then changes the cells to their new states and displays them. Some cells are born, others die, others continue to live. Each calculation-display sequence is called a *generation.*

The fascinating thing about Life is that these simple rules can give rise to very complex displays of pattern growth and change from generation to generation. Some simple patterns behave in predictable ways. For example, a four-by-four block of living cells is stable; since every cell has three living neighbors, they all continue to live. However, a line of three cells (called a *semaphore*) will flip back and forth between vertical and horizontal; the cell in the middle lives, the ones at the ends die, and new cells are born next to the middle. Other fairly simple patterns, such as the one used in the program, can grow into patterns of hundreds of cells, shifting and moving in fantastic kaleidoscopic animation. Figure 18-6 shows some possibilities.

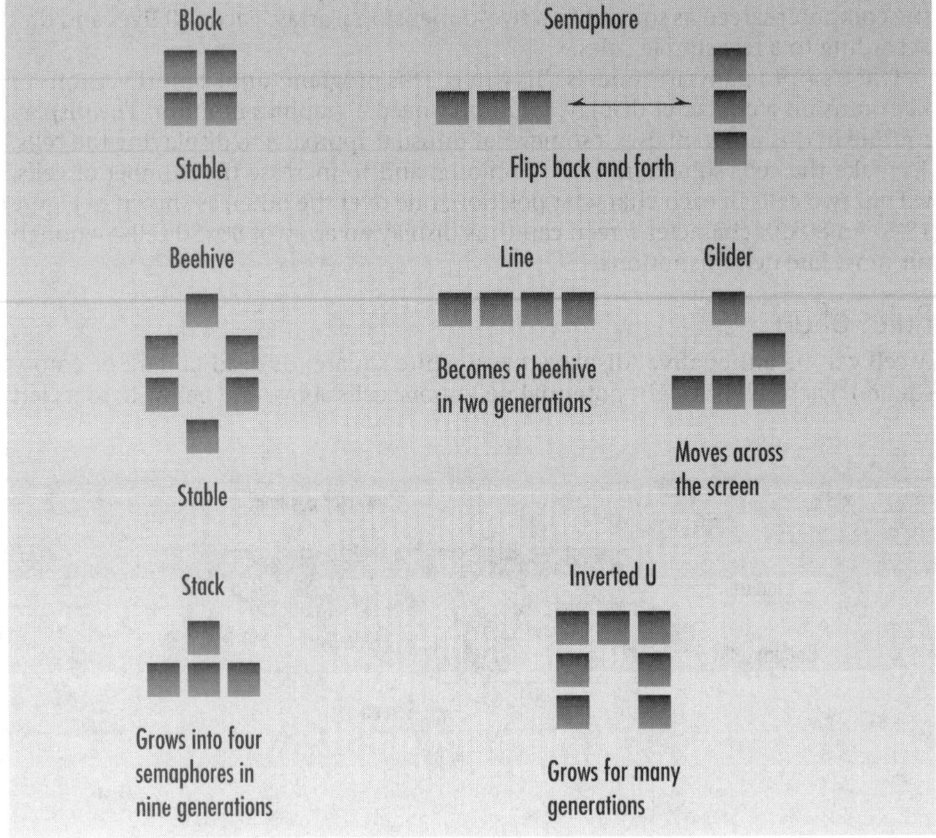

Figure 18-6 Patterns from Life

Considerable research has been done on Life, which is far richer than we have space to discuss here. To learn more, read *Wheels, Life, and Other Mathematical Amusements*, by Martin Gardner (listed in Appendix E).

Running LIFE

When you start LIFE, you'll see a simple pattern: an inverted "U" shape made of seven cells, as shown in Figure 18-7.

Pressing any key causes this pattern to start evolving. This particular pattern grows for several hundred generations before reaching a stable state. An intermediate state in its evolution is shown in Figure 18-8. To stop the program, press any key.

Architecture of LIFE

The LIFE program uses only one class, called `Cell`. We define a two-dimensional array of objects of this class, each object representing a cell on the screen. Each cell has four items of private data: its x and y coordinates and two variables representing the `state` of the cell. The `state` variable is defined in an `enum` definition to have the possible values `alive` or `dead`. Here's the listing for LIFE.

Figure 18-7 Initial Position in LIFE Program

Figure 18-8 Intermediate Position in LIFE Program

```
// life.cpp
// recreates Conway's "Game of Life"
#include <conio.h>                  // for kbhit(), getch(), etc.
const unsigned char top =  '\xDF';  // square in upper half
const unsigned char bot =  '\xDC';  // square in lower half
const unsigned char both = '\xDB';  // square in both halves
const unsigned char none = '\x20';  // square in neither half
const int maxCols = 80;             // screen width
const int maxRows = 50;             // two squares per character
const int maxRealRows = 25;         // really only 25 rows

enum state { dead, alive };

class Cell
   {
   private:
      int xCo, yCo;                       // coordinates of cell
      state oldState, newState;           // dead or alive
   public:
      void InitCell(int, int);            // initialize cell
      void SetLive(void);                 // to set initial pattern
      state GetState(void);               // to check neighbors
      void Calc(void);                    // calculate new state
      void Display(void);                 // display the cell
   };
Cell c[maxCols][maxRows];                 // define array of cells

void Cell::InitCell(int x, int y)         // initialize cell
   {
   xCo = x;                               // set coordinates
   yCo = y;
   oldState = newState = dead;            // set to dead
   }

void Cell::SetLive()                      // set cell to alive
   {
   newState = alive;
   }

state Cell::GetState(void)                // get state of cell
   {
   return(oldState);
   }

void Cell::Calc()                         // calculate new state
   {                        // find number of neighbors alive
   int neighbors =  c[xCo-1][yCo-1].GetState() +   // nw
                    c[xCo  ][yCo-1].GetState() +   // n
                    c[xCo+1][yCo-1].GetState() +   // ne
                    c[xCo-1][yCo  ].GetState() +   // w
                    c[xCo+1][yCo  ].GetState() +   // e
                    c[xCo-1][yCo+1].GetState() +   // sw
                    c[xCo  ][yCo+1].GetState() +   // s
                    c[xCo+1][yCo+1].GetState();    // se

   newState = dead;        // cell is dead unless
```

```
                              // it's alive and has 2 or 3 neighbors
   if( oldState==alive && (neighbors==2 || neighbors==3) )
      newState = alive;
                              // or it's dead and has 3 neighbors
   else if( oldState==dead && neighbors==3 )
      newState = alive;
   }

// display the cell
// ( yCo goes from 0 to 49, screenRow from 0 to 24 )
void Cell::Display(void)
   {
   char chbuff[1];              // one-character buffer
   oldState = newState;         // update oldState
   if( newState==alive )        // if cell is alive, display it
      {
      int screenRow = yCo / 2;  // find actual row on screen
      int botrow = yCo % 2;     // top row = 0, bottom row = 1
                                // get screen character (two cells)
      gettext(xCo, screenRow, xCo, screenRow, chbuff);
      int ch = chbuff[0];
                                // find character (two cells)
      if(botrow)                      // if our cell on bottom row,
         if(ch==none || ch==bot)      // and if neither or bottom,
            ch = bot;                 //    set bottom only
         else                         // if both or top,
            ch = both;                //    set both
      else                      // if our cell on top row,
         if(ch==none || ch==top)      // and if neither or top half,
            ch = top;                 //    set top only
         else                         // if both or bottom halves,
            ch = both;                //    set bottom
                                // set new screen character
      gotoxy(xCo, screenRow);         // move cursor
      putch(ch);                      // insert character
      }
   }

main()
   {
   int x, y;
   clrscr();                          // clear screen
   _setcursortype(_NOCURSOR);         // turn off cursor
   for(x=0; x<maxCols; x++)           // initialize to dead
      for(y=0; y<maxRows; y++)
         c[x][y].InitCell(x, y);

   c[39][24].SetLive();               // set inverted U pattern
   c[40][24].SetLive();
   c[41][24].SetLive();
   c[39][25].SetLive();
   c[41][25].SetLive();
   c[39][26].SetLive();
   c[41][26].SetLive();
```

(continued on next page)

(continued from previous page)

```
   for(x=0; x<maxCols; x++)              // display initial cells
      for(y=0; y<maxRows; y++)
         c[x][y].Display();

   getch();                              // wait for keypress

   while( !kbhit() )                     // continue until keypress
      {
      for(x=1; x<maxCols-1; x++)         // find new states
         for(y=1; y<maxRows-1; y++)
            c[x][y].Calc();

      clrscr();                          // erase screen

      for(x=0; x<maxCols; x++)           // display cells
         for(y=0; y<maxRows; y++)
            c[x][y].Display();
      }  // end while
   _setcursortype(_NORMALCURSOR);        // restore cursor
   }  // end main()
```

Two states, represented by `oldState` and `newState`, are necessary for each cell, because calculating the new state of all the cells is a two-step process. First the new state of each cell is calculated, based on the old state of its neighbors. Until this is carried out for all cells, no cell may change its old state. Then the old state is set to the value of the new state, and all the old states are displayed.

Initializing the Cells

Each cell must know where it is so that it knows what neighbors to query to find out if it lives or dies. A member function, `InitCell()`, executed once for each cell at the beginning of the program, tells each cell its coordinates and sets its states to *dead*.

Getting and Setting the State

The member function `GetState()` returns the state, alive or dead, of a cell. It's used to calculate the number of living neighbors. The `SetAlive()` function sets the new state of the cell to *alive*, and is used in `main()` to set the initial cell pattern.

Calculating the New State

The member function `Calc()` determines whether the cell will live or die. This function finds the state of all eight neighboring cells and adds them together to obtain the number of living neighbors. A living cell will die unless it has two or three living neighbors, and a dead cell will be born if it has three living neighbors. This function changes the cell's `newState` variable accordingly. The `Calc` member function is unusual in that it assumes the existence of objects of its own class, namely `c[x][y]`.

Displaying the Cell

Before displaying the cell, the `Display()` function first sets the `oldState` variable equal to `newState`. It can do this because it knows that `Calc()` has finished calculating the new state for all the variables. `Display()` uses the library function `gotoxy()` to cause a cell to display itself at the correct position.

Because the screen is erased just before all the cells display themselves, they need do nothing if they are dead. If a cell is alive, it must figure out what character on the screen to modify. It determines the existing character with the `gettext()` function.

Since each character has two cell positions, some logic is devoted to figuring out the correct graphics character to insert. There are four possibilities: a blank character (a space), a character with a cell on the bottom but not on the top, a character with a cell on the top but not on the bottom, and a character with cells on both the top and the bottom. The choice depends on the character that was there before (stored in the variable `ch`) and whether the cell that we want to display is on the top row of the character or on the bottom row. The nested `if else` statements take care of this. Figure 18-9 shows the possibilities.

The `main()` Function

The `main()` function erases the screen, using the `clrscr()` function. Then it initializes all the cells to *dead*, and sets some of them back to *alive* to form the initial pattern. It displays this initial pattern and waits for a keypress.

Following this keypress, the program enters a loop (which can be terminated with a second keypress). Three actions take place in the loop. First the new state

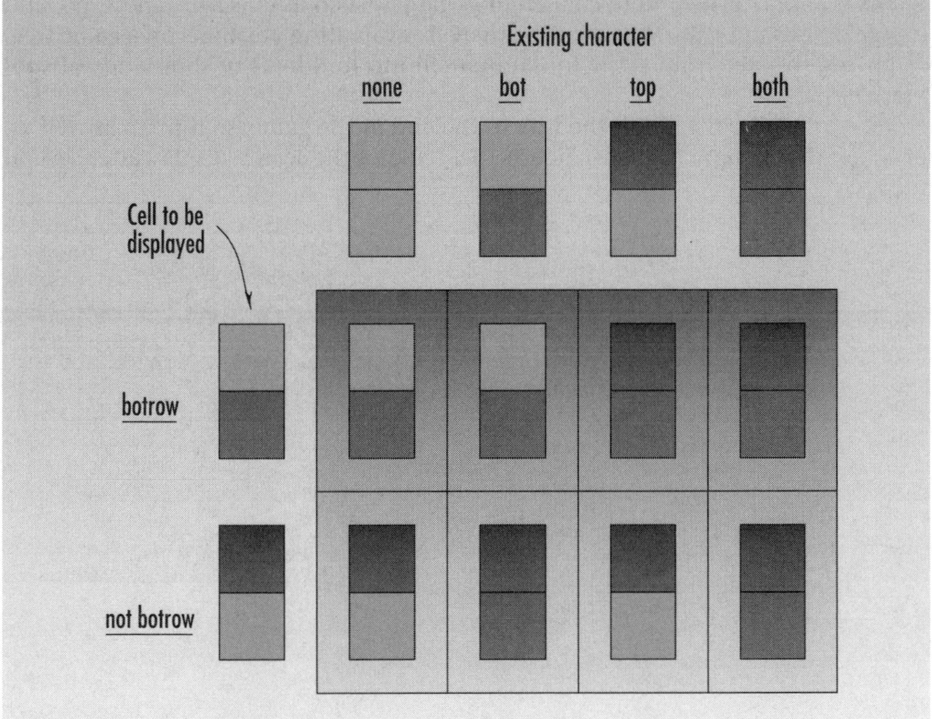

Figure 18-9 Combining a Cell with a Character

of all the cells is found, using `Calc()`. Notice that the cells on the outer edges of the array are not calculated (the index variables go from 1 to the maximum–1). This avoids out-of-bounds array references when a cell examines its neighbors. Next the screen is erased, and finally all cells are displayed using `Calc()`.

The present version of LIFE requires you to rewrite the calls to `SetLive()` in `main()` if you want to change to a new initial pattern. This simplifies the program but makes it rather inflexible. It would be easy to modify this program so the user could type in initial patterns using cell coordinates. This would give it much more flexibility. Even better would be a routine that allows the user to input cell positions using the cursor keys.

A Tic-Tac-Toe Program

Tic-tac-toe is a classic pencil-and-paper game in which each of two opponents tries to get three marks, usually represented by O and X, in a row. Figure 18-10 shows such a game, where X (due to an unfortunate lapse in concentration by O) wins.

The next program, TICTAC, enables the computer to play tic-tac-toe against a human opponent. This program actually demonstrates a minor form of artificial intelligence. In terms of OOP, it provides another example of recursion. A member function in one object creates another object of the same type, the same member function in the second object creates a third object, and so on.

You may think that tic-tac-toe is too simple a game to merit serious analysis. However, the approach used in TICTAC is fundamentally the same as that of programs that play other, more challenging, games, such as checkers, chess, go, and bridge. It uses the same strategy of recursively evaluating positions on a game tree, following the tree from a few initial branches to hundreds or thousands of sub-branches.

TICTAC "thinks ahead" all the way to the end of the game, so it plays as well as, or better than, many humans. Figure 18-11 shows the screen display after several moves.

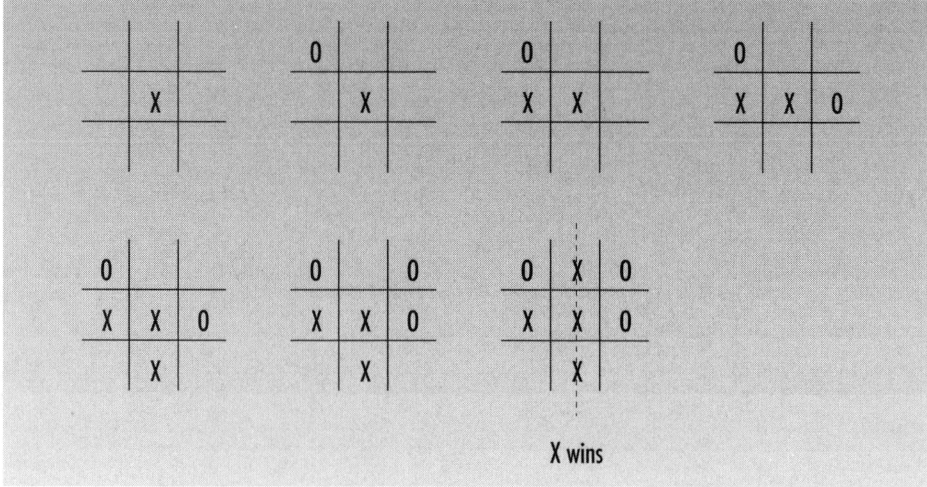

Figure 18-10 Moves in a Typical Tic-Tac-Toe Game

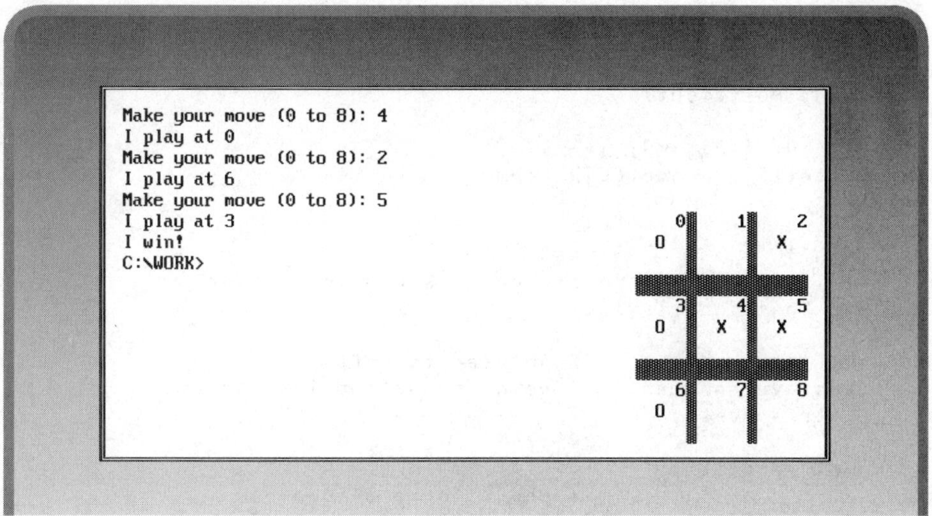

Figure 18-11 The TICTAC Program

Here's the listing for TICTAC:

```
// tictac.cpp
// tic-tac-toe game
#include <iostream.h>     // for cout, etc
#include <conio.h>        // for gotoxy()
#include <process.h>      // for exit()

enum whoplays { human, machine };
enum cell { empty, full };
enum boolean { false, true };

int deep = 0;             // recursion depth

class Position            // represents one board position
   {
   private:
      cell mcell[9];      // cells marked with machine moves
      cell hcell[9];      // cells marked with human moves
      whoplays player;    // human or machine to play next
   public:
      Position();                       // constructor
      boolean IsWin();                  // win in this position?
      boolean IsLegal(int);             // move is legal?
      void MakeMove(int);               // make move
      void SetPlayer(whoplays);         // swap player and machine
      static void InitDisplay();        // displays lines & numbers
      void Display();                   // display board position
      int Evaluate(int&);               // score this position
   };
```

(continued on next page)

(continued from previous page)

```
// Position()
// constructor: reset all cells to empty
Position::Position()
   {
   for( int j=0; j<9; j++ )
      mcell[j] = hcell[j] = empty;
   }

// IsWin()
// see if the current position is a win for player
boolean Position::IsWin()
   {
   cell *ptr;            // pointer to cells
   if( player==human ) // point to appropriate array
      ptr = hcell;
   else
      ptr = mcell;
                         // check for a 3-in-a-row
   if( (ptr[0] && ptr[1] && ptr[2]) ||  // horizontal
       (ptr[3] && ptr[4] && ptr[5]) ||
       (ptr[6] && ptr[7] && ptr[8]) ||
       (ptr[0] && ptr[3] && ptr[6]) ||  // vertical
       (ptr[1] && ptr[4] && ptr[7]) ||
       (ptr[2] && ptr[5] && ptr[8]) ||
       (ptr[0] && ptr[4] && ptr[8]) ||  // diagonal
       (ptr[2] && ptr[4] && ptr[6]) )
      return(true);
   else
      return(false);
   }

// IsLegal()
// find if move is legal in this position
boolean Position::IsLegal(int move)
   {
   if( move>=0 && move<=8 &&
                mcell[move]==empty && hcell[move]==empty )
      return(true);
   else
      return(false);
   }

// MakeMove()
// make move in current position with current player
void Position::MakeMove(int move)
   {
   if( player==human )     // player is human
      hcell[move] = full;
   else                    // player is machine
      mcell[move] = full;
   }

// SetPlayer()
// set player to human or machine
```

```
void Position::SetPlayer(whoplays p)
   {
   player = p;
   }

// InitDisplay()
// Draws lines, numbers squares
void Position::InitDisplay()
   {
   const unsigned char block = '\xB2';        // gray block

   void Insert(unsigned char, int, int);      // prototype
   int row, col;

   clrscr();                                  // clear screen
   for(row=0; row<11; row++)                  // vertical lines
      {
      Insert( block,  5, row);
      Insert( block, 11, row);
      }
   for(col=0; col<17; col++)                  // horizontal lines
      {
      Insert( block, col, 3);
      Insert( block, col, 7);
      }
   for(int j=0; j<9; j++)                     // number squares
      Insert( (char)(j+'0'), (j%3)*6+4, (j/3)*4 );
   }  // end InitDisplay()

// Display()
// displays board
void Position::Display()
   {
   void Insert(unsigned char, int, int);      // prototype
   int row, col;

   for(int j=0; j<9; j++)                     // for each square
      {
      if( hcell[j] )                          // human move
         Insert('X', (j%3)*6+2, (j/3)*4+1);
      else if( mcell[j] )                     // machine move
         Insert('O', (j%3)*6+2, (j/3)*4+1);
      else                                    // no move
         Insert(' ', (j%3)*6+2, (j/3)*4+1);
      }
   gotoxy(1, 23);                             // restore cursor pos
   }  // end Display()

// Insert()
// inserts character ch at col, row
void Insert(unsigned char ch, int col, int row)
   {
   // start 5 lines down, 50 cols over
   gotoxy(col+50+1, row+5+1);          // insert the character
```

(continued on next page)

(continued from previous page)

```
   putch(ch);
   }

// Evaluate()
// set score to chance of win, return the best move
int Position::Evaluate( int& score )
   {
   int const winscore = 100;         // score for a win (lose=0)
   int const drawscore = 50;         // score for a draw
   int returnmove;                   // move to be returned
   Position *posptr;                 // pointer to new position
   int legalmoves = 0;               // count legal moves
   int totalscore = 0;               // cumulative score
   int highscore = 0;                // highest score to date
   int avgscore;                     // average score
   int score2;                       // score from recursive call
   boolean waswin = false;           // true if at least one win
   boolean wasother = false;         // if at least one non-win

   ++deep;                           // down one recursion level
   for(int move=0; move<9; move++)   // for each of 9 moves
      {                              // 'player' can make
      if( IsLegal(move) )            // if no one played there yet
         {
         if( legalmoves==0 )         // set returnmove to first
            returnmove = move;       //   legal move
         ++legalmoves;               // count a legal move
         posptr = new Position;      // make new position
                                     //    for this move
         *posptr = *this;            // transfer this pos to posptr
         posptr->MakeMove(move);     // make the move
         if (deep < 3)               // display, if in first two
            posptr->Display();       // levels of recursion
         if( posptr->IsWin() )        // check if it's a win
            {
            waswin = true;            // there was a win
            highscore = winscore;     // win is highest score
            totalscore += winscore;   // update total
            returnmove = move;        // return this move
            }
         else                           // no win, so check deeper
            {
                                        // swap human/machine
            whoplays newp = (player==machine) ? human : machine;
            posptr->SetPlayer(newp);  // in new position

                                        // recursive call
            posptr->Evaluate(score2); // to new position

            if(score2==winscore)        // if wining score,
               waswin = true;           // remember there was a win
            else
               wasother = true;         // remember non-win
            totalscore += score2;       // add new score to total
```

```
            if( score2 > highscore )  // remember the move that
               {                      // produced the
               highscore = score2;    // highest score, and
               returnmove = move;     // the score
               }
            }  // end else (no win)
         delete posptr;               // delete the position
         }  // end if IsLegal
      }  // end for
                              // summarize results of all moves
   if( legalmoves==0 )        // if there are no legal moves
      {
      score = drawscore;      // it must be a draw
      --deep;                 // go up one recursion level
      return(99);             // return nonsense move
      }
   else                              // there were some legal moves
      {
      avgscore = totalscore / legalmoves;   // find average
      if( waswin && wasother )           // if wins and non-wins,
         score = winscore - (winscore-avgscore)/5;  // favor wins
      else
         score = avgscore;  // otherwise, use the average score
      score = 100 - score;  // invert: bad for them, good for us
      --deep;               // go up one recursion level
      return(returnmove);   // return best move
      }  // end else (legal moves)
   }  // end Evaluate()

// main()
// get human move, get machine move, etc.
void main(void)
   {
   int move;                              // store moves
   int sc;                                // for Evaluate()
   int movecount = 0;                     // number of move-pairs
   Position current;                      // create current position
   int cursrow = 0;                       // cursor row for text
   Position::InitDisplay();               // display the board
   while(1)                               // cycle until game over
      {
      current.SetPlayer(human);           // set player to human
      current.Display();                  // display the position
      gotoxy(1, ++cursrow);
      cout << "Make your move (0 to 8): ";  // get human move
      cin >> move;
      if( ! current.IsLegal(move) )
         {
         gotoxy(1, ++cursrow);
         cout << "Illegal move.";
         continue;                        // return to top of loop
         }
      current.MakeMove(move);             // make human move
      current.Display();
```

(continued on next page)

(continued from previous page)

```
      if( current.IsWin() )           // check for human win
         {
         gotoxy(1, ++cursrow);
         cout << "You win!";
         exit(0);
         }
      if( ++movecount==5 )            // if human move was
         {                            // the last possible move
         gotoxy(1, ++cursrow);
         cout << "It's a draw";
         exit(0);
         }                            // now machine can play
      current.SetPlayer(machine);     // set player to machine
      move = current.Evaluate(sc);    // get machine move
      gotoxy(1, ++cursrow);
      cout << "I play at " << move;
      current.MakeMove(move);         // make machine move
      current.Display();
      if( current.IsWin() )           // check for machine win
         {
         gotoxy(1, ++cursrow);
         cout << "I win!";
         exit(0);
         }
      } // end while
   } // end main()
```

The `Position` Class

TICTAC uses objects of the class `Position`. Each object of this class represents a board position—that is, some arrangement of Xs and Os on the 3-by-3 matrix of squares. Besides recording the X and O moves made to date, a `Position` object also includes a variable that specifies the player with the next turn.

The `main()` program creates a single object of class `Position` called `current`. This position records the current state of the game, and is displayed so the user can see what's happening.

Member Functions of `Position`

Let's look at each member function of `Position` in turn. This will serve to explain how TICTAC works.

The `Position()` Constructor

The constructor for `Position` initializes all the cells in a given position to `empty`. A single array could be used to represent the board, but it turns out to be simpler to use two arrays: one for human moves (`hcell`) and one for machine moves (`mcell`). The elements of these arrays are of type `cell`, which is declared in an `enum` statement to have two possible values: `empty` and `full`.

The cells are numbered from 0 in the upper-left corner down to 8 in the lower-right corner.

The `IsWin()` Function

The `IsWin()` function figures out if a particular position represents a win. If the human is playing, a win is three `hcell` (for *human cell*) elements in a row; if the player is the machine, it's three `mcell` elements in a row. `IsWin()` sets a pointer to the appropriate array, and then checks each of the eight possible three-in-a-rows to see if its cells are occupied. It returns the Boolean value of `true` if it finds a win, or `false` if it doesn't.

The `IsLegal()` Function

The `IsLegal()` function checks to see if a move, sent to it as an argument, is legal. A move is legal if it is a number between 0 and 8 and if neither human nor machine has already played in the specified cell.

The `MakeMove()` Function

The `MakeMove()` function changes the contents of the specified cell from `empty` to `full`. This happens in `mcell` or in `hcell`, depending on whether the player in the position is the machine or the human.

The `SetPlayer()` Function

The `SetPlayer()` function changes the player in a particular position. The `main()` program uses it to switch back and forth between the human—who always plays first—and the machine, as they alternate moves in the `current` position.

The `InitDisplay()` Function

When the program is first executed, it calls `InitDisplay()` to draw the crossed lines that form the tic-tac-toe game board, and to number each of the resulting nine squares, so the human knows what they are. The squares are numbered from 0 to 8, as shown in the program output. `InitDisplay()` starts by clearing the screen with `clrscr()`. It uses the `Insert()` function to actually place characters on the screen.

The `Display()` Function

The `main()` program displays the moves made on the board by calling `Display()` as a member function of the `current` position. This function translates the contents of `hcell` and `mcell` into the X and O display. `Display()` is also used by the `Evaluate()` function to show—very briefly—the positions it's thinking about as it looks ahead. `Display()` places characters on the screen by calling the `Insert()` function.

The `Insert()` Function

The `Insert()` function inserts a character at a fixed column-row position on the screen, using the `gotoxy()` and `putch()` library functions. `Insert()` uses a coordinate system that starts 5 lines down and 50 columns over from the upper-left corner of the screen; that's where the game board is drawn.

The `Evaluate()` Function

We now come to the "brains" of the program. The `Evaluate()` function evaluates a particular position to see how likely it is to lead to a win for a particular player. It also returns the best move in a particular position.

The `main()` function calls `Evaluate` to determine the best machine move, and makes the machine's move based on the recommendations of this function. How does `Evaluate()` figure out the best move? Its overall strategy is to create a new `Position` object (using `new`) for each move that can be made legally from its position. Each of these positions is then evaluated. For instance, the human has the first move and selects one of the nine choices. Thus on its first move the machine is faced with eight possible moves. Which is the best? To decide, it evaluates each of the eight moves. For each of the eight moves it creates a new `Position`. From this position it then calculates a score, based on how likely the move is to lead to a win. When all possible moves have been evaluated, it returns the move with the highest score, and `main()` then executes this move.

How is each of the eight possible moves evaluated? For the position corresponding to each move, `Evaluate()` calls itself again. For each of the eight moves the machine can make, the human has seven possible responses. When `Evaluate()` is called for one of the machine's eight moves, it generates a position for each of the seven possible human responses. Each of these seven positions then uses `Evaluate()` again to determine the best move. This involves creating six positions for each possible machine move, and calling `Evaluate()` for each of the six moves. The resulting branching of nine initial moves, each with eight responses, and so on, is partially shown in Figure 18-12. Since there are 9! (9 factorial, or 9*8*7*6*5*4*3*2*1, or more than 300,000) possible move combinations, we can't show them all. We show the first few, and several toward the end of the tree.

Eventually, as the `Evaluate()` function works its way down lower and lower into the move tree, one of several things happens. The first possibility is that somebody wins—that is, they get three in a row. This is the end of that branch of the move tree, since the game ends at that point. (Thus there are actually somewhat fewer possible positions than 9!, since the tree stops branching when there's a win, although this does not reduce the size of the tree substantially.) The `Evaluate()` function assigns a number, called a *score*, to each possible outcome so that the various moves can be compared. A win results in a score of 100; this is the highest score. A score of 0 represents a loss.

The other possibility when the move tree is followed to the end is that no more moves can be made; all the squares have been filled by Xs or Os, and the game is a draw. A draw results in a score of 50.

The `Evaluate()` function is set up in the form of a loop that cycles through nine possible moves. In each cycle through the loop, it checks to see if the move is legal. If so, it creates a new position, transfers the current position into it, and makes the move in the new position. It then checks to see if making this move results in a win. If so, it places 100 in the `highscore` variable, and adds 100 to a running total. It also remembers the move that generated the score.

If the move didn't generate a win, `Evaluate()` must look deeper, so it calls the `Evaluate()` function that is a member of the new position. This function will eventually return a score, either because there's a win or because the game ends. This score is again added to the running total. If the score is the highest seen so

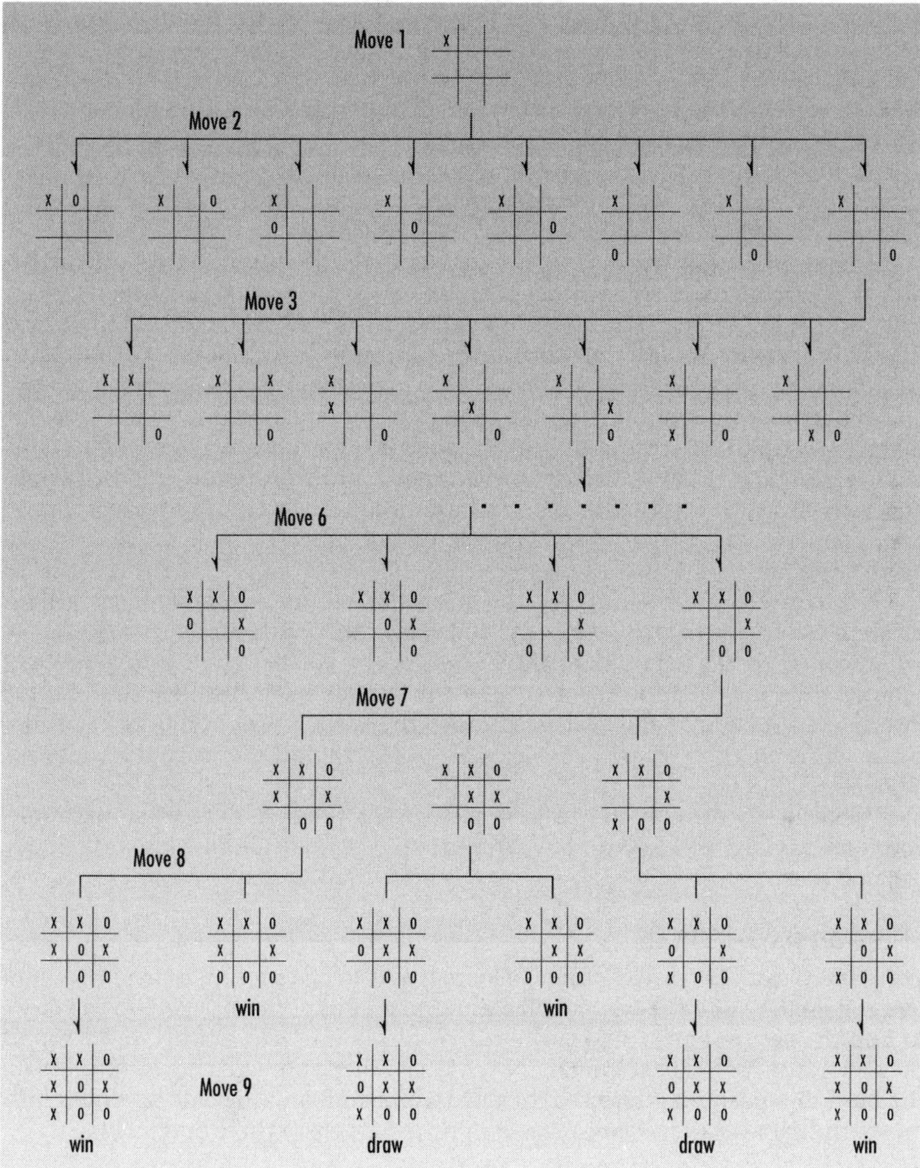

Figure 18-12 The Move Tree

far, it is placed in the `highscore` variable, and the return move is set to this new high-scoring move.

Evaluating a Position

When all the moves have been evaluated, the loop ends and `Evaluate()` figures out a total score for its position. You can approximate this calculation by saying that it averages the scores of the opponent's moves. `Evaluate()` then inverts the average to obtain the score. The inversion is necessary because a win for our opponent is a loss for us. For instance, if our opponent has four moves—say three wins and a draw—the total score is close to 100 for them, but close to 0 for us, since there's a good chance we'll lose. A draw, on the other hand, is a draw for both players, and 50 subtracted from 100 is still 50.

This inversion of the score each time the player changes is called the *minimax* approach. We assume we'll do what's good for us, but we also assume our opponent will do what's bad for us.

Combining several scores into one is actually a little more complicated than simply averaging them. To see the reason for this, imagine that our opponent can make one of four moves. One of the moves leads to a win for them, and three lead to losses for them. What's the score for these four moves? The average would be 100+0+0+0, or 25, which is less than a draw. However, our opponent won't choose one of the moves at random; they'll choose the best one for them. So the score for them is close to 100. It's not quite 100, since it's not quite as good as four wins (which would score 100), but it's still up there. For us (as opposed to our opponent) the situation is reversed. We don't want to make the move that will lead to our opponent having four possible moves, one of which is a win, so we score the move close to 0.

These considerations—and trial and error—lead to the following scoring algorithm: If our opponent has some wins and some other outcomes (draws, losses, or other scores), then we start with 100 (the `winscore` constant in the program) and subtract from it 100 minus the average score, divided by 5. For the win and three losses described above, the average is 25, so the score is 100 – (100–25)/5, or 85. For a win and three draws, the average is 62, so the score would be 100 – (100–62)/5, or 92.

If there are no wins, or all wins, the average can be used without modification. Four draws is 50, two losses and two draws is 25 (75 for us), four wins is 100 (0 for us), and so on.

The `main()` Function

The `main()` function cycles around a loop. It asks the user for his or her move, and makes it on the `current` position. It then displays this position, calls `Evaluate()` to find the best response, makes this move, displays it, and returns to the top of the loop to ask for the next human move. After either a human or a machine move, the `current` position is checked for a win. If the human has made his or her fifth move, the game is a draw. Messages are printed for these three outcomes.

Further Thoughts

You may have noticed how long it takes the program to make its first move (actually the second move of the game) when it has eight choices, and how much more quickly it figures out its next move (the fourth move of the game) when it has only six choices. Not only is eight larger than six, but the branches of the move tree that start at the second move are far larger than those starting at the fourth move. There are about 8! choices for the second move, but only 6!, or 56 times fewer, for the fourth. If we changed the program to let the machine play first, its first move would take nine times as long as the current first move.

Thus, you can see that if the tic-tac-toe game were even slightly more complicated than it is, we could not use the approach of following the move tree to the end. For more complex games a different strategy must be used. One approach is to follow the move tree downward only a fixed number of moves. At an appropriate depth no more positions are created. Instead, the position is evaluated in other ways. In a chess game, for example, an evaluation is based on such factors as the number of pawns occupying center squares and the total value of the pieces on the board. Also, branches that lead to unlikely situations are not explored; this is called "pruning" the tree. Such topics are beyond the scope of this book.

Summary

This chapter has explored some diverse applications of C++ programming. If nothing else, these examples demonstrate that the uses to which you can put C++ are limited only by your imagination (or perhaps the spur of necessity). The object-oriented approach can be applied to most programming problems. Now that you understand how to use this new approach, as embodied in C++, you have at your disposal one of the most powerful programming tools yet created. We hope you enjoyed this introduction to OOP and C++, and that your use of these tools is amusing as well as profitable.

Questions and Exercises

Because this chapter is just for fun, there are no questions or exercises.

Appendices

A: ASCII TABLE

B: BORLAND C++ KEYWORDS

C: STAND-ALONE GRAPHICS PROGRAMS

D: ANSWERS TO QUESTIONS AND EXERCISES

E: BIBLIOGRAPHY

F: DEBUGGING

ASCII Table

DEC	HEX	Symbol	Key
0	00	(NULL)	CTRL 2
1	01		CTRL A
2	02		CTRL B
3	03		CTRL C
4	04		CTRL D
5	05		CTRL E
6	06		CTRL F
7	07		Beep
8	08		BACKSPACE
9	09		TAB
10	0A		Newline
11	0B		Vertical Tab
12	0C		Form Feed
13	0D		ENTER
14	0E		CTRL N
15	0F		CTRL O
16	10		CTRL P
17	11		CTRL Q
18	12		CTRL R
19	13		CTRL S
20	14		CTRL T
21	15		CTRL U
22	16		CTRL V
23	17		CTRL W
24	18		CTRL X
25	19		CTRL Y
26	1A		CTRL Z
27	1B		ESC
28	1C		CTRL \
29	1D		CTRL]
30	1E		CTRL 6
31	1F		CTRL -
32	20		SPACEBAR
33	21	!	!
34	22	"	"
35	23	#	#
36	24	$	$
37	25	%	%
38	26	&	&
39	27	϶	'
40	28	(	(
41	29	)	)
42	2A	*	*
43	2B	+	+
44	2C	,	,
45	2D	–	-
46	2E	.	.
47	2F	/	/
48	30	0	0
49	31	1	1
50	32	2	2
51	33	3	3
52	34	4	4
53	35	5	5
54	36	6	6
55	37	7	7
56	38	8	8
57	39	9	9
58	3A	:	:
59	3B	;	;
60	3C	<	<
61	3D	=	=
62	3E	>	>
63	3F	?	?
64	40	@	@
65	41	A	A
66	42	B	B
67	43	C	C

DEC	HEX	Symbol	Key
68	44	D	D
69	45	E	E
70	46	F	F
71	47	G	G
72	48	H	H
73	49	I	I
74	4A	J	J
75	4B	K	K
76	4C	L	L
77	4D	M	M
78	4E	N	N
79	4F	O	O
80	50	P	P
81	51	Q	Q
82	52	R	R
83	53	S	S
84	54	T	T
85	55	U	U
86	56	V	V
87	57	W	W
88	58	X	X
89	59	Y	Y
90	5A	Z	Z
91	5B	[	[
92	5C	\	\
93	5D	]	]
94	5E	^	^
95	5F	_	_
96	60	`	`
97	61	a	a
98	62	b	b
99	63	c	c
100	64	d	d
101	65	e	e
102	66	f	f
103	67	g	g
104	68	h	h
105	69	i	i
106	6A	j	j
107	6B	k	k
108	6C	l	l
109	6D	m	m
110	6E	n	n
111	6F	o	o
112	70	p	p
113	71	q	q
114	72	r	r
115	73	s	s
116	74	t	t
117	75	u	u
118	76	v	v
119	77	w	w
120	78	x	x
121	79	y	y
122	7A	z	z
123	7B	{	{
124	7C		¦
125	7D	}	}
126	7E	~	~
127	7F	Δ	CTRL ←
128	80	Ç	ALT 128
129	81	ü	ALT 129
130	82	é	ALT 130
131	83	â	ALT 131
132	84	ä	ALT 132
133	85	à	ALT 133
134	86	å	ALT 134
135	87	ç	ALT 135
136	88	ê	ALT 136
137	89	ë	ALT 137
138	8A	è	ALT 138
139	8B	ï	ALT 139
140	8C	î	ALT 140
141	8D	ì	ALT 141
142	8E	Ä	ALT 142
143	8F	Å	ALT 143
144	90	É	ALT 144
145	91	æ	ALT 145
146	92	Æ	ALT 146
147	93	ô	ALT 147
148	94	ö	ALT 148
149	95	ò	ALT 149

DEC	HEX	Symbol	Key	DEC	HEX	Symbol	Key
150	96	û	(ALT) 150	191	BF		(ALT) 191
151	97	ù	(ALT) 151	192	C0		(ALT) 192
152	98	ÿ	(ALT) 152	193	C1		(ALT) 193
153	99	Ö	(ALT) 153	194	C2		(ALT) 194
154	9A	Ü	(ALT) 154	195	C3		(ALT) 195
155	9B	¢	(ALT) 155	196	C4		(ALT) 196
156	9C	£	(ALT) 156	197	C5		(ALT) 197
157	9D	¥	(ALT) 157	198	C6		(ALT) 198
158	9E	Pt	(ALT) 158	199	C7		(ALT) 199
159	9F	*f*	(ALT) 159	200	C8		(ALT) 200
160	A0	á	(ALT) 160	201	C9		(ALT) 201
161	A1	í	(ALT) 161	202	CA		(ALT) 202
162	A2	ó	(ALT) 162	203	CB		(ALT) 203
163	A3	ú	(ALT) 163	204	CC		(ALT) 204
164	A4	ñ	(ALT) 164	205	CD		(ALT) 205
165	A5	Ñ	(ALT) 165	206	CE		(ALT) 206
166	A6	ª	(ALT) 166	207	CF		(ALT) 207
167	A7	º	(ALT) 167	208	D0		(ALT) 208
168	A8	¿	(ALT) 168	209	D1		(ALT) 209
169	A9		(ALT) 169	210	D2		(ALT) 210
170	AA		(ALT) 170	211	D3		(ALT) 211
171	AB		(ALT) 171	212	D4		(ALT) 212
172	AC		(ALT) 172	213	D5		(ALT) 213
173	AD		(ALT) 173	214	D6		(ALT) 214
174	AE		(ALT) 174	215	D7		(ALT) 215
175	AF		(ALT) 175	216	D8		(ALT) 216
176	B0		(ALT) 176	217	D9		(ALT) 217
177	B1		(ALT) 177	218	DA		(ALT) 218
178	B2		(ALT) 178	219	DB		(ALT) 219
179	B3		(ALT) 179	220	DC		(ALT) 220
180	B4		(ALT) 180	221	DD		(ALT) 221
181	B5		(ALT) 181	222	DE		(ALT) 222
182	B6		(ALT) 182	223	DF		(ALT) 223
183	B7		(ALT) 183	224	E0	α	(ALT) 224
184	B8		(ALT) 184	225	E1	β	(ALT) 225
185	B9		(ALT) 185	226	E2	Γ	(ALT) 226
186	BA		(ALT) 186	227	E3	π	(ALT) 227
187	BB		(ALT) 187	228	E4	Σ	(ALT) 228
188	BC		(ALT) 188	229	E5	σ	(ALT) 229
189	BD		(ALT) 189	230	E6	µ	(ALT) 230
190	BE		(ALT) 190	231	E7	τ	(ALT) 231

DEC	HEX	Symbol	Key	DEC	HEX	Symbol	Key
232	E8	Φ	ALT 232	244	F4	⌠	ALT 244
233	E9	Θ	ALT 233	245	F5	⌡	ALT 245
234	EA	Ω	ALT 234	246	F6	÷	ALT 246
235	EB	δ	ALT 235	247	F7	≈	ALT 247
236	EC	∞	ALT 236	248	F8	°	ALT 248
237	ED	φ	ALT 237	249	F9	•	ALT 249
238	EE	ε	ALT 238	250	FA	·	ALT 250
239	EF	∩	ALT 239	251	FB	√	ALT 251
240	F0	≡	ALT 240	252	FC	η	ALT 252
241	F1	±	ALT 241	253	FD	²	ALT 253
242	F2	≥	ALT 242	254	FE	■	ALT 254
243	F3	≤	ALT 243	255	FF	(blank)	ALT 255

Note that IBM Extended ASCII characters can be displayed by holding down the ALT key and then typing the decimal code of the character on the keypad. Always type exactly three digits, using an initial 0 (or 00) if necessary.

Borland C++ Keywords

Keywords implement specific C++ language features. They cannot be used as names for variables or other user-defined program elements. Most of the keywords are common to both C and C++, but some are specific to C++. A few are specific to MS-DOS computers and are not found in other C++ implementations, such as Unix.

```
asm
_asm
__asm
auto
break
case
catch
cdecl
_cdecl
__cdecl
char
class
const
continue
_cs
__cs
default
delete
do
double
_ds
__ds
else
enum
_es
__es
__except
_export
__export
extern
far
_far
__far
_fastcall
__fastcall
__finally
float
for
friend
goto
huge
_huge
__huge
if
_import
__import
inline
int
interrupt
_interrupt
__interrupt
_loadds
__loadds
long
near
_near
__near
new
operator
pascal
_pascal
__pascal
private
protected
public
register
return
__rtti
_saveregs
__saveregs
_seg
__seg
short
signed
sizeof
_ss
__ss
static
_stdcall
__stdcall
struct
switch
template
this
__thread
throw
try
__try
typedef
union
unsigned
virtual
void
volatile
while
```

C

Stand-Alone Graphics Programs

In Chapter 11, on graphics, we described a simple approach to creating graphics programs. Unfortunately, in order for a program to run, this approach requires the existence of the Borland C++ or Turbo C++ development system on your computer's hard disk. This is not very satisfactory if you plan to distribute a program to users who are not running Borland C++ or Turbo C++.

However, by using the project feature, described in Chapters 2 and 15, we can make *stand-alone* graphics programs—that is, graphics programs that run on any MS-DOS computer, not just one in which the Borland or Turbo development system is installed.

Special Files

The approach to graphics that we used in Chapter 11 relies on the existence of the directory \BC45\BGI (or \TC\BGI, if you're using Turbo C++) in the system. The last argument to the `initgraph()` function specifies the path to this directory, and the graphics functions expect to find various files there. One of these files is the graphics driver. If you're using an EGA or VGA display mode, then this driver is the file EGAVGA.BGI. If you're using CGA, it's CGA.BGI.

If you're using fonts, then your program will need other files from \BGI. These files have the .CHR extension. TRIP.CHR is necessary if you use the triplex font, LITT.CHR for the small font, SANS.CHR for the sans serif font, and GOTH.CHR for the Gothic font. Since your program depends on one or more of these files, it won't run in a computer that doesn't already have them installed in the appropriate directory.

There are several ways to create a stand-alone program that will run on any machine. Here's one of the simplest.

Three steps are necessary. First insert into your source file certain functions to *register* the drivers and fonts you use. Next convert any .BGI or .CHR files your program needs to .OBJ files. And finally link these .OBJ files to your program using the project facility. Let's look at these steps in more detail.

Registering Drivers and Fonts

To create a stand-alone program you must link various files together. Some of these files are derived from the drivers and font files that are normally in the BGI directory. The graphics system must be told that these files are supplied at link time and are therefore not found in the BGI directory. Telling this to the graphics system is called *registering* the files.

Two functions are used for this purpose. The `registerbgidriver()` function registers drivers like CGA.BGI and EGAVGA.BGI. However, these filenames themselves are not used as arguments to this function. What Borland calls *symbolic* filenames are used instead. For the files shown, these are `CGA_driver` and `EGAVGA_driver`.

The `registerbgifont()` function registers font files like SANS.CHR. Table C-1 shows the correspondence between some of the filenames and the names to be supplied to this function. The registration functions go just before `initgraph()`.

Let's assume that we want to create a stand-alone version of the CALC program presented in Chapter 15. (The process would be similar with other graphics programs.) Here's how to rewrite the CALC_APP.CPP file:

```
registerbgidriver(EGAVGA_driver); // register driver
registerbgifont(sansserif_font);  // register font
int driver, mode;
driver = EGA;
mode = EGAHI;
initgraph(&driver, &mode, "");    // initialize graphics system
```

The pathname in `initgraph()` is not necessary when the driver is registered, and can be left blank as shown.

Converting the .BGI and .CHR Files

In order for drivers and font files to be linked with your application files, they must be converted to object form. Use the BGIOBJ.EXE utility to convert .BGI or .CHR files to .OBJ files. Simply enter `BGIOBJ`, followed by the name of the file, without the extension. In CALC we convert EGAVGA.BGI to EGAVGA.OBJ, and SANS.CHR to SANS.OBJ. You would enter

```
C>bgiobj egavga
```

and

```
C>bgiobj sans
```

Linking Multiple Files

Now we're ready to compile and link the various files we've created into a final executable file, using the project facility. Make sure all the files you need are in the same directory. (Actually you can put the files wherever you want, but it's simpler

Filename	Symbolic name
TRIP.CHR	triplex_font
LITT.CHR	small_font
SANS.CHR	sansserif_font
GOTH.CHR	gothic_font

Table C-1 Symbolic Font Names

if they're all in one place.) These files include all the .OBJ files generated from .BGI and .CHR files, and the .CPP source file (or files) for your program. In CALC these are CALC.CPP, CALC_APP.CPP, EGAVGA.OBJ, and SANS.OBJ.

In Borland C++, add the new files, EGAVGA.OBJ and SANS.OBJ, to the project by clicking on the CALC_APP icon in the project window with the right mouse button, and then selecting *Add Node* from the resulting menu.

In Turbo C++, create a project file for all the files, as described in Chapter 15. Give it the name of your main .CPP file, such as CALC_APP.PRJ. Then create the final .EXE file by selecting *Make EXE File* from the Compile menu.

In the CALC example you'll emerge with a CALC_APP.EXE file that can be executed on any MS-DOS computer (provided it has an EGA or VGA display).

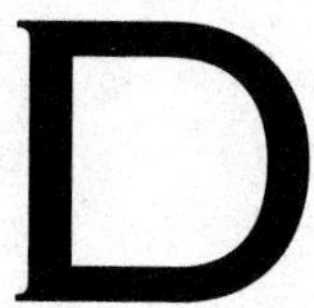

Answers to Questions and Exercises

Chapter 1

Answers to Questions

1. procedural, object-oriented
2. b
3. data, act on that data
4. a
5. data hiding
6. a, d
7. objects
8. False; the organizational principles are different.
9. encapsulation
10. d
11. False; most lines of code are the same in C and C++.
12. polymorphism
13. d
14. b

Chapter 3

Answers to Questions

1. b, c
2. parentheses
3. braces { }
4. It's the first function executed when the program starts
5. statement
6.
```
// this is a comment
/* this is a comment */
```
7. a, d
8. a. 2

   b. 10

   c. 4

   d. 4

9. False
10. a. integer constant
    b. character constant
    c. floating-point constant
    d. variable name (could also be something else)
    e. function name
11. a. `cout << 'x';`
    b. `cout << "Jim";`
    c. `cout << 509;`
12. False; they're not equal until the statement is executed.
13. `cout << setw(10) << george;`
14. IOSTREAM.H
15. `cin >> temp;`
16. IOMANIP.H
17. string constants, preprocessor directives, comments
18. true
19. 2
20. assignment (=) and arithmetic (like + and *)
21. `temp += 23;`
    `temp = temp + 23;`
22. 1
23. 2020
24. to provide declarations and other data for library functions, overloaded operators, and objects
25. CS.LIB

Solutions to Exercises

1.
```
// ex3_1.cpp
// converts gallons to cubic feet
#include <iostream.h>

void main()
   {
   float gallons, cufeet;

   cout << "\nEnter quantity in gallons: ";
   cin >> gallons;
   cufeet = gallons / 7.481;
   cout << "Equivalent in cublic feet is " << cufeet;
   }
```

2.
```
// ex3_2.cpp
// generates table
#include <iostream.h>
```

```
#include <iomanip.h>

main()
   {
   cout << endl << 1990 << setw(8) << 135
        << endl << 1991 << setw(8) << 7290
        << endl << 1992 << setw(8) << 11300
        << endl << 1993 << setw(8) << 16200;
   }
```

3.
```
// ex3_3.cpp
// exercises arithmetic assignment and decrement
#include <iostream.h>

void main()
   {
   int var = 10;
   cout << endl << var;       // var is 10
   var *= 2;                  // var becomes 20
   cout << endl << var--;     // displays var, then decrements it
   cout << endl << var;       // var is 19
   }
```

Chapter 4

Answers to Questions

1. b, c
2. `george != sally`
3. –1 is true; only 0 is false.
4. The initialize expression initializes the loop variable, the test expression tests the loop variable, and the increment expression changes the loop variable.
5. c, d
6. True
7.
```
for(int j=100; j<=110; j++)
   cout << endl << j;
```
8. braces (curly brackets)
9. c
10.
```
int j = 100;
while( j <= 110 )
   cout << endl << j++;
```
11. False
12. At least once.
13.
```
int j = 100;
do
   cout << endl << j++;
while( j <= 110 );
```
14.
```
if(age > 21)
   cout << "Yes";
```
15. d

16.
```
if( age > 21 )
    cout << "Yes";
else
    cout << "No";
```
17. a, c
18. `'\r'`
19. preceding, surrounded by braces
20. reformatting
21.
```
switch(ch)
{
case 'y':
   cout << "Yes";
   break;
case 'n':
   cout << "No";
   break;
default:
   cout << "Unknown response";
}
```
22. `ticket = (speed > 55) ? 1 : 0;`
23. d
24. `limit == 55 && speed > 55`
25. unary, arithmetic, relational, logical, conditional, assignment
26. d
27. the top of the loop
28. b

Solutions to Exercises

1.
```
// ex4_1.cpp
// displays multiples of a number
#include <iostream.h>
#include <iomanip.h>                        // for setw()

void main()
   {
   unsigned long n;                         // number
   cout << "\nEnter a number: ";
   cin >> n;                                // get number
   for(int j=1; j<=200; j++)                // loop from 1 to 200
      {
      cout << setw(5) << j*n << "  ";       // print multiple of n
      if( j%10 == 0 )                       // every 10 numbers,
         cout << endl;                      // start new line
      }
   }
```
2.
```
// ex4_2.cpp
// converts fahrenheit to celsius, or
// celsius to fahrenheit
```

```
#include <iostream.h>

void main()
   {
   int response;
   double temper;
   cout << "\nType 1 to convert fahrenheit to celsius,"
        << "\n     2 to convert celsius to fahrenheit: ";
   cin >> response;
   if( response == 1 )
      {
      cout << "Enter temperature in fahrenheit: ";
      cin >> temper;
      cout << "In celsius that's " << 5.0/9.0*(temper-32.0);
      }
   else
      {
      cout << "Enter temperature in celsius: ";
      cin >> temper;
      cout << "In fahrenheit that's " << 9.0/5.0*temper + 32.0;
      }
   }
```

3.
```
// ex4_3.cpp
// makes a number out of digits
#include <iostream.h>
#include <conio.h>                          // for getche()
void main()
   {
   char ch;
   unsigned long total = 0;                 // this holds the number
   cout << "\nEnter a number: ";
   while( (ch=getche()) != '\r' )           // quit on Enter
      total = total*10 + ch-'0';            // add digit to total*10
   cout << "\nNumber is: " << total;
   }
```

4.
```
// ex4_4.cpp
// models four-function calculator
#include <iostream.h>
#include <conio.h>                    // for getche()
void main()
   {
   double n1, n2, ans;
   char oper, ch;
   do
      {
      cout << "\nEnter first number, operator, second number: ";
      cin >> n1 >> oper >> n2;
      switch(oper)
         {
         case '+':  ans = n1 + n2;  break;
         case '-':  ans = n1 - n2;  break;
         case '*':  ans = n1 * n2;  break;
         case '/':  ans = n1 / n2;  break;
```

(continued on next page)

(continued from previous page)
```
          default:    ans = 0;
          }
       cout << "Answer = " << ans;
       cout << "\nDo another (y/n)? ";
       ch = getche();
       } while( ch != 'n' );
    }
```

Chapter 5

Answers to Questions

1. b, d
2. True
3. semicolon
4. ```
   struct time
      {
      int hrs;
      int mins;
      int secs;
      };
   ```
5. False; only a variable definition creates space in memory.
6. c
7. `time2.hrs = 11;`
8. 18 (3 structures times 3 integers times 2 bytes)
9. `time time1 = { 11, 10, 59 };`
10. True
11. `temp = fido.dogs.paw;`
12. c
13. `enum players { B1, B2, SS, B3, RF, CF, LF, P, C };`
14. ```
    players joe, tom;
    joe = LF;
    tom = P;
    ```
15. a. No

    b. Yes

    c. No

    d. Yes
16. 0, 1, 2
17. `enum speeds { obsolete=78, single=45, album=33 };`
18. Because false should be represented by 0.

Solutions to Exercises

1. ```
   // ex5_1.cpp
   // uses structure to store phone number
   #include <iostream.h>
   ```
   ```

```
struct phone
   {
   int area;          // area code (3 digits)
   int exchange;      // exchange (3 digits)
   int number;        // number (4 digits)
   };

void main()
   {
   phone ph1 = { 212, 767, 8900 };  // initialize phone number
   phone ph2;                       // define phone number
                                    // get phone no from user
   cout << "\nEnter your area code, exchange, and number";
   cout << "\n(Don't use leading zeros): ";
   cin >> ph2.area >> ph2.exchange >> ph2.number;

   cout << "\nMy number is "        // display numbers
        << '(' << ph1.area << ") "
        << ph1.exchange << '-' << ph1.number;

   cout << "\nYour number is "
        << '(' << ph2.area << ") "
        << ph2.exchange << '-' << ph2.number;
   }
```

2.
```
// ex5_2.cpp
// structure models point on the plane
#include <iostream.h>
struct point
   {
   int xCo;      // X coordinate
   int yCo;      // Y coordinate
   };

void main()
   {
   point p1, p2, p3;                           // define 3 points

   cout << "\nEnter coordinates for p1: ";  // get 2 points
   cin >> p1.xCo >> p1.yCo;                    // from user
   cout << "Enter coordinates for p2: ";
   cin >> p2.xCo >> p2.yCo;

   p3.xCo = p1.xCo + p2.xCo;                   // find sum of
   p3.yCo = p1.yCo + p2.yCo;                   // p1 and p2

   cout << "Coordinates of p1+p2 are: "        // display the sum
        << p3.xCo << ", " << p3.yCo;
   }
```

3.
```
// ex5_3.cpp
// uses structure to model volume of room
#include <iostream.h>

struct Distance
```

(continued on next page)

(continued from previous page)

```
   {
   int feet;
   float inches;
   };

struct Volume
   {
   Distance length;
   Distance width;
   Distance height;
   };

void main()
   {
   float l, w, h;
   Volume room1 = { { 16, 3.5 }, { 12, 6.25 }, { 8, 1.75 } };

   l = room1.length.feet + room1.length.inches / 12.0;
   w = room1.width.feet  + room1.width.inches  / 12.0;
   h = room1.height.feet + room1.height.inches / 12.0;

   cout << "\nVolume = " << l*w*h << " cubic feet";
   }
```

Chapter 6

Answers to Questions

1. d (half credit for b)
2. definition
3. `void foo()`
   ```
   {
   cout << "foo";
   }
   ```
4. declaration, prototype
5. body
6. call
7. declarator
8. c
9. False
10. To clarify the purpose of the arguments.
11. a, b, c
12 Empty parentheses mean the function takes no arguments.
13. one
14. True
15. At the beginning of the declaration and declarator.
16. `void`

17.
```
main()
    {
    int times2(int);           // prototype
    int alpha = times2(37);    // function call
    }
```

18. d
19. To modify the original argument.
20. a, c
21. `int bar(char);`

    `int bar(char, char);`
22. faster, more
23. `inline float foobar(float fvar)`
24. a, b
25. `char blyth(int, float=3.14159);`
26. visibility, lifetime
27. Those functions defined following the variable definition.
28. The function in which it is defined.
29. b, d
30. On the left side of the equal sign.

Solutions to Exercises

1.
```
// ex6_1.cpp
// function finds area of circle
#include <iostream.h>

float circarea(float radius);

void main()
   {
   double rad;
   cout << "\nEnter radius of circle: ";
   cin >> rad;
   cout << "Area is " << circarea(rad);
   }

float circarea(float r)
   {
   const float PI = 3.14159;
   return r * r * PI;
   }
```

2.
```
// ex6_2.cpp
// function raises number to a power
#include <iostream.h>

double power( double n, int p=2);    // p has default value 2
```

(continued on next page)

(continued from previous page)

```
void main()
   {
   double number, answer;
   int pow;
   char yeserno;

   cout << "\nEnter number: ";       // get number
   cin >> number;
   cout << "Want to enter a power (y/n)? ";
   cin >> yeserno;
   if( yeserno == 'y' )              // user wants a non-2 power?
      {
      cout << "Enter power: ";
      cin >> pow;
      answer = power(number, pow);  // raise number to pow
      }
   else
      answer = power(number);        // square the number
   cout << "Answer is " << answer;
   }

// power()
// returns number n raised to a power p
double power( double n, int p )
   {
   double result = 1.0;              // start with 1
   for(int j=0; j<p; j++)            // multiply by n
      result *= n;                   // p times
   return result;
   }
```

3.
```
// ex6_3.cpp
// function sets smaller of two numbers to 0
#include <iostream.h>

void main()
   {
   void zeroSmaller(int&, int&);
   int a=4, b=7, c=11, d=9;

   zeroSmaller(a, b);
   zeroSmaller(c, d);
   cout << "\na=" << a << " b=" << b
        <<  " c=" << c << " d=" << d;
   }

// zeroSmaller()
// sets the smaller of two numbers to 0
void zeroSmaller(int& first, int& second)
   {
   if( first < second )
      first = 0;
   else
      second = 0;
   }
```

4.
```
// ex6_4.cpp
// function returns larger of two distances
#include <iostream.h>

struct Distance                        // English distance
   {
   int feet;
   float inches;
   };
                                       // declarations
Distance bigengl(Distance, Distance);
void engldisp(Distance);

void main()
   {
   Distance d1, d2, d3;                // define three lengths
                                       // get length d1 from user
   cout << "\nEnter feet: ";  cin >> d1.feet;
   cout << "Enter inches: ";  cin >> d1.inches;
                                       // get length d2 from user
   cout << "\nEnter feet: ";  cin >> d2.feet;
   cout << "Enter inches: ";  cin >> d2.inches;

   d3 = bigengl(d1, d2);               // d3 is larger of d1 and d2
                                       // display all lengths
   cout << "\nd1="; engldisp(d1);
   cout << "\nd2="; engldisp(d2);
   cout << "\nlargest is "; engldisp(d3);
   }

// bigengl()
// compares two structures of type Distance, returns the larger
Distance bigengl( Distance dd1, Distance dd2 )
   {
   if(dd1.feet > dd2.feet)             // if feet are different, return
      return dd1;                      // the one with the largest feet
   if(dd1.feet < dd2.feet)
      return dd2;
   if(dd1.inches > dd2.inches)         // if inches are different,
      return dd1;                      // return one with largest
   else                                // inches, or dd2 if equal
      return dd2;
   }

// engldisp()
// display structure of type Distance in feet and inches
void engldisp( Distance dd )
   {
   cout << dd.feet << "\'-" << dd.inches << "\"";
   }
```

Chapter 7

Answers to Questions

1. A class specifier describes how objects of a class will look when they are created.

2. class, object
3. c
4.
```
class leverage
   {
   private:
      int crowbar;
   public:
      void pry();
   };
```
5. False; both data and functions can be private or public.
6. `leverage lever1;`
7. d
8. `lever1.pry();`
9. `inline` (also `private`)
10.
```
int getcrow()
{ return crowbar; }
```
11. defined (created)
12. the class of which it is a member
13.
```
leverage()
   { crowbar = 0; }
```
14. True
15. a
16. `int getcrow();`
17.
```
int leverage::getcrow()
{ return crowbar; }
```
18. member functions and data are, by default, public in structures but private in classes
19. three, one
20. calling one of its member functions
21. b, c, d
22. False; trial and error may be necessary.

Solutions to Exercises

1.
```
// ex7_1.cpp
// uses a class to model an integer data type
#include <iostream.h>

class Int                           // (not the same as int)
   {
   private:
      int i;
   public:
      Int()                         // create an Int
         { i = 0; }
      Int(int ii)                   // create and initialize an Int
```

```
      { i = ii; }
   void add(Int i2, Int i3)  // add two Ints
      { i = i2.i + i3.i; }
   void display()            // display an Int
      { cout << i; }
};

void main()
   {
   Int Int1(7);              // create and initialize an Int
   Int Int2(11);             // create and initialize an Int
   Int Int3;                 // create an Int
   Int3.add(Int1, Int2);              // add two Ints
   cout << "\nInt3 = "; Int3.display();  // display result
   }
```

2.
```
// ex7_2.cpp
// uses class to model toll booth
#include <iostream.h>
#include <conio.h>
const char ESC = 27;       // escape key ASCII code
const double TOLL = 0.5;   // toll is 50 cents

class tollBooth
   {
   private:
      unsigned int totalCars;  // total cars passed today
      double totalCash;        // total money collected today
   public:
      tollBooth()                            // constructor
         { totalCars = 0; totalCash = 0.0; }
      void payingCar()                       // a car paid
         { totalCars++; totalCash += TOLL; }
      void nopayCar()                        // a car didn't pay
         { totalCars++; }
      void display()                         // display totals
         { cout << "\nCars=" << totalCars
                << ", cash=" << totalCash; }
   };

void main()
   {
   tollBooth booth1;            // create a toll booth
   char ch;
   cout << "\nPress 0 for each non-paying car,"
        << "\n      1 for each paying car,"
        << "\n      Esc to exit the program.\n";

   do
      {
      ch = getche();            // get character
      if( ch == '0' )           // if it's 0, car didn't pay
         booth1.nopayCar();
      if( ch == '1' )           // if it's 1, car paid
         booth1.payingCar();
```

(continued on next page)

(continued from previous page)

```
      } while( ch != ESC );        // exit loop on Esc key
   booth1.display();               // display totals
   }
```

3.
```
// ex7_3.cpp
// uses class to model a time data type
#include <iostream.h>

class time
   {
   private:
      int hrs, mins, secs;
   public:
      time()                                 // no-arg constructor
         { hrs = mins = secs = 0; }

      time(int h, int m, int s)              // 3-arg constructor
         { hrs=h; mins=m; secs=s; }

      void display()                         // format 11:59:59
         { cout << hrs << ":" << mins << ":" << secs; }

      void add_time(time t1, time t2)        // add two times
         {
         secs = t1.secs + t2.secs;           // add seconds
         if( secs > 59 )                     // if overflow,
            { secs -= 60; mins++; }          //    carry a minute
         mins += t1.mins + t2.mins;          // add minutes
         if( mins > 59 )                     // if overflow,
            { mins -= 60; hrs++; }           //    carry an hour
         hrs += t1.hrs + t2.hrs;             // add hours
         }
   };

void main()
   {
   time time1(5, 59, 59);                    // creates and initialze
   time time2(4, 30, 30);                    //    two times
   time time3;                               // create another time

   time3.add_time(time1, time2);             // add two times
   cout << "\ntime3 = "; time3.display(); // display result
   }
```

Chapter 8

Answers to Questions

1. d
2. same
3. `double doubleArray[100];`
4. 0, 9
5. `cout << doubleArray[j];`

6. c
7. `int coins[] = { 1, 5, 10, 25, 50, 100 };`
8. d
9. `twoD[2][4]`
10. True
11. `float flarr[3][3] = { {52,27,83}, {94,73,49}, {3,6,1} };`
12. memory address
13. a, d
14. an array with 1000 elements of structure or class `employee`
15. `emplist[16].salary`
16. d
17. `bird manybirds[50];`
18. False
19. `manybirds[26].cheep();`
20. array, `char`
21. `char city[21]` (An extra byte is needed for the null character.)
22. `char dextrose[] = "C6H1206-H20";`
23. True
24. d
25. `strcpy(blank, name);`
26.
```
class dog
   {
   private:
      char breed[80];
      int age;
   };
```

Solutions to Exercises

1.
```
// ex8_1.cpp
// reverses a string
#include <iostream.h>
#include <string.h>                   // for strlen()

const int MAX = 80;

void main()
   {
   void reversit( char[] );          // prototype
   char str[MAX];                    // string

   cout << "\nEnter a string: ";     // get string from user
   cin.get(str, MAX);

   reversit(str);                    // reverse the string
```

(continued on next page)

(continued from previous page)
```
   cout << "Reversed string is: ";  // display it
   cout << str;
   }

// reversit()
// function to reverse a string passed to it as an argument
void reversit( char s[] )
   {
   int len = strlen(s);              // find length of string
   for(int j = 0; j < len/2; j++)    // swap each character
      {                              //    in first half
      char temp = s[j];              //    with character
      s[j] = s[len-j-1];             //    in second half
      s[len-j-1] = temp;
      }
   }
```

2.
```
// ex8_2.cpp
// employee object uses a string as data
#include <iostream.h>

const int LEN = 80;

class employee
   {
   private:
      char name[LEN];
      long number;
   public:
      void getdata()                       // get data from user
         {
         cout << "\nEnter name: ";  cin >> name;
         cout << "Enter number: "; cin >> number;
         }
      void putdata()                       // display data
         {
         cout << "\n   Name: " << name;
         cout << "\n   Number: " << number;
         }
   };
void main()
   {
   employee emparr[100];        // an array of employees
   int n = 0;                   // how many employees
   char ch;                     // user response

   do                           // get data from user
      {
      cout << "\nEnter data for employee number " << n+1;
      emparr[n++].getdata();
      cout << "Enter another (y/n)? "; cin >> ch;
      }
   while( ch != 'n' );

   for(int j=0; j<n; j++)      // display data in array
```

```
      {
      cout << "\nEmployee number " << j+1;
      emparr[j].putdata();
      }
   }
```

3.
```
// ex8_3.cpp
// averages an array of Distance objects input by user
#include <iostream.h>

class Distance                          // English Distance class
   {
   private:
      int feet;
      float inches;
   public:
      Distance()                        // constructor (no args)
         { feet = 0; inches = 0; }
      Distance(int ft, float in)        // constructor (two args)
         { feet = ft; inches = in; }

      void getdist()                    // get length from user
         {
         cout << "\nEnter feet: ";  cin >> feet;
         cout << "Enter inches: ";  cin >> inches;
         }

      void showdist()                   // display distance
         { cout << feet << "\'-" << inches << '\"'; }
      void add_dist( Distance, Distance );    // declarations
      void div_dist( Distance, int );
   };
                                        // add Distances d2 and d3
void Distance::add_dist(Distance d2, Distance d3)
   {
   inches = d2.inches + d3.inches;  // add the inches
   feet = 0;                        // (for possible carry)
   if(inches >= 12.0)               // if total exceeds 12.0,
      {                             // then decrease inches
      inches -= 12.0;               // by 12.0 and
      feet++;                       // increase feet
      }                             // by 1
   feet += d2.feet + d3.feet;       // add the feet
   }
                                    // divide Distance by int
void Distance::div_dist(Distance d2, int divisor)
   {
   float fltfeet = d2.feet + d2.inches/12.0;  // convert to float
   fltfeet /= divisor;                        // do division
   feet = int(fltfeet);                       // get feet part
   inches = (fltfeet-feet) * 12.0;            // get inches part
   }

void main()
    {
   Distance distarr[100];           // array of 100 Distances
```

(continued on next page)

(continued from previous page)

```
   Distance total(0, 0.0), average;      // other Distances
   int count = 0;                       // counts Distances input
   char ch;                             // user response character
   do
      {
      cout << "\nEnter a Distance";          // get Distances
      distarr[count++].getdist();            // from user, put
      cout << "\nDo another (y/n)? ";        // in array
      cin >> ch;
      }
   while( ch != 'n' );

   for(int j=0; j<count; j++)                // add all Distances
      total.add_dist( total, distarr[j] );   // to total
   average.div_dist( total, count-1 );       // divide by number

   cout << "\nThe average is: ";             // display average
   average.showdist();
   }
```

Chapter 9

Answers to Questions

1. a, c
2. `x3.subtract(x2, x1);`
3. `x3 = x2 - x1;`
4. True
5. void operator -- () { count--; }
6. None.
7. b, d
8.
```
void Distance::operator ++ ()
   {
   ++feet;
   }
```
9.
```
Distance Distance::operator ++ ()
   {
   int f = ++feet;
   float i = inches;
   return Distance(f, i);
   }
```
10. It increments the variable prior to use, the same as a non-overloaded ++ operator.
11. c, e, b, a, d
12. twice, same
13. b, c
14.
```
String String::operator ++ ()
   {
   int len = strlen(str);
   for(int j=0; j<len; j++)
```

```
      str[j] = toupper( str[j] )
   return String(str);
   }
```

15. d
16. False if there is a conversion routine; true otherwise.
17. b
18. True
19. constructor
20. True, but it will be hard for humans to understand.

Solutions to Exercises

1.
```
// ex9_1.cpp
// overloaded '-' operator subtracts two Distances
#include <iostream.h>

class Distance                            // English Distance class
   {
   private:
      int feet;
      float inches;
   public:
      Distance()                          // constructor (no args)
         { feet = 0; inches = 0.0; }
      Distance(int ft, float in)          // constructor (two args)
         { feet = ft; inches = in; }

      void getdist()                      // get length from user
         {
         cout << "\nEnter feet: ";  cin >> feet;
         cout << "Enter inches: ";  cin >> inches;
         }

      void showdist()                     // display distance
         { cout << feet << "\'-" << inches << '\"'; }

      Distance operator + ( Distance );   // add two distances
      Distance operator - ( Distance );   // subtract two distances
   };
                                          // add d2 to this distance
Distance Distance::operator + (Distance d2)   // return the sum
   {
   int f = feet + d2.feet;                // add the feet
   float i = inches + d2.inches;          // add the inches
   if(i >= 12.0)                          // if total exceeds 12.0,
      {                                   // then decrease inches
      i -= 12.0;                          // by 12.0 and
      f++;                                // increase feet by 1
      }                                   // return a temporary Distance
   return Distance(f,i);                  // initialized to sum
```

(continued on next page)

(continued from previous page)

```
   }
                                          // subtract d2 from this dist
Distance Distance::operator - (Distance d2)  // return the diff
   {
   int f = feet - d2.feet;                // subtract the feet
   float i = inches - d2.inches;          // subtract the inches
   if(i < 0)                              // if inches less than 0,
      {                                   // then increase inches
      i += 12.0;                          // by 12.0 and
      f--;                                // decrease feet by 1
      }                                   // return a temporary Distance
   return Distance(f,i);                  // initialized to difference
   }
void main()
   {
   Distance dist1, dist3;                  // define distances
   dist1.getdist();                        // get dist1 from user
   Distance dist2(3, 6.25);                // define, initialize dist2
   dist3 = dist1 - dist2;                  // subtract
                                           // display all lengths
   cout << "\ndist1 = ";  dist1.showdist();
   cout << "\ndist2 = ";  dist2.showdist();
   cout << "\ndist3 = ";  dist3.showdist();
   }
```

2.
```
// ex9_2.cpp
// overloaded '+=' operator concatenates strings
#include <iostream.h>
#include <string.h>          // for strcpy(), strcat()
const int SZ = 80;           // size of all String objects
class String                 // user-defined string type
   {
   private:
      char str[SZ];                       // holds a string
   public:
      String()                            // constructor, no args
         { strcpy(str, ""); }
      String( char s[] )                  // constructor, one arg
         { strcpy(str, s); }
      void display()                      // display the String
         { cout << str; }
      String operator += (String ss) // add a String to this one
         {                                // result stays in this one
         if( strlen(str) + strlen(ss.str) < SZ )
            {
            strcat(str, ss.str);          // add the argument string
            return String(str);           // return temp String
            }
         else
            cout << "\nString overflow";
         }
   };
```

```
void main()
   {
   String s1 = "\nMerry Christmas!  ";   // uses constructor 2
   String s2 = "Happy new year!";        // uses constructor 2
   String s3;                            // uses constructor 1

   s3 = s1 += s2;          // add s2 to s1, assign to s3
   cout << "\ns1="; s1.display();         // display s1
   cout << "\ns2="; s2.display();         // display s2
   cout << "\ns3="; s3.display();         // display s3
   }
```

3.
```
// ex9_3.cpp
// overloaded '+' operator adds two times
#include <iostream.h>

class time
   {
   private:
      int hrs, mins, secs;
   public:
      time()                            // no-arg constructor
         { hrs = mins = secs = 0; }

      time(int h, int m, int s)         // 3-arg constructor
         { hrs=h; mins=m; secs=s; }

      void display()                    // format 11:59:59
         { cout << hrs << ":" << mins << ":" << secs; }

      time operator + (time t2)         // add two times
         {
         int s = secs + t2.secs;        // add seconds
         int m = mins + t2.mins;        // add minutes
         int h = hrs + t2.hrs;          // add hours
         if( s > 59 )                   // if secs overflow,
            { s -= 60; m++; }           //    carry a minute
         if( m > 59 )                   // if mins overflow,
            { m -= 60; h++; }           //    carry an hour
         return time(h, m, s);          // return temp value
         }
   };

void main()
   {
   time time1(5, 59, 59);               // creates and initialze
   time time2(4, 30, 30);               //    two times
   time time3;                          // create another time

   time3 = time1 + time2;               // add two times
   cout << "\ntime3 = "; time3.display(); // display result
   }
```

4.
```
// ex9_4.cpp
// overloaded arithmetic operators work with type Int
#include <iostream.h>
#include <process.h>       // for exit()

class Int
   {
   private:
      int i;
   public:
      Int()                               // no-arg constructor
         { i = 0; }
      Int(int ii)                         // 1-arg constructor
         { i = ii; }                      //    (int to Int)
      void putInt()                       // display Int
         { cout << i; }
      void getInt()                       // read Int from kbd
         { cin >> i; }
      operator int()                      // conversion function
         { return i; }                    //    (Int to int)
      Int operator + (Int i2)             // addition
         { return checkit( long(i)+long(i2) ); }
      Int operator - (Int i2)             // subtraction
         { return checkit( long(i)-long(i2) ); }
      Int operator * (Int i2)             // multiplication
         { return checkit( long(i)*long(i2) ); }
      Int operator / (Int i2)             // division
         { return checkit( long(i)/long(i2) ); }
      Int operator % (Int i2)             // remainder
         { return checkit( long(i)%long(i2) ); }

      Int checkit(long answer)            // check results
         {
         if( answer > 32767 || answer < -32768L )
            { cout << "\nError: overflow"; exit(1); }
         return Int( int(answer) );
         }
   };

void main()
   {
   Int alpha = 20;
   Int beta = 7;
   Int gamma;

   gamma = alpha + beta;                   // 27
   cout << "\ngamma="; gamma.putInt();
   gamma = alpha - beta;                   // 13
   cout << "\ngamma="; gamma.putInt();
   gamma = alpha * beta;                   // 140
   cout << "\ngamma="; gamma.putInt();
   gamma = alpha / beta;                   // 2
   cout << "\ngamma="; gamma.putInt();
   gamma = alpha % beta;                   // 6
```

```
cout << "\ngamma="; gamma.putInt();
gamma = alpha * alpha * alpha * beta;  // overflows (56,000)
}
```

Chapter 10

Answers to Questions

1. a, c
2. derived
3. b, c, d
4. `class Bosworth : public Alphonso`
5. False
6. `protected`
7. yes (assuming `basefunc` is not private)
8. `BosworthObj.alfunc();`
9. True
10. the one in the derived class
11. `Bosworth() : Alphonso()  { }`
12. c, d
13. True
14. `Derv(int arg) : Base(arg)`
15. a
16. True
17. c
18. `class Tire : public Wheel, public Rubber`
19. `Base::func();`
20. False

Solutions to Exercises

1.
```
// ex10_1.cpp
// publication class and derived classes
#include <iostream.h>

const int LEN = 80;

class publication                          // base class
   {
   private:
      char title[LEN];
      float price;
   public:
      void getdata()
         {
         cout << "\nEnter title: "; cin >> title;
```

(continued on next page)

(continued from previous page)

```
          cout << "Enter price: "; cin >> price;
          }
       void putdata()
          {
          cout << "\nTitle: " << title;
          cout << "\nPrice: " << price;
          }
    };

class book : private publication      // derived class
    {
    private:
       int pages;
    public:
       void getdata()
          {
          publication::getdata();
          cout << "Enter number of pages: "; cin >> pages;
          }
       void putdata()
          {
          publication::putdata();
          cout << "\nPages: " << pages;
          }
    };

class tape : private publication      // derived class
    {
    private:
       float time;
    public:
       void getdata()
          {
          publication::getdata();
          cout << "Enter playing time: "; cin >> time;
          }
       void putdata()
          {
          publication::putdata();
          cout << "\nPlaying time: " << time;
          }
    };

void main()
    {
    book book1;                           // define publications
    tape tape1;

    book1.getdata();                      // get data for them
    tape1.getdata();

    book1.putdata();                      // display their data
    tape1.putdata();
    }
```

2.
```
// ex10_2.cpp
// inheritance from String class
#include <iostream.h>
#include <string.h>        // for strcpy(), etc.

const int SZ = 80;         // size of all String objects

class String                           // base class
   {
   protected:                          // Note: can't be private
      char str[SZ];                    // holds a string
   public:
      String()                         // constructor 0, no args
         { str[0] = '\0'; }
      String( char s[] )               // constructor 1, one arg
         { strcpy(str, s); }           //    convert string to String
      void display()                   // display the String
         { cout << str; }
      operator char*()                 // conversion function
         { return str; }               //    convert String to string
   };

class Pstring : public String          // derived class
   {
   public:
      Pstring( char s[] );             // constructor
   };

Pstring::Pstring( char s[] )           // constructor for Pstring
   {
   int len = strlen(s);                // check length of argument
   if(len > SZ-1)                      // if too long,
      {
      for(int j=0; j<SZ-1; j++)        // copy the first SZ-1
         str[j] = s[j];                // characters "by hand"
      str[j] = '\0';                   // add the null character
      }
   else                                // not too long,
      strcpy(str, s);                  // so copy entire string
   }

void main()
   {                                              // define String
   Pstring s1 = "This is a very long string which is probably--\
no, certainly--going to exceed the limit set in SZ.";
   cout << "\ns1="; s1.display();                 // display String

   Pstring s2 = "This is a short string.";  // define String
   cout << "\ns2="; s2.display();                 // display String
   }
```

3.
```
// ex10_3.cpp
// multiple inheritance with publication class
#include <iostream.h>
```

(continued on next page)

(continued from previous page)

```
const int LEN = 80;
const int MONTHS = 3;

class publication
   {
   private:
      char title[LEN];
      float price;
   public:
      void getdata()
         {
         cout << "\nEnter title: "; cin >> title;
         cout << "   Enter price: "; cin >> price;
         }
      void putdata()
         {
         cout << "\nTitle: " << title;
         cout << "\n   Price: " << price;
         }
   };
class sales
   {
   private:
      float sales[MONTHS];
   public:
      void getdata();
      void putdata();
   };

void sales::getdata()
   {
   cout << "   Enter sales for 3 months\n";
   for(int j=0; j<MONTHS; j++)
      {
      cout << "      Month " << j+1 << ": ";
      cin >> sales[j];
      }
   }
void sales::putdata()
   {
   for(int j=0; j<MONTHS; j++)
      {
      cout << "\n   Sales for month " << j+1 << ": ";
      cout << sales[j];
      }
   }

class book : private publication, private sales
   {
   private:
      int pages;
   public:
      void getdata()
```

```
            {
            publication::getdata();
            cout << "   Enter number of pages: "; cin >> pages;
            sales::getdata();
            }
         void putdata()
            {
            publication::putdata();
            cout << "\n   Pages: " << pages;
            sales::putdata();
            }
      };
   class tape : private publication, private sales
      {
      private:
         float time;
      public:
         void getdata()
            {
            publication::getdata();
            cout << "   Enter playing time: "; cin >> time;
            sales::getdata();
            }
         void putdata()
            {
            publication::putdata();
            cout << "\n   Playing time: " << time;
            sales::putdata();
            }
      };
   void main()
      {
      book book1;          // define publications
      tape tape1;
      book1.getdata();     // get data for publications
      tape1.getdata();
      book1.putdata();     // display data for publications
      tape1.putdata();
      }
```

Chapter 11

Answers to Questions

1. a, b, c, d
2. `window()`
3. False
4. `int driver=VGA, mode=VGAHI;`
   `initgrzph(&driver, &mode, "\\tc\\bgi");`
   (Use `borlandc` in place of `tc` for Borland C++.)
5. 16
6. True

7. b, d
8. `circle(99, 44, 13);`
9. True
10. `line(2, 7, 5, 11);`
11. b, c
12. `setlinestyle(CENTER_LINE, 0, NORM_WIDTH);`
13. b
14. ```
    int arrayname[] = { 0, 10, 5, 0, 10, 10 };
    fillpoly(3, arrayname);
    ```
15. b, d
16. `sound(1000); delay(2000); nosound();`
17. produce the same sequence of random numbers
18. erase
19. c
20. current position

Solutions to Exercises

1.
```
// ex11_1.cpp
// adds size to ball
#include <graphics.h>            // for graphics functions
#include <conio.h>               // for getch()

class ball                       // ball class
   {
   private:
      int xCo, yCo;              // coordinates of center
      int rad;
   public:
      ball()                     // no-argument constructor
         { xCo=0; yCo=0; rad=0; }
      void set(int x, int y, int r)  // set position
         { xCo=x; yCo=y; rad=r; }
      void draw()                // draw the ball
         { circle(xCo, yCo, rad); }
   };

void main()
   {
   int driver, mode;
   driver = DETECT;              // set to best graphics mode
   initgraph(&driver, &mode, "\\bc45\\bgi");

   ball b1;                      // create three balls
   ball b2;
   ball b3;

   b1.set(250, 150, 50);         // position and size them
   b2.set(300, 150, 75);
   b3.set(350, 150, 100);
```
```

```
   b1.draw();                      // draw them
   b2.draw();
   b3.draw();

   getch();             // wait for keypress
   closegraph();        // close graphics system
   }
```

2.
```
// ex11_2.cpp
// adds size data to shape class
#include <graphics.h>            // for graphics functions
#include <conio.h>               // for getch()

class shape                      // base class
   {
   protected:
      int xCo, yCo;              // coordinates of center
      int width, height;         // width and height
      int linecolor;             // color of outline
      int fillcolor;             // color of interior
   public:
      shape()                    // no-arg constructor
         {
         xCo=0; yCo=0; width=0; height=0;
         linecolor=WHITE; fillcolor=WHITE;
         }                                      // set data
      void set(int x, int y, int w, int h, int lc, int fc)
         {
         xCo=x; yCo=y; width=w; height=h;
         linecolor=lc; fillcolor=fc;
         }
      void draw()
         {
         setcolor(linecolor);                        // line color
         setlinestyle(SOLID_LINE, 0, THICK_WIDTH); // line width
         setfillstyle(SOLID_FILL, fillcolor);   // set fill color
         }
   };

class ball : public shape
   {
   public:
      ball() : shape()           // no-arg constr
         { }
      void set(int x, int y, int r, int lc, int fc) // set data
         { shape::set(x, y, r, r, lc, fc); }
      void draw()                // draw the ball
         {
         shape::draw();                         // set colors
         circle(xCo, yCo, width/2);             // draw circle
         floodfill(xCo, yCo, linecolor);        // fill circle
         }
   };
class rect : public shape
```

(continued on next page)

(continued from previous page)

```
   {
   public:
      rect() : shape()          // no-arg constr
         { }                                       // set data
      void set(int x, int y, int w, int h, int lc, int fc)
          { shape::set(x, y, w, h, lc, fc); }
      void draw()               // draw the rectangle
         {
         shape::draw();                            // set colors
         rectangle( xCo-width/2, yCo-height/2,     // draw rectangle
                    xCo+width/2, yCo+height/2 );
         floodfill(xCo, yCo, linecolor);           // fill rectangle
         }
   };

void main()
   {
   int driver, mode;
   driver = DETECT;                       // set to best graphics mode
   initgraph(&driver, &mode, "\\bc45\\bgi");
   rect windowbox;                        // create top part of car
   rect bodybox;                          // create bottom part of car
   ball wheel1, wheel2;                   // create wheels

   windowbox.set(300, 75, 40, 20, YELLOW, BLUE);  // set size,
   bodybox.set(320, 100, 100, 30, YELLOW, BLUE);  // position,
   wheel1.set(290, 117, 27, YELLOW, BROWN);       // and colors
   wheel2.set(350, 117, 27, YELLOW, BROWN);

   windowbox.draw();                      // draw the car parts
   bodybox.draw();
   wheel1.draw();
   wheel2.draw();

   getch();                               // wait for keypress
   closegraph();                          // close graphics system
   }
```

3.
```
// ex11_3.cpp
// makes a car class out of various shapes
#include <graphics.h>           // for graphics functions
#include <conio.h>              // for getch()

class shape
   {
   protected:
      int xCo, yCo;             // coordinates of center
      int width, height;        // width and height
      int linecolor;            // color of outline
      int fillcolor;            // color of interior
   public:
      shape()                   // no-arg constructor
         {
         xCo=0; yCo=0; width=0; height=0;
         linecolor=WHITE; fillcolor=WHITE;
```

```
      }                                        // set data
   void set(int x, int y, int w, int h, int lc, int fc)
      {
      xCo=x; yCo=y; width=w; height=h;
      linecolor=lc; fillcolor=fc;
      }
   void draw()
      {
      setcolor(linecolor);                        // line color
      setlinestyle(SOLID_LINE, 0, THICK_WIDTH); // line width
      setfillstyle(SOLID_FILL, fillcolor);  // set fill color
      }
   };
class ball : public shape
   {
   public:
      ball() : shape()           // no-arg constr
         { }
      void set(int x, int y, int r, int lc, int fc)  // set data
         { shape::set(x, y, r, r, lc, fc); }
      void draw()                // draw the ball
         {
         shape::draw();                          // set colors
         circle(xCo, yCo, width/2);              // draw circle
         floodfill(xCo, yCo, linecolor);         // fill circle
         }
   };
class rect : public shape
   {
   public:
      rect() : shape()           // no-arg constr
         { }                                    // set data
      void set(int x, int y, int w, int h, int lc, int fc)
         { shape::set(x, y, w, h, lc, fc); }
      void draw()                // draw the rectangle
         {
         shape::draw();                          // set colors
         rectangle( xCo-width/2, yCo-height/2,  // draw rectangle
                    xCo+width/2, yCo+height/2 );
         floodfill(xCo, yCo, linecolor);         // fill rectangle
         }
   };

class car
   {
   private:
      rect windowbox;            // create top part of car
      rect bodybox;              // create bottom part of car
      ball wheel1, wheel2;       // create wheels
   public:
      void set(int x, int y)
         {                       // set size, position, and colors
         windowbox.set(x+10, y, 40, 20, YELLOW, BLUE);
         bodybox.set(x+30, y+25, 100, 30, YELLOW, BLUE);
```

(continued on next page)

(continued from previous page)

```
         wheel1.set(x, y+42, 27, YELLOW, BROWN);
         wheel2.set(x+60, y+42, 27, YELLOW, BROWN);
         }
      void draw()
         {
         windowbox.draw();      // draw the car parts
         bodybox.draw();
         wheel1.draw();
         wheel2.draw();
         }
   };

void main()
   {
   int driver, mode;
   driver = DETECT;                    // set to best graphics mode
   initgraph(&driver, &mode, "\\bc45\\bgi");

   car car1, car2, car3;               // create three cars
   car1.set(100, 100);                 // position them
   car2.set(200, 200);
   car3.set(300, 300);
   car1.draw();                        // draw them
   car2.draw();
   car3.draw();

   getch();                            // wait for keypress
   closegraph();                       // close graphics system
   }
```

Chapter 12

Answers to Questions

1. `cout << &testvar;`
2. 4 bytes
3. c
4. `&var, *var, var&, char*`
5. constant; variable
6. `float* ptrtofloat;`
7. name
8. `*testptr`
9. pointer to; contents of the variable pointed to by
10. b, c, d
11. No. The address `&intvar` must be placed in the pointer `intptr` before it can be accessed.
12. any data type
13. They both do the same thing.

14.
```
for(int j=0; j<77; j++)
    cout << endl << *(intarr+j);
```
15. Because array names represent the address of the array, which is a constant and can't be changed.
16. reference; pointer
17. a, d
18. `void func(char*);`
19.
```
for(int j=0; j<80; j++)
    *s2++ = *s1++;
```
20. b
21. `char* revstr(char*);`
22. `char* numptrs[] = { "One", "Two", "Three" };`
23. a, c
24. wasted
25. memory that is no longer needed
26. `p->exclu();`
27. `objarr[7].exclu();`
28. a, c
29. `float* arr[8];`
30. b

Solutions to Exercises

1.
```
// ex12_1.cpp
// finds average of numbers typed by user
#include <iostream.h>

void main()
   {
   float flarr[100];                    // array for numbers
   char ch;                             // user decision
   int num = 0;                         // counts numbers input
   do
      {
      cout << "Enter number: ";         // get numbers from user
      cin >> *(flarr+num++);            // until user answers 'n'
      cout << "   Enter another (y/n)? ";
      cin >> ch;
      }
   while(ch != 'n');
   float total = 0.0;                   // total starts at 0
   for(int k=0; k<num; k++)             // add numbers to total
      total += *(flarr+k);
   float average = total / num;         // find and display average
   cout << "Average is " << average;
   }
```

2.
```
// ex12_2.cpp
// member function converts String objects to upper case
#include <iostream.h>
#include <string.h>        // for strcpy(), etc
#include <ctype.h>         // for toupper()

class String               // user-defined string type
   {
   private:
      char* str;                       // pointer to string
   public:
      String(char* s)                  // constructor, one arg
         {
         int length = strlen(s);       // length of string argument
         str = new char[length+1];     // get memory
         strcpy(str, s);               // copy argument to it
         }
      ~String()                        // destructor
         { delete str; }
      void display()                   // display the String
         { cout << str; }
      void upit();                     // uppercase the String
   };

void String::upit()                    // uppercase each character
   {
   char* ptrch = str;                  // pointer to this string
   while( *ptrch )                     // until null,
      {
      *ptrch = toupper(*ptrch);        // uppercase each character
      ptrch++;                         // move to next character
      }
   }
void main()
   {
   String s1 = "He who laughs last laughs best.";
   cout << "\ns1=";        // display string
   s1.display();
   s1.upit();              // uppercase string
   cout << "\ns1=";        // display string
   s1.display();
   }
```

3.
```
// ex12_3.cpp
// sort an array of pointers to strings
#include <iostream.h>
#include <string.h>              // for strcmp(), etc.

const int DAYS = 7;              // number of pointers in array
void main()
   {
   void bsort(char**, int);      // prototype
                                 // array of pointers to char
   char* arrptrs[DAYS] = { "Sunday", "Monday", "Tuesday",
                           "Wednesday", "Thursday",
                           "Friday", "Saturday"  };
```

```
   cout << "\nUnsorted:\n";
   for(int j=0; j<DAYS; j++)     // display unsorted strings
      cout << *(arrptrs+j) << endl;

   bsort(arrptrs, DAYS);         // sort the strings

   cout << "\nSorted:\n";
   for(j=0; j<DAYS; j++)         // display sorted strings
      cout << *(arrptrs+j) << endl;
   }

void bsort(char** pp, int n)     // sort pointers to strings
   {
   void order(char**, char**);   // prototype
   int j, k;                     // indexes to array

   for(j=0; j<n-1; j++)          // outer loop
      for(k=j+1; k<n; k++)       // inner loop starts at outer
         order(pp+j, pp+k);      // order the pointer contents
   }

void order(char** pp1, char** pp2)  // orders two pointers
   {                             // if string in 1st is
   if( strcmp(*pp1, *pp2) > 0)   // larger than in 2nd,
      {
      char* tempptr = *pp1;      // swap the pointers
      *pp1 = *pp2;
      *pp2 = tempptr;
      }
   }
```

4.
```
// ex12_4.cpp
// linked list includes destructor
#include <iostream.h>

struct link                            // one element of list
   {
   int data;                           // data item
   link* next;                         // pointer to next link
   };

class linklist                         // a list of links
   {
   private:
      link* first;                     // pointer to first link
   public:
      linklist()                       // no-argument constructor
         { first = NULL; }             // no first link
      ~linklist();                     // destructor
      void additem(int d);             // add data item (one link)
      void display();                  // display all links
   };

void linklist::additem(int d)          // add data item
```

(continued on next page)

(continued from previous page)

```
   {
   link* newlink = new link;          // make a new link
   newlink->data = d;                 // give it data
   newlink->next = first;             // it points to next link
   first = newlink;                   // now first points to this
   }

void linklist::display()              // display all links
   {
   link* current = first;             // set ptr to first link
   while( current != NULL )           // quit on last link
      {
      cout << endl << current->data;  // print data
      current = current->next;        // move to next link
      }
   }

linklist::~linklist()                 // destructor
   {
   link* current = first;             // set ptr to first link
   while( current != NULL )           // quit on last link
      {
      link* temp = current;           // save ptr to this link
      current = current->next;        // get ptr to next link
      delete temp;                    // delete this link
      }
   }

void main()
   {
   linklist li;          // make linked list

   li.additem(25);       // add four items to list
   li.additem(36);
   li.additem(49);
   li.additem(64);

   li.display();         // display entire list
   }
```

Chapter 13

Answers to Questions

1. d
2. True
3. base
4. `virtual void dang(int);` or `void virtual dang(int);`
5. late binding or dynamic binding
6. derived
7. `virtual void aragorn()=0;` or `void virtual aragorn()=0;`
8. a, c

9. `dong* parr[10];`
10. c
11. True
12. c, d
13. `friend void harry(george);`
14. a, c, d
15. `friend class harry;` or `friend harry;`
16. c
17. It performs a member-by-member copy.
18. `zeta& operator = (zeta&);`
19. a, b, d
20. False; the compiler provides a default copy constructor.
21. a, d
22. `Bertha(Bertha&);`
23. True, if there was a reason to do so.
24. a, c
25. True; trouble occurs if it's returned by reference.
26. They operate identically.
27. a, b
28. The object of which the function using it is a member.
29. No; since `this` is a pointer, use `this->da=37;`.
30. `return *this;`

Solutions to Exercises

1.

```
// ex13_1.cpp
// publication class and derived classes
#include <iostream.h>

const int LEN = 80;

class publication
   {
   private:
      char title[LEN];
      float price;
   public:
      void getdata()
         {
         cout << "\nEnter title: "; cin >> title;
         cout << "Enter price: "; cin >> price;
         }
      virtual void putdata()
         {
         cout << "\nTitle: " << title;
```

(continued on next page)

(continued from previous page)

```
         cout << "\nPrice: " << price;
         }
   };

class book : public publication
   {
   private:
      int pages;
   public:
      void getdata()
         {
         publication::getdata();
         cout << "Enter number of pages: "; cin >> pages;
         }
      void putdata()
         {
         publication::putdata();
         cout << "\nPages: " << pages;
         }
   };

class tape : public publication
   {
   private:
      float time;
   public:
      void getdata()
         {
         publication::getdata();
         cout << "Enter playing time: "; cin >> time;
         }
      void putdata()
         {
         publication::putdata();
         cout << "\nPlaying time: " << time;
         }
   };

void main()
   {
   publication* pubarr[100];         // array of ptrs to pubs
   book* bookptr;                    // pointer to books
   tape* tapeptr;                    // pointer to tapes
   int n = 0;                        // number of pubs in array
   char choice;                      // user's choice

   do
      {
      cout << "\nEnter data for book or tape (b/t)? ";
      cin >> choice;
      if( choice=='b' )              // if it's a book
         {
         bookptr = new book;         // make a new book
```

```
         bookptr->getdata();          // get book's basic data
         pubarr[n++] = bookptr;       // put pointer in array
         }
      else                            // it's a tape
         {
         tapeptr = new tape;          // make a new tape
         tapeptr->getdata();          // get tape's basic data
         pubarr[n++] = tapeptr;       // put pointer in array
         }
      cout << "   Enter another (y/n)? ";  // another pub?
      cin >> choice;
      }
   while( choice =='y');              // cycle until not 'y'

   for(int j=0; j<n; j++)             // cycle thru all pubs
      pubarr[j]->putdata();           // print data for pub
   }
```

2.
```
// ex13_2.cpp
// friend square() function for Distance
#include <iostream.h>

class Distance                        // English Distance class
   {
   private:
      int feet;
      float inches;
   public:
      Distance()                      // constructor (no args)
         { feet = 0; inches = 0.0; }
      Distance(float fltfeet)         // constructor (one arg)
         {
         feet = int(fltfeet);           // feet is integer part
         inches = 12*(fltfeet-feet);    // inches is what's left
         }
      Distance(int ft, float in)      // constructor (two args)
         { feet = ft; inches = in; }
      void showdist()                 // display distance
         { cout << feet << "\'-" << inches << '\"'; }
      friend Distance operator * (Distance, Distance); // friend
   };
                                      // multiply d1 by d2
Distance operator * (Distance d1, Distance d2)
   {                                  // argument
   float fltfeet1 = d1.feet + d1.inches/12;  // convert to float
   float fltfeet2 = d2.feet + d2.inches/12;
   float multfeet = fltfeet1 * fltfeet2;     // find the product
   return Distance(multfeet);         // return temp Distance
   }

void main()
   {
   Distance dist1(3, 6.0);            // make some distances
```

(continued on next page)

(continued from previous page)

```
   Distance dist2(2, 3.0);
   Distance dist3;

   dist3 = dist1 * dist2;         // multiplication
   dist3 = 10.0 * dist3;          // mult and conversion
                                  // display all distances
   cout << "\ndist1 = "; dist1.showdist();
   cout << "\ndist2 = "; dist2.showdist();
   cout << "\ndist3 = "; dist3.showdist();
   }
```

3.
```
// ex13_3.cpp
// creates array class
// overloads assignment operator and copy constructor
#include <iostream.h>

class Array
   {
   private:
      int* ptr;                   // pointer to "array" contents
      int size;                   // size of array
   public:
      Array()                     // no-argument constructor
         { }
      Array(int s)                // one-argument constructor
         {
         size = s;
         ptr = new int[s];
         }
      Array(Array&);              // copy constructor
      ~Array()                    // destructor
         { delete ptr; }
      int& operator [] (int j)  // overloaded subscript op
         { return *(ptr+j); }
      Array& operator = (Array&);  // overloaded = operator
   };

Array::Array(Array& a)            // copy constructor
   {
   size = a.size;                 // new one is same size
   ptr = new int[size];           // get space for contents
   for(int j=0; j<size; j++)      // copy contents to new one
      *(ptr+j) = *(a.ptr+j);
   }

Array& Array::operator = (Array& a)  // overloaded = operator
   {
   size = a.size;                 // new one is same size
   ptr = new int[size];
   for(int j=0; j<size; j++)      // copy contents to new one
      *(ptr+j) = *(a.ptr+j);
   return *this;                  // return this object
   }
```

```
void main()
   {
   const int ASIZE = 10;          // size of array
   Array arr1(ASIZE);             // make an array

   for(int j=0; j<ASIZE; j++)     // fill it with squares
      arr1[j] = j*j;

   Array arr2(arr1);              // use the copy constructor
   cout << endl;
   for(j=0; j<ASIZE; j++)         // check that it worked
      cout << arr2[j] << "  ";

   Array arr3;                    // make an empty Array
   arr3 = arr1;                   // use the assignment operator
   cout << endl;
   for(j=0; j<ASIZE; j++)         // check that it worked
      cout << arr3[j] << "  ";
   }
```

Chapter 14

Answers to Questions

1. b, c
2. `ios`
3. `ifstream`, `ofstream`, and `fstream`
4. `ofstream salefile ("SALES.JUN");`
5. True
6. `if(foobar)`
7. d
8. `fileOut.put(ch);`
9. c
10. `ifile.read( (char*)buff, sizeof(buff) );`
11. a, b, d
12. the byte location at which the next read or write operation will take place
13. False; *file pointer* can be a synonym for *current position.*
14. `f1.seekg(-13, ios::cur);`
15. b
16. a
17. `skipws` causes whitespace characters to be ignored on input so that `cin` will not assume the input has terminated.
18. `void main(int argc, char *argv[] )`
19. PRN, LPT1, etc.
20. `istream& operator >> (istream&, Sample& )`

Solutions to Exercises

1.
```
// ex14_1.cpp
// write array
#include <iostream.h>
#include <fstream.h>                    // for file streams

class Distance                          // English Distance class
   {
   private:
      int feet;
      float inches;
   public:
      Distance()                        // constructor (no args)
         { feet = 0; inches = 0.0; }
      Distance(int ft, float in)  // constructor (two args)
         { feet = ft; inches = in; }
      void getdist()                    // get length from user
         {
         cout << "\n   Enter feet: ";  cin >> feet;
         cout << "   Enter inches: ";  cin >> inches;
         }
      void showdist()                   // display distance
         { cout << feet << "\'-" << inches << '\"'; }
   };

void main()
   {
   char ch;
   Distance dist;                       // create a Distance object
   fstream file;                        // create input/output file
                                        // open it for append
   file.open("DIST.DAT", ios::binary | ios::app |
                         ios::out | ios::in );
   do                                   // data from user to file
      {
      cout << "\nDistance";
      dist.getdist();                   // get a distance
                                        // write to file
      file.write( (char*)&dist, sizeof(dist) );
      cout << "Enter another distance (y/n)? ";
      cin >> ch;
      }
   while(ch=='y');                      // quit on 'n'
   file.seekg(0);                       // reset to start of file
                                        // read first distance
   file.read( (char*)&dist, sizeof(dist) );
   int count = 0;
   while( !file.eof() )                 // quit on EOF
      {
      cout << "\nDistance " << ++count << ": "; // display dist
      dist.showdist();
      file.read( (char*)&dist, sizeof(dist) );  // read another
      }                                         // distance
   }
```

2.
```
// ex14_2.cpp
// imitates COPY command
#include <fstream.h>              // for file functions
#include <process.h>              // for exit()

void main(int argc, char* argv[] )
   {
   if( argc != 3 )
      { cerr << "\nFormat: ocopy srcfile destfile"; exit(-1); }
   char ch;                       // character to read
   ifstream infile;               // create file for input
   infile.open( argv[1] );        // open file
   if( !infile )                  // check for errors
      { cerr << "\nCan't open " << argv[1]; exit(-1); }

   ofstream outfile;              // create file for output
   outfile.open( argv[2], ios::noreplace );  // open file
   if( !outfile )                 // check for errors
      { cerr << "\nCan't open " << argv[2]; exit(-1); }

   while( infile )                // until EOF
      {
      infile.get(ch);             // read a character
      outfile.put(ch);            // write the character
      }
   }
```

3.
```
// ex14_3.cpp
// displays size of file
#include <fstream.h>              // for file functions
#include <process.h>              // for exit()

void main(int argc, char* argv[] )
   {
   if( argc != 2 )
      { cerr << "\nFormat: filesize filename"; exit(-1); }
   ifstream infile;               // create file for input
   infile.open( argv[1] );        // open file
   if( !infile )                  // check for errors
      { cerr << "\nCan't open " << argv[1]; exit(-1); }
   infile.seekg(0, ios::end);           // go to end of file
                                        // report byte number
   cout << "Size of " << argv[1] << " is " << infile.tellg();
   }
```

Chapter 15

Answers to Questions

1. a, b, c, d
2. `#include` directive
3. the project feature to compile the .CPP file and link the resulting .OBJ files
4. b, c
5. class library

6. True
7. c, d
8. True
9. b, d
10. a, c

Chapter 16

Answers to Questions

1. b and c
2. class
3. False. Different functions are created at compile time.
4.
```
template<class T>
T times2(T arg)
   {
   return arg*2;
   }
```
5. b
6. True
7. instantiating
8. c
9. fixed data type, any data type
10. store data
11. a or c
12. `try`, `catch`, and `throw`
13. `throw BoundsError();`
14. False. They must be part of a try block.
15. d
16.
```
class X
   {
   public:
      int xnumber;
      char xname[MAX];
      X(int xd, char* xs)
         {
         xnumber = xd;
         strcpy(xname, xs);
         }
   };
```
17. False
18. a and d
19. d
20. True

Solutions to Exercises

1.
```
// ex16_1.cpp
// template used for function that averages array

#include <iostream.h>

template <class atype>                    // function template
atype avg(atype* array, int size)
   {
   atype total = 0;
   for(int j=0; j<size; j++)              // average the array
      total += array[j];
   return (atype)total/size;
   }

int intArray[] =          {1, 3, 5, 9, 11, 13};
long longArray[] =        {1, 3, 5, 9, 11, 13};
double doubleArray[] = {1.0, 3.0, 5.0, 9.0, 11.0, 13.0};
char charArray[] =        {1, 3, 5, 9, 11, 13};

void main()
   {
   cout << "\navg(intArray)=" << avg(intArray, 6);
   cout << "\navg(longArray)=" << avg(longArray, 6);
   cout << "\navg(doubleArray)=" << avg(doubleArray, 6);
   cout << "\navg(charArray)=" << (int)avg(charArray, 6);
   }
```

2.
```
// ex16_2.cpp
// implements queue class as a template

#include <iostream.h>
const int MAX = 3;

template <class Type>

class Queue
   {
   private:
      Type qu[MAX]; // array of any type
      int head;     // index of start of queue (remove item here)
      int tail;     // index of end of queue (insert item here)
   public:
      Queue()                      // constructor
         { head = -1; tail = -1; }
      void put(Type var)           // insert item at queue tail
         {
         qu[++tail] = var;
         if(tail >=MAX-1)          // wrap around if past array end
            tail = -1;
         }
      Type get()                   // remove item from queue head
```
(continued on next page)

(continued from previous page)

```
         {
         Type temp = qu[++head]; // store item
         if(head >= MAX-1)       // wrap around if past array end
            head = -1;
         return temp;            // return item
         }
   };

void main()
   {
   Queue<float> q1;     // q1 is object of class Queue<float>

   q1.put(1111.1);                         // put 3
   q1.put(2222.2);
   q1.put(3333.3);
   cout << "1: " << q1.get() << endl;   // get 2
   cout << "2: " << q1.get() << endl;
   q1.put(4444.4);                         // put 2
   q1.put(5555.5);
   cout << "3: " << q1.get() << endl;   // get 1
   q1.put(6666.6);                         // put 1
   cout << "4: " << q1.get() << endl;   // get 3
   cout << "5: " << q1.get() << endl;
   cout << "6: " << q1.get() << endl;

   Queue<long> q2;      // q2 is object of class Queue<long>

   q2.put(123123123L);  // put 3 longs, get 3 longs
   q2.put(234234234L);
   q2.put(345345345L);
   cout << "1: " << q2.get() << endl;
   cout << "2: " << q2.get() << endl;
   cout << "3: " << q2.get() << endl;
   }
```

3.
```
// ex16_3.cpp
// implements queue class as a template
// uses exceptions to handle errors in queue

#include <iostream.h>
const int MAX = 3;

template <class Type>
class Queue
   {
   private:
      Type qu[MAX]; // array of any type
      int head;     // index of front of queue (remove old item)
      int tail;     // index of back of queue (insert new item)
      int count;    // number of items in queue
   public:
      class full  {  };          // exception classes
      class empty  {  };

      Queue()                    // constructor
```

```
         { head = -1; tail = -1; count = 0; }

      void put(Type var)          // insert item at queue tail
         {
         if(count >= MAX)         // if queue already full,
            throw full();         //    throw exception
         qu[++tail] = var;        // store item
         ++count;
         if(tail >=MAX-1)         // wrap around if past array end
            tail = -1;
         }

      Type get()                  // remove item from queue head
         {
         if(count <= 0)           // if queue empty,
            throw empty();        //    throw exception
         Type temp = qu[++head]; // get item
         --count;
         if(head >= MAX-1)        // wrap around if past array end
            head = -1;
         return temp;             // return item
         }
   };

void main()
   {
   Queue<float> q1;       // q1 is object of class Queue<float>
   float data;            // data item obtained from user
   char choice = 'p';     // 'x', 'p' or 'g'

   do                     // do loop (enter 'x' to quit)
      {
      try                 // try block
         {
         cout << "\nEnter 'x' to exit, 'p' for put, 'g' for get: ";
         cin >> choice;
         if(choice=='p')
            {
            cout << "Enter data value: ";
            cin >> data;
            q1.put(data);
            }
         if(choice=='g')
            cout << "Data=" << q1.get() << endl;
         } // end try
      catch(Queue<float>::full)
         {
         cout << "Error: queue is full." << endl;
         }
      catch(Queue<float>::empty)
         {
         cout << "Error: queue is empty." << endl;
         }
      } while(choice != 'x');
   } // end main()
```

Chapter 17

Answers to Questions

1. b
2. `\bc4\include\classlib`
3. True
4. `\classlib\time.h, \classlib\arrays.h`
5. b, c
6. `cout << st;`
7. d
8. ```
   stack1.Push(obj);
   obj = stack1.Pop();
   ```
9. ```
   while( !stack1.IsEmpty() )
      { }
   ```
10. False
11. b
12. `array1.AddAt(obj1, 3);`
13. True
14. associations
15. a, b
16. A Fundamental Data Type is a simpler container than an Abstract Data Type, with few member functions, and ADTs are usually derived from FDTs.
17. `d1.GetItemsInContainer()`
18. `Find()`
19. True
20. A key and a value.

Solutions to Exercises

1. ```
   // ex17_1.cpp
   // tests the TStackAsVector class with type TDate
   #include <classlib\stacks.h>        // for TStackAsVector class
   #include <classlib\date.h>          // for TDate class
   #include <iostream.h>

   void main()
      {
      TStackAsVector<TDate> stada;     // stack for type TDate

      stada.Push( TDate(10, 1, 91) );  // push dates onto stack
      stada.Push( TDate(20, 2, 92) );  //    (day, month, year)
      stada.Push( TDate(30, 3, 93) );

      while( !stada.IsEmpty() )        // pop dates off stack
         cout << stada.Pop() << endl;
      }
   ```
   ```

2.
```
// ex17_2.cpp
// TListImp class stores object of string class
#include <classlib\listimp.h>        // for TListImp class
#include <cstring.h>                 // for string class
#include <iostream.h>

void Display(string&, void*);        // prototype

void main()
   {
   TListImp<string> liststr;         // list of strings

   liststr.Add("Harriet");           // add strings to list
   liststr.Add("Beecher");
   liststr.Add("Stowe");

   liststr.ForEach(Display, 0);      // display all strings
   cout << endl;

   liststr.Detach("Beecher");        // remove a string
   liststr.ForEach(Display, 0);      // display remaining strings
   }

void Display(string& i, void*)       // function displays string
   {                                 // passed as argument
   cout << i << " ";
   }
```

3.
```
// ex17_3.cpp
// tests the TStackAsVector class with type int
#include <classlib\stacks.h>
#include <iostream.h>
void main()
   {
   TStackAsVector<int> stint; // instantiate stack for type int
   unsigned int total_items;

   stint.Push(11);            // push items onto stack
   stint.Push(12);
   stint.Push(13);
   stint.Push(14);
   stint.Push(15);
                              // find number of items
   total_items = stint.GetItemsInContainer();
                              // pop items off stack
   for(int j=0; j<total_items; j++)
      cout << stint.Pop() << endl;
   }
```

Bibliography

Here are some books that might prove interesting to students of object-oriented programming who are using Borland C++ or Turbo C++.

The classic tutorial for C++ is *The C++ Programming Language* by Bjarne Stroustrup (Addison Wesley, Reading, MA, 1991). The author is the designer of C++, and this is, not surprisingly, a definitive work, loaded with information. It is not easy going, especially for beginners, but it is an essential reference after you've learned the fundamentals of the language.

The ultimate reference to the C++ language is *The Annotated C++ Reference Manual*, by Margaret Ellis and Bjarne Stroustrup (Addison Wesley, Reading, MA, 1990). This is a highly technical book, but as you become more proficient in C++ you will probably want to have it around to resolve obscure points of the language.

Most C++ books are weak on their coverage of the I/O streams library. Fortunately, you can find out all you want to know about streams in the *C++ IOStreams Handbook*, by Steve Teale (Addison Wesley, Reading, MA, 1993).

If you want to learn more about the C language, try *The Waite Group's C Programming Using Turbo C++*, by Robert Lafore (Howard W. Sams & Co., Carmel, IN, 1990). This book explains many details of how to program in the MS-DOS environment, including details of keyboard use and the process of speeding up the screen display with direct memory access. It also describes hardware-oriented language features that are common to both C and C++ but do not appear in *Object-Oriented Programming in C++, second edition*, such as bit-wise operators.

The Waite Group's Turbo C++ Bible, by Nabajyoti Barkakati (Howard W. Sams & Co., Carmel, IN, 1990), provides a complete list and descriptions, with examples, of Turbo C++ (and Borland C++) library functions.

No one book, including the present one, can cover every detail of C++. Here are several tutorial books that approach C++ from slightly different angles. *C++ for C Programmers*, by Ira Pohl (Benjamin/Cummings, Redwood City, CA, 1989), and *Teach Yourself C++*, by Al Stevens (MIS Press, Portland, OR, 1990), both assume you already know C, but *Object-Oriented Programming in C++, second edition* gives you all the background you need to understand them. *C++ Primer* by Stanley B. Lippman (Addison Wesley, Reading, MA, 1991) doesn't assume you know C, but it moves pretty fast (a discussion of pointer types in Chapter 1, for example).

For more on data structures such as linked lists, queues, and hash tables, not to mention all sorts of other topics such as searching and sorting, read *Algorithms* by Robert Sedgewick (Addison Wesley, Reading, MA, 1988).

Computers, Pattern, Chaos and Beauty, by Clifford A. Pickover (St. Martin's Press, New York, 1990), is filled with fascinating material, not only on fractals, but on using computer graphics to show chaos, the Mandelbrot set, and other mathematical ideas. The illustrations make it fun to read, and program listings make it easy to reproduce the results on your computer.

If you're interested in fractals, try *The Waite Group's Fractal Creations,* by Tim Wegner and Mark Peterson (Waite Group Press, Corte Madera, CA, 1991). This is an addicting software product that demonstrates fractals and the Mandelbrot set. It's accompanied by a sizable book that explores many byways of the fractal world, while also explaining the operation of the program.

You can read about Conway's Game of Life, among other topics (many of which are related in some way to computer programming), in *Wheels, Life, and Other Mathematical Amusements* by Martin Gardner (W. H. Freeman Co., New York, 1983).

Debugging

In this appendix we provide a very brief introduction to the use of the debuggers in Borland C++ and Turbo C++. We cover several of the most important features, which should help you get started.

Of course one of the most effective debugging techniques doesn't involve a debugger at all, but another kind of software: your brain. Sit down and think about the problem. Imagine which part of your code is causing the bug, and then mentally step through the code line by line. It's amazing how many bugs can be discovered simply by studying the listing. This approach is often much faster than using a debugger, which tends to overwhelm you with data.

However, some problems are simply too weird and obscure to discover through mental analysis. When this happens, a debugger's linear approach will (in most cases) eventually lead you to the bug.

Borland Integrated Debugger

Debugging features are built into the Borland C++ IDE, where they are easily accessible from the normal menu bar. This debugger works on EasyWin programs (or Windows programs), but not on programs written for DOS. Since this integrated debugger is the most convenient debugger to use, we'll describe its main features first. Later we'll summarize these features for the Turbo Debugger built into Borland C++, and for the integrated debugger built into Turbo C++.

Single-Stepping

The simplest, but also one of the most revealing, things you can do with a debugger is to single-step through your program. In the integrated debugger this is easy. Open the project for your program. Then press the F7 or the F8 key. The first time you do this, the program will be recompiled with debugging information included in it. Then the program will start "running" in single-step mode. You'll see that the first executable line of the program, probably `main()`, is highlighted.

As you continue to press F7 or F8, the highlighted line will move through the listing, following the path of program control. The highlight marks the line *about to be* executed.

Step Over Versus Trace Into

The F8 key will cause control to *step over* any function call it encounters, treating the call as a single line of code. Conversely, the F7 key will cause control to *trace into* the function, so that you can single-step through all the function's statements.

You can switch between these two keys whenever you want, so you can trace into some functions but not others.

Sometimes just finding out where the control goes in a program is enough to find a bug. Once you know that a program is wandering off somewhere it's not supposed to, the reason is often easy to discover and fix.

Incidentally, you can't trace into C++ library functions like `strcpy()` or `atoi()`, even with the F7 key. It's not clear why you would want to anyway, since they are (presumably) already debugged.

Starting Over

If you want to start over at the beginning of the program, select *Terminate Program* from the Debug menu.

Endless Loops

In most cases you can terminate a program you're debugging by selecting *Terminate Program* from the Debug menu. However, if the program is running full speed in an endless loop, you'll need to press CTRL-ALT-DEL to have Windows terminate it.

A C++ Peculiarity

The debugger has a limitation specific to C++, at least in its default configuration: You can't single-step through an inline function. This includes class member functions that are defined within the class specification (as shown in many examples in this book). The debugger treats such functions as a single line of code, even with the F7 key. This is frustrating, especially if the bug lies within such a function.

You can fix this by forcing all functions to be "out-of-line" (that is, to be real functions instead of inline functions), even if they are defined inside a class specification. To do this, select *Project* from the Options menu, double-click on the *Compiler* topic, double-click on the *Debugging* subtopic, and check the box called *Out-of-line Inline Functions*. Now you can trace into any member function, no matter where it's defined.

Breakpoints

Sometimes it's not practical to single-step from the beginning of the program to the place where the bug is. Suppose you have a loop that does something 10,000 times, and you know the bug is somewhere in the program lines following the loop. No one has time to single-step around a loop 10,000 times, or even 100. The solution to this is the breakpoint. In the situation just described you should install a breakpoint after the loop but before the section of code with the bug in it. Then you can run the program full speed through the loop, and it will stop at the breakpoint. From there, you can start single-stepping.

To install a breakpoint, position the cursor on the line where you want control to stop. Then select *Toggle Breakpoint* from the Debug menu. The selected line will be highlighted (in a different color than the line about to be executed). Now select *Run* from the Debug menu. The program will run full speed until it reaches the breakpoint, then stop.

Program Output

While you're debugging a program you may want to see what kind of output it is generating. Since the EasyWin program being debugged is actually a separate Windows program, you can examine its window by switching to the *Windows Task List* and double-clicking on its name. This will bring its window into view. The cursor in the program's window will be a stop sign, indicating that the program is temporarily stopped (by the debugger). You can see whatever output the program has sent to the window up to that point.

Watches

Usually you need to know not only where your program goes, but also what is happening to one or more variables. You can monitor a variable's value by setting a *watch* on it. You can think of a watch as a little TV camera focused on the variable.

To set a watch, position the cursor on the variable's name anywhere in the listing. Then select *Add Watch* from the Debug menu. A dialog called *Watch Properties* will appear. The variable name should already be displayed in the *Expressions* field. If it's not, you can type it in. Click on *OK* to make the dialog go away. Another—faster—approach to setting a watch is to click the right mouse button and select *Add Watch* from the speed menu that appears.

When you set the first watch, a new window called *Watch* will appear, with the variable name and the value of the variable shown in it. As you single-step through the program, this value will change. You can place as many variables in the *Watch* window as you want, and monitor them all simultaneously.

The most effective way to use the *Watch* window is to size it so you can see it and your program's *Edit* window at the same time. This way you can see where program control is from the highlighted line in the *Edit* window, and also see the corresponding values of the watch variables.

Incidentally, you can switch to whatever window you want (*Edit, Watch, Message*, etc.) by making the appropriate selection in the Window menu.

Turbo Debugger in Borland C++

If you use Borland C++ to write a DOS (as opposed to an EasyWin) program, you will find that the integrated debugger doesn't work. If you try to use it, a box appears saying *BCW can debug only 16-bit Windows applications*. However, all is not lost. You can use another debugger instead: Turbo Debugger. This is a DOS debugger that can be accessed by selecting *Turbo Debugger* from the Tool menu.

When you start this debugger, you'll see a DOS-type window with the target program's source file in it. The following table shows how to access the major features of Turbo Debugger.

Step over	Press F8
Trace into	Press F8
Output screen	Select *Window/User* screen, or press ALT-F5
Set breakpoint	Position cursor on program line, select *Breakpoints/Toggle*
Set watch	Position cursor on variable name, select *Data/Add* watch
Run at full speed	Select *Run/Run*
Reset program	Select *Run/Program* reset

You can also use Turbo Debugger by exiting Windows entirely and calling it up directly from DOS. Type the name of its .EXE file, which is TD, along with the name of the .EXE file being debugged, at the DOS prompt:

```
c>tc myprog
```

This will bring up the compiler with the target program already displayed.

Turbo C++ Integrated Debugger

The Turbo C++ compiler's IDE also contains an integrated debugger. The following table summarizes its features.

Step over	Press F8
Trace into	Press F7
Output screen	Select *Window/Output* or press ALT-F5
Set breakpoint	Position cursor on program line, select *Debug\Toggle breakpoint*
Set watch	Position cursor on variable name, select *Debug\Watches\Add watch*
Run at full speed	Select *Run/Run*
Reset program	Select *Run/Program* reset

Of course all the debuggers have many more features than we have room to describe in this appendix. The reference manuals that accompany your compiler, online help, and some experimentation will acquaint you with their capabilities.

Index

ENVIRONMENTAL AWARENESS

Books have a substantial influence on the destruction of the forests of the Earth. For example, it takes 17 trees to produce one ton of paper. A first printing of 30,000 copies of a typical 480-page book consumes 108,000 pounds of paper which will require 918 trees!

Waite Group Press™ is against the clear-cutting of forests and supports reforestation of the Pacific Northwest of the United States and Canada, where most of this paper comes from. As a publisher with several hundred thousand books sold each year, we feel an obligation to give back to the planet. We will therefore support organizations which seek to preserve the forests of planet Earth.

This is a legal agreement between you, the end user and purchaser, and The Waite Group®, Inc. and the authors of the programs contained in the disk. By opening the sealed disk package, you ar agreeing to be bound by the terms of this Agreement. If you do not agree with the terms of thi Agreement, promptly return the unopened disk package and the accompanying items (including th related book and other written material) to the place you obtained them for a refund.

SOFTWARE LICENSE

1. The Waite Group, Inc. grants you the right to use one copy of the enclosed software pro grams (the programs) on a single computer system (whether a single CPU, part of a license network, or a terminal connected to a single CPU). Each concurrent user of the program mus have exclusive use of the related Waite Group, Inc. written materials.

2. The program, including the copyrights in each program, is owned by the respective autho and the copyright in the entire work is owned by The Waite Group, Inc. and they are therefor protected under the copyright laws of the United States and other nations, under internationa treaties. You may make only one copy of the disk containing the programs exclusively fo backup or archival purposes, or you may transfer the programs to one hard disk drive, usin the original for backup or archival purposes. You may make no other copies of the program and you may make no copies of all or any part of the related Waite Group, Inc. written mate rials.

3. You may not rent or lease the programs, but you may transfer ownership of the programs an related written materials (including any and all updates and earlier versions) if you keep n copies of either, and if you make sure the transferee agrees to the terms of this license.

4. You may not decompile, reverse engineer, disassemble, copy, create a derivative work, o otherwise use the programs except as stated in this Agreement.

GOVERNING LAW

This Agreement is governed by the laws of the State of California.

LIMITED WARRANTY

The following warranties shall be effective for 90 days from the date of purchase: (i) The Waite Group, Inc. warrants the enclosed disk to be free of defects in materials and workmanship under normal use; and (ii) The Waite Group, Inc. warrants that the programs, unless modified by the purchaser, will substantially perform the functions described in the documentation provided by The Waite Group, Inc. when operated on the designated hardware and operating system. The Waite Group, Inc. does not warrant that the programs will meet purchaser's requirements or that operation of a program will be uninterrupted or error-free. The program warranty does not cover any program that has been altered or changed in any way by anyone other than The Waite Group, Inc. The Waite Group, Inc. is not responsible for problems caused by changes in the operating characteristics of computer hardware or computer operating systems that are made after the release of the programs, nor for problems in the interaction of the programs with each other or other software.

THESE WARRANTIES ARE EXCLUSIVE AND IN LIEU OF ALL OTHER WARRANTIES OF MERCHANTABILITY OR FITNESS FOR A PARTICULAR PURPOSE OR OF ANY OTHER WARRANTY, WHETHER EXPRESS OR IMPLIED.

EXCLUSIVE REMEDY

The Waite Group, Inc. will replace any defective disk without charge if the defective disk is returned to The Waite Group, Inc. within 90 days from date of purchase.

This is Purchaser's sole and exclusive remedy for any breach of warranty or claim for contract, tort, or damages.

LIMITATION OF LIABILITY

THE WAITE GROUP, INC. AND THE AUTHORS OF THE PROGRAMS SHALL NOT IN ANY CASE BE LIABLE FOR SPECIAL, INCIDENTAL, CONSEQUENTIAL, INDIRECT, OR OTHER SIMILAR DAMAGES ARISING FROM ANY BREACH OF THESE WARRANTIES EVEN IF THE WAITE GROUP, INC. OR ITS AGENT HAS BEEN ADVISED OF THE POSSIBILITY OF SUCH DAMAGES.

THE LIABILITY FOR DAMAGES OF THE WAITE GROUP, INC. AND THE AUTHORS OF THE PROGRAMS UNDER THIS AGREEMENT SHALL IN NO EVENT EXCEED THE PURCHASE PRICE PAID.

COMPLETE AGREEMENT

This Agreement constitutes the complete agreement between The Waite Group, Inc. and the authors of the programs, and you, the purchaser.

Some states do not allow the exclusion or limitation of implied warranties or liability for incidental or consequential damages, so the above exclusions or limitations may not apply to you. This limited warranty gives you specific legal rights; you may have others, which vary from state to state.

Disk Order Form

Receive a 3.5-inch, 1.44MB disk with solutions to all the questions and exercises in *Object-Oriented Programming in C++, Second Edition.*

To order by phone, call 800-368-9369 or fax this form to 415-924-2576

or send to Waite Group Press, 200 Tamal Plaza, Corte Madera, CA 94925

College professors and instructors who wish to receive the companion disk to *Object-Oriented Programming in C++, Second Edition,* please see A Note to Teachers at the beginning of the book.

Name

Company

Address

Street Address Only, No P.O. Box

City State ZIP –

Telephone

Quantity and Type

Name	Quantity	Price	
OOP in C++, Second Edition companion disk		x $9.95 =	
		Sales Tax	
		Shipping	
		Total Due	

Sales tax — California addresses add 7.25% sales tax.

Shipping — Add $5 USA, $10 Canada or Mexico, or $15 foreign for shipping and handling. Standard shipping is US mail. Allow 2 to 3 weeks for delivery.

Method of Payment

Checks or money orders, payable to Waite Group Press. To pay by credit card, complete the following:

Visa Mastercard Card Number

Cardholder's Name ______________________ Exp. Date

Cardholder's Signature ______________________

Phone Number ______________________

SATISFACTION REPORT CARD

Please fill out this card if you wish to know of future updates to *Object-Oriented Programming in C++, Second Edition*, or to receive our catalog.

mpany Name: ____________________

vision/Department: ____________________ **Mail Stop:** ____________________

st Name: ____________________ **First Name:** ____________________ **Middle Initial:** ____________________

eet Address: ____________________

y: ____________________ **State:** ____________________ **Zip:** ____________________

ytime telephone: (   ) ____________________

te product was acquired: Month   Day   Year   Your Occupation: ____________________

erall, how would you rate *Object-Oriented Programming in +, Second Edition?*

Excellent ☐ Very Good ☐ Good
Fair ☐ Below Average ☐ Poor

at did you like MOST about this book? ____________________

at did you like LEAST about this book? ____________________

ase describe any problems you may have encountered with talling or using the disk: ____________________

w did you use this book (problem-solver, tutorial, reference...)? ____________________

at is your level of computer expertise?

New ☐ Dabbler ☐ Hacker
Power User ☐ Programmer ☐ Experienced Professional

at computer languages are you familiar with? ____________________

ase describe your computer hardware:

mputer ____________ Hard disk ____________
5" disk drives ____________ 3.5" disk drives ____________
leo card ____________ Monitor ____________
nter ____________ Peripherals ____________
und Board ____________ CD ROM ____________

Where did you buy this book?

☐ Bookstore (name): ____________________
☐ Discount store (name): ____________________
☐ Computer store (name): ____________________
☐ Catalog (name): ____________________
☐ Direct from WGP ☐ Other ____________

What price did you pay for this book? ____________________

What influenced your purchase of this book?

☐ Recommendation ☐ Advertisement
☐ Magazine review ☐ Store display
☐ Mailing ☐ Book's format
☐ Reputation of Waite Group Press ☐ Other

How many computer books do you buy each year? ____________

How many other Waite Group books do you own? ____________

What is your favorite Waite Group book? ____________

Is there any program or subject you would like to see Waite Group Press cover in a similar approach? ____________

Additional comments? ____________________

Please send to: **Waite Group Press**
Attn: *OOP in C++, Second Edition*
200 Tamal Plaza
Corte Madera, CA 94925

☐ **Check here for a free Waite Group catalog**

SATISFACTION CARD

BEFORE YOU OPEN THE DISK OR CD-ROM PACKAGE ON THE FACING PAGE, CAREFULLY READ THE LICENSE AGREEMENT.

Opening this package indicates that you agree to abide by the license agreement found in the back of this book. If you do not agree with it, promptly return the unopened disk package (including the related book) to the place you obtained them for a refund.